Reflecting on
White-Collar and
Corporate Crime

Discerning Readings

David Shichor
Emeritus, California State University, San Bernardino

Larry Gaines
California State University, San Bernardino

Andrea Schoepfer
California State University, San Bernardino

WAVELAND

PRESS, INC.

Long Grove, Illinois

For information about this book, contact:
 Waveland Press, Inc.
 4180 IL Route 83, Suite 101
 Long Grove, IL 60047-9580
 (847) 634-0081
 info@waveland.com
 www.waveland.com

Contents

Part 3 — Wall Street Crimes — 173

Part 4 — Other Forms of White-Collar Crime — 259

Part 5 — Social Response — 359

Preface

Most of us have been victims of white-collar crime. In most cases, we were probably unaware of our victimization—whether in the form of price fixing, hidden fees, or the manipulation of stock prices. The manufacture of dangerous or unsafe products may eventually become public knowledge, as do the effects of pollution. Newspapers trumpet large-scale debacles, but details are confusing or scarce. The public is aware of white-collar crime in general terms but has little understanding of it.

The lack of attention to white-collar crime allows it to flourish. If people recognized that white-collar crime is far more costly and harmful than drug or street crime, we might develop more effective responses for dealing with it. Corporate and Wall Street crimes have the most notoriety and result in the greatest amount of public condemnation, especially after the collapse of the mortgage industry, failure of the big banks, and Washington's bailout of large corporations.

This collection provides an overview of the problem of white-collar crime. Part I looks at exactly what constitutes white-collar crime—in order to understand it, we need to be able to define it. Some definitions focus on the characteristics of the offense, others on the characteristics of the offender, and still others on the culture of organizations.

Criminal law was established as a means of social control over individuals and was eventually extended to corporations, which were perceived as persons before the law. The personification of corporations is reflected in widely used terms such as "corporate responsibility" and "corporate crime." Part II looks at the crimes committed by officers and employees acting in the name of the corporation.

The global economic recession of the first decade of the twenty-first century was triggered by the subprime mortgage crisis, multibillion-dollar Ponzi schemes, fraudulent risk taking by large financial institutions, and insider trading. The crimes of Wall Street are the topic of Part III.

Part IV expands the concept of white-collar crime beyond the corporate boardroom and Wall Street. These crimes are not committed by political and corporate elites, but the consequences can be just as great if not more dangerous. The articles in this section look at identity theft, political corruption, terrorism financing, crime and the Internet, and environmental crime.

Social response to white-collar crimes is often different than for other crimes. White-collar crimes are more complex than street crimes and are harder to prove; offenders often can afford a strong legal defense. The public usually does not identify with the victims of white-collar crime, frequently assuming the victims were as driven by greed as the perpetrators. In the wake of the recent corporate and financial crimes, attitudes may be changing. Part V explores social response to white-collar criminality.

White-collar crime is pervasive and touches all facets of life. Regulatory agencies and current laws are often inadequate to address white-collar crime. We hope the articles in this book help to improve and expand understanding of its ramifications.

Part 1

Defining White-Collar Crime

In order to understand white-collar crime, one must be able to define it. Unfortunately, this is easier said than done as no formal consensus exists on how to specifically define the phenomenon. Definitions vary according to their orientation; some focus on the characteristics of the offense, others the characteristics of the offender, and still others on the organizational culture itself. When Sutherland (1940:1) coined the term "white-collar crime," he was referring to the criminal behavior of "respectable" upper class citizens. More recent definitions have moved away from distinguishing socioeconomic status and instead focus on the opportunity to engage in the behavioral aspects. In fact, definitions of white-collar crime have become so broad that a new category has been created—identifying activities that lie just outside of the margins of traditionally defined white-collar crimes as "hybrid" white-collar crime. For example, contrepreneurial crime (a combination of "con artist" and "entrepreneur") is a term used to refer to white-collar con artists who engage in swindling and other various frauds (Francis, 1988) while technocrime refers to crimes facilitated by any sophisticated form of technology, including computers (Friedrichs, 2010). These hybrid white-collar crimes do not necessarily require the offense to occur during the course of a legitimate occupation, which was once an essential requirement for white-collar crimes. This section of the book presents several articles that address the definitional and measurement issues facing white-collar crime and how they affect our understanding of the phenomenon.

The first chapter in this section by Gilbert Geis also appeared in the first edition of this book. We included it again due to its timeless relevance in the definitional controversies surrounding white-collar crime. Geis traces the definition of white-collar crime from Sutherland's Presidential Address to subsequent definitions that have had an impact on the definitional debate. He also addresses issues such as whether or not "white-collar crime" is a legal term. Geis concludes that perhaps the best way to proceed is to stick with Sutherland's original definition.

Stuart Green's article examines the "meaning" of white-collar crime, how it is defined, how it should/could be defined, and how law enforcement and legal scholars use the term. Green points out that although the term "white-collar crime" has been used in the United States for over half a century and is frequently used in other countries, the term has seldom been included in written legislation. The author goes on to discuss how "white-collar crime" is too vague a concept for legal theory; yet, ironically, the term conveys such power that it is continually invoked.

The article by Neal Shover and Francis Cullen examines what they identify as two competing perspectives for viewing and studying white-collar crime, the Populist and Patrician perspectives. The Populist perspective, much like the conflict paradigm, views white-collar crime as a struggle against socioeconomic inequality. The Patrician perspective, on the other hand, examines white-collar crime through the characteristics of the offense itself by focusing on social organization as opposed to political or economic organization. While the authors argue that these two competing perspectives are not mutually exclusive, scholars do tend to frame their questions and understanding about the phenomenon through one of these two perspectives, thus leading to conflicting views of white-collar crime.

The chapter by Andrea Schoepfer and Stephen Tibbetts questions why the white-collar crime research prior to Sutherland's 1939 American Sociological Society Presidential Address is largely ignored in the literature. While it is clear that Sutherland brought much needed attention to the study of white-collar crime and jump-started the surge of white-collar crime research, he was not the first to study the phenomenon. The second half of their chapter includes an overview of the theoretical research on white-collar crime, which has largely consisted of applying conventional crime theories to white-collar crime. The authors conclude that white-collar crime is indeed a uniquely different form of crime and thus poses challenges within the field of criminology.

Mary Dodge's chapter examines the increasing role of female offenders in white-collar crime. Historically, female participation in crime has been, and still is, less than male participation; due to increased opportunities, however, females are engaging in crimes at a higher rate than in the past. Dodge focuses on the increased opportunities in the corporate and political realm while emphasizing that females are still treated differently from their male counterparts in the workforce. The author notes that several recent shifts in the female offender literature suggest that motivations for female involvement in white-collar crimes may be more similar to male motivations than they were in the past (i.e., a shift from family needs to greed). Similarly, Dodge questions the long-held idea that women are more "ethical, generous, and caring" than men given the recent trends in female offending patterns.

REFERENCES

Francis, D. (1988). *Contrepreneurs*. Toronto: Macmillan of Canada.

Friedrichs, D. (2010). *Trusted Criminals: White-Collar Crime in Contemporary Society*, 4th ed. Belmont, CA: Thomson.

Sutherland, E. H. (1940). White Collar Criminality. *American Sociological Review, 5*, 1–12.

1

White-Collar Crime

What Is It?

— Gilbert Geis

Few, if any, legal or criminological terms are surrounded by as much dispute as white-collar crime. Sociologists, who dominate the field of academic criminology, are wont to insist that by "white-collar crime" they mean to pinpoint a coterie of offenses committed by persons of reasonably high standing in the course of their business, professional, or political work. Especially clear illustrations would be an antitrust conspiracy among vice presidents of several major corporations, the acceptance of a bribe by a member of the national cabinet, and Medicare fraud by a surgeon.

Persons with criminal law or regulatory law backgrounds, for their part, are likely to point out that no such designation as "white-collar crime" is to be found in the statute books and that the kinds of criminal offenses that sometimes are embraced within the term—such as insider trading, embezzlement, and a large variety of frauds—are committed by persons who might be located anywhere on a status hierarchy. While antitrust conspiracies are not likely to be carried out by lower-echelon employees (though they could in theory involve executives' secretaries), bribery transactions often include lower-level go-betweens, and fraud against medical insurance programs is perpetrated by pharmacy employees and ambulance drivers as well as medical doctors. Why, it is asked, should a distinction be drawn between persons who have committed the same type of offense merely because they hold different occupational positions? This is but one of the disputes about definition that both plague and invigorate research and writing on white-collar crime.

Source: Gilbert Geis, White-Collar Crime: What Is It? *Current Issues in Criminal Justice*, 3(1), 9–24. Copyright © 1991 by Sydney Institute of Criminology. Reprinted with permission.

Cynics are apt to view jousting about the definition of white-collar crime the same way they regard disputes about the definition of pornography: We all can recognize it when we see it, so why bother overmuch with attempting to pinpoint precise parameters? Those rejecting this viewpoint maintain that it is vital to establish an exact meaning for a term so that everyone employing it is talking about the same thing and so that scientific investigations can build on each other rather than going off in various directions because of incompatible definitions of their subject matter.

On the debit side in this long-standing debate is the fact that a great deal of energy and ingenuity has been dedicated to defending one or another of the supposed characteristics of the term "white-collar crime" that could have been employed to increase our understanding of the behaviors involved and to determine more satisfactory methods for dealing with them. The credit side lists improved insight and understanding that result when good minds ask hard questions regarding precisely what is meant by words and terms that appear to be employed imprecisely. In the remainder of this chapter, I want to indicate the course of the intellectual fray regarding the definition of white-collar crime, so that readers might be better able to decide for themselves what resolution satisfies them.

Sutherland and His Early Disciples

The term "white-collar crime" was introduced to the academic world by Edwin H. Sutherland in 1939 during his presidential address to the American Sociological Society in Philadelphia. Fifty-six years old at the time, Sutherland was at the peak of a distinguished career marked primarily by his authorship of a sophisticated textbook, *Criminology*, that had first been published in 1924. Though he had lapsed from the orthodox religious faith of his father, a Baptist minister and college president, Sutherland had intensely strong moral convictions about commercial, political, and professional wrongdoing. He also had been deeply influenced by the populist ideas that permeated the Nebraska of his youth (Cherney, 1981), ideas that depicted corrupt business practices as undermining the well-being of the hard-working, God-fearing frontier people among whom Sutherland had been brought up.[1]

In Sutherland's presidential address, he insisted that he had undertaken his work on "crime in the upper, white-collar class, which is composed of respectable, or at least respected, business and professional men" only "for the purpose of developing the theories of criminal behavior, not for the purpose of muckraking or of reforming anything except criminology" (Sutherland, 1940, p. 1). This patently disingenuous disclaimer was primarily a bow to the ethos of sociology at the time, an ethos that insisted on a "value-free" and "neutral" research stance. A proper definition of his subject matter did not occupy Sutherland's attention in this paper; rather, he used anecdotal stories of rapacious acts by America's notorious "robber barons" and their successors to flay then-popular explanations of criminal activity such as poverty, low intelligence, and offender psychopathy.

Ten years later, in *White Collar Crime,* Sutherland (1949) fleshed out his presidential address, but did little to pin down with any more precision the definition of his subject matter. That he buried part of his definition in a footnote attests to his indifference to the matter. In the text, Sutherland declared that a white-collar crime "may be defined approximately as a crime committed by a person of respectability and high social status in the course of his occupation" (p. 9). He then added that the definition consequently "excludes many crimes of the upper class, such as most of their cases of murder, adultery, and intoxication, since these are not customarily a part of their occupational procedures" (p. 9). The footnoted observation added that "'white collar' is used here to refer principally to business managers and executives, in the sense that it was used by a president of General Motors who wrote *An Autobiography of a White Collar Worker*" (p. 9). However, within two pages of this pronouncement Sutherland illustrated white-collar crime with examples of thefts by employees in chain stores and overcharges by garage mechanics and watch repairers. It may have been a dearth of material at his disposal that led Sutherland to use these illustrations; more likely, it was the inconstancy of his definitional focus. Sutherland believed that all crime could be understood by a single interpretative scheme—his theory of differential association—and therefore, this being so, he saw no compelling reason to distinguish sharply between various forms of illegal activity.

Besides the ill-considered use of fudge words such as "approximately" and "principally" in his definition, Sutherland further muddied the semantic waters by planting here and there other equally amorphous clues to what he might have had in mind. The year before he published *White Collar Crime,* in a speech at DePauw University in Indiana, Sutherland had said:

> I have used the term white-collar criminal to refer to a person in the upper socioeconomic class who violates the laws designed to regulate his occupation. The term white-collar is used in the sense in which it was used by President Sloan of General Motors, who wrote a book titled *The Autobiography of a White Collar Worker*. The term is used more generally to refer to the wage-earning class that wears good clothes at work, such as clerks in stores. (Sutherland, 1956, p. 79)

The fact that Sutherland, usually a meticulous scholar in such matters, wrongly cites the Sloan book (it was *Adventures of a White Collar Man*) (Sloan and Sparkes, 1941) and that Sloan's book offers no further definitional enlightenment adds to the confusion. A strict constructionist might argue that the fact that Sutherland abandoned the final sentence in the foregoing quotation about the wage-earning class and its dress when he incorporated this material into his monograph the following year indicates that he had second thoughts and that he intended to confine his focus to upper-class offenders.

The most straightforward definition that Sutherland offered has rarely been noted. It appeared in the *Encyclopedia of Criminology* (1949, p. 511) almost co-terminously with the publication of *White Collar Crime.* Here, Sutherland wrote that "the white collar criminal is defined as a person with high socioeconomic status who violates the laws designed to regulate his occupational activities." Such laws, Sutherland added, can be found in the penal code but also included federal and state trade regulations, as well as special war regulations and laws regarding advertising, patents, trademarks, and copyrights. Thereafter, he observed:

> The white collar criminal should be differentiated, on the one hand, from the person of lower socio-economic status who violates the regular penal code or the special trade regulations which apply to him; and, on the other hand, from the person of high socio-economic status who violates the regular penal code in ways not connected with his occupation. (p. 511)

It has to be an uncertain exegetic exercise to comb these different proclamations in order to try to state what was "truly" meant as the definition of the phenomenon Sutherland had so effectively called to academic and public attention. Certainly, the definitions are uncrystallized and, at times, contradictory. For me, though, what stands out is a sense that Sutherland was most concerned with the illegal abuse of power by upper-echelon businessmen in the service of their corporations, by high-ranking politicians against their codes of conduct and their constituencies, and by professional persons against the government and against their clients and patients.

Particularly significant, I find, is Sutherland's specific exclusion in the last of the definitions quoted of a person from the lower socioeconomic class who violates "special trade regulations which apply to him." It must be granted, however, that this phrase too has its ambiguities. Did Sutherland mean to include lower socioeconomic-class persons who violated regulations that applied *both* to them and to those above them in the power structure—such as the printer's devil and the corporate president who trade on insider information? Was it the law or the status of the perpetrator—or both linked together—that concerned him? It is said that Sutherland once was asked by Edwin Lemert, a noted criminologist, whether he meant by white-collar crime a type of crime committed by a special class of people, and he replied that "he was not sure" (Sparks, 1979, p. 17). Given its progenitor's alleged uncertainty, it is not surprising that those who try to perform as glossarists on the Sutherland definitional text often are befuddled. Besides, it should be stressed that Sutherland's definition, whatever its essence, has no necessary standing if more useful conceptualizations of the subject matter emerge.

In Sutherland's Wake

The focus of this chapter will almost exclusively be on definitional issues raised in the United States, primarily because most writers outside America have rather sanguinely ignored the question of the "proper" parameters for white-collar crime. In part, this is probably because it typically requires a large corps of communicants for some to devote their time to matters that have no immediate utilitarian result. Also, criminology outside the United States has only recently emerged as a social science enterprise distinctive from law and medical faculties, and the concept of white-collar crime is a characteristically social science formulation.

The term "white-collar crime" itself has been widely incorporated into popular and scholarly language throughout the world, though the designation "economic crime" tends to be preferred in socialist countries and is also widely used elsewhere. The United Nations, for its part, has adopted the phrase "abuse of power" for those behaviors that correspond to white-collar crimes. In addition, other designations, such as "upper-world crime," "crimes by the powerful," "crime in the suites," and "organizational crime" have their devotees.

Sutherland's position on white-collar crime elicited some early stinging but off-target critiques from two sociologists (Tappan, 1947; Caldwell, 1958), both of whom also held law degrees. Rather than focusing on Sutherland's definitional imprecision, both castigated him for what they saw as his anti-business bias and his use of a conceptual brush to tar persons who had not been convicted by a criminal court. Sutherland got much the better of this debate by arguing that it was what the person actually had done in terms of the mandate of the criminal law, not how the criminal justice system responded to what they had done, that was essential to whether they should be regarded as criminal offenders (Sutherland, 1945, pp. 132–139).

The pioneering empirical studies that followed in the wake of Sutherland's enunciation of a new area of inquiry did little to clarify the definitional uncertainty. Marshall Clinard (1952), studying black-market offenses during the Second World War, devoted his attention to the issue of whether what he had investigated truly was a crime rather than whether it might mesh with the ingredients necessary to characterize the behaviors as white-collar crime. Clinard also argued that the personalities of the perpetrators—such as egocentricity, emotional insecurity, and feelings of personal inadequacy—were at least as significant as Sutherland's differential association theory in accounting for the black-market violations.

Donald Cressey's (1953) interviews with embezzlers in federal prisons led him to question whether these offenders met the criteria for categorization as white-collar offenders, since they typically cheated their employers, and "[w]hile, with a few exceptions, the persons interviewed were in no sense poverty stricken, neither can they be considered as persons of high social status in the sense that Sutherland uses the phrase."[2]

As had Clinard, Frank Hartung (1950), in the third early major study of white-collar crime, addressed almost all of his definitional remarks to the debate over whether what the violators of the wartime regulations in the meat industry had done could be considered criminal (he believed, with solid evidence, that it could), and not whether, if so, the perpetrators were white-collar criminals. What particularly marked Hartung's contribution, however, was the feisty response it drew from a preeminent sociologist, Ernest Burgess (1950). Burgess insisted that persons violating regulatory laws, such as black marketers, could not be regarded as criminals because they did not so view themselves and were not so viewed by the public. Besides, Burgess maintained, this would mean that half the country's population, given the widespread disregard of rationing during the war, were criminals, a conclusion he apparently found intellectually intolerable. Hartung tried to assuage Burgess, a power in the discipline, but had understandable difficulty with the idea that a person is not a criminal unless that person thinks of himself or herself as a criminal.

Summarizing these early days of white-collar crime scholarship, Donald Newman (1958) maintained that the chief criterion for a crime to be white-collar is that it occurs as a part of or as a deviation from the violator's occupational role. "Technically," Newman insisted, "this is more crucial than the type of law violated or the relative prestige of the violator, although these factors have necessarily come to be major issues in the white-collar crime controversy" (p. 737). This had happened, he argued, because most of the laws involved were not part of the traditional criminal codes and because most of the violators were a cut above the ordinary criminal in social standing. Yet, in the same article, Newman notes that "[w]hether he likes it or not, the criminologist finds himself involved in an analysis of prestige, power, and differential privilege when he studies upperworld crime" (p. 746). Writing slightly later, Richard Quinney (1964) maintained that the concept of white-collar crime lacked conceptual clarity and thought that it ought to embrace the derelictions of persons in all kinds of occupations. This, however, created another dilemma for Quinney—the question of what constitutes an occupational act. Is the filing of a tax return part of a retired person's occupation?[3] Is a welfare recipient who cheats the social services engaged in a white-collar crime because being on the dole is an occupational pursuit? Quinney, thus, added some more riddles, but, like those who had written before him, he was unable to put forward a definitional manifesto that could elicit widespread agreement.

The Middle Years

After the first burst of creative research on white-collar crime, the subject was virtually abandoned by scholars in the United States during the 1960s. Undoubtedly, this was in large part because of the reluctance to tackle iconoclastic ventures with the threat of McCarthyism hanging over the country (Schrenker, 1986). Ultimately, the surge for power by blacks, the challenge to the Vietnam conflict, Watergate, and similar events served to refocus attention on abuses of power. At the same time, as the study of crime in countries other than the United States moved away from being solely an enterprise conducted by black-letter lawyers and medical doctors, scholars throughout the world began to turn their attention to white-collar crime.[4]

On the definitional front, there was, first, an ineffectual and probably ill-conceived attempt in 1962 by the present author to restrict the term "white-collar crime" to the realm of corporate violations (Geis, 1962). Then, in 1970, Herbert Edelhertz, at the time the chief of the fraud section of the federal Department of Justice, offered a definition that drew exclusively upon legal understanding and, as he indicated, one that differed "markedly" from that advanced by Sutherland, which Edelhertz believed was "far too restrictive." "White collar crime is democratic," Edelhertz asserted, and "can be committed by a bank teller or the head of his institution" (pp. 3–4). Edelhertz proposed that a useful definition of white-collar crime would be "an illegal act or series of illegal acts committed by nonphysical means and by concealment or guile, to obtain money or property, to avoid the payment or loss of money or property, or to obtain business or personal advantage" (p. 3). He set out four subdivisions to embrace diverse forms of white-collar crime: (1) crimes by persons operating on an individual, ad hoc basis, for personal gain in a nonbusiness context; (2) crimes in the course of their occupations by those operating inside businesses, government, or other establishments, or in a professional capacity, in violation of their duty of loyalty and fidelity to employer or client; (3) crimes incidental to and in furtherance of business operations, but not the central purpose of such business operations; and (4) white-collar crime as a business, or as the central activity of the business. The last, Edelhertz indicated, referred to confidence games as forms of crime (pp. 19–20).

Criticism of the Edelhertz position predictably came from sociologists who regretted his slighting of the idea of abuse of power as the key aspect of white-collar offenses and his expansive extension of the term to such a variegated range of behaviors. They were puzzled by the excision of violence from the realm of white-collar crime, noting that crimes such as unnecessary surgical operations, the manufacture of unsafe automobiles, and the failure to label poisonous substances at the workplace could be regarded as white-collar crimes with a strong component of violence.

Miriam Saxon (1980), for instance, in challenging Edelhertz's viewpoint, noted that the MER/29 case involved a pharmaceutical corporation that knowingly sold an anti-cholesterol drug that subjected at least five thousand persons to such serious side effects as cataracts and hair loss. Later, the American Bar Association would adopt the term "economic offense" for behaviors within the white-collar crime realm set forth by Edelhertz, and would modify the term "nonviolent" with the footnoted observation that this referred to "the means by which the crime is committed" even though "the harm to society can frequently be described as violent" (p. 5).

In 1973, Clinard and Quinney (p. 188) put forward what has become a widely accepted distinction in scholarship on white-collar crime, that between (1) occupational criminal behavior and (2) corporate criminal behavior. The former is meant to include persons at all levels of the social structure and was defined as the "violation of the criminal law in the course of activity of a legitimate occupation." The category included offenses of employees against their employers. Corporate crime for its part was to consist of offenses committed by corporate officials for their corporation and the offenses of the corporation itself[5] (p. 189).

Seven years later—in 1980—Albert Reiss and Albert Biderman, two particularly sophisticated scholars, suggested the following definition of white-collar crime in a monograph that sought, with a singular lack of success, to establish some basis for counting in a systematic manner the number of such offenses committed annually:

> White-collar violations are those violations of law to which penalties are attached that involve the use of a violator's position of significant power, influence, or trust in the legitimate economic or political institutional order for the purpose of illegal gain, or to commit an illegal act for personal or organizational gain. (p. 4)

What is notable about this stab at achieving definitional order is the return to what I see as Sutherland's clarion point, that the offense involve "the use of a violator's position of significant power, influence, or trust."

Another contribution of note was that by Richard Sparks (1979), who preferred to abandon the law as the essential ingredient of a white-collar offense and, instead, to incorporate both deviancy and illegality within its purview. By white-collar crime (or, as he preferred, "crime as business"), Sparks wrote that he meant acts possessing "all or most of the following features":

1. They are carried out primarily for economic gain, and involve some form of commerce, industry, or trade.
2. They necessarily involve some form of organization, in the sense of more or less formal relationships between the parties involved in committing the criminal acts. This organization is either based on, or adapted to, the commission of crimes.

3. They necessarily involve either the use or the misuse, or both, of legitimate forms and techniques of business, trade, or industry. What distinguishes such things as price-fixing conspiracies, invoice faking, and bankruptcy fraud from robbery, burglary, and shoplifting is that the former do, but the latter typically do not, involve methods and techniques that are also used for legitimate business purposes. (p. 172)

Perhaps the most interesting aspect of Sparks's definitional venture is his linkage of what has been called "organized crime" with white-collar crime. Dwight Smith (1981), in particular, has long insisted, though for the most part he has remained a lone voice, that conceptually there is little to distinguish the two forms of lawbreaking.

Current Controversies

Sentencing Studies

Science, both the social and natural varieties, progresses by testing ideas empirically, preferably by experimental means that utilize control or comparison groups. Some ideas—that there is resurrection after life, for instance—remain impervious to scientific scrutiny; others can be tested with greater or lesser difficulty. The field of white-collar crime, for its part, is notably resistant to experimental work. In some measure, this is because the standing of the perpetrators protects them from the kinds of manipulations that constitute so large a portion of experimental research.

A number of Sutherland's ideas concerning possible judicial favoritism towards white-collar offenders, however, have been converted into testable propositions in ways that have had an important impact on the manner in which white-collar crime is defined. In these instances, the nature of the available information dictated the definition employed.

One of the major studies, by John Hagan, Ilene Nagel, and Celesta Albonetti (1980), used college education and income as proxies for white-collar status in its review of the sentences handed out in ten American federal courts. The roster of white-collar offenses was initially derived intuitively from all acts in the statute books that plausibly might fit the category. Then it was refined by asking U.S. attorneys for their views. Ultimately, thirty-one offenses came to be regarded as white-collar offenses. The list included such arguable acts as failure to file a tax return, embezzlement or theft by bank employees, mail fraud swindles, and fraudulent acceptance of veterans' benefit payments. The research then was directed toward determining whether offenders convicted of committing such acts got tougher sentences than persons who had committed non-white-collar offenses—it was found that they did. In the other major sentencing study, Stanton Wheeler, David Weisburd, and Nancy Bode

(1982) employed eight broad categories of federal offenses for their representation of white-collar crime: securities fraud, antitrust violations, bribery, tax offenses, bank embezzlement, postal and wire fraud, false claims and statements, and credit- and lending-institution fraud. They directed their inquiry toward discovering whether persons with higher social status were sentenced more leniently for such offenses than those with lower social status—it was found that they were not.[6]

The conclusions of the Wheeler study have been disputed on the ground, among others, that they fail to take into account the considerable screening that takes places in regard to white-collar offenses prior to the point where the remaining perpetrators go to court to plead or to be tried and, if found guilty, to be sentenced.[7] Perhaps a more basic issue is whether or not either team of researchers truly was studying persons who might reasonably be regarded as white-collar criminals. Kathleen Daly (1989), reanalyzing the data used in the Wheeler et al. investigation to determine the fate of women who committed white-collar crimes, came to the paradoxical conclusion that it was "occupational marginality" that best explained such offenses; virtually all of the bank embezzlers in her sample, for instance, were clerical workers, and as many as a third of the women in some offense categories were unemployed. For the men, Wheeler and his colleagues had reported that among the credit-fraud, false-claim, and mail-fraud offenders, fewer than half were steadily employed and a quarter were unemployed at the time of their offenses (Wheeler et al., 1988). At the end of her study, Daly, in an aside almost plaintive in nature, mused, "The women's socioeconomic profile, coupled with the nature of their crimes, makes one wonder if 'white-collar' aptly describes them or their illegalities."[8]

Responding in part to the criticism that he had corrupted the essential nature of white-collar crime in his sentencing study (Geis, 1984, p. 146), Hagan, in collaboration with Patricia Parker (1985), later refocused his attention on securities violations during a seventeen-year period in the province of Ontario in Canada. He now employed as the determinant of white-collar power what he called "relational indicators," such as ownership and authority, which located individuals in class positions directly relevant to the perpetration of their offenses. Hagan and Parker also looked at regulatory enforcement under the Securities Act, arguing that the majority of the offenses in which they were interested never came before the criminal courts. This research overturned the earlier counterintuitive conclusion that white-collar offenders are treated less leniently; instead, it was found that employers often escaped both criminal-court appearance and regulatory punishment for Securities Act violations and that managers bore the heaviest burden of the sanctioning process. Regarding the importance of their different definitional focus, Hagan and Parker noted: "Empirical results of our work suggest that the substitution of class for status measures [for example, education and income] is crucial."

Organizational Foci

Parallel to the contretemps regarding the definitional boundaries of white-collar crime elicited by the sentencing studies, there has been an increasing focus on offenses by organizations as part of the territory of white-collar crime. Sutherland himself had devoted a major portion of his monograph to a compilation of the official records of wrongdoing by the seventy largest American corporations (and, as a result, had labeled most of them "criminal recidivists"), and Clinard and Quinney had established corporate crime as a separable unit of white-collar crime analysis.

Chief among the proponents of an organizational focus are M. David Ermann and Richard Lundman (1978) who note in their definitional framework that, among other things, to be considered deviant an organizational act must be contrary to norms maintained outside the organization and must have support from the dominant administrative coalition of the organization. Laura Schrager and James F. Short, Jr., (1977) define organizational crime in the following manner:

> The illegal acts of omission or commission of an individual or a group of individuals in a formal organization in accordance with the operative goals of the organization, which have a serious physical or economic impact on employees, consumers, or the general public. (p. 408)

The inclusion of a measure of the consequence of the offense ("a serious . . . impact") as an aspect of its definition seems puzzling, since various forms of illegal economic activity, such as some kinds of antitrust activity (for example, pooling resources by different companies to finance research on serious diseases), are at best arguably detrimental to economic health and vitality, but have been outlawed as a consequence of the force of a particular marketplace philosophy (Kadish, 1963).

Attention to organizational activity in white-collar crime studies has drawn heavy criticism from Donald R. Cressey (1989), who argued that the idea that corporations commit crimes is merely a legal fiction. Cressey maintained that "so-called organizational crime (another name for corporate crime) is committed by corporation executives, not by organizations." Cressey's position, for its part, has been criticized by John Braithwaite and Brent Fisse (1990). They argued that "sound scientific theories can be based on a foundation of corporate action," and noted that "[b]ecause the makeup of a corporation is different from that of a human being, it can do things that are not humanly possible, such as growing from infant to adult in a year, securing immortality." The essence of Braithwaite and Fisse's position appears in the following paragraph:

> The notion that individuals are real, observable, flesh and blood, while corporations are legal fictions, is false. Plainly, many features of corporations are observable (their assets, factories, decision-making procedures), while many features of individuals are not (e.g., personality, intention, unconscious minds).[9] (p. 19)

Finally, Braithwaite and Fisse insist that "[t]he products of organizations are more than the sum of the products of individual actions" (p. 22). Albert K. Cohen (1990) recently has supported the Braithwaite and Fisse viewpoint, and offered some guidelines to white-collar crime students for a better understanding of the "organization as an actor."

General Theory and Abuse of Trust

Two major forays into the definitional realm regarding white-collar crime have emerged in the past few years. Both offer strong arguments for the idiosyncratic stances they adopt. Whether either will have more than a passing influence on the manner in which white-collar crime comes to be viewed seems uncertain.

Travis Hirschi and Michael Gottfredson (1987) maintain that white-collar crime is nothing more than another form of lawbreaking—like rape, vandalism, and simple assault—and readily can be incorporated into an explanatory framework that accounts for the causes of all criminal behavior. For them, there is no relevant distinction that would necessitate white-collar crime being regarded as a special category of offense. They argue that focusing on the class position of the offender precludes all theories except those based on psychological differences between lawbreakers as an explanation for what they have done. Hirschi and Gottfredson maintain that persons studying juvenile delinquency have found no utility in examining as separate entities vandalism, arson, rape, or burglary, and that, therefore, "there is little reason to think that the idea of specialization in white-collar offenses will bear fruit."[10] They also argue, apropos white-collar crime, that crimes have in common features that make those engaging in any one of them extremely likely to engage in others as well, a proposition that could be upheld in regard to white-collar offenders only if the category of behavior is defined extremely broadly, as it is by these authors. Critics of Hirschi and Gottfredson maintain that the pursuit of a single explanation that will permit understanding of all forms of criminal activity is a chimera, doomed to eternal failure.

The second call to reconceptualize white-collar crime—or, as she terms it, to "liberate" the term—is that offered by Susan Shapiro (1990), who insists that white-collar crime ought to refer specifically and only to the violation of trust by which persons are enabled "to rob without violence and burgle without trespass" (p. 346). Such persons manipulate norms of disclosure, disinterestedness, and role competence. Their behaviors involve lying, misrepresentation, stealing, misappropriation, self-dealing, corruption, and role conflict. As a whimsical example of misrepresentation, Shapiro tells the story of "Zoogate"—that the zoo in Houston advertised live cobras but actually displayed rubber replicas, since live cobras could not live under the lights in the area where they would have to be kept. Prosecution of crimes involving abuse of trust is handicapped, Shapiro points out, because of the ambiguity that renders victims unwitting and therefore unable to assist in prosecution, and the fact that the suspects tend to have custody of the crucial evidence against them. Shapiro grants that the Sutherland definitional heritage is not readily cast aside, because the concept of white-collar crime is "polemically powerful" and "palpably self-evident" (p. 357). She also grants that her redesign of the concept has its own problems—for instance, that it excludes antitrust crimes as well as corporate violence that grows out of deliberate decisions or negligence. Nonetheless, Shapiro concludes with a resounding indictment of the consequences of the usual way of looking at white-collar crime, which is said to have

> created an imprisoning framework for contemporary scholarship, impoverishing theory, distorting empirical inquiry, oversimplifying policy analysis, inflaming our muckraking instincts, and obscuring fascinating questions about the relationships between social organization and crime. (p. 362)

Conclusion

I proposed at the outset of the chapter to set forth a sample of the major contributions directed toward providing a satisfactory definition of white-collar crime so that readers might be helped to adjudicate the debate for themselves. Most certainly, I have intruded into the presentation of viewpoints a relatively strong indication of my personal preferences. In this final section, I want to formalize how I see some of the issues that have been considered in this chapter.

In writing for newspapers, reporters often strive to tie their stories into a more significant or at least more recognizable overarching framework. This search for a "news peg" has its analog in scientific work: all of us generally attend more readily to things that relate to matters about which we already are concerned rather than to unfamiliar issues. The extensive and excellent work of Wheeler and his colleagues at Yale University was funded by the U.S. Department of Justice as a response to concern with what was known as "white-collar crime." Therefore, it was incumbent upon the grant recipients to place their research under that heading and, when they gained access to federal court data, to insist that such data represented white-collar crime rather than to regard them as a collection of information about certain kinds of offenses against federal law.

Similarly, Shapiro's contribution most basically asks that a new line of inquiry—one that focuses on abuse of trust—be pursued in scholarly work. There is no compelling reason that this call-to-arms be allied to the abandonment of traditional research on white-collar crime. Her blueprint may produce worthwhile scholarly and policy products. Shapiro's argument against the traditional study of white-collar crime, however, seems gratuitous, since it is not—and probably cannot be—accompanied by a demonstration of the truth of the assertion that intellectual, political, or social life would be better served by attending to abuses of trust rather than abuses of power.

My personal belief is that, whatever the loss incurred by the mounting of wayward inquiries, the preferred situation is that which encourages research and policy people to pursue those kinds of inquiries that strike them as offering the greatest personal, professional, and public reward. That position, of course, so stated, has elements both of the platitudinous and the pious, but I know of no other way to convey it. In regard to white-collar crime, I remain persuaded that Sutherland, however errantly, focused on a matter of singular practical and intellectual importance—the abuse of power by persons who are situated in high places where they are provided with the opportunity for such abuse. To my mind, the excellent study by Hagan and Parker of the punishment of securities fraud in Canada illustrates how adherence to the Sutherland tradition can produce valuable findings. In my more ardent, youthful days I predicted that unless the term "white-collar crime" was accorded a tighter definition it would remain "so broad and indefinite as to fall into inevitable desuetude" (Geis, 1962, p. 171). Instead, as this chapter indicates, in my more ancient state, almost thirty years down the line, the concept remains vital and compelling. I find myself today in agreement with John Braithwaite's (1985, p. 19) suggestion that "[p]robably the most sensible way to proceed . . . is to stick with Sutherland's definition." This, he points out, at least excludes welfare cheats and credit-card frauds from the territory. Thereafter, Braithwaite would "partition the domain into major types of white collar crime" in order to generate sound theory (p. 3). If his were a legislative motion, and I a member, I would second it. Then, during debate, I would be certain to read into the record Robert Nisbet's (1965) advice:

> Beyond a certain point, it is but a waste of time to seek tidy semantic justifications for concepts used by creative minds. The important and all-too-neglected task in philosophy and social theory is that of observing the ways in which abstract concepts are converted by their creators into methodologies and perspectives which provide new illumination of the world. (p. 39)

NOTES

[1] For biographical details regarding Sutherland, see Gilbert Geis and Colin Goff, "Introduction," in Edwin H. Sutherland, *White Collar Crime: The Uncut Version* (New Haven, CT: Yale University Press, 1983), *ix–xxxiii*.

[2] Daniel Bell similarly excludes embezzlers from the white-collar territory because of their middle-class status: "Crime as an American Way of Life," in *The End of Ideology* (New York: Free Press, 1960), 382.

[3] It has been argued that tax evasion ought to be regarded as a white-collar crime, and that all persons, regardless of their social positions, who evade taxes ought to be studied together. Robert Mason and Lyle D. Calvin, "A Study of Admitted Income Tax Evasion," *Law and Society Review*, 13 (1978), 73–89.

[4] A brief sample of non-American writings includes Lin Dong-Mao, *The Study of Economic Crime* (Taipei: Central Police College, 1984); Andrew Hopkins, *Crime, Law and Business: The Sociological Aspects of Australian Monopoly Law* (Canberra, Australia: Australian Institute of Criminology, 1978); Georges Kellens, *Banqueroute et Banqueroutiers* (Brussels: Dessart et Mardaga, 1974); Michael Levi, *The Phantom Capitalists: The Organisation and Control of Long-Firm Fraud* (London: Heinemann, 1981). The most comprehensive white-collar crime bibliography has been produced in Germany: Hildegard Liebl and Karlhans Liebl, *Internationale Bibliographie zur Wirtschaftskriminalität* (Pfaffenweiler, Germany: Centaurus-Verlagsgesellschaft, 1985).

[5] The two American textbooks on white-collar crime employ slight variants of the Clinard and Quinney position. James S. Coleman defines white-collar crime as a "violation of the law committed by a person or group of persons in the course of their otherwise respected and legitimate occupation or financial activity" (*The Criminal Elite*, 2d ed., New York: St. Martin's Press, 1989, 5). Gary S. Green entitled his text *Organizational Crime* (Chicago: Nelson Hall, 1990), and defined its subject as (1) acts punishable by law; and (2) those committed through opportunity created by an occupational role that is legal (p. 13).

[6] A replication of the study using different courts has reached somewhat different conclusions: Michael Benson and Esteban Walker, "Sentencing the White-Collar Offender," *American Sociological Review*, 53 (1988), 294–302.

[7] For a defense of the sample, see Stanton Wheeler and Mitchell Rothman, "The Organization as Weapon in White-Collar Crime," *Michigan Law Review*, 80 (1982), 1403–1426.

[8] Another writer has more aptly described such offenders as "frayed-collar criminals." Jane Roberts Chapman, *Economic Realities and the Female Offender* (Lexington, MA: Lexington Books, 1980), 68.

[9] See also John Braithwaite and Brent Fisse, "Varieties of Responsibility and Organizational Crime," *Law & Policy*, 7 (1985), 315–343.

[10] A critique is found in Darrell Steffensmeier, "On the Causes of 'White-Collar' Crime," *Criminology*, 27 (1989), 345–358.

REFERENCES

Bell, D. (1960). Crime as an American way of life. In *The end of ideology*. New York: Free Press.

Benson, M. L., and Walker, E. (1988). Sentencing the white-collar offender. *American Sociological Review*, 53, 294–302.

Braithwaite, J. (1985). White collar crime. In R. H. Turner and J. F. Short, eds. *Annual review of sociology*, 1–25. Vol. 11. Palo Alto, CA: Annual Reviews.

Braithwaite, J., and Fisse, B. (1985). Varieties of responsibility and organizational crime. *Law & Policy*, 7, 315–343.

Braithwaite, J., and Fisse, B. (1990). On the plausibility of corporate crime theory. In W. S. Laufer and F. Adler, eds. *Advances in criminological theory*, Vol. 2, 15–38. New Brunswick, NJ: Transaction Books.

Burgess, E. W. (1950). Comment, and concluding comment. *American Journal of Sociology*, 56, 32–34.

Caldwell, R. G. (1958). A re-examination of the concept of white-collar crime. *Federal Probation*, 22, 30–36.

Chapman, J. R. (1980). *Economic realities and the female offender.* Lexington, MA: Lexington Books.

Cherney, R. W. (1981). *Populism, progressivism and the transformation of Nebraska politics, 1885–1915.* Lincoln: University of Nebraska Press.

Clinard, M. B. (1952). *The black market: A study of white collar crime.* New York: Rinehart.

Clinard, M. B., and Quinney, R. (1973). *Criminal behavior systems: A typology* (2d ed.). New York: Holt, Rinehart and Winston.

Cohen, A. K. (1990). Criminal actors: Natural persons and collectivities. In School of Justice Studies, Arizona State University, ed. *New direction in the study of justice, law, and social control,* 101–125. New York: Plenum.

Coleman, J. W. (1989). *The criminal elite: The sociology of white collar crime* (2d ed.). New York: St. Martin's Press.

Cressey, D. R. (1953). *Other people's money: A study in the social psychology of embezzlement.* Glencoe, IL: Free Press.

———. (1989). The poverty of theory in corporate crime research. In W. S. Laufer and E. Adler, eds. *Advances in criminological theory,* Vol. 1, 31–56. New Brunswick, NJ: Transaction Books.

Daly, K. (1989). Gender and varieties of white-collar crime. *Criminology,* 27, 769–793.

Edelhertz, H. (1970). *The nature, impact and prosecution of white-collar crime.* Washington, DC: Law Enforcement Assistance Administration, U.S. Department of Justice.

Ermann, M. D., and Lundman, R. J. (1978). Deviant acts by complex organizations: Deviance and social control at the organizational level of analysis. *The Sociological Quarterly,* 19, 56–67.

Geis, G. (1962). Toward a delineation of white-collar offenses. *Sociological Inquiry,* 32, 160–171.

———. (1984). White-collar and corporate crime. In R. E Meier, ed. *Major forms of crime,* 137–166. Beverly Hills: Sage.

Green, G. S. (1990). *Organizational crime.* Chicago: Nelson Hall.

Hagan, J., Nagel-Bernstein, I. H., and Albonetti, C. (1980). The differential sentencing of white-collar offenders in ten federal district courts. *American Sociological Review,* 45, 802–820.

Hagan, J., and Parker, P. (1985). White-collar crime and punishment: The class structure and legal sanctioning of securities violations. *American Sociological Review,* 50, 302–316.

Hartung, F. E. (1950). White-collar offenses in the wholesale meat industry in Detroit. *American Journal of Sociology,* 56, 25–44.

Hirschi, T., and Gottfredson, M. (1987). Causes of white-collar crime. *Criminology,* 25, 957.

Hopkins, A. (1978). *Crime, law and business: The sociological aspects of Australian monopoly law.* Canberra, Australia: Australian Institute of Criminology.

Kadish, S. H. (1963). Some observations on the use of criminal sanctions in enforcing economic regulations. *University of Chicago Law Review,* 30, 423–449.

Kellens, G. (1974). *Banqueroute et banqueroutiers.* Brussels: Dessart et Mardaga.

Levi, M. (1981). *The phantom capitalists: The organisation and control of long-firm fraud.* London: Heinemann.

Liebl, H., and Liebl, K. (1985). *Internationale bibliographie zur wirtschaft-skriminalitat.* Pfaffenweiler, Germany: Centaurus-Verlagsgesellschaft.

Lin, Dong-Mao (1984). *The study of economic crime.* Taipei: Central Police College.

Mason, R., and Calvin, L. D. (1978). A study of admitted income tax evasion. *Law and Society Review,* 13, 73–89.

Newman, D. J. (1958). White-collar crime: An overview and analysis. *Law and Contemporary Problems,* 23, 737.

Nisbet, R. A. (1965). *Makers of modern social science: Emile Durkheim.* Englewood Cliffs, NJ: Prentice Hall.

Pepinsky, H. E. (1976). *Crime and conflict: A study of law and society.* New York: Academic Press.

Quinney, R. (1964). The study of white collar crime: Toward a reorientation in theory and research. *Journal of Criminology, Criminal Law, and Police Science,* 55, 208–214.

Reiss, A. J., Jr., and Biderman, A. D. (1980). *Data sources on white-collar lawbreaking.* Washington, DC: Government Printing Office.

Rheingold, P. D. (1968). The MER/29 story: An instance of successful mass disaster litigation. *California Law Review,* 56, 116–148.

Saxon, M. S. (1980). *White collar crime: The problem and the federal response.* Washington, DC: Congressional Research Service, Library of Congress.

Schrager, L. S., and Short, J. F. Jr. (1977). Toward a sociology of organizational crime. *Social Problems,* 25, 407–419.

Schrenker, E. W. (1986). *No ivory tower: McCarthyism and the universities.* New York: Oxford University Press.

Shapiro, S. P. (1985). The road not taken: The elusive path to criminal prosecution for white-collar offenders. *Law and Society Review,* 19, 179–217.

———. (1990). Collaring the crime, not the criminal: Liberating the concept of white-collar crime. *American Sociological Review,* 55, 346.

Sloan, A. P., Jr., and Sparkes, B. (1941). *Adventures of a white collar man.* New York: Doubleday Doran.

Smith, D. C., Jr. (1981). White-collar crime, organized crime, and the business establishment: Resolving a crisis in criminological theory. In P. Wickman and T. Dailey, eds. *White-collar and economic crime: Multidisciplinary and cross-national perspectives,* 23–38. Lexington, MA: Lexington Books.

Sparks, R. F. (1979). "Crime as business" and the female offender. In F. Adler and R. J. Simon, eds. *The criminology of deviant women,* 171–179. Boston: Houghton Mifflin Company.

Steffensmeier, D. (1989). On the causes of "white-collar" crime. *Criminology,* 27, 345–358.

Sutherland, E. H. (1940). White collar criminality. *American Sociological Review,* 5, 1–12.

———. (1945). Is "white collar crime" crime? *American Sociological Review,* 10, 132–139.

———. (1949). The white collar criminal. In V. C. Branham and S. B. Kutash, *Encyclopedia of Criminology,* 511–515. New York: Philosophical Library.

———. (1949). *White collar crime.* New York: Dryden Press.

———. (1956). Crime of corporations. In A. K. Cohen, A. Lindesmith, and K. Schuessler, eds. *The Sutherland Papers,* 78–96. Bloomington: Indiana University Press.

———. (1983). *White collar crime: The uncut version.* New Haven, CT: Yale University Press.

Tappan, P. W. (1947). Who is the criminal? *American Sociological Review,* 12, 96–102.

Wheeler, S., and Rothman, M. (1982). The organization as weapon in white-collar crime. *Michigan Law Review,* 80, 1403–1426.

Wheeler, S., Weisburd, D., and Bode, N. (1982). Sentencing the white-collar offender: Rhetoric and reality. *American Sociological Review,* 47, 641–659.

Wheeler, S., Weisburd, D., Waring, E., and Bode, N. (1988). White collar crimes and criminals. *American Criminal Law Review,* 25, 346.

2

The Concept of White Collar Crime in Law and Legal Theory

— Stuart P. Green

Use of the term "white collar crime" to refer to some category of illegal, or at least deviant, conduct is now a common feature of our linguistic landscape. Sociologists and criminologists, though disagreeing among themselves about exactly what the term means, have been talking about white collar crime for more than sixty years. The majority of American law schools have a course in the subject. Journalists and politicians refer to it regularly. Law enforcement agencies, prosecutors, and defense attorneys all claim expertise in the area. And the term is increasingly being used outside the United States, both in English and in translation.

Yet, despite its currency in the academic, professional, and popular culture, the term "white collar crime" occurs only rarely in substantive criminal law. The term appears in only a handful of relatively obscure criminal statutes, and the question whether an offense should be considered a white collar crime is one that has arisen in even fewer cases. Or at least that was the case until recently. For it is striking that, in the recently-enacted Sarbanes-Oxley Act—one of the most important pieces of federal criminal law legislation in many years, and the subject of this symposium—the term makes a prominent appearance.

Source: Stuart P. Green, The Concept of White Collar Crime in Law and Legal Theory. *Buffalo Criminal Law Review*, (8)1, 1–34 (April 2004). © 2004 by the Buffalo Criminal Law Center. Published by the University of California Press. Reprinted with permission.

The aim of this article is to inquire into the many meanings of white collar crime. I begin by identifying three fault lines upon which disagreement over use of the term has developed, particularly among social scientists. Here, we find a remarkably wide range of both proposed definitions and terminological alternatives. I then turn to the various ways in which the term has been used by law enforcement officials, prosecutors, and the defense bar, and in law school curricula and legal scholarship. In these contexts, we find a much narrower range of variation than in the social sciences. Next, I consider the use of the term in substantive criminal law, including under the Sarbanes-Oxley Act. I identify five such contexts in which the term has been used, and argue that in only one, or possibly two, of these is such use unproblematic. Finally, I inquire into the appropriate use of the term in the context of legal theory. My contention is that, despite the various problems it poses, the term "white collar crime" remains indispensable. But, I suggest, it needs to be used with care. To this end, I offer the legal theorist a preliminary, context-specific, "family-resemblance"-based framework for thinking about "white collar crime."

I. THE MEANINGS OF "WHITE COLLAR CRIME"

The meaning of white collar crime, like that of other abstract terms in legal, social science, and philosophical discourse (think, for example, of "coercion," "violence," "victim"), is deeply contested.[1] Definitions vary both across and within disciplines and linguistic practices. White collar crime scholars have sometimes sought to find an agreed-upon meaning of the term; other times, they have looked for substitutes. But none of these efforts has been successful: Whatever definitions have been offered have failed to find general acceptance; whatever alternatives have been suggested have proved inadequate. Despite its fundamental awkwardness, the term "white collar crime" is now so deeply embedded within our legal, moral, and social science vocabularies that it could hardly be abandoned. The term persists and proliferates not so much in spite of its lack of definitional precision, but because of it. Speakers attribute to it those meanings that correspond to their own particular analytical or ideological concerns.

My aim in this part is to examine several contexts in which the term white collar crime has been used: by social scientists; among law enforcement officials, prosecutors, and defense attorneys; in the law schools; and in substantive criminal law legislation.

A. Critical Issues in the Battle over the Definition of "White Collar Crime"

One interesting difference between white collar crime and many other contested concepts in law, the humanities, and the social sciences is that its origins are so easily known and so widely acknowledged. The term was first used only sixty-five years ago by Edwin Sutherland, the most influential American criminologist of his day, in a presidential address to the American Sociological Association.[2] Sutherland was famously vague and inconsistent in saying exactly what the term should mean. But even if he had been precise and consistent in his usage, it seems likely that the term would still have generated uncertainty and misunderstanding among other users of the term. The concept that Sutherland was the first to put a label on is one that is so inherently complex and multifaceted that it seems unlikely that one single definition could ever prevail.

The story of how the social sciences have used the term "white collar crime" has been told on many occasions.[3] Rather than repeating that history here, I would like to focus on three critical issues that have arisen in the battle over the meaning of white collar crime: (1) Should the term refer only to activity that is actually criminal, or also to other forms of non-criminal "deviance"?; (2) Should the term refer to behavior (whether criminal or not) engaged in exclusively or primarily by particular kinds of actors, such as those who occupy certain jobs or have a high socioeconomic status; or should it refer instead to some particular kinds of acts?; (3) Assuming that the term should refer to a particular category of criminal acts or other deviant behavior (rather than to actors), what factors should determine which such acts will be included?

1. Should "White Collar Crime" Refer Only to Activity That Is Actually Criminal or Also to Other Forms of Non-Criminal "Deviance"?

To lawyers, the term "crime" denotes a legal category. It refers to particular kinds of conduct that our legal institutions recognize as criminal. Such conduct must be defined in a particular manner, employing certain characteristic concepts such as actus reus and mens rea; it must have a certain public character in the sense that a wrong is committed against the public as a whole and charges are brought in the name of the government or the people; the question whether a crime has been committed must be adjudicated in a particular manner, with various actors playing distinctive roles, employing distinctive procedures and burdens of proof, and recognizing distinctive procedural rights; and it must entail certain characteristic forms of punishment.[4] To lawyers, therefore, it seems obvious that when one talks about "white collar crime," one should be talking about some subcategory of conduct that reflects such criminal law-like characteristics.

To social scientists, this point is less clear. Sociologists and criminologists are concerned less with legal labels and categories than with describing patterns of behavior, its causes, and society's attitudes towards it. Thus, for Sutherland and many of his fellow sociologists, white collar crime is not "crime" in the legal sense of the term.[5] At the time he was writing, much of the activity he was concerned with—such as restraint of trade, violation of patents, unfair labor practices, and adulteration or misbranding of food and drugs—either was not subject to criminal sanctions at all, or, if it was, was rarely prosecuted as such. Indeed, this was precisely Sutherland's point: a good deal of conduct that is at least as, or even more, harmful or wrongful than what has traditionally been viewed as criminal is subject to a range of procedures and penalties that differ from those used for (and is largely excluded from official statistics on) traditional crime.

This is not to say, however, that everyone has agreed with Sutherland's approach to defining white collar crime. Indeed, there have been two distinct responses to the confusion caused by including in the notion of white collar "crime" conduct that is not regarded as criminal by the law. The first is simply to insist, as Paul Tappan and others have done, that only conduct regarded as criminal by the law should be included in the notion of white collar crime.[6] The second is to set aside the term white collar crime and instead use terms such as "elite deviance" to refer not only to actual crimes committed by the elite but also to deviant activities of the elite that do not violate the criminal law.[7]

From a sociological perspective, this second alternative makes some sense. Much of the conduct we are dealing with here could be treated either as: (1) a crime (whether a serious felony or a relatively minor misdemeanor); (2) a non-criminal violation of law (e.g., a tort, breach of contract, or statutory violation); or (3) a merely "deviant," aggressive, or antisocial act which is violative of some informal norm but is not contrary to either criminal or civil law.[8] For example, there is a great deal of conduct falling within the scope of the Securities Exchange Act of 1934, Sherman Act, Clean Water Act, Bankruptcy Code, Tax Code, Truth in Lending Act, False Claims Act, and Federal Food, Drug and Cosmetic Act in which precisely the same conduct can be treated either as a crime or as a civil violation.[9] In light of such overlaps, one can easily imagine a sociological study in which the distinction between deviant activity that is criminal and that which is not would seem arbitrary.

Moreover, to the extent that one is concerned with *reforming* the criminal law—so that currently non-criminalized behavior is made criminal, or currently criminalized behavior is decriminalized—there is much to be said for a general term that refers to both kinds of conduct. Indeed, there is a significant polemical or reformist strain that runs through a good deal of the sociological literature on white collar crime.[10]

From the perspective of law and legal theory, however, the term "elite deviance" is highly problematic. The discipline of criminal law is defined by what is criminal. A wide range of critically important procedural questions turns on whether conduct alleged is violative of the criminal law. To replace the concept of white collar crime with the concept of deviant behavior is thus to blur a distinction that, at least in legal discourse, is foundational.

Moreover, not only is there deviant behavior that is not criminalized, there is also criminal activity that is not generally regarded as deviant. For example, a good deal of regulatory crime involves so-called *malum prohibitum* conduct, which is wrongful only, or primarily, in virtue of its being prohibited.[11] And there are other forms of conduct that may well be regarded as deviant in one social setting (e.g., courtside at Wimbledon), but not in another (say, the trading floor of the Chicago Board of Trade).

A final problem with substituting the term "elite deviance" for "white collar crime" is that much white collar crime is not committed by elites at all. For example, many people would consider insider trading to be the quintessential white collar offense. Yet, as one scholar has noted, the Supreme Court first addressed the subject in a case in which the defendant was not a high-level corporate executive, but rather a "markup man" for a printing press.[12] It thus seems obvious that many cases not only of insider trading, but also of perjury, obstruction of justice, mail fraud, bribery, extortion, and tax fraud involve defendants who cannot be said, in any meaningful sense of the term, to be elite.

2. Should White Collar Crime Refer to Conduct Engaged in by Particular Kinds of Actors, or Only to Particular Sorts of Acts?

To refer to a crime as "white collar" is to draw attention to the characteristics of the person (or entity) that committed it. Indeed, it was the qualities of the offender, rather than those of the offense, that were the main focus of Sutherland's critique. Sutherland sought to question the then-prevalent theory that associated crime with the activities of the lower classes and emphasized poverty as its principal cause. He argued that because there is a significant category of crimes that are committed by persons of wealth, "respectability," and social status, poverty cannot be viewed as the sole, or main, cause of crime.[13] And, in fact, recent cases involving the likes of super-wealthy alleged white collar criminals such as Martha Stewart, Kenneth Lay, Bernard Ebbers, Richard Scrushy, and Dennis Kozlowski seem to demonstrate the truth of such an assertion.

From the perspective of the criminal law, however, such an approach is once again problematic. Deeply rooted equal protection-type norms forbid us from distinguishing among offenders on the basis of wealth, occupation, race, gender, ethnicity, or other personal characteristics.[14] To be sure, there are special immunity rules that apply to certain kinds of governmental actors. But outside of such narrow exceptions, the law is not ordinarily permitted to take account of a defendant's social status in determining criminal liability. Nor, ordinarily, is legal theory.

One alternative is to change the focus of the inquiry from social class to occupation. Thus, Marshall Clinard and Richard Quinney suggest that the term "white collar crime" be replaced with two constitutive terms: "corporate crime" and "occupational crime."[15] The first category is meant to include offenses committed by corporations and their officials for the benefit of the corporation.[16] The second kind of crime is defined as that which is committed "in the course of activity in a legitimate occupation" and is meant to apply to offenses involving persons at all levels of the social structure. As such, occupational crimes can be committed by employees against employers (as in the case of embezzlement), employers against employees (as in the case of workplace safety violations), and by those who provide services and goods to the public (e.g., consumer fraud, health care fraud, procurement fraud, and environmental pollution).[17]

In somewhat more precise legal terminology, we might say that white collar crimes are those offenses that require, as an element, that the offender be (1) a corporate entity or officer of such entity, or (2) performing a particular job or serving in a particular position at the time she committed the offense. And, indeed, such an approach is not at all foreign to the criminal law. For example, one cannot commit the offense of receiving a bribe unless one is performing an act as a member of Congress, a juror, a witness, or "an officer or employee or person acting on behalf of the United States, or any department, agency or branch of Government thereof."[18]

Such an approach would likely forestall the anomaly of having to include under the category of white collar crime cases in which a person of high social status and wealth commits a presumptively non-white collar crime such as murder, rape, or possession of a controlled substance. But it would at the same time create a host of other problems. Much of what could presumably be included within the category of "occupational" crime— including theft of office equipment, workplace assaults, police brutality, and serial killings of patients by doctors and nurses—would not ordinarily be regarded as white collar crime.[19] Even more problematic is the fact that a great many white collar crimes have nothing at all do with either corporations or a defendant's occupation. Indeed, perjury, obstruction of justice, the offering of bribes, extortion, false statements, criminal contempt, tax evasion, and most intellectual property offenses are only rarely committed by employees against employers, employers against employees, or by those who provide goods and services to the public; and only rarely involve corporations.[20] In short, there is a vast range of presumptively white collar crime that falls outside the categories of both corporate and occupational crime.

3. Assuming that White Collar Crime Should Refer to Some Particular Group of Criminal Offenses, What Factors Should Determine Which Offenses Will Be Included?

For the remainder of this article, let us assume that, at least in the limited context of law and legal theory, the term "white collar crime" should refer neither to non-criminalized, deviant behavior, nor to crimes committed by offenders holding particular kinds of jobs or enjoying a particular social status. Instead, let us use "white collar crime" to refer exclusively to a category of criminal offenses that reflects some particular group of legal or moral characteristics.

Not surprisingly, this is the approach taken by various lawyers and law enforcement officials interested in formulating a standard definition of white collar crime. For example, in 1970, U.S. Department of Justice official Herbert Edlehertz described white collar crime as "an illegal act or series of illegal acts committed by nonphysical means and by concealment or guile, to obtain money or property, or to obtain business advantage."[21] Nineteen years later, the FBI defined white collar crime as

> those illegal acts which are characterized by deceit, concealment, or violation of trust and which are not dependent upon the application or threat of physical force or violence. Individuals and organizations commit these acts to obtain money, property, or services; to avoid the payment or loss of money or services; or to secure personal or business advantage.[22]

One of the most influential formulations has been offered by the U.S. Department of Justice, Bureau of Justice Statistics, which defines white collar crime as:

> [n]onviolent crime for financial gain committed by means of deception by persons whose occupational status is entrepreneurial, professional or semi-professional and utilizing their special occupational skills and opportunities; also, nonviolent crimes for financial gain utilizing deception and committed by anyone having special technical and professional knowledge of business and government, irrespective of the person's occupation.[23]

From the perspective of legal analysis, an act-focused definitional approach such as these is much preferable to the actor-focused approach discussed above.[24] Nevertheless, each of the particular definitions offered presents significant problems: First, it is unclear what it means to commit a crime by "nonphysical" means, since it is generally assumed that every crime commission requires, at a minimum, a physical act.[25] Nor is it clear even what is meant for a crime to be "nonviolent."[26] For example, would the release of toxic chemicals into a public water source in violation of the Clean Water Act, or the sale of adulterated drugs in violation of the Federal Food, Drug, and Cosmetic Act, qualify as such?

Second, there is virtually no explanation for why the definition of white collar crime should be limited to those offenses committed for the purpose of obtaining "money," "property," or "services," or to secure "financial gain" or "business advantage." To the extent that such an approach would exclude many cases of presumptively core white collar offenses such as perjury, bribery, and obstruction of justice; and at the same time include presumptively nonwhite collar offenses such as larceny, robbery, and embezzlement, it would seem to require some justification. Indeed, this may explain why some scholars now prefer the term "economic" or "business crime" to "white collar crime."[27]

Third, and even more problematic, is the unexplained use of the terms "deception," "concealment," "guile," and "violation of trust." Even if the meaning of such terms were not highly contested (as it is), one could not help but wonder whether this limited list of moral wrongs would fully capture the moral content of white collar offenses such as insider trading, tax evasion, extortion, blackmail, obstruction of justice, and many regulatory and intellectual property crimes. This is a question that I have addressed extensively elsewhere and to which I return briefly at the end of this article.[28]

B. Law Enforcement, Prosecutors, and the Defense Bar

Having looked broadly at the kinds of definitional issues that have revolved around the term "white collar crime," we can now focus more narrowly on how the term is used in a number of important, specifically law-related contexts which the definitional literature has, for the most part, ignored.[29] Let us consider, first, the defense bar. Hundreds of law firms and thousands of private lawyers throughout the United States and, to a lesser extent, Great Britain, now hold themselves out as specialists in what they refer to as "white collar" criminal defense work (although there does not yet appear to be any official certification as such).[30] One indication of the prominence of white collar crime as a criminal law subspecialty is the existence of the American Bar Association's Section on Criminal Justice Committee on White Collar Crime. Another is the monthly column on white collar crime in the *Champion*, the magazine of the National Association of Criminal Defense Lawyers. Moreover, there is a growing industry in continuing legal education programs, newsletters, books, and other materials designed for the white collar criminal law practitioner.[31]

The emergence of white collar crime as a distinct practice area can also be seen among prosecutorial offices and law enforcement agencies.[32] Specialists in white collar crime can be found in numerous prosecutorial offices at the federal, state, and local level;[33] at the FBI and in local police departments;[34] and in the U.S. Department of Justice Criminal Division's Section on Fraud, which is "charged with directing the Federal law enforcement effort against fraud and white-collar crime."[35] The National White Collar Crime Center, a federally funded, non-profit corporation whose membership comprises primarily law enforcement agencies, state regulatory bodies with criminal investigative authority, and state and local prosecution offices, has as its focus the assistance of state and local prosecutors in the battle against high tech and economic crime.[36] And some agencies, including the Department of Justice, even have offices that deal specifically with the *victims* of fraud and other white collar offenses.[37]

Not surprisingly, the definition of exactly what constitutes "white collar crime" tends to vary within and among these various constituencies, though to a lesser extent than in the case of the social scientists. Law enforcement officials, prosecutors, and defense attorneys are all more inclined than sociologists to use the term to refer to acts rather than actors, and to real crime rather than mere deviance.[38]

Some white collar criminal defense lawyers emphasize their experience in representing individual and corporate defendants in criminal cases. Others highlight their skill in establishing and administering corporate compliance programs and conducting internal investigations. Almost all claim expertise in dealing with the complex procedural and evidentiary contexts in which many white collar crime prosecutions occur. Among the specific "white collar" areas in which expertise is frequently claimed are securities fraud and insider trading; health care fraud and False Claims Act cases; antitrust; banking, financial, and accounting fraud; environmental and health and safety violations; RICO; trade secret theft; and customs violations.[39]

A similar range of usage can be observed among prosecutors and law enforcement agencies. The *White Collar Crime Reporter,* perhaps the leading practice-oriented publication in the field, covers insider trading, forfeiture, fraud, money laundering, foreign corrupt practices, health care fraud, perjury, espionage, and trade secrets. The U.S. Sentencing Commission, in its Sourcebook of Federal Sentencing Statistics, defines its "non-fraud white collar category" to "include the following offense types: embezzlement, forgery/counterfeiting, bribery, money laundering, and tax."[40] And the Department of Justice speaks of its section on white collar crime as being concerned with various forms of fraud—corporate, financial institution, securities, insurance, telemarketing, government program, Internet, and banking; identity theft; and the bribery of foreign officials.[41]

C. Legal Education and Scholarship

Within the last generation, white collar crime has developed into a standard subject in the curriculum of most American law schools. There are now at least four major casebooks, two hornbooks, an anthology, an annual student-edited law review survey, and scores of law school courses expressly devoted to the subject.[42] Indeed, white collar, federal, business, and environmental crime are among the most rapidly proliferating subjects in the curricula of American law schools.[43]

Law professors are clearly less inclined than their social science counterparts to think of white collar crime in terms of either offender characteristics or mere deviance. Almost all law school courses and texts in white collar crime deal with the general principles of corporate criminality and with the specific offenses of mail and wire fraud, perjury, obstruction of justice, conspiracy, and RICO. But beyond that there is little consensus. Many courses emphasize white collar crime as a body of substantive law, while others focus on the procedures associated with its prosecution, particularly in the federal courts. Some, but by no means all, of the courses emphasize constitutional issues raised by the supposedly increasing federalization of criminal law. Others cover grand jury and forfeiture proceedings. Still others deal with specific offenses such as insider trading and other forms of securities fraud, computer crimes, bribery, gratuities, money laundering, environmental and other regulatory crimes, extortion, false claims, bank fraud, and tax crimes.

The almost universal inclusion of conspiracy and RICO in the law school white collar crime curriculum is, in some respects, surprising. Both are essentially inchoate or procedural crimes, in which the predicate offense is often far removed from the domain of what would ordinarily be considered white collar crime. (Under RICO, for example, the definition of "racketeering activity" includes, among many other offenses, both sexual exploitation of children and the use of interstate commercial facilities in the commission of murder for hire[44]—neither of which could even remotely be considered a white collar crime.) The reason for such inclusion seems to be simply that such law school courses are designed to prepare students for the complex procedural context in which white collar criminal law is practiced, regardless of the actual substance of offenses studied.

In any event, given the tortuous definitional history of white collar crime in the social sciences, it is somewhat surprising that legal academics have expended relatively little effort in defining white collar crime or explaining the criteria upon which specific offenses are included in a given curriculum. Most of the textbooks and law review literature deal with the definitional question only briefly,[45] and some not at all.[46] Rather, there seems to be an assumption that the subject matter of white collar criminal law can be defined simply by reference to the offenses that are actually covered in a given course or casebook.

D. Substantive Criminal Law

In 1992, the sociologist Gilbert Geis, perhaps the most influential scholar of white collar crime since Edwin Sutherland, wrote that "no such designation as 'white collar crime' is to be found in the statute books."[47] By this, Geis presumably meant that "white collar crime" is not a category of offenses in substantive criminal law and has no specific doctrinal significance. But, in fact, Geis was only half right. Though its use as such is admittedly rare, there are at least five contexts in which "white collar crime" appears in substantive criminal law.

First, the term has been used to identify aggravating circumstances that are relevant to sentencing. California Penal Code section 186.11 imposes what it refers to as a "white collar crime enhancement" for "[a]ny person who commits two or more related felonies, a material element of which is fraud or embezzlement."[48] The enhancement consists of potentially higher fines and other penalties than would otherwise apply.[49]

Second, the term has been used to define a class of victims who are entitled to certain rights. Florida Statutes section 775.0844 authorizes various remedies (including restitution) for victims of "white collar crime," defined as including computer-related crimes, fraudulent practices, issuing worthless checks, bribery and corruption, forgery and counterfeiting, abuse and exploitation of the elderly and disabled, and racketeering.[50]

Third, the term has been used to define the jurisdiction of certain state prosecuting officials. Mississippi Code section 7-5-59(2) gives the Mississippi Attorney General jurisdiction to conduct "official corruption investigations and such other white-collar crime investigations that are of statewide interest or which are in the protection of public rights."[51] Subsection (1) in turn defines "white-collar crime and official corruption" to consist of a range of frauds (mail, wire, radio, television, computer), false advertising, extortion, bribery, and embezzlement by public officials. Similarly, Virgin Islands Code title 3, section 118 establishes within the Department of Law a White Collar Crime and Public Corruption Section "to institute aggressive prosecution of white collar crime and corruption."[52]

Fourth, the term has been used in the creation of funding mechanisms for law enforcement programs and research facilities. Title 42 U.S.C. § 3722(c)(2)(F) establishes a National Institute of Justice within the Department of Justice, which is charged with, among other things, developing programs to improve the ability of states and local governments to "combat and prevent white collar crime," a term that is elsewhere defined to refer to "an illegal act or series of illegal acts committed by nonphysical means and by concealment or guile, to obtain money or property, to avoid the payment or loss of money or property, or to obtain business or personal advantage."[53] Similarly, California Penal Code section 13848(b)(1) creates a statewide program to assist local enforcement and district attorneys in the fight against "white-collar crime, such as check, automated teller machine, and credit card fraud, committed by means of electronic or computer-related media."[54]

Finally, the term has been used in the title or section heading of various substantive criminal law provisions. A good example is the District of Columbia Theft and White Collar Crimes Act of 1982, the stated goal of which is to "reform the criminal laws of the District of Columbia relating to theft, receipt of stolen property, fraud, forgery extortion, blackmail, bribery, perjury, obstruction of justice, and criminal libel."[55] Here, the term "white collar crime" has no specific doctrinal significance; rather, it is used as a label to signify a general legislative intent that white collar crime be distinguished from mere street crime.

Near the end of this paper, I will offer a critique of each of these five uses.[56]

E. The Sarbanes-Oxley Act

The most significant piece of legislation ever to use the term "white collar crime" is undoubtedly the Sarbanes-Oxley Act. The Act was passed amidst a sense of urgency, one might even say panic, that surrounded a string of spectacular corporate crime scandals that came to light during 2001 and 2002, involving firms such as WorldCom, Adelphia, Tyco, Arthur Andersen, and, most infamously, Enron. The statute enacts a multi-pronged approach to the prevention and punishment of white collar criminality: It creates a variety of new offenses, imposes stiffer penalties for existing offenses, requires companies to have audit committees, creates a board to regulate auditors, imposes new duties on CEOs and CFOs, makes it easier to file class actions against corporations and directors, imposes new regulatory compliance requirements, and expands the authority of the SEC over corporate governance matters.[57]

Title IX of the Act, which has five substantive sections, is entitled "White-Collar Crime Penalty Enhancements." Sections 902, 903, and 904 increase the penalties for attempt and conspiracy, mail and wire fraud, and violation of section 501 of ERISA, respectively. Section 906 makes it a crime for CEOs and CFOs to fail to submit certain financial statements required by the Securities Exchange Act of 1934. Section 905, entitled "Amendment to Sentencing Guidelines Relating to Certain White-Collar Offenses," is the provision that is of particular relevance here.

Section 905 directed the U.S. Sentencing Commission to "review and, as appropriate, amend the Federal Sentencing Guidelines and related policy statements to implement the provisions of this Act."[58] In carrying out this mission, the Commission was specifically instructed to "ensure that the sentencing guidelines and policy statements reflect the serious nature of the offenses and the penalties set forth in this Act, the growing incidence of serious fraud offenses which are identified above, and the need to modify the sentencing guidelines and policy statements to deter, prevent, and punish such offenses."[59]

The legislative history to section 905, which was cosponsored by Senators Orrin Hatch and Joseph Biden, clearly reflects the view that there is a disparity in how white collar and street crimes are treated under federal law, and that such disparity should be reduced or eliminated. According to Senator Biden:

> One thing most of our hearing witnesses agreed on was that there is a "penalty gap" between white collar crimes and other crimes. For example, if a kid steals your car and drives it over the 14th Street Bridge into Northern Virginia, he could get up to 10 years in jail under the Federal interstate auto theft law. Yet, if a corporate CEO steals your pension and commits a criminal violation under ERISA, he is only subject to 1 year in jail.[60]

Earlier, Senator Hatch had remarked:

> A person who steals, defrauds, or otherwise deprives unsuspecting
> Americans of their life savings—no less than any other criminal—
> should be held accountable under our system of justice for the full
> weight of the harm he or she has caused. Innocent lives have been
> devastated by the crook who cooks the books of a publicly traded
> company, the charlatan who sells phony bonds, and the confidence
> man who runs a Ponzi scheme out there. These sorts of white-collar
> criminals should find no soft spots in our laws or in their ultimate
> sentences, but all too often have done so.[61]

Whether there really is a disparity in the way comparable street and
white collar crimes are punished,[62] and whether title IX and the Sentencing Guidelines that were promulgated in response to it[63] are the right
way to deal with such a disparity are surely matters that are open to
debate.[64] My concern here, however, is less with evaluating the wisdom
of the Act than with observing how it deals with the concept of white collar crime; and here I want to make four observations: First, Congress
seems to have thought that the concept of "white collar crime" was sufficiently well-recognized that it could be used in the title of an important
federal statute. Second, it saw no need to define the concept anywhere in
the Act. Third, it did not assign the term any specific doctrinal significance. Finally, its use of the term seems to have been primarily rhetorical—as a way to signal a shift in attitudes towards the disposition of such
offenses. As such, the Sarbanes-Oxley Act represents a significant step in
the development of the concept of white collar crime.

F. Outside the United States

As we have seen, the term "white collar crime" was invented and
propagated primarily by American scholars in the social sciences. Given the
serious definitional controversy it has spawned, however, it is surprising
that the term has been used so broadly outside the United States as well.
The idea that there is some distinct category of crimes that corresponds to
one or another conception of white collar crime seems to have struck a
chord in a remarkably wide range of legal, academic, and popular cultures.

The term "white collar crime" has been translated literally into
French (*crime en col blanc*[65]), German (*Weisse-Kragen-Kriminalität*[66]), Ital-
ian (*criminalità dei colletti bianchi*[67]), Norwegian (*hvit krageforbrytelse*[68]),
Portuguese (*crime branco de colarinho*[69]), and Spanish (*crimen blanco del
collar*[70]). In addition, it has appeared in English-language commentary
referring to criminal activity in countries as diverse as Australia,[71]
China,[72] Greece,[73] India,[74] Israel,[75] Malaysia,[76] Mexico,[77] South Africa,[78]
Tanzania,[79] and Zimbabwe.[80]

Outside the United States, however, the term has been favored more
by social scientists and journalists than by academic lawyers.[81] Perhaps

for the reasons discussed above, foreign legal academics have been reluctant to use "white collar crime" as an umbrella term for a category of crimes broad enough to include the range of offenses dealt with in a typical American law school casebook. Indeed, few British or European law schools offer a course in white collar crime. Instead, the usual practice has been to speak of "corporate," "economic," "business," or "administrative" crime, each as a separate category, rather than of a unified category of white collar crime.[82]

II. SALVAGING "WHITE COLLAR CRIME" AS A CONCEPT OF LAW AND LEGAL THEORY

If one were starting from scratch, "white collar crime" is hardly the term one would choose to describe the concept we have been dealing with here. The term was vague and imprecise when first conceived, and seems even more so today. Frequently, it means exactly the opposite of what it says, as when it is used to refer to merely deviant, non-criminalized activity. Sometimes it has been used overinclusively, such as when it refers to RICO, conspiracy, and corporate homicide. At other times it has been used underinclusively, as when it excludes various regulatory crimes and non-business-related offenses such as perjury and obstruction of justice. It has been used to refer to characteristics of persons rather than of offenses in a manner that is unacceptable within the framework of equal protection norms. Its ideological overtones are significant and, in the pursuit of objective scientific and legal analysis, unforgivable. And although it was coined only sixty years ago, the point at which all parties might agree on a definition has long since passed.

In light of all these problems, is there any justification for continuing to talk about white collar crime? It would be presumptuous of me, an academic lawyer, to offer advice to social scientists, law enforcement officials, practicing attorneys, social activists, or journalists, among others, on whether and, if so, how, the term should be used. From the perspective of legal theory, however, it seems to me that—in the absence of any viable alternative, and in light of its powerful cultural resonances—the term white collar crime *is* worth preserving, provided that certain features are understood, and various caveats observed.

A. "White Collar Crime" as a Family Resemblance Category

We would do better to think of "white collar crime" as entailing a collection of what philosophers call "family resemblances," rather than as susceptible to definition through a precise set of necessary and sufficient conditions.[83] According to linguist George Lakoff, under the traditional, Aristotelian, or classical approach to classification, categories are "assumed to be abstract containers, with things either inside or outside the category. Things [are] assumed to be in the same category if and only if they ha[ve] certain properties in common. And the properties they ha[v]e in common [are] taken as defining the category."[84] Under the classical model, then, categories are thought to have clear boundaries and be defined by common properties. Such an approach seems appropriate in the context of defining criminal offenses. We want to know, to the extent possible, precisely which acts will fall within the category of, say, "murder," "rape," or "theft," and which will not.

But many concepts in the social sciences, the humanities, the arts, and in our daily lives are simply not susceptible to such precise in-or-out definition. Such concepts have "fuzzy" boundaries that do not fit into the classical model. Wittgenstein gives the example of the category "game."[85] Some games involve competition and strategizing (like chess and capture the flag). Others involve merely amusement (like ring-around-the-rosy). With categories of this sort, it seems impossible to find any single collection of properties that all members (and only those members) share. Instead, categories like "game" seem to consist of a collection of members who share what Wittgenstein called "family resemblances."[86] Just as family members may resemble each other in a variety of different traits (say, hair or eye color, facial features, or physical stature), what defines the category of games is not some single well-defined collection of common properties, but rather a collection of different resemblances, a whole series of similarities and relationships shared by the class.[87]

It seems obvious that, at least for purposes of legal theory, "white collar crime" is better approached as a family resemblance-, rather than classical-, type category. As the discussion above suggests, it is probably impossible to find consensus on any single, well-defined collection of properties that all members of the category (and only those members) share. Instead, the term "white collar crime" should be understood to refer to a loosely defined collection of criminal offenses, forms of deviance, kinds of offenders, and moral concepts that share a series of similarities and relationships.

B. Use of "White Collar Crime" in Substantive Criminal Law Legislation

If I am correct that "white collar crime" is best thought of as a family resemblance-type category, then it would seem to follow that the term would be mostly unsuitable in the realm of substantive criminal law. We expect our criminal offense categories to be sharply defined. Citizens and decision makers need to know, as precisely as can be made out, what it is that constitutes "murder," a "felony," or "self-defense," and what does not. We aspire to precision in defining mens rea and actus reus elements, defenses, jurisdictional elements, and procedural rights. The fuzzier the boundaries of such concepts, the weaker, it would seem, is the moral authority of our law.

Let us reconsider each of the five ways in which the term "white collar crime" has been used in substantive criminal law legislation. The first is as a label for aggravating circumstances relevant to sentencing.[88] As a matter of policy, we might well want to enhance punishments for crimes (such as certain thefts) when they are committed by white collar-like means such as deception or breaches of trust. (Alternatively, we might wish to *reduce* punishments for crimes that are committed through white collar-like, non-violent means.) Without a specific provision defining which offenses are to be covered, however, reference to a prototypical category such as white collar crime is likely to lead to obvious problems of legality, as it surely did in the case of the Alaska provision referred to above, in which the court was forced to refer to a dictionary in determining whether to apply the white collar crime aggravator.[89]

A related problem would occur under statutes that use the term to define a class of victims entitled to compensation or other procedural rights.[90] Although the doctrine of *nulla poena sine lege* would not directly be implicated (since no issue of criminal punishment would be at stake), the vague quality of the term would nevertheless result in a serious problem of statutory ambiguity. Likewise are those statutes in which an otherwise undefined group of white collar crimes delineates the prosecutor's jurisdiction.[91]

In each of these three cases, problems of statutory ambiguity and legality could be avoided only if the term "white collar crime" were defined explicitly, by referring to covered offenses either by name or, better yet, specific statutory provision. (This, in fact, is precisely the approach that has been followed in the Florida and Mississippi statutes, though apparently not under the Virgin Islands and Alaska statutes.) In cases in which the term *is* so defined, it would perform no real doctrinal function, however. Rather, it would be intended primarily to add rhetorical force to the statutes in which it appears.

The problem of definitional ambiguity seems to me considerably less serious, however, in the case of statutes that create funding mechanisms for law enforcement programs and research facilities, as under the federal and California schemes.[92] One can easily imagine why a state or the federal government would want to provide special resources for the fight against some collection of complex business frauds, corruption, and the like. In such circumstances, a strict, classical category would be unnecessary, since no cognizable legal rights would likely be affected by the determination that a particular offense is or is not a white collar crime. Indeed, given the likelihood that some investigations will target persons suspected of committing both white collar and non-white collar crimes, a certain amount of fuzziness in defining an agency's responsibilities would probably be welcome.[93] Thus, this seems to me a sensible use of the term.

As for statutes such as the Sarbanes-Oxley and District of Columbia Theft and White Collar Crimes Acts, it appears that the term "white collar crime" is serving what is essentially a signaling or symbolic function, rather than a definitional one. Once again, no specific legal rights are affected by how the term is defined. In each case, the legislature is doing nothing more than sending a message that it regards the offenses covered as part of a loosely defined moral or political, rather than legal, category.

C. Use of "White Collar Crime" in Legal Theory

In this concluding section, I want to consider the extent to which the term "white collar crime" might provide a useful label in criminal law theory. Given the substantial disagreement over its meaning, one might well wonder whether it would make sense to abandon the term entirely and rely instead on some alternative term or collection of terms, such as "economic," "business," "corporate," or "occupational" crime. To put it another way, we need to ask whether there is some defining group of family resemblances that is characteristic of white collar crime and is not adequately captured by the alternatives.

In approaching this question, my aim is not to offer yet another alternative definition of white collar crime. Instead, I want to suggest an appropriate *methodology* for developing such a definition. And, inasmuch as legal theory is concerned with the moral content of criminal offenses, it is in that realm that we will want to look in developing such a methodology.

As I have described elsewhere,[94] the moral content of criminal offenses can be divided into three basic elements: *Culpability* reflects the mental element with which an offense is committed, such as intent, knowledge, or belief. *Harmfulness* reflects the degree to which a criminal act causes, or risks causing, harm to others or self. And *moral wrongfulness* involves the way in which the criminal act entails a violation of moral norms. Following this approach, then, one way to determine which offenses should be included within the category of white collar crime would be to ask whether—in terms of culpability, harmfulness, and wrongfulness—a particular offense "resembles" other offenses within that category.

Drawing on work I have published elsewhere,[95] I would argue that white collar crime does differ from non-white collar crime in all three of the dimensions identified: First, the harms that white collar crimes cause (think, for example, of bribery, tax evasion, and insider trading[96]) tend to be more diffuse and aggregative than in the case of conventional crime; and it is often harder to say who (or what, in the case of governmental institutions or corporations) has been victimized, and how. Second, white collar crime tends to involve certain distinctive forms of moral wrongfulness: not only deception and breach of trust,[97] but also cheating, exploitation, coercion, promise-breaking, and disobedience. Third, white collar offenses frequently reflect a distinctive role for mens rea: They either require no mens rea at all (as is the case with many regulatory offenses), or make proof of mens rea so important that conduct performed without it not only fails to expose the actor to criminal liability, but may not be regarded as wrongful at all.

My point, of course, is not that all white collar offenses (and only such offenses) exhibit such qualities. If we expect to find some fixed and universally-agreed-upon collection of necessary and sufficient conditions that define the category of white collar crime across all disciplines, we are bound to be disappointed.[98] Nevertheless, I believe that it would be a mistake to give up on the term entirely. Provided that we recognize its context-specific, family-resemblance-like-quality, "white collar crime" remains for the legal theorist a term both powerfully evocative and ultimately indispensable.

NOTES

[1] Kip Schlegel has compared the controversy over the meaning of "white collar crime" to that over the meaning of "privacy." Recalling Status, Power and Respectibility [*sic*] in the Study of White-Collar Crime, at 98, in National White Collar Crime Center Workshop, Definitional Dilemma: Can and Should There be a Universal Definition of White Collar Crime?, at http://www.nw3c.org/research_topics.html (last visited Oct. 22, 2004).

[2] Edwin H. Sutherland, White-Collar Criminality, 5 *Am. Soc. Rev.* 1 (1940), reprinted in *White-Collar Crime* (Gilbert Geis & Robert F. Meier eds., rev. ed. 1977); see also Edwin H. Sutherland, *White Collar Crime: The Uncut Version* (1983).

[3] See, e.g., Gilbert Geis, White-Collar Crime: What Is It?, in *White-Collar Crime Reconsidered* 31–52 (Kip Schlegel & David Weisburd eds., 1992); David Weisburd et al., *Crimes of the Middle Classes: White-Collar Offenders in the Federal Courts* 3–9 (1991); Stanton Wheeler & Dan Kahan, White-Collar Crime: History of an Idea, in 4 *Encyclopedia of Crime & Justice* (2d ed. 2002); Proceedings of the Academic Workshop, National White Collar Crime Center, Definitional Dilemma: Can and Should There Be a Universal Definition of White Collar Crime? (1996).

[4] See generally Antony Duff, Theories of Criminal Law, Stanford Encyclopedia of Philosophy, at http://plato.stanford.edu/entries/criminal-law (last substantive content change Oct. 14, 2002).

[5] Sutherland acknowledged this point in his essay, Is "White Collar Crime" Crime?, 10 *Am. Soc. Rev.* 132 (1945).

[6] Paul W. Tappan, Who Is the Criminal?, 12 *Am. Soc. Rev.* 96 (1947); see also Robert G. Caldwell, A Re-Examination of the Concept of White-Collar Crime, in *White-Collar Criminal: The Offender in Business and the Professions* 376 (Gilbert Geis ed., 1968); Herbert Edelhertz, *The Nature, Impact and Prosecution of White-Collar Crime* (1970).

[7] See, e.g., David Simon & D. Stanley Eitzen, *Elite Deviance* (1982).

[8] I have previously described the wide range of means—informal, institutional, civil, and criminal—with which society deals with the "deviant" act of plagiarism. Stuart P. Green, Plagiarism, Norms, and the Limits of Theft Law: Some Observations on the Use of Criminal Sanctions in Enforcing Intellectual Property Rights, 54 *Hastings L. J.* 167 (2002). On the narrower overlap between civil and criminal law, see John E.

Conklin, *"Illegal But Not Criminal": Business Crime in America* (1977); Stuart P. Green, Moral Ambiguity in White Collar Criminal Law, 18 *Notre Dame J.L. Ethics & Pub. Pol'y* 501 (2004).

[9] See, e.g., Margaret V. Sachs, Harmonizing Civil and Criminal Enforcement of Federal Regulatory Statutes: The Case of the Securities Exchange Act of 1934, 2001 *U. Ill. L. Rev.* 1025, 1027. See also Andrew Ashworth, Is the Criminal Law a Lost Cause?, 116 *L.Q. Rev.* 225, 234-35 (2000) (on blurring of civil and criminal categories in intellectual property and competition law); Lawrence M. Solan, Statutory Inflation and Institutional Choice, 44 *Wm. & Mary L. Rev.* 2209 (2003).

[10] See, e.g., Susan P. Shapiro, The New Moral Entrepreneurs: Corporate Crime Crusaders, 12 *Contemp. Soc.* 304 (1983) (criticizing this tendency). Although Sutherland himself claimed that his theory was "for the purpose of developing the theories of criminal behavior, not for the purpose of muckraking or reforming anything except criminology," see Sutherland, White-Collar Criminality, supra note 2, at 1, his real motives surely included the latter. To be sure, many students of white collar crime cannot help but be incensed by the fact that such conduct, which is often more harmful than traditional street crime, has traditionally been dealt with more leniently.

[11] I have explored this concept in Stuart P. Green, Why It's a Crime to Tear the Tag Off a Mattress: Overcriminalization and the Moral Content of Regulatory Offenses, 46 *Emory L. J.* 1533 (1997); see also Douglas Husak, *Malum Prohibitum* and Retributivism, in *Defining Crimes: Essays on the Criminal Law's Special Part* (R. A. Duff & Stuart P. Green eds., 2005).

[12] J. Kelly Strader, The Judicial Politics of White Collar Crime, 50 *Hastings L. J.* 1199, 1207 (1999) (citing *United States v. Chiarella*, 455 U.S. 222 (1980)).

[13] Sutherland, White-Collar Criminality, supra note 2.

[14] Cf. Kenneth S. Abraham & John C. Jeffries, Jr., Punitive Damages and the Rule of Law: The Role of the Defendant's Wealth, 18 *J. Leg. Stud.* 415, 423 (1989) ("Punishment based on the characteristics of the actor, rather than on specific misconduct, threatens fundamental notions of freedom from governmental constraint.")

[15] Marshall B. Clinard & Richard Quinney, *Criminal Behavior Systems: A Typology* (2d ed. 1973); see also Gilbert Geis, Toward a Delineation of White-Collar Offenses, 32 *Soc. Inquiry* 160 (1962).

[16] Geis, supra note 15, at 189. I address the limits of corporate criminality in Stuart P. Green, The Criminal Prosecution of Local Governments, 72 *N.C. L. Rev.* 1197 (1994).

[17] Geis, supra note 3, at 39–40.

[18] 18 U.S.C. § 201(a)(1) (2004). I address the question of who can be a "bribee" more generally in Stuart P. Green, What's Wrong With Bribery, in *Defining Crimes: Essays on the Criminal Law's Special Part*, supra note 11.

[19] Here, it should be pointed out that there is a range of ways in which the term "occupational crime" has been used. For example, David O. Friedrichs has suggested that the term should be restricted to illegal and unethical activities committed for individual financial gain in the context of a legitimate occupation—thereby excluding crimes such as workplace assault. Occupational Crime, Occupational Deviance, and Workplace Crime: Sorting Out the Difference, 2 *Crim. Just.* 243 (2002). Others, such as Gary Green, have used the term much more broadly. *Occupational Crime* (2001). My point is simply that the term is a poor substitute for "white collar crime."

[20] Cf. Edelhertz, supra note 6 (arguing that we ought not to exclude from the definition of white collar crime offenses such as tax evasion, receiving illegal social security payments, and consumer fraud).

[21] Id. at 3 (emphasis omitted).

22 U.S. Department of Justice, Federal Bureau of Investigation, *White Collar Crime: A Report to the Public* 3 (1989).

23 Bureau of Justice Statistics, U.S. Dep't of Justice, *Dictionary of Criminal Justice Data Terminology* 215 (2d ed. 1981).

24 Cf. Susan P. Shapiro, Collaring the Crime, Not the Criminal: Reconsidering the Concept of White-Collar Crime, 55 *Am. Soc. Rev.* 346 (1990) (endorsing act-based approach).

25 See generally Michael Moore, *Act and Crime: The Philosophy of Action and Its Implications for Criminal Law* (1993).

26 "Violence," of course, is another famously contested term. See, e.g., C.A.J. Coady, The Idea of Violence, 3 *J. Applied Phil.* 3 (1986); Robert Paul Wolff, On Violence, 66 *J. Phil.* 601 (1969).

27 See, e.g., Harry First, *Business Crime: Cases and Materials* (1990); Frank O. Bowman, III, Coping With "Loss": A Re-Examination of Sentencing Federal Economic Crimes under the Guidelines, 51 *Vand. L. Rev.* 461 (1998); Jayne W. Barnard, Allocution for Victims of Economic Crimes, 77 *Notre Dame L. Rev.* 39 (2001). In my view, the problem with the term "economic" crime is that it fails to capture the crucial moral distinction between presumptively white collar crimes such as fraud and ordinary street crimes such as larceny. For a discussion of this distinction, see Stuart P. Green, Deceit and the Classification of Crimes: Federal Rule of Evidence 609(a)(2) and the Origins of *Crimen Falsi*, 90 *J. Crim. L. & Criminology* 1087, 1093–94 & n.21 (2000). For a contrary view, see Bowman, supra, at 490–97.

28 See infra note 95 and accompanying text.

29 See sources cited supra note 3.

30 See generally Larry Smith, Jury Split on Status of White-Collar Practice at Major Firms, 10 *Inside Litig.* 1 (1996); Larry Smith, Fastest-Growing Practice Areas, 17 *Of Counsel* 1 (1998). Even elite corporate firms that have not traditionally been engaged in criminal defense work now claim expertise in white collar criminal law. See, e.g., David Polk & Wordwell, White Collar Crime, at http://www.dpw.com/practice/litwhitecollar.htm (last visited Dec. 1, 2004); and Arnold & Porter, White Collar Crime, at http://www.arnoldporter.com/practice.cfm?practice_ld=34 (website of Arnold & Porter) (last visited Oct. 25, 2004).

31 See, e.g. *White Collar Crime Reporter* (published by Thomson West legal publisher); see also *Business Crimes Bulletin* (published by Law Journal Newsletters); Practicing Law Institute, *Advanced White Collar Criminal Practice* (1983); American Bar Association, *White Collar Crime* (1997); Joel M. Androphy, *White Collar Crime* (2003); F. Lee Bailey & Henry B. Rothblatt, *Defending Business and White Collar Crimes* (2d ed. 1984); Otto G. Obermaier & Robert G. Morvillo, *White Collar Crime: Business and Regulatory Offenses* (2001).

32 As the Supreme Court recognized in *Braswell v. United States*, 487 U.S. 99, 115–16 (1988), white collar crime cases present distinctive challenges to government prosecutors in terms of discovery and proof. Thanks to Peter Henning for bringing this case to my attention.

33 See, e.g., Norfolk District Attorney's Office, White Collar Crime Unit, at http://www.state.ma.us/da/norfolk/special_whitecollarcrime.html (Norfolk District Attorney's Office, Massachusetts) (last visited Oct. 25, 2004); Thirteenth Judicial Circuit District Attorney, White Collar Crime Team, at http://www.mobileda.org/team-white_collar.htm (Mobile, Alabama, District Attorney) (last visited Oct. 25, 2004); City of St. Louis Circuit Attorney, White Collar Crime and Fraud Unit, at http://sticin.missouri.org/circuitattorney/wcfraud.cfin (St. Louis Circuit Attorney) (last visited Oct. 25, 2004) (white collar crimes defined as theft and embezzlement, identify theft, elder abuse, bribery and kickback schemes, computer crimes, and public integrity crimes).

[34] See, e.g., Federal Bureau of Investigation, Phoenix Division, White Collar Crime Program, at http://phoenix.fbi.gov/pxwcc.htm (Phoenix, Nevada, FBI office, focusing on bank, telemarketing, and bankruptcy fraud) (last visited Oct. 25, 2004); Dakota County Sheriff Department, Criminal Investigation—White Collar Crime Division, at http://www.co.dakota.mn.us/sheriff/investigation/whitecollar.htm (Dakota County, Minnesota, Sheriff Department) (last visited Oct. 25, 2004).

[35] U.S. Dept of Justice, Criminal Division, Fraud Section, at http://www.usdoj.gov/criminal/fraud.html (last visited Oct. 25, 2004).

[36] See NW3C, National White Collar Crime Center, at http://www.nw3c.org (last visited Oct. 25, 2004). The NW3C also sponsors a White Collar Crime Research Consortium, whose members are mostly social scientists. See NW3C Research, at http://www.nw3c.org/research_wccrc.html (last visited Oct. 25, 2004).

[37] U.S. Dept of Justice, Office for Victims of Crime, White Collar Crime, at http://www.ojp.usdoj.gov/ovelhelp/wc.htm (last visited Oct. 25, 2004).

[38] Of course, to the extent that highly paid white collar criminal defense practitioners wish to have clients who are wealthy enough to pay their bills, they will give some attention to the socio-economic status of the alleged offender. And their legal strategy may well be to convince jurors and the public that the conduct in which their clients engaged was not criminal, but at most deviant. See Green, Moral Ambiguity, supra note 8, at 517.

[39] The ABA group sponsors white collar programs on subjects such as health care, tax, bank, insurance, and government procurement fraud, gaming, false claims, money laundering, antitrust offenses, corporate criminal liability, environmental crimes, the federal rules of criminal procedure, forfeiture, and public corruption. American Bar Association, Criminal Justice Section, Substantive Committees, at http://www.abanet.org/crimjust/committees/comlist.html#substantive (last visited Oct. 25, 2004).

[40] U.S. Sentencing Commission, 1998 Sourcebook of Federal Sentencing Statistics.

[41] According to the Department of Justice's website, the Fraud Section "plays a unique and essential role in the Department's fight against sophisticated economic crime. The Section is a front-line litigating unit that acts as a rapid response team, investigating and prosecuting complex white collar crime cases throughout the country." U.S. Dep't of Justice, Criminal Division, Fraud Section, at http://www.usdoj.gov/criminal/fraud.html (last visited Oct. 25, 2004).

[42] See Kathleen Brickey, *Corporate and White Collar Crime: Cases and Materials* (3d ed. 2002); Pamela H. Bucy, *White Collar Crime: Cases and Materials* (2d ed. 1998); Jerold H. Israel et al., *White Collar Crime: Law and Practice* (2d ed. 2003); Julie R. O'Sullivan, *Federal White Collar Crime: Cases and Materials* (2d ed. 2003); see also Leonard Orland, *Corporate and White Collar Crime: An Anthology* (1995); Ellen S. Podgor & Jerold H. Israel, *White Collar Crime in a Nutshell* (2d ed. 1997); J. Kelly Strader, *Understanding White Collar Crime* (2002). There are also several casebooks dealing with "federal criminal law" and "business crime" that cover many of the same topics. E.g., Norman Abrams & Sara Sun Beale, *Federal Criminal Law and Its Enforcement* (3d ed. 2000). The annual student-written white collar crime survey of the *American Criminal Law Review* deals with antitrust, computer crimes, corporate criminal liability, employment-related crimes, false claims, false statements, criminal conflicts of interest, conspiracy, food and drug violations, financial institutions fraud, foreign corrupt practices, health care fraud, intellectual property crimes, mail and wire fraud, money laundering, obstruction of justice, perjury, RICO, securities fraud, and tax violations.

[43] Deborah Jones Merritt & Jennifer Cihon, New Course Offerings in the Upper-Level Curriculum: Report of an AALS Survey, 47 *J. Legal Ed.* 524 (1997).

[44] 18 U.S.C. § 1961(1)(B).

[45] See Israel et al., supra note 42, at 1–9; O'Sullivan, supra note 42, at 1–7; Strader, supra note 42, at 1–3; Podgor, supra note 42, at 1–3. Richard Posner, interestingly, relies on a status-, rather than offense-, based approach to definition. Richard A. Posner, Optimal Sentences for White-Collar Criminals, 17 *Am. Crim. L. Rev.* 409, 409 (1980).

[46] See, e.g., Dan M. Kahan & Eric A. Posner, Shaming White-Collar Criminals: A Proposal for Reform of the Federal Sentencing Guidelines, 42 *J.L. & Econ.* 365 (1999); Kenneth Mann et al., Sentencing the White-Collar Offender, 17 *Am. Crim. L. Rev.* 479, 481 & n.8 (1980); Robert F. Meier, Understanding the Context of White-Collar Crime: A Sutherland Approbation, at 204, in National White Collar Crime Center Workshop, "Definitional Dilemma: Can and Should There Be a Universal Definition of White Collar Crime?," at http://www.nw3c.org/research_topics.html (last visited Oct. 25, 2004) ("[Kathleen Brickey] fails to offer a definition of white collar crime; in fact, the term is not even listed in the index of [her casebook]. Neither are the names of Sutherland or Geis.").

[47] Geis, supra note 3, at 31 (attributing this view to "[p]ersons with criminal law or regulatory law backgrounds").

[48] Cal. Penal Code. § 186.11(a)(1) (2004).

[49] Similarly, Alaska Statutes sections 12.55.155(c)(16) and (17) identify as aggravating circumstances that the "defendant's criminal conduct was designed to obtain substantial pecuniary gain and the risk of prosecution and punishment for the conduct is slight" and "the offense was one of a continuing series of criminal offenses committed in furtherance of illegal business activities from which the defendant derives a major portion of the defendant's income." Alaska Stat. §§ 12.55.155(c)(16) & (17) (2004). The commentary to the code, in turn, declares that the legislature intended these two aggravators to be applied to "white collar" criminals. 1980 *Alaska Senate J.*, Supp. No. 44, at 25 (May 29, 1980), cited in *Landon v. State of Alaska*, 941 P.2d 186, 193 (Alaska Ct. App. 1997). Thus, in *Landon*, the Alaska Court of Appeals determined that the sentence for a defendant who was convicted of various drug-related offenses was not subject to enhancement because he had not been convicted of a "white collar" crime, which the court, relying on the dictionary, defined as involving "fraud or deceit" or the "surreptitious steal[ing of] anyone's property." 941 P.2d at 193.

[50] Fla. Stat. § 775.0844 (2004).

[51] Miss. Code Ann. § 7-5-59(2) (2004).

[52] 3 V.I. Code Ann, § 118 (2004).

[53] 42 U.S.C. § 3722(c)(2)(F) (2004).

[54] See also Cal. Penal Code § 1203.044(g)(1) (2004) (requiring defendants convicted of certain offenses to pay a "surcharge" to the county in which the crime was committed "to be used exclusively for the investigation and prosecution of white collar crime offenses").

[55] D.C. Law 4-164 (1982) (codified in various sections of D.C. Code).

[56] See infra text accompanying notes 88–93.

[57] Sarbanes-Oxley Act of 2002, Pub. L. 107–204, 116 Stat. 745.

[58] Sarbanes-Oxley Act, § 905(a).

[59] Id. § 905(b)(1).

[60] Accounting Reform and Investor Protection, S. Hrg. 107–948 (2003), at 1325 (statement of Mr. Biden).

[61] Id. at 1318 (statement of Mr. Hatch).

[62] U.S. Sentencing Commission statistics indicate that, during 2001, the average sentence for white collar crime (defined to include embezzlement, forgery/counterfeiting, bribery, money laundering, and tax evasion) was just over twenty months, while the average sentence for drug and violent crimes was 71.7 and 89.5 months, respectively. U.S. Sentencing Commission, Sourcebook of Federal Sentencing Statistics 32, fig. E (2001). Admittedly, such aggregate figures can tell us only so much. To accurately assess the inconsistent treatment of "comparable" white collar and non-white collar crimes, we would obviously need some reliable measure of "comparability." Cf. National White Collar Crime Center, National Public Survey on White Collar Crime (2000) (asking survey participants to compare seriousness of crimes such as armed robbery causing serious injury vs. neglecting to recall a vehicle that results in serious injury); Francis T. Cullen et al., The Seriousness of Crime Revisited: Have Attitudes Toward White-Collar Crime Changed?, 20 *Criminology* 83, 88 (1982); Ilene Nagel & John Hagan, The Sentencing of White-Collar Criminals in Federal Courts: A Socio-legal Exploration of Disparity, 80 *Mich. L. Rev.* 1427 (1982).

[63] In 2003, the Sentencing Commission responded to Congress's directive, first in a set of "emergency" sentencing guidelines, see United States Sentencing Commission, Emergency Guidelines Amendments, 15 *Fed. Sent. Rep.* 281 (2003), and later in more permanent amendments, see *U.S. Sentencing Guidelines Manual* § 2B1.1(a) (2003). The amendments included significant sentencing enhancements for white collar offenses that affect a large number of victims or endanger the solvency or financial security of publicly traded corporations, other large employers, or one hundred or more individual victims. For example, an officer of a publicly traded company who defrauds more than 250 employees or investors of more than $1 million will receive a sentence of more than ten years in prison, almost double the term of imprisonment previously provided by the guidelines. Officers and directors of publicly traded corporations who commit securities violations are targeted for particularly substantial increases in penalties. The amendments also contain provisions imposing significantly increased penalties for offenders who obstruct justice by shredding either a substantial number of documents or especially probative documents; such offenders will receive a guideline sentencing range of approximately three years imprisonment, up from as low as eighteen months in prison under prior guidelines. Id.

[64] For a critique, see Frank O. Bowman, III, *Pour encourager les autres?* The Curious History and Distressing Implications of the Criminal Provisions of the Sarbanes-Oxley Act and the Sentencing Guidelines Amendments That Followed, 1 *Ohio St. J. Crim. L.* 373 (2004) (arguing that various provisions of the Act, including § 905, are vague in their language, overbroad in their scope, detrimental to the Sentencing Commissions independence, and unnecessary in light of earlier sentencing increases). See also Testimony of Frank Bowman before U.S. Senate Committee on the Judiciary, Penalties for White Collar Offenses: Are We Really Getting Tough on Crime?, Committee Print J-107-87, at http://judiciary.senate.gov/print_testimony.cfm?id=280&wit_id647 (last visited Oct. 25, 2004); Jennifer S. Recine, Note, Examination of the White Collar Crime Penalty Enhancements in the Sarbanes–Oxley Act, 39 *Am. Crim. L. Rev.* 1535 (2002).

[65] André Normandeau, Les Deviations en Affaires et la "Crime en Col Blanc," 19 *Rev. Intl. Crim. & Police Tech.* 247 (1965). This and several of the other citations to older works were taken from Gilbert Geis & Colin Goff, Introduction, Edwin H. Sutherland, *White Collar Crime: The Uncut Version* xi–xiii (1983).

[66] Markus Binder, Weisse-Kragen-Kriminalitat, 16 *Kriminalistik* 251 (1962).

[67] La criminalità dei colletti bianchi, at http://criminologia.advcom.it/unaricerca.htm (last visited Dec. 1, 2004).

[68] Bill Evans, "My Turn," Says Jon Johansen, P2Pnet (Jan. 28, 2004), at http://p2pnet.net/story/656 (last visited Oct. 25, 2004).

[69] Claúdia Maria Cruz Santos, *O crime de colarinho branco: da origem do conceito e sua relevância criminológica à questão da desigualdade na administração da justiça penal* (2001).

[70] Mario Permuth and Associates, Other Services, at http://www.permuth.com/newlook/services/other_areas_list. asp (website of Guatemalan law firm) (last visited Dec. 1, 2004).

[71] Geis & Goff, supra note 60, at xiii (referring to headline in *Sydney Morning Herald:* State Attorney General "Predicts Rapid Increase in White-Collar Crime").

[72] David Lague and Susan V. Lawrence, White-Collar Crime in China: Rank Corruption, *Far Eastern Econ. Rev.* (Oct. 31, 2002) at http://www.fsa.ulaval.ca/personnel/vernag/EH/F/noir/lectures/white–collar_crime_in_china.htm (last visited Oct. 25, 2004).

[73] Hieros Gamos, Sarantitis and Partners, Law Firm Overview, http://www.hierosgamos.org/hg/db_lawfirms.asp?action=page&pcomp=35418&page=1&country=Greece&SubCategory=White|Collar|Crime (last visited Oct. 25, 2004).

[74] DGP Denies Involvement in Stamp Scam, *The Hindu*, Jan. 22, 2004.

[75] See Jerusalem Criminal Justice Study Group, Report on the Jerusalem Criminal Justice Study Group's White Collar Crime Project, at http://law.mscc.huji.ac.il/lawl/newsite/CrimeGroup/white/simcha.htm (last visited Oct. 25, 2004).

[76] Lim Kit Siang, Will Ministers, Deputy Ministers, Parliamentary Secretaries, Mentri-Mentri Besar and Chief Ministers Be Required to Undergo Psychological Tests to Reduce the Incidence of Corruption?, at http://www.malaysia.net/ dap/sg336.htm (last visited Oct. 25, 2004).

[77] Symposium, US–Mexico White Collar Crime, 11 *U.S.–Mexico L.J.* 128 (2003).

[78] Lala Camerer, White-Collar Crime in South Africa: A Comparative Perspective 5 *Afr. Security Rev.*, No. 2 (1996), available at http://www.iss.co.za/ Pubs/ASR/5No2/5No2/WhiteCollarcrime.html (last visited Oct. 25, 2004).

[79] Business Times, Tanzania: Reserve Sharia Law for White-Collar Thieves, *Afr. News*, Oct. 3, 2003.

[80] House Slams Corruption, *AllAfrica*, Jan. 21, 2004. See also Gilbert Geis & Ezra Stotland, *Introduction, White-Collar Crime: Theory and Research* 9–10 (1980) (describing studies of white collar crime in Canada, France, Germany, Australia, Asia, Africa, and the former Soviet Union); David Nelken, White-Collar Crime, in the *Oxford Handbook of Criminology* 892 (Mike Maguire et al. eds., 2d ed. 1997) ("The equivalent term for white-collar crime is also widely found in other languages, and even used in foreign court proceedings.") The 2000 annual meeting of the American Sociological Association included a panel on "White Collar Crime in Comparative Perspective," which featured papers and commentaries on white collar crime in the Netherlands, Finland, Taiwan, and Spain. See White Collar Crime in Comparative Perspective, at http://www.asc41.com/www/2000/wc6.htm (last visited Oct. 25, 2004).

[81] See, e.g., Hazel Croall, *Understanding White Collar Crime* (2001) (book by British sociologist).

[82] See, e.g., September 25, 2003 email message to the author from Professor Jesper Lau Hansen, Law Faculty, University of Copenhagen (on file with the author) (explaining usage in Denmark and elsewhere in Scandinavia).

[83] In this paragraph and the next, I rely liberally on my discussion in Prototype Theory and the Classification of Offenses in a Revised Model Penal Code: A General Approach to the Special Part, 4 *Buff. Crim. L. Rev.* 301, 305–16 (2000).

[84] George Lakoff, *Women, Fire, and Dangerous Things* 6 (1987).

[85] Ludwig Wittgenstein, *Philosophical Investigations* 66–71 (G.E.M. Anscombe trans., 3d ed. 1968).

[86] Id.

[87] Green, supra note 83.

[88] See supra note 48.

[89] See supra note 49.

[90] See supra note 50.

[91] See supra notes 51–52.

[92] See supra notes 53–54.

[93] For example, former Tyco CEO Dennis Kozlowski was charged not only with the presumptively white collar offenses of enterprise corruption, securities fraud, conspiracy, and falsifying business records, but also with the more mundane street offense of grand larceny.

[94] See Green, supra note 11.

[95] Green, supra note 18; Lying, Misleading, and Falsely Denying: How Moral Concepts Inform the Law of Perjury, Fraud, and False Statements, 53 *Hastings L.J.* 157 (2001); Cheating, 23 *Law & Phil.* 137 (2004); Uncovering the Cover–up Crimes, 42 *Am. Crim. L. Rev.* (forthcoming 2005); Theft by Coercion: Extortion, Blackmail, and Hard Bargaining, 44 *Washburn L.J.* (2005). See also my forthcoming book, *A Moral Theory of White Collar Crime.*

[96] In formulating such an argument, we need to acknowledge the serious potential for circularity that exists in any such definitional enterprise: namely, that in deciding which offenses fall within the category of white collar crime, we will be forced to assume that certain paradigmatic qualities define the category; and in determining which qualities define the category, we will be forced to assume that certain offenses fall within it.

[97] Cf. sources cited supra notes 21–24.

[98] Thus, I am in agreement with the sociologist David Friedrichs, who has suggested that any definition of white collar crime is ultimately meaningful only in relation to its stated purpose. David O. Friedrichs, *Trusted Criminals* 4–12 (2d ed. 2004); David O. Friedrichs, White-Collar Crime and the Definitional Quagmire: A Provisional Solution, 3 *J. Hum. Just.* 5 (1992).

3

White-Collar Crime

Interpretive Disagreement and Prospects for Change

— *Neal Shover and Francis T. Cullen*

The concept *white-collar crime* has become securely rooted in lay and scholarly lexicons, but public interest in the crimes of respectable citizens and organizations waxes and wanes. It peaks when evidence suggests these offenders have been unusually active and harmful, and it diminishes when either the targets of their interest are laying low or the entertainment/news media are paying little attention to respectable crime. Thus the countless crimes that helped kindle and stoke the Great Recession raised public awareness, anger, and concern to a high if not unprecedented level. There were calls for public officials and agencies to move boldly and aggressively against privileged criminal offenders who played a part in causing financial havoc and destruction (Shover and Grabosky, 2010). As many see it, an enforcement campaign aimed at upperworld criminals, especially in the wake of the Great Recession, is more than justified by commitment to equal justice and notions of just desserts. In addition, deterrence theory principles, which underpin the wars on street crime and drugs, are cited as theoretical justification.

[handwritten margin note: "rich can be held accountable too"]

The public has been treated to extensive media coverage of unusually gluttonous white-collar defendants who received lengthy prison sentences, but a handful of severe sentences does not a crackdown make. Almost certainly this would require a significant and sustained increase in the proportion of suspected offenders singled out for official attention.

An original article written for this publication.

[handwritten: Reason why WCC isn't using same principles as traditional crime]

That in turn would also require substantially increased resources and imaginative procedures to avoid replicating the pitiable record of enforcement actions that followed the Savings and Loans crime and collapse of the 1980s (Calavita, Pontell, and Tillman, 1997). Dissatisfaction with the criminal justice response to white-collar crime remained high in the months following the worst of the economic downturn.

There is frustration also for those who stump instead for a substantially different approach to oversight. Broadly known as "responsive regulation," this approach de-emphasizes criminal threats and penalties in favor of increased reliance on voluntary, consultative, and non-state oversight (Ayres and Braithwaite, 1992). Responsive regulation has been on the march for two decades or more, and its supporters occupy center stage in the oversight debate. Seen through the eyes of many advocates for this approach, deterrence-based approaches to oversight are harmful to entrepreneurship, public welfare, and much that lies at the base of collective economic fortunes and forecasts. Its original formulation was critical of the deterrence-based approach to enforcement for its failure to make more effective use of criminal threats and prosecution; responsive regulation argues that regulations can be a productive combination of persuasion and sanctions, chiefly by shifting more attention to use of educative and voluntary strategies.

[handwritten margin note: punishing actions instead of preventing them]

Among scholars, policy makers and state managers there is substantial disagreement over key issues in interpreting and responding to white-collar crime (Shover and Cullen, 2008). The launching point for this article is the belief that awareness and understanding of this diversity of thought is a context for and helps make sense of state responses to white-collar crime. Diverse or conflicting notions about white-collar crime have resulted in polarized factions: one pushing for government regulation and the other for free markets. Those determined to see tough and sustained action taken against upperworld crime meet with limited success; likewise, those seeking reductions in state oversight and minimal use of criminal penalties draw only momentary satisfaction from their victories until the battle is rejoined.

Most of this article lays out core components of two ways of seeing and thinking about white-collar crime—Populist and Patrician—drawn from publications by academicians to identify and describe these perspectives, which likely are paralleled in the beliefs held by a substantial proportion of the public at large. The two perspectives are clear also in the diverse approaches to oversight of white-collar crime favored by managers and line workers of agencies charged with the task. Given this diversity, there is little reason to forecast an end to public confusion and dissatisfaction with how white-collar crime is responded to by regulatory and crime-control bureaucracies. This article's elaboration of points of contrast between Populist and Patrician ways of thinking about white-collar crime is focused in four areas: how white-collar crime is to be defined;

the essential criminality of white-collar offenses; the level of attention paid to the victims and costs of white-collar crime; and the importance of choice in causal explanations for variation in white-collar crime.

Populist and Patrician Perspectives

Both Populist and Patrician approaches to identifying and interpreting problems of white-collar crime are evident in scholarly publications on the subject matter: The former perspective situates white-collar crime and responses to it in the struggle for equal justice, while the latter is characterized by a more narrow, technical, and less reform-oriented view of the problem. Populist and Patrician perspectives are contrasting ways to conceptualize and think about white-collar crime. The focus is on ways of seeing, interpreting, and evaluating rather than on individuals. In distinguishing Populist and Patrician perspectives, we do not imply that they are incommensurable; some individuals find merit in aspects of both.

What Is White-Collar Crime?

Sutherland (1983), the intellectual midwife for the concept white-collar crime, regarded the respectable social status of its perpetrators as its defining characteristic. Following his lead, many others have suggested that white-collar crime consists of offenses committed by those of wealth, privilege, and respectable status. They "are privileged most importantly by freedom from daily preoccupation with meeting basic material needs; fiscal precariousness and unceasing concern about it are largely alien to [their experience]." The privileged "do not live in families where injury to the breadwinner can plunge all into material desperation in a matter of days" (Shover and Hochstetler, 2006:11).

Seen though Populist eyes, white-collar criminals are privileged also by their location on the hierarchy of respectability. They hail from worlds where people do not do "dirty work"—work or tasks that most people understand must be carried out despite their undesirable and morally "dirty" nature. Those located near the bottom of the respectability hierarchy work under conditions structured and monitored by others. Their income is derived not from a salary but from wages; if they miss work, they are not paid. The conditions of well-paid, respectable employment differ conspicuously from this. Last, many white-collar criminals are privileged by holding positions of authority in state or private organizations; they can "make things happen" by directing or suggesting need for action by subalterns and departments.

A preference for offender-based definitions of white-collar crime is the foundation of the Populist way of seeing it, and commitment to this approach generally is made with the intent of netting criminal offenders who are extremely wealthy and highly placed in powerful organizations whether private or public. These offenders contrast demographically with the general population, and they contrast starkly with those normally selected for criminal justice attention; they are older, wealthy, almost exclusively white, and well educated.

focuses on offender

Investigators who see white-collar crime through Patrician eyes find little value in offender-based definitions, and they opt instead for ones that highlight the formal characteristics of crimes without regard to the status of those who commit them. Herbert Edelhertz (1970) suggests that white-collar crime is "an illegal act or series of illegal acts committed by nonphysical means and by concealment or guile, to obtain money or property, to avoid the payment or loss of money or property, or to obtain business or personal advantage" (p. 3). Edelhertz makes clear his belief that "the character of white-collar crime must be found in its modus operandi and its objectives rather than in the nature of the offenders" (p. 4). Others likewise contend that the most promising analytic approach is "collaring the crime, not the criminal" (Shapiro, 1990).

focuses on crime itself

The wealth-leveling and demographically homogenizing effects of defining white-collar crime on the basis of crime characteristics are clear. Seen in this way, it can be committed by citizens who wear blue collars as well as white ones, because it lumps together for theoretic and policy purposes fraud committed by itinerant door-to-door vinyl siding installers and the crimes of international bankers. It casts as white-collar criminals both the single mother who fraudulently receives $1,000 welfare assistance and the chief executive officer of a large multinational corporation who knowingly deceives potential investors and shareholders about company earnings. Street-level heroin addicts and Enron executives are equally white-collar criminals.

Broader sense of white collar crime

When defined by crime characteristics, white-collar crime no longer is the province solely of the wealthy, the remote, and the powerful. The consistent pattern of findings from studies in which white-collar crime is defined on the basis of conviction offense, led some investigators to suggest that white-collar crime amounts to "crimes of the middle classes" (Weisburd et al., 1991). It is unavoidable; when offense-based definitions of white-collar crime are employed, the wealth, power, and respectable status of those who commit it are de-emphasized theoretically, reduced empirically, and generally ignored or discounted. Unusually privileged offenders thereby blend with and become less conspicuous among their more numerous middle-class criminal cousins.

Whether it is defined on the basis of offender or crime characteristics clearly makes a world of difference in the demographic face of white-collar crime. That said, however, some white-collar offenders are criminal by any definition. They are individuals of high wealth or authority in powerful organizations who commit felony-level economic white-collar offenses. Because most of their crimes may go either undetected or unre-

only overlap

ported, they remain unknown to authorities and the public. Their numbers are undeterminable, and the parameters of their criminal careers are unknown. These upperworld offenders stand out from ordinary white-collar criminals represented by retail sales clerks, small business owners, and other offenders of modest economic circumstance whose crimes by comparison are unremarkable.

Apart from their preference for offender-based definitions, many Populist interpreters prefer to focus attention on narrow types of white-collar crime. "Corporate crime" is crime committed by officers, managers, or employees of profit-seeking organizations or firms in pursuit of employer objectives (Yeager, 2007). The chief rationale for distinguishing this and other subtypes of organizational crime is the belief that some organizations are unusually criminogenic or that causal conditions are more characteristic of them and their environments. The emphasis in for-profit organizations, for example, of unalloyed economic calculation coupled with possibly distinctive structural and cultural features may make them unusually criminogenic (Pearce, 2001). Among the first to assert this belief, at the dawn of the twentieth century, Edward Ross (1907) indicted them as entities that "transmit the greed of investors, but not their conscience" (p. 109). Other rationales for isolating and examining corporate crime include the pervasiveness and power of large corporations, the high cost of corporate crime to victims and the larger community, and the distinctive and difficult control challenges it presents.

Populist interpretations of white-collar crime accommodate easily, if not inspire, the belief that the meaning of the concept of "crime" is construed too narrowly by public officials and most scholars. Calls to broaden the meaning sound two themes (albeit underlying both is the belief that conventional definitions reflect power imbalances and inequality). One would expand the meaning of crime to include regulatory infractions, conduct that generally does not require demonstration of willfulness or recklessness by violators (Clinard and Yeager, 1980; Sutherland, 1983). The other proposal would expand the meaning of crime to include violations of human rights, avoidable harms, and many forms of socially injurious conduct (Schwendinger and Schwendinger, 1975; see also Box, 1984). Those who view the matter through Patrician eyes adamantly reject calls for a broadened definition of crime (Baucus and Dworkin, 1991) and label those who do "moral entrepreneurs" (Shapiro, 1983) with an "antimiddle-class bias" (Toby, 1979:520). In truth the bias was directed almost exclusively at large corporations and citizens ensconced at or above the highest levels of middle-class material comfort.

But Is It Crime?

Seen from the Populist vantage point, public sentiment is one of the most compelling reasons for the theoretical and policy importance of white-collar crime. Investigators point to findings from public opinion surveys to show that adults regard many forms of white-collar crime as no less, if not more, serious than some street crimes (Evans, Cullen, and Dubeck, 1993; Kane and Wall, 2006; Piquero, Carmichael, and Piquero, 2008; Unnever, Benson, and Cullen, 2008). This is a bedrock exercise in Populist efforts to demonstrate to larger audiences the urgency and priority of paying more attention to white-collar crime. Both its manifest harmfulness and public opinion legitimize white-collar crime as a pressing problem, and Populist investigators are noticeably disinclined to see it as anything less than serious *crime*. Moreover, no moral or legal distinctions are drawn between white-collar crime and street crime when the former is examined with a Populist cast; the appellation "crime" is employed equally to describe offenses committed by the high-placed and powerful and by ordinary citizens.

Appeals to heed public opinion on problems of white-collar crime are conspicuous by their absence entirely from Patrician interpretations. In the Patrician view of matters, conduct by white-collar citizens that violates criminal statutes is approached obliquely when it is approached at all. For the most part, "crime" is folded into concepts and analytic categories with softer and less accusatory labels. With this conceptual reworking, the conduct becomes a "mistake," "dubious behavior," "unlawful behavior," "deviance," "misconduct," "illegal behavior," "violation," "law-breaking," "questionable behavior," or a form of "risky behavior" (Baucus and Near, 1991; Bromiley and Marcus, 1989; Reiss and Biderman, 1980; Szwajkowski, 1986; Vaughan, 1999).

Whether or not the drive for more formal theory, which essentially removes talk of *crime* from investigators' analysis, unwittingly helps white-collar criminals deny moral and legal responsibility for their crimes is unclear. It appears, however, that the distinctive nature of their criminal acts is obscured in the process. The use of morally and legally ambiguous categories divorces analysis of white-collar crime from theory and investigation of crimes committed by less reputable offenders.

Victims and Costs

Moral condemnation is an unmistakable if sometimes obscured component of the Populist perspective on white-collar crime. Ross (1907) dubbed white-collar offenders "criminaloids" and likened them to "wolves." Sutherland compared them to Nazis (Geis and Goff, 1983). In the Populist view of matters, moral reproach is more than justified by the toll white-collar crime exacts from victims and the wider community. No one can determine or estimate these costs with confidence; this would require systematically collected data on the prevalence of white-collar crime, the numbers of victims, and their losses. These data do not exist and would be extremely difficult to collect in any case. In marked contrast to street crime, data on white-collar offenses and offenders in the United States are not routinely collected, collated, and disseminated by offices of state or federal government. The result is incomplete and potentially biased estimates of white-collar crime.

Against the backdrop of limited empirical data, case studies of especially egregious and harmful crimes occupy a prominent place in the corpus of white-collar crime research. Reports span decades, from the heavy electric equipment conspiracy cases of the 1960s (Geis, 1967) to the University of California fertility clinic scandal (Dodge and Geis, 2003) to the abuse and torture of prisoners at Abu Ghraib (Rothe, in press). In the Populist perspective, some reports become landmark narratives that are cited repeatedly by successive investigators as evidence of the seriousness of white-collar crime and the callousness of respectable offenders (Lee and Ermann, 1999). That the interpretations based on them sometimes are unsupported empirically or based on exaggerated interpretations may be important since they evoke in some readers a sense of moral indignation. A substantial proportion of white-collar crimes, however, are not complex, they have few victims, and they result in modest harm (Shapiro, 1984).

All who examine the patchy data on the aggregate costs of white-collar crime report a toll that is both staggering in size and much greater than losses to street crime (Cullen et al., 2006). Some white-collar crimes have hundreds or thousands of victims, and losses from only a few highly publicized incidents can surpass the total annual monetary cost of burglaries, robberies, and other such crimes. The number of workplace casualties and illnesses caused by criminal action or neglect cannot be determined, but few doubt it is high. In all likelihood, employer failure to provide a safe and healthful working environment exacts a heavier toll than interpersonal violence. Arguably, crimes committed by state officials or agencies victimize a nation's entire population.

As seen through Populist eyes, white-collar crime also has a corrosive effect on trust and other social psychological supports of civil society. Because much of it violates trust, white-collar crime may breed distrust, lower social morale and "attack the fundamental principles of [social] institutions" (Sutherland, 1983:10). When high public officials act indifferently toward lawful constraints on their discretion or use their office for illicit enrichment, the result may be eroded public trust in government and loss of confidence in public institutions, leaders, and processes (Meier and Short, 1982). Likewise, when public officials and agencies appear to tolerate or condone white-collar crime, it may complicate the task of convincing citizens they should be honest. Highly visible white-collar crime can corrode public morality and commitment to conformity if citizens come to believe that everyone is acting only from narrow self-interest.

There is also the possible effect of pervasive white-collar crime on confidence in economic institutions (Meier and Short, 1982). Trust is "truly the foundation of capitalism." In its absence, "people would not delegate discretionary use of their funds to other entrepreneurs . . . [and] capitalism would break down as funds were stuffed into mattresses, savings accounts, and solo business enterprises rather than invested in the business ventures of . . . corporations" (Shapiro, 1984:2). In short, when it goes unchecked, white-collar crime may lead to loss of legitimacy for political and economic institutions, a process that may stimulate increased crime (LaFree, 1998). For those who view white-collar crime from a Populist perspective, its high and diverse costs are reason enough for examining and subjecting it to more rigorous oversight.

The obvious and immediate impacts of white-collar crime on victims include possible death or physical injuries, as well as loss of money and property. Others include pain, emotional suffering, and reduced quality of life. Damage to health generally is incremental and long-term rather than catastrophic. High levels of workplace carcinogens, for example, take time off the end of lives, long after employees have retired or otherwise been replaced. The effects of victimization by white-collar crime can ripple far beyond immediate victims to harm families and the larger community. When organizations dispose of hazardous materials in reckless or willfully criminal fashion, the costs may include increased risk of health problems for innocent parties and the financial costs of cleaning up toxic legacies (Barnett, 1994; Pearce and Tombs, 1998). A high proportion of economic white-collar crimes probably leave victims more angry and inconvenienced following modest financial losses than emotionally devastated and destitute. That said, there is little doubt that for some victims of white-collar crime, the impact of victimization matches or exceeds in intensity and duration the experiences of street-crime victims (Shichor, Sechrest, and Doocy, 2001; Shover, Fox, and Mills, 1994).

Victims of white-collar crime who find their way to the police, to prosecutors, or to regulatory officials generally meet with experiences remarkably similar to and no less frustrating than the experiences of street-crime victims. They may be required to negotiate a maze of agencies and institutions, most of uncertain jurisdiction and commitment. In addition, local-level front-line troops in the war on crime generally receive little training on how to recognize and respond to any but the simplest white-collar crimes. Research into the practical problems faced by victims of white-collar crime lags well behind the more numerous and methodologically sophisticated studies of responses to street-crime victims by the state apparatus.

While individuals and families receive most of the attention in research on victims of white-collar crime, organizations also are victimized (Association of Certified Fraud Examiners, 2010; Bussmann, 2006). Less is known about institutions and their reactions to the experience in part because many organizational victims probably have an interest in keeping quiet about it; insurance costs might be increased, for example. It is not difficult to imagine a host of potentially harmful effects. Small businesses may be forced into bankruptcy and their employees onto unemployment rolls. Charitable organizations, for whom public trust is a powerful determinant of financial contributions, may suffer in their capacity to assist or protect the young, disabled, and infirm; when scandal occurs and evidence suggests charitable contributions have been mishandled, public giving suffers. Where public bureaucracies are victimized by white-collar crime, the larger community of taxpaying citizens may be the ultimate victim. Moral condemnation is less prominent if not missing entirely from the Patrician interpretation. In addition, save for a modicum of attention to organizational victims, the disregard shown for victims of white-collar crime by those who examine it from a Patrician perspective stands in sharp contrast to the focus placed on them in Populist interpretations.

White-Collar Crime as Choice

In the United States, the closing decades of the twentieth century witnessed a major shift in dominant theoretical interpretations of crime and policy options by elite academics and policy makers. Cultural explanations, which had enjoyed support for decades, were supplanted by rediscovery of and rekindled favor for rational-choice theory. This interpretive approach depicts offenders as actors who choose to commit crime after weighing systematically its potential gains and losses. The resurrection of rational-choice theory stimulated many investigations of decision making by burglars, robbers, drug dealers, and street criminals generally, and a great deal has been learned about the way they choose to commit crime and select suitable targets. Studies consistently show, however, that their rationality is bounded severely; street-level thieves and hustlers are anything but careful or systematic decision makers (Shover and Copes, 2010). Reasons start with the fact that they predominantly are young males who typically weigh potential transgression while high on drugs or desperate to regain a state of drug-induced comfort and while in company of others like them. The last makes them highly susceptible to interpersonal influences and erodes careful thought processes. Evidence suggests that the potential monetary rewards of potential criminal acts count heavily in the calculus of street offenders, and many are surprisingly inattentive to risk when choosing to commit crime.

Intuition suggests that white-collar criminals should be capable of employing greater rationality than street offenders. Their decision-making contexts are strikingly unlike what is commonplace for the latter; many white-collar criminals live and work in worlds where rational conduct is expected, promoted, monitored, and rewarded. Also, when they choose to commit crime, few white-collar criminals are in company with young males high on drugs or materially desperate (Shover and Copes, 2010). On the face of it, rational-choice theory would seem well-suited for explaining crime committed by white-collar offenders.

decisions consciously made

When white-collar crime is viewed through Patrician eyes, the taken-for-granted moral equivalence of all felonies and the explanatory utility of rational-choice theory are denied or ignored. Because the focus generally is on behavioral categories that de-emphasize even that crime is included, there is little interest in what has been learned about criminal decision making in studies of street offenders. Examination of how the decision was made to launch the ill-fated Challenger space shuttle suggests there was an organizational bias at the National Aeronautics and Space Administration toward risky decisions and maintaining deadlines, which ultimately led officials to authorize the shuttle launch under dangerous conditions (Vaughan, 1996, 2006). The lesson drawn from this is that the rationality of white-collar decision makers is bounded by culture and circumstances. The launch decision was not criminal, and the probative value of these findings for understanding *criminal* decisions is unclear and cannot be assumed. That said, conclusions about the bounded rationality of white-collar criminals and their use of culturally based subjective preferences is remarkably similar to what has been learned about decision making by burglars and robbers (Shover and Honaker, 1992).

Still, in stark contrast to the large number of investigations into decision making by street criminals, there are few comparable studies of white-collar criminals. Strategies and methodologies used to study street-criminal decision making may be more difficult to employ with white-collar criminals. Burglars and robbers do not take umbrage or argue when asked questions premised on their assumed criminality. Everything is different with white-collar criminals; questions exemplified by "tell me how you decided to do this crime" elicit denials of criminal intent and, therefore, of *criminal* decision making. Their refusal to acknowledge that they committed or were fairly convicted of crime means that white-collar criminals' decision making cannot be approached in the straightforward manner employed with muggers and burglars; circumspection is required (Shover and Hunter, 2010). The upshot of methodological obstacles and limited research, however, is that where white-collar offenders are concerned, "we have little evidence about [their] beliefs or knowledge of [possible criminal penalties] *at the time they contemplated their offences*" (Levi, 2010:117, emphasis in the original).

In addition to explaining why some individuals choose to commit crime but others do not, the challenge faced by theories of crime causation includes explaining why crime rates vary temporally and spatially. While this variation in white-collar crime cannot be measured with precision, no one doubts the importance of understanding its causes. Explanations are found in a variety of theories, but Populist approaches typically build on structural and historical interpretations. Analysis, for example, of historical transformations of the forces, relations and dynamics of production are pointed to as fundamental causes of aggregate-level variation in crime. The rapid growth of global economic relationships, its causes and its consequences also are featured in Populist interpretations. Attention is paid also to structural sources of pressures and inducements to commit crime. Populist-grounded interpretations have a critical edge; hierarchy, inequality, and conflict are common building blocks.

Historical structural analysis and explanatory concepts at the core of Populist perspectives are largely absent from Patrician approaches to white-collar crime. Efforts of the former kind, moreover, are seen as "grandiose" when viewed from the Patrician vantage point (Shapiro, 1980). The causes of white-collar crime are thought to lie in historical conditions that unfold or emerge without human intervention. The importance and effects of power, authority, and agency are obscured when change in white-collar crime is attributed to evolving transaction systems or the growth of fiduciary relationships (Shapiro, 1990; Vaughan, 1982).

The explanatory concept *organizational culture* exemplifies the obfuscation process while showing also that theories of white-collar crime and theories of street crime diverge in Patrician perspectives (Shover and Hochstetler, 2002). Although initial explication of the notion of organizational culture is nearly 50 years old (Jacques, 1951), it did not attract attention until nearly three decades later. The animus for its appeal to scholars and policy makers is the belief that organizational culture is a "social force that controls patterns of organizational behavior by shaping members' cognitions and perceptions of meanings and realities" (Ott, 1989:69). Hypothetical defects in organizational culture were seized upon as the principal sources of untoward behavior by corporate managers and employees.

In the closing decades of the twentieth century as political leaders and policy analysts re-embraced the notion that street offenders are rational actors, white-collar criminals were cast as decision-making pawns of forces largely beyond their control. Cultural explanations for white-collar crime gained support even as they were displaced as the dominant explanation for street crime (Zimring, 1993). This reflects a larger pattern in causal interpretations of white-collar crime from a Patrician vantage point that singles out impersonal causal forces, although generally they do not make mention of inequality, power differentials, or domination.

The essential elements of the Populist and Patrician perspectives are summarized in Table 1.

So What?

It should be clear from this comparison of Populist and Patrician perspectives that white-collar crime can be seen in conspicuously contrasting fashion. There is disagreement on and occasional controversy on many points. This would not be noteworthy save for belief it is not confined to occupants of ivory towers and the lay public; likely it is commonplace among policy makers, public officials, and the apparatchiks of

Table 1.

Summary of Populist and Patrician Perspectives on White-Collar Crime

Issue	Populist	Patrician
Basis of Definition of White-Collar Crime	Focus on the status of the criminal	Focus on the nature of the crime
Keen Focus on Hierarchy and Power	Yes	No
Make Moral/Legal Distinction between White-Collar Crime and Street Crime	No—see both types of offenses as serious	Yes—depress the seriousness of white-collar crimes
Include Regulatory Offenses as White-Collar "Crimes"	Yes—the acts are seen as illegal and criminal	No—the acts are seen as illegal but not criminal
Moral Condemnation of White-Collar Offenders	Strong	Weak
Focus on Costs of White-Collar Crime to Victims	Strong—emphasize case studies showing large and damaging effects of white-collar crime to victims	Weak
Explanation of Criminal Decision-Making	See criminal decision-making of white-collar and street offenders as similar (although unequally applied)	Do not compare the decision-making of white-collar and street criminals
Critical Perspective on Causes of White-Collar Crime	Yes—emphasis on structural roots of white-collar crime	No
Academic/Intellectual Roots	Sociology and Criminal Justice	Business and elite institutions

oversight. Their day-to-day decisions build on or give life alternatively to Populist or Patrician assumptions and interpretations.

Disagreement over key aspects of white-collar crime, as exemplified by the split between scholars who work from Populist and Patrician perspectives, is intractable. It is also immensely useful; it can be used by officials to obfuscate public efforts to gain a clear picture of their adversary. Generally, the understanding of white-collar crime employed by oversight officials aligns seamlessly with Patrician definitions of the concept. In the eyes of officialdom, what characterizes them is the use of "deceit, concealment, or violation of trust, [meaning they] are not dependent upon the application or threat of physical force or violence. . . . [They are committed] to obtain personal or business advantage" (U.S. Department of Justice, 2005:A1). Use of this offense-based definition enables public officials to mount campaigns against white-collar crime that nab primarily ordinary offenders but less than a handful from the highest ranks of privileged and respectable citizens. Officials can proclaim they are acting against white-collar criminals while looking no further than identity thieves (U.S. Department of Justice, 2007) and criminal telemarketers (Shover, Coffey, and Sanders, 2004). This makes it difficult for the public to gage knowledgeably their commitment to oversight of white-collar crime. The entertainment/news media and its depiction of white-collar criminals further obfuscates or even mystifies problems of white-collar crime for many (Levi, 2009).

What is the lesson for citizens angered by white-collar crime and wishful of seeing more effective oversight? Conflict and dissatisfaction is woven into the very nature of white-collar crime. It is ineradicable. Inevitably, the challenge of how to craft and enforce oversight of the extremely privileged is contentious and unsettled. The reasons for this are prosaic, but they include dissemination of information about white-collar crime that perhaps obfuscates it for many citizens and leaves them poorly prepared to assess state oversight. Dissatisfaction gave birth to the concept white-collar crime seven decades ago, and it was no less the spawning bed for the flood tide of kinder and gentler oversight policies that has developed in recent decades. Moreover, given the persistence and strength of parties opposed to rigorous oversight of white-collar crime, reforms will be incremental, not transformative. Reformers must be prepared for a complex and endless campaign, one that likely will produce only short-term and politically vulnerable advances. Confusion about and high levels of discontent with official responses to white-collar crime are no guarantee that limp oversight of those who commit these offenses will change anytime soon.

REFERENCES

Association of Certified Fraud Examiners. 2010. *2010 Report to the Nation on Occupational Fraud and Abuse.* http://www.acfe.com/rttn/2010–rttn.asp. Accessed October 20, 2010.

Ayres, Ian, and John Braithwaite. 1992. *Responsive Regulation.* Cambridge, UK: Cambridge University Press.

Barnett, Harold C. 1994. *Toxic Debts and the Superfund Dilemma.* Chapel Hill: University of North Carolina Press.

Baucus, Melissa S., and T. M. Dworkin. 1991. "What is corporate crime? It is not illegal corporate behavior." *Law & Policy* 13:231–44.

Baucus, Melissa S., and Janet P. Near. 1991. "Can illegal corporate behavior be predicted? An event history analysis." *Academy of Management Journal* 34:9–36.

Box, Steven. 1984. *Power, Crime, and Mystification.* London: Tavistock.

Bromiley, Philip, and Alfred Marcus. 1989. The deterrent to dubious corporate behavior: Profitability, probability, and safety recalls. *Strategic Management Journal* 10:233–50.

Bussmann, Kai-D. 2006. "Addressing crime in companies: First findings from a global survey of economic crime." *British Journal of Criminology* 46:1–17.

Calavita, Kitty, Henry N. Pontell, and Robert H. Tillman. 1997. *Big Money Crime: Fraud and Politics in the Savings and Loan Crisis*. Berkeley: University of California Press.

Clinard, Marshall B., and Peter C. Yeager. 1980. *Corporate Crime*. New York: Free Press.

Croall, Hazel. 1992. *White Collar Crime*. Philadelphia: Open University Press.

Cullen, Francis T., Gray Cavender, William J. Maakestad, and Michael L. Benson. 2006. *Corporate Crime under Attack: The Fight to Criminalize Business Violence* (2nd ed.). Newark, NJ: Lexis/Nexis-Anderson.

Dodge, Mary, and Gilbert Geis. 2003. *Stealing Dreams: A Fertility Clinic Scandal*. Boston: Northeastern University Press.

Edelhertz, Herbert. 1970. *The Nature, Impact, and Prosecution of White Collar Crime*. Washington, DC: U.S. Department of Justice, National Institute of Law Enforcement and Criminal Justice.

Evans, T. David, Francis T. Cullen, and Paula J. Dubeck. 1993. "Public perceptions of corporate crime." In *Understanding Corporate Criminality*, edited by Michael B. Blankenship. New York: Garland.

Geis, Gilbert. 1967. "The heavy electric equipment conspiracy cases of 1961." In *Criminal Behavior Systems*, edited by Marshall B. Clinard and Richard Quinney. New York: Holt, Rinehart and Winston.

Geis, Gilbert, and Colin Goff. 1983. "Introduction" to Edwin Sutherland, *White Collar Crime: The Uncut Version*. New Haven, CT: Yale University Press.

Jacques, Elliott. 1951. *The Changing Culture of the Factory*. London: Tavistock.

Kane, John, and April D. Wall. 2006. *The 2005 National Survey on White Collar Crime*. Fairmont, WV: National White Collar Crime Center.

LaFree, Gary. 1998. *Losing Legitimacy: Street Crime and the Decline of Social Institutions in America*. Boulder, CO: Westview.

Lee, Matthew T., and M. David Ermann. 1999. "Pinto 'madness' as a flawed landmark narrative: An organizational and network analysis." *Social Problems* 46:30–47.

Levi, Michael. 2009. "Suite revenge? The shaping of folk devils and moral panics about white-collar crimes." *British Journal of Criminology* 49:48–67.

———. 2010. "Hitting the suite spot: Sentencing frauds." *Journal of Financial Crime* 17:116–32.

Meier, Robert F., and James F. Short, Jr. 1982. "The consequences of white-collar crime." In *White-Collar Crime: An Agenda for Research*, edited by Herbert Edelhertz. Lexington, MA: Lexington.

Ott, S. J. 1989. *The Organizational Culture Perspective*. Pacific Gove, CA: Brooks/Cole.

Pearce, Frank. 2001. "Crime and capitalist business corporations." In *Crime of Privilege: Readings in White-Collar Crime*, edited by Neal Shover and John P. Wright. New York: Oxford University Press.

Pearce, Frank, and Steve Tombs. 1998. *Toxic Capitalism: Corporate Crime and the Chemical Industry*. Aldershot, UK: Ashgate.

Piquero, Nicole L., Stephanie Carmichael, and Alex R. Piquero. 2008. "Research note: Assessing the perceived seriousness of white-collar and street crime." *Crime and Delinquency* 54:291–312.

Reiss, Albert J., Jr., and A. D. Biderman. 1980. *Data Sources on White-Collar Law-Breaking*. Washington, DC: U.S. Department of Justice, National Institute of Justice.

Ross, Edward A. 1907. *Sin and Society*. Boston: Houghton Mifflin.

Rothe, Dawn. In press. "Policy, lies, and denial: Abu Ghraib and state crime." *Crime, Media, Culture*.

Schwendinger, Herman, and Julia Schwendinger. 1975. "Defenders of order or guardians of human rights?" In *Critical Criminology*, edited by Ian Taylor, Paul Walton, and Jock Young. London: Routledge and Kegan Paul.

Shapiro, Susan P. 1980. *Thinking about White Collar Crime: Matters of Conceptualization and Research*. Washington, DC: U.S. Department of Justice, National Institute of Justice.

———. 1983. "The new moral entrepreneurs: Corporate crime crusaders." *Contemporary Sociology* 12:304 07.

———. 1984. *Wayward Capitalists: Target of the Securities and Exchange Commission*. New Haven, CT: Yale University Press.

———. 1990. "Collaring the crime, not the criminal: Reconsidering 'white-collar crime.'" *American Sociological Review* 55:346–65.

Shichor, David, Dale K. Sechrest, and Jeffrey Doocy. 2001. "Victims of investment fraud." In *Contemporary Issues in Crime and Criminal Justice: Essays in Honor of Gilbert Geis*, edited by Henry N. Pontell and David Shichor. Upper Saddle River, NJ: Prentice Hall.

Shover, Neal, Glenn S. Coffey, and Clinton R. Sanders. 2004. "Dialing for dollars: Opportunities, justifications, and telemarketing fraud." *Qualitative Sociology* 27:59–75.

Shover, Neal, and J. H. Copes. 2010. "Decision making by persistent thieves and crime-control policy." In *Crime and Public Policy: Putting Theory to Work* (2nd ed.), edited by Hugh Barlow and Scott Decker. Philadelphia: Temple University Press.

Shover, Neal, and Francis T. Cullen. 2008. "Studying and teaching white-collar crime: Populist and Patrician perspectives." *Journal of Criminal Justice Education* 19:155–74.

Shover, Neal, Greer L. Fox, and Michael Mills. 1994. "Long-term consequences of victimization by white-collar crime." *Justice Quarterly* 11:301–24.

Shover, Neal, and Peter Grabosky. 2010. "White-collar crime and the Great Recession." *Criminology and Public Policy* 9:429–34.

Shover, Neal, and Andy Hochstetler. 2002. "Cultural explanation and organizational crime." *Crime, Law and Social Change* 37:1–18.

———. 2006. *Choosing White-Collar Crime*. New York: Cambridge University Press.

Shover, Neal, and David Honaker. 1992. "The socially bounded decision making of persistent property offenders." *Howard Journal of Criminal Justice* 31:276–93.

Shover, Neal, and Ben W. Hunter. 2010. "Blue-collar, white-collar: Crimes and mistakes." In *Offenders on Offending: Learning about Crime from Criminals*, edited by Wim Bernasco. Collompton, UK: Willan.

Sutherland, Edwin H. 1940. "White-collar criminality." *American Sociological Review* 5:1–11.

———. 1983 [1949]. *White-Collar Crime: The Uncut Version*, with an introduction by Gilbert Geis and Colin Goff. New Haven, CT: Yale University Press.

Szwajkowski, E. 1986. "The myths and realities of research on organizational misconduct." In James E. Post (Ed.), *Research in Corporate Social Performance and Policy*. New York: JAI.

Toby, Jackson. 1979. "The new criminology is the old sentimentality." *Criminology* 16:516–26.

Unnever, James D., Michael L. Benson, and Francis T. Cullen. 2008. "Public support for getting tough on corporate crime: Racial and political divides." *Journal of Research in Crime and Delinquency* 45:163–90.

U.S. Department of Justice. 2005. *Financial Crimes Report to the Public*. Washington, DC: Federal Bureau of Investigation. http://www.fbi.gov/stats-services/publications/fcs_report2005. Accessed October 20, 2010.

———. 2007. *Identity Theft, 2005*. Washington, DC: Bureau of Justice Statistics. http://www.justice.gov/criminal/fraud/websites/idtheft.html. Accessed October 20, 2010.

Vaughan, Diane. 1982. "Transaction systems and unlawful organizational behavior." *Social Problems* 29:373–79.

———. 1996. *The Challenger Launch Decision: Risky Technology, Culture, and Deviance at NASA*. Chicago: University of Chicago Press.

———. 1999. "The dark side of organizations: Mistake, misconduct, and disaster." *Annual Review of Sociology* 25:271–305.

———. 2006. "NASA revisited: Theory, analogy, and public sociology." *American Journal of Sociology* 12:353–93.

Weisburd, David, Stanton Wheeler, and N. Bode. 1991. *Crimes of the Middle Classes.* New Haven, CT: Yale University Press.

Yeager, Peter C. 2007. "Understanding corporate lawbreaking: From profit seeking to law finding." In *International Handbook of White-Collar and Corporate Crime*, edited by Henry N. Pontell and Gilbert Geis. New York: Springer.

Zimring, Franklin E. 1993. "Crime, justice and the savings and loan crisis." In *Beyond the Law: Crime in Complex Organizations*, edited by Michael Tonry and Albert J. Reiss, Jr. Chicago: University of Chicago Press.

4

From Early White-Collar Bandits and Robber Barons to Modern-Day White-Collar Criminals

A Review of the Conceptual and Theoretical Research

— *Andrea Schoepfer and Stephen G. Tibbetts*

Wherever the victorious race had forced its way, it sowed the seeds of hate and industrial crime.

Robert Herrick, *A Life for a Life*
(in *The Cry for Justice*, edited by Upton Sinclair, 1921)

This article begins with a review of the earliest documented examinations of various concepts of white-collar crime of the late 1800s and early 1900s, which preceded Sutherland's widely cited presidential address at the American Sociological Society in Philadelphia on December 27, 1939.

An original article written for this publication.

63

The address was published in February 1940 in *The American Sociological Review*. This article will discuss a large amount of scientific literature that examined a wide range of issues in the area of corporate and occupational crime that has largely been acknowledged, but subsequently ignored by most criminologists regarding the study of white-collar crime. It will become clear that, despite virtually all recent reviews, Sutherland did not innovate the study of white-collar crime, but he did have a strong impact in criminology/sociology by identifying white-collar crime as a primary issue to be studied, and the key portions of his address will be examined in detail. Next, this article provides a comprehensive review of the primary theoretical concepts and perspectives, as well as the findings of numerous studies, from mid-nineteenth century to present, that have been applied to the study of white-collar crime, with an emphasis on the findings that show the unique, categorical differences that white-collar and corporate crimes pose for our discipline.

Virtually all scientific and book sources specifically name Edwin H. Sutherland as the scholar who innovated the concept of white-collar crime. Although Sutherland was likely the scholar who coined the term "white-collar crime," he certainly did not innovate the concept nor did he create the initial attention to the study of white-collar offending; he simply brought more awareness to the already existing topic. Although his presidential address led to an increase in attention regarding scholarly work in this area of study, for which he should be credited, we will show in this section that the study of white-collar offending by legal scholars, criminologists, and other social scientists existed and was quite active decades before Sutherland acknowledged it in his presidential address.

A search of the extant literature shows numerous references to "white-collar bandits," "robber barons," "criminaloid," "corporate crime," and "industrial crime," for many years prior to Sutherland's address and subsequent studies on the topic of white-collar crime. The meaning of all these references is virtually synonymous with "white-collar crime." Sutherland's coining of the latter term appears to be more about semantics than the actual innovation of a new concept or unique topic of study in criminology. Specifically, the concept of "white-collar bandits" was the focus of a number of scholarly works in studies prior to Sutherland's 1939 address. For example, the first paragraph of H. J. Kenner's (1926) article in *The ANNALS of the American Academy of Political and Social Science* emphasized the need to examine white-collar bandits and also defined the concept:

> Business men are now taking a hand in checking the "rising tide of crime" and the "growing disrespect for law." While one national group is studying the problem of curbing crimes of violence, others locally and nationally are continuing action against the *white collar bandit*, the gentleman thief who steals the savings of the uninformed or the gullible by stock-swindling and fraudulent brokerage practices. (emphasis added to the original, p. 54)

Kenner was the first manager of the Better Business Bureau. He claimed: "The money loss caused by the white collar bandits is each year many times that resulting from crimes of violence" (p. 54). Kenner went on to examine several important aspects of this type of crime, such as lists of "outstanding perils" to victims and society and "essentials to fraud prevention" (pp. 54–55), as well as numerous anecdotes of key cases that the Better Business Bureaus of New York City and Florida had dealt with in recent years. He provided extensive details and information regarding such white-collar bandits more than a decade prior to Sutherland's address.

Another example of scholarly study of the white-collar bandit can be found in the August 1929 issue of the *Commercial Law League Journal*, in which a judge, the Honorary George E. Q. Johnson, U.S. District Attorney for the Northern District of Illinois, emphasized the financial impact of white-collar offenders. "The White Collar Bandit has been [a] particular problem, and indeed it is a problem" (Johnson, 1929, p. 432). He elaborated about the extremely large amounts of funds lost to such offenders and explored various strategies of addressing the problem of white-collar bandits. Bertram K. Wolfe (1938), an associate professor in law at Temple University, wrote a journal article in which he claimed that "the 'white collar bandit' may still attempt a 'profitable' bankruptcy" (p. 1). He then discussed how such bandits could profit from the existing bankruptcy laws/policies.

Another early term for white-collar criminals was "robber baron," which was largely promoted by Matthew Josephson in his book *The Robber Barons: The Great American Capitalists,* first published in 1934 during the Great Depression. Josephson first attributed this label to a pamphlet in the 1880s in which farmers in Kansas had used the term to describe railroad magnates. Josephson applied the label to many other businessmen believed to have used improper or illegal practices in order to gain profits for their companies or themselves. Although the term originally derived from the middle ages, specifically Germanic practices in which lords would charge large fees against sea vessels traveling on the Rhine, Josephson applied this term to current (at that time) businessmen, such as Rockefeller, Carnegie, and Vanderbilt, for their business practices in the oil, railroad, and steel companies. Regardless of the validity of his claims, he presented research on the topic of white-collar crime in his book.

It is interesting to note that the term "robber baron" was used in Sutherland's address (1940, p. 2), but he (or the editors of the journal in which it was published) did not credit Josephson or others who had previously used the same label or examined such corporate criminals. For example, Sutherland said in his address: "The 'robber barons' of the last half of the nineteenth century were white-collar criminals, as practically everyone now agrees" (p. 2).

Sutherland's use of "robber baron" highlights the fact that he did not pioneer the study of white-collar crime. Rather, he highlighted a type of crime—white-collar crime—that had been examined by other research-ers in previous years. His terminology in the presidential address put more focus on this topic than did the previous publications and scholarly works. Ironically, and as often occurs in criminology, the attention to cer-tain concepts and theories reappears decades later. For example, "robber baron" was the term used to describe the unregulated selfishness and greed of modern CEOs and other corporate "sharks" during the financial meltdown that began in 2008.

Media exposure is likely one of the reasons, if not the most impor-tant reason, why Sutherland is credited with innovating or introducing the concept of white-collar crime. Gilbert Geis (2007) reviewed significant news headlines after Sutherland's 1939 speech. The *New York Times* ran a story about the conference proceedings with the headline: "Hits Crimi-nality in White Collars" and subheadlines of "Robber Barons' Outdone" and "Dr. Sutherland Says the Cost of Duplicity in High Places Exceeds Burglary Losses" (p. 15). It was (and still is) quite rare for a nationally rec-ognized publication such as the *New York Times* to run a major story on proceedings from a professional conference. According to Geis (2009), "His observations got extended coverage in the NY Times where they heralded it as dazzling the audience."

Another term used for white-collar criminals prior to Sutherland's address was "criminaloid," credited to Edward A. Ross (1907). Ross claimed that criminaloids "want nothing more than all of us want—money, power, consideration—in a word, success; but they are in a hurry and they are not particular about the means" (quoted in Geis, 2007, p. 12). Sutherland used the term "criminaloid" in his early works. "These white-collar criminaloids are by far the most dangerous to society . . . from the point of view of effects on private property and social institutions" (Sutherland, 1934, p. 2). So it is clear that Sutherland recognized previous conceptualization and theorizing by other social scientists about offend-ers he subsequently labeled "white collar." Various terms and concepts that were equivalent to white-collar crime were in existence before Sutherland's address, and he incorporated some of these labels in his ear-lier work and in his address.

A recent search of the extant literature found the term "corporate crime" was used over a dozen times in scholarly articles before Suther-land's 1939 address. For example, the *Yale Law Journal* published an arti-cle by Henry W. Edgerton (1926), titled "Corporate Criminal Responsibility," in which he used the term "corporate crime." *Columbia Law Review* published an article by Frederic P. Lee (1928), who not only used the term "corporate crime" but also defined it "as a crime comprised of acts of members of the corporation" (p. 282). The *Oregon Law Review* also published the term "corporate crime" in an article by James Barnett (1937) titled "The Criminal Liability of American Municipal Corpora-tions." Even earlier, Ernst Freund (1897), an associate professor at the

University of Chicago in the late 1800s, published a book entitled *The Legal Nature of Corporations*, which discussed the concept of "corporate crime" at length and used the term repeatedly (e.g., see page 69). Another book that used the term in discussing the concept of corporate crime was *The Consolidation of Gas Companies in Boston* by George Anderson (1905) at Harvard University, which presented an extensive review of such violations. All of these examples indicate that the study of white-collar crime existed prior to Sutherland's 1939 address.

Geis (1988) reviewed the history of deceptive marketing—particularly the *caveat emptor* doctrine—from biblical times to modern day. He explored issues from the Roman times to the "South Sea Bubble" case in the early 1700s, which involved a British monopoly company manipulating investments. Geis and Joseph DiMento (2002) provided a comprehensive review of a multitude of legal issues and cases regarding corporate crime that existed prior to Sutherland's address in 1939. Additional references by Geis to historical reactions to white-collar crime can be found in Part III ("Wall Street Crimes") of this book. There are many other examples of the study of corporate crime and corporate liability before Sutherland's address in 1939. Both legal scholars and social scientists had been aware of and acknowledged the importance of white-collar crime years before the ASS address.

Another common term for white-collar crime is "industrial crime," which was also used in scholarly publications before 1939. For example, Benjamin Wood wrote a book in 1901 (*Bugle Calls: Awake, Educate, Agitate, Act!*) that discussed the concept of industrial crime at length. Charles Henderson (1911) discussed the concept of industrial crime in *Pay-Day*. In *The Cry for Justice*, Upton Sinclair (1915; see p. 101) used the term industrial crime and explored various topics regarding such offenses. There are other sources that discussed industrial crime, corporate crime, and white-collar bandits before 1939, but we will not review them here due to space limitations.

There are also many dozens of scholarly works prior to Sutherland's address regarding "bribery," which involves giving compensation to persons in power to overlook certain violations or taking "kickbacks" for certain decisions regarding governmental contracts, etc. For example, M. D. Naar (1880) included an entire chapter on bribery and corruption (before Sutherland was born). The term "corporate fraud" appears numerous times in scholarly works prior to Sutherland's address. C. Wood Davis (1891) noted various forms of such fraud committed by companies.

Geis (2007) traces fraud and bribery back to the ancient Greeks. A decree issued about 476 B.C.E. state: "If anyone prevents grain from being imported . . . or forces up prices of imported grain, that man shall die both himself and his family" (cited in Garnsey, 1986, p. 76). Given the severity of the penalty (extending to the family of the perpetrator), this type of offense must have been quite prevalent. Geis (2007) goes on to provide multiple examples of references to various forms of white-collar crime in ancient Rome, in Judeo-Christian precepts, in early English law, and up to the muckrakers in the early 1900s. President Theodore Roosevelt castigated "muckrakers who rake up so much" (pp. 66–67). Again, it is clear that white-collar crime was studied and acknowledged prior to Sutherland's 1939 address, yet criminologists often ignore previous research, crediting Sutherland with innovating or introducing the concept of white-collar crime.

It is rather surprising that Sutherland is characterized as pioneering the study of white-collar crime when it had been written about for almost 60 years before he made it the primary focus of his 1939 presidential address. Virtually all sources—across the sociological, criminological and business literature—cite his ASS address as innovating the concept of white-collar crime. Sutherland should certainly be credited for helping to bring far more attention to this area of research, but it is also important to recognize earlier research and studies.

For example, one of the current criminology textbooks in the field states that "The concept of white-collar crime was formally born in 1939 when Edwin H. Sutherland . . . used the term as the title of his presidential address to the American Sociological Society" (Brown, Esbensen, and Geis, 2007, p. 504). Many other sources claim the same, such as Geis' article in this book (see p. 6, which refers to Sutherland's "introduction of the concept of 'white-collar crime'"). We are not taking issue with Sutherland's coining of the term "white-collar crime," but we are addressing the inaccuracy of the idea that Sutherland introduced this concept.* The same assumption exists in the business literature, where Sutherland is recognized as the scholar who "did the pioneering research on the subject" (Heath, 2008, p. 601).

We asked Gilbert Geis, perhaps the most respected criminologist on the history of white-collar crime, to read this article. We also asked his opinion about why he (as well as virtually all criminologists—including the authors of this article) continued to write that Sutherland introduced the concept of white-collar crime. He explained: "I believe that what we wrote was essentially a *shorthanded* and perhaps *misleading* way of saying that Sutherland was the one who put the concept front and center in the world of social science" (Geis, 2009; emphasis added). We agree—we have all overlooked previous studies because Sutherland's address was vitally important in attracting media and professional attention. We believe,

---

* It should be noted that publications by the two authors of this article have also made claims that Sutherland "first introduced the concept of white-collar crime" (Tibbetts and Hemmens, 2010; also see a similar claim in Schoepfer and Piquero, 2006). In this article, we are not attacking particular criminologists; rather, we are questioning all criminologists, including ourselves, regarding why Sutherland has been given so much credit for innovating the concept of white-collar crime, which existed before his 1939 address.

however, that criminologists who study white-collar issues should examine earlier documents from the nineteenth and early twentieth centuries, as well as ancient documents.

Sutherland's Presidential Address to the American Sociological Society in 1939

Sutherland (1940) deserves credit for placing more emphasis on white-collar crime and for emphasizing that fellow criminologists had neglected this area when developing theories of crime causation. "The criminal statistics show unequivocally that crime, *as popularly conceived and officially measured*, has a high incidence in the lower class and a low incidence in the upper class" (p. 1). Sutherland went on to say that "the conception and explanations of crime which have just been described are misleading and incorrect, that crime is in fact not closely correlated with poverty or with the psychopathic and sociopathic conditions associated with poverty, and that an adequate explanation of criminal behavior must proceed along quite different lines" (p. 2). His argument was based on his belief that the conventional [at that time] explanations of crime were "invalid principally because they are derived from biased samples . . . that they have not included vast areas of criminal behavior of persons not in the lower class" (p. 2). Rather, Sutherland points out that "one of these neglected areas is the criminal behavior of business and professional men" (p. 2).

Sutherland's presidential address goes on to detail various forms of white-collar crime from that of "robber barons" (such as Vanderbilt), leaders of finance/industry (such as Whitney), those involving tax fraud (such as Capone), as well as other types involving those in the medical profession (Sutherland, 1940, pp. 2–3). He outlined and gave many details regarding the data from the Federal Trade Commission in the 1920s that showed commercial bribery was a common practice in many industries (p. 3). He also gave specific examples of illegal acts by many companies, such as distributing impure foods and the activities of most banks and financial institutions during the early 1900s (p. 4). Sutherland went on to note the impact of white-collar crimes in politics, which he claimed was "generally recognized as fairly prevalent" (p. 4).

Sutherland's address goes on to report anecdotes that support his claim that "the financial cost of white-collar crime is probably several times as great as the financial cost of all the crimes which are customarily regarded as the 'crime problem'" (Sutherland, 1940, pp. 4–5). This fact is currently undisputed by experts in this area. Sutherland also notes the fact that such white-collar crimes damage social relations with the populace, claiming that "white-collar crimes violate trust . . . which lowers social morale and produces social disorganization on a large scale" (p. 5).

Sutherland noted that such white-collar crime is even more important to the overall well-being of society by claiming, "Other crimes produce relatively little effect on social institutions or social organization" (p. 5). So it is clear that Sutherland believed that white-collar and corporate crimes actually cost society more, in terms of both financial and emotional consequences, than street crimes. Later studies agreed with this assessment and estimated that white-collar crime cost society between $300 and $600 billion annually (Kane and Wall, 2006), while the financial costs of conventional crime were estimated at $105 billion annually (Miller, Cohen, and Wiersema, 1996). More recent estimations suggest that the financial costs of white-collar crime are ten to fifty times greater than the costs of conventional crimes (Friedrichs, 2010).

One of the most revealing quotations from Sutherland's presidential address is "White-collar crime is real crime" (Sutherland, 1940, p. 5). In current times, that goes without saying. But at the time of his speech in 1939, it is clear that many (perhaps most) criminologists did not believe that white-collar offenses represented actual criminal offending. His conclusion called for a "theory of criminal behavior which will explain both white-collar criminality and lower class criminality" (p. 12).

Thus, it is important to recognize the importance that Sutherland's address had for placing an emphasis on researching and understanding white-collar crime. He clearly brought the concept of white-collar crime to the attention of most criminologists, whereas it may have been neglected for many years had he not emphasized this type of crime. Also, as noted previously, his address was highly recognized and touted by national publications, such as the *New York Times*, which increased public attention to this type of criminal offending. Furthermore, he specifically noted the need to create a theory that would explain such white-collar crime. Notably, he readily provided his own theory to explain this concept—differential association theory.

It is likely that previous research in this area strongly influenced Sutherland—especially regarding "robber barons"—and may have provided an important stimulus in his emphasizing this concept for further study in his 1939 presidential address. The early, pre-1939 research on white-collar bandits, robber barons, corporate/industrial crime, etc., should be recognized as vital in the development of our understanding of white-collar crime.

Theoretical Overview of White-Collar Crime from 1939 to Present

The study of white-collar crime has not occupied a prominent position in the field of criminology. Even after Sutherland's presidential address, empirical research on the topic has been hesitant. There are several reasons for the lack of research and attention to the field of white-collar crime. Perhaps the most important reason is the lack of consensus regarding how white-collar crime should be defined. White-collar crime was originally defined by offender characteristics (Sutherland, 1940). Over time, definitions evolved to include terms such as position of power and trust; almost all definitions required the offender to commit the act through opportunities provided by a legitimate occupation. More modern definitions focus on the offense itself and have moved away from the requisite employment factor by focusing on the skills and knowledge required to engage in the crimes as opposed to opportunities afforded through a career. Paul Tappan (1947) argued that the definitions had become much too broad, creating complications in the ability of researchers to thoroughly explain the phenomenon.

A second stumbling block in the study of white-collar crime is the lack of applicable data. Most of our in-depth information about white-collar crime comes from case studies with results that cannot be generalized to the larger white-collar population. Gaining access to corporations to collect data or access to convicted white-collar offenders is difficult if not impossible. Self-report studies are flawed in the fact that many may not willingly divulge their involvement in white-collar crime if they have not been caught or if they are awaiting appeals. When trying to explain white-collar crime, many tend to favor explanations of greed and rational choice. The argument is that white-collar offenders are already well-off, have jobs, are successful, and are simply engaging in crime because they are greedy. Even the news tends to portray these actors as avaricious, excessive, with no regard for others (e.g., former Tyco CEO Dennis Kozlowski's $6,000 shower curtain). David Weisburd, Stanton Wheeler, Elin Waring, and Nancy Bode (1991; see also Wheeler, 1992) have discussed the idea of the fear of failure to explain that it is not greed per se, but the fear of losing what one has worked so hard to obtain. Even Dennis Kozlowski admitted not needing (or necessarily wanting) extravagant items but they were necessary to keep up appearances (Curran, 2007). These lines of reasoning follow the rational choice perspective in which offenders rationally calculate the costs vs. the benefits of the offense. It is certainly possible to argue that educated, middle- to upper-class individuals are capable of rational thinking.

If white-collar crime simply boiled down to the motivations of greed or keeping up with appearances, then one would expect extremely low to negligible amounts of white-collar crime in noncapitalist societies where there is presumably less pressure for monetary success or power. This, however, is not the case. Gilbert Geis (1982) and John Braithwaite (1988) found that white-collar crime existed at a higher than expected level in socialist and communist countries. James Coleman (1988) suggested that even with cultural expectations for equality, it appears as though individuals still desire personal gain. Furthermore, if white-collar crime is an issue of rational choice in which benefits are weighed against the costs of the crime, then theoretically, deterrence theory should work to reduce white-collar offending. Studies so far have found little support for the successful deterrence of white-collar crime (Elis and Simpson, 1995; Moore, 1987; Piquero, Tibbetts, and Blankenship, 2005b; Stevens and Payne, 1999; Weisburd, Waring, and Chayet, 1995), but this may largely be due to the lack of consistency in white-collar crime enforcement and punishment. Various studies have looked at the effectiveness of deterrence under certain circumstances, including levels of moral inhibitions (Paternoster and Simpson, 1996) and feelings of guilt or shame (Makkai and Braithwaite, 1994; Murphy and Harris, 2007). However, deterrence by itself, and overall, has not been successful at reducing white-collar crime. In fact, research suggests that corporate managers place more emphasis on the benefits of the potential crime than on the consequences (Simpson and Koper, 1992). Oftentimes, the costs of the crime (i.e., fines) are simply seen as the costs of doing business.

White-collar crime has become a hot topic in the business field in recent years, yet business leaders/researchers rarely consult criminologists in their efforts to explain the phenomenon. In his search of 25 years of articles in the *Journal of Business Ethics*, Joseph Heath (2008) found only one reference to Cressey's (1953) classic study of convicted embezzlers' motivations for stealing, *Other People's Money*. (Interestingly, Danny DeVito's movie *Other People's Money* was cited more often in the journal than Cressey's study of the same name.) While criminologists have been studying the phenomenon for decades, the actual term "white-collar crime" rarely appeared in criminal statutes until the Sarbanes-Oxley Act of 2002 (Green, 2005). This is not to say that white-collar crimes have been ignored in the business literature or in criminal statutes, but it may be safe to say that interest in the field is growing once again as the damage from these crimes is becoming apparent on a much wider scale.

Overall, the business literature tends to point to ethics/morals and regulatory and corporate climates as the main cause of white-collar crime. The latter is in line with criminology research and will be discussed later in the article. In respect to the former, one of the main focuses has been on ethics training at the university level. While many business schools require students to enroll in ethics courses, research on the effectiveness of such courses has not been consistent. Some studies find that ethics training in college effectively increases moral awareness (Arlow and Ulrich, 1980; Cohen and Cornwell, 1989; Gauthschi and Jones 1998; Smith, Skalnik and Skalnik, 1999); some have found the opposite effect among business students (McCabe, Dukerich, and Dutton, 1994); and others have found no significant effects (Martin, 1981–1982; Wynd and Maget, 1989). In addition, one study has shown that cheating among business students in college lead to deceptive practices in actual business practices later in their careers (Sims, 1993).

Ultimately, though, in regards to quality or quantity of administration, ethics training may not be effective if the individual cares more about self-interest than moral righteousness. Similarly, while ethical considerations may play a role, they are by no means the main cause (or deterrent) of white-collar crime. According to William Black (2005), people are capable of behaving immorally while at the same time believing themselves to be morally superior; this is largely accomplished through the use of rationalizations and neutralizations.

The idea that people rationalize their criminal behaviors in order to neutralize the contradictions between their actions and societal norms was first introduced in conjunction with Sutherland's differential association theory. Donald Cressey (1953) argued that rationalizations are learned through associations with deviant others and are formed before the act takes place and therefore contribute to the motivation. Four years later Gresham Sykes and David Matza (1957) introduced a formal version of these rationalizations—techniques of neutralization—that include denial of responsibility, denial of injury, denial of victim, condemnation of condemners, and appeals to higher loyalties.

One study involved both MBA students and Executive MBA students who were presented with a scenario and asked if they would promote a drug that would likely hurt people who used it (Piquero et al., 2005b). In this study, participants who said they would market and/or sell the drug used several techniques of neutralization. Specifically, the participants who believed that governmental authorities exaggerate dangers to the consumer (i.e., denial of injury/denial of victim) and that profit is the most important priority (i.e., appeal to higher loyalty) were significantly more likely to engage in marketing the dangerous drug. It is notable that the subjects in the Executive MBA program, with more experience in the business world, were more likely to employ such techniques of neutralization in decisions to market the drug, especially regarding the profit motive.

Other researchers investigating the topic of white-collar crime have found additional techniques of neutralization. William Minor (1981) identified the *defense of necessity:* "If an act is perceived as necessary, then one need not feel guilty about its commission, even if it's considered morally wrong in the abstract" (p. 298). This type of neutralization technique may be common among white-collar criminals working in a corporate culture under constant pressure to make a profit using whatever tactics are "necessary." This neutralization technique reduces guilt by supporting perceptions that the act was integral to the company's success.

Carl Klockars (1974) identified a neutralization technique he called the "metaphor of the ledger," which involves the concept of balancing "good" and "bad" acts for the better good. If an individual can produce a large contribution to the "bottom line" (profits), it is likely that certain illegal activities or "shortcuts" will be rewarded, not punished, by the company. As the previous neutralization technique showed, the focus is on perceptions of what the corporation wants and not on what individuals actually believe. The corporate culture convinces individuals that they are acting in the best interests of the company.

Geis (1967) found that managers in the heavy electrical equipment manufacturing industry claimed that their criminal behavior served a worthwhile purpose because it helped stabilize industry prices. Cressey (1953) found that embezzlers rationalized their behavior by claiming that they were simply "borrowing" the money. Neal Shover, Glenn Coffey, and Dick Hobb's (2003) study found that telemarketers rationalized their illegal acts by identifying the customers as greedy, ignorant, and careless with their money—therefore, the customers were not really victims at all. Blaming victims for their greed and ignorance dovetails nicely with routine activities theory in which a motivated offender, suitable target, and lack of a capable guardian converge in time and space. Fraud in particular is an interesting form of white-collar crime in that it requires consensual participation from the victim; the victim willingly gives information to the offender. Because individuals in fraud cases are not properly guarding themselves and their money, predators are able to neutralize their behaviors by blaming the victim.

As with conventional crimes, the opportunity to offend plays a prominent role in white-collar crime. One cannot steal from an employer without opportunity. One cannot market an unsafe product without opportunity. One thing that makes white-collar crime different from conventional crime is that those committing the crimes are often the "capable guardians," or as Geis (1973) put it, they are the foxes guarding the chicken coop.

In his 1939 address, Sutherland discussed his differential association theory as an explanation for white-collar and all other crime.

> The hypothesis which is here suggested . . . is that white-collar criminality, just as other systematic criminality, is learned; that it is learned in direct or indirect association with those who already practice the behavior; and that those who learn this criminal behavior are segregated from frequent and intimate contacts with law-abiding behavior. Whether a person becomes a criminal or not is determined largely by the comparative frequency and intimacy of his contacts with the two types of behavior. This may be called the process of differential association. It is a genetic explanation both of white-collar criminality and lower class criminality. . . . A second general process is social disorganization in the community. Differential association culminates in crime because the community is not organized solidly against that behavior. The law is pressing in one direction, and other forces are pressing in the opposite direction. In business, the "rules of the game" conflict with the legal rules. (pp. 10-11)

Sutherland (1940) argued that just as with conventional crime, white-collar crime is fostered through the learning of deviant definitions and rationalizations through interactions/associations with deviant others. This may explain why certain industries tend to have more violators than others (Baucus and Near, 1991). One criticism to Sutherland's general theory of differential association is that it does not explain individualistic crimes like embezzlement when actors generally work alone in the commission of such crimes. A second criticism to differential association is that it is a tautological explanation—which comes first, deviant associations or deviant inclinations?

In the study that looked at marketing a harmful drug, the researchers also examined various differential association theory variables in determining which factors were important in the decisions made by the MBA students (Piquero et al., 2005b). The results clearly showed that the decision to market the drug was inversely and significantly related to perceptions the subjects had of whether their close friends and business professors would agree with their decision. The subjects placed a stronger emphasis on how their company and bosses (e.g., Board of Directors) would think about their decision to continue marketing the drug versus what friends would think. Differential association theory was supported to the extent that participants followed what they perceived to be the corporate climate; however, the theory was also questioned because participants did not follow what they perceived their closest friends or professors would have done.

White-collar crime presents a unique category for theorizing and understanding decision making by employees of corporations. Individuals may confront a difference between the values of their social world (e.g., friends) and the values of their employment culture (e.g., their boss/Board of Directors). To clarify, while most street criminals may be more highly influenced by their friends, white-collar employees seem to be far more likely influenced by their employers. Theoretically, these findings lend some support to the fact that deviant associations may come before deviant inclinations; after all, the deviant inclinations were likely not due to previous relationships of friends or business professors, but more likely came from their employers once they were employed. There is little doubt that the climate in a given corporation can lead to more (or less) corporate crime, which fits with Sutherland's theory of differential association. Individuals will adapt to the various norms to which they are currently exposed—the norms of the persons they most respect and/or depend on the most (often their employer).

Another popular general theory used to explain white-collar crime is Michael Gottfredson and Travis Hirschi's (1990) general theory of crime, or theory of low self-control. The general theory of crime has received extensive support in conjunction with conventional crime (see Pratt and Cullen, 2000), yet it has not received the same consistent support when used with white-collar crime. Some studies have not found support for low self-control and white-collar crime (Simpson and

Piquero, 2002; Piquero, Schoepfer, and Langton, 2010), while others have found support (Nagin and Paternoster, 1994; Weisburd et al., 1995). Although low self-control has not consistently explained the reasons why one would engage in white-collar crime, it has been found to significantly increase one's likelihood of fraud victimization (Holtfreter, Reisig, and Pratt, 2008). One of the main tenants of the theory of low self-control is that individuals with low self-control are impulsive, quick tempered, prefer simple tasks and physical activity to mental activity, are shortsighted, and like to take risks.

A theory from psychology—desire for control theory—has been pitted against the general theory of crime, and the results so far seem promising. The theory posits a general wish to be in control of everyday life events. It is characterized by assertion, decisiveness, a desire to influence others, and manipulation to avoid unpleasant situations (Burger and Cooper, 1979)—characteristics that appear to be at odds with the traits associated with low self-control. The limited research thus far has shown significant support for the desire-of-control theory and white-collar crime (Piquero, Exum, and Simpson, 2005a). Nicole Piquero, Andrea Schoepfer, and Lynn Langton (2010) found the desire for control to be a better predictor of white-collar crime than the general theory of crime.

Hirschi's (1969) social control theory has also been used to explain white-collar crime (Lasley, 1988). The general theory of crime contends that individuals with low self-control are—among other traits—self-centered and do not think about the consequences of their actions. Social control theory, however, contends that individuals do think about others, and they do contemplate the consequences of their actions. Strong bonds to conventional others—in the form of attachments, commitments, involvements, and beliefs—restrain individuals from engaging in crime. Essentially, social control theory suggests that individuals think about the consequences of their actions and refrain from negative behaviors that would disappoint those to whom they are bonded. However, if social control theory is correct, and strong bonds to conventional others is the key, then one could expect that individuals who are strongly bonded to their job (a conventional other), would be more likely to offend in order to see themselves (or their company) succeed. Again, we see that company culture may be more important than outside cultural influences when looking at white-collar crime.

Strain theories have also played a role in the explanation of white-collar crime. Robert Merton's (1938) strain theory focused on the American idea of equal opportunity for success with the reality that not everyone can achieve this success. This disjunction between wanting wealth and not being able to achieve it would lead individuals to create their own ways (including crime) to gain access to the things they desire. Merton suggested that the lower class would be most affected by strain. Addressing criticisms of the class distinction, Robert Agnew's (1992) general strain theory (GST) suggests that everyone experiences strain regardless of socio-economic status, but how one deals with the emotions created by strain is what really matters. GST has rarely been applied to white-collar crime (for an exception see Langton and Piquero, 2007), but as Ruth Kornhauser (1978) suggested, those with wealth might experience as much strain from trying to acquire more wealth as those who have less wealth to begin with.

Another variant of strain theory, institutional anomie theory (IAT), has also received very little attention in regards to white-collar crime (for an exception, see Schoepfer and Piquero, 2006) and conventional crime in general. IAT suggests that the American cultural value of monetary success is held much higher than the emphasis on family, education, and polity and it is this overwhelming emphasis on the economy that leads to such high crime rates in the United States. As greed is often associated with white-collar crime motivation, it would seem that IAT would have applications in the study of white-collar crime. Unfortunately IAT lacks empirical support largely due to the difficulties in concept operationalization.

Strain not only affects individuals, it also affects corporations. Organizational strain emanates from factors both internal (i.e., size, performance) and external to the organization (i.e., regulations, economic conditions). In terms of internal sources of strain, it might be expected that poorly performing firms would experience more strain and therefore be more likely to offend, but empirical research has not supported this idea (Clinard and Yeager, 1980; Simpson, 1986; Baucus and Near, 1991; Jenkins and Braithwaite, 1993). By their very nature, corporations are strongly goal-oriented. Regardless of their performance, firms may experience strain from wanting or expecting more. Another source of organizational strain is size; increased size can lead to communication and coordination breakdowns, increased number of employees, decentralization, and increased opportunities for offending. Other sources of strain may emanate from both the internal and external culture pressures discussed below.

Cultural theories are perhaps one of the more widely accepted explanations in both criminology and business literatures, despite the inherent weaknesses of conceptualizing and examining "culture" (Shover and Hochstetler, 2002). Cultural theories in terms of white-collar crime generally focus on corporate culture and government and regulatory climate. James Coleman (1992) argued for a theory emphasizing organizational goals (profit), organizational environment, and internal culture and structure. Similarly, Diane Vaughan (1992) proposed a theory focusing on the organization's competitive environment, the organizational characteristics that provide opportunities to offend, and the regulatory environment. Neal Shover and Kevin Bryant (1993, p. 152) suggested that "the supply of corporate offenders varies directly with the strength of cultures of non-compliance." Unfortunately there is a lack of empirical research testing these claims, largely due to the difficulties of obtaining applicable data and conceptualizing "culture." Another issue is the idea that corporate culture is not necessarily static or uniform across organizations; over time, goals (aside from profit) may shift, economic climates may change, executives and managers retire or leave, regulatory enforcement may vary, and industry demands evolve.

Cultural pressures also come from regulatory agencies that reorganize over time with different government administrations. For example, democrats tend to favor a deterrence style of corporate control. The deterrence style assumes that corporations are greedy and respond only to profit and power; therefore, state coercion through strict regulation is needed to control them. On the other hand, republicans tend to favor the compliance style that suggests that corporations should be left alone and de-regulated. The compliance style of corporate control assumes that the market will fix itself through healthy competition and the good will of industry. Shifts between deterrence style and compliance style can be seen with changes in presidential administrations (Friedrichs, 2010). Corporate actors know when regulatory enforcement is low, and they know what they can get away with. Likewise, they know when enforcement is high and when they need to be careful. Governmental emphasis on control may help corporate actors rationalize their behaviors one way or the other.

There is no reason to think that a corporate culture of compliance or noncompliance would not affect decisions to offend, but it is not the only factor. Perhaps cultural support for noncompliance makes it easier to rationalize one's behaviors. As Joseph Heath (2008) suggested, it is not simply an issue of morals or ethics; rather, it is an issue of how people think about the situations they are presented with and what they expect others to think about their situations. If the corporate climate supports (or does not punish) unethical activity, then individuals may be more likely to perceive such behaviors as acceptable.

Another aspect of cultural explanations is conflict theory. Conflict theory assumes that crime is an inevitable product of capitalist societies, and the worst form of crime is the exploitation of the working class. This exploitation generally occurs during the pursuit of profit maximization and cost reduction. When the benefits of the crime outweigh the costs in the pursuit of profit maximization, illegalities are more likely to occur (Slapper and Tombs, 1999). Some examples include crimes against consumers where companies market unsafe products or engage in price-fixing. Another example includes crimes against employees in which companies provide unsafe working conditions, inadequate compensation, discrimination, etc. Conflict theory can also be seen in corporate and political crimes when those with economic or political power create laws to benefit their own interests—laws that further their own goals or laws that marginalize a threatening group (Quinney, 1974). Furthermore, during times of economic crisis in capitalist societies, pressures to commit crime increases as resources become scarce (Reiman and Headlee, 1981). A criticism to conflict theory's explanation of white-collar crime is that it cannot explain why some companies do not offend.

The majority of empirical research in white-collar crime thus far has been built off traditional theories that were originally developed to explain conventional crimes. However, white-collar and conventional offenders, for the most part, are distinctly different (Weisburd et al., 1991), and we shouldn't necessarily expect the same explanations to apply. While the use of conventional theoretical explanations is an important step in the study of white-collar crime, our next step should be to move beyond conventional explanations.

Conclusion

This article began with an examination of the pre-Sutherland research on various forms of white-collar crime in the late nineteenth and early twentieth centuries, which has largely been ignored by criminologists. While it is clear that Sutherland did not "innovate" the study of white-collar crime, he did have a strong impact in criminology/sociology by identifying white-collar crime as a primary issue in the field. The article concluded with a review of the various theoretical concepts and perspectives, as well as the findings of numerous studies, that show the unique and categorical differences that white-collar and corporate crimes pose for our discipline.

It appears that the inclusion of cultural influences may be imperative to any explanation of white-collar crime, yet it is only one small part of the explanation. As we have seen, white-collar crime still exists in communist countries; despite cultural expectations, people still want to be successful. This negates the simple cultural explanation theory, but does perhaps point to cultural support as a tool that may make it easier to rationalize our behaviors (thus explaining why there is more white-collar crime in capitalist societies). Therefore, integrated theories, while relatively new, may provide the most promising approach to the study of white-collar crime and corporate crime in particular. Explanations that encompass cultural influences and individual level factors may prove to have an increased explanatory power than either theoretical focus on its own. While integrated theories have been proposed (e.g., Braithwaite, 1989; Coleman, 1987), there is still a rather sizeable lack of empirical investigation.

Obviously, there is no one-size-fits-all explanation of white-collar crime, and there really is no reason to think that we will find one or even need to find one. As David Friedrichs (2010) points out, white-collar crimes are fundamentally different from conventional crimes and may therefore require different explanations; even the different white-collar crimes may need their own theories. As of yet, there are no solid theories of white-collar crime, there are only theories of crime that have been applied to white-collar crime, and suggested theories that are close to impossible to conceptualize. This is not a fault of researchers per se but rather an inherent flaw in the white-collar crime phenomenon itself. If we can't define it, we can't measure it, if we can't measure it, we can't explain it.

The study of white-collar crime seems to be in a holding pattern due to complications of defining, measuring, and explaining the phenomenon, and there does not appear to be any easy or quick fixes on the horizon. This is not to say we should give up on finding answers, but perhaps it is time for more interdisciplinary collaboration as a way to see the problem from different perspectives in the hopes of fostering innovative solutions. As highlighted by our initial discussion, the topic of white-collar crime has been a concern for centuries. Sutherland's 1939 address encouraged criminology/sociology to study white-collar criminals rather than limiting their efforts to crime committed by the less privileged. Sutherland may not have initiated the topic of white-collar crime, but he advanced the study of an age-old problem. The study of white-collar crime has ebbed and flowed, and we still have a long way to go. Whether anyone will have as large an impact as Sutherland did, remains to be seen.

REFERENCES

Agnew, R. (1992). "Foundation for a General Strain Theory of Crime and Delinquency." *Criminology, 30*, 47–88.

Anderson, G. W. (1905). *Consolidation of Gas Companies in Boston.* Boston: Public Franchise League.

Arlow, P., and Ulrich, T. (1980). "Business Ethics: Social Responsibility and Business Students: An Empirical Comparison of Clark's Study." *Akron Business and Economic Review, 11*, 17–22.

Barnett, J. D. (1937). "The Criminal Liability of American Municipal Corporations." *Oregon Law Review, 17*, 289–302.

Baucus, M., and Near, J. (1991). "Can Illegal Corporate Behavior Be Predicted? An Event History Analysis." *Academy of Management Journal, 34*, 9–36.

Black, W. (2005). *The Best Way to Rob a Bank Is To Own One.* Austin: University of Texas Press.

Braithwaite, J. (1988). "White-Collar Crime, Competition, and Capitalism: Comment on Coleman." *American Journal of Sociology, 94*, 632–636.

Braithwaite, J. (1989). "Criminological Theory and Organizational Crime." *Justice Quarterly, 6*, 333–358.

Brown, S., Esbensen, F., and Geis, G. (2007). *Criminology: Explaining Crime and Its Context* (6th ed.). Cincinnati, OH: Lexis-Nexis Anderson.

Burger, J., and Cooper, H. (1979). "The Desirability of Control." *Motivation and Emotion, 3*, 381–393.

Clinard, M., and Yeager, P. (1980). *Corporate Crime.* New York: The Free Press.

Cohen, E., and Cornwell, L. (1989). "A Question of Ethics: Developing Information System Ethics." *Journal of Business Ethics, 8*, 431–437.

Coleman, J. (1987). "Toward an Integrated Theory of White-Collar Crime." *American Journal of Sociology, 93*, 406–439.

Coleman, J. (1992). "The Theory of White-Collar Crime: From Sutherland to the 1990s." In K. Schlegel and D. Weisburd (Eds.), *White-Collar Crime Reconsidered* (pp. 53–77). Boston: Northeastern University Press.

Cressey, D. (1953). *Other People's Money: A Study in the Social Psychology of Embezzlement*. Belmont, CA: Wadsworth (1971 ed.)

Curran, D. (Producer). (2007, March 25). *60 Minutes: Ex-Tyco Chief Behind Bars* [Television broadcast]. New York: Central Broadcasting Service.

Davis, C. W. (1891). *A Compendium of the World's Food Production and Consumption*. Wichita, KS: Eagle Printing House.

Edgerton, H. W. (1926). "Corporate Criminal Responsibility." *Yale Law Journal, 36,* 827–838.

Elis, L., and Simpson, S. (1995). "Informal Sanction Threats and Corporate Crime: Additive versus Multiplicative Models." *Journal of Research in Crime and Delinquency, 32*(4), 399–424.

Freund, E. (1897). *The Legal Nature of Corporations*. Chicago: University of Chicago Press.

Friedrichs, D. (2010). *Trusted Criminals: White-Collar Crime in Contemporary Society* (4th ed.). Belmont, CA: Cengage.

Garnsey, P. (1986). *Famine and Food Supply in the Greco-Roman World: Responses to Risk and Crisis*. Cambridge, England: Cambridge University Press.

Gautsch, F., and Jones, T. (1998). "Enhancing the Ability of Business Students to Recognize Ethical Issues: An Empirical Assessment of the Effectiveness of a Course in Business Ethics." *Journal of Business Ethics, 17,* 205–216.

Geis, G. (1967). "White-Collar Crime: The Heavy Electrical Equipment Antitrust Cases of 1961." In M. Clinard and R. Quinney (Eds.) *Criminal Behavior Systems: A Typology* (pp. 139–151). New York: Holt, Reinhart, and Winston.

Geis, G. (1973). "Deterring Corporate Crime." In R. Nader and M. Green (Eds.) *Corporate Power in America* (pp. 185–187). New York: Grossman.

Geis, G. (1982). *On White-Collar Crime*. New York: Dryden Press.

Geis, G. (1988). "From Deuteronomy to Deniability: A Historical Perlustration on White-Collar Crime." *Justice Quarterly, 5,* 7–32.

Geis, G. (2007). *White-Collar and Corporate Crime*. Upper Saddle River, NJ: Pearson.

Geis, G. (2009). Personal communication via e-mail on 10/19/09. Available from Stephen Tibbetts, California State University, San Bernardino.

Geis, G., and DiMento, F. C. (2002). "Empirical Evidence and the Legal Doctrine of Corporate Criminal Liability." *American Journal of Criminal Law, 29,* 341–375.

Gottfredson, M., and Hirschi, T. (1990). *A General Theory of Crime*. Stanford, CA: Stanford University Press.

Green, S. (2005). "The Concept of White-Collar Crime in Law and Legal Theory." *Buffalo Criminal Law Review, 8,* 1–34.

Heath, J. (2008). "Business Ethics and Moral Motivation: A Criminological Perspective." *Journal of Business Ethics, 83,* 595–614.

Henderson, C. H. (1911). *Pay-Day*. Boston: Houghton Mifflin Company.

Hirschi, T. (1969). *Causes of Delinquency*. Berkeley: University of California Press.

Holtfreter, K., Reisig, M., and Pratt, T. (2008). "Low Self-Control, Routine Activities, and Fraud Victimization." *Criminology, 46*(1), 189–220.

Jenkins, A., and Braithwaite, J. (1993). "Profits, Pressure and Corporate Lawbreaking." *Crime, Law and Social Change, 20,* 221–232.

Johnson, G. E. Q. (1929). "Enforcement and Administration of the Criminal Law." *Commercial Law League Journal, 34,* 432–441.

Josephson, M. (1934). *The Robber Barons: The Great American Capitalists*. New York: Harcourt Brace.

Kane, J., and Wall, A. (2006). *The 2005 National Public Survey on White Collar Crime*. Fairmount, WV: The National White Collar Crime Center.

Kenner, H. J. (1926). "The Fight on Stock Swindlers." *The ANNALS of the American Academy of Political and Social Science, 125,* 54–58.

Klockars, C. B. (1974). *The Professional Fence.* New York: The Free Press.

Kornhauser, R. (1978). *Social Sources of Delinquency.* Chicago: University of Chicago Press.

Langton, L., and Piquero, N. (2007). "Can General Strain Theory Explain White-Collar Crime? A Preliminary Investigation of the Relationship between Strain and Select White-Collar Offenses." *Journal of Criminal Justice, 35,* 1–15.

Lasley, J. (1988). "Toward a Control Theory of White-Collar Offending." *Journal of Quantitative Criminology, 4,* 347–362.

Lee, F. P. (1928). "Corporate Criminal Liability." *Columbia Law Review, 28*(1), 1–28.

Makkai, T., and Braithwaite, J. (1994). "The Dialectics of Corporate Deterrence." *Journal of Research in Crime and Delinquency, 31*(4), 347–373.

Martin, T. (1981–1982). "Do Courses in Ethics Improve the Ethical Judgment of Students?" *Business and Society Review, 20 & 21,* 17–26.

McCabe, D., Dukerich, J., and Dutton, J. (1994). "The Effects of Professional Education on Values and the Resolution of Ethical Dilemmas: Business School vs. Law School Students." *Journal of Business Ethics, 13,* 693–700.

Merton, R. (1938). "Social Structure and Anomie." *American Sociological Review, 3,* 672–682.

Miller, T., Cohen, M., and Wiersema, B. (1996). *The Extent and Costs of Crime Victimization: A New Look.* Washington, DC: National Institute of Justice.

Minor, W. (1981). "Techniques of Neutralization: A Reconceptualization and Empirical Examination." *Journal of Research in Crime and Delinquency, 18,* 295–318.

Moore, C. (1987). "Taming the Giant Corporation? Some Cautionary Remarks on the Deterrability of Corporate Crime." *Crime and Delinquency, 33*(3), 379–402.

Murphy, K., and Harris, N. (2007). "Shaming, Shame, and Recidivism: A Test of Reintegrative Shaming Theory in the White-Collar Crime Context." *British Journal of Criminology, 47,* 900–917.

Naar, M. D. (1880). "Bribery and Corruption." Chapter XI, *The Law of Suffrage and Elections* (pp. 215–227). Trenton, NJ: Naar, Day & Naar.

Nagin, D., and Paternoster, R. (1993). "Enduring Individual Differences and Rational Choice Theories of Crime." *Law and Society Review, 27,* 467–496.

Paternoster, R., and Simpson, S. (1996). "Sanction Threats and Appeals to Morality: Testing a Rational Choice Model of Corporate Crime." *Law and Society Review, 30*(3), 549–583.

Piquero, N., Exum, M., and Simpson, S. (2005a). "Integrating the Desire for Control and Rational Choice in a Corporate Crime Context." *Justice Quarterly, 13,* 481–510.

Piquero, N., Schoepfer, A., and Langton, L. (2010). "Completely Out of Control of the Desire to Be in Complete Control?" *Crime & Delinquency, 56,* 627-647.

Piquero, N., Tibbetts, S., and Blankenship, M. (2005b). "Examining the Role of Differential Association and Techniques of Neutralization in Explaining Corporate Crime." *Deviant Behavior, 26,* 159–188.

Pratt, T., and Cullen, F. (2000). "The Empirical Status of Gottfredson and Hirschi's General Theory of Crime: A Meta-Analysis." *Criminology, 38,* 931–964.

Quinney, R. (1974). *Critique of Legal Order: Crime Control in a Capitalist Society.* Boston: Little, Brown.

Reiman, J., and Headlee, S. (1981). "Marxism and Criminal Justice Policy." *Crime and Delinquency, 27,* 24–47.

Ross, E. A. (1907). "The Criminaloid." *Atlantic Monthly, 99,* 44–53.

Schoepfer, A., and Piquero, N. (2006). "Exploring White-Collar Crime and the American Dream: A Partial Test of Institutional Anomie Theory." *Journal of Criminal Justice, 34,* 227–235.

Shover, N., and Bryant, K. (1993). "Theoretical Explanations of Corporate Crime." In M. Blankenship (Ed.), *Understanding Corporate Criminality* (pp. 141–176). New York: Garland.

Shover, N., Coffey, G., and Hobbs, D. (2003). "Crime on the Line: Telemarketing and the Changing Nature of Professional Crime." *British Journal of Criminology, 43,* 489–505.

Shover, N., and Hochstetler, A. (2002). "Cultural Explanation and Organizational Crime." *Crime, Law and Social Change, 37,* 1–18.

Simpson, S. (1986). "The Decomposition of Antitrust: Testing a Multi-Level, Longitudinal Model of Profit Squeeze." *American Sociological Review, 51,* 859–875.

Simpson, S., and Koper, C. (1997). "The Changing of the Guard: Top Management Characteristics, Organizational Strain, and Antitrust Offending." *Journal of Quantitative Criminology, 13,* 373–404.

Simpson, S., and Piquero, N. (2002). "Low Self-Control, Organizational Theory, and Corporate Crime." *Law and Society Review, 36,* 509–548.

Sims, R. (1993). "The Relationship between Academic Dishonesty and Unethical Business Practices." *Journal of Education for Business, 69,* 207–211.

Sinclair, U. (1915). *The Cry for Justice: An Anthology of the Literature of Social Protest.* New York: John C. Winston Company.

Slapper, G., and Tombs, S. (1999). *Corporate Crime.* United Kingdom: Pearson Education Ltd.

Smith, D., Skalnik, R., and Skalnik, P. (1999). "Ethical Behavior of Marketing Managers and MBA Students: A Comparative Study." *Teaching Business Ethics, 3,* 323–337.

Stevens, E., and Payne, B. (1999). "Applying Deterrence Theory in the Context of Corporate Wrongdoing: Limitations on Punitive Damages." *Journal of Criminal Justice, 27*(3), 195–207.

Sutherland, E. (1934). *Principles of Criminology* (2nd ed.). Philadelphia: Lippincott.

Sutherland, E. (1940). "White-Collar Criminality." *American Sociological Review, 5,* 1–12. http://www2.asanet.org/governance/PresidentialAddress1939.pdf

Sykes, G., and Matza, D. (1957). "Techniques of Neutralization: A Theory of Delinquency." *American Sociological Review, 22,* 664–670.

Tappan, P. (1947). "Who Is the Criminal?" *American Sociological Review, 12,* 96–102.

Tibbetts, S., & Hemmens, C. (2010). *Criminological Theory: A Text/Reader.* Thousand Oaks, CA: Sage.

Vaughan, D. (1992). "The Macro-Micro Connection in White-Collar Crime Theory." In K. Schlegel and D. Weisburd (Eds.), *White-Collar Crime Reconsidered* (pp. 124–145). Boston: Northeastern University Press.

Weisburd, D., Waring, E., and Chayet, E. (1995). "Specific Deterrence in a Sample of Offenders Convicted of White-Collar Crimes." *Criminology, 33*(4), 587–607.

Weisburd, D., Wheeler, S., Waring, E., and Bode, N. (1991). *Crimes of the Middle Class.* New Haven, CT: Yale University Press.

Wheeler, S. (1992). "The Problem of White-Collar Motivation." In K. Schlegel and D. Weisburd (Eds.), *White-Collar Crime Reconsidered* (pp. 108–123). Boston: Northeastern University Press.

Wolfe, B. K. (1938). "Detection of Fraud under the New Bankruptcy Law." *Temple University Law Quarterly, 13*(1), 1–28.

Wood, B. (1901). *Bugle Calls: Awake, Educate, Agitate, Act!* New York: Brentanos.

Wynd, W., and Maget, J. (1989). "The Business and Society Course: Does it Change Student Attitudes?" *Journal of Business Ethics, 8,* 486–491.

5

What about Women and White-Collar Crime?

— *Mary Dodge*

White-collar crime is rife with masculine imagery that reflects the hegemonic nature of the offenders and offenses. Profiles and definitions of white-collar criminals focus on powerful, wealthy men in positions of trust (see e.g., Sutherland, 1949; Geis, Meier, & Salinger, 1995). Corporate and occupational crime studies include numerous cases of wrongdoing by a respected person in a high social status in the course of *his* occupation. Consider the following examples of white-collar crime.

- A corporate executive decides to dump stock based on inside information that a newly developed and highly lucrative cancer drug will not be approved by the Food and Drug Administration.
- High ranking company officials conspire with competitors to control the market price with the sole purpose of increasing profits and defrauding consumers.
- A company president bills personal expenses and extravagant redecorating costs to subsidiary businesses.
- A state senator accepts bribes and kickbacks from companies bidding on a government contract.

Typically, these offenders and offenses evoke images of men such as Enron's Ken Lay and Jeffery Skilling, Tyco's Dennis Kozlowski, or Qwest's Joe Nacchio.

Un-gendered considerations of the offender may bring to mind visions of Martha Stewart, Leona Helmsley, Diane Brooks, or Lea Fastow,

An original article written for this publication.

all of whom entered the elite world of white-collar crime. Stewart was accused of insider trading after she received information that a new cancer drug would be rejected by the Food and Drug Administration. Helmsley was convicted of tax evasion after evidence emerged that she billed costly estate renovations to other business holdings. Diane Brooks of Sotheby's art house conspired with top executives at Christie's, an auction house in London, to control the market and defraud investors. Though few in numbers, women are engaging in illegal and unethical acts in the corporate, professional, and political realms. Many commentators speculate that the gender gap in white-collar crimes is narrowing as women increasingly participate in illegal and unethical behavior, despite traditions and tendencies to ignore or minimize the illicit behavior of women in the workplace (Dodge, 2009). *[handwritten margin note: probably because there are more women in the work force in general]*

Studies related to women and white-collar crimes are rare, though the actions of female offenders who commit such offenses merit investigation. Quantitative research on women and elite deviance is scarce, in part, because of the low number of incidents. Additionally, some evidence suggests women are more likely to engage in financial fraud involving less significant amounts of money compared to men—a conclusion that implies such acts are unworthy of serious attention. In fact, early speculations about the participation of women in white-collar crime discovered that their crimes were relatively inconsequential, primarily because of the overly masculine nature of the public sphere. Female upward occupational mobility and higher arrest rates, however, indicate a need for further analysis. Opportunity, not gender, is the key to understanding white-collar offending (Simon & Ahn-Redding, 2005). The landscape of white-collar crime and gender is changing as an increasing number of females in high-level positions are afforded greater opportunities to steal, lie, and cheat—elite deviance committed by women is no longer unique or trivial. *[handwritten: ↳ populist view?]*

The vast number of corporate executives, Fortune 500 board members, politicians, judges, lawyers, and doctors are men. Women, however, are making inroads into the corporate world and taking their place in male dominated professions. In 2010, 15 women were chief executive officers (CEOs) in the largest 500 publicly traded companies, and Ursula Burns at Xerox became the first woman to replace a woman CEO (CNN, 2010). In 2009, women accounted for 51.5 percent of all workers in management, professional, and related occupations. According to the annual averages, 24 percent of chief executives and more than 55 percent of financial managers are women (Bureau of Labor Statistics, 2009).

The increased number of women who hold high-level positions may be seen as good news, but it comes amid great defeat. Despite some findings that companies with female leadership perform better, women remain at the lower spectrum of the pay scale (Jones, 2009). Ironically, female leaders are rated by peers as tenacious and emotionally intelligent;

though, at all levels of the organization colleagues reported they lacked vision (Ibarra & Obodaru, 2009). Deborah Rhode (1989) argued: "Women are criticized for being 'too feminine' or 'not feminine' enough. Those who conform to accepted stereotypes appear to lack ideas or initiative, while women who take a more assertive stance are judged arrogant, aggressive, or abrasive" (pp. 169–170). Indeed, doing gender in the corporate world equates to being tough, taking risks, and acting aggressively. Traits that are desirable in business become liabilities when applied to women. Undoubtedly, women in the corporate world engage in the same tactics and risks as their male colleagues, but descriptions of women who have committed white-collar crime become derogatory, stereotypical descriptions of negative feminine behavior: bitchy, pushy, and manipulative. Successful women often are placed in no-win situations when making legal and illegal business decisions. Unlike male counterparts, women are castigated by the public and press for alleged unfeminine behavior, both as company executives and criminals (Dodge, 2009).

Opportunity is an essential aspect of white-collar crimes. Undoubtedly, societal structures have limited the types of criminal offenses committed by women. In 1975, research on women and crime by Freda Adler and Rita Simon noted the paucity of female participation in illegal activities, but predicted, correctly so, an increase in deviant behavior patterns. Adler, a celebrated scholar and criminologist, noted the connection between opportunity and female criminality:

> The kinds of crimes one commits are related to the illegal opportunities to commit them. While a shopper might pilfer from commercial establishments, it is not possible to be involved in insider trading, unless one is "inside" the corporate community. White-collar criminals inhabit the upper echelons of the American economic system— prestigious positions in the ranks of government, various professions and industry. As great proportions of wealth and power pass through female hands, most will be dealt with responsibly. But, just as with males, some will find its way into the illegitimate world (Dodge, 2009, p. 180).

Motives to engage in white-collar crime vary; more often than not, however, greed ranks at the top. Some studies suggest that women are less motivated to commit crimes solely based on greed. Mark Koebrich and Quynah Nguyen (2004) surveyed women and found that they tended to place a higher value on family/home, fairness/equity, friends/relationships, and recognition/rewards. In contrast, the men in the study valued pay/money/benefits and power/status/authority. Women may bring a higher ethical standard to the workplace that includes a more "caring" or "intuitive" perspective of doing business. Judith Collins examined incarcerated female executives and discovered that women tended to act in ways that are "other directed" and rationalized their crimes as attempts to help friends and family (Associated Press, 1987; Judith Collins, personal communication, February 28, 2005). Other commentators and researchers note that many women claim their crimes were committed to help a family member or for a male lover (Gerencher, 2001; Zietz, 1981).

The pressure and need to achieve success in a male-dominated environment represents a powerful motive that may easily trump any notion of the nurturing "other." Financial pressures are a powerful justification to engage in fraud. Women working full-time earned a median weekly income of $657 compared to the $819 median weekly earnings of men (Bureau of Labor Statistics, 2009). Lower incomes and perceptions of unfair treatment may easily develop into rationalizations or justifications for criminal activities. Rationalizations of "helping others" seem less plausible as white-collar crimes committed by women begin to mirror men's seemingly self-centered and compulsive behavior. Numerous examples of women who commit crimes to achieve a lavish lifestyle or engage in gambling shed some doubt that males and females have dissimilar motives related to criminal behavior.

→ ...so then which reasoning is more common?

Corporate Crime

The number of women involved in corporate crime appears to be increasing, though details of misdeeds can only be gleaned through case studies. The rise in female CEOs in corporate America, on the one hand, will likely change the masculine nature of the crimes. The small number of women in charge, on the other hand, often results in unparalleled scrutiny of their job performance and may prevent widespread criminal activity. In 2005, Carly Fiorina, named by *Fortune* magazine as the "Most Powerful Woman in Business" for six consecutive years, stepped down as CEO at Hewlett-Packard. Fiorina described her chagrin at being labeled a "female CEO" and noted the barrage of inquiries and criticisms she faced in a male-dominated profession. The media focused on her dress, hair, or clothing rather than her business acumen; colleagues described her as a "bimbo," who was either "too soft" or "too hard," or "too ambitious" (Fiorina, 2006). Women at the top echelon of the corporate world often are isolated and face insurmountable barriers that result in marginalization and disenfranchisement. In some respects, the social and financial pressure placed on women in elite positions may push them toward risk taking, criminal behavior.

→ wouldn't being under a microscope deter it?

One problem in determining the motivations and participation of women in corporate crime is the biased and harsh treatment women face after a white-collar offense is discovered. Linda Wachner, the former CEO of Warnaco, was well known on Wall Street as a strong business leader who transformed the company into a $2.2 billion-a-year business. *Fortune* dubbed her "America's most successful businesswoman." After the company filed for bankruptcy in 2001, Wachner, labeled the "iron maiden of lingerie," was denigrated by colleagues for her lavish lifestyle, aggressive tactics, and tough business demeanor (McDonald, 2001). Calvin Klein's lawsuit against Warnaco claimed Wachner was a "cancer" and noted that she ran the business "like a monarchy."

how does this justify a lawsuit

A woman allowed into the inner circle of the corporate world may find it difficult to abide by legal and regulatory mandates. Legal and illegal behavior often depends on accepted norms that have become embedded in the corporate culture. The fear of failing or job loss is likely to induce men and women into committing white-collar crime, though corporate crime remains entrenched in masculinities. The primary issue facing the future of women and white-collar crime is not about taking on male characteristics in order to succeed; it's about human motives associated with greed, power, and success—no matter what the cost (Dodge, 2009).

Financial Fraud

Embezzlement represents the one crime in which women equal men. Not surprisingly, the higher number of managerial and administrative jobs held by women provides greater opportunity to commit fraud, embezzlement, and forgery (Simon & Ahn-Redding, 2005). Craig Forsyth and Thomas Marckese (1995) found the number of fraud, embezzlement, and forgery/counterfeiting offenses by females from 1943 to 1991 was almost equal to men. Federal data show arrests of women for embezzlement increased about 49 percent between 1995 and 2008 (FBI, 2009). In 2008 women (18 and older) represented almost 52 percent of all arrests for embezzlement. The statistical trends for women embezzlers indicate that greater opportunity and less traditional socialization related to domesticity may explain increasing levels of wrongdoing (Forsyth & Marckese, 1995; Hoffman-Bustamente, 1973; Simon & Ahn-Redding, 2005). The high number of female embezzlers also implies that given the chance women will engage in other financial frauds at levels commensurate with male colleagues.

Dorothy Zietz (1981) and Kathleen Daly (1989) were the first scholars to attempt to quantify the role of women in white-collar crime. Zietz interviewed 100 inmates at the California Institution for Women identified as embezzlers (honest women who violated financial trust) or fraudulent operators (women who intended to steal or defraud). The honest women group revealed four distinct types: Obsessive Protectors engaged in criminal activity to meet their responsibilities as wives or mothers; Romantic Dreamers sought to please husbands or lovers; Greedy Opportunists were women addicted to a lavish lifestyle; and Victims of Pressure were forced to embezzle by demands or threats. In contrast, women who intended to steal were Vindictive Self-servers or Asocial Entrepreneurs. The former embezzled as a result of lives of hardship and deprivation; whereas the later viewed their fraudulent acts as a career.

Daly (1989) discovered that female fraudsters were more likely to be in low-level positions that afforded the opportunity to steal only petty amounts. The research, though methodologically sound and informative, created a framework that placed women in the role of pink-collar offenders and portrayed them as figures so desperate to help their families and lovers that they were willing to turn to crime as an altruistic means of solving financial problems. Daly's study noted significant differences between male and female white-collar offenders. Women offenders were younger and less educated than males, held lower-status positions, and received less pay. Overall, Daly found that financial crimes by women were almost always petty.

Current trends indicate that embezzlement schemes by women appear to be increasing in size. The theft of small amounts of money is becoming less characteristic of the offenses. In one of the largest frauds every perpetrated against the state of Colorado, Michelle Cawthra was accused of stealing $11 million from taxpayers. Cawthra worked as a tax supervisor and funneled bogus tax refunds into the business accounts of Hysear Randell (her former boyfriend) and his wife (Lindsay, 2008). In February 2008, Cawthra pled guilty to one count of racketeering and was sentenced to 24 years in prison. As part of the plea bargain other counts involving theft, forgery, and conspiracy were dropped, and she agreed to testify against Randell, who was sentenced to 58 years in prison. Women in the workplace have greater access to larger sums of money and often are committing embezzlement for less altruistic reasons. Cawthra claimed to have stolen the money primarily for love, though she also received jewelry from her married boyfriend.

Female embezzlers in high-ranking occupations are stealing dollar amounts comparable to male fraudsters. An examination of 40 nonrandom female embezzlement cases shows that the majority of the women held mid-level management positions, stole money ranging from $10,000 to over $1 million, and 50 percent were motivated by the need to support a lavish lifestyle or gambling habit (Dodge, 2009). Two bank tellers, for example, who were convicted of stealing $1.2 million dollars from customers' accounts, admitted to buying new cars every six months and taking five trips to Las Vegas in one year (Pankratz, 2008). In a wide-reaching organized crime scheme involving $80 million, three women were charged with using credit lines to obtain loans and products that they never intended to pay back, including the purchases of luxury vehicles (Cardona, 2009). A paralegal who worked for a Connecticut law firm pleaded guilty to stealing $1.7 million between 2003 and 2007 to cover gambling debts (*Hartford Courant*, 2008). In the new millennium, motivations for embezzling may differ little between males and females; if men embezzle for "babes, booze, and bets" it may be fair to say that women engage in the offense for "cars, clothing, and casinos" (Dodge, 2009; Bloch & Geis, 1962; Nettler, 1974).

Political Transgressions

Women have made headway in the political realm, though they remain underrepresented and have suffered several recent setbacks. Political crime often involves bribery of government officials and includes actions committed by state agents who accept money, gifts, or favors in exchange for influencing a favorable outcome for the payees (Coleman, 1994; Ross, 2003). Estimations of bribery among elected officials range from $3 billion to $1 trillion annually (Baird, 2006; Coleman, 1994). Bribery, according to David Shichor and Gilbert Geis (2007), "involves the violation of a trust, explicit or implicit, bestowed upon the public official, but it need not require a situation of trust between the briber and bribe taker; both are said to be committing a criminal act" (p. 408). Government corruption violates the most basic sense of trust between citizens and elected politicians; according to Vanessa Baird, political crime "saps the lifeblood of a society," deepens inequality and, often "kills." Bribery and corruption are separate but related acts that are "ingrained in the political machinery of local and state governments" (Adler, Mueller, & Laufer, 2010, p. 308).

There is no reason to think that women in political positions are beyond taking bribes, and many may well succumb to political crimes at levels comparable to men when given the opportunity. Presidential candidate Hillary Clinton (D) and vice presidential candidate Sarah Palin (R) both emerged as strong leaders who became targets of accusations and innuendos involving corruption. Clinton's unsuccessful bid for the presidency occurred in the shadow of her husband's illicit sexual behavior while in the White House and her suspected participation in the Whitewater scandal. The Whitewater affair was a convoluted case involving a land deal with the Clintons and Jim and Susan McDougal. In fact, the Senate Banking Committee and House Banking Committee issued reports that no laws had been broken in the property investment. In early 1996, however, Hillary Clinton was accused of withholding key documents related to the case. Though her role in the unsavory land deal appeared to be minimal, her motives for investment were clearly prompted by financial gain.

Sarah Palin's alleged illegal and unethical behavior received widespread attention as media reports besieged her character. Scandals related to the misuse of power haunted Palin's tenure as mayor of Wasilla and governor of Alaska. According to Todd Purdum (2009), in a blistering article published in *Vanity Fair*, Palin "takes disagreements personally, and swiftly deals vengeance on enemies, real or perceived." Palin's misuse of authority was widely known among constituents in Alaska. During her initial rise to political fame, Mayor Palin created a great deal of turbulence in the small community located outside of Anchorage. The firing of Police Chief Irl Stambaugh and Chief Librarian Mary Ellen Emmons occurred under a cloud of suspect motives. The former police chief filed a lawsuit and claimed he was fired in retaliation for supporting the ex-mayor. The unsuccessful lawsuit also claimed gender discrimination. Stambaugh argued that Palin publicly vilified him when she stated that the chief was physically much larger than her and tried to intimidate her at meetings (Harper, 2008). The librarian was fired amid controversy over Palin's alleged penchant for book banning. Additionally, under the Palin reign, Wasilla gained the unique distinction of being the only community in Alaska that required ⇒ what... rape victims to pay for their own medical exams (Harper, 2008). Her actions as mayor appeared to be a harbinger of her tenure as governor.

Palin's involvement in Troopergate became headline news again after she was chosen as the vice presidential running mate by John McCain, and the scandal was a constant backdrop during the campaign. Newspaper columnists took great delight in featuring the vice presidential candidate's "Taser-toting, moose-shooting, beer-swilling ex-brother-in-law," who served as a key figure in the Troopergate probe. Palin allegedly misused her position to fire the state public commissioner Walt Monegan. Monegan claimed his firing was pay-back for refusing to dismiss state trooper Mike Wooten, Palin's ex-brother-in-law. Palin accused Wooten of threatening harm to family members, driving drunk on duty, using an electronic control device on his stepson, and shooting a moose without a permit. Whether or not Palin abused her executive power is debatable, though the slew of ethics charges that emerged seemed to indicate some form of wrongdoing.

State and city political scandals often exemplify the worst in corruption. In Baltimore, Mayor Sheila Dixon was indicted on 12 counts that included perjury, theft, fraudulent misappropriation by a fiduciary, and misconduct in office. Few would argue that Dixon was acting for the good of the citizens, who placed their trust in her ability to better the community. In perhaps her most callous act, she stood accused of taking gift cards intended for needy families and using the money to buy electronics and clothes. She accepted illegal gifts for travel and fur coats. Sara Bost, former mayor of Irvington, New Jersey, was well known for her unorthodox leadership style. In one incident, she prayed for divine intervention at a gospel service hoping to fix the city's $7 million deficit (Paonita, 2004). In April 2002, Bost was indicted for taking bribes from developers and engaging in witness tampering. In another case, Georgia's school superintendent Linda Schrenko was charged with over 40 counts involving conspiracy and money laundering. Schrenko admitted to stealing money from school children to fund her growing political ambitions to run for governor.

Changing Roles

In 1997, Patricia Pearson faced caustic criticism after the publication of her book *When She was Bad* in which she persuasively argued that vio-

lence among women is more than a fluke, and our inability to acknowledge female aggression undermines attempts to understand an entire
culture of crime. Indeed, women engage in all types of crime when
opportunity and motive coalesce. In 2009, for example, three women
finally made their way to the world's most wanted list (Reiss, 2009).
Omana Edan, an eye doctor from India, is being sought for allegedly poisoning her lover. Authorities believe that she cut his body into pieces and
stuffed them in a suitcase. Slovakian Lucia Kanis remains on the lam after
being indicted for bringing illegal workers into the United States and
exploiting their labor. Denise Sinankwa, ex-finance minister of Burundi,
fled after being charged with stealing $6.5 million from the government.

everyone does...

Women commit less crime than men. The higher number of male
offenders is a trend that holds true across all types of crime except for
embezzlement. The idea that women are increasingly conducting illegal
and unethical business, however, is controversial, and Stacy Teicher
(2004) describes the "contentious debate" as filled with "ifs and buts—
and few hard facts." Studies have found that women are more likely than
men to exhibit "helping" behavior, demonstrate higher levels of ethical
behavior and integrity, and act in an unselfish manner (see e.g., Bampton
& Maclagan, 2009; Betz, O'Connell, & Shepard, 1989; Eagly & Crowley,
1986; Eckel & Gorssman, 1998; Ones & Viswesvarn, 1998; Reiss & Mitra,
1998). David Dollar, Raymond Fisman, and Roberta Gatti (1999) discovered lower levels of corruption in government when the rate of female
representation in parliamentary positions was high. The most palatable
explanation for gender differences in offending is the lack of opportunity
rather than ingrained socialization skills.

The notion that women are more ethical, generous, and caring than
men in the public sphere is questionable. Phyllis Atkinson (2006) illustrated the increasing trends and offered numerous incidents to support
the assertion that women may represent 40 percent of all white-collar
criminals. Women convicted in state fraud felonies increased 55 percent
from 1990 to 1996 and, in 1996, 41 percent of the convicted forgery, fraud,
and embezzlement defendants were female. In 2006, women accounted
for 37 percent of forgery convictions and 38 percent of fraud convictions,
which included embezzlement (Cohen & Kycklehahn, 2010). Returning to
the federal data, women accounted for 39 percent of the arrests (18 years
or older) for forgery, fraud, and embezzlement in 2008 (FBI, 2009).

Some empirical findings support intuitive notions that women are
more involved in white-collar crime. Jay Albanese (1993) discovered a
dramatic increase in the number of women involved in white-collar
offenses during the 1970s and 1980s. Research sponsored by the National
White-Collar Crime Center reported a pronounced increase in the
involvement of women in elite offenses (Haantz, 2002). According to the
report, nearly one in four of the 1,016 federal prisoners incarcerated for
white-collar crime in 2000 was a woman. Kristy Holtfreter (2005) found

no gender differences between asset misappropriation and corruption offenses; the high number of female asset misappropriation/embezzlement is closely connected to occupational opportunity. The role of women in occupational crimes can no longer be labeled as crimes of the powerless committed for altruistic purposes. Undoubtedly, women are just as capable as their male counterparts of engaging in illegal acts, particularly when placed in positions that demand they "do gender" common to any offender (Messerschmidt, 1986, 1993).

(handwritten note:) Whole article contradicts itself repeatedly...

REFERENCES

Adler, F. (1975). *Sisters in crime: The rise of the new female criminal.* New York: McGraw-Hill.

Adler, F., Mueller, G. O. W., & Laufer, W. S. (2010). *Criminology* (7th ed.). New York: McGraw-Hill.

Albanese, J. (1993). Women and the newest profession: Females as white-collar criminals. In C. C. Culliver (Ed.), *Female criminality: The state of the art* (pp. 119–131). New York: Garland.

Associated Press (1987, July 27). Corporate crime low for women, *The Record*, p. C2.

Atkinson, P. (2006, November 13). Women and white collar crime. Unpublished. Author was Senior Asset Recovery Specialist at the Deloitte Forensic & Dispute Services office in Cape Town, South Africa.

Baird, V. (2006, December). Can the rot be stopped? *New Internationalist*, pp. 2–5.

Bampton, R., & Maclagan, P. (2009). Does a "care orientation" explain gender differences in ethical decision making? A critical analysis and fresh findings. *Business Ethics: A European Review*, 18(2), 179–191.

Betz, M., O'Connell, L., & Shepard, J. M. (1989). Gender differences in proclivity for unethical behavior, *Journal of Business Ethics*, 8, 321–324.

Bloch, H. A., & Geis, G. (1962). *Men, crime and society.* New York: Random House.

Bureau of Labor Statistics (2009, October), "Labor Force Statistics from the Current Population Survey." Household Data Annual Averages, table 39: Median weekly earnings of full-time wage and salary workers by detailed occupation and sex. Retrieved from ftp://ftp.bls.gov/pub/special.requests/lf/aat39.txt

Cardona, F. (2009, August 20). Three accused in Colorado fraud get bail. *Denver Post.*

CNN. (2010). "Women CEOs." Retrieved from http://money.cnn.com/magazines/fortune/fortune500/2010/womenceos/

Cohen, Thomas H., & Kycklehahn, T. (2010). "Felony defendants in large urban counties, 2006." Retrieved from http://bjs.ojp.usdoj.gov/content/pub/pdf/fdluc06.pdf

Coleman, J. W. (1994). *The criminal elite: The sociology of white collar crime.* New York: St. Martin's Press.

Daly, K. (1989). Gender and varieties of white-collar crime. *Criminology*, 27, 769–793.

Dodge, M. (2009). *Women and white-collar crime.* Upper Saddle River, NJ: Prentice Hall.

Dollar, D., Fisman, R., & Gatti, R. (1999, October). Are women really the "fairer" sex? Corruption and women in government. Policy Research Report on Gender and Development, Working Paper Series, No. 4. Retrieved from http://www.sec.lt/pages/alfdiskusijos/pages/discuss3/docs/gender%20and%20corruption.pdf.

Eagly, A. H., & Crowley, M. (1986). Gender and helping behavior: A meta-analytic review of the social psychological literature. *Psychological Bulletin*, 100, 283–308.

Eckel, C. C., & Grossman, P. J. (1998). Are women less selfish than men? Evidence from dictator experiments. *Economic Journal*, 108, 726–735.

Federal Bureau of Investigation (2009). *Crime in the United States, 2008*. Table 33. Retrieved from http://www.fbi.gov/ucr/cius2008/data/table_33.html

Fiorina, C. (2006). *Tough choices*. New York: Penguin Group.

Forsyth, C. J., & Marckese, T. A. (1995). Female participation in three minor crimes: A note on the relationship between opportunity and crime. *International Journal of Sociology of the Family*, 25, 127–132.

Geis, G., Meier, R. F., & Salinger, L. M. (1995). *White-collar crime: Classic and contemporary views* (3rd ed.). New York: The Free Press.

Gerencher, K. (2001, July 18). Skimming from the top: More women committing white-collar crime. Retrieved from http://www.marketwatch.com/story/more-women-committing-white-collar-crimes.

Haantz, S. (2002). Women and white-collar crime. National White Collar Crime Center. Retrieved from http://www.nw3c.org/research/site_files.cfm?mode=p

Harper, T. (2008, September 13). Palin's political track record marked by bitter clashes. *The Toronto Star*.

Hartford Courant (2008, October 13). Paralegal pleads guilty to taking $1.7 million from firm. Retrieved from http://www.law.com/jsp/law/sfb/lawArticleSFB.jsp?id=1202425185546

Hoffman-Bustamente, D. (1973). The nature of female criminality. *Issues in Criminology*, 8, 117–136.

Holtfreter, K. (2005). Is occupational fraud "typical" white-collar crime? A comparison of individual and organizational characteristics. *Journal of Criminal Justice*, 33, 353–365.

Ibarra, H., & Obodaru, O. (2009). Women and the vision thing. *Harvard Business Review*. www.hbr.org

Jones, D. (2009). Women CEOs slowly gain on corporate America. *USA Today*. Retrieved from http://www.usatoday.com/money/companies/management/2009-01-01-women-ceos-increase_N.htm

Koebrich, M., & Nguyen, Q. (2004, July 21). Gender role found in workers' health. *Denver Post*, pp. C1, 5.

Lindsay, S. (2008, February 2). State tax supervisor pleads guilty to racketeering. *Rocky Mountain News*, p. 6.

Messerschmidt, J. (1986, 1993). *Masculinities and crime*. Lanham, MD: Rowman & Littlefield.

McDonald, M (2001). Lingerie's iron maiden is undone. *U.S. News & World Report*, p. 37.

Nettler, G. (1974). Embezzlement without problems. *The British Journal of Criminology*, 14, 70–77.

Ones, D. S., & Viswesvarn, C. (1998). Gender, age, and race differences on overt integrity tests: Results across four large-scale job applicant data sets. *Journal of Applied Psychology*, 83(1), 1581–1593.

Paonita, A. (2004, January). Crime wave. *More*, pp. 110–113, 114.

Pankratz, H. (2008, February 22). "Steamboat tellers accused of stealing $1.2 million." *Denver Post*. Retrieved from http://www.denverpost.com/search/ci_8336422

Pearson, P. (1997). *When she was bad*. New York: Penguin Books.

Purdum, T. S. (2009, August). It came from Wasilla. *Vanity Fair*.

Reiss, B. (2009, February 8). Who are the world's most wanted? *Parade*, pp. 6–7.

Reiss, M. C., & Mitra, K. (1998). The effects of individual difference factors on the acceptability of ethical and unethical workplace behaviors. *Journal of Business Ethics*, 17(14), 1581–1593.

Rhode, D. L. (1989). *Justice and gender: Sex discrimination and the law.* Cambridge, MA: Harvard University Press.

Ross, J. I. (2003). *The dynamics of political crime.* Thousand Oaks, CA: Sage.

Shichor, D., & Geis, G. (2007). The itching palm: The crimes of bribery and extortion. In H. Pontell and G. Geis (Eds.), *International handbook of white-collar and corporate crime* (pp. 405–423). New York: Springer.

Simon, R. J. (1975). *Women and crime.* Lexington, MA: Lexington Books.

Simon, R. J., & Ahn-Redding, H. (2005). *The crimes women commit, the punishments they receive* (3rd ed.). Lanham, MD: Lexington Books.

Sutherland, E. H. (1949). *White collar crime.* New York: Dryden Press.

Teicher, S. A. (2004, March 15). Do female execs have cleaner hands? *Christian Science Monitor.* Retrieved from http://www.csmonitor.com/2004/0315/p14s03-wmgn.html

U.S. Department of Labor (2009, September). *Women in the labor force: A databook.* Report 1018. Retrieved from http://www.bls.gov/cps/wlf-databook-2009.pdf

Zietz, D. (1981). *Women who embezzle or defraud: A study of convicted felons.* New York: Praeger Publishers.

Part 2

Corporate Crimes

In modern Western societies, corporations have a major presence. They are involved in all facets of complex economic activities. Modern corporations trace their roots to the mercantile period in Europe that developed with the spread of international trade and the decline of the feudal social and economic system.

As corporations grew in importance, the potential for social harm also evolved (Clinard & Yeager, 1980). Criminal law was established as a means of social control of individuals. In order to extend criminal law to corporations, they were perceived as persons before the law. The widespread personification of corporations is reflected in widely used terms such as "corporate responsibility" and "corporate crime." This approach is pragmatic, but it is also problematic because it implies that corporations think, make decisions, plan, and even make mistakes as individuals do (Cressey, 1989). A necessary element in making a criminal case against individuals is criminal intent (*mens rea*). It is problematic to attribute criminal intent to corporations. Accordingly, corporate crimes are illegal acts committed by officers and employees acting in the name of the corporation.

Kai-D. Bussmann and Markus M. Werle from the Economy and Crime Research Center in Germany analyze the findings of a global survey of 5500 companies worldwide to determine the prevalence of economic crime and the prevention measures applied. Particularly interesting in this study is the focus on the global nature of corporate crime and the efforts to control it. With the increased pace of political and economic globalization, there is growing interest in learning about the various forms and patterns of criminal activity and prevention around the world. This issue may be especially important regarding corporate crime considering the increased economic interconnectedness, the rapid rise in the numbers of large multinational corporations, the growing competition among corporations, the rapid pace of technological inventions, the informational technology explosion, and the cyber revolution.

David O. Friedrichs analyzes the first major corporate scandals that emerged in the twenty-first century. This wave of corporate wrongdoing involved well-known corporations such as Enron, WorldCom, Adelphia, Tyco, Qwest, Global Crossing, Rite Aid, and Xerox. The criminal activities related to these companies and their top executives included misrepresentation of financial statements, fraudulent accounting practices, inflated sales figures, inflated numbers of customers, inflated profits, concealed expenses, bonuses, and large loans to executives. While executives received extraordinary compensation, stockholders often experienced large losses. The revelation of these fraudulent practices resulted in the erosion of confidence in the stock market. In the concluding part of his article, Friedrichs relates these scandals to Sutherland's original definition of white-collar crime.

David Shichor, in a chapter written for this volume, elaborates on the concept of "looting" or "collective embezzlement" of corporations that was developed by Kitty Calavita and Henry Pontell (1990) in their well-known analysis of the Savings and Loan debacle of the 1980s. This concept was defined as "the siphoning of funds from a savings and loan institution for personal gain, at the expense of the institution itself and with the implicit or explicit sanction of its management" (Pontell & Calavita, 1993: 223). Shichor shows how top executives often violate the trust and fiduciary obligation to their companies' shareholders in pursuing their own personal benefits.

The Annual Report to Congress on Foreign Economic Collection and Industrial Espionage in 2005 by the Office of the National Counterintelligence Executive reported that 108 countries made efforts to collect information on sensitive US technologies. These efforts hurt US national security by revealing technologies that took years to develop. In addition, foreign companies gaining access to technology developed at the expense of US companies was damaging economically.

The report explains that the most likely perpetrators of these offenses are not spies of foreign agencies but "respectable," often foreign-born professionals such as professors, scientists, researchers, engineers, students, and businessmen who become involved in unlawful information gathering in the course of their occupational activities.

REFERENCES

Calavita, K. and Pontell, H. N. (1990). "Heads I win, tails you lose:" Deregulation, crime, and crisis in the savings and loan industry. *Crime and Delinquency,* 36: 309–341.

Clinard, M. B. and Yeager, P. C. (1980). *Corporate crime.* New York: Free Press.

Cressey, D. R. (1989). The poverty of theory in corporate crime research. *Advances in Criminological Theory* (1): 31–55.

Pontell, H. N. and Calavita, K. (1993). The savings and loan industry. In Tonry, M. and Reiss Jr., A. J. (Eds.), *Beyond the law: Crime in complex organizations.* Chicago, IL: The University of Chicago Press.

6

Addressing Crime in Companies

First Findings from a Global Survey of Economic Crime

— *Kai-D. Bussmann and Markus M. Werle*[1]

Methodology

Between May and September 2005, we asked more than 5,500 companies worldwide about their experiences with economic crime, how they control and prevent it, and how they respond to actual cases. Findings reported here are based on a combined dataset from two simultaneous studies partly conducted in collaboration between the Economy & Crime Research Centre and PricewaterhouseCoopers International. The collaborative study (n = 3,600; PricewaterhouseCoopers 2005)[2] focused on trends in the prevalence of economic crime as well as control and prevention measures. The second study by the authors (n = 1,900) examined the impact of the German and (US) American criminal justice systems on the control and prevention practices of companies. Because the use of these practices is more widespread and advanced in the United States, we were particularly interested in innovative trends in Germany due, for example, to a knowledge transfer from the United States.[3] This second study used the same set of items as the collaborative study and included a number of additional questions. This article presents combined findings from both studies, which both also yielded in-depth information on a total of 2,900 criminal cases. Managers in both studies were asked to select the two most serious offenses that their company had suffered in the recent past, and to provide further information on detection, causes, processing of the crime, characteristics of the offenders, and alleged causes for them.

The target persons selected for the victimization surveys received advance notice of the telephone interviews. The data for the collaborative study were collected in a standardized computer-assisted telephone interview (CATI) of company managers in 34 countries.[4] National selections of companies were multi-layered random samples taking into account such factors as the number of employees, annual turnover, the industry sector as well as business rankings (e.g. Forbes) and listings on the major international stock exchanges.[5] In some segments of smaller national economies, like Tanzania or Kenya, this was sometimes almost a complete census. Information on companies was gathered through data mining in several international databanks. Although the 34 participant nations were selected to provide a global overview, only small numbers were available for detailed analyses within some individual regions (e.g. Africa: $n = 175$ companies; Australia: 101; South and Central America: 334). Merging the two studies therefore had the advantage that data from other regions and particularly Western Europe (3,038 companies of which 1,512 came from Germany alone) and North America (694) could be analyzed in much more detail.[6]

Interviews were carried out in either the native language or English with those target subjects who claimed responsibility for crime prevention and detection in their company. These managers were selected in advance from several public and private data banks like Hoppenstedt, the Internet and other publications, and their responsibility for economic crime was checked when screening for the interview.[7]

Almost half of these managers worldwide (53 percent) were members of the executive board or the management of a company, and 43 percent worked mainly in the field of finance as Chief Finance Officer or directors of financial departments. Twenty-five percent of companies worldwide were major international companies with more than 5,000 employees. However, more than one-third of respondents also came from smaller companies with fewer than 200 employees on the national level. As a result, the sample is representative of top companies worldwide, and represents a mixture of industry branches and company size structure, both in the global overview and individually in most of the regions.

Risk Perception and Prevalence of Economic Crime

Companies were asked to report on seven types of economic crime perpetrated against them by internal or external offenders:[8]

- asset misappropriation (e.g. theft, embezzlement);
- false pretences (i.e. deception);
- financial misrepresentation (accounting fraud or manipulation);
- corruption and bribery (e.g. "kickbacks");[9]
- insider trading;
- money laundering; and
- counterfeiting (including product piracy, industrial espionage).

Throughout the world, nearly every ~~second company~~ <u>←every other</u> (45 percent; see Figure 1) reported having been a victim of one of these seven types of economic crime during the last two years (2004/05).[10] This replicates the findings of other recent studies on the same subject (e.g. Ernst & Young 2003; KPMG 2003; PricewaterhouseCoopers 2003; Control Risks Group 2002).

Figure 1 shows major differences between single regions and nations. These can be attributed to three main reasons:

1. Real variations in crime rates, perhaps assisted by differing "techniques of neutralization."
2. Cultural/national differences in managers' openness in discussing economic crimes committed against them.
3. Only successful control and detection systems in the companies can pick up on the misconduct, and there may be national/regional differences in detection.

Because the number of control and detection measures in African companies was below average, their high detected economic crime rate (77 percent) may be accompanied by a comparably high undetected rate as well. In contrast, the high Australian (63 percent) and North American (54 percent) economic crime rates probably also reflect their higher number of control and detection mechanisms.[11] Multivariate analyses support this hypothesis, showing that the number of control and detection measures was one of the most powerful explanatory variables for the detection of economic crimes. Companies that reported no victimization possessed significantly fewer control and security measures, but they also estimated their risk of becoming a victim of economic crime as being far lower.

In contrast to most regions worldwide, there was a conspicuously lower rate of reported economic crime at 32 percent in Asian countries,[12] with Singapore (16 percent), Hong Kong (22 percent), Malaysia (23 percent) and Japan (37 percent) making major contributions to the number of

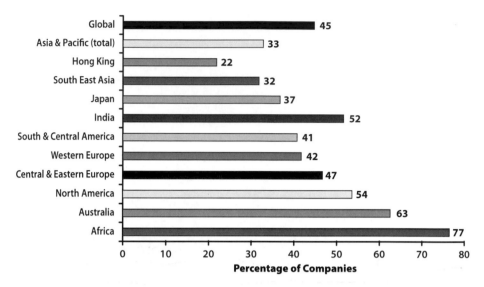

Figure 1 — Economic crime rates worldwide

cases. Moreover, the reported financial impact of cases of economic crime in Japanese companies, in terms of financial losses (33,000 US dollars) amounted to only a fraction of the reported international average of 2 million US dollars, so that these were disproportionately "petty" crimes. In Japan, 71.4 percent of frauds were reported as being below 10,000 US dollars, while, globally, 23 percent were in this category,[13] and most of the offenders in Japanese companies were reportedly from lower ranks of staff (see below). We assume that this finding in Japan (and in Asia in general) can be attributed to less willingness on part of the subjects to report economic crime or, at least, to a stronger inclination to avoid defining such offenses as economic crime and also to deal with them informally (see, also, Pontell and Geis 2007 and the section on coping strategies below).

Victimization from corruption and bribery globally ranked fourth on the list of victimizations at 11 percent, together with financial misrepresentation.[14] Higher victimization rates worldwide were only reported for asset misappropriation (30 percent), false pretenses (22 percent) and counterfeiting (12 percent). Insider trading (4 percent) and money laundering (3 percent) tended to be rare from the perspective of companies. For corruption, reported victimization rates varied greatly from between 1 and 3 percent in Hungary, Italy, Japan, Singapore, Spain and Switzerland to about 30 percent in the African nations, the Czech Republic, Indonesia and Russia. The mean level was 12 percent in Asia and 7 percent in Western Europe (see Table 1). Asian companies suffer more from corruption, although Japan stands out, with its rate below average.

The Corruption Perception Index of Transparency (CPI) provided the opportunity for external validation of our respective findings. In our survey, the correlation between victimization through corruption (prevalence rate) and managers' perceptions of corruption and bribery as the most prevalent economic crime risks in their own country[15] was highly significant at $r = 0.63$. We tested the external validity of this finding by correlating our prevalence rates with Transparency Internationals Corruption Perception Index of 2005. This was of similar size at $r = -0.65$, and since our own perception measure was strongly related to the CPI,[16] our survey with both prevalence and perception measures is clearly in line with those that form the basis of the CPI. Therefore, we assume that companies' perceptions of general victimization risks through corruption and bribery may be more valid than the low regional rates that result from their reporting of these crimes. The rather strong correlation between perception and actual victimization, however, shows that the latter reflects the general problem as it is perceived. We cannot be sure whether this extends to other types of victimization as well, but would not rule out such a possibility. Regional characteristics also need to be taken into account when assessing the validity of the prevalence measures. With regard to the level of corruption perception in our study as well as in the CPI, Japan is on the same level as North America and most Western European countries. According to the CPI, many other Asian countries reveal even higher rates, suggesting that the low level of corruption reported in this and other surveys is inaccurate. There are several indications that the actual economic crime rate in Asia is unlikely to be lower than in North America and most Western European countries (see Transparency International 2005; for Japan in particular: Pontell and Geis 2007).[17]

A comparison of this survey with a previous one in 2003 shows that, globally, there has been an average increase in economic crime of 8 percent since then (PricewaterhouseCoopers 2003). One major reason for this may well be the trend that more companies throughout the world are arming themselves with prevention and control mechanisms (Ernst & Young 2003; KPMG 2003; PricewaterhouseCoopers 2003), and, as a result, the increase might have been to a considerable extent caused by higher rates of detection.[18] The increasing sensitivity in companies has certainly been encouraged by media reports on spectacular cases of economic crime such as Enron and WorldCom (Friedrichs 2004b). With the reinforcement of publicity campaigns by non-governmental organizations (NGOs) such as Transparency International, public opinion now seems to be taking certain forms of economic crime increasingly more seriously (Rebovich and Kane 2002: 7–9; European Commission 2004). In addition, law enforcement authorities, national legislators (overviewed in Friedrichs 2004a: 218–41) and international organizations such as the World Bank, the United Nations, the OECD and the International Monetary Fund have been alerted and mobilized.

Table 1.
Corruption Worldwide

	Africa	Australia	S & C America	North America	Asia and Pacific					Western Europe	C & E Europe	Global
					Hong Kong	India	Japan	SE Asia	Total			
Corruption rate*	31	15	12	9	15	20	2	15	12	7	17	11
Corruption perception**	30	7	30	9	18	31	15	25	22	15	29	19

* % of companies; ** percentage of companies, multiple answers.

Table 2.
Frequency of Whistleblowing Systems

	Africa	Australia	S & C America	North America	Asia and Pacific					Western Europe	C & E Europe	Global
					Hong Kong	India	Japan	SE Asia	Total			
Present in the company*	49	61	47	74	26	52	77	34	43	31	26	40
Detection of serious offenses**	8	2	3	10	0	19	9	6	9	5	5	7
(Very) Satisfied with**	61	65	66	79	32	67	52	61	55	54	63	62

* % of companies; ** percentage of companies with whistleblowing systems.

Paths to Detection

The selection of cases and further information on how these were handled within the companies allowed for detailed analyses and comparisons on how companies had discovered their victimization. More than 95 percent of all investigations into these cases worldwide were not instigated by law enforcement authorities but by internal and external tip-offs or by accident (36 percent).[19] Generally, the companies themselves detected the perpetrators, as the proportion detected by law enforcement agencies is only 4 percent (see Figure 2). Law enforcement authorities were more active in countries and regions with less well developed risk awareness and internal audits, and, accordingly, a lower willingness on the part of the companies to tackle economic crime as, for example, in Asia and also Central and Eastern Europe. In Japan, reported economic crimes were detected disproportionately more often by law enforcement authorities (22 percent). In North America, in contrast, authorities played only a minor role, with involvement in 1.5 percent of the cases. There are two possible reasons for these differences. First, with their low willingness to report economic crime (see above), Asian companies tend to report only cases they consider to be, in any case, public knowledge, in our survey as well as to authorities. Second, our data indicate that North American companies have more control systems in place than the global average, and probably a very high detection rate.[20] Consequently, they are generally the first to detect economic crime through their internal mechanisms of control.

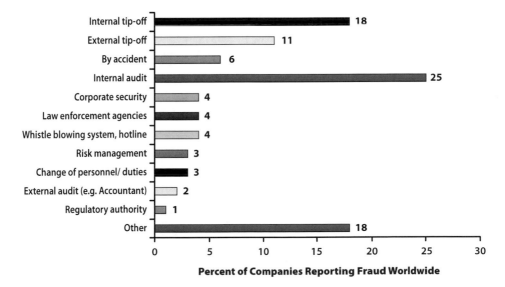

Figure 2 — Means by which economic crime was originally detected

Whistleblowing systems are of particular interest. Even if only 4 percent of all cases are detected through such systems, installing a whistleblowing system provided companies with an important source of information. Worldwide, companies with whistleblowing systems tend to have higher detection rates; however, it cannot be resolved whether this was due to the whistleblowing system or to a generally higher awareness in these companies (that motivated them to adopt whistleblowing systems). Whistleblowing systems had a different impact on the detection of different types of crime. They proved to be most effective for detecting corruption and bribery, but insignificant for money laundering and illicit insider trading. In Australia, whistleblowing systems were reported to have detected all cases of reported corruption compared with 50 percent in India, 25 percent in the United Kingdom and 25 percent in the United States (global: 15 percent). Comparing companies which have implemented a whistleblowing system with those which have not shows that whistleblowing seems to substitute for external or internal tip-offs as well as accidental detections. This is supported by a detection rate for corruption through tip-offs or by accident of 18 percent in companies with whistleblowing systems compared with 50 percent in companies without.

Notwithstanding such indications of a beneficial impact, a considerable minority of company managers expressed some dissatisfaction with the system (see Table 2). A pivotal weakness is the lack of protection for the "whistleblower." Our survey in the United States and Germany showed that only approximately 15 and 9 percent, respectively, of internal and external tip-offs were anonymously processed. Only 63 percent of companies in the United States and 34 percent in Germany reported having completely secure protection in place, regardless of whether informants used a whistleblowing system or not. Improving the protection of informants might considerably increase the utility of these sources of information and uncover more of the tip of the iceberg of undetected crime.[21]

Profile of the Perpetrators

Information on the perpetrators was collected as part of the inquiry into the two cases of victimization of which in-depth reports were given by the subjects. Little more than half of the offenders (52 percent) came from the company's own staff and management. In the global survey, the only sector significantly deviating was financial services, in which 34 percent were internal and 64 percent external perpetrators.

Back in 1949, Edwin Sutherland used high social standing as part of the definition of white-collar crime—a notion that has given rise to much misunderstanding with which we are not concerned here. Our study showed that in fact, high social status is a consistent characteristic of

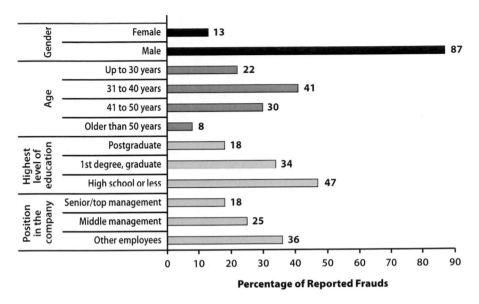

Figure 3 — Sociodemographic profile of offenders

offenders across cultures (Figure 3). Eighteen percent of identified perpetrators worldwide belonged to the senior/top management and 25 percent to the middle management of their company. A total of 18 percent had postgraduate qualifications and 34 percent a first academic degree. With hardly any national variations, perpetrators of economic crime had an above-average education. These results show that although economic crime is not committed exclusively by elites, senior/top management is overrepresented. Further, globally, common characteristics were gender (male) and age of the offenders. The average age was at about 40 years, and only 22 percent were under the age of 30. From the age of 30, the risk of offending increased continuously with career advancement until about the age of 50. The proportion of women was 13 percent.[22]

Moreover, the financial loss and collateral damage (loss of reputation) due to economic crime increased with the perpetrator's status in the company. Throughout the world, companies emphasized the greater risk of serious damage to reputation and impaired business relations when a perpetrator had been entrusted with a highly responsible post.

Reported Causes of Crimes and Motives of Offenders

The crimes of economic elites are attributed particularly to a lack of moral awareness (Coleman 1998: 181–3; Green 1997: 248–9; Simon and

Hagan 1999: 136–7). Research has shown that these offenders are risk seekers (Wheeler 1992) and also very decisive, strongly career-, success-, publicity-oriented (see, for overviews, Simon and Hagan 1999; Löw 2002) and extroverted personalities (Coleman 1998). These are precisely the "achiever" traits so highly valued in management recruitment and development (Steinmann and Schreyögg 2000; Shover and Hochstetler 2006: 57–72). Managers need to be particularly creative and flexible, and both personality traits are equally advantageous for illegal and legal business (Coleman 1998). We asked our subjects to expand on the reasons that they thought had been important in committing the offense; they were presented with a list[23] including "expensive lifestyle," "denial of financial consequences for the company," "overriding responsible staff," "easy to tempt" or "lacking awareness of values or wrongdoing." In order to examine connections with and involvement in an organizational and management milieu that condones such acts (Coleman 1998: 187; Sutherland 1949), we also included "internal collaboration (collusion) with other employees or members of the management" and "collaboration (collusion) with external parties."

According to social bond theory (Hirschi 1969), a climate of distance and anonymity in a company may increase the probability of fraud, whereas the formation of strong attachment to a company will provide a degree of protection. Social psychological studies on equity point to the crime-facilitating impact of disappointment and unfairness (Greenberg 1990; Marcus 2000: 107–12). Research on procedural justice shows that for individuals, being treated fairly is often more important than a positive outcome (see Tyler 1990). We therefore included company-related reasons such as "occupational/career disappointment," "dissatisfaction with the company," "anonymity in the staff/management," "layoff/redundancy" and "differing foreign business customs/ethics."

When naming the most frequent individual reasons for economic crime, more than half of all companies worldwide (53 percent) reported that offenders lacked any awareness of wrongdoing, and half (50 percent) gave low resistance to temptation as a reason. Forty-four percent attributed economic crime to insufficient controls and security measures within the company. This was a global pattern of our findings, with hardly any regional variation. If only offenders from within the company are taken into account, individual attributes and motives were mentioned in 38 percent of all cases, and insufficient controls on the part of the company itself gained in importance (46 percent). In addition, offenses were attributed to internal and external collaboration/ collusion (28 percent). Managers reported that perpetrators frequently did not work alone; several others were involved or at least knew what was going on—suggesting the impact of a general organizational culture. Managers assigned 12 percent (a comparatively minor—though not insignificant—role) to various other company-related reasons.

Table 3 reports the categories of alleged reasons for different management levels. The reasons given for senior/top managers clearly differed from the other levels. The crimes were more frequently attributed to their personal high status, to collusion and insufficient company controls. When talking about such offenders, respondents mentioned their lack of awareness of values and of self-discipline and, above all, their exploitation of a high position of trust. Company-related causes were also reported more frequently for middle and top/senior management than for other employees.

The disproportionate involvement of senior and middle management indeed raises questions about corporate culture and ethics (Bussmann 2003; Wieland 2003). The global comparison showed that the majority of companies in our survey had implemented a set of ethical guidelines (global 79 percent) and, in Canada and the United States, nearly every company reported having ethical guidelines or a code of conduct (94 percent; see Table 4).[24] United States-specific regulations such as the Federal Sentencing Guidelines and the Sarbanes Oxley Act may well be partially responsible for this (see Hefendehl 2004; Steinherr et al. 1998; see also McBarnet in this issue).

Earlier surveys in the 1980s indicated that half of North American corporations consider such ethics programs to be effective in preventing crime (Steinherr et al. 1998: 199). Our survey showed that the proportion of those who were satisfied with such systems was very high. Seventy-nine percent of the respondents in companies in North America and, worldwide, 70 percent were satisfied with how their own guidelines worked in practice. However, this might give a too optimistic picture. Thus, in our US and German sample, only 63 percent of managers in the United States and 38 percent in German companies are very well informed about the ethical guidelines in their companies. Further, business ethics should not just address general values but should offer concrete guidelines for actions and include distinct consequences for failure to respect them (Bussmann 2003). Therefore, they need explicitly to communicate norms of criminal law. In our sub-sample, we found that only 50 percent of US and a mere 23 percent of German companies reported that their ethical codes contained detailed information on what is prohibited by criminal law. It seems that companies perceive of business ethics as on top of legal obligations, and therefore might miss out on the more mundane references to criminal law.

Coping Strategies

In relation to the reported cases, we probed into how companies proceeded after they had discovered that they had been victimized (Table 5). After first suspicions of serious economic crime had arisen, companies generally launched an internal investigation (82 percent of all cases worldwide), commissioned an external investigator (73 percent) or called in law enforcement officers (62 percent). There seemed to be distinct differences

Table 3.
Reasons for Crime According to Management Level

	Individual-related	Company-related	Lack of	Internal and External Collaboration
Senior/top	44	16	55	41
Middle management	39	15	51	31
Other employees	35	10	39	22

Percentage of reported frauds of internal fraudsters—multiple answers.

Table 4.
Business Ethics

	Africa	Australia	S & C America	North America	Asia and Pacific					Western Europe	C & E Europe	Global
					Hong Kong	India	Japan	SE Asia	Total			
Implemented*	88	95	80	94	70	92	89	86	84	76	63	79
(Very) satisfied with**	68	75	83	79	57	74	67	65	65	66	69	70

* Percentage of companies worldwide; ** percentage of companies with business ethics.

Table 5.
Actions Brought Against Internal Perpetrators

	Africa	Australia	S & C America	North America	Asia and Pacific					Western Europe	C & E Europe	Global
					Hong Kong	India	Japan	SE Asia	Total			
Warning/reprimand	11	18	15	10	38	14	19	16	19	19	14	15
Transfer	2	2	1	<1	13	6	19	5	10	2	—	3
Dismissal	84	86	87	81	75	81	62	67	68	85	82	82
Criminal charge	58	51	50	50	25	19	15	35	26	46	55	46
Civil action	27	16	28	20	—	11	8	13	10	34	38	26
Other consequence	1	—	1	3	—	3	8	8	7	4	6	3
No action	5	18	3	6	—	11	19	18	16	8	4	8

Percentage of reported frauds—multiple answers.

Table 6.
Perpetrators Sentenced

	Africa	Australia	S & C America	North America	Asia and Pacific					Western Europe	C & E Europe	Global
					Hong Kong	India	Japan	SE Asia	Total			
Sentenced	34	25	24	32	14	20	36	24	26	34	21	30

Percentage of reported frauds.

in legal cultures between (economic) regions. This was particularly obvious in the widely differing practices regarding criminal charges. Globally, approximately half (51 percent) of all internal and external suspects were charged. However, the importance of criminal charges is drastically reduced when offenders from within the company are involved. Companies took advantage of a wider range of options that also allowed them to protect their reputation. Generally, such perpetrators were dismissed (worldwide 82 percent), and criminal charges were brought only against less than half of them (46 percent). Culture-specific treatment of offenders was also more obvious for internal perpetrators. In Asia, criminal charges were only brought against 26 percent of perpetrators from the ranks of the company, while dismissal increased to two-thirds (68 percent). Asian companies overwhelmingly preferred discreet responses, and consequently they more frequently only warned internal perpetrators (19 percent, globally 15 percent), transferred them within the company (10 percent, globally 3 percent) or twice as often than the global average did nothing (16 percent, globally 8 percent) (see, also, Pontell and Geis 2007).

As controversial as the deterrent impact of criminal charges on economic crime offenders may be,[25] companies have to react and if they are concerned about legitimacy, need to be seen to apply the same standards to all their staff—managers as well as other employees. This was often not the case, because companies clearly took the offenders position into account when reporting an offender to the authorities. If he or she came from top management, criminal charges were brought in only 40 percent of cases worldwide compared with 55 percent against employees below the middle management. It is also notable that companies worldwide far more frequently reported having taken no action against high-status offenders (17 percent) than against those of lower status (middle management 10 percent; other employees 8 percent).

New insurance packages against the risk of economic crime might contribute to this pattern. Half of the companies worldwide purchased fidelity insurance to cover the financial risks of economic crime. The standard conditions of company fidelity insurances do not require criminal charges as long as a suspect is named, and insurance terms only specify that criminal charges must be brought in investigations of persons unknown. As a result, companies retain full discretion when responding to perpetrators from their own ranks, and apply this discretion as they see fit. These types of insurance basically favor and support procedures of self-regulation in dealing with such cases without bringing criminal charges.

In addition, our study revealed a strong dissatisfaction with law enforcement agencies, their investigations and their success throughout the world. Managers thought little of the justice system. Only 28 percent were satisfied with its procedures, with the lowest rates in Africa (16 percent), Japan (17 percent), Central and Eastern Europe (23 percent) and South and Central America (24 percent). Moreover, as Table 6 shows, companies worldwide reported that only 30 percent of the perpetrators they knew about were actually sentenced (internal perpetrators 21 percent, external perpetrators 32 percent); sentencing of alleged and detected offenders was least frequent in Central and Eastern Europe (21 percent) and most frequent in the United States and Japan[26] (36 percent). Our data further indicate preferential treatment for offenders from the top management. Even if transferred to the criminal justice system, on average, only 26 percent of offenders from top management were sentenced compared with 34 percent from lower-ranking staff. Taken together, these can be deemed strong incentives for the internal settlement of the cases.

Conclusion

Our study shows that despite the observed regional and probably also cultural differences throughout the world, we find very similar patterns of reasons given for the perpetration (and victimization) of economic crime and equally similar ways of handling it. Companies worldwide prefer internal settlements of cases when they have been victimized through economic crime, and business globally develops a set of strategies of prevention and control in the shadow of the criminal justice system. Interest in research findings from this branch of criminology is growing just as fast as the awareness in companies of the risks that they have to face.

REFERENCES

Bussmann, K-D. (2003), "Business Ethics und Wirtschaftsstrafrecht: Zu einer Kriminologie des Managements," *Monatsschrift für Kriminologie und Strafrechtsreform*, 86: 90–104.

Coleman, J. W. (1998), *The Criminal Elite: Understanding White-Collar Crime*. New York: St. Martin's Press.

Control Risks Group (2002), *Facing Up to Corruption: Survey Results 2002*, available online at www.crg.com.

Ernst & Young (2003), "Fraud: The Unmanaged Risk," 8th Global Survey, available online at www.ey.com.

European Commission (2004), *Attitudes Related to Defrauding the European Union and its Budget: CC-EB 2003.4*, available online at http://europa.eu.int.

Friedrichs, D. O. (2004a), *Trusted Criminals: White Collar Crime in Contemporary Society*, 2nd ed. Belmont: Wadsworth.

——— (2004b), "Enron et al.: Paradigmatic White Collar Crime Cases for the New Century," *Critical Criminology* 12: 113–132.

Green, G. S. (1997), *Occupational Crime*. Chicago: Nelson-Hall Publishers.

Greenberg, J. (1990), "Employee Theft as a Reaction to Underpayment Inequity: The Hidden Costs of Pay Cuts," *Journal of Applied Psychology*, 75: 561–8.

Hefendehl, R. (2004), "Enron, WorldCom, and the Consequences: Business Criminal Law between Doctrinal Requirements and the Hopes of Crime Policy," *Buffalo Criminal Law Review*, 8: 51–88.

Hirschi, T. (1969), *Causes of Delinquency*. Berkeley: University of California Press.

KPMG (2003), "Fraud Survey 2003," available online at www.kpmg.com.

Levi, M. (2002), "Suite Justice or Sweet Charity? Some Explorations of Shaming and Incapacitating Business Fraudsters," *Punishment and Society*, 4: 147–63.

Löw, A. (2002), *Multiperspektivische Analyse der Wirtschaftskriminalität: Konsequenzen für die Gestaltung des integrierten Risikomanagement*. St Gallen: IVW 43.

Marcus, B. (2000), *Kontraproduktives Verhalten im Betrieb*: Göttingen et al. Hogreve.

Nelken, D. (1997), "White-Collar Crime," in M. Maguire, R. Morgan and R. Reiner, eds., *The Oxford Handbook of Criminology*, 891–924. Oxford: Oxford University Press.

Paternoster, R. and Simpson, S. (1996), "Sanction Threats and Appeals to Morality: Testing a Rational Choice Model of Corporate Crime," *Law and Society Review*, 30: 549–83.

Pontell, H. and Geis, G. (2007), "The Paradox of Economic Crime in Japan," *Monatsschrift für Kriminologie und Strafrechtsreform*, spezial Vols 1 and 2, forthcoming.

PricewaterhouseCoopers (2003), "Global Economic Crime Survey 2003," available online at www.pwcglobal.com.

—— (2005), "Global Economic Crime Survey 2005," available online at www.econcrime.unihalle.de, www.pwcglobal.com.

Rebovich, D. J. and Kane, J. L. (2002), "An Eye for an Eye in the Electronic Age: Gauging Public Attitude toward White Collar Crime and Punishment," *Journal of Economic Crime Management*, available online at www.jecm.org.

Shover, N. (1998), "White-Collar Crime," in M. Tonry, ed., *International Handbook of Crime and Punishment*, 133–58. Oxford: University Press.

Shover, N. and Hochstetler, A. (2006), *Choosing White-Collar Crime*. Cambridge: Cambridge University Press.

Simon, R. S. and Hagan, F. E. (1999), *White-Collar Deviance*. Boston: Allyn and Bacon.

Simpson, S. S. (2002), *Corporate Crime, Law and Social Control*. Cambridge: Cambridge University Press.

Steinherr, C., Steinmann, H. and Olbrich, T. (1998), "Die U.S.-Sentencing Commission Guidelines: Eine Dokumentation," in H. Alwart, ed., *Verantwortung and Steuerung von Unternehmen in der Marktwirtschaft*. München: Hampp.

Steinmann, H. and Schreyogg, G. (2000), *Management: Grundlagen der Unternehmensführung; Konzepte, Funktionen, Fallstudien*. Wiesbaden: Gabler.

Sutherland, E. H. (1949), *White Collar Crime*, Reprint (1983). New Haven, CT: Yale University Press.

Transparency International (2005), "Corruption Perceptions Index 2005," www.transparency. org.

Tyler, T. R. (1990), *Why People Obey the Law*. New Haven, CT: Yale University Press.

Wheeler, S. (1992), "The Problem of White Collar Crime Motivation," in K. Schlegel and D. Weisburd, eds., *White-Collar Crime Reconsidered*, 108–23. Boston: Northeastern University Press.

Wieland, J., ed. (2003), *Standards and Audits for Ethics Management Systems: The European Perspective*. Berlin: Springer.

APPENDIX 1: DEFINITION OF CRIME TYPES

Asset misappropriation (including embezzlement by employees): the theft of company assets (including monetary assets/cash or supplies and equipment) by company directors, others in fiduciary positions or an employee for their own benefit.

Corruption and bribery (including racketeering and extortion): typically, the unlawful use of an official position to gain an advantage in contravention of duty. This can involve the promise of an economic benefit or other favor, the use of intimidation or blackmail. It can also refer to the acceptance of such inducements.

False pretences (confidence game): the intentional action of a perpetrator to deceive those in fiduciary positions and make a personal or financial gain.

Financial misrepresentation: company accounts are altered or presented in such a way that they do not reflect the true value or financial activities of the company.

Insider trading: trading of securities by a person inside a company based on non-public information.

Money laundering: actions intended to legitimize the proceeds of crime by disguising their true origin.

Counterfeiting (including product piracy, industrial espionage): this includes the illegal copying and/or distribution of fake goods in breach of patent or copyright and the creation of false currency notes and coins with the intention of passing them off as genuine. It also includes the illegal acquisition of trade secrets or company information.

NOTES

1   Martin-Luther-University Halle-Wittenberg, Economy and Crime Research Center: werle@jura.uni-halle.de; bussmann@jura.uni-halle.de. We are grateful to Jonathan Harrow, Bielefeld, for translating the manuscript and to the editors Susanne Karstedt and Michael Levi for their advice.

2   Alongside the internationally staffed editorial board, Steven Skalak (New York), Claudia Nestler (Frankfurt), James Parker (London) and Steffen Salvenmoser (Frankfurt) from PwC were particularly involved in this survey.

3   The study "Crime Prevention and Intervention in Corporations" was funded by the German Volkswagen Foundation. Aside from the survey, we also analyzed business ethics documents and guidelines on company procedures for dealing with suspects; in addition, we carried out 100 interviews with top managers of German companies.

4   Data were collected by TNS Emnid. Interviewers received special training and were provided with handouts particularly detailing the offenses.

5   Not all sources of information were available in each of the 34 countries.

6   For the global analysis, national data were assigned to five differently sized sample classes on the basis of national gross domestic product (GDP) and weighted accordingly.

7   If responsibility or the organization had changed, a list of potential departments and posts in the company was used to find the final target person (e.g. CEO, CFO, Head of risk management, Head of human resources department).

8   Due to the wide range of different legal terms worldwide, we used standardized definitions of offenses (see Appendix 1).

9   The survey asked about offenses committed by internal and external offenders against the company, but not for corporate crimes committed by the company. This includes, for example, the acceptance of bribes for sales that put their own company at a disadvantage.

10   Original question: "How many incidents of economic crime has your organization been subject to over the past 2 years in . . . [own country]?"

11   We asked respondents about 15 control and prevention measures, and whether they had been established in the company or not. These included, for example, "corporate security," "internal/external audits," "risk management (concerning fraud)" and "forensic analysis techniques." From this information, a sum score was computed for each company, and respective aggregate measures for countries and

regions. These categories are broadly defined, and give little guidance as to how tightly operationally the measures were applied. Enron might have employed all of these, or said that they did.

12 In the following discussion, we focus on Asia, because other than for Africa and Australia, the high number of participating Asian countries and companies, respectively, allows for more regional differentiation.

13 These are average sums of financial losses from all reported incidents of asset misappropriation, false pretenses and counterfeiting that a company has suffered during the last two years. Losses due to corruption, insider trading, financial misrepresentation and money laundering were not surveyed because these would have been hard for interviewees to estimate.

14 See definition in Appendix 1. According to this definition, corruption does not imply in every case a financial loss for the company, but in many cases, they experience damage in other forms, such as bad or overpriced services or goods from suppliers, due to the elimination of any real competition.

15 Question: "Which type of economic crime would you consider to be the most prevalent in business in [own country]?" Corruption and bribery were named as the most prevalent types of economic crime in, for example, South and Central America (30 percent) and Central and Eastern Europe (29 percent; see Table 1).

16 This correlation is negative because high indices in CPI stand for low levels of corruption. As to be expected, the correlation between our perception measure and the CPI 2005 was also very high, at $r = -0.93$.

17 Another aspect is that private companies do not yet perceive corruption problems as applying to themselves as much as to administration and government. Although the CPI did not distinguish between the private and public business sectors, it is obvious that corruption is about exchanges that often involve both business and government.

18 As causes of a real increase globalization, increased competition, the great number of technical innovations and changing values have been named (see, e.g., Friedrichs 2004b; Nelken 1997; Shover 1998: 155–7).

19 Question: "How was the case initially detected?" The list of response categories included a variety of control and security measures as well as the items "internal tip-off," "external tip-off" and "by accident."

20 The much stricter legislation following Enron and WorldCom has probably also contributed to this (see, e.g., the Sarbanes Oxley Act 2002). For details on surveying control and prevention measures, see footnote 11.

21 According to our survey results from the United States and Germany, less than 3 percent of companies in both countries reported any resistance to the introduction of whistleblowing systems.

22 Further results from the survey in the United States and Germany show that economic offenders had worked for their company for an average of 6.5 (United States) or 10 years (Germany), and had held the same post for about 4.5 or 8 years, respectively.

23 Original question: "To what extent would you say that the following reasons have played a role in the offenses you mentioned?"

24 We attribute the relatively high rates in Africa and India as reported in Table 4 to the fact that the sample consists of a disproportionately high number of international companies.

25 See, e.g., Friedrichs 2004a 296–318; Levi 2002; Paternoster and Simpson 1996; Shover and Hochstetler 2006; Simpson 2002.

26 The reported high sentencing rate in Japan is probably due to the practice of reporting only petty cases for lower-ranking employees.

7

Enron et al.

Paradigmatic White Collar Crime Cases for the New Century

— David O. Friedrichs

Enron as Metaphor

The Enron et al. cases of 2001–2004 are the largest scale white collar crime cases since the S & L and insider trading cases of the 1980s. The Microsoft antitrust case of the late 1990s could also be classified as a major white collar crime case, although it was pursued by federal and state antitrust lawsuits that did not attempt to convict Microsoft executives of criminal charges (Auletta 2001; Heilemann 2001). In terms of overall impact on the economy, the political and legal environment, and public perceptions of business-related crime and ethical lapses, it was evident from quite early on in 2002 that the Enron case, in conjunction with related cases, was overshadowing many earlier cases of white collar crime, and at least potentially could have transformative effects. These cases involved an exceptionally broad range of leading corporate and financial executives and institutions.

The term "Enron et al." is invoked here to refer to the specific cases involving the Enron corporation and some of its top personnel, but also to the linked case of the Andersen accounting firm, and a series of cases that surfaced in the wake of the Enron case. Enron, then, becomes a metaphor for a series of other cases, part of a domino effect: these cases, in

Source: David O. Friedrichs, Enron et al.: Paradigmatic White Collar Crime Cases for the New Century. *Critical Criminology*, Vol. 12, No. 2, pp. 113–132. Copyright © 2004 by Springer Science. Reprinted with permission.

alphabetical order, include Adelphia Communications, Computer Associates, Dynergy, Global Crossing, Qwest, Rite Aid, Tyco International, WorldCom, and Xerox (Berenson 2002b). In the case of each of these corporations, either the corporation itself and/or top executives were under criminal and/or civil investigation for some form of gross misrepresentation on financial statements or outright accounting fraud, typically involving inflation of sales, numbers of customers and profits, sham off-the-books partnerships, transactions and trades, concealment of expenses, bonus payments or loans to top executives, or some combination of these activities. A common thread in at least most of these cases was the extraordinary levels of compensation for top executives, and large paper losses for investors following revelations of the misrepresentations or misstatements (Oppel and Atlas 2001; Barboza 2002a; Greider 2002). Questions were subsequently raised about the financial statements of other major corporations (e.g., see Berenson 2003; Morgenson 2003). The legitimate fear that there might be many corporations that issued misleading financial statements contributed to a precipitous erosion of investor confidence and dramatic declines in stock market indices, despite claims of some analysts that many market fundamentals were relatively positive (Berenson 2002a; Morgenson 2002a). The common thread of inflating apparent profits or concealing losses and costs, in the interest of pushing the stock price up or avoiding a decline in the stock price, is more striking than the various devices or techniques to achieve this end (McLean 2001; Barboza 2002b). The immense rewards in various forms enjoyed by the top insiders in these corporations, significantly based upon basic misrepresentation of the corporation's financial balance sheet, are another common thread (Leonhardt 2002a, b). The cooperative involvement of a broad network of other parties—including independent boards of directors, accounting firms, law firms, investment banking firms, and stock analysts—is still another common theme (Eichenwald and Barboza 2002; Madrick 2002).

Enron et al. as Crime

In addition to massive civil lawsuits, the Enron et al. cases have inspired numerous criminal investigations, leading to some guilty pleas, indictments and pending trials (Eisenberg 2002b; Thomas 2002; Eichenwald 2004; Feder and Eichenwald 2004). Claims of criminal conduct have been vigorously contested in most cases, although some concessions of such conduct have been forthcoming as a part of plea negotiations. In the narrow, technical sense, willful violation of criminal laws will have to be demonstrated to make the case that crimes occurred. Alternative constructs on the misrepresentations of corporate financial balance sheets are likely to include the following: the various accounting strategies were technically legal and generally accepted practices, or were so certified by professionals (accountants and lawyers) overseeing the process; judgment calls, as opposed to willful intent to defraud, were involved; unanticipated circumstances and bad luck, rather than criminal conduct, can be blamed for the financial meltdowns (Eichenwald 2002b; Toobin 2003). The inherent ambiguity of some of the relevant laws, the complexity of the schemes themselves, and the resources of first-class legal talent to challenge government characterizations of these activities, all contribute to the difficulties inherent in successfully applying a legal designation of crime to the Enron et al. activities.

The crime question can also be considered more broadly. Sutherland (1949), in his original study of corporate crime, adopted the broader conception of corporate crime to encompass violations of civil law and regulatory law, as well as criminal law, on the premise that the corporations disproportionately influence the adoption of criminal laws in ways that favor their interests. This claim certainly still has merit. More broadly still, progressive criminologists would characterize the activities of Enron et al. as criminal simply on the basis that policies were adopted that can be shown to have had demonstrably exploitative and harmful consequences (for workers; for consumers; for investors; for citizens; and so on) (Henry and Lather 2001; Tifft and Sullivan 2001). Indeed, the actual and potential scope of demonstrable harm attributable to Enron et al. is extraordinary, and includes: for tens of thousands of people, lost jobs; lost pensions; lost opportunities for higher education; higher prices; higher rates of interest; less money for investment in legitimate businesses; less money for charities; and so on (Fusaro and Miller 2002). To the extent that government resources have to be directed toward addressing these activities, government resources for other concerns (including socially beneficial programs) can be affected. Somewhat more abstract but very real costs are possible, and include: enhanced physical and mental distress for those most directly affected; erosion of trust in major institutions; and intensification of inter-group resentment and conflicts. Of course, those who adopt some version of a Marxist perspective would regard the activities of Enron et al. as simply the more manifestly obvious forms of crime that are inherent to capitalist enterprise (Lynchy, et al. 2000; Russell 2002). In sum: While there are many indications of criminal conduct in the narrowest legal sense, crime may also be said to be involved in the Enron et al. cases in terms of broader conceptions of the term crime.

Applying Criminological Theory to Enron et al.

Greed is a term commonly used as an explanation for Enron et al. and surely greed played a role. But such a simplistic, one-dimensional explanation does not take us very far. At the other end of the spectrum, Enron et al. can be explained as an outcome of a complex interaction of many different factors and variables, operating on various levels. Accordingly, an integrated theoretical approach is called for in these cases (Barak 1998; Vold et al. 2002). If we aspire to understand Enron et al. on a truly sophisticated level, it is useful to identify as many potentially applicable variables and factors as possible, with at least some such factors either eliminated or relegated to a minor role in the development of a comprehensive explanatory scheme.

Structural Level

Enron et al. occurs within the context of a capitalist political economy that establishes the fundamental conditions for the operation of private corporations, and is linked with certain cultural values promoting free market competition, the pursuit of profit, and the expansion of markets, or growth, among other things. Russell's (2002) brief on behalf of the on-going relevance of a Marxist framework applies here. In the wake of the collapse of the Soviet Union, capitalism was widely celebrated as triumphant, and a political and cultural environment of intensified celebration of capitalist values prevailed throughout the 1990s and into the new century. Mitchell (2001) has critiqued the current form of orientation of American corporate capitalism as favoring stock price maximization over values. The focus on short-term enhancement of stock price has many harmful consequences, but top corporate executives who make the often ruthless decisions (e.g., laying off thousands of workers) are relatively insulated from confronting the painful human costs of these decisions.

The late 1990s bull market created expectations of substantial stock price growth, and put CEOs under immense pressure to produce numbers that would promote such price growth, or at a minimum would not lead to a decline in stock price. If reported quarterly numbers were below expectations, the corporate stock price would fall dramatically, generating substantial losses and making it more difficult to raise further capital. During the same period of time, the expansion of stock option plans, bonuses and other forms of rewarding top executive personnel were much more fully developed. An escalating stock price was arguably the surest way to riches for corporate managers, and provided strong additional incentives for encouraging aggressive or blatantly fraudulent accounting in connection with the production of corporate financial statements.

The political and legal context of the present era must also be taken into account. Although many political leaders and legislators expressed outrage over Enron et al., they also played a key role in creating the legal environment that facilitated the illegal and unethical activities of these corporations (Labaton 2002a). For example, legislation in 1995 was passed shielding companies and accountants from investor lawsuits, and in 2000 regulators were forced to dilute proposed restrictions on accountants. Altogether, during this period of time, legislation relating to investor lawsuits imposed tougher burdens of proof on plaintiffs; shortened the statute of limitations for filing such suits; put limits on pretrial discovery, and on accountant liability; and imposed the obligation on plaintiffs who lost such suits to pay the legal costs. The sum effect of such legislation was to provide corporations and their auditors with a sense of relative immunity for any financial manipulations they might undertake causing losses to investors.

Deregulatory legislative initiatives cannot be understood independently of the political environment. In an era of costly political campaigns, political office-holders have become increasingly dependent upon the donations of major corporations and wealthy corporate executives, who in return expect favorable responses to their lobbying on behalf of laws favorable to their economic well-being. Indeed, the entire Enron et al. phenomenon could be said to lend support to Mills' (1959) thesis about the power elite: that the top corporate, political, and military people make the important decisions for the rest of us, are closely linked with each other and engage in "higher immorality" in the pursuit of their own interests. Although these propositions apply to both political parties, and all recent administrations, the extent of these interlocks and mutual interests are especially pronounced in the administration of President George W. Bush, as has been widely documented (Duffy and Dickerson 2002; Fusaro and Miller 2002). The earlier career and actions of the President, the Vice President, and other high-level officials in this administration raised questions in many quarters about the depths of their commitment to address emerging corporate scandals.

One can also argue that an emerging postmodern cultural environment fostered an increasing disconnect between traditional criteria for reality toward hyperreal orientations privileging simulations and abstract projections as real (Schwartz and Friedrichs 1994). This postmodern dimension of the Enron et al. cases is explored more fully in the section that follows; however, it can be observed here that high-level executives in Enron et al. may have become increasingly insulated from a conventional form of a real world, creating a self-delusional and mutually reinforcing world of ever-expanding opportunities for profit and growth (Wolff 2002). Financial deals and the use of financial instruments such as derivatives became so complex the executives involved may no longer have fully comprehended what was involved (Altman 2002b). The distribution of very large political donations and the cultivation of political connections could have also contributed to an illusion of immunity from political or justice system interference in their schemes (Greider 2001; Van Natta 2002). If high-level executives did not on some level buy into these various illusions, they were consciously engaged in profoundly self-destructive activities.

Networks and Interlocks

Contemporary capitalist corporations such as Enron are best understood as operating as part of a network of organizations and entities with
which they establish ties of mutual interdependence. In the public
realm—as noted above—corporations develop ties with political leaders
and parties upon whom they are dependent for favorable policy decisions, and who are dependent on them, in turn, for political campaign
donations. The interconnections between public and private interests,
then, incorporate fundamental conflicts of interest, with the practical benefits of accommodating corporate donors often trumping other considerations by political decision-makers. In the private sector, entities include
accounting firms, investment banking houses, stock brokerages, stock
analysts, and law firms. These networks are increasingly structured to
have inherent conflicts of interest that lead to enabling fraudulent activity
as opposed to acting as checks and balances on such activities (Gullotta
2001; Atlas 2002; Berenson 2002b; Levin 2002; Morgenson 2002b).

Two of the more blatant conflicts of interest highlighted in the wake
of the exposure of Enron et al. are as follows: Auditing firms derive a substantial proportion of their income from consulting contracts with the
corporations they are auditing; a fear of losing these lucrative consulting
contracts inhibits the accounting firms from pressing the corporation on
financial statement discrepancies, or leads to willing participation in the
production of misrepresented financial statements. As another example,
stock analysts are affiliated with investment banking operations that
derive their principal income from underwriting and consulting deals
with corporate clients, as opposed to truly independent and honest evaluation of the corporation's stock. As the top people in the corporation have
much to lose if the stock price declines, stock analysts serve their own
firm best by evaluating the stock of corporate clients (or prospective clients) in positive terms.

The notion of independent boards overseeing corporate financial
arrangements was also severely compromised by the various benefits
derived by board members from not challenging or seriously questioning
corporate practices (Stellin 2002). Even investors and employees were not
strongly inclined to challenge the actions of the corporate leadership as
long as they seemed to be reaping high rates of return on their investments.
Altogether, effective preventive checks and balances on unwarranted or
outright fraudulent activities were largely absent. External entities did not
adequately compensate for the conflicts of interest and lack of internal
oversight: e.g., credit rating agencies failed to identify misrepresentations
in corporate financial statements; the SEC was neither adequately staffed
nor appropriately organized to proactively investigate these corporate
financial statements; and the media—disproportionately owned and controlled by large corporations—also largely failed to reveal the financial

misrepresentations of these corporations, until they became self-evident as the corporate finances began unraveling (Lewis 2002; McNamee et al. 2002; White 2002). Criminologists have to attend to the various ways in which these networks, interlocks, inherent conflicts of interest, and inadequate forms of oversight promote a criminogenic environment.

Organizational Factors

On an organizational level, an environment of intense competitiveness, intimidation toward compliance with the organizational agenda established by company leadership, and the promotion of a strong ethos of corporate pride, loyalty, and superiority was also significant. At Enron, for example, a "rank and yank" system of evaluating employees' performance was put into place: employees who fell below a certain ranking at the periodic evaluation points would lose their jobs (Fusaro and Miller 2002: 51). Employees who failed to comply with corporate directives were also in jeopardy. On the positive side, employee loyalty was promoted by much celebratory activity and rhetoric within the corporation, all geared to promoting the perception that the corporation was superior to most others, had an excellent business plan and outstanding prospects for the future, and so forth.

The pay incentive structures adopted at Enron et al. are another organizational feature of these cases. At Enron, specifically, huge bonuses were paid in 2000 to executives who made stock-price targets; these bonuses exceeded $300 million (Eichenwald 2002a). The period of these bonus awards coincides with the period when Enron was engaged in various accounting maneuvers to inflate the appearance of profits from its operations. Accordingly, one has evidence of a financial motivation for these maneuvers, and to the extent that they turn out to be illegal, criminal intent. Furthermore, generous loans in the millions were made to many top executives at these companies, enabling the executives to increase their pay while satisfying demands to increase their holding in the corporation's stock (Leonhardt 2002a). These loans gave executives incentives to pursue risky strategies to keep the stock price up, since this would make it easier to repay the loans with higher value stocks, profiting greatly from the difference in the original price of the stock. By paying back loans with stocks, executives avoided having to report that they were selling shares in their own corporation; and generous stock option plans provided such executives with parallel incentives to do whatever was necessary to drive up stock price.

Some of these corporate organizations—and again, Enron in particular—proudly proclaimed themselves to be models of a new, more creative, more visionary form of management than was true of "old economy" corporations, and they were praised in some quarters for pioneering new approaches to business in a rapidly evolving information age (Barboza 2001). In the case of Ford Motor Company, it is clear what business they are in: they produce automobiles. In the case of Enron (and some of the other companies) the nature of their business was far less clear, and the stress was on trades and deals, not products and assets. In hindsight, this form of corporate organization is especially likely to foster management obfuscation and illegal financial manipulations.

Modern corporate organizations have become increasingly complex in terms of how they are organized. Transnational conglomerates are going to be far more complex than traditional, domestic corporations with a single, core product or service. In addition, highly complex financial instruments have been adopted by these corporations. "Derivatives" exemplify such instruments. According to Altman (2002b) "derivatives are contracts that promise payments from one investor, and 'counter-party,' to another, depending on future events. These events can be as ephemeral as changes in the prices of securities or commodities from which the contracts are derived—hence the name—or as concrete as weather changes . . . ." Derivatives were developed as a useful hedge on certain types of business-related risks, and can serve a legitimate purpose, but they also tend to be highly complex, are not transparent, and incorporate risks that may not be well understood. Enron specifically used derivative trades as a means of hiding loans. Accordingly, the complexity of many of the new corporate organizations—especially those in emerging businesses such as telecommunications and energy trading—created expanded opportunities for illegal and unethical financial manipulations.

Dramaturgic Level

On a dramaturgic level, the Enron corporation was for some time very successful in conveying an image of ultra-respectability that largely insulated it from external challenge, and also reinforced an internal legitimation of its business practices. This projection of ultra-respectability was fostered by: the cultivation of and friendship with top political leaders (including both Presidents Bush) by Chairman Kenneth Lay; the construction of an emblematic headquarters in Houston; the naming of Houston's stadium as Enron Field; the conspicuous local philanthropy; and so on. Lay, the son of a Baptist minister, as the "face" of Enron, projected an image of decency, generosity, charm, and—or so it seemed—integrity (Thomas and Murr 2002). Enron was able to capitalize on an especially high level of trust that was in turn, in important ways, a function of its image of ultra-respectability.

Individualistic Level

Sutherland (1949) dismissed the notion that personality or individual attributes could significantly explain white collar crime, and this has generally been the line adopted ever since. But character and personality should not be wholly irrelevant. The top personnel at Enron et al.—or those most directly implicated in wrongful conduct—are quite uniformly described as lacking in basic integrity, and greedy. It seems excessively cynical to declare that integrity is irrelevant, and that any executive operating in the environment in which the Enron et al. executives operated would make exactly the same decisions. But to the extent that these individuals had any ethical bearings or concerns, they seem to have been clearly trumped by other considerations, and priorities. The media has also reported on the greed, in the traditional sense, of at least some of the key executives in these cases: multi-million dollar mansions, extravagant vacation homes, yachts, private jets or helicopters, fancy art collections, and so on (Eichenwald 2002a; Leonhardt 2002a, b). Many of these executives (who in some cases came from very humble circumstances) were also greedy for acceptance by political and social elites, and surely some of their campaign contributions and philanthropic endeavors were inspired by the desire for acceptance. Finally, in an oft-cited proposition, money becomes a way of "keeping score": that is, at least some of these executives seemed to have a bottomless need to run up the numbers of their compensation simply as a way of proving to themselves (and others) their superior place in the society's "scoreboard" of winners and losers.

Of course many highly successful corporate leaders who do not get in trouble with the law have some mixture of such attributes. These attributes by themselves may not necessarily lead to engaging in unlawful and unethical practices, but in conjunction with some of the conditions described earlier may well facilitate law-breaking. These high-level executives may be more fearful of failing, of losing their position and losing face, than of what may be quite unthinkable or unimaginable to them: that they might be indicted for crimes and go to prison (Schwartz 2002). Accordingly, they engage in risky strategies. The process of getting into trouble with high-risk decisions is often incremental, and gradual. In a vein somewhat parallel to the thinking of embezzlers, who first embezzle small sums fully expecting to replace the embezzled money, and then due to unanticipated losses get in deeper and deeper, so it is with at least some of these executives (Cressey 1953). Their past success has imbued them with an unwarranted optimism, and an assumption that they will be able to overcome any crisis, with a combination of various factors working in their favor. Things get out of control, however. Ever since the Watergate case, it has been a commonly advanced axiom that the cover-up is worse (and more damaging) than the original crime (Eichenwald 2002d; Schwartz 2002). Some efforts at cover-up continue to be the norm in Enron et al. cases, however, and may reflect a fundamental unwillingness to face up to losing one's privileged position and all that goes with it, and the inherently arrogant sense that one is too smart to get caught.

One of the striking—and arguably especially disheartening—aspects of the Enron et al. cases was the absence of individuals who took a stand against illegal or unethical practices, refused to cooperate, or reported such matters to the proper authorities (McLean and Elkind 2003). In the case of Enron, one high-level official had apparently expressed some concerns about the irregular financial arrangements, resigned, and then appears to have committed suicide when the public scandal surfaced (although some suspicion remains that it wasn't a suicide) (Fusaro and Miller 2002; Yardley 2002). In his suicide note this individual expressed his unbearable pain over the turn of events; but such a response seems to have been highly atypical.

Enron et al.:
Modern or Postmodern White Collar Crime?

The question now turns to whether the Enron/Andersen case—or Enron et al. cases—is best understood as a modern or a postmodern phenomenon; whether it is something new in white collar crime, or simply an exemplification of long-standing, familiar forms of white collar crime. This question, I believe, does not have a single, straightforward answer, but it is surely worth addressing.

It is not uncommon to differentiate between traditional, modern, and emerging future (or postmodern) societies (Friedrichs and Friedrichs, 2004). Traditional societies are characterized by agriculture as the central form of productive activity, hand-tool technology, farming villages as the typical community, the family structure as the dominant form of organization for farms and shops, interpersonal communication, and social and geographical stability as the normative expectation. In modern societies, industrial activity is the central form of productive activity, the machine displaces hand tools in the technological realm, urbanization and city life dominate, bureaucracies displace families as the dominant form of organization, mass communication becomes increasingly important, and both social and geographical mobility are normative expectations. In an emerging postmodern society, information services (broadly defined) increasingly become central to productive activity, the computer displaces the machine at the center of modern technology, the megalopolis and virtual communities become increasingly important, adhocracies (or more flexible, adaptable forms of bureaucracy) emerge, interactive communication (exemplified by video, cable, the Internet, and television/computer linkups) spreads, and social and geographical fluidity—i.e., moving in and out, back and forth—is increasingly internalized as an expectation.

Needless to say, the foregoing is a broad, generalized, and selective characterization of social change. Furthermore, it makes sense to acknowledge that traditional, modern, and postmodern patterns of social existence co-exist, that tensions and conflicts between these patterns are central elements of our social existence, and that the schematic comparison of traditional, modern, and postmodern societies reflects mainly a matter of degree in the existence of different elements at a particular point in time. Any attempt to demarcate a specific time frame for the transformation from a traditional to a modern, or from a modern to a postmodern, society is necessarily arbitrary. Nevertheless, if one accepts such qualifications and caveats, the comparative endeavor is a necessary and useful exercise.

Instances of white collar crime, broadly defined, can be found in the earliest historical records, and various forms of fraud have been a persistent feature of human history. But white collar crime as it has been conventionally conceived of—since Sutherland—is principally a modern phenomenon, because the conditions of modernity promote the amplification of such crime. Many forms of corporate crime, in particular, reflect in some form the conditions generated by a modern, industrial society. The literature on corporate crime has especially attended to corporate violence in the forms of crimes against citizens (e.g., pollution), crimes against workers (e.g., unsafe working conditions, such as exposing workers to asbestos), and crimes against consumers (e.g., unsafe products, such as the Pinto and the Dalkon Shield). Corporate crime also takes the form of abuses of power, fraud, and economic exploitation, including crimes against taxpayers (e.g., defense contract fraud), crimes against consumers (e.g., price fixing), crimes against employees (e.g., economic exploitation), crimes against competitors (e.g., theft of trade secrets), and crimes against owners and creditors (e.g., managerial self-dealing and strategic bankruptcy).

In certain respects, the Enron et al. crimes are manifestations of frauds with a long lineage. The South Sea Bubble case of the 18th century is one example of such fraud (Robb 1992; Balen 2003). The South Sea Company was chartered in London in 1711 to engage in slave trade and commerce in South America. Over a period of about 10 years, investors lost large fortunes because the whole enterprise was quite fraudulent, driven by bribery, false financial statements, and stock manipulation. In some interpretations, the Enron et al. cases simply exemplify—on a grand scale—the classic, enduring "pump and dump" schemes where insiders drive up stock prices on the basis of some form of misrepresentation, and then bail out of their own positions at the top, with other investors incurring huge losses when the scheme inevitably collapses. On the other hand, it is also possible to identify some dimensions of the Enron et al. cases that are at least relatively novel, and may be taken to reflect emerging postmodern attributes of social existence.

First, the corporate crime literature to date has principally focused on corporations that manufacture some type of product. The Enron et al. cases disproportionately involve corporations engaged in the provision of some form of service (e.g., relating to energy, telecommunications, entertainment, and the like). In the case of corporations like Exxon, Ford, Johns-Manville, or A.H. Robbins, everyone understands the core nature of their business; in the cases of Enron, Global Crossings, WorldCom and

Tyco International, however, the real nature of what they do or what kind of business they are in is far less clear. Second, those involved in the Enron et al. cases can in many cases be characterized as "paper entrepreneurs." Unlike Henry Ford they did not make their fortune by developing (or inventing) and producing a product for which there was a large and expanding public demand so much as that they found ways of acquiring and manipulating financial assets. Third, the companies involved are increasingly likely to be transnational in their operations, and organized to take advantage in every way (e.g., on corporate tax liability) of this transnational character.

The concept of hyperreality introduced by Baudrillard (1994) can usefully be applied to the Enron et al. cases. Hyperreality has been characterized as a circumstance wherein images breed incestuously with each other without reference to reality or meaning. When we increasingly experience our world in terms of simulations, and can no longer clearly differentiate between conventional reality and simulations, then we have entered the realm of hyperreality. The related term "hyper-modernism" has been applied to the hyper-intensification of modernism, and a circumstance where technology and economics merge (Appignanesi and Garratt 1995: 126). Hyperreal finance is a world of 24 hour hook-ups between worldwide financial markets, where transactions in cyberspace become dominant.

In the various accounts of the Enron et al. cases, one is struck by a fundamental disconnect between the presumed modernist assumptions of most ordinary investors—that they are investing in something real, in an appropriately assessed product or service with a good potential for growth—and the apparent postmodernist or "hyperreal" orientation of some of the central figures in these cases, whose primary concern seemed to be the manipulation of assets and numbers in ways that maximized their own short-term gain, with almost complete indifference to the demonstrable value of the product or service at the center of their business. The question of whether the key figures in these cases were deliberately and consciously engaging in transactions they knew to be fraud, or that on some level they were no longer able to clearly discriminate between simulated transactions and transactions of substance, is not entirely resolved. In more colloquial terms, did these key figures on some level confuse the "smoke and mirrors" they were generating with something of substance? Did they operate in an environment promoting a "dematerialization of the real," and a disconnect with the conventional reality of capitalist economy?

The concept of intertextuality as it has emerged from postmodernist discourse may also have some relevance here. This term refers to the idea that there is a complex and infinite set of interwoven relationships, "an endless conversation between the texts with no prospect of ever arriving at or being halted at an agreed point" (Bauman 1990: 42). Absolute intertextuality assumes that everything is related to everything else. In the Enron et al.

cases, as they have been emerging, one is struck first by the complexity of the many suspect deals, financial arrangements and instruments (e.g., derivatives), to the point that it seems possible that at a certain juncture, none of the key players can any longer fully grasp the scope and character of the financial edifice they have constructed. Second, and relatedly, one is struck by the direct and indirect intertwined involvement of so many different parties in these transactions: i.e., corporate executives, corporate boards, auditors, investment bankers, stock analysts, lawyers, credit rating agencies, and the like. On the one hand, none of these different entities may have a complete handle on all aspects of the complex financial transactions involved; on the other hand, these different entities may mutually reinforce on at least some level the basic disconnect with conventional reality.

None of the propositions stated in the previous paragraph should be interpreted as excusing the culpability of the different parties from their fiduciary responsibilities; denying the significant forms of conscious wrongdoing, unethical or illegal activity involved; or overlooking the role of greed and personal enrichment as motivating factors in individual and collective involvement in fraudulent transactions. But at the same time, a deeper understanding of the Enron et al. crimes calls for attention to the potential role of an emerging postmodern environment in the corporate world.

Challenges for Criminology

What specific contribution can criminologists make to the understanding of these cases? First, if the term crime is to be applied here, it is criminologists who should be best qualified to clarify different ways in which this term is most appropriately applied to these cases (Henry and Lather 2001). More specifically, criminologists can clarify what forms of white collar crime are involved in these cases. In another vein, Snider's (2000) work on the decriminalization of corporate crime, in the recent era, provides an important point of departure for critical criminologists addressing the definitional issues.

Second, criminologists can engage in what Barak (1998: 294) calls "newsmaking criminology." The media coverage of Enron et al.—variously characterized as corporate scandals, corporate transgressions, or a corporate crime wave—has arguably been the most substantial, pervasive, and sustained coverage of white collar crime (in some form) in American history. Criminologists can engage in the systematic study of this media coverage and its influence on public policy. On the applied level, criminologists can contribute more directly to the popular media coverage of Enron et al. crimes, challenging some of the common misrepresentations of such crime in the media. Criminologists are especially well-qualified to address the question of the real costs of these crimes in relation to more conventional forms of crime.

Third, criminologists can initiate the systematic criminological study of Enron et al. cases, through the exploration of primary data, and ethnographic or participant observer studies. The present articles relies largely on journalistic sources, in part because as a practical matter—with many legal cases pending—primary data and interviews with participants are not yet a feasible option. Over time, this should change, and articles such as this can hopefully provide a useful point of departure for such directly engaged research. In this connection, as well, criminologists will face challenges of obtaining funding for this type of research.

Fourth, there is the question of theory and explanation: Which theories—most typically, developed to explain conventional forms of crime and delinquency—are usefully applied to the understanding of the Enron et al. cases? This article has attempted to make a preliminary contribution to this endeavor. But much further work is called for, especially in terms of the application of sophisticated forms of critical theories of the political economy to an understanding of this type of crime. The relevance of some significant work being done within the framework of mainstream approaches, such as an emerging network science, has to be considered. Altogether, refinements of existing initiatives toward the development of integrated criminological theories will be necessary if we are to obtain a profound understanding of Enron et al. crime.

Finally, criminologists are especially qualified to identify some of the challenges of policing and prosecuting the Enron et al. cases. They can identify what has been learned about the prevention and control of other forms of crime that is applicable to crimes of this nature. Furthermore, they can build upon pioneering work of Benson and Cullen (1998) on the prosecution of corporate crime, studying the complex decision-making process involved in the pursuit of the Enron et al. cases.

In sum, a specifically criminological analysis of the Enron et al. cases should complement and enrich analyses generated by commentary and interpretation coming from many other sources.

Conclusion

Enron et al. might well be described as a paradigmatic form of white collar crime, because they incorporated in almost pure form some of the key—and sometimes contradictory—attributes that Sutherland had in mind when he promoted the concept of white collar crime: The crimes were committed by privileged, respectable members of society, violating a fundamental trust, through major corporations, for purposes of financial gain (and to avoid financial loss), with devastating economic consequences for many ordinary members of society. Sutherland's interest in white collar crime was significantly inspired by his revulsion with the manipulations of financial elites during the 1920s, culminating in the stock market crash of 1929 and contributing to the depression of the 1930s. At the same time, the Enron et al. cases also incorporate some elements distinctive to an emerging postmodern information age.

One can envision a number of different outcomes for the Enron et al. cases. First, it is possible they will largely recede from public consciousness; prosecutors will encounter insurmountable barriers to successfully pursuing most of these cases, or convictions will be reversed on appeal; various lobbying entities will successfully defeat any serious efforts for new laws and regulatory initiatives; and the cases will simply become part of an evolving list of white collar crime cases, devoid of a special status. The likelihood of such a scenario is importantly linked with other developments in the larger world, including the course of international terrorism and the response to it. More specifically, if major new terrorist attacks along the lines of 9/11 occur, or the occupation of Iraq becomes increasingly costly and chaotic, governmental and public attention (and resources) are proportionally less likely to focus on corporate crime cases.

In a second scenario, Enron et al. will continue to be a focus of some on-going public interest. They will lead to some successful prosecutions, focused principally on individual executives identified as having initiated illegal actions, and convictions will generally be upheld. But in this scenario, the stress will be on the enforcement of existing laws and regulations, with some possible fine-tuning, but no fundamental reforms. This might be described as the scenario generally favored by the administration of President George W. Bush and the Republican congressional leadership.

In a third scenario, Enron et al. will reemerge as matters of significant on-going public interest. They will produce major prosecutions of not only individual executives but errant corporations as well, and convictions will be quite uniformly upheld. These cases will lead to the adoption of laws and regulations tougher in fundamental ways in response to the types of activities involved in these cases. This is a scenario most likely to be embraced by liberal democrats.

Finally, there is this: Enron et al. might hypothetically evolve into criminal cases so large in scope that they will lead to a fundamental transformation of the public perception of white collar crime, and a structural transformation of the political and economic system fostering these forms of white collar crime. Such a transformation could lead to broad support for preventive measures and basic deterrence of Enron et al. types of crime. Those of a progressive orientation have long awaited the white collar crime "tsunami," a white collar crime wave so devastating and broad in scope that it will produce just such a transformation.

If past history is any guide, perhaps the expectation of a minor or moderate impact of the Enron et al. cases is the most probable scenario. However, the fostering of a broader consciousness in the direction of a major or transformative impact of the Enron et al. cases is a worthwhile objective toward which white collar crime criminologists—and especially those with a critical criminological orientation—should orient themselves.

REFERENCES

Altman, D. (2002a). Finding gems of genius among Enron's crumbs. *The New York Times* (February 3), Wk3.

Altman, D. (2002b). Contracts so complex they imperil the system. *The New York Times* (February 24), 3/1.

Appignanesi, R. and Garratt, C. (1995). *Introducing Postmodernism.* New York: Totem Books.

Atlas, R. (2002). Market place. *The New York Times* (June 13), C3.

Auletta, K. (2001). *World War 3.0: Microsoft and Its Enemies.* New York: Random House.

Balen, M. (2003). *The Secret History of the South Sea Bubble: The World's First Great Financial Scandal.* New York: HarperCollins.

Barak, G. (1998). *Integrating Criminologies.* Boston: Allyn & Bacon.

Barak, G. (2001). Crime and crime control in an age of globalization: A theoretical discussion. *Critical Criminology* 10, 57–72.

Barboza, D. (2001). Victims and champions of a Darwinian Enron. *The New York Times* (December 12), C4.

Barboza, D. (2002a). Officials got a windfall before Enron's collapse. *The New York Times* (June 18), Cl.

Barboza, D. (2002b). Former officials say Enron had gains during crisis in California. *The New York Times* (June 23), Al.

Barboza, D. and Schwartz, J. (2002). The financial wizard ties to Enron's fall. *The New York Times* (February 6), Al.

Baudrillard, J. (1994). *Simulacra and Simulation.* Ann Arbor: University of Michigan Press.

Bauman, Z. (1990). Philosophical affinities of postmodern sociology. *Sociological Review* 38, 411–444.

Benson, M. and Cullen, F. T. (1998). *Combating Corporate Crime: Local Prosecutors at Work.* Boston: Northeastern University Press.

Berenson, A. (2002a). The biggest casualty of Enron's collapse: Confidence. *The New York Times* (February 10), 4/1.

Berenson, A. (2002b). Three-decade-old echoes, awakened by Enron. *The New York Times* (February 24), Cl.

Berenson, A. (2003). Report says Freddie Mac misled investigators. *New York Times* (July 24), Cl.

Bradley, W. (2002). Enron's end. *The American Prospect* (January 1–14), 30–31.

Callahan, D. (2002). Private sector, public doubts. *The New York Times* (January 15), A21.

Cressey, D. R. (1953) *Other People's Money.* Glencoe, IL: Free Press.

Duffy, M. and Dickerson, J. F. (2002). Enron spoils the party. *Time* (February 4), 19–25.

Eichenwald, K. (2002a). Enron paid huge bonuses in '01: Experts see a motive in cheating. *The New York Times* (March 1), Al.

Eichenwald, K. (2002b). White-collar defense stance: The criminal-less crime. *The New York Times* (March 3), Wk/3.

Eichenwald, K. (2002c). How the trial at Andersen could hurt a fraud case. *The New York Times* (May 24), C1.

Eichenwald, K. (2002d). Andersen guilty of shredding files in Enron scandal. *The New York Times* (June 16), Al.

Eichenwald, K. (2002e). Ex-Enron official admits payments to finance chief. *The New York Times* (August 22), AI.

Eichenwald, K. and Barboza, D. (2002). Enron criminal investigation is said to expand to bankers. *The New York Times* (June 13), Al.

Eisenberg, D. (2002a). Dennis the Menace. *Time* (June 17), 48–49.

Eisenberg, D. (2002b). Jail to the chiefs? *Time* (August 12), 24–25.

Friedrichs, D. O. (2004), *Trusted Criminals: White Collar Crime in Contemporary Society,* 2nd edition. Belmont, CA: Wadsworth.

Friedrichs, D. O. and Friedrichs, J. (2004). Postmodernist theory. In A. Thio and T. Calhoun (eds.), *Readings in Deviant Behavior,* 3rd ed. Boston: Pearson, pp. 70–76.

Fusaro, P. C, and Miller, R. M. (2002). *What Went Wrong at Enron.* New York: John Wiley.

Greider, W. (2001). Enron's rise and fall. *The Nation* (December 24), 5–6.

Greider, W. (2002). Crime in the suites. *The Nation* (February 4), 11–14.

Gullotta, M. (2001). The SEC's auditor independence rule. Missing the boat on independence. 42 *Santa Clara Law Review,* 221–245.

Heilemann, J. (2001). *Pride Before the Fall: The Trials of Bill Gates and the End of the Microsoft Era.* New York: HarperCollins.

Henry, S. and Lanier, M. (eds.) (2001). *What is Crime? Controversies over the Nature of Crime and What to do About It.* Lanham, MD: Rowman & Littlefield.

Labaton, S. (2002a). Now who, exactly, got us into this? *The New York Times* (February 3), 3/1.

Labaton, S. (2002b). Downturn and shift in population feed boom in white-collar crime. *The New York Times* (June 2), A1.

Leonhardt, D. (2002a). A prime example of anything goes executive pay. *The New York Times* (June 4), Cl.

Leonhardt, D. (2002b). Slivers of support for shackling corporate pay. *The New York Times* (July 13), C1.

Levitt, A. (2002). Who audits the auditors? *The New York Times* (January 17), A29.

Lewis, R. (2002). Media, mostly big businesses, fail to report on big business. *The Scranton Times* (February 4), Editorial page.

Lynch, M. J., Michalowski, R. and Groves, W. B. (2000). *The New Primer in Radical Criminology: Critical Perspectives on Crime, Power, and Identity.* Monsey, NY: Criminal Justice Press.

Madrick, J. (2002). Enron: Seduction and betrayal. *The New York Review of Books* (March 14), 21–24.

McLean, B. (2001). Why Enron went bust. *Fortune* (December 24), 59–68.

McNamee, M., Borrus, A. and Henry, D. (2002). The reluctant reformer. *Business Week* (March 25), 72–82.

Mills, C. W. (1959). *The Power Elite.* New York: Oxford University Press.

Mitchell, L. (2001). *Corporate Irresponsibility: America's Newest Export.* New Haven, CT: Yale University Press.

Morgenson, G. (2002a). Worries of more Enrons to come give stock prices a pounding. *The New York Times* (January 30), C11.

Morgenson, G. (2002b). Requiem for an honorable profession. *The New York Times* (May 5), 3/1.

Morgenson, G. (2003). Financial disclosure the Barry Diller way. *New York Times* (July 24), Cl.

New Republic (2002). The real Enron scandal. *The New Republic* (January 28), 7.

Oppel, R. A. Jr. and Atlas, R. (2001). Enron struggles to find financing to remain in business. *The New York Times* (December 1), Cl.

Rich, F. (2002). All the president's Enrons. *The New York Times* (April 6), A13.

Robb, G. (1992). *White-Collar Crime in Modern England: Financial Fraud and Business Morality—1845–1929*. Cambridge, UK: Cambridge University Press.

Russell, S. (2002). The continuing relevance of Marxism to critical criminology. *Critical Criminology* 11, 113–135.

Sargent, M. A. (2002). The real scandal, *Commonwealth* (March 8), 10–12.

Schwartz, J. (2002). Choosing whether to cover-up or come clean. *The New York Times* (July 1), Cl.

Schwartz, M. and Friedrichs, D. (1994). Postmodern thought and criminological discontent: New metaphors for understanding violence. *Criminology* 32, 221–246.

Scott, J. (2002). Once bitten, twice shy: A world of eroding trust. *The New York Times* (April 21), Wks.

Snider, L. (1999). Relocating law: Making corporate crime disappear. In. E. Comack (ed.), *Locating Law*. Halifax, NS: Fernwood Publishing Co, 183–207.

Snider, L. (2000). The sociology of corporate crime: An obituary. *Theoretical Criminology* 4, 169–206.

Stellin, S. (2002). Directors ponder new, tougher rules. *The New York Times* (June 30), 3/16.

Sutherland, E. H. (1940). White collar criminality. *American Sociological Review* 5, 1–12.

Sutherland, E. H. (1949). *White Collar Crime*. New York: Holt, Rinehart & Winston.

Thomas, C. B. (2002). Called to account. *Time* (June 24), 52.

Thomas, E. and Murr, A. (2002). The gambler who blew it all. *Newsweek* (February 4), 19–24.

Tifft, L. and Sullivan, D. (2001). A needs-based, social harms definition of crime. In S. Henry and M. Lanier (eds.), *What Is Crime? Controversies over the Nature of Crime and What to Do About It*. Lanham, MD: Rowman & Littlefield, 179–206.

Van Natta, D. Jr. (2002). Enron spread contributions on both sides of the aisle. *The New York Times* (January 21), A13.

Vold, G. B., Bernard, T. J. and Snipes, J. B. (2002). *Theoretical Criminology*. 5th edition. New York: Oxford University Press.

White, L. (2002). Credit and credibility. *The New York Times* (February 24), Wk 13.

Wilentz, S. (2002). A scandal for our time. *The American Prospect* (February 25), 20–22.

Wolff, M. (2002). Spread thin. *New York* (March 4) 1, 20–21.

Yardley, J. (2002). Critic who quit top Enron post is found dead. *The New York Times* (January 26), A1.

Zweig, P. (2002). Learning old lessons from a new scandal. *The New York Times* (February 2), A11.

Criminal and Legal "Looting" in Corporations

— David Shichor

The earliest Anglo-American corporations, "proto-corporations" as Stone (1975: 11) referred to them, were churches, municipalities, guilds, and universities. These early corporations were not of major interest to the law; their activities rarely brought them before the courts. In the beginning, these corporations mainly held property. The church, for instance, owned property, and towns were granted land by the king and were given the right to establish courts and to collect customs.

Modern corporations can be traced to the mercantile period in Europe. Trade and international commerce replaced the land-based feudal economy. Starting in the seventeenth century, and especially after the Industrial Revolution, corporations increasingly became the flag bearers of the capitalist system.

The Nature of Corporations

A corporation is a legal construct, a fictitious "personality" that is formally "owned" by its shareholders who supply capital by purchasing stock. Executives and managers conduct the everyday business of the cor-

An original article written for this publication. The author would like to thank Gil Geis for his suggestions on an earlier version of this article and is especially thankful for his editorial comments that involved the use of a lot of red ink.

poration. This is the essence of an "agency relationship" in which individuals (executives/managers) act on behalf of others (principals). Executives are not controlled by the principals, although management has a fiduciary obligation to serve the interests of the shareholders (Shapiro, 1990; Heimer, 1988). The executives and managers are supposed to be supervised and controlled by a board of directors whose members also have a fiduciary obligation to the shareholders. The agency relationship in which there is a separation between the owners and the managers (executives) is one of the most important defining characteristics of modern corporations.

According to one view, corporations were created to protect shareholders' fiscal liability and to provide them total legal immunity. These legal "constructs" allow shareholders to seek profit by pressuring the managers/executives to satisfy their interests. This argument claims that the above described organizational characteristic of corporations opens the door for socially irresponsible ways (legal or illegal) to pursue profits (Glasbeek, 2007). Following this view, stockholders relinquish operational control and decision making to managers/executives and to the board in exchange for no legal liability.

Illegal Looting

The second half of the twentieth century witnessed several major corporate scandals. The Equity Funding Insurance scandal in the early 1970s was an egregious corporate fraud preceding the notorious Savings and Loan debacle. The management of the company devised a scheme to issue fictitious insurance policies to inflate sales and used other falsified records to show high profits, thereby attracting large numbers of investors. Executives eventually looted the company and sent it into bankruptcy in 1973 (Seidler, Andrews & Epstein, 1977; Ermann & Lundman, 1982).

"Data diddling" is illegal or unauthorized alteration of data (Kabay, 2002). Equity Funding Corporation of America was a publicly traded firm that became highly successful after it implemented a "leveraging dollars" concept in which customers would invest in a mutual fund and then borrow against the fund shares to pay a life insurance premium. After ten years, the customer would repay the loan with any insurance cash values or by redeeming the appreciated value of the mutual fund shares (Hancox, 1997). The price of Equity's stock grew dramatically through the 1960s. The data diddling began in 1964 when the head of data processing discovered he could not access financial figures from the computer to prepare the annual report. He told the president they would have to delay publication, but the president said to show $10 million in profits and to make the other figures agree (Kabay, 2002). The profit never materialized.

Mutual fund sales sagged, and in 1969 executives decided to keep the stock price high by booking false insurance policies (*Time*, 1973). They entered information about nonexistent policyholders into their records. The scheme was successful, and the management then decided to sell the fake policies to reinsurers, who would pay the company $1.80 for every $1 it received in premiums the first year. To pay the premiums, Equity had to invent more insurance policies every year. Equity carried more than $6.5 billion worth of insurance on its books by the end of 1972—up to $1 billion in fictitious policies. It also "killed off" nonexistent policy-holders, filing for death benefits.

Auditors accepted the manufactured records without checking, just as they accepted lists of deposit certificates as assets without checking their existence. The scheme ended after a disgruntled employee reported the sham transactions to an insurance specialist at a Wall Street firm. Rumors swirled through the financial community, and large sharehold-ers unloaded their stock. The price dropped from $25 to $14 in 8 days before trading was halted.

In 1973, Equity and its largest insurance subsidiary were charged with false bookkeeping, issuing bogus insurance policies, and insider trading to sell stock before the fraud became public—at that time it was one of the biggest business scandals in history, with the fraud exceeding $300 million (Trumbore, 2003). The story became the basis for a 1976 movie, *The Billion Dollar Bubble*. Twenty-two people, including officers and directors, were convicted (five received sentences ranging from three to seven years); the chairman was sentenced to eight years in prison and fined $20,000.

The Savings and Loan debacle of the 1980s was to a large degree the outcome of the ideologically motivated deregulatory policies of the Rea-gan administration (Calavita & Pontell, 1990; Waldman, 1990). The dereg-ulatory trend was presaged in Reagan's first inaugural address (1981) when he declared that "the government is not the solution to our problem, government is the problem." This statement reflected the president's belief in Adam Smith's premise (1776) that the free enterprise system reg-ulates itself and works best without government interference. Deregula-tion in the thrift industry opened the door for individuals to buy up financially troubled thrifts at bargain prices. Many of these individuals not only lacked any previous experience in the banking or savings and loan industries but some of them also had checkered backgrounds.

Deregulation also lifted many established limits on the types of investments that these financial institutions were allowed to make (origi-nally they were chartered only to make mortgage loans to individual bor-rowers). The institutions had to attract a large number of deposits to remain solvent; to achieve this goal, they paid increasingly higher interest rates to depositors. As Kitty Calavita and Henry Pontell (1990) noted in their frequently cited article, these policies were coupled with the increase of federal insurance (FSLIC) of deposits from $40,000 to $100,000 for each account—creating a situation ripe for large-scale criminal activities in the thrift industry. Calavita and Pontell categorized the major forms of lawbreaking that became common and led to the savings and loan scandals: (1) unlawful risk-taking; (2) collective embezzlement; and (3) cover up. Unlawful risk-taking involved making high-risk investments that extended the limits permissible under the already loose standards of regulation, by inadequate marketability studies and/or by poor supervision of loan disbursement. Collective embezzlement or looting referred to "the siphoning off of funds from a savings and loan institution for personal gain, at the expense of the institution itself and with the implicit or explicit sanction of its management" (Pontell & Calavita, 1993: 223). Pontell and Calavita claim that this kind of violation is tantamount to "robbing of one's own bank." Many of the thrifts made transactions that did not serve the company's interest; rather, the transactions were for the personal benefits of the company executives.

In this article, looting or collective embezzlement refers to the legal or illegal actions taken by executives for their own benefit—generally against the interest of the firm itself and ultimately against its stockholders. These kinds of actions involve the violation of trust of the owners (e.g., the stockholders) by the executives, often with the tacit approval or active participation of the directors of the firms.

Donald Cressey (1953) in his landmark study of male embezzlers characterized embezzlement as a violation of trust by an employee who was experiencing a non-shareable financial problem (alcohol abuse, gambling debt, womanizing, etc.). Embezzlers, despite knowing that they are committing a crime, try to rationalize their actions by claiming that they are only "borrowing" from their employer and will repay the money taken or that the sums taken were owed to them because they were underpaid.

In the Savings and Loan fiasco, looting or collective embezzlement took various forms, such as buying personal luxury goods for directors with corporate funds, paying for extravagant vacations and trips for executives and their families, and even buying properties for private ownership. In many cases, the executives used their institutions as personal ATMs.

There were systematic cover ups to conceal looting and to hide the firms' actual financial situations from regulators, current and prospective shareholders, and depositors. The most common practice of masking insolvency and personal gain was the manipulation of the company's financial records. Some efforts involved sophisticated transactions, making it difficult to track actual earnings. Other attempts involved outright forgery—fabricating or changing figures in the accounting records (see Calavita & Pontell, 1990).

William Black (2001), who served in a regulatory position to address the Savings and Loan debacle, used the term "control fraud" to describe cases in which the firm defrauded creditors and shareholders and converted firm resources to the personal use of the top executives (see article 9). These actions are similar to the ones that Calavita and Pontell (1990) called collective embezzlement or looting. Referring to this phenomenon, Black (2001: 67) suggested that "the best way to rob any organization is to be the guy or gal in charge of it."

Looting of firms by executives occurs not only in the United States but in other industrial countries as well. For example, in the United Kingdom the crime statistics list "fraud by company directors" and "false accounting" as separate categories. These offenses are included in the British Theft Act of 1968. The false accounting clause includes "faking, altering, and hiding company documents." According to this law company directors are liable for deceptive statements intended to increase the price of the company's stock (Doig, 2006: 31). One of the major illegal looting cases in England involved Robert Maxwell, who controlled publishing and newspaper companies that were implicated in fraudulent dealings. After his mysterious death in 1991, investigations revealed that Maxwell had taken funds from his companies (the Mirror Group Pension Fund in particular) because he had massive debts (Punch, 1996: 6).

Trust

Trust is essential in the existence and maintenance of a healthy business environment and a well functioning financial system. Susan Shapiro (1984) emphasized the centrality of trust in the operation of the securities market—an integral component of the American economic system. She defined trust in this context as "the impersonal guarantee that representation of expertise or risk or financial condition can be taken at face value and that fiduciaries are not self-interested," and she concluded that trust is "truly the foundation of capitalism" (p. 2). Reinforcing this view, business and financial columnist Robert Samuelson, referring to the recent collapse of several giant financial firms and the steep decline of the stock market in the wake of the global economic crisis spurred by the subprime mortgage debacle, stated that: "Every financial statement depends on trust. We are in a full-blown crisis because investors and financial managers have lost that trust" (Samuelson, 2008: 31).

In another article, Shapiro (1990) extended her emphasis on the importance of trust and argued that the central attribute of all forms of white-collar crime is the violation of trust. She suggested that the "agency" arrangement is often a breeding ground of white-collar crime. According to her argument, "in agency relationships individuals or organizations act on the behalf of another" (p. 348). Agents provide professional knowledge for the principals who lack this kind of expertise. The lack of knowledge, in turn, makes it unlikely that the principals will be able to evaluate the quality of the service provided to them by the agents. The relationship becomes even more complex because often there are intervening agents such as accounting firms—hired by and reporting to agents in terms that principals probably do not understand. When executives breach their fiduciary obligation to act on behalf of shareholders, they violate the trust between the principal and the agent—the core of the agency relationship. In the agency context, the problem of violation of trust is acute. As noted earlier, shareholders have little or no influence over managers/executives. Thus, those who have the decision-making power over the interests of the shareholders (the agents) are not controlled by them. Independence and freedom from control create and maintain an asymmetrical relationship between executives and stockholders.

Robert Meier and James Short (1995) emphasized the importance of trust on the societal level. In a modern complex society, trust implies "the expectancy that institutions can be relied on to meet the expectations constituents have for them." Meier and Short saw a major risk for the breakdown of social cohesion in society that may result in anomie. If "expectations are not met constituents may become alienated from these institutions, and may reduce or eliminate participation in them" (Meier & Short, 1995: 94). One of the most important impacts of white-collar crime is its harm against the "fabric of society."

A Recent Wave of Looting

In the early 2000s, several major financial scandals involved the false and fraudulent reporting of income, debts, and assets by corporations. These crimes cost hundreds of millions of dollars and harmed thousands of investors, stockholders, and employees who had their 401ks invested in the companies' stocks. In addition to illegal manipulations, executives in most cases also "looted" their own company and its shareholders, reducing the equity of the firm often by making tens of millions of dollars in salaries, bonuses, stock options, and various other perks. The most egregious of these scams was the Enron case involving fraudulent bookkeeping concocted by executives that included the creation of limited partnerships—straw companies to hide the firm's debt and to show profitability on the books. These manipulations were overlooked by Arthur Andersen, one of the largest and most prestigious accounting firms working for Enron (Geis, 2007; Rosoff, Pontell, & Tillman, 2004).

Other major cases in which "looting" took place included the WorldCom phone company that involved false financial statements overstating cash flow by booking $3.8 billion in operating expenses as capital expenses. Founder Bernard Ebbers received $400 million in off-the-books loans. Similar patterns were found at Adelphia Communications Company (John Rigas, the CEO, and his family received $3.1 billion in off-balance-sheet loans backed by Adelphia; overstated financial results by hiding debt), at Global Crossing (a voice and data carrier that inflated revenue and shredded documents related to accounting practices; the company declared bankruptcy in 2002), at Qwest Communications (a long-distance carrier that inflated revenue and engaged in improper accounting), and at Tyco (a manufacturing conglomerate) (Patsuris, 2002).

As a vivid example of "looting," the CEO of Tyco, Dennis Kozlowski, and the CFO, Mark Swartz, were convicted in 2005 of 22 counts of grand larceny, conspiracy, securities fraud, and falsifying business records (Hamilton and Mulligan, 2005). They used $150 million of company funds for personal use, including Kozlowski's famous purchase of a $6000 shower curtain and a $15,000 umbrella stand (Graybow, 2008). He was fined $70 million, and Swartz was fined $35 million. Each man was sentenced to 8–25 years in prison. In the Tyco case, one of the outside directors received an unauthorized payment of $20 million, while several other executives also enjoyed exorbitant salaries, perks, and other forms of compensation.

During the same time period, there were also many less publicized instances of accounting manipulations—including at Halliburton, whose CEO was Dick Cheney until he became vice president of the United States. Halliburton improperly booked $100 million annual cost overruns before customers had agreed to the payments (Patsuris, 2002). All of the manipulations amounted to looting of the firms (reducing the equity of the stockholders) by executives for their own personal benefit. In most cases not only did shareholders suffer serious losses, but company employees also lost their jobs, their pensions, and the value of their 401ks plummeted.

Accounting firms acting as company auditors have an important role not only to protect shareholders' interests by detecting and preventing corporate fraud and illegal looting but also to maintain the public trust in the economic system (Bologna, 1993; Sorensen, Grove & Sorensen, 1980). The SEC requires audits, but accounting firms are hired and paid by the companies that they audit and do not always fulfill their obligations to the shareholders and to the public. Thirty years before the Enron scandal, the SEC initiated legal actions against certain auditors because of their failure to detect management fraud by corporations. In the wake of the Equity Funding insurance scandal mentioned earlier, three auditors were indicted and their firms eventually paid $39 million to the shareholders as compensation for their losses. In 1977 a Congressional hearing and report "have emphasized the importance of restoring public confidence in the usefulness and integrity of corporate financial reports certified by independent auditors" (Sorenson, Grove & Sorenson, 1980: 247). Nonetheless auditors continued to be implicated in major financial fraud cases. Arthur Andersen, auditor for Enron, was found guilty of complicity with Enron's criminal activities, and the firm collapsed.

Stock Options Backdating

Another form of corporate financial wrongdoing involves "looting" through stock options granted to executives and selected key employees in publicly traded corporations. Granting stock options to executives as a part of their compensation package became a widespread practice during the "dot com" boom of the 1990s. In that era many start-up (mainly high-tech) companies did not have substantial income, and they were searching for ways to compensate executives and to attract talented employees. Indeed, a large number of executives of successful new companies subsequently became multi-millionaires in a very short time by exercising stock options bought at a low price and sold for a much higher one when their companies became profitable. To increase the value of the stock options, they were often backdated to a date when the price of the company's stock was especially low. These manipulations allowed the recipients to gain a larger profit at the company's and stockholders' expense by basing the gain on a lower stock price than existed at the actual time the options were granted. In many start-up firms, stock options provided incentives for creativity and advancement. When these options were backdated, it was hidden from the shareholders so that they were not aware that the value of their holdings had been reduced by the fraudulent pricing of options at a lower cost than should have been the case. For example, the Securities Exchange Commission (SEC) found that the books and records of Broadcom, which produces semiconductors for communications companies, "falsely and inaccurately reflected, among other things, the dates of option grants, the company's stock-based compensation expenses, the company's operating results, and at least one employee's hiring date" (Reckard, Christensen, & Elliott, 2008: A21). As an outcome of the discovery of this fraudulent reporting, the company restated its financial results and made public more than $2.2 billion in additional compensation paid out. These added expenses diluted substantial value from the company; the stock lost 40% of its value, seriously reducing the equity of the stockholders. This revelation followed Broadcom's previous agreement of April 22, 2008 to pay $12 million to settle another SEC lawsuit that alleged that the backdating went on between 1998 and 2003 during a period of rapid growth ($5.5 billion in earnings) in its first years as a public company.

While option backdating was most prevalent in the fast growing high-tech industry, it was by no means restricted to that segment alone. Companies in other branches of the economy that flourished during the real estate boom were vulnerable to this kind of looting. For example, Bruce Karatz, the former CEO of KB Homes (one of the leading home building companies in California), was charged with backdating his own stock options, netting him more than $7 million (Pfeifer, 2009). In April 2010 he was found guilty of option backdating.

It was reported in October 2006 shortly after the backdating scandals became public that the cost of option backdating in 153 firms under investigation was $10.3 billion. By that time, 44 executives and directors in 24 different companies had been fired or resigned as a result of investigations. Two thirds of the companies involved were in the technology sector—primarily software and semiconductor firms (bizjournals.com: October 25, 2006). It was estimated that 18.9 percent of the options granted to top executives during the period of 1996–2005 were backdated or otherwise manipulated. It also was found that there was a greater frequency of backdating in high-tech companies, small firms, and in firms that had considerable stock price volatility (Heron & Lie, 2007). The high volatility increased the potential for yielding substantial profits for those who benefited from backdating and led to substantial decreases in the companies' balance sheets and consequently in shareholder's equity.

The widespread stock backdating was a form of illegal looting of firms by their own executives and managers. These manipulations also might have enhanced the executives' control over the company by enabling them to purchase a large amount of stock for a lower price, thus increasing their ability to acquire a bigger stake in the firm than they would have otherwise. Stock option backdating is considered to be an act of fraud since as Neal Shover and Andy Hochstetler (2006: 10) stated: "Fraud is committed when misrepresentation or deception is used to secure unfair or unlawful gain."

Corporate Governance

Not all forms of "looting" of a firm are formally considered to be criminal. Certain practices that have similar effects as illegal looting, namely the sizeable reduction of the equity of the shareholders by the top executives of the company, is not against the law.

As a result of corporate scandals and recent financial turbulence, the remuneration of top corporate executives has increasingly come under public scrutiny. There is a growing criticism of the high salaries, including the previously mentioned stock options granted to executives. A great deal of attention has focused on the large bonuses, severance pay, and various perks accorded to executives in addition to their salaries.

An increasing number of people—economists, social scientists, investors, and politicians—see the exorbitant compensation of executives and corporate officials as a decisive factor in the current financial crisis. For example, in early 2007 there was a public uproar when the CEO of Home Depot, Bob Nardelli, who abruptly resigned because of stockholders' criticism of his performance reflected in the weak stock price of the company, received a $210 million severance package (his lagging performance at Home Depot did not deter Chrysler Corporation, where he became CEO in August of the same year; Chrysler declared bankruptcy in 2009.) David Friedrichs (2009) sees the exorbitant compensation of CEOs as a form of stealing and states that "extravagant CEO compensation can be usefully framed as a criminological issue, and such exorbitant compensation can be regarded as a form of white-collar crime" (p. 69).

Bonuses were traditionally given in addition to the salary of the receiver as a reward for an exceptionally good performance. Lately, however, many executives were granted bonuses while the companies under their direction did not do well at all. For example, in 2007 CBS CEO Leslie Moonves received $18.5 million in cash bonuses on top of his $5.3 million salary and more than $12.5 million in stock options. His compensation increased 28 percent over his 2006 package. During the same period, CBS's revenue declined by 2 percent, and its net income fell by 24 percent. The value of the shares of the company declined during that period, and CBS had to cancel several programs and lay off more than 160 employees, including news anchors, reporters, and technicians (James, 2008).

The multimillion-dollar bonuses added to the already exorbitant salaries and options for executives whose company lost large sums of money defies the principle of meritocracy that is touted as integral to the free market system of a capitalist economy. Even in cases when companies show profits and the executives' performance is considered to be good, their compensation often exceeds the level of the company's accomplishment. For example, Larry Ellison is the cofounder and CEO of Oracle (a software company) and reportedly the fourth richest person in the United States. He demanded and received a 38 percent increase in his pay package from the firm's compensation committee, raising it to $72 million for 2008. This compensation was in addition to the $544 million that he made in the previous year by exercising stock options. Oracle also awarded 7 million additional options to Ellison, who already owned 1.15 billion shares. While Oracle did show a 29 percent increase of profit in the previous year, Ellison's compensation increased by a higher percentage (*Los Angeles Times*, 2008). After criticism by shareholders, Ellison decided to work for $1 in base salary in 2010; he owns 23.4% of Oracle's stock (McIntyre, 2009). Increasingly more shareholders, especially large investment funds, raise objections to excessive executive compensation and in some cases vote down executive pay plans not only in the United States but in Europe as well (Chazan & Lublin, 2009).

Board of Directors

Executive compensation is determined and approved by the Board of Directors of the corporation. In *Directors: Myth and Reality*, Myles Mace (1971) described boards as being to large degree rubber stamps for the actions of the company management since they almost always approve recommendations made by the executives. Over 40 years ago, William Dill (1965) noted that corporate boards "no longer serve as effective representatives of shareholders to make an independent check on the performance of management because, even in cases where they are outsiders, they are usually nominated and elected upon the recommendation of the management" (p. 1082).

In the wake of major scandals involving U.S. corporations, increased scrutiny of the criminal liability of corporations focuses on the concept of "corporate governance." Gilbert Geis (2007) pointed out that "corporate governance guidelines call for sufficient oversight by the board of directors to assure that the business obeys the law and that the interests of customers and shareholders are adequately protected" (p. 101). Geis also cited Warren Buffet's opinion in his 2002 Annual Report of Berkshire-Hathaway, Inc. that there is a need to monitor the "fidelity" of managers because "so many people in recent years have behaved badly at the office, fudging numbers, and drawing obscene pay for mediocre business achievement" (quoted in Geis, 2007: 101). Buffet suggested that company executives should not be present at board meetings in order to encourage discussions among board members and to allow for more objective decision making. However, boards usually include insiders such as company executives who participate in the board's deliberations and have a say in its decisions. That is the case even in Buffett's Berkshire Hathaway corporation (see, Berkshire Hathaway, 2008).

While there is some variety in the views concerning the roles and responsibilities of a board of directors, most share some common themes. In general, the board of directors is the body that has the legal authority and responsibility to govern a corporation. In for-profit corporations this body is responsible to the stockholders who are the "owners" of the corporation. A recent *"Notice of Annual Meeting of Stockholders"* of CVS/Caremark Corporation (2008), a multibillion-dollar retail pharmacy and pharmacy benefit company, described the functions of its Board to the shareholders:

> The Company's Board of Directors acts as the ultimate decision-making body of the Company and advises and oversees management, who are responsible for the day-to-day operations and the management of the Company. In carrying out its responsibilities, the Board reviews and assesses the Company's long-term strategy and its strategic, competitive and financial performance (p. 4).

This description makes clear that the members of the board have a fiduciary obligation to serve the benefit of the corporation. Among the major duties of the board are the selection and appointment of a chief executive and subsequently the review and evaluation of his/her performance. In for-profit corporations the number one performance criterion is the profitability of the corporation. In general the boards have an audit committee and a special compensation committee that decides the salary and other compensation of executives, including fringe benefits, bonuses, severance pays, retirement benefits and the granting of stock options. An increasing number of boards employ compensation consultants to determine executives' compensation packages. While these consultants are supposed to be objective and independent, more often than not they are neither. Similar to the board of directors, they seem more interested in pleasing executives than in working for the good of the entire corporation and its stockholders.

A report prepared for the Committee on Oversight and Government Reform of the United States House of Representatives (2006: 4) concluded that "compensation consultant conflicts of interest are pervasive," meaning that the consultants were providing other lucrative services for the companies that they advised besides consulting on executive compensation. In most cases, the fees that they earned for other services far exceeded what they received for executive compensation advice. According to the report, Fortune 250 companies paid on the average 11 times more to consultants for other services than for compensation advice. For example, in 2006 some of the consultants received over $10 million for other services. These figures cast serious doubts regarding the objectivity of their advice on executive salaries, since it is likely that the consultants would risk losing lucrative business opportunities if the executives were not satisfied with the compensation recommendations. It was also found that many companies did not disclose that the compensation consultants had conflicts of interest. Furthermore the data showed a positive correlation between the extent of the consultants' conflicts of interest and the level of the CEOs' compensation package—the larger the conflict of interest, the higher the CEO salaries. In many cases, executive salaries in companies that hired consultants with substantial conflicts of interest increased twice as fast as in companies that did not use consultants with similar conflicts (U.S. House of Representatives, 2006).

Management generally submits the slate of board members for election at the annual shareholders' meeting. Unless a board member resigns or decides not to continue to serve, he/she is very likely to be re-nominated and re-elected by the shareholders, who tend to accept the nominations almost automatically. Most shareholders do not know the candidates, do not attend the meeting, and own only a relatively small number of shares, limiting their impact on the election. Rarely are competing slates presented.

Occasionally the recommendations for the election of board members are contested when a major investor or a major investment group wants to gain influence in the management of the company and to put a representative on the board. In the wake of the "mortgage crisis" that prompted the global depression, there is somewhat more willingness by shareholders to challenge slates suggested by the executives. In most cases, however, the slate supported by management is approved.

Most outside or independent board members either are currently executives of other corporations or have held corporate executive positions in the past. Many of them concurrently serve on more than one corporate board. Board members usually own stock in the companies for which they serve as directors and receive remuneration for their services. Regarding the effectiveness of boards, Christopher Stone (1975) pointed out that so many things are going on in a complex organization that outside directors who meet only once a month or even less frequently cannot be familiar with everything that is happening in the company. Thus, they are dealing with issues and problems framed and presented to them by the management and based on information prepared by company personnel. Board members seldom "rock the boat" by seriously challenging executive actions (Braithwaite, 1985).

Since many board members serve on more than one board, they might create linkages between corporations leading to what is often referred to as "interlocking directorates"—networks of shared directorships (Useem, 1984). Interlocking directorates have been studied since the Progressive Era at the beginning of the twentieth century. Some journalists of that period as well as the future Supreme Court Justice Louis Brandeis observed that "a few large commercial and investment banks controlled most major corporations" (Domhoff, 2005: 1). G. William Domhoff (2005) claimed that interlocking directors tend to develop shared perspectives and interests that serve their economic power base; he referred to them as the real "power elite." The shared perspective of the directors favors executives' actions and policies over the protection of the interests of the shareholders. Thus, "directors are often allies of or beholden to the CEO, and in any case they are not especially well positioned to police the managers" (Friedrichs, 2010: 88).

In sum, boards of directors are often co-opted by the executives of corporations and are not very vigilant in supervising executive actions and protecting the interests of the shareholders. Rather than fulfilling their fiduciary obligation to shareholders, boards of directors are often rubber stamping management decisions. Since many board members are themselves executives of other companies, they often have more affinity and even common interests with company executives than with shareholders.

Insider Trading

Insider trading became a major white-collar offense during the 1980s. As one of the authors dealing with this subject stated, this offense was "the representative white-collar crime" of that period (Coffee, 1988: 121). Individuals having knowledge of the detailed business activities of corporations have been trading and investing on the basis of information known to them but unknown to other investors and to the general public.

For a long time, trading based on privileged information was not forbidden. Its prohibition emerged with federal regulations of the marketplace following the market crash of 1929 (Friedrichs, 2010). The rationale behind the prohibition of insider trading is that it creates an unfair marketplace favoring those who know what is happening in the company. Accordingly, insider trading laws were aimed to neutralize advantages provided by privileged information and to create an even playing field for all investors.

Insider trading is a complex issue. It is usually encouraged that executives, directors, as well as others who work for a corporation should own its stock. The practice of giving stocks or granting stock options to executives and some employees was intended as an incentive to increase motivation for better performance (Szockyj, 1993).

The reasoning that led to making insider trading illegal was that it represented a breach in the relationship required of the involved parties (Reichman, 1993). According to the theory formulated by the Supreme Court, "insider trading is wrongful because it involves a breach of fiduciary duty—either to the shareholder from whom the stock was purchased or to the person from whom confidential information was misappropriated" (Green, 2007: 233).

Insider trading is not always perpetrated by executives or directors of a company. For example, stockbroker Dennis Levine used inside information about corporate takeovers to trade by himself and also to sell information to Ivan Boesky, a major figure in the junk bond scandal of the 1980s. However, most cases of insider trading involve company higher ups who have access to useful information.

Executives selling stocks based on insider information about negative performance may save themselves millions of dollars. Angelo Mozilo, CEO of Countrywide (a major mortgage lender), is under investigation by the SEC for selling $145 million in stocks a short time before the steep decline of the company's shares. Reacting to Mozilo's action, Senator Charles Schumer of New York released the following statement: "Mr. Mozilo spent a good part of his career hurting homeowners, now it appears he's been hurting his stockholders too" (Kristof, 2007: C1). Insider trading by executives has the effect of looting, since it substantially dilutes the value of the company and the value of the shares held by the rest of the shareholders—while personally benefitting the insider.

The Sarbanes-Oxley Act

The major corporate scandals that unfolded at the beginning of the new century (Enron, WorldCom, Global Crossing, Adelphia, Tyco, and others) indicated that large scale corporate fraud is not an uncommon phenomenon. In addition to the major losses accrued to the shareholders, these cases also caused public outrage that prompted some legislators to address fraudulent corporate manipulations, false profit statements sanctioned by major accounting firms, and excesses by some corporate executives. In 2002 the Sarbanes-Oxley Act (officially the "Public Company Reform and Investor Protection Act") was enacted. It tightens oversight of public companies by forbidding auditing firms to provide non-auditing services for a client company without the explicit approval of the company's board of directors.

The act required CEOs and CFOs to guarantee that the quarterly financial report of the company is correct. Accordingly, if the report is found to be false, the officers have to reimburse the company for any equity-based compensation and profits made from sales of company stocks executed following the report. The act also extends the statute of limitation for corporate wrongdoing from two years to five years (see, Geis, 2007). As the official title of this legislation implies, the new rules are aimed at protecting shareholders by improving the accuracy of corporate disclosures and providing better transparency for corporate activity. In addition the Sarbanes-Oxley Act enhanced penalties for corporate executives involved in fraudulent manipulation of financial records (U.S. Sentencing Commission, 2003). The law was a response to scandals that endangered confidence in the economy (Shover & Hochstetler, 2006). This act was not without its critics from the business sector and also from academics claiming that it involved over-criminalization of corporate offenses. They also pointed to some of the failings of the deterrence doctrine concerning white-collar crime (see, for example, Nicholson, 2007).

In the more notorious criminal looting cases, the penalties meted out to top executives were severe prison and financial sentences (see, for example, the punishments of the executives of Enron, WorldCom, Adelphia, and Tyco). Geis and Joseph DiMento (2002) pointed out that "higher status offenders, while they might benefit initially based on their prestige, are likely to be treated more severely than ordinary defendants when the violation is egregious" (p. 369).

On the other hand, the corporate executives' "legalized looting" in regard to astronomical salaries, severance payments, retirement benefits, golden parachutes, and various perks are not only sanctioned by the board of directors but often seen as a status symbol qualifying them to be a part of the most prestigious elite groups of society (Friedrichs, 2009).

Conclusion

This article elaborates on the concept of "collective embezzlement" or "looting" suggested by Calavita and Pontell (1990) in their research on the Savings and Loan scandal of the 1980s. They used those terms to describe the actions of CEOs and top company executives in violating their fiduciary obligation to the investors and shareholders of the company for their own benefit. The term "looting" was preferred to describe the actions and manipulations of executives by which their personal gain is put before the interest of the company, their shareholders and employees.

Originally, the concept of looting referred to outright fraudulent manipulations. This article, however, argues that the concept of looting has a wider applicability and should refer to executive actions that are not considered clearly criminal. Even if the exaggerated compensations of executives are not formally criminal they often cause serious harm by reducing shareholders' equity and by reducing the viability of the company.

According to this approach, the concept of looting is relevant in analyzing corporate leadership and the relationships among executives, directors, and shareholders. The crux of the matter is that corporations are based on an "agency relationship" that entails a fiduciary obligation by the managers to the owners and the investors who do not have a direct supervisory capability over them. This arrangement opens the door for violation of the trust by top executives in the form of "looting." Looting, the financial exploitation of a company by its own managers and top executives, is often done through illegal methods (e.g., stock manipulations, false reports, "cooking" the books, option backdating, etc.). As noted, it is also done legally by granting exorbitant compensation packages to top executives that often do not have any logical and realistic relation to the performance of the company in the marketplace. These compensation packages are approved by the board of directors, whose members also have a fiduciary obligation to shareholders. The board is much more likely to support the decisions and policies of management than to watch out for the interests of the shareholders.

The "subprime mortgage" debacle that prompted several investigations into fraudulent manipulations and unlawful looting was a major factor in the collapse of the U. S. housing and financial markets. This crisis reached its crescendo in 2008 and resulted in one of the most severe recessions since the depression of the 1930s—not only in the United States but in the entire global economy. Hundreds of thousands were losing their homes; major financial institutions lost billions in shaky investments, and some went bankrupt; stockholders saw the value of their investments plummet; tens of thousands lost their retirement accounts; and thousands upon thousands were laid off. At the same time, some top executives who were actively involved in creating the economic crisis walked away with millions of dollars in compensation packages—successfully looting their companies.

It might be only a vain hope that the current economic crises fueled by deregulation, lax oversight, and low levels of "corporate social responsibility" (see, for example, Smith & Lenssen, 2009) would bring more effective government controls of illegal looting and stronger shareholders' demand for effective independent boards to prevent large scale "legalized looting" by top executives. Demands for control of looting could be particularly effective if powerful institutional investors (pension funds, mutual funds, etc.) would forcefully demand more transparency, more realistic compensation policies, and stronger shareholders' representation in decision making. Over a quarter of century ago M. David Ermann and Richard Lundman (1982) predicted that by the year 2000 "more than half of corporate stocks probably will be controlled by institutional investors" (p. 52). They claimed that during the 1970s many institutional investors "set up proxy committees to decide how to vote on the various issues put before stockholders for a vote. Typically, they vote negatively on proposals that they feel unduly enrich management at stockholders expense or dilute the relative value of a share of stock." In light of the criminal looting by fraudulent manipulations and the legal looting by exorbitant executive compensations that continued and even accelerated since Ermann's and Lundman's statement, their observation proved to be overly optimistic and mistaken. The fact that large institutional investors were not able to or did not want to exert enough influence and oversight over executive behavior makes them to a degree a "silent partner" in the looting.

REFERENCES

Black, W. K. (2001). Control fraud and control freaks. In H. N. Pontell & D. Shichor (Eds.), *Contemporary issues in crime and criminal justice: Essays in honor of Gilbert Geis* (pp. 67–80). Upper Saddle River, NJ: Prentice-Hall.

Berkshire Hathaway. (2008). *Berkshire Hathaway Inc. 2007 annual report.* Retrieved from http://www.berkshirehathaway.com/2007ar/2007ar.pdf

Bologna, J. (1993). *Handbook on corporate fraud.* Stoneham, MA: Butterworth-Heinemann.

Braithwaite, J. (1985). Taking responsibility seriously: Corporate compliance systems. In B. Fisse & P. A. French (Eds.), *Corrigible corporations and unruly law.* San Antonio, TX: Trinity University Press.

Calavita, K., & Pontell, H. N. (1990). "Heads I win, tails you lose": Deregulation, crime, and crisis in the savings and loan industry. *Crime and Delinquency, 36,* 309–341.

Chazan, G., & Lublin, J. S. (2009, May 20). Shell investors revolt over executive pay plan. *The Wall Street Journal,* B1–B2.

Coffee, J. Jr. (1988). Hush! The criminal status of confidential information after McNally and Carpenter and the enduring problem of overcriminalization. *American Criminal Law Review, 26,* 121–154.

Cressey, D. R. (1953). *Other people's money.* Glencoe, IL: Free Press.

CVS Caremark Corporation. (2008). *Notice of annual meeting of stockholders.* Woonsocket, RI.

Dill, W. R. (1965). Business organizations. In J. G. March (Ed.), *Handbook of organizations* (pp. 1071–1114). Chicago, IL: Rand McNally.

Doig, A. (2006). *Fraud.* Cullompton, UK: Willan Publishing.

Domhoff, G. W. (2005, August). Power in America: Interlocking directorates in the corporate community. *Who rules America?* Retrieved from http://sociology.uscs.edu/whorulesamerica/power/corporate-community.html

Ermann, M. D., & Lundman, R. J. (1982). *Corporate deviance.* New York: Holt, Rinehart and Winston.

Friedrichs, D. O. (2010). *Trusted criminals: White collar crime in contemporary society* (4th ed.). Belmont, CA: Wadsworth Publishing Company.

Friedrichs, D. O. (2009). Exorbitant CEO compensation: Just reward or grand theft? *Crime, Law and Social Change, 51,* 45–72.

Geis, G. (2007). *White-collar and corporate crime.* Upper Saddle River, NJ: Prentice-Hall.

Geis, G., & DiMento, J. F. C. (2002). Empirical evidence and the legal doctrine of corporate criminal liability. *American Journal of Criminal Law, 29*(3), 341–375.

Glassbeek, H. (2007). The corporation as a legally created site of irresponsibility. In H. N. Pontell & G. Geis (Eds.), *International handbook of white-collar and corporate crime* (pp. 248–278). New York: Springer.

Graybow, M. (2008. October 16). Conviction of ex-Tyco CEO Kozlowski upheld. Retrieved from http://www.reuters.com/article/idUSTRE49F5DR20081016

Hamilton, W., & Mulligan, T. S. (2005, June 18). Ex-chiefs convicted of looting Tyco. *Los Angeles Times.* Retrieved from http://articles.latimes.com/2005/jun/18/business/fi-tyco18

Hancox, D. R. (1997). Could the equity funding scandal happen again? Retrieved from http://findarticles.com/p/articles/mi_m4153/is_n5_v54/ai_20057314/

Kabay, M. E. (2002, January 21). The equity funding fraud. *Network World Security Newsletter.* Retrieved from http://www.networkworld.com/newsletters/sec/2002/01190226.html

Green, S. P. (2007). A normative approach to white-collar crime. In H. N. Pontell & G. Geis (Eds.), *International handbook of white-collar and corporate crime* (pp. 223–247). New York: Springer.

Heimer, C. A. (1988, March). Dimensions of the agency relationship. Paper presented at the Public Choice Meeting, San Francisco.

Heron, R. A., & Lie, E. (2007). What fraction of stock option grants to top executives have been backdated or manipulated? *Journal of Financial Economics, 83,* 271–295.

James, M. (2008, April 12). '07 golden for CBS' Moonves. *Los Angeles Times,* C1.

Kristof, K. (2007, August 29). Report: Mozilo sales probed. *Los Angeles Times,* C1.

Kristof, K. (2008). Oracle investors want say on pay. *Los Angeles Times,* C2.

Mace, M. L. (1971). *Directors: Myth and reality.* Cambridge, MA: Harvard University Graduate School of Business Administration.

Mann, K. (1985). *Defending white-collar crime.* New Haven, CT: Yale University Press.

Meier, R. F. & Short, Jr., J. F. (1995). The consequences of white-collar crime. In G. Geis, R. F. Meier, & L. M. Salinger (Eds.), *White-collar crime: Classic and contemporary views* (3rd ed., pp. 80–104). New York: The Free Press.

McIntyre, D. A. (2009, August 24). Larry Ellison: The return of the dollar a year man. *The Wall Street Journal.* Retrieved from http://247wallst.com/2009/08/24/larry-ellison-the-return-of-the-dollar-a-year-man/

Nicholson, L. (2007). Sarbanes-Oxley's purported over-criminalization of corporate offenders. *Journal of Business and Technology Law, 2,* 43.

Patsuris, P. (2002, August 26). The corporate scandal sheet. Retrieved from http://www.forbes.com/2002/07/25/accountingtracker.html

Pfeifer, S. (2009, March 31). Karatz enters plea in stock case. *Los Angeles Times,* B2.

Pontell, H. N., & Calavita, K. (1993). The savings and loan industry. In M. Tonry & A. J. Reiss, Jr. (Eds.), *Beyond the law: Crime in complex organizations* (pp. 203–246). Chicago: University of Chicago Press.

Punch, M. (1996). *Dirty business: Exploring corporate misconduct.* London: Sage.

Reckard, E. S., Christensen, K., & Elliott, H. (2008, May 15). Broadcom founders accused by SEC of stock option fraud. *Los Angeles Times,* A1, A21.

Richman, N. (1993). Insider trading. In M. Tonry & A. J. Reiss, Jr. (Eds.), *Beyond the law: Crime in complex organizations* (pp. 55–96). Chicago: The University of Chicago Press.

Rosoff, S. M., Pontell, H. N., & Tillman, R. H. (2004). *Profit without honor: White-collar crime and the looting of America* (3rd ed.). Upper Saddle River, NJ: Prentice-Hall.

Samuelson, R. J. (2008, September 28). The great confidence game. *Newsweek*, 31.

Seidler, L. J., Andrews, F., & Epstein, M. J. (1977). *The equity funding papers: The anatomy of a fraud*. Santa Barbara, CA: Wiley.

Shapiro, S. P. (1990). Collaring the crime, not the criminal: Reconsidering "white-collar crime." *American Sociological Review, 55*(3), 346–365.

Shapiro, S. P. (1984). *Wayward capitalists: Targets of the Securities and Exchange Commission*. New Haven, CT: Yale University Press.

Shover, N., & Hochstetler, A. (2006). *Choosing white-collar crime*. New York: Cambridge University Press.

Smith, A. (1776). *An inquiry into the nature and causes of the wealth of the nations*. London: W. Strahan and T. Caudel.

Smith, N. C., & Lenssen, G. (Eds.). (2009). *Mainstreaming corporate responsibility*. Chishester, UK: Wiley.

Snider, L. (2007). "This time we really mean it!" Cracking down on consumer fraud. In H. N. Pontell & G. Geis (Eds.), *International handbook of white-collar and corporate crime* (pp. 627–647). New York: Springer.

Sorensen, J. E., Grove, H. D., & Sorensen, T. L. (1980). Detecting management fraud: The role of the independent auditor. In G. Geis & E. Stotland (Eds.), *White-collar crime: Theory and research*. Beverly Hills, CA: Sage.

Stone, C. D. (1975). *Where the law ends: The special control of corporate behavior*. New York: Harper and Row.

Szockyj, E. (1993). *The law and insider trading: In search for a level playing field*. Buffalo, NY: Hain.

Time (1973, April 16). Scandals: Ghostly insurance. Retrieved from http://www.time.com/time/magazine/article/0,9171,878566,00.html

Trumbore, B. (2003). Ray Dirks and the equity funding scandal. Retrieved from http://www.buyandhold.com/bh/en/education/history/2004/ray_dirks.html

United States House of Representatives. (2007). *Executive pay: Conflict of interest among compensation consultants*. Washington, DC: Committee of Oversight and Government Reform.

United States Sentencing Commission. (2003). *Increased penalties under the Sarbanes-Oxley Act of 2002*. Washington, DC.

Useem, M. (1984). *The inner circle*. New York: Oxford University Press.

Waldman, M. (1990). *Who robbed America? A citizen's guide to the savings & loan scandal*. New York: Random House.

August 2006

Annual Report to Congress on Foreign Economic Collection and Industrial Espionage—2005

One of the essential objectives of the Presidentially approved National Counterintelligence Strategy of the United States is to safeguard our vital national security secrets, critical assets, and technologies against theft, covert foreign diversion, or exploitation. This includes both helping to protect the sensitive technologies that are the backbone of our security and seeking to ensure a level economic playing field so that business and industry are not disadvantaged by foreign intelligence operations.

Amb. Eric J. Boswell
Former Acting National Counterintelligence Executive

Source: This assessment was prepared by the Office of the National Counterintelligence Executive. www.ncixinfo@ncix.gov.

The Threat to US Technologies

The Damaging Theft of US Technology and Trade Secrets

Foreign entities continued to aggressively target and acquire sensitive and protected US technologies in fiscal year 2005 (FY 2005).[1] Evidence amassed by the Counterintelligence (CI) Community showed a record number of countries—108—were involved in collection efforts. The Federal Bureau of Information (FBI) opened 89 economic espionage cases during the year and had 122 cases pending at year-end. In addition, the US Immigration and Customs Enforcement initiated more than 1,050 export investigations and conducted more than 2,400 export investigations involving violations of the Arms Export Control Act, International Traffic in Arms Regulations, Export Administration Regulations, International Emergency Economic Powers Act, and the Trading With the Enemy Act. These investigations resulted in 101 arrests, 70 criminal indictments, and 85 criminal convictions. The Department of Commerce, Bureau of Industry and Security, initiated more than 1,300 export investigations resulting in 31 criminal convictions and the imposition of almost $8 million in criminal fines and $9 million in civil penalties.

The CI Community is unanimous in the view that this illegal outflow of technology imposed huge costs on the United States. A sample of the types of technologies lost during the year indicates the potential extent of damage.[2] Recent losses have hurt the United States by:

- Enabling foreign militaries to leapfrog technological hurdles and to acquire sophisticated capabilities that might have otherwise taken years to develop. A former Department of Defense (DoD) contractor provided China and a number of other countries with access to classified and export-controlled infrared signature suppression technologies developed for the B-2 Stealth Bomber. Such acquisitions would provide foreign militaries with an invaluable jump in developing stealth aircraft of their own or in countering the US advantage.

- Making it possible for foreign firms to gain a competitive economic edge over US competitors, thereby undermining the US economy. For example, in 2005, a major Japanese firm was fined more than $400 million after it was found guilty of stealing a US company's trade secrets and selling them to a competitor.

As in years past, entities from a relatively small number of countries accounted for the majority of foreign targeting of US technologies in FY 2005. China and Russia are two of the most aggressive collectors. The major collectors have been repeatedly identified targeting multiple US Government organizations and all types of technologies since at least 1997, when the CI Community first began systematically reporting on targeting efforts.

Globalization Expands Access to Sensitive Technologies

Foreign businessmen, scientists, engineers, students, and academics were major collectors of sensitive US technology in FY 2005. The openness of the US economy and the forces of globalization provide both opportunities and powerful natural incentives for this private-sector technology theft. The sheer number of visitors explains, in large part, why most of the opportunities devolved to the private sector. More than 30 million foreigners entered the United States on nonimmigrant visas in 2004, according to the most recent Department of Homeland Security's Office of Immigration statistics (see table 1). Most visitors came as tourists and had limited access to sensitive technologies. Almost 5 million, however, came on business visas, and many would have had access to sensitive US technologies or trade secrets. The number far exceeded the 350,000 official foreign visitors to the United States in 2004. US companies seeking to develop overseas markets sometimes employ first-generation immigrants who are bilingual and who

Table 1.   *(Number of visitors)*

Nonimmigrants from Selected Countries Admitted to the United States, 2004

Rank	Country of Last Residence	Business	Pleasure	Other	All Classes
	All Countries	**4,593,124**	**22,802,907**	**3,385,299**	**30,781,330**
1	United Kingdom	606,398	4,042,056	132,561	4,781,015
2	Mexico[a]	443,802	3,779,304	206,178	4,429,284
3	Japan	381,281	3,648,711	178,248	4,208,240
4	Germany	301,361	1,139,036	78,095	1,518,492
5	France	187,769	832,883	51,735	1,072,387
6	China[b]	177,323	278,941	103,242	559,506
7	Korea	164,674	431,726	118,420	714,820
8	Brazil	108,711	336,596	67,685	512,992
9	Australia	107,787	458,139	30,980	596,906
10	Netherlands	105,969	386,966	16,023	508,958
11	Italy	103,942	486,541	33,347	623,630
12	Canada	97,960	346,641	139,953	584,554
13	India	88,011	185,854	168,463	442,328
14	Israel	74,679	218,104	24,103	316,886
15	Venezuela	68,771	262,658	31,273	362,702

[a] The increased use of Department of Homeland Security Form 1-94 for the inspection of Mexican nationals helps explain the increased number of admissions after 1997.

[b] Includes People's Republic of China and Taiwan.

Source: Office of Immigration, *Yearbook of Immigration Statistics, 2004.*

maintain connections in their home countries. Such individuals, especially those with advanced degrees in scientific and technological fields, are well placed to broker illegal technology transfers from the United States.

The vast majority of these visitors—businessmen, scientists, and tourists—do not come here with the intent to collect sensitive technologies or economic information. Of the small percentage that eventually did steal US trade secrets, we doubt that foreign governments were directly involved in tasking these collectors (see text box). Instead, profits, patriotism to their home countries, and the desire to achieve academic or scientific acclaim appear to be the natural drivers—the so-called invisible hand behind most private-sector technology theft.[3] Indeed, most of those arrested for stealing US technology appear to have become involved in the theft after finding, serendipitously, that they had access to information that was in great demand in their home countries.

Globalization has intertwined US and foreign businesses in ways that have generated huge economic gains for both sides but that also have made it increasingly difficult to protect commercial and dual-use trade secrets. In 2004, the latest year for which data were available, foreign direct investment in the United States rose 8 percent—the fastest growth since a 32-percent increase in 2000—to $1,526 billion at the end of 2004.[4] A couple of the notable foreign acquisitions of US high-tech companies in the past few years included the purchase of fiber-optic network provider Global Crossing by Singapore Technologies Telemedia and the more recent takeover of IBMs personal computer (PC) business by China's computer giant Lenovo.[5]

Increasingly, foreign entities may not even need to come to the United States to access key US technologies. US firms increasingly feel compelled to move design specifications and even sensitive source code overseas in an effort to take advantage of foreign tax incentives or to shorten the supply cycle.[6] Just-in-time inventories and the speed necessary to bring new items to market to meet rapidly changing international demands also work to break down barriers to the outflow of sensitive technology. Once abroad, this information—previously considered too sensitive to share with foreign partners—becomes difficult to protect. In late 2004, for example, a US software manufacturer reported that portions of its source code and confidential design documents of one of its key products had been stolen from a recently opened research and development (R&D) center in Mumbai, India, according to press reports. The firm's security practices quickly uncovered the theft, but the organization had difficulty finding legal recourse to stop further dissemination of the information.

This enmeshing of US and foreign firms is also creating supply-chain vulnerabilities. Foreign firms are increasingly becoming the primary or even sole providers of key information technology (IT) components, both hardware and software, for US industry. This dependence raises the possibility that components could be altered to allow clandestine access to IT systems and the trade secrets and technologies that they hold. The ability to

Figure 9.1 — How Much Private, How Much Government Directed?

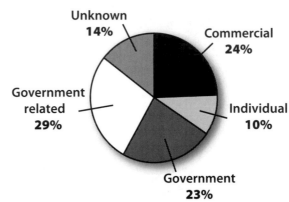

**Types of Foreign Collectors Targeting
US Defense Technology, 2005** (DSS data)

Because of the complex nexus between public- and private-sector players in the theft of technology, it is virtually impossible to accurately
gauge exactly how much collection can be attributed to the various
players. Defense Security Service (DSS) data, however, provides one
measure of the activity. The DSS data comes from reporting by cleared
defense contractors. Because foreign state-sponsored organizations
probably target US defense contractors more heavily than do foreign
commercial entities, the DSS figures may show a larger government
role than would similar statistics derived from US commercial firms.
Even here, though, DSS data shows a significant portion of the activity
comes from commercial enterprises or from private individuals.

insert altered IT components into US supply chains presents other threats
to national security as well, such as creating opportunities for asymmetric
warfare, espionage, and for degrading US critical national infrastructure.

The openness of the US economy has also given foreign individuals
unprecedented access to high-tech US research facilities.

- Almost 30 percent of the science and engineering faculty
  employed at US universities and colleges are foreign born,
  according to National Science Foundation statistics.[7]

- Annual foreign student attendance at US institutes of higher education has averaged more than 570,000 since the beginning of the
  2000 academic year, compared to an average of 460,000 students
  during the previous decade. More than 40 percent of PhDs
  awarded in science and engineering in the United States in 2004
  went to foreign citizens; in physics and mathematics, the shares
  were around 55 percent.

Most of the foreign students and academics working in US research institutes are not involved with US technology theft. In fact, many significantly contribute to the advancement of research at their respective universities and institutes. However, the sheer size of the population and the access that some have to key R&D projects make it inevitable that this group will serve as an important funnel abroad for technologies.

At the same time that foreign access to sensitive US technologies is expanding, rapid advances in IT have vastly simplified the illegal retrieval, storage, and transfer of massive amounts of information, including trade secrets and proprietary data. Compact storage devices the size of a finger are now capable of handling up to five gigabytes of memory. Cell phones with digital photographic capability and the ability to wirelessly connect to the Internet are some of the other new facilitators in technology transfer. Sophisticated information systems that create, store, process, and transmit sensitive information are vulnerable to cyber exploitation. Many nations have formal programs for gathering our networked information, and foreign competitors are developing the capability to exploit those vulnerabilities.

The fact that the US technology is acquired by the private sector in no way slows its flow to foreign governments or inhibits its use in military applications. This transfer from the private to the public sector often happens voluntarily and seamlessly in countries like China and Russia, where there are hand-in-glove relationships between industry and government.[8] But even in most Asian and European countries, the CI Community sees continued evidence of cooperative information sharing between the public sector and the private firms that have acquired sensitive US technology.

Government Collectors Learn To Ride Private Coattails . . .

Although the private sector played an important role in collection last year, foreign governments were by no means out of the picture. In fact, there was ample evidence in FY 2005 that foreign intelligence services, defense establishments, and other government organizations remained aggressive in two ways. First, they became more effective in capitalizing on the increased private-sector collection activity underway, letting the invisible hand drive the collection process and then tapping the technology collected to meet official needs. Second, foreign government entities continued their own direct operations to collect technologies that commercial sources seemed unable to provide.

Foreign governments and intelligence organizations have created quasi-official organizations to enable them to capitalize on the private-sector theft that is underway. Indeed, the CI Community believes that foreign governments are major beneficiaries of the private-sector technology flow (see text box). To elicit sensitive information from those attending these quasi-official organizations, government officials may appeal to the professional egos of the private sector contacts, to their patriotism, or to their commercial sensibilities, by offering domestic business deals to accomplish the technology transfer. Coercion is also an option in countries like Russia and China, where security services still hold considerable sway over the private sector.

. . . But Foreign Government Organizations Also Directly Target US Technology

Although they have had significant success in capitalizing on the private-sector theft, foreign government organizations—including intelligence and security services—also mounted their own targeting and collection operations in FY 2005. Instances of official collection efforts were plentiful during the year.

The Problem of Deemed Exports

The "deemed export" rule of the Export Administration Regulations (EAR) applies to the release of "technology"—as defined in the EAR—to a foreign national in the United States. Such release is deemed to be an export to the country in which the foreign national holds citizenship status. Technology, in the context of EAR, means specific information required for the development, production, or use of a product. It may take the form of technical data or technical assistance. "Release" may occur in visual inspection by foreign nationals of US-origin equipment and facilities, oral exchanges of information in the United States or abroad, or in the application to situations abroad of personal knowledge or technical experience acquired in the United States. Naturalized US citizens and foreign nationals holding valid permanent resident status in the United States (green card holders) are not subject to the deemed export rule.

Although the CI Community believes that a significant amount of protected US technology leaves the country each year after being released to foreign nationals in the United States, so far, there has been only one case tried for violation of the deemed export law. In 2004, a US company, whose primary shareholder was a Chinese firm controlled by the People's Republic of China Government, failed to obtain export licenses for three Chinese nationals who worked at the company and were trained in manufacturing technology controlled by the EAR. The result was the transfer to China of knowledge concerning the manufacture of export-controlled products with direct military applications.

In our view, the reason so few cases have been prosecuted under the deemed export law is the difficulty in observing deemed exports. With no observable movement of goods, the transfer is virtually impossible to detect, let alone prosecute. The absence of prosecutions, in turn, may be a factor in lowering the awareness of the US scientific community to the extent of the problem.

The steady flow of foreign officials and organizations to US military bases and laboratories in FY 2005 created opportunities for foreign intelligence efforts against US technologies. During FY 2005, delegations from several countries that are considered to be major collectors against US technology requested almost 900 visits to US military bases and more than 2,700 visits to DoD industries—a 35-percent increase from the previous year. During the same period, more than 9,000 foreign visitors from the same countries visited the Department of Energy (DOE) National Nuclear Security Administration (DOE/NNSA) facilities (see tables 2 and 3). Foreign intelligence and security services also continued to clandestinely exploit a variety of other commercial collectors. For example, they:

- Continued to clandestinely employ commercial firms in technology collection activities. The large volume of genuine commercial activity serves to mask the activity of front companies and other intermediaries.

- May also be developing techniques for inserting collectors inside US companies to facilitate technology-acquisition efforts.

- On occasion, employed students, professors, scientists, and researchers in the technology collection effort.

Few Changes in Tools Used To Acquire Technology

In the FY 2004 *Annual Report*, we devoted considerable attention to detailing the major techniques used to target cleared defense contractors. Although those techniques vary during long periods of time—for example,

Table 2.   *(Number of visitors)*
Countries Sending the Most Foreign Visitors to DOE/NNSA Facilities, FY 2005

Rank	Country	All DOE/NNSA Facilities	Weapons Labs
	Total	**10,477**	**1,458**
1	China	4,011	404
2	India	2,202	300
3	Russia	2,150	403
4	Taiwan	459	85
5	Ukraine	348	31
6	Israel	336	76
7	France	256	47
8	Japan	231	25
9	Pakistan	174	44
10	South Korea	156	22
11	Kazakhstan	80	21
12	Iran	34	0

Table 3.

Requests for Visits to US Military Facilities and Department of Defense Industries[a]

FY 2004				FY 2005			
Country	Total Military and Industry	Military Facilities	DoD Industry	Country	Total Military and Industry	Military Facilities	DoD Industry
Germany	2,389	1,847	542	Germany	2,896	1,399	1,497
China	72	72	0	China	97	96	1
Taiwan	286	246	36	Taiwan	2,585	647	1,938
Colombia	64	64	0	Colombia	2,546	2,546	0
Japan	1,076	953	123	Japan	2,284	2,120	164
India	68	65	3	India	485	457	28
Israel	1,283	1,086	197	Israel	1,419	896	523
Egypt	146	122	24	Egypt	1,346	1,146	200
France	649	552	97	France	823	633	190
Russia	19	19	0	Russia	114	111	3
All Countries	14,276	5,954	1,158	All Countries	22,916	11,548	4,690

[a] CIFA Cornerstone data.

Note: Recorded in the foreign visitors database. A single request may have multiple visitors.

with the advent of the Internet—there is little indication of sharp deviation from year to year. As a result, in this report for FY 2005, we provide only a brief summary of recent developments along with data for comparison purposes (see table 4).

Given that a significant portion of technology theft took place through commercial channels, it is not surprising that the cheapest, easiest, and least risky methods were the most heavily employed. As in previous years, **direct requests** were the most often used methods to acquire sensitive US technologies in FY 2005, far outnumbering any other approach, according to Defense Security Service (DSS), Air Force Office of Special Investigations (AFOSI), and Army Counterintelligence Center (ACIC) data. For the most part, these were requests for classified, sensitive, or export-controlled information that were not sought or encouraged by cleared contractors. Also included in this category were efforts by foreign entities to purchase US components or technologies. In some cases, a single would-be foreign buyer was observed sending multiple requests to a variety of US companies, probably in search of a seller willing to ignore export-licensing requirements. Since most requests were made using e-mail or telephone solicitation, search costs were virtually zero.

The more costly **exploitation of relationships** was a much less frequently used method of operation in FY 2005. This technique involved foreign firms forming ventures with US firms in the hope of placing collectors in proximity to sensitive technologies or else establishing foreign research facilities and software development companies outside the United States to work on commercial projects related to protected programs. AFOSI data showed a sharp decline in the use of this technique in FY 2005, while DSS data showed the figure constant but at only 5 percent of all suspicious incidents.

Table 4. *(Percent share of total)*

Methods of Operation—Comparing ACIC, AFOSI, and DSS Data

DSS			AFOSI			ACIC	
	FY 2005	FY 2004		FY 2005	FY 2004		FY 2005
Direct request [a]	68	68	Direct request [a]	53	66	Direct request [a]	69
Exploitation of relationships	5	5	Joint ventures	9	15		
Solicitation of marketing services	10	13	Solicitation and seeking employment [b]	13	6	Solicitation of business or services	2
Foreign visits to United States and targeting at conventions, expos, and seminars	10	8	Foreign visitors and targeting at conferences [c]	26	13	Official visits and targeting at conferences or exhibitions	10
Suspicious internet activity	5	3				Computer network intrusion, exploitation of unclassified Website	6
Other	3	2					
						Request to participate in research/scientific exchange	4
						Elicitation through liaison	6
						Unknown	3

[a] The Direct request category used here combines two categories broken out by DSS and AFOSI and three categories broken out by ACIC. Their specificity is based on the amount of detail that the foreign entities ask for in making their requests. For this paper, that specificity was considered unnecessary.

[b] Combines the Solicitation and Seeking employment categories in OSI data to make the data more comparable with DSS.

[c] Combines Foreign visits and Targeting at conventions, and so forth, categories.

In the **solicitation of marketing services,** foreign entities offered their technical services to US research facilities or to cleared defense contractors in the hope of gaining access to protected technologies. The FY 2005 AFOSI and DSS data presented a conflicting picture of the trends in the use of this method. AFOSI data showed stepped-up use of the solicitation of marketing services in FY 2005, while DSS data—which looked at all cleared defense contractors—showed the opposite. Although no clear conclusions about this trend can be drawn from the data, the fact that roughly 10 percent of all suspicious incidents for DSS and AFOSI relied on this approach was evidence of its continued viability as a tool for extracting technology.

Two other related approaches that remained in favor by those attempting to attract US technologies in FY 2005 were **exploitation of foreign visits** to the United States and **targeting at conventions and expositions.** The large number of foreign visitors each year from the major collecting nations indicates, in our view, that these visits continued to yield useful information for collectors. Conventions, expositions, and seminars offered rich collection and targeting opportunities for foreign entities because they directly linked foreign experts with US specialists, programs, and technologies. Furthermore, these venues gave foreign specialists the opportunity to compare and contrast the various technologies and to ask technical questions to fill intelligence gaps. On the basis of DSS and ACIC data, collection at these venues accounted for around 10 percent of all suspicious incidents in FY 2005. Because of the prominence of international air shows in the AFOSI data, this tool accounted for 14 percent of suspicious incidents in FY 2004 and almost twice that share in FY 2005.

The Internet—Coming Into Its Own as a Tool for Technology Collection

The CI Community believes that the Internet will be a tool increasingly relied on to help acquire sensitive US technologies. Threats come from both state and nonstate actors. Of major concern is the fact that the nations best poised to use cybertools to access US technologies are also the countries that traditionally have been the most aggressive collectors in the United States.

No one is certain how much technology and sensitive proprietary information are lost annually to cybertheft. Detection of intrusions is difficult. Moreover, a recent private US survey indicated that, even when intrusions are detected, more than half of the impacted firms do not report the breach for fear of tarnishing their public image. In addition, the Internet has given foreign interests an easy, inexpensive, and anonymous way to spot, assess, and target US firms and individuals who may be willing to ignore or short-circuit export restrictions on sensitive US technologies.

Cyberespionage Crossing International Boundaries

One of the most interesting recent cases of Internet espionage demonstrated the international nature of the problem. In early 2005, a British programmer sold customized copies of his spy software to three Israeli private investigation firms. Those firms, in turn, worked for a number of blue-chip Israeli firms, which allegedly used the software to spy on dozens of their international competitors, including at least one major high-tech firm. The software tempted victims into installing it by posing as a package of confidential documents delivered via e-mail. Once installed, the software recorded every keystroke and collected business documents and e-mails on a victim's personal computer and transmitted information to a server computer registered in London.

A recent FBI survey provided additional weight to the observation that Internet espionage may be on the rise. According to the study, nearly nine out of 10 US businesses suffered from a computer virus, spyware, or other online attack in 2004 or 2005 despite widespread use of security software. The study concluded that viruses, spyware, computer theft, and other computer-related crimes cost US businesses $67 billion a year, according to an online press report. Detecting the origins of such attacks—even determining for certain whether they originate outside the United States—is difficult, since the probes can be routed through multiple foreign countries. And the real concern for the CI Community is how many such attacks may have gone undetected.

We believe that foreign governments, including intelligence services, also increasingly use the Internet as a tool for collecting a wide variety of information, including targeting information on US experts and the technologies with which they deal. There is no question that targeting is taking place but determining the specific source of the attack is difficult (see text box).

All Technologies Targeted

As has been the case in previous years, collectors targeted the entire range of items on the Militarily Critical Technology List (MCTL) in FY 2005 (see table 5). Biomedical technology and weapon effects were only lightly targeted, according to all reporters. Each of the major collecting countries targeted most militarily critical technologies during the year. China, for example, targeted all but the three least targeted categories, according to DSS statistics, while Russia targeted 14 of the 20 categories.

Comparing the DSS, AFOSI, and ACIC data is difficult because the three organizations do not categorize the technologies in the same way. In addition, this is the first year in which ACIC data was reported, making

Table 5.   *(Percent of total incidents)*

US Militarily Critical Technologies Targeted in FY 2005[*]

DSS Data			AFOSI Data				ACIC Data	
	FY 2005	FY 2004		FY 2005		FY 2004		FY 2005
Information technology	22	21	Information technology	11	Information systems	15	Information technology	4
							Telecommuni-cations	3
			Information security and information warfare	18			Communica-tions and data links	21
Lasers and optics	11	8					Lasers, optics, supporting technology	10
Aeronautics	10	12	Aeronautics	15	Aeronautics	7	Aeronautics	4
Sensors	9	13	Sensors	6	Sensors and lasers	11	Sensors	5
Armaments and energetic materials	9	10	Armaments and energetic materials	17	Armaments and energetic materials	11	Armaments and energetic materials	16
Electronics	7	11	Electronics	3	Electronics	11		
Space systems	6	3	Space systems	12	Space systems	7		
Marine systems	5	2	Marine systems	2	Marine systems	5		
Materials and processing	4	3	Materials and processing	5	Materials	9	Materials and processing	3
Signature-control technology	4	5					Signature-control technology	3
Chemical technology	3	3					Chemical systems	4
Biological technology	3	2						
Positioning, navigation, and time technology	3	2	Positioning, navigation, and time technology	3	Guidance	6		
Manufacturing and fabrication	2	2	Manufacturing and fabrication	4	Manufacturing	7		

DSS Data			AFOSI Data				ACIC Data	
	FY 2005	FY 2004		FY 2005		FY 2004		FY 2005
Energy systems	1	2	Energy systems	1	Power systems	3		
Nuclear technology	1	0	Nuclear, chemical systems, and technology	2	Nuclear, biological, and chemical systems	5		
Directed-energy and kinetic-energy systems	1	0	Directed-energy and kinetic-energy systems	3	Directed-kinetic energy	5		
Weapons effects	0	0						
Biomedical technology	0	1						
Ground systems technology	0	1					Ground systems technology	12
							Defensive protection systems	3
							Imaging and remote sensing	4
							Soldier systems technologies	8

* Categories differ because originators either modify or use different versions of the standard militarily critical technologies list.

trend analysis problematic. Nevertheless, it is possible to draw a few broad conclusions on the basis of the data. For example, as was the case in FY 2004, the 2005 data shows that IT-related technologies were again the most heavily targeted items on the MCTL, accounting for almost 30 percent of suspicious incidents for all reporters.[9] The other technologies that were heavily targeted in FY 2004—lasers and optics, aeronautics, sensors and armaments, and energetic materials—were again near the top of the collection list in FY 2005 for all of the organizations reporting suspicious incidents.

Both AFOSI and DSS data showed a significant increase in the targeting of space systems technology, a category not shown in ACIC data. The National Reconnaissance Office concurs with those findings and agrees that this trend has been underway for several years and will most likely become more pronounced as a number of state and nonstate actors seek to achieve parity with the United States on space technologies or to gain insight into the vulnerabilities of US space systems. The CI Community believes that more than 30 countries targeted US space-related technology or information, though a small number of core countries accounted for around three-fourths of all known and suspect collection efforts since 1997. China by itself accounted for almost half the attempts.

The Road Ahead

The road ahead is a challenging one when it comes to protecting sensitive US technologies from foreign theft. There will be no slackening in demand for state-of-the-art US technology and production know-how. Globalization is shining an increasingly bright light on the potential gains associated with technology acquisition. At the same time, the openness of the US economy to both trade and labor flows continues to make the United States a near ideal location for illicit technology acquisition.

China will continue to absorb vast amounts of US technology, though it is also pushing hard for indigenous development of many advanced technologies. As its civilian and military sectors become more sophisticated, demand for more advanced technology will concomitantly rise. Then too, its access to sensitive US technologies is likely to improve in the years ahead. The number of scientists, engineers, and academics working in the United States from China shows no signs of abating. As the number of US students working in the hard sciences levels off, Chinese experts are likely to make up an even larger share of the US and global technology workforces. It is likely, moreover, that the informal organizations that have been set up in the United States to help Beijing track the access of these experts will be refined in the years ahead, further facilitating the flow of technology abroad.

At the same time, improving economic conditions in China and elsewhere mean that a larger share of experts studying and working overseas probably will return to work in their homelands. When they do, they will take with them their US educations, their accumulated scientific and commercial expertise, and—in some instances—trade secrets and protected technologies as well. Ironically, the United States, which has long benefited from its ability to attract some of the best and brightest minds from around the world, could experience a significant brain drain of its own during the next few years.

The demand for US technology will most likely not level off in the other major targeting countries. If anything, the appetites for technology will increase. On the commercial side, globalization will continue to serve as a driver for technology theft. Current market forces—including the demand for globally integrated manufacturing processes and for shorter production cycles—require that competing firms acquire the latest technologies either through direct purchase or using surreptitious means.

Similarly, the military benefits associated with acquisition of US technology will remain a dominant driver for a number of countries, including both Russia and China. The applications of nanotechnology in the military arena, the continued importance of lasers and sensors and armaments and energetic materials in maintaining military superiority all ensure continued demand for the latest military and dual-use technologies.

Third-country venues may also become increasingly important locations for acquisition of US technology. There is little doubt that Chinese and Russian companies have acquired US technology from third countries in both Asia and elsewhere. As the two countries' military and economic relations improve globally, both will have increased collection opportunities.

At the same time that the forces of globalization prod firms toward legal and illegal technology acquisition, they will also continue to facilitate that acquisition. The shift of US R&D facilities overseas appears to be accelerating as US firms attempt to take advantage of the large, cheap, and increasingly sophisticated foreign engineering and scientific communities. Microsoft will invest $1.7 billion dollars in India during the next four years, according to press reports, making India a major hub of Microsoft's research, product and application development, services, and technical support. Japan and China are likely to be two other major beneficiaries of this flow. Governments in these countries encourage foreign R&D investment by offering a range of preferential policies that include tax rebates, construction loans, access to modern facilities, and other incentives. They also use the lure of their large potential market as leverage to encourage technology transfer and R&D investment from abroad. Protecting technologies in these environments will continue to prove difficult. Although we expect gradual improvements in both security awareness and in the legal infrastructure protecting US patents and copyright in places like China and India, the speed at which technology moves overseas will probably continue to outpace the protections.

Other factors are combining to make it more difficult to protect US technologies:

- Cybertheft appears to be on the rise. As quickly as new protections evolve, fresh vulnerabilities are discovered, leaving firms vulnerable to technology theft. The creation of international supply chains—where foreign firms become the major providers of key software and hardware components—opens the door to even greater possible vulnerabilities.

- Devices that can be used for stealing technology are becoming increasingly commonplace within the workforce and are becoming significantly more powerful. Cell phones with digital photographic capability and Personal Digital Assistants with significant storage capability are available for data collection by those who gain even serendipitous access to corporate trade secrets or sensitive technologies.

Looking further down the road, it seems likely that, as profits continue to drive technology theft, markets will develop to move technology to the highest global bidder. At present, ethnic Chinese and Russian middlemen generally funnel US technologies toward their home countries; the entrepreneurs of the future may work as global merchants. The global linkages are made even more probable as the Internet removes the need for personal interaction in the marketing of goods abroad. In such an environment, nonstate players, including terrorist organizations, might find it even easier than now to acquire sensitive US technology.

APPENDIX:
EXAMPLES OF FOREIGN TECHNOLOGY ACQUISITION EFFORTS—LISTED BY SUSPECTED END-USER COUNTRY

Selected Technology Acquisition Efforts in FY 2005:

- In October 2004, a naturalized US citizen and a Chinese citizen were sentenced to three years probation for false statements in connection with illegally exporting to China 25 low-noise amplifier chips that have applications in the US Hellfire missile. According to the indictment, the defendants falsely labeled the amplifier chips in export documents as transistors worth some $20. One of the individuals was a former employee of a major US defense contractor, and the other worked at a US research institute that designed software for military and warfare simulations.

- In November 2004, a New Jersey company was charged with attempted violation of the Iranian embargo in connection with an effort to export oil-burner nozzles to Germany, knowing that the devices would subsequently be illegally diverted to Iran.

- In November 2004, a federal judge fined a US aircraft parts supplier for illegally exporting components for the HAWK missile, the F-4 Phantom fighter jet, and the F-5 Phantom/Tiger fighter jet to China. The conviction was the 11th to result from a 5-year undercover US Immigration and Customs Enforcement investigation that targeted aircraft parts suppliers that sold defense articles over the Internet to foreign buyers without obtaining the required US export licenses or complying with the arms embargoes.

- In December 2004, a US citizen pleaded guilty to conspiracy to violate the Arms Export Control Act after purchasing from US vendors sensitive US military items, including components for HAWK missiles, military radars, and F-4 Phantom fighter jet aircraft for export to Israel. The individual knowingly failed to obtain the required export license. The individual has previously exported items via Israel to Iran. Israeli authorities that cooperated in the investigation do not believe the final destination of the shipments was Israel.

- In early 2005, a Singapore company on multiple occasions shipped US export-controlled items, including GPS components and radiofrequency power meters, to Iran Electronics Industries, according to press.

- In early 2005, the FBI arrested two employees of a US auto parts manufacturer on charges that they leaked trade secrets to a Chinese firm, according to press reporting. The Chinese company, Chongqing Huafa Industry Co., used the information to manufacture metal connecting rods and undercut the US manufacturers' prices.

- In January 2005, a Japanese national pleaded guilty in federal court to conspiracy to violate the Arms Export Control Act after attempting to purchase and illegally export military laser sights for M-16 and M-5 rifles.
- In February 2005, a UK citizen was indicted for violating the US embargo on Iran after allegedly attempting to illegally export an experimental, single-engine aircraft from the United States to Iran via the United Kingdom. The aircraft was intercepted in the United Kingdom. The individual, who also allegedly exported electrical components from the United States to Iran via Austria on four occasions between 2000 and 2004, was arrested in Warsaw, Poland, by Polish authorities acting on a US arrest warrant.
- In February 2005, a US citizen pleaded guilty to illegally exporting sensitive night-vision lenses to Iran.
- In February 2005, managers of two United Arab Emirates (UAE)-based companies were charged with conspiring to illegally export goods to Iran via the UAE. The indictment alleges that the defendants shipped computer goods from a Texas company to an entity in Iran affiliated with that nation's ballistic missile program. It also alleges that they illegally exported a satellite communication system and other goods to Iran.
- In March 2005, a federal grand jury indicted the sales director of a US company with attempting to illegally export sensitive US technology to Iran in violation of the US embargo. According to the indictment, the individual attempted to export a machine that measures the tensile strength of steel and related software technologies.
- In March 2005, a US company pleaded guilty to exporting digital oscilloscopes to Israel without a license. The items were capable of being utilized in development of weapons of mass destruction and in missile delivery fields.
- In October 2005, an engineer working for a cleared defense contractor attempted to transfer US Navy Quiet Electric Drive (QED) technology to China, according to press reports. The engineer transferred QED information to a compact disk with the assistance of his wife and then delivered the disk to his brother. The brother encrypted the QED information and was arrested at the airport as he prepared to leave the United States for China with the data.

NOTES

[1] From 1 October 2004 to 30 September 2005.
[2] Calculating a precise dollar figure for these losses would be difficult. Any such estimate must make fair market value estimates of the technologies lost by firms and the value of replacement technologies necessary to remain competitive. The figure must also consider factors such as lost sales as well as marketing and shipping costs. One of the challenges that makes calculating the cost of industrial espionage particularly difficult is that the technology losses often are not readily apparent. The only indication a US company may have that its research and development plans or its marketing strategies have been stolen is a shrinking or even a more slowly growing market share as foreign and domestic firms take advantage of price and product

information to win customers. Likewise for national security secrets, often the only evidence of a loss of a key military technology is the emergence of a new or more sophisticated weapon or countermeasure in a foreign arsenal years later.

3   Adam Smith originally coined the term "invisible hand" in his 1776 book *An Inquiry into the Nature and Causes of the Wealth of Nations*. The term was Smith's way of describing the mechanism by which he felt economic society operated. Smith noted that each individual in society strives to become wealthy intending only his own gain by providing what others in society value. Thus an invisible hand produces what is best for society even though the individual is driven only by self-interest. Nowadays, something much more general is meant by the expression. An invisible hand process is one in which the outcome to be explained is produced in a decentralized way, with no explicit agreements between the acting agents. The second essential component is that the process is not intentional. The agent's aims are neither coordinated nor identical with the actual outcome, which is a byproduct of those aims. The process is invisible because it works without the agents having knowledge of it.

4   Valued at historical cost—the book value of foreign direct investors' equity in, and outstanding loans to, their US affiliates.

5   The United States has a mechanism in place to prevent foreign investment that is deemed to threaten US strategic interests. The Committee on Foreign Investments in the United States reviews such investments and can recommend that the President suspend or prohibit a foreign acquisition or, in the event that a takeover has already occurred, recommend he request the Attorney General to seek appropriate relief—including divestiture—in the district courts of the United States. Similarly, US federal laws require firms that have access to US classified information to be generally free from foreign ownership, control, or influence.

6   In December 2004, for example, another major US firm announced its intent to open a $12 million research and development center in Tokyo, Japan. The new center will focus on developing Internet Protocol-based networking technologies. In late 2005, according to press reports, a major US chipmaker announced plans to spend $3.5 billion to build a new state-of-the-art chip-making plant in Israel.

7   Several of the countries that send the most students to the United States are also among the top foreign collectors of US technology, and all experienced increases in enrollment during 2004-05.

8   A Chinese Web site advertising a technology exhibit in April 2006 in Chongqing, China, highlights the emphasis Beijing places on facilitating the transfer of technology from civil to military uses. According to the Web site, the exhibit has three objectives: breaking down the barriers to sharing technology among industries, bureaucratic entities, and state and private sectors; facilitating coordinated development between the civilian hi-tech sector and the military; serving as a technology-exchange platform for civilian and military technologies.

9   The DSS data breaks out IT as a separate category. For AFOSI, the IT-related category includes both "Information Technology" and "Information Security and Information Warfare." For the ACIC data, the IT-related category includes, "Information Technology," "Telecommunications," and "Communications and Data Links."

Part 3

Wall Street Crimes

The subprime mortgage crisis, multibillion-dollar Ponzi schemes, extraordinarily high and often fraudulent risk taking by large financial institutions, and stock market manipulations including insider trading triggered the global economic recession of the first decade of the twenty-first century.

Gilbert Geis, one of the preeminent scholars of white-collar crime, wrote an article for this collection that gives a general overview of the economic meltdown that began in 2007. He describes the fraudulent manipulations of major banks, prestigious Wall Street firms, mortgage brokers, and affiliated businesses (e.g., bond rating companies, appraisers). Combined with misguided monetary policies, lax or ineffective regulatory agencies, and naïve or devious borrowers, the manipulations played a major role in the collapse of the housing market and ultimately global depression. Geis also analyzes fraudulent schemes that the SEC failed to recognize and that caused investors to lose trust in Wall Street.

William Black, a former regulator and a current professor of law and economics frequently contacted by the media to comment on the economic "meltdown," wrote a special analysis for this volume about the subprime mortgage debacle. Black describes the dynamics of how the financial bubble created by the easily available money, the lack of effective regulation, the greed of lending institutions, the dishonesty of mortgage brokers, and the gullibility of many of the borrowers led to the housing bubble and ultimately to the crisis in which hundreds of thousands of people could not afford their payments and lost their homes. At the same time, unscrupulous bankers and mortgage brokers made huge profits in the poorly regulated market.

Elizabeth Szockyj and Gilbert Geis explore the widespread practice of insider trading, which occurs when a person with access to information not available to the public trades on the stock market on the basis of that information. The rationale for prohibiting insider trading is that it creates an unfair market favoring those who have access to information that others do not have. The laws prohibiting insider trading were intended to create an "even playing field." Szockyj and Geis studied 452 defendants charged by the federal government with involvement in insider trading. They provide information about the characteristics of offenders, the type of information used, and the sentences imposed for this illegal activity.

10

The Great American Economic Meltdown of 2007 and Onward

— Gilbert Geis

The economic collapse that brought the United States to its knees beginning in the summer of 2007 has most commonly been tied to profligate real estate practices in what became known as the subprime lending market. Subprime lending involved mortgage brokers courting potential home buyers who ordinarily could not qualify for traditional 30-year, 20 percent down loans. The sellers offered these people seductively easy terms, low interest rates that later escalated steeply, interest only terms, and low or nonexistent down payments. They fraudulently reported incomes for the potential buyers far above what they actually earned. The lenders themselves profited mightily as they exploited what they heralded as the American Dream of home ownership (Rivlin, 2010).

Banks and other lending organizations participated in the seducing of persons to purchase homes that they could not afford with the idea that the stunning escalation in real estate values would continue indefinitely and the new home owners would be able to meet their payments by withdrawing cash based on the value of a home that in short order would be worth a great deal more than what they had paid for it. This led to the great Refi (refinancing) boom during which families used the wildly increasing value of their homes like an ATM machine. Some brokers would push buyers into higher interest subprime loans even though they could qualify for traditional terms because the broker received a higher

An original article written for this publication.

175

fee (Gross, 2009). In a particularly nefarious ploy a team of brokers in San Diego, California, combed through the list of persons who had been turned down for loans by their company and sold them homes by forging appraisals and other loan documents, earning in the process incomes of more than a million dollars a year (Muolo & Padilla, 2008, pp. 86–88).

The bubble burst when houses went "under water," the term indicating that they now were worth less than what was owed on them. The elements of the wild joy ride that led up to this disaster have been pinpointed by Gillian Tett: "Bankers were becoming like the inhabitants of the cave in Plato's tale who at best could see only shadows, not tangible reality" (Tett, 2009, p. 99). Put another way, the investment industry, driven by a lust for lucre, irresponsibly and stupidly took risks that they did not have the capacity or the willingness to appreciate. As a result the world economy was driven to its knees (Gasparino, 2009).

When the economy slowed and home prices stagnated, a <u>domino effect</u> played out relentlessly. Unemployment rose, further incapacitating home owners without standby assets. Credit card payments could not be made, and consumers became wary of going (further) over their head financially. Automobile sales plummeted. Businesses became strapped for cash, and those dependent on bank loans found lending institutions short of funds and reluctant to give up what they had. And in the wake of the foundering economic conditions, the public became aware that large businesses had rewarded their executives with what many regarded as obscene salaries and bonuses even while the balance sheets of the companies showed staggering losses. These multimillion dollar bonus payouts were arranged by boards of directors that had been chosen by the very executives who "earned" the huge sums paid to them (Friedrichs, 2009).

It did not take long before the collapse of the American economic system was matched by similar financial catastrophes in countries around the globe. In the fall of 2008, for instance, Iceland's government declared that it was bankrupt, that it no longer was able to meet its foreign debts, and that the krona (the national currency) had become virtually without value so that there was no way to pay for the imports that were essential to existence on the isolated island (Jónsson, 2009). In the United States, the federal government, first during the lame duck days near the end of the administration of George W. Bush and subsequently in the Barack Obama presidency, poured billions of dollars into banks and other financial giants in an attempt to revitalize commerce, or, at least, to keep matters from getting worse (Wessel, 2009).

As these dire events unfolded, students of white-collar crime might well have said: "We told you so." Their work on white-collar crime, some of the best of which is featured in this book, had always challenged the myth, most notably promulgated by the Scottish economist Adam Smith (1776), that under capitalism excesses would in time self-correct and that the world of business functions best when unencumbered by government oversight and regulations. Adherence to that position in the United States had led to deregulation and nonexistent or lax oversight of business enterprises, allowing them to engage unmolested by the law in the excesses that triggered the economic meltdown (Posner, 2009).

Suspicion of capitalism, a hallmark of white-collar crime studies, was not a new thing, although it has failed to take substantial root in American policy, primarily because that policy is set by those with power, the persons who benefit most from the hands-off doctrine of lais-sez-faire. It takes great sums of money to obtain and keep an elective political position, and those who contribute these sums—the haves and not the have-nots—expect to get their way, to obtain a significant return on the money that they have paid out for political campaigns.

Since the beginning of recorded time there have been jeremiads against the greed and rapaciousness of business. St. Jerome, a fifth century Catholic ascetic, wrote *Homo mercator vix aut numquam potest Deo placere:* a man who is a merchant can seldom please God (Tuchman, 1978, p. 37). Echoing this theme centuries later, Pope Pius XI declared: "The worst injustices and frauds take place beneath the obscurity of the common name of a corporate firm" (Pius XI, 1931, para. 32). Jewish theology sums up the importance of impeccable commercial ethics by claiming that the first question a person will be asked in the hereafter during judgment is: "Hast thou been honest in business?" (Friedman, 1980, p. 49).

Mercantile corruption has been associated with all the major American wars, most notoriously in regard to arms procurement in the First World War. An agent for a manufacturer of arms told a Congressional committee that selling weapons abroad in the war period had "brought into play the most despicable side of human nature, lies, deceit, hypocrisy, greed and graft occupying a most prominent place in the transactions (United States Senate, 1936, p. 11). The construction of the railroads marked a time of extraordinary rapacity. One writer described the so-called "robber barons," the owners of the railroads, as "cold-hearted, selfish, sordid men" (Boardman, Jr., 1977, p. 62). Another commented that these men were "scrupulously dishonest" (Lewis, 1938, p. 11). When he introduced the concept of white-collar crime in 1939, Edwin H. Sutherland quoted a former Solicitor General of the United States whose words then would aptly characterize conditions today: "Diogenes would have been hard pressed to find an honest man in the Wall Street that I knew as a corporation lawyer" (Sutherland, 1940, p. 4). Diogenes, a philosopher in ancient Greece, was said to prowl the streets of Athens carrying a lamp, in search of an honest man. By choice, Diogenes lived a life of poverty, allegedly inhabiting a tub instead of a house.

The Corporate Culprits

Bear Stearns

The first major meltdown scandal involved the collapse in March 2008 of New York-based Bear Stearns, a company founded in 1923 that had become the fifth largest investment bank in the United States. Bear Stearns had never, until then, registered a quarterly loss. In 2005, for the second time in three years, it was honored by *Fortune* magazine as the "Most Admired" securities firm, based on employee talent, the quality of risk management, and its business innovations. But by 2008, Bear Stearns' risk management team, while taking home spectacular paychecks, had run up a $1.5 billion company debt. "The holy grail of investment banking had become increasing short-term profits and short-term bonuses at the expense of long-term health of the firm and its shareholders" (Cohan, 2009, p. 1996). There was too much money to be made as the housing bubble continued to expand before it burst. Greed readily trumped prudence.

Prodded and aided by the federal government, Bear Stearns merged with JPMorgan Chase, which paid $10 for a share that once had sold at a high of $172.69 (Bamber & Spencer, 2009; Cohan, 2009; McDonald, 2009). It did not escape the public and most certainly not Bear Stearns' shareholders that company assets had been eviscerated by a magnificently compensated management team that had engaged in reckless and irresponsible behavior. Michael Siconolfi of the *Wall Street Journal* blended the Wall Street theme of bulls and bears with a basketball metaphor—linking the five top executives of Bear Stearns to the 1996 NBA champions, the Chicago Bulls. He noted that the Bear Stearns "starting five" paid themselves $23.3 million more than the entire roster of the Chicago Bulls and stated "Bears sometimes can beat the Bulls" (Cohan, p. 283).

From a white-collar crime perspective, perhaps the most telling observation was made by the son of Salim (Cy) Lewis, the onetime managing partner of Bear Stearns, in a comment on the firm's culture: "Few came honest. None leave honest" (Cohan, 2009, p. 188). The Board meetings at Bear Stearns were so scripted that the minutes were often written out in advance, and directors were asked to read from prepared comments. One observer noted: "It became a dictatorship as opposed to a corporation" (Kelly, 2009, p. 69).

The senior managers of the company's hedge fund, Ralph Cioffi and Matthew Tannin, were criminally indicted on charges of security fraud, conspiracy, and wire fraud. Cioffi also was charged with insider trading for taking $2 million of his own money out of a hedge fund without informing investors. For eighteen months the pair had indicated in their monthly statement to investors that only six percent of their holdings were in subprime mortgages when the true figure was sixty percent. But both men were acquitted after a three-week jury trial in late 2009. The jury based its verdict on a judgment that the men had made poor investment decisions but that doing so was not a criminal offense.

Countrywide Financial

Companies kept falling. Countrywide Financial Corporation (CFC), the largest American mortgage lender which at its height financed one out of every five American home loans, had to be rescued with a $4 billion takeover (or, as some put it, a takeunder) purchase by the Bank of America in the summer of 2008. Founded in 1969, and located in the city of Calabasis, an hour drive north of Los Angeles, Countrywide occupied a sprawling Mediterranean-style headquarters at the foot of the Santa Monica Mountains. The company's stock had risen 23,000 percent between 1982 and 2003, largely by the resale on the secondary market of subprime mortgages (Bruck, 2009). This meant that an investment of $1,000 in Countrywide stock in 1982 was worth $230,000 in 2003. As Adam Michaelson, a senior vice president, would subsequently note, Countrywide's "new system of loans and Refis awarded to anyone with a pulse was, in retrospect, long-term madness driven by short-term profit" (Michaelson, 2009, p. 133). He described Countrywide as "a profit-hungry corporate beast" (p. 242). Countrywide's stated mission was to "Help All Americans Achieve the Dream of Home Ownership." Unstated were two other elements of that aspiration: "At a Magnificent Profit for Us" and "Without Being Concerned that They Could Readily Lose Their Home Ownership."

The financial hanky-panky by Countrywide executives resulted in charges by the Securities and Exchange Commission and the Department of Justice in 2009. The most prominent of those cited was Angelo Mozilo, who had co-founded CFC and was its chief executive officer and chairman of the board. Mozilo had worked in his father's butcher shop in the Bronx when he was ten years old and would often tell audiences that his family had been unable to afford a home and that his goal at Countrywide was to see to it that other Americans could purchase a house of their own.

The Department of Justice charged Mozilo with insider trading and securities fraud for an alleged failure to disclose CFC's lax lending standards in its annual report. Mozilo himself between 2005 and 2007, when he was or should have been well aware that the business was going south, had sold some of his own company shares for a profit of $129 million. His combined salary, bonuses, and stock options between 2001 and 2006 came to $400 million. In a press release, the SEC portrayed Mozilo as a man who bet the chips of investors in his company on ever-crazier schemes while quietly pocketing personal wealth.

The case against Mozilo was based in considerable measure on the discrepancy between his public statements about the health of CFC and the private messages he had dispatched to insiders regarding the true condition of the subprime loans that were massacring the company's profit and loss statements. One internal e-mail read: "In all my years in the business I have never seen a more toxic product." In another he wrote: "Frankly, I consider that product line to be the poison of our time" (Reckard & Puzzanghera, 2009, p. 15A).

The case of Edward Jordan, a retired postal worker living in New York City, puts a human face on the predatory Countrywide tactics. Jordan was close to paying off his home when a broker told him that he was paying altogether too much interest on his loan. She offered a one percent rate. Jordan refinanced his house, ending up with a fee of $20,000 for doing so. He soon found that the interest rate would quickly escalate to a high of 9.9 percent. Charles Morris, who discusses the case, says bluntly about the Jordan case: "On any construction of the deal, he was robbed by Countrywide" (Morris, 2008, pp. 70–71).

The Federal Bureau of Investigation also was looking into a setup known as FOA—"Friends of Angelo." Prominent politicians, including Christopher Dodd, chair of the Senate Banking Committee, and Kent Conrad, chair of the Senate Finance Committee, were given sweetheart loans by CFC that waived fees and carried low interest rates. Dodd, for instance, had gotten a mortgage on houses in Washington and in Connecticut, his home state, which was $75,000 less than it would have been under normal conditions. A Senate Ethics committee investigation found no wrongdoing on Dodd's part except that he should have "avoided the appearance of impropriety." At the end of 2009, Dodd announced that he would not run for re-election, a decision in part triggered by a wave of constituent disapproval regarding his dealings with Countrywide.

The *New York Post* learned that Mozilo and his codefendants had hired a brigade of 19 lawyers to mount their defense and that at least indirectly American taxpayers would foot the estimated $50 million attorneys' fees. The Bank of America, which received $45 billion in bailout money from the federal government, had agreed when taking over CFC that for six years it would be responsible for the legal expenses incurred by the company and its officers (Tharp & Scanlan, 2009).

Fannie Mae and Freddie Mac

In September 2008, Fannie Mae (the colloquial term for the Federal National Mortgage Association) and Freddie Mac (standing for Federal Home Loan Mortgage Corporation), both in desperate financial condition, were placed under the conservatorship of the Federal Housing Finance Agency in a move that was tantamount to nationalization and was described as "one of the most sweeping government interventions in the private financial markets" (Goldfarb, Cho & Binyamin, 2008, p. A01).

Fannie Mae and Freddie Mac were nongovernmental agencies created during the Great Depression to assist low-income persons to secure housing by assuring that banks would have sufficient liquidity to provide them with loans. The two agencies before their fall either owned or had guaranteed $1.4 trillion worth of mortgages or forty percent of the entire total in the United States (Christie, 2006; Wallison, 2001). Their shares had suffered a loss of $100 billion in 2008. The entities enjoyed federal backing and were known as GSEs (government-sponsored enterprises). They are the only companies among the Fortune 500 roster of the leading U.S. businesses that are not required to inform the public about any financial difficulty they might be experiencing.

Henry M. Paulson, Jr., George W. Bush's Treasury Secretary, blamed the need for the takeover on a "flawed business model," a euphemism for inept and irresponsible business management (Paulson, Jr., 2010). The government rationale for the injection of taxpayer funds into the floundering credit agencies was that to allow them to fail would have repercussions more severe than the financial cost necessary to keep them afloat. White-collar crime scholars wondered whether the same considerations might excuse the incompetence or shady activities of a Mafia boss or a small business owner supporting a large family.

Notable was the fact that two former chief executive officers of Fannie Mae, James Johnson and Franklin Raines, had benefited from the good graces of Countrywide's Friends of Angelo favoritism program (Simpson & Hagerty, 2008).

Lehman Brothers Holdings

The rescue operations stalled momentarily when Lehman Brothers, a company founded in the 1850s by three brothers from Bavaria as a dry goods store and cotton trader in Montgomery, Alabama, went broke. The company had moved to New York in 1868 and grew to be the country's fourth largest investment bank. Then in 2007, in dire financial straits, it failed to find a buyer and was allowed by the government to go under. Lehman Brothers had been fudging its balance sheet, inflating its asset position by means of accounting chicanery, and was short $650 billion (McDonald & Robinson, 2009). The casino capitalism of Lehman Brothers was aided and abetted by the rating agencies that gave top scores to the company's toxic holdings. A pair of observers had their idea about what was up with the rating agencies: "Maybe it was something spectacularly dishonest, like taking that colossal amount of fees in return for doing what Lehman and the rest wanted, giving those [bonds] an utterly undeserved rating" (McDonald & Robinson, 2009, p. 200).

While the disappearance of Lehman Brothers did not produce the catastrophic level of widespread financial disorder that seemingly would have occurred had Bear Stearns been allowed to go into bankruptcy, the company was not rescued in part because for the moment—and only for the moment—Wall Street and the government had lost their appetite for bailing out distressed investment houses.

The other part of the failure to come to Lehman's aid lay in an aspect of its culture. The company, led by Richard S. (Dick) Fuld, Jr., was an insular entity, lacking close connections with the other Wall Street players and internally riven. Fuld operated his fiefdom as if he were engaged in a war with competitors rather than an enterprise in which they could jointly become famously wealthy. He was dubbed the "gorilla" because he seemed to grunt rather than speak in full sentences. He told his underlings: "Every day is a battle. You've got to kill the enemy." To make his point, he handed out plastic swords to staffers. For his own part, Fuld had taken home some $480 million during the six years before 2007 and owned six houses, including a twenty-room mansion in Greenwich, Connecticut.

The vastness of the Lehman Brothers empire can be realized by the fact that after it had to evacuate three floors of the World Trade Center when the building was destroyed on September 11, 2001 (one Lehman employee was killed), it rented offices throughout Manhattan, including 650 rooms in the Sheraton Hotel, so that it could continue operating.

The company's downfall was the consequence of its reckless indulgence in subprime lending and its failure to finalize a buyout by either of two suitors, Barclay's Bank of England and the Bank of America, both of whom backed off when a final takeover decision had to be made (Fishman, 2008; Ward, 2010).

American International Group (AIG)

Next came AIG, the largest insurance company in the United States and the eighteenth largest public company in the world. AIG had a colorful background. It had been founded in Shanghai in China in 1919 by Cornelius Vander Starr, a young expatriate American who, among other things, correctly presumed that a fortune could be made by insuring Chinese people because improved hygiene and other amenities would enable them to live a good deal longer than current estimates of longevity. The company opened a branch in New York in 1926 that insured only risks to Americans working or traveling overseas. In 1939, with the Japanese targeting China, AIG relocated its headquarters to New York City (Shelp & Ehrbar, 2009).

Maurice Raymond Greenberg, nicknamed Hank Greenberg after a well-known former Detroit Tigers home run slugger, subsequently ran AIG for thirty-seven years, the longest term of any contemporary leader of a major corporation. In time, Greenberg's personal holdings in AIG stock were worth more than three billion dollars, placing him forty-seventh on the *Fortune* roster of the richest Americans. One of Greenberg's working maxims was: "All I want from life is an unfair advantage" (Shelp & Ehrbar, 2009, p. 146). He was forced to resign as AIG's chief executive officer in 2005 when the company admitted intentionally giving false information to regulators and misrepresenting earnings. The board of directors turned against Greenberg when it learned that he planned to take the Fifth Amendment against self-incrimination when called to testify before a Congressional committee.

In August 2009, Greenberg and Howard Smith, AIG's former chief financial officer, paid $15 million to the SEC to settle the charge that they had misstated the financial condition of the company. Had the truth been revealed, AIG would have failed to meet key earnings and growth targets. Greenberg did not admit guilt and insisted that had he been charged criminally for securities fraud he would have fought the case rather than settle. Earlier, four former executives of General Re, a reinsurance company, and one AIG executive were convicted following six days of jury deliberation of inflating AIG's reserves by $500 million through fraudulent dealings, thereby artificially boosting AIG's stock price. Christian Milton, head of AIG's reinsurance division, received a four-year prison sentence (Efrati & Pleven, 2009).

AIG had been deeply involved in the credit derivative market (for details on these complex risk-ridden instruments see Goodman, et al., 2008; Bomfim, 2005). Warren Buffet, the second richest man in American (Bill Gates of Microsoft is the richest), had called derivatives "weeds priced as flowers" and branded them as "financial weapons of mass destruction" (McDonald & Robinson, 2009, p. 161). Financier Felix Rohatyn similarly derided them as "financial hydrogen bombs, built on personal computers by twenty-six-year olds with MBAs" (Tett, 2009, p. 31). Derivatives, complex packaged deals, became the hottest items around, due to their risky nature, they paid hefty commissions. AIG, in addition to its exposure to derivative losses, was found to have placed reinsurance funds with companies that it misrepresented to regulators as independent, although they were totally owned by AIG. In the fall of 2008, the government bailed AIG out of its dire liquidity crisis to the tune of $173 billion. The government now owned nearly 80 percent of the company, and the trustees appointed to oversee AIG named the majority of the board of directors.

Two subsequent AIG acts came to epitomize the belief that huge organizations such as AIG exist in a world spectacularly different from that inhabited by more ordinary people and entities.

The first was an eight-day company "outing" for favored employees that took place at the St. Regis Monarch Beach Resort in Dana Point, California, just five days after the company accepted a huge sum of taxpayer money. The total cost came to almost half a million dollars (excluding airfares to the site) and included $139,000 for hotel rooms (an ordinary St. Regis room is priced at $425 a night plus tax; an ocean view room at $565), $147,301 on banquets, and $23,380 for spa treatments. The company's carefully-crafted response to revelations of the celebration is worth parsing. It read:

This type of gathering is standard practice in the industry and was planned a year in advance of the Federal Reserve loan to AIG. We recognize, however, that even activities that have long been considered practice may be perceived negatively. As a result, we are reevaluating various aspects of our operations in the light of the new times in which we operate.

The defense that something is acceptable because everybody in the industry does the same thing is much like a burglar saying that his thievery is fine because all the burglars he knows are engaged in the same activity. And that this has been going on for a long time would seem to demonstrate added culpability rather than excusatory evidence. The statement that AIG will be thinking twice about continuing the enormously expensive indulgence is grudging, as evidenced by the phrase "may be perceived" rather than a flat-out admission that the spending orgy was inexcusable.

The second episode involved the expenditure by AIG of $165 million in bonuses. The top payout to one person was $6.4 million while 73 employees received at least one million dollars each. The action led to comments in Congress that AIG was like an Alice in Wonderland business, that its behavior was surreal and demonstrated unbridled greed, that the bonuses boggled the mind, and that they rewarded incompetence.

Merrill Lynch & Co

The implosion of financial institutions began to assume a familiar pattern. On December 5, 2008, shareholders of Merrill Lynch, a company founded in 1914, approved a buyout by the Bank of America that itself had received bailout money from the federal government. Subsequently, it was learned that Merrill Lynch, apparently unbeknownst to the Bank of America, had lost some $138 billion during the last three months of 2008. Not surprisingly the Bank of America had to return to the federal trough to get its hands on more taxpayer money.

Only later did it become known that right before the merger Merrill had paid 170 executives a total of $3.6 billion in bonuses despite the fact that the company had lost $28 billion during the year. The response to criticism was that such staggering sums were necessary to retain the best and the brightest. The critics wondered how bright a person needed to be in order to inflict losses of billions of dollars on a company. Or as one wisecrack had it: "As a general rule, only the very smartest people can make catastrophic mistakes" (Morris, 2008, p. 49).

When the agreement to take over Merrill Lynch was reached, Bank of America (BOA) needed the approval of its stockholders to complete the merger. But the proxy statement it sent to those who held its shares knowingly omitted the bonuses Merrill Lynch would pay out and the extent of its losses. The Securities and Exchange Commission negotiated a $33 million penalty with Bank of America. That agreement had to be endorsed by a federal district judge. Judge Jed S. Rakoff refused to approve the agreement, ruling that it did not "comport with the most elementary notions of justice and morality." He wanted to know why the SEC was allowing Bank of America to pass the fine onto its shareholders rather than pinpointing those persons who had violated the law by omitting critical information from the proxy statement. Bank of America claimed that lawyers had put together the proxy. The judge asked: Then why not go after the lawyers? And what about Bank of America executives who presumably were being paid, very well, to see that the company's affairs were conducted legally? The bank officials also maintained that they had arranged the settlement because to go to court would probably cost them more than $33 million. The judge thought that absurd and implied that perhaps they were reluctant to have their behavior revealed in a public forum. He pointed out that "it is quite something for the very management that is accused of having lied to its shareholders to determine how much of the victims' money should be used to make the case against the arrangement go away" (*Securities and Exchange Commission v. Bank of America*, 2009).

Five months after his original decision, on February 22, 2010, Rakoff reluctantly agreed to a $150 million settlement, thereby expropriating even more of the shareholders' money than in the original plan. In the 2010 ruling, he noted:

> A fine assessed against the Bank, taken by itself, penalizes the shareholders for what was, in effect if not in intent, a fraud by management on the shareholders. This was among the major reasons the Court rejected the earlier proposed settlement. Where management deceives its own shareholders, a fine most directly serves its deterrent purposes if it is assessed against the persons responsible for the deception. If such persons acted out of negligence, rather than bad faith, that should be a mitigating factor, but not a reason to have the shareholder victims pay the fine instead. (*Securities and Exchange Commission v. Bank of America*, pp. 11–12)

He conceded that the new agreement was "far from ideal" but felt that his first ruling had gone too far in ignoring the doctrine of judicial restraint, but he also stated the greatest defect of the agreement was that it provided

> very modest punitive, compensatory, and remedial measures that are neither directed at the specific individuals responsible for the nondisclosures nor appear likely to have more than a very modest impact on corporate practices or victim compensation. While better than nothing, this is half-baked justice at best. (*Securities and Exchange Commission v. Bank of America*, 2010)

New York Attorney General Andrew Cuomo filed civil charges against Bank of America and its two top executives in February 2010. The suit alleged that Bank of America was "motivated by self-interest, greed, hubris, and a palpable sense that the normal rules of fair play did not apply to them." It further alleged that BOA management regarded itself as too big to play by the rules and too big to tell the truth (Goldfarb, 2010).

The Automobile Manufacturers

In 2009, it was the turn of the big three auto companies—Ford, Chrysler, and General Motors—to confront their massive losses. The American auto industry had once led the world, but in recent times it had been strikingly outpaced by foreign vehicles, particularly cars from Japan. When gas prices soared, the heavy guzzlers such as American-made SUVs took a heavy hit. When the overall economy went south, the big three had to come to Washington hat in hand begging for financial subsidies. They traveled to the Congressional hearings in pampered style aboard company jets—and that created an uproar.

The reaction to the executives' means of transportation is informative in regard to public opinion concerning the economic meltdown and white-collar crime. Almost all Americans have at best a limited understanding of the arcane economics of Wall Street and its financial affiliates, but they could understand and get exercised about company bonuses that in a year for some CEOs would be higher than their own earnings over their entire working life. And they could appreciate that travel on expensive company-owned jets is a luxury that is financed by stockholders and also by taxpayers, since the planes are written off as corporate business expenditures. Yet, despite obvious public antipathy and distaste directed at the automobile company CEOs, executives with other corporations that had been propped up with huge sums of bailout funds continued to use company jets not only for business purposes but also for vacation jaunts for themselves and their families. Investigative reporters with the *Wall Street Journal* documented numerous flights on company planes by numerous executives to vacation spots in Europe, Mexico, the Caribbean, and the ski resorts in Aspen, Colorado. The Regions Financial Corporation in Birmingham, Alabama, for instance, had received $3.5 billion in bailout money from the federal Treasury Department's Troubled Asset Relief Program (TARP) on November 14, 2008. Twelve days later, the day before Thanksgiving, two company jets flew from Birmingham, bound for the posh Greenbriar Resort in West Virginia where the company's CEO and members of his family spent four nights over the holiday. The round-trip cost was estimated to be in the range of $17,000 (Drucker & Maremont, 2009).

These were not white-collar crimes, of course, because they violated no laws except perhaps the somewhat amorphous legal concept that corporate executives have a fiduciary responsibility to act in the best interests of their shareholders. The jet-setting illustrated again the power of those in executive positions to influence the shape that the criminal law will take. Daniel Gross, looking carefully at the evidence, concluded that "in the case of the biggest and most expensive failures—Lehman Brothers, AIG, Fannie and Freddie—managers were craven, stupid, and incompetent, but not probably criminal" (Gross, 2009, p. 97). A crusading Illinois Senator put it well: The only reason that contributions by lobbyists to persons in Congress are not defined as bribery is because those with political power determine what is bribery. It seems important that the study of white-collar crime must focus not only on violations of the letter of the law but also acts by those in positions of power who in their occupational roles seriously harm others. That the wrongdoer may not have intended injury often is not permitted as a defense in law when a reasonable person should have known that his or her self-serving actions had a strong likelihood of harming others.

On Ponzi's Pathway

Charles Ponzi (1882–1949) gave his name to a form of white-collar crime—the Ponzi scheme—that characterized two of the major scandals during the economic breakdown, one involving Bernard Madoff and the second R. Allen Stanford. The basic ingredients of a Ponzi scheme are very simple. You have to get enough people interested in putting money into whatever investment you are promoting by promising them outstanding profits. Then you pay off the initial investors with the funds that keep coming in as other people are attracted by the rewards reaped by the first investors. It is likely that those original investors will be so delighted with their gains that they will leave the money they have "earned" with you in order to reap even greater returns. So for a time a great deal of money will be coming in and not much going out. A Ponzi scheme demonstrates the truth of one of the oldest maxims in the financial world. If something is offered that flagrantly flies in the face of common sense, it is very likely to be nonsensical—and probably crooked.

Italian-born Charles Ponzi had stumbled about after migrating to the United States until he hit upon the idea that he could in theory buy postage stamps issued internationally to facilitate commerce for one price abroad and sell them at a significant profit in the United States. Investors swamped the company he originated. He never quite got around to purchasing the stamps, which in actual fact could not have come close to financing the scheme he advertised. When he was exposed, Ponzi received a five-year prison sentence. After his release, he set up another scam, this time based on Florida land sales. It ended with seven more years in prison and, thereafter, deportation to Italy, where he died impoverished (Dunn, 2004; Zuckoff, 2006).

Bernard L. Madoff Investment Securities

For forty years, Bernie Madoff, an affable crook who mingled with the country club elite, operated a Ponzi scheme that was estimated to have defrauded investors of $25 to $65 billion, depending on which source you accept. Madoff enticed the careless and the gullible with a campaign that, among other claims, maintained that Madoff Investment used sophisticated computer systems "to monitor prices" and to "identify trading opportunities around the world." Much business was generated by word of mouth endorsements from customers who were paid dividends with money invested by other customers. By the time the law caught up with Madoff he owned apartments on New York's Upper East Side and near Wall Street, a house in Montauk on Long Island, three properties in Palm Beach, a house in Key Largo in Florida, and another in Antibes in France. To gain political advantages, between 1997 and 2008 Madoff spent $590,000 on lobbying efforts, plus another quarter of a million on campaign contributions from 1991 forward.

Madoff was arrested on December 11, 2008, and raised bail of $10 million that allowed him to remain under house arrest in his penthouse apartment. He had been turned in by his sons Andrew and Mark, who worked for the investment company, and reported to their attorney their father's confession to them of peculation. The attorney informed the authorities. Speculation was widespread that this was a planned scenario designed to keep Madoff's wife and his sons as well as his brother, Peter, who had long worked for the investment company, from facing criminal charges. All of them, many believed, must have known that the company was crooked. Critics were appalled that the SEC had never investigated Madoff's company even though Harry Markopolos, a financier who had concluded that the "profits" heralded by Madoff were too good to be true (and weren't) had alerted the SEC and the media multiple times over nine years (Markopolos, 2010). Madoff's gigantic enterprise was audited by a hole-in-the-wall store front accounting company, Friehling & Horowitz, that had but one active member, David G. Friehling. He had invested $14 million with Madoff, but by 2000 had withdrawn $5.5 million. In November 2009, Friehling pleaded guilty for conspiring with Madoff and is awaiting sentence. Also facing criminal charges were the two men—Jerome O'Hara and George Perez—who set up the elaborate computer software program that allowed Madoff to generate phony earnings statements to be sent to his clients.

Among the gullible who were robbed by Madoff were filmmaker Steven Spielberg, husband and wife actors Kyra Sedgwick and Kevin Bacon, Nobel Prize author Elie Wiesel, Fred Wilson, owner of the New York Mets baseball team, and media mogul Mort Zuckerman. Madoff also swindled a large roster of Jewish schools, including Yeshiva University (losses of $110 million), New York University (out $24 million), and Tufts University (out $20 million) in addition to a host of foreign investment funds that, often without informing their customers, took in money, charged a hefty fee, and put all of the money into Madoff's scam operation. René-Thierry Magnon de la Villehuchet, a co-founder of Access International Advisors, who had lost $1.4 billion of his own and his clients' money, committed suicide two weeks after Madoff's ruse became public knowledge. Austria's Bank Medici had placed $2.1 billion at Madoff's disposal. The Bank Medici had touted itself as employing "the most unusual mixture of financial strength and tradition, of sophisticated know how and technological expertise." In the wake of the Madoff disaster, the Austrian government took over the Bank Medici (Sander, 2009). As always in such cases it was the lawyers who would reap the juiciest financial harvest. The firm that was charged by the court with cleaning up Madoff's business billed $15.5 million for five months' work, with the attorney leading the work charging $700 for each hour he said he put in on the job.

The hammer fell in June 2009 on some of the persons who had steered billions of dollars into the Madoff scam—so-called "feeders"— when the government filed a civil fraud suit against Stanley Chais, a prominent money manager for some forty years with an office in Beverly Hills. Chais was charged with a breach of fiduciary duty by deceiving his investors and ignoring obvious signs of fraud. In December 2009, the civil suit was put on hold until the following June while the government determined whether to pursue a criminal action. One of Chais' victims, Mark Pelle, part owner of an upscale restaurant, offered his view of Chais' actions: "He thought he had some great scheme where he didn't have to do anything and everybody would love him. He got caught up in a huge way by his arrogance and hubris" (Pfeifer, 2009: B4).

Another SEC case was against three executives of the Cohmad Securities Corporation, a small brokerage firm housed in the same building as the Madoff enterprise. They had turned over their clients' money to Madoff, unbeknownst to the clients. The SEC pointed out that the rewards to the executives never were taken from the amounts allegedly accrued by the clients, a sign that the SEC believed made clear that the Cohmad executives knew that these profits were fictitious. In addition to the SEC actions, Andrew Cuomo, the New York State Attorney General, filed a civil suit against J. Ezra Merkin, who ran a Madoff feeder firm, while Massachusetts went after Fairfield Greenwich on the same grounds. The company, while not admitting guilt, agreed to pay $8 million to its Massachusetts investors.

Madoff pled guilty on March 3, 2009 to eleven criminal charges. His lawyer noted that at age 71 his client had a life expectancy of thirteen years and asked the judge to impose a twelve-year sentence. Ignoring the defense recommendation, on June 29, 2009 federal district court judge Denny Chin Sain imposed the maximum possible sentence of 150 years on Madoff, declaring that the defendant was "extraordinarily evil." He granted that the 150 years was symbolic, an overkill of a sentence to life in prison, but he said he considered it a symbol that ought to convey a lesson to other actual or potential white-collar criminals. The sentence was not a record for a financial fraud perpetrator. In the past decade there have been sentences as high as 350 and 845 years (Frank & Efrati, 2009). Madoff was placed in the medium-security section of the Federal Correctional Complex in Butner, North Carolina. There he could enjoy the company of a coterie of other white-collar crooks, including former Rite-Aid vice chairman Franklin C. Brown and Al Parrish, who also was convicted of operating a Ponzi scheme.

During the Madoff sentencing session there were wrenching presentations to the court by victims of his nefarious acts. One victim said that the funds deposited with Madoff were to be used for the care of his mentally disabled brother. "I hope Madoff's sentence is long enough so that his jail cell will become his coffin," the victim declared. One woman told the judge: "I now live on food stamps. I scavenge in dumpsters at the end of the month." Others labeled Madoff a "monster" and a "low life" (Lattman & Lobb, 2009, p. A12).

Debora and Gerald Strober interviewed numerous victims of the Madoff rip-off. The Strobers ask (but never answer) a trio of interpretive questions: (1) Is Bernie Madoff mentally disturbed?; (2) Is he a sociopath?; or (3) Is he completely rational but totally amoral? (Strober & Strober, 2009, p. 47). They stress that what differentiated Madoff from most all other white-collar malefactors was that he cold-bloodedly betrayed and fleeced intimates, including relatives and his closest friends.

For others, there was scant satisfaction in seeing Madoff get his due while those who directly contributed to the economic meltdown not only escaped untouched by the criminal justice system but were raking in even more exorbitant incomes. At the firm of Goldman Sachs, the average employee salary had risen to $700,000 a year, higher than before the meltdown. For Frank Rich, a *New York Times* columnist, Madoff's offenses were small potatoes compared to "the esoteric (and often legal) heists by banks and bankers. They gamed the entire system, then took the money and ran before the bubble burst, sticking the rest of us with that fear, panic and loss" (Rich, 2009, p. 8).

Stanford Financial Group

The Madoff case was instrumental in leading law enforcement authorities to the Stanford Financial Group (SFG). The Securities Exchange Commission had gone on the alert when SFG lied to it, declaring that it had no exposure to Madoff's schemes. Earlier, American enforcement agencies had ignored a scathing denunciation of SFC by Alex Dalmady (2009) in a Venezuelan magazine. Two employees of SFG had also testified in a 2008 discrimination suit about various unethical and illegal business practices engaged in by their employer.

Finally, in June 2009, the Department of Justice filed a 21-count criminal indictment against financier R. Allen Stanford, a 59-year-old Texas billionaire, and five others. Stanford was accused of masterminding a Ponzi scheme that bilked some 30,000 investors, a large portion of them from Latin American countries, out of an estimated $7 billion. As is common in prosecutions that involve co-defendants, the government convinced one of the secondary participants, James M. Davis, SFG's chief financial officer, to plead guilty to charges of fraud and conspiracy in return for a lesser sentence than he would have received if convicted and to testify against Stanford. Davis and Stanford had been close; they first met as college roommates at Baylor University in Waco, Texas.

SFG had its headquarters on the Caribbean island-nation of Antigua and Barbuda with investment offices in Venezuela, Houston, Panama, and Miami. *Forbes* magazine had listed Stanford as the 250th wealthiest person in the United States. In 2006, he had been the first American to be knighted in Antigua. The head of the Antiguan Financial Services Authority, Leroy King, indicted with Stanford, allegedly was paid more than $100,000 to abstain from auditing SFG and for supplying confidential information to the company. When SEC investigators requested reports about Stanford's operation from King he notified the company of these suspicions and helped craft a response that said that SFG was "in compliance with all areas of depositor safety and solvency, as well as all other applicable laws and regulations." The enforcement head of the SEC used a football analogy to convey the character of the Stanford-King relationship: "While Stanford quarterbacked his massive Ponzi scheme, he paid the referee to spy on the huddles and provide an insider's play-by-play of the SEC investigation" (Krauss, 2009, p. B6).

In February 2009, the SEC had filed a civil suit that charged Stanford and Laura Pendergest-Holt, the company's chief investment officer, with two instances of obstruction of a federal investigation and with complicity in the Ponzi scheme. The Stanford company was said to offer certificates of deposit paying ten percent interest (Perez, 2009). Among its other scams, the company had engaged in "round-trip" real estate transactions, buying undeveloped Antiguan real estate for $63.5 million and then "selling" the property to its own subsidiaries for $2 billion, and carrying that sum on its books as an asset. In the company magazine, Stanford made the following declaration, which an SEC spokeswoman declared to be "improbable, if not impossible."

> Our world is far different than the world my grandfather lived in when the first Stanford company was founded. . . . As a company founded in the midst of the Great Depression—an environment of despair—we have a long-proven record of how even the most severe downcycles can bring opportunities that yield significant benefits in the long run.

Instead, in the words of the SEC spokeswoman, Stanford had operated "a fraud of shocking magnitude that has spread its tentacles throughout the world." Unlike Madoff, Stanford was denied bail on the ground that he posed a serious risk of fleeing the country because he had high-placed connections in foreign lands. At the bail hearing, a pilot testified that he had recently flown Stanford to Libya and Switzerland, and an auditor told the court that $100 million had been withdrawn from a Swiss bank that Stanford controlled. In addition, Stanford had recently requested a friend to bring him his Antigua passport. Stanford's trial is scheduled for early 2011.

Conclusion

The economic meltdown that began in the fall of 2007, as Gillian Tett observes, "was not triggered by a war, a widespread recession, or any external shock": it was self inflicted. She notes that "the entire financial system was wrong as a result of flawed incentives within banks and investment funds, as well as the rating agencies; warped regulatory structures; and a lack of oversight" (Tett, 2009, p. x). On an individual level, we can note the comment of a Citicorp trader who responded to information that the housing market was riddled with corruption: "What's the worst that can happen? We make $200 million and then we get fired" (Gasparino, 2009: 146).

These allegations are certainly true, but they do not go far enough. They imply that structural conditions inevitably allowed—indeed, encouraged—humans in a position to do so to take advantage of these economic fault lines. White-collar crime research over the years had documented in great detail the greed and rapaciousness of many of those in power or clawing their way up the ladder to financial wealth. There is no gainsaying the general truth of Lord Acton's famous maxim that "power tends to corrupt and absolute power corrupts absolutely" (Creighton, 1904, Vol. 1, p. 37). We can also note the observation of novelist Isaac Beshevis Singer: "Power kills all ideals" (Singer, 2008, p. 54). Considerably more pungent is the observation of Francis Bacon, the sixteenth century English philosopher and statesman. "He who rides without a lid," said Bacon apparently referring to self-control and self-discipline, "doth like the ape, the higher he climbs the more he shows his ars" (quoted in Pope, 1975). Power must be held in check by restraining mechanisms, by diligent oversight, and by tough responses to its abuse.

The economic meltdown proved something more than the failure of unbridled and underregulated capitalism. It revealed the failure of a social system to have taught enough of its citizens, most notably those in the top echelons, principles of honesty and transparency in their dealings and to have inculcated them with a goodly dosage of selflessness. As one writer has noted in regard to the recent business disasters: "The scent of money deadens all other sensory and ethical organs." He adds that "the securities laws assume that lawyers, accountants, and credit raters will not allow monetary incentives to override their professional ethics—an assumption that draws little support from the abysmal recent record" (Morris, 2008, pp. 31, 150). That record offered a backdrop for a writer who sought to understand the public support accorded John Dillinger, a bank robber at work during the Great Depression of the 1930s. "As our own day's story of stupid policies and lax regulations, of great money-men, free-market hucksters, white-collar thieves, and self-serving politicians unfolds, and banks foreclose on millions of families' homes, workers lose their jobs, and life savings disappear, it becomes clear why an outlaw who could be said to rob those who became rich by robbing the poor might channel a people's sense of rage at a system that had failed them" (Gorn, 2009, p. 213).

Many students who are reading this book will appreciate that they too were embroiled in the meltdown when it was revealed that the privatized student loan sector had bribed campus counselors and exploited government subsidies (Collinge, 2009). The study of white-collar crime alerts us to the flaws in human beings and in social systems that permit—even encourage—such abuses of power.

REFERENCES

Bamber, Bill & Spencer, Andrew (2009). *Bear Trap: The Fall of Bear Stearns and the Panic of 2008*. New York: Brick Tower Press.

Boardman, Fon W., Jr. (1977). *America and the Robber Barons*. New York: Henry Welck.

Bomfim, Antilo N. (2005). *Understanding Credit Derivatives and Other Instruments*. Amsterdam, The Netherlands: Elsevier Academic Press.

Bruck, Connie (2009, June 29). Angelo's Ashes: The Man Who Became the Face of the Financial Crisis. *The New Yorker*, 46–55.

Business Wire (2005). *FORTUNE* Magazine Names Bear Stearns 'Most Admired' Securities Firm." http://findarticles.com/p/articles/mi_m0EIN/is_2005_Feb_25/ai_n10302819/

Christie, James R. (Ed.). (2006). *Fannie Mae and Freddie Mac: Scandal in U.S. Housing*. New York: Nova.

Cohan, William D. (2009). *House of Cards: A Tale of Hubris and Wretched Excess on Wall Street*. New York: Doubleday.

Collinge, Alan Michale (2009). *The Student Loan Scam: The Most Oppressive Debt in U.S. History and How We Can Fight Back*. Boston: Beacon Press.

Creighton, Louise (1904). *Life and Letters of Mandell Creighton*. London: Longmans Green.

Dalmady, Alex (2009, January). Duck Tales. *VerEconomy Magazine*, 11–15.

Drucker, Jesse & Maremont, Mary (2009, June 19). CEOs of Bailed-Out Banks Fly to Resorts on Firms' Jets. *Wall Street Journal*, pp. A1, A12.

Dunn, Donald H. (2004). *Ponzi: The Incredible Story of the King of Financial Con*. New York: Broadway Books.

Efrati, Amir & Pleven, Liam (2009, August 7). Greenberg to Pay $15 Million in SEC Case. *Wall Street Journal*, p. C1, C3.

Fishman, Steve (2008, December 1). Burning Down His House: Is Lehman's CEO Dick Fuld the Villain in the Collapse of Wall Street, Or Is He Being Sacrificed for the Sins of His Peers? *New York, 29,* 39–48.

Frank, Robert & Efrati, Amir (2009, June 30). "Evil" Madoff Gets 150 Years in Epic Fraud. *Wall Street Journal,* pp. A1, A12.

Friedman, Hershey H. (1980, Winter). Talmudic Business Ethics: An Historical Perspective, *Akron Business and Economic Review, 11,* 45–49.

Friedrichs, David O. (2009). Exorbitant CEO Compensation: Just Reward or Grand Theft? *Crime, Law and Social Change, 51,* 45–72.

Gasparino, Charles (2009). *How Three Decades of Wall Street Greed and Government Mismanagement Destroyed the Global Financial System.* Cambridge, MA: Harvard Business.

Goldfarb, Zachary A. (February 23, 2010). "Judge Criticizes, but Approves, Settlement with Bank of America." *The Washington Post.* http://www.washingtonpost.com/wp-dyn/content/article/2010/02/22/AR2010022202062.html

Goldfarb, Zachary A., Cho, David & Bloomberg, Binyamin (2008, September 8). Treasury to Rescue Fannie and Freddie: Regulators Seek to Keep Firms' Troubles from Setting Off Wave of Bank Failures. *Washington Post,* p. A1.

Goodman, Lauie S., Shumin, Li, Zimmerman, Thomas A. & Lucas, Douglas J. (2008). *Subprime Mortgage Credit Derivatives.* Hoboken, NJ: John Wiley.

Gorn, Elliott J. (2009). *Dillinger's Wild Ride: The Year That Made America's Public Enemy Number One.* New York: Oxford University Press.

Gross, Daniel (2009). *Dumb Money: How Our Greatest Financial Minds Bankrupted the Nation.* New York: Free Press.

Jónsson, Ásgeir (2009). *Why Iceland?* New York: McGraw-Hill.

Kelly, Kate (2009). *Street Fighters: The Last 72 Hours of Bear Stearns, the Toughest Firm on Wall Street.* New York: Portfolio.

Krauss, Clifford (2009, June 20). How Stanford Financial Dodged Regulators. *New York Times,* pp. B1, B6.

Lattman, Peter & Lobb, Annelena (2009, June 30). Victims' Speeches in Court Influence Verdict. *Wall Street Journal,* p. A12.

Lewis, Oscar (1938). *The Big Four: The Story of Huntington, Stanford, Hopkins and Croker and the Building of the Central Pacific.* New York: Knopf.

Markapolos, Harry (2010). *No One Would Listen to Me: A True Financial Thriller.* Hoboken, NJ: John Wiley.

McDonald, Lawrence G. & Robinson, Patrick (2009). *A Colossal Failure of Common Sense: The Inside Story of the Collapse of Lehman Brothers.* New York: Crown.

Michaelson, Adam (2009). *The Foreclosure of America: The Inside Story of the Rise and Fall of Countrywide, Home Loans, the Mortgage Crisis, and the Default of the American Dream.* New York: Berkley Books.

Morris, Charles R. (2008). *The Two Trillion Dollar Meltdown: Easy Money, High Rollers, and the Great Credit Crunch* (Rev. ed.). New York: Public Affairs.

Muolo, Paul & Padilla, Matthew (2008). *Chain of Blame: How Wall Street Caused the Mortgage and Credit Crisis.* Hoboken, NJ: John Wiley.

Perez, Evan (2009, June 19). Stanford Is Indicted in Fraud, Surrenders. *Wall Street Journal,* p. C1,

Paulson, Henry M., Jr. (2010). *On the Brink: Inside the Race to the Collapse of the Global Finance System.* New York: Business Plus/Grand Central.

Pfeifer, Start (2009, December 12). Feds Pursue Criminal Case Against Chais. *Los Angeles Times,* pp. B1, B4.

Pius XI (1931). *After Forty Years.* Ann Arbor, MI: Pieran Press.

Pope, Alexander (1975/1728). *Dunciad I, 1728.* New York: Garland.

Posner, Richard A. (2009). *A Failure of Capitalism: The Crisis of '08 and the Descent into Depression.* Cambridge, MA: Harvard University Press.

Reckard, E. Scott & Puzzanghera, Jim (2009, June 5). Countrywide's CEO Charged with Fraud. *Baltimore Sun*, p. 15A.

Rich, Frank (2009, July 5). Bernie Madoff is No John Dillinger. *New York Times*, Week in Review, p. 8.

Rivlin, Gary (2010). *Broke, USA: Pawnshop to Poverty, Inc.: How the Working Poor Became Big Business.* New York: Harper.

Sander, Peter (2009). *Madoff: Corruption, Deceit, and the Making of the World's Most Notorious Ponzi Scheme.* New York: Lyon Press.

Securities and Exchange Commission v. Bank of America (2009). 653 F.2d 507 (S.D.N.Y.)

Securities and Excange Commission v. Bank of America (2010). 09 CIV 6829 (JSR) (S.D.N.Y.)

Shelp, Ronald & Ehrbar, Al (2009). *Fallen Giant: The Amazing Story of Hank Greenberg and the History of AIG* (2nd ed.). Hoboken, NJ: John Wiley.

Simpson, Glen R. and Hagerty, James R. (2008, June). "Countrywide Friends Got Good Loans." *Wall Street Journal.* http://online.wsj.com/article/SB121279970984353933.html

Singer, Isaac Bashevis (2008). *Shadows on the Hudson.* Translated by Joseph Sherman. New York: Farrar, Straus Giroux.

Smith, Adam (1776). *An Inquiry into the Nature and Causes of the Wealth of Nations.* London: W. Strahan and T. Caudel.

Strober, Debora & Strober, Gerald (2009). *Catastrophe: The Story of Bernard L. Madoff, the Man Who Swindled the World.* Beverly Hills, CA; Phoenix Books.

Sutherland, Edwin H. (1940). White-Collar Criminality. *American Sociological Review,* 5, 1–12.

Tett, Gillian (2009). *Fool's Gold: How the Bold Dream of a Small Tribe at J.P. Morgan was Corrupted by Wall Street Greed and Unleashed a Catastrophe.* New York: Free Press.

Tharp, Paul & Scanlan, Matthew (2009, June 10). $50M Toxic Avenger: Bailed-Out B of A Footing Mozilo's Legal Bills. *New York Post*, p. 34.

Tuchman, Barbara W. (1978). *A Distant Mirror: The Calamitous 14th Century.* New York: Knopf.

United States Senate (1936). *Report* Special Committee on the Investigation of the Munitions Industry. 74 Congress, 2d Session. Washington, DC: Government Printing Office.

Wallison, Peter J. (Ed.) (2001). *Serving Two Masters, Yet Out of Control: Fannie Mae and Freddie Mac.* Washington, DC: AEI Press.

Ward, Vicky (2010). *The Devil's Casino: Betrayal and the High-Stakes Games Played Inside Lehman Brothers.* Hoboken, NJ: John Wiley

Wessel, David (2009). *In Fed We Trust: Ben Bernanke's War on the Great Panic.* New York: Crown.

Zuckoff, Mitchell (2005). *Ponzi's Scheme: The True Story of a Financial Legend.* New York: Random House.

11

Epidemics of "Control Fraud" Lead to Recurrent, Intensifying Bubbles and Crises

— *William K. Black*

Abstract

"Control frauds" are seemingly legitimate entities controlled by persons who use them as a fraud "weapon." A single control fraud can cause greater losses than all other forms of property crime combined. This article focuses on the role of control fraud in causing financial crises. Financial control frauds' "weapon of choice" is accounting. Fraudulent lenders produce guaranteed, exceptional short-term "profits" through a four-part strategy: extreme growth (Ponzi-like), lending to uncreditworthy borrowers, extreme leverage, and minimal loss reserves. These exceptional "profits" render "private market discipline" perverse, often defeat regulatory restrictions, and allow the CEO to convert firm assets to his personal benefit through seemingly normal compensation mechanisms. The short-term profits also cause the CEO's stock options holdings to appreciate. Fraudulent CEOs who follow this strategy are guaranteed to obtain extraordinary income while minimizing the risks of detection and prosecution.

The optimization strategy for lenders that engage in accounting control frauds explains why such firms fail and cause catastrophic losses.

An original article written for this publication.

Each element of the strategy dramatically increases the eventual loss. The record "profits" allow the fraud to continue and grow rapidly for years, which is devastating because the firm grows by making bad loans. The "profits" allow the managers to loot the firm through exceptional compensation, which increases losses.

The accounting control fraud optimization strategy hyperinflates and extends the life of financial bubbles, which causes extreme financial crises. The most "criminogenic environment" in finance for accounting control fraud will attract an initial cluster of frauds. The factors that make a finance sector most criminogenic are the absence of effective regulation and the ability to invest in assets that lack a readily verifiable asset value. Unless those initial frauds are dealt with effectively by the regulators or prosecutors, they will produce record profits and other firms will mimic them. Those control frauds can be a combination of "opportunistic" and "reactive" (moral hazard). If entry is relatively easy, opportunistic control fraud is optimized. If the finance sector is suffering from severe distress, reactive control fraud is optimized. Both conditions can exist at the same time, as in the early years of the savings and loan (S&L) debacle.

When many firms follow the same optimization strategy in the same financial field, a financial bubble will arise, extend, and hyperinflate. This further optimizes accounting control fraud because the rapid rise in values allows the frauds to hide the real losses by refinancing the bad loans. Mega bubbles can produce financial crises.

Modern Finance Theory and Its Implications for the Developing New Criminology

Traditional economics and modern finance theory have failed to understand or counter even hyperinflated financial bubbles, the financial crises they cause, and the resultant severe recessions. This failure arises from a more basic failure—modern finance theory is fatally flawed. The theory is premised on the existence (indeed, the virtual inevitability) of "efficient markets" absent government "interference." While there are variant definitions of "efficient markets," even the weakest meaningful definition requires that the markets (1) not make systematic pricing errors and (2) move consistently toward more accurate pricing when there are random pricing errors.

"Private market discipline" was the dynamic asserted to make contracts efficient. Creditors are assumed to understand the risk of fraud, to have the ability to protect by contract against the risk, and to take effective action to protect against fraud. Honest, low-risk borrowers (and issuers of stock) are assumed to have the incentive to "signal" their status to lenders and investors and to have the *unique* ability to send such signals. Lenders and purchasers of stock are presumed to be rational. Rational lenders and purchasers do not want to be defrauded. Modern finance theory, therefore, presumed that lenders and purchasers of stock would only deal with companies that sent "honesty" "signals." It follows that "control fraud" is impossible. "Control fraud" (a new criminology theory) refers to frauds in which those who control (typically, the CEO) an entity use it as a "weapon" to defraud (Black, 2005; Wheeler and Rothman, 1982). Among finance firms, accounting is the "weapon of choice." Accounting control frauds grossly inflate their accounting "profits" in order to enrich the senior officers. If markets are efficient, accounting control fraud should be impossible because the fraudulent firms could not send the requisite "honesty" "signals." Rational lenders and purchasers of shares would not deal with an accounting control fraud. This is an example of "private market discipline" and it would—even if there were no rules, laws, regulators, or prosecutors—prevent all accounting control fraud.

Criminologists' research has documented that accounting control fraud can "mimic" the "honesty" signals and that each of the signals that economists asserted could only be sent by honest companies were routinely sent by accounting control frauds. Moreover, the accounting control frauds used these signals to aid their frauds and turned private market discipline into an oxymoron (Black, 2005).

These new criminology theories also showed what conditions could produce an intensely criminogenic environment that would lead to an epidemic of accounting control fraud. Criminologists borrowed the economics/finance concept of optimization to examine how lenders engaged in accounting control fraud would operate and why an epidemic of accounting control fraud would likely hyperinflate financial "bubbles." The term "bubble" refers to situations in which the prices of certain assets, e.g., homes, inflate rapidly in excess of the asset's fundamental values. Bubbles are impossible if markets are efficient because they represent systematic pricing errors (values are consistently overstated) and bubbles expand because market-pricing errors increase. Under the efficient markets hypothesis, errors should be random and the markets should consistently reduce pricing errors. Bubbles, however, do exist and they sometimes hyperinflate and cause catastrophic damage. Bubbles, therefore, falsify the claims that "free" markets (and contracts) are inherently "efficient" (Black, 2005). The housing bubble that triggered "The Great Recession" is only the most recent example.

White-Collar Criminology's Struggle to Address Elite Financial Frauds

Finance scholars could have avoided modern finance theory's fundamental errors had they read the white-collar crime literature. Sutherland, in his 1939 presidential address to the American Sociological Association, first created the term (and concept of) white-collar crime: "A crime committed by a person of respectability and high social status in the course of his occupation." We will see that each of these three elements represented a vital insight into what produced uniquely dangerous crimes: respectability, high social status, and crime done in the course of one's occupation. Sutherland demonstrated that large corporations frequently violated the law. Control frauds are the epitome of white-collar crime. The recent global crisis falsified modern finance theory, which is premised on the efficient markets hypothesis. The remarkable fact, however, is that Sutherland's work falsified the efficient markets hypothesis 60 years ago—roughly 30 years before modern finance theory triumphed.

Unfortunately, criminology did not advance rapidly from Sutherland's creation of a new field of study. Few criminologists studied white-collar crime and many of those who did revolted against Sutherland's use of class in his definition ("high social status"). Cressey (1973), one of Sutherland's students, interviewed embezzlers imprisoned in the 1940s. He found that they were disproportionately female, rarely had college degrees, and were relatively low social status. The low status embezzlers caused minor losses compared to more senior embezzlers.

Cressey's research taught us a great deal about minor embezzlers, but it had two unfortunate consequences. First, white-collar criminologists, from virtually the birth of the field, began to spend much of their time studying minor occupational crime rather than white-collar crime. There have never been large numbers of white-collar criminologists, so the diversion of such a high proportion of its scholars to the study of minor occupational crimes minimized advances in white-collar criminology. The diversion also reflected the continuation of precisely the perverse distortion of law enforcement priorities that Sutherland sought to change. A single high-status embezzler will often embezzle more funds than 100 low-status embezzlers combined. Financial institutions commonly refused to make criminal referrals when they discovered embezzlement by senior officers because they feared adverse publicity. When white-collar criminologists focused on low-status employees, they inherently focused on relatively minor financial crimes and reinforced instead of challenged the normal law enforcement predisposition to concentrate on relatively minor occupational crimes. Worse, it led many scholars to redefine "white-collar crime" by removing Sutherland's third element ("high social status") from the definition. This redefinition made it easier for scholars to consider themselves white-collar criminologists even though they rarely studied the elite white-collar offenders who cause the vast bulk of all financial fraud losses.

Second, Cressey's interviews of embezzlers led him to develop what he eventually termed the "fraud triangle." He viewed embezzlers as engaging in fraud when three factors came together: a non-shareable need (i.e., an embarrassing financial need that they could not discuss with their superiors), the opportunity to commit the crime, and the ability to rationalize the fraud. Embezzlers are unique fraud offenders. They frequently confess upon being confronted and often indicate relief that they have been caught and can end their lies. Embezzlement is a crime in which women are the majority of those imprisoned (which is why it is sometimes called "pink collar crime"). The embezzlers Cressey studied were overwhelmingly from lower social classes. In sum, the embezzlers he studied are exceptionally unlike the elites about whom Sutherland was concerned because he recognized that their violations of law caused massive losses—often with impunity from prosecution. Nevertheless, Cressey generalized from his study of lower social class embezzlers to apply his "fraud triangle" theory to all fraudsters.

Cressey was so famous and well respected that the accounting profession enshrined his fraud triangle in its auditing standards—even though the fraud triangle's predictive failures are at their worst when applied to accounting control fraud. Outside auditors' central priority should be accounting control fraud—which causes greater losses than all other forms of corporate fraud combined and which can cause the failure of massive corporations. "Fraud triangle" analysis leads outside auditors to ignore what should be their central priority because it predicts that fraudsters are low status, poorly educated, and in embarrassing, personal financial crises. Cressey urged us to look at the bottom of the organizational chart to find fraud. The *last* employee or officer that an auditor would suspect of fraud under Cressey's analysis is the CEO. Even if the auditor overcame Cressey's presumption that senior officers, particularly the CEO, will rarely if ever engage in fraud, an auditor relying on the fraud triangle would only suspect that a CEO would engage in fraud if he were in a personal financial crisis. Even if the auditor were willing to consider that the CEO might engage in fraud and even if the auditor found that the CEO was engaged in a hidden, personal financial crisis, the fraud triangle would still mislead the auditor because it predicts that such CEOs will defraud the company through embezzlement. None of the fraud triangle's factors would help an outside auditor in most cases. First, control frauds, not embezzlers, cause the vast bulk of corporate fraud losses. Control frauds are led by elites—not lower social class embezzlers. Second, wealthy CEOs engage in accounting control fraud. They do not need any personal financial crisis to engage in fraud. Third, accounting control fraud inherently poses a far lower risk of prosecution for a CEO than does embezzlement while providing greater gains in income and status. This is why accounting, not embezzlement, is a control fraud's "weapon of choice." The officers who lead control frauds have always thought "outside the triangle"—it is time for criminologists, economists, finance specialists, auditors, and regulators to join (and combat) them.

As scholars who considered themselves white-collar criminologists increasingly chose to study minor occupational crimes by lower status offenders, the dismissive phrase "so-called white-collar crimes" became widespread. Some blue-collar criminologists sought to trivialize white-collar criminology on the bases that (1) all criminality arises from common genetic or environmental factors and (2) so-called white-collar criminals are overwhelmingly lower-status individuals who commit minor property crimes. James Q. Wilson and Richard Herrnstein (1985) blamed criminality on genetics (gender, intelligence—which they saw as primarily determined by genetics—and body-type, i.e., dumb, hulking males), age (young), and personality (aggressive, fearless, and impulsive). Their title: *Crime and Human Nature* reflects their claim that their theories explain all criminality (or at least all criminality worthy of study). In *The Bell Curve*, Herrnstein and Murray (1994) made clear their belief that intelligence was largely determined by genetics and that blacks were less intelligent than Asians and whites. They explicitly endorsed the link between low intelligence and criminality.

Wilson (political science) and Herrnstein (psychology) had little use for criminologists or their research. They viewed adult criminals as sharply distinct from normal human beings. Their theories imply that an experienced police officer could identify any "criminal" within minutes of meeting them. The police officer could tell from looking at them that their gender, age, and body type fit the profile of the classic offender. Even a brief conversation would reveal their low intelligence, high aggressiveness, and impulsiveness. "Criminals" could not rise to positions of authority in an honest business. They could not pass for respectable people. They would not be smart enough to be promoted; their aggressiveness would lead to constant altercations; their inability to control their impulses would cause recurrent embarrassing blunders, violence, or thefts that would get them fired. Even so-called white-collar criminals were not like "us." Wilson and Herrnstein's message to criminologists, policy, and policy makers was to look at losers at the bottom of the organization chart to find the criminal risk in any business. The CEO was the last person to suspect of criminality.

In *The General Theory of Crime* (1990), Michael Gottfredson and Travis Hirschi argued that their "control theory" explained all crime. Criminals have extremely poor control over their impulses. They are not like normal adults, who learn to control their impulses. Their poor impulse control marks them not only as criminals but also as more general failures in life. They lack the self-discipline essential to making the investments (e.g., saving money and getting a good education) that are increasingly essential to employment success, and they are more likely to engage in extremely risky and self-destructive behavior. Relying in part on "occupational crime" scholars, Gottfredson and Hirschi argued that so-called white-collar criminals were really low-status employees with poor impulse controls. Again, the message was to look for criminality only at the bottom rung of a company's employees.

Sutherland, of course, falsified Wilson's and Herrnstein's claim that low intelligence and poor impulse control were factors in predicting all criminality 45 years before publication of their work. He falsified Gottfredson's and Hirschi's claim that poor impulse control was a universal cause of crime over 50 years before their publication. Elite white-collar criminals are generally highly intelligent and older. They demonstrate higher impulse control than the general population. On many dimensions, elite white-collar criminals are the antithesis of Wilson's and Herrnstein's and Gottfredson's and Hirschi's supposed universal criminal traits.

Sutherland's work showed great sophistication along several related dimensions relevant to the later control theorists' claims that criminality was the sole province of the underclass and "organizational crime" scholars' findings that incarcerated "white-collar criminals" were frequently from lower social classes. First, he emphasized that the damage a relatively small number of elite white-collar criminals could do was immense—far exceeding that of all of the lower-class offenders. Second, he explained that incarceration should never be the measure of criminality given how rare it was to imprison elite white-collar criminals. Third, he made the logical point that the ultimate triumph of elite white-collar criminals is to have the state define actions as at most unlawful—not criminal. This is a moderately subtle distinction that all criminologists must master. An action that is criminal can be punished by criminal prosecution and, generally, by imprisonment (though Sutherland noted that elites were commonly fined or given probation instead of being imprisoned). An action that is unlawful can only be sanctioned by a civil or administrative order, e.g., that a bank "cease and desist" from a particular "unsafe and unsound" practice. In general, corporations that violate federal rules are acting unlawfully, but not criminally.

Sutherland never claimed that only high-status individuals committed crimes in the course of their employment. He defined "white-collar crime" to describe a type of criminal behavior that he felt was uniquely harmful, poorly understood and reported, and rarely prosecuted.

Wheeler and Rothman Point the Way

Few white-collar criminologists explored the significance of the third element of Sutherland's definition: "respectability." The powerful exceptions were Stanton Wheeler and Michael Rothman. They wrote persuasively about the large losses that seemingly legitimate organizations can cause (Wheeler and Rothman, 1982). Their work filled an odd gap in Sutherland's conceptualization of white-collar crime. As they note, Sutherland's research into white-collar crime was in the organizational context, but his definition ignored the conduct of the organization as an entity, focusing only on the individual "in the course of his occupation." The organization as a whole can cause even more damage. Under Sutherland's logic (and consistent with his research findings), "respectable" elite officers would use organizations as a "weapon" and cause exceptional harm. Geis' classic work on the heavy electrical equipment cartel (1967) had shown how elites created corrupt corporate cultures and deniability designed to make it more difficult to prosecute the senior officers.

Many white-collar scholars, particularly Geis and his colleagues and students, kept alive Sutherland's emphasis on how much greater damage elites could cause and researched the crimes of organizations, but the theories of organizational criminality either implied that it should be omnipresent (because it was prompted by the profit motive itself) or found primarily among failing firms and industries (where prior frauds were implicitly assumed not to have caused the failure). Wheeler and Rothman (1982) decried what they described as the "confusion" in the literature:

> Unfortunately, no one has specified what difference it makes when a crime is committed under the cover of an organization or in some occupational context. (pp. 1405–1406)

White-collar criminologists did not systematically study how an organization could be used as a weapon—they lacked expertise in accounting, finance, corporate governance, economics, and executive compensation. Traditional criminology has not even attempted to explain financial bubbles and crises. Wheeler and Rothman did not have this expertise and did not study the components of what makes a seemingly legitimate organization such a destructive weapon. This makes their ability to infer that there must be something special about seemingly legitimate organizations' ability to cause exceptionally large losses worthy of careful study by criminologists all the more impressive.

Wheeler and Rothman used an empirical methodology that was inherently crude due to the Department of Justice's failure to compile comprehensive data on crimes by organizations. That failure continues. Wheeler and Rothman's work was done as part of the immensely fruitful Yale studies in white-collar crime—the only time in recent (29 years ago!) history when the National Institute of Justice (NIJ) has funded a comprehensive study of white-collar crime. NIJ's continuing failure to fund research into elite white-collar crime is scandalous.

Wheeler and Rothman's (1982) empirical work used data drawn from a sample of presentence investigative reports (PSIs) of eight "presumptively white-collar crimes" (p. 1406). Wheeler and Rothman do contemplate that crimes committed by the organization may be more severe, but they did not envision control fraud, and they did not design their study to research situations in which the person controlling a seemingly legitimate organization would hone it as a "weapon." They made clear that they wanted to study the most *common* uses of the organization as weapon—not necessarily the most *destructive* uses. Their empirical findings are entirely consistent with control fraud theory, but because of their study design these findings offer only modest empirical information relevant to control fraud. Their findings also support Sutherland's definition of white-collar crime and further falsify the "control theorists'" claimed general theory of crime. Senior corporate officials who commit white-collar crimes in organizations are older and well educated. They cause "vastly greater" financial losses (pp. 1420–1421).

Wheeler and Rothman (1982) made insightful comments about the need for regulators to develop means of controlling corporate crime other than the criminal justice system.

> [M]ore thought should be given to alternative mechanisms of control. Is it possible, for example, to develop better warning signs that would indicate when a company is in financial trouble and, therefore, more likely to adopt illegal solutions to its problems? Given the power of the organizational form, should we create more windows into the organization so that outsiders can see more clearly what insiders are doing? Can we make better use of the accountants and lawyers whose presence lends legitimacy to organizational conduct? Maybe we can predict under what circumstances organizations will be more likely to violate the law. Perhaps more sophisticated indicators can be developed, allowing regulatory and other enforcement workers to focus all-too-limited investigative resources in areas where they will be most effective. (pp. 1425–1426)

Wheeler and Rothman (1982) deserve special praise for their innovative suggestions on the research topics that were most needed and methodological steps to redress the crippling data problems. They urged the creation of analogs to "ballistics laboratories" to analyze major crimes by organizations.

> The areas for research are fertile. What are the most crucial features of organization for the commission of specific white-collar offenses? Can we develop the organizational equivalent of the ballistics unit for common crime to identify readily features that link characteristic attributes of organizational style to particular offenses? These and related questions are prompted by viewing the organization as the white-collar criminal's most powerful weapon. (p. 1426)

The Confluence of Research Streams that Generated a New Approach to the Study of Elite White-Collar Criminology

The S&L Regulators (and an introduction to the economics a criminologist needs)

Wheeler and Rothman's work was brilliantly timed, for it came out just as an epidemic of accounting control fraud was about to cause the savings and loan (S&L) debacle. The S&L regulators began, in late 1983, to realize that interest rate risk was no longer the industry's primary problem and that a new type of S&L (the "high flier") and their CEOs were the problem. In 1984, the agency began to "reregulate" the industry and launched a campaign against the CEOs who were destroying "their" S&Ls.

The regulators came primarily from financial and legal backgrounds. Their primary influences were those fields and closely related fields such as economics, accounting, fraud, fiduciary duties, and corporate governance. I served as one of the regulators. We were often critical of the conventional wisdom and dominant methodologies in these fields, but we drew heavily on financial concepts in understanding accounting control fraud and developing regulatory strategies to counter the epidemic. In so doing, we demonstrated the utility of many of Wheeler and Rothman's insights and created a new type of white-collar criminology that added key financial concepts to explain *how* the people who controlled seemingly legitimate organizations used them as fraud weapons. To understand this new approach to the study of elite white-collar criminology, it is necessary to understand some key financial concepts. This section of the article assumes that the reader is unfamiliar with such concepts. It introduces new economics terms in **bold** and explains their meaning briefly (without mathematics or graphs). This level of detail is sufficient to enable even the beginning reader to understand how these economic concepts and terms helped produce a new criminology that can explain how those controlling seemingly legitimate firms can use them as a "weapon" to produce not only massive individual failures but also enormous financial bubbles and global financial crises.

Wheeler and Rothman published their "weapon" article in the *University of Michigan Law Review* (the law school from which I graduated); their suggestions could have greatly aided the regulators. Sadly, I was not aware of their article until 1993. Without their guidance, we were forced to rely primarily on economic discussions of fraud, which were rare, and the applicability to our problems was not obvious. Gary Becker (1968) wrote about the economics of deterring crime. Virtually all of his writings dealt with blue-collar crime. He asserted, incorrectly, that his model was applicable to white-collar crime (it is not because his optimal deterrence model requires knowing the incidence of each crime—which is impossible to know in the case of fraud). He did, however, champion two points that proved useful in studying elite white-collar crimes. First, he viewed those who commit crimes as normal humans instead of a distinct criminal class. Second, he assumed that criminals **optimized.**

George Akerlof (1970) wrote about anti-consumer control frauds in his famous article about markets for "lemons." A **"lemons" market** is a market in which the seller exploits its superior information (**"asymmetrical information"**) to defraud the customer by misleading him into believing that inferior quality goods (e.g., cars that are "lemons") are superior quality. Akerlof discussed the costs of this "dishonesty." He provided several insights critical to our success in developing the concept of control fraud and understanding how CEOs optimize accounting control fraud.

- The corporation has superior information about its operations ("asymmetrical information")

- Some seemingly legitimate firms are able and willing to maximize profits by committing fraud

- If a seller gains a competitive advantage through fraud, markets will drive honest competitors out of the industry—Akerlof (1970) termed this a "**Gresham's dynamic**" because bad cars and bad ethics drive good cars and good ethics out of the marketplace (pp. 489–490). A dishonest used car dealer could buy "lemons" at a very low price, use deceit to make customers pay a very high price for the car because they believed that it was a high quality car, and make large profits that no honest used car dealer could match.

- Lemons markets are **inefficient**—they misallocate capital and reward the dishonest. They harm not only the customer but also honest competitors.

Becker and Akerlof were awarded the Nobel Prize in economics in 1992 and 2001, respectively, so while the economic literature on fraud was sparse, the field's top scholars provided it.

The S&L regulators added elements drawn from their knowledge of economics, accounting, regulation, corporate governance, and executive compensation to these economic concepts in order to develop a theory of accounting control fraud. The three most important economics principles that we drew on were adverse selection, moral hazard, and agency cost theory.

- **Adverse selection:** when a lender cannot determine the credit risk that borrowers pose, it will charge an interest rate that is grossly inadequate to compensate for making loans to fraudulent or high risk borrowers. It will suffer large losses and eventually fail.

- **Moral hazard:** when rewards and risks are asymmetrical, an individual or company has a **perverse incentive** to engage in fraud or imprudent risks. For example, shareholders have "**limited liability.**" That means that if a corporation becomes **insolvent**—its **liabilities** (debts) exceed its **assets**—its shareholders can take advantage of the asymmetry of risk and reward. The formula has three parts: assets minus liabilities = **capital.** The shareholders own corporations and (theoretically) control them. The shareholders have the claim to the corporation's capital (if it is positive). If the corporation has no capital, its shareholders' financial interest is wiped out. They lose whatever they paid for their shares if the shares become worthless. If the corporation becomes deeply insolvent the shareholders are not responsible for any of those additional losses (that is what "limited liability" means)—the **creditors** suffer all the additional losses. (Creditors are the entities, usually banks, which lend money to the corporation.) The result is that shareholders of insolvent corporations have no downside risk. If the shareholders still control the insolvent corporation, they have a perverse incentive to cause it to engage in control fraud or wildly imprudent risks. Control fraud is a "sure thing"—if optimized, it produces guaranteed, record "profits." The great bulk of these exceptional profits will go to the shareholders—not the creditors. The same is true of taking (honest) extreme risks, but the greater the risk the lower the chance that it will succeed. Moral hazard occurs when a party insulated from risk behaves differently than if fully exposed to the risk; the benefits of a behavior outweigh the costs. The shareholders of an insolvent corporation have no downside risk and immense upside potential. This creates powerful, perverse incentives to engage in accounting control fraud.

- **Agency cost theory:** shareholders own corporations, therefore, they are its **principals.** Officers and directors run corporations as "**agents**" for the shareholders. It is very difficult for the shareholders to monitor these agents, so there is a serious danger that the agents will act "**unfaithfully**" to further their own interests at the expense of the shareholders. (Traditionally, the law has imposed **fiduciary duties of loyalty and care** on officers and directors in order to induce them to act faithfully.) Agency cost theory predicts that shareholders will bear costs designed to increase the chance that the officers and directors will act in the shareholders' interests, e.g., by providing bonuses based on performance.

While the regulators drew heavily on economic theories relevant to control fraud, they did so selectively. They disregarded the core principles of modern finance and economics and their defining methodology. The core principle of modern finance is "**the efficient markets hypothesis**" **(EMH).** There are multiple versions ("weak," "semi-strong," and "strong") of the EMH. The technical details are not critical for these purposes. The key is that accounting control fraud would inherently make the stock markets grossly inefficient under any version of EMH. Virtually everything in modern finance assumes that stock markets are efficient, so control fraud theory falsifies modern finance.

The "**efficient contracts**" **hypothesis** is not microeconomics' sole pillar, but it is one of the core assumptions underlying the study of the price system. It predicts that lenders will accurately evaluate the **credit risk** of lending to particular classes of borrowers and will price the risk appropriately to compensate themselves. In plain English, lenders will charge riskier borrowers higher interest rates.

Economics and finance are supremely proud of their reliance on quantitative analysis. They believe it demonstrates that they are hard sciences. Economists refer to their use of statistics as **econometrics.** The greatest methodological insult an economist can make is to call someone's work

"merely anecdotal." The central problem the regulators faced with econometrics is that it provides the worst possible information about accounting control fraud. This article explains why optimizing accounting control fraud produces guaranteed, record "income." Econometric studies typically use either income or stock price as the outcome variable (and accounting "income" is the key driver of stock prices). If an economist were asked in 2005 to study whether it was good public policy to permit banks to make mortgage loans without verifying and documenting the borrower's income, employment, and assets she would design an econometric study to test whether banks that made such loans produced higher income (profit). If making "no doc" loans optimized accounting fraud (and this article shows why it did), then the econometric study would have to show a strong *positive correlation* between making "no doc" loans and increased profitability. The economist would then conclude that there was strong empirical evidence that allowing lenders to make "no doc" loans would be desirable. In reality, "no doc" loans were known in the trade as "liar's loans." These loans eventually caused the massive losses characteristic of accounting control fraud. A study done now would reveal that the true "sign" of the correlation has emerged and that it is the reverse of that found by prior econometric studies. (Making "no doc" loans is *negatively correlated* with bank income, i.e., banks that made "no doc" loans were deeply unprofitable.)

The regulators used an alternative methodology. We conducted an "autopsy" of each S&L placed in **conservatorship** or **receivership** to determine the causes. The regulators can take over failing or failed banks and appoint an official (a conservator) to manage the bank and attempt to stabilize it or to sell its assets (receivership). The number of takeovers of failed S&Ls was so great that it created a substantial research opportunity. The "sample" of S&Ls that we reviewed was not random. The agency attempted to prioritize for takeover the worst accounting control frauds. The results of our analyses demonstrated that accounting control frauds exhibited a distinctive operational pattern that would have been profoundly irrational for any honest firm. The identification of the pattern led the agency to be even more effective in targeting accounting control frauds for early closure. This made the sample consist over time even more heavily of accounting control frauds.

The formula for a lender optimizing accounting control fraud has four parts:

1. Grow extremely rapidly (Ponzi-like)
2. Lend to the **uncreditworthy** (borrowers who have high **credit risk,** i.e., they are unlikely to repay their loans—a borrower who does not make scheduled payments "**defaults**" on the loan)
3. Extreme **leverage** (the firm finances itself primarily by borrowing money instead of by raising capital through the sale of stock or retaining profits)

4. Grossly inadequate **loss reserves** (the lender does not set aside funds it will need to pay for future **defaults**—this creates fraudulent "income" or profits in the early years and leads to catastrophic losses in later years)

The autopsies revealed other aspects of the distinctive pattern that arises from accounting control fraud:

- The frauds were led from the top by those controlling the S&L
- The frauds invested overwhelmingly in a small category of assets that were optimal for accounting fraud (because it was easy to inflate their market values)
- The first two parts of the formula are intertwined: it is very difficult to grow extremely rapidly as a lender in a mature, competitive market by making high quality loans, but it is easy to grow rapidly by making bad loans (and the lender can charge a premium interest rate for such loans)
- In order to make large quantities of bad loans a lender must gut its underwriting and suborn its **internal and external controls** (e.g., the credit committee, the internal auditor, and the external audit firm)
- They invariably chose top tier audit firms and typically were able to get "**clean**" **audit opinions** "blessing" financial statements showing high profitability and minimal losses even when the S&L was insolvent and deeply unprofitable (a clean audit opinion certifies that a business has prepared its financial statements in accordance with **generally accepted accounting principles (GAAP)**
- They covered up their losses on bad loans by refinancing those loans
- The large, guaranteed "profits" allowed CEOs to use normal corporate compensation mechanisms to convert firm assets to the CEO's benefit

The reader may have noted how closely our actions resemble Wheeler and Rothman's (1982) methodological and policy recommendations:

> What are the most crucial features of organization for the commission of specific white-collar offenses? Can we develop the organizational equivalent of the ballistics unit for common crime to identify readily features that link characteristic attributes of organizational style to particular offenses?

> Perhaps more sophisticated indicators can be developed, allowing regulatory and other enforcement workers to focus all-too-limited investigative resources in areas where they will be most effective. (pp. 1425–1426)

In addition to being able to identify the accounting control frauds while they were still reporting record profits and minimal losses, understanding the fraud pattern allowed the regulators to target the frauds' Achilles' heel. A Ponzi scheme must grow rapidly or collapse. The agency passed a rule restricting growth, which caused the control frauds to implode.

The regulators also recognized that the Ponzi nature of the frauds, the CEOs' efforts to optimize accounting fraud, and the fact that certain assets and particular states (due to exceptionally weak regulation) combined to make an epidemic of accounting control fraud the perfect device for hyperinflating a **financial bubble** (a sharp rise in the price of a category of assets not caused by economic fundamentals). The regulators deliberately burst the Southwest regional bubble in commercial real estate.

Criminologists, Regulators and Economists Combine to Create a New Criminology of Elite White-Collar Crime

Wheeler and Rothman proved influential with a group of sociologists (Calavita, Pontell, and Tillman, 1997) with expertise in white-collar crime who received a rare NIJ grant to study an epidemic of elite white-collar crime—the S&L debacle. Pontell and his colleagues interviewed a large number of regulatory and law enforcement officials and wrote extensively about the role of elite white-collar criminology. They realized that the debacle demonstrated Wheeler and Rothman's primary thesis that the organization was used as a "weapon" to cause enormous damage to the nation and profit to the senior officers.

The criminologists/sociologists did not, however, have expertise in accounting, economics, finance, law, or corporate governance, and they struggled to find regulators and prosecutors who could explain *how* the frauds were using the S&L as a weapon. They attempted to use (1) the existing white-collar crime categories and (2) to fit the regulators' motif in explaining the debacle—"risk"—into a criminological framework. The first attempt led them to coin the term "collective embezzlement." This term proved both vague and misleading. It was vague because it was unclear what the "collective" was, and it was misleading because the key to accounting control fraud is that it closely approaches a perfect crime because the large, guaranteed (albeit fictional) "profits" allow the person controlling the corporation to convert its assets to his personal benefit through seemingly normal corporate compensation mechanisms (bonuses, salaries, perks, stock options, and the appreciation in value of stock owned by the CEO). Embezzlement, by contrast, requires the employee to take an unlawful action to convert the firm's assets to the employee's benefit, e.g., by writing an unauthorized check on the firm's bank account for his own benefit.

The term "unlawful risk taking" was also misleading. The criminologists argued that it described what was known as the "heads, I win; tails, FSLIC loses" (or "gambling for resurrection") strategy. (FSLIC was the acronym for Federal Savings and Loan Insurance Corporation.) The purported strategy was an example of "moral hazard." The idea was that an insolvent S&L would take extreme (imprudent) risks knowing that if it won its gamble the shareholders would win, while if it lost the gamble the creditors (in the first instance) would bear the losses. Ultimately, however, because the S&L was insolvent and because an S&L's creditors are overwhelmingly depositors, the federal insurance fund for S&Ls (FSLIC in that era) would bear the cost because it guaranteed that insured depositors would suffer no loss when an S&L failed. There were two difficulties with the concept of unlawful risk taking. First, it wasn't unlawful. Taking imprudent risks can be a civil and a regulatory wrong, but it is not a crime. Second, it didn't describe a real strategy. The conventional economic wisdom was that (honest) "gambling for resurrection" caused the second phase of the S&L debacle, but that was inaccurate (as the criminologists' research confirmed).

In 1993, the criminologists repeatedly interviewed me because I was the regulator who had been responsible for the autopsies of the failed S&Ls and provided the staff leadership of the reregulation of the industry in 1984–87. I was also serving as the Deputy Staff Director of the National Commission on Financial Institution Reform, Recovery and Enforcement, which was charged with researching and reporting on the causes of the S&L debacle. In that capacity, I met and collaborated with economists George Akerlof and Paul Romer, who were independently investigating the role of elite fraud in the debacle. The result of these discussions was a multi-disciplinary cross-fertilization. The criminologists and I shared extensive scholarship about the debacle and engaged in detailed discussions about the causes. This alerted me for the first time to these critical criminological concepts:

- The organization as a weapon
- "Criminogenic environment"
- "Systems capacity"
- "Neutralization"

I also engaged in detailed discussions and exchanged scholarship about the debacle (and about Drexel Burnham Lambert and Michael Milken) with Akerlof and Romer (1993). In particular, I emphasized the actual mechanisms that accounting control frauds used, why these mechanisms optimized accounting fraud, and the tradeoff between the amounts of corporate funds the CEO could convert to his personal benefit versus the risk of prosecution. I also explained why the control frauds' distinctive lending practices would never be used by an honest S&L "gambling for resurrection." Akerlof and Romer's endorsement of the concept of control fraud and the ability of widespread control fraud to hyperinflate financial bubbles was of great importance because it represented a refutation of the conventional economic wisdom about the debacle by economists of impeccable reputations.

The criminologists gained both a coherent explanation of the mechanisms that accounting control frauds used and confirmation that what they were observing at the most expensive S&L failures were criminal frauds. They had always been uncomfortable with the conventional economic wisdom ("gambling for resurrection") about the debacle and now they had a firm basis (1) from the regulators' findings, (2) from two top economists, and (3) from the National Commission on Financial Institution Reform, Recovery and Enforcement rejecting the conventional wisdom and confirming the decisive role of elite white-collar criminals at the most expensive S&L failures. They also confirmed the importance of systems capacity and criminogenic environments in explaining why the epidemic of accounting control fraud occurred in the S&L industry during the 1980s. The cross-fertilization demonstrated the enormous advantages of multi-disciplinary and multi-methodological research.

The Conventional Economic Wisdom Did Not Recognize that Criminology had Falsified the Efficient Markets Hypothesis

White-collar criminology falsified the efficient market hypothesis over a half century prior to the housing bubble. Savings and loan (S&L) regulators and criminologists recognized the decisive role that fraud played in causing the worst losses during the S&L debacle and the fact that these frauds were led by the CEOs and used accounting as their "weapon of choice." Fraudulent S&Ls always used accounting fraud to overstate asset values and to hide real losses, producing inflated market values for their stocks. This is impossible if markets are efficient. The regulators (NCFIRRE, 1993), and two prominent economists, (Akerlof and Romer, 1993) showed how these frauds hyperinflated the regional bubble in commercial real estate. The existence of the bubble and the S&L frauds' role in causing it to hyperinflate further falsified the efficient markets and contracts hypotheses.

Unfortunately, Akerlof and Romer assumed that the inefficiency was caused by the existence of federal deposit insurance and did not falsify the general efficiency of markets and contracts. Their logic was that private market discipline is expensive for creditors and that if the creditors (depositors in the S&L context) were protected from loss by deposit insurance they would not exert effective discipline (Akerlof and Romer, 1993). More traditional economists simply ignored the research by the criminologists and regulators.

White-collar criminologists and regulators writing about the S&L "control frauds" never accepted the claim that deposit insurance caused the failure of private market discipline. "Control frauds" are seemingly legitimate entities used as fraud "weapons" by the individuals who control them (Black, 2005; see also Wheeler and Rothman, 1992). They saw that *uninsured* creditors (including subordinated debt holders—who traditional economics presumes are the ideal source of discipline due to their financial exposure and greater risk exposure)—and shareholders failed to exercise effective discipline against any S&L control fraud. Criminologists argued that control frauds did not simply evade effective private market discipline, but actually profited from it because even uninsured creditors and shareholders funded the control frauds' growth.

Economists, however, ignored the criminologists' and the regulators' findings, theories, and methodologies. Their belief in efficient markets and contracts became even more fervent as the housing bubble hyperinflated. Their failure to consider criminologists' findings is ironic because criminologists have built control fraud theory in substantial part on economic theory.

Criminologists Have Developed Unique Expertise in Understanding:

- Which environments are most "criminogenic" for accounting control fraud
- Why individual accounting control frauds can cause massive losses
- How control frauds optimize accounting fraud
- Why accounting control frauds produce guaranteed, extreme "profits"
- How executive compensation optimizes CEO looting via accounting fraud
- How executive compensation aids accounting fraud
- How executive compensation reduces whistle blowing
- Why control frauds routinely defeat private market discipline
- Why control frauds defeat regulators who do not understand how they operate
- How control frauds suborn internal and external controls and make them allies
- Why control fraud epidemics occur
- Why control fraud epidemics extend and hyperinflate financial bubbles
- Why econometric studies are perverse when a bubble is inflating
- Why accounting control frauds follow a distinctive operational pattern
- Why accounting control frauds have an "Achilles' heel"
- Why accounting control frauds erode trust and can shut down markets

Criminology has a comprehensive set of theoretical, methodological, and policy findings that could be of critical help in avoiding or minimizing financial bubbles and financial crises. It is well past time for economists and policy makers to learn from criminologists and to develop a comprehensive theory of control fraud. Economics offers many of the building blocks to create such a theory. Whether or not economists make the intellectual journey to use these building blocks to build a comprehensive theory, modern criminologists have recognized that they must understand economics, finance, and accounting if they are to understand the most harmful white-collar crimes.

Optimizing Accounting Control Fraud

Recall that the formula for a lender optimizing accounting control fraud has four parts:

- Grow extremely rapidly (Ponzi-like)
- Lend to the uncreditworthy
- Extreme leverage
- Grossly inadequate loss reserves

The central fact that must be understood is that this formula produces nearly immediate, extraordinary, and guaranteed short-term "profits." The formula is simple accounting mathematics. Accounting fraud is a sure thing—not a "risk" as we think of that term in finance (Akerlof and Romer, 1993; Black, 2005). Accounting frauds rarely engage in fraud for the purpose of slightly increasing reported profits. They typically engage in fraud to report exceptional profits.

The reason that extreme growth optimizes accounting fraud is obvious, but the concept that *deliberately* making uncreditworthy loans optimizes short-term accounting profits is counter-intuitive. The first two ingredients in the accounting fraud formula are related. Lenders in a mature market such as home mortgages cannot simply decide to grow rapidly by making *good* loans. Lenders can grow rapidly by making good loans through two means. They can acquire competitors (a strategy that inherently cannot be followed by a very large number of lenders), or they can drop their yields and seek to compete on the basis of price (i.e., their mortgage interest rate in this context). Their competitors are almost certain to match any reduction in mortgage interest rates, so the latter strategy generally fails to provide substantial growth while the lower price leads to reduced "profit" margins.

Lending to the uncreditworthy, however, allows exceptional growth and allows one to charge a higher interest rate. The combination maximizes accounting income. As James Pierce, Executive Director of the National Commission on Financial Institution Reform, Recovery and Enforcement (NCFIRRE) explained:

> Accounting abuses also provided the ultimate perverse incentive: it paid to seek out bad loans because only those who had no intention of repaying would be willing to offer the high loan fees and interest required for the best looting. It was rational for operators to drive their institutions ever deeper into insolvency as they looted them. (NCFIRRE, 1993, pp. 10–11)

"Bo" Cutter, former managing partner of the prestigious Wall Street firm Warburg Pincus, describes the same phenomenon during the nonprime lending crisis:

> In fact, by 2006 and early 2007 everyone thought we were headed to a cliff, but no one knew when or what the triggering mechanism would be. The capital market experts I was listening to all thought the banks were going crazy, and that the terms of major loans being offered by the banks were nuttiness of epic proportions. (Black, 2009)

When competitors mimic this optimization strategy, the net effect of this competition further optimizes accounting fraud. This perverse competitive effect is also counterintuitive. As more firms emulated the initial accounting control fraud strategy of making subprime and "liar's loans" to buyers who could not repay the loans, the competition among the lenders reduced nonprime mortgage interest rates. That effect, of course, reduced their accounting profits. "Alt A" loans were (falsely) represented by their issuers as equivalent in risk to (extremely low risk) "prime" loans. They were made without verifying the borrower's most important representations. (In the trade, they were known as "liar's loans" because failing to verify such information maximizes "adverse selection" and leads to pervasive deceit.) The dominant effects of rapidly expanding nonprime lending, however, were to massively expand growth and to extend and hyperinflate the housing bubble. The net effect of increased competition among nonprime lenders was to substantially increase short-term "profits."

The greater a firm's leverage, the higher the ratio of its debt to its capital, the greater its return on capital. The greater its return on capital, the more likely its stock is to increase in value, and the larger the executive compensation.

If the lender were to place the loss reserves appropriate to lending (and required by generally accepted accounting principles) primarily to the borrowers least likely to repay the loans, its "profits" would disappear and it would report that it was insolvent and unprofitable. The executives would not be paid any bonuses, and their stock options and shares would be worthless. It would also make it impossible to sell their nonprime mortgages to others. Accounting control frauds therefore do not comply with GAAP and record proper loss reserves. This optimizes their short-term "profits" but constitutes securities fraud if they are publicly traded. A.M. Best warned in its 2005 report that "the industry's reserves-to-loan ratio has been setting new record lows for the past four years."

Optimizing the Ability to Make Bad Loans

The glaring difficulty with a lender adopting a strategy of deliberately making an enormous number of bad loans is that an honest lender's entire institutional structure and culture is designed to prevent bad loans. Large lenders (and bubbles are inherently the product of the actions of large lenders) have multiple layers of internal and external controls that are typically extremely effective in preventing bad home mortgage loans. Losses on prime home mortgage loans are generally well under one percent.

The internal controls at large lenders are supposed to include the loan officer, the loan officer's supervisor, loan underwriters, internal appraisers, the credit committee, the senior risk manager, the internal auditor, the audit committee, the chief operations officer (COO), CFO and CEO, the asset/liability committee, and the board of directors. The external controls include the outside auditor, rating agencies, and appraisers. A large lender will have roughly a dozen overlapping controls that are supposed to stop any practice that leads to significant numbers of preventable bad loans.

Each of these control layers must fail—contemporaneously—to permit an overall strategy of making tens of thousands of bad loans. The odds against each of these controls failing contemporaneously and independently due to random events are miniscule. The odds that the controls will all fail independently and the failures will continue for five years without being restored are essentially zero.

Lenders that engage in accounting control fraud need to end normal, prudent underwriting and to pervert multiple layers of "controls" into non-controls that will (1) endorse a lending strategy of making bad loans, (2) fail to book loss reserves that will cover the resultant losses, (3) produce and "bless" fraudulent accounting statements that purport to show that making bad loans is exceptionally profitable, and (4) pay extraordinary bonuses premised on the fraudulent profits. It is impossible to produce and maintain such a pervasively fraudulent firm (and suborn the external controls) without the active support of the senior officers controlling the firm (Black, Calavita, and Pontell, 1995; Calavita et al., 1997).

Creating a Corrupt "Tone at the Top" Suborns Internal Controls

A large firm obviously cannot send a memorandum or e-mail message to a thousand employees instructing them to commit accounting fraud. The firm can, however, send the same message without any risk of criminal prosecution through its compensation system.

Modern executive compensation systems suborn internal controls. (Control frauds do not "defeat" controls—they turn them into oxymoronic allies.) The Business Roundtable is made up of the nation's 100 largest firms. In response to the series of accounting control fraud failures (e.g., Enron and WorldCom) in 2001 and 2002, the Roundtable chose Franklin Raines, then Fannie Mae's CEO, as its spokesman to explain why that epidemic of fraud had occurred. In a *Business Week* interview he was asked:

> [*Businessweek:*] We've had a terrible scandal on Wall Street. What is your view?
>
> [Raines:] Investment banking is a business that's so denominated in dollars that the temptations are great, so you have to have very strong rules. My experience is where there is a one-to-one relation between if I do X, money will hit my pocket, you tend to see people doing X a lot. You've got to be very careful about that. Don't just say: "If you hit this revenue number, your bonus is going to be this." It sets up an incentive that's overwhelming. You wave enough money in front of people, and good people will do bad things. (*Business Week*, 2003)

Unfortunately, Raines' insights stemmed from his implementation of just such a system. Raines knew that the unit that should have been most resistant to this "overwhelming" financial incentive, Fannie Mae's Internal Audit department, had succumbed to it. Mr. Rajappa, its head, instructed his internal auditors in a formal address in 2000 (and provided the text to Raines, who praised it):

> By now every one of you must have 6.46 [the earnings per share bonus target] branded in your brains. You must be able to say it in your sleep, you must be able to recite it forwards and backwards, you must have a raging fire in your belly that burns away all doubts, you must live, breath and dream 6.46, you must be obsessed on 6.46. . . . After all, thanks to Frank [Raines], we all have a lot of money riding on it. . . . We must do this with a fiery determination, not on some days, not on most days but day in and day out, give it your best, not 50%, not 75%, not 100%, but 150%. Remember, Frank has given us an opportunity to earn not just our salaries, benefits, raises, ESPP, but substantially over and above if we make 6.46. So it is our *moral obligation* to give well above our 100% and if we do this, we would have made tangible contributions to Frank's goals [emphasis in original]. (Office of Federal Housing Enterprise Oversight, 2006, p. 4)

Internal audit is the "anti-canary" in the corporate "mines"; by the time it is suborned every other unit is corrupted.

The CEO does not have to order, or be aware of, the specific frauds—some employees will do whatever is needed to "earn" their top bonus. The CEO simply communicates—by paying large bonuses based on fictional profits—that he does not care how they meet the target. This can create a perfect crime, for it gives the CEO ideal deniability. The most common example of this in the housing crisis was the nearly universal practice among nonprime lenders of paying loan officers bonuses on the basis of loan volume irrespective of loan quality. As their peers see that the worst loan officers who make the worst loans maximize their bonuses (and that the "controls" approve even horrific loans), many of them will mimic the worst loan officers' practices. The most moral loan officers leave. This is one example of a Gresham's dynamic in which bad ethics drive good ethics out of the marketplace.

By paying large bonuses even to junior officers if extreme "profits" are obtained, the CEO also minimizes the risk of whistleblowers. Whistleblowers are the most common means by which authorities learn of these elite frauds. They pose a special risk to the senior officers running an accounting fraud because they can place the officers on notice of the firm's fraudulent accounting practices by communicating the frauds to the officers. Ignoring the fraudulent practices, or covering them up, can establish the senior officers' knowledge of the frauds and their intent to permit or assist the fraud. Even if the whistleblower communicates the fraud only to junior officers they may inform the senior managers or the internal or external auditors in the belief that it reduces their risk of prosecution. Some potential whistleblowers may be discouraged from blowing the whistle because they will lose their bonuses. More, however, are likely to be discouraged from blowing the whistle if scores of their friends and peers will lose their bonuses and cease to be their friends.

When the CEO leads the fraud and uses executive compensation to suborn internal "controls," he and his subordinate officers can also use the power to hire, fire, reward, and discipline to break any resistance to making bad loans. The best employees will reject bad loans—and be criticized and overruled by their superiors. If they persist in rejecting bad loans they can be disciplined or fired—and their vacant cubicle will serve as a warning to their peers. It is less grisly than the King placing his enemy's head on a pike but probably more effective in deterring undesired (desirable) behavior.

Using Compensation to Suborn External Controls

Accounting control frauds optimize their frauds not by "defeating" external controls, but rather by suborning them and turning them into their most valuable allies. U.S. accounting control frauds typically retain top tier audit firms precisely because these firms' reputations are so valuable in assisting their frauds. The value of a top tier audit firm "blessing" fraudulent financial statements is obvious. The blessing helps the control fraud deceive creditors, investors, and regulators. It also makes it difficult to prosecute the CEO who "relied" on the outside auditors.

The value of having one of the top three rating agencies give a collateralized debt obligation (CDO) "tranche" backed by "liar's loans" a "AAA" rating is even more obvious. (CDOs are a variety of "structured finance" in which the cash flows from the underlying mortgages in order of priority to the owners of different layers of financial derivatives. The top CDO layer (tranche) has the first claim to cash flows and is the least toxic of an extraordinarily toxic instrument. A tranche rated "AAA" (while the nonprime secondary market was still operating), was considerably more valuable and more liquid. The "AAA" rating also appears to validate the "high" quality of the nonprime assets and demonstrate that the nonprime mortgage lenders must be prudent.

Appraisers cannot provide substantial reputation advantages to a control fraud because no appraisal firm has a national reputation remotely analogous to a top tier audit or ratings firm. Nevertheless, outside appraisers can appear to provide an independent, expert, and professional opinion of the market value of the pledged real estate. That opinion, if materially inflated, offers two advantages to accounting control frauds. It allows the lender to make a substantially larger loan (which increases fees and "income"), and it allows the lender to claim that the loan is prudent even if the borrower defaults. Appraisers can make horrific loans appear to be good loans.

Control frauds suborn each of these controls primarily by using compensation to create a Gresham's dynamic. In the case of audit firms, they also exploit "agency" problems. It is important to understand that while a Gresham's dynamic can lead to endemic corruption of these "controls," they can cause a crisis by suborning only a small portion of the professionals. The senior officers at the control fraud choose the professionals the lender will employ, and they can choose the weakest link to provide the opinions they need to aid their accounting fraud.

The existence of a strong Gresham's dynamic has been confirmed in each of these three external "controls." The National Commission on Financial Institution Reform Recovery and Enforcement (NCFIRRE, 1993) reported on the causes of the S&L debacle. It documented the distinctive pattern of business practices that lenders typically employ to optimize accounting control fraud.

> The typical large failure was a stockholder-owned, state-chartered institution in Texas or California where regulation and supervision were most lax. . . . [It] had grown at an extremely rapid rate, achieving high concentrations of assets in risky ventures. . . . [E]very accounting trick available was used to make the institution look profitable, safe, and solvent. Evidence of fraud was invariably present as was the ability of the operators to "milk" the organization through high dividends and salaries, bonuses, perks and other means. (pp. 3–4)
>
> [A]busive operators of S&L[s] sought out compliant and cooperative accountants. The result was a sort of "Gresham's Law" in which the bad professionals forced out the good. (p. 76)

The typical large S&L fraud invariably used a top tier audit firm and was successful in getting "clean" opinions for several years. Enron, World-Com and their ilk were consistently able to obtain clean opinions from top tier audit firms, as were the large nonprime specialty lenders.

A major rating agency has confirmed that customers created a Gresham's dynamic during the current crisis. Raymond W. McDaniel, chairman and CEO of Moody's Corporation, referred to a "slippery slope" of events.

> What happened in '04 and '05 with respect to subordinated tranches is . . . our competition, Fitch and S&P, went nuts. Everything was investment grade. We tried to alert the market. We said we're not rating it. This stuff isn't investment grade. No one cared because the machine just kept going. (Woellert and Kopecki, 2008)

Moody's lost 50% of its business share when it sought to give more realistic (i.e., lower) ratings to the most toxic tranches of toxic CDOs. However, one should not have too much sympathy for Moody's loss of market share on "subordinated tranches." The real money for the agencies on CDOs was the top tranche. The agencies (ludicrously) helped their clients structure their CDO tranches such that the overwhelming bulk of CDOs composed of nonprime loans was purportedly top tier. Moody's joined its peers in giving virtually all of the (toxic) top tier "AAA" or "AA" ratings even though that was factually absurd. Its competitors, by giving even the toxic subordinated tranches "investment grade" ratings, misled pension funds and governments that acquired billions of dollars of ultra-toxic assets that eventually suffered nearly total losses in market value.

The Gresham's dynamic in appraisals has been established repeatedly in surveys of appraisers.

> A new survey of the national appraisal industry found that 90 percent of appraisers reported that mortgage brokers, real estate agents, lenders and even consumers have put pressure on them to raise property valuations to enable deals to go through. That percentage is up sharply from a parallel survey conducted in 2003, when 55 percent of appraisers reported attempts to influence their findings and 45 percent reported "never." Now the latter category is down to just 10 percent. . . .
>
> The survey found that 75 percent of appraisers reported "negative ramifications" if they refused to cooperate and come in with a higher valuation. Sixty-eight percent said they lost the client—typically a mortgage broker or lender—following their refusal to fudge the numbers, and 45 percent reported not receiving payment for their appraisal. . . .
>
> Though mortgage brokers were ranked the most common source of pressure—71 percent of appraisers said brokers had sought to interfere with their work—agents came in a close second at 56 percent. Both numbers were up significantly from where they were in the 2003 survey. Also identified as sources of pressure were consumers—typically home sellers (35 percent)—as well as mortgage lenders (33 percent) and appraisal management companies (25 percent). (Harney, 2007)

Appraisal profession leaders have been remarkably open about the destructive effects of Gresham's dynamic.

> Given the decline in mortgage activity, appraisers are scrambling for work in a way that's testing the industry's moral fiber, especially in hard-hit markets such as South Florida. It's getting to the point where, says Faravelli [Manager of the California Association of Real Estate Appraisers], with unusual candor for a trade-group official, "You show me an honest appraiser and I'll show you a [financially] poor one" (Pummer, 2007).

The intimidation can be extreme. Mr. Inserra, an Illinois appraiser, testified before Congress about a physical threat:

> Inserra knows how intense the pressure to inflate values can get. Three years ago, he found himself battling one of his largest clients. The bank's senior vice president in charge of mortgage lending tried to get Inserra to "hit a number," industry parlance for inflating the appraisal. He wouldn't do it.

> "The discussion got so heated," recalled Inserra, "that he threatened to do harm to my family if I didn't cooperate. I really thought he might do it. I got a restraining order from a judge."

> In the end, the banker didn't hurt his family, but he did punish Inserra by depriving him of the $200,000 in annual business he had been getting from the bank (Pummer, 2007).

Inflating an appraisal is an act of fraud and the only reason that a lender would seek an inflated appraisal—or tolerate inflated appraisals—is if it is an accounting control fraud. Lenders and their trade associations emphasize this point.

> "We have absolutely no incentive to have appraisers inflate home values," Washington Mutual said in a release. "We use third-party appraisal companies to make sure that appraisals are objective and accurate." (Gormley, 2007)

The Mortgage Bankers Association (MBA) first noted why it would be irrational for a lender to inflate appraised values, particularly during a mortgage fraud epidemic.

> If the appraisal contains inflated, inaccurate or material omissions related to the value of the property, the lender will likely suffer a greater loss if the loan goes into foreclosure. Furthermore, a borrower who obtains financing based on an inflated value may be less likely to continue making payments when he or she discovers the value of their home is lower than the outstanding loan balance.

> MBA recognizes that mortgage fraud is a burgeoning crime that is impacting more and more companies and communities.

> MBA opposes all fraud that affects the mortgage industry, and it is important to understand that mortgage lending institutions do not benefit from inflated appraisals. (MBA, 2007b)

MBA's logic is impeccable, but it does not explain why lenders were a significant direct source of pressure to inflate appraisals and why they permitted their agents (e.g., loan brokers) to be an even larger source of appraisal intimidation given their incentive and ability to ensure that appraisals they relied on were not inflated. Why did so many lenders directly, or indirectly through their agents, push for inflated appraisals when inflated appraisals are disastrous for the lender? Why did the nonprime specialty lenders routinely pay their loan officers and brokers primarily through compensation systems that created an intense incentive for them to pressure the appraisers to inflate the appraisals? The answer is accounting control fraud. Inflating the appraisal allowed the lender to make more, and larger, loans to uncreditworthy borrowers who would pay a premium interest rate. That maximized short-term accounting "profits" and the senior officers' compensation. Accounting control frauds do not act to further the best interests of the lender. They maximize the CEO's interests at the expense of the lender. The CEO loots the firm through accounting fraud.

The New York Attorney General's investigation of Washington Mutual (WAMU) (one of the largest nonprime mortgage lenders) and its appraisal practices supports this dynamic.

> New York Attorney General Andrew Cuomo said [that] a major real estate appraisal company colluded with the nation's largest savings and loan companies to inflate the values of homes nationwide, contributing to the subprime mortgage crisis.
>
> "This is a case we believe is indicative of an industrywide problem," Cuomo said in a news conference.
>
> Cuomo announced the civil lawsuit against eAppraiseIT that accuses the First American Corp. subsidiary of caving in to pressure from Washington Mutual Inc. to use a list of "proven appraisers" who he claims inflated home appraisals.
>
> He also released e-mails that he said show executives were aware they were violating federal regulations. The lawsuit filed in state Supreme Court in Manhattan seeks to stop the practice, recover profits and assess penalties.
>
> "These blatant actions of First American and eAppraiseIT have contributed to the growing foreclosure crisis and turmoil in the housing market," Cuomo said in a statement. "By allowing Washington Mutual to hand-pick appraisers who inflated values, First American helped set the current mortgage crisis in motion."
>
> "First American and eAppraiseIT violated that independence when Washington Mutual strong-armed them into a system designed to rip off homeowners and investors alike," he said (Gormley, 2007).

Note particularly Attorney General Cuomo's claim that WAMU "rip[ped] off . . . investors." That is an express claim that it operated as an accounting control fraud and inflated appraisals in order to maximize accounting "profits." Pressure to inflate appraisals was endemic among nonprime lending specialists.

> Appraisers complained on blogs and industry message boards of being pressured by mortgage brokers, lenders and even builders to "hit a number," in industry parlance, meaning the other party wanted them to appraise the home at a certain amount regardless of what it was actually worth. Appraisers risked being blacklisted if they stuck to their guns. "We know that it went on and we know just about everybody was involved to some extent," said Marc Savitt, the National Association of Mortgage Banker's immediate past president and chief point person during the first half of 2009 (White, 2009).

Modern Executive Compensation Minimizes the CEO's Risk of Prosecution

In addition to creating the perverse incentives discussed above, modern executive compensation allows CEOs running accounting control frauds to become enormously rich while minimizing the risk of detection and prosecution. Modern executive compensation is premised on the claim that senior officers must be paid extremely high bonuses to incentivize them to remain with the firm. Proponents claim that such compensation "aligns" the CEO's interests with those of the shareholders (Easterbrook and Fischel, 1991). Control fraud theory demonstrates that it can do the opposite—further misalign the interests of fraudulent CEOs, encouraging them to loot the firm and providing an optimal means for that looting. I have discussed both aspects in some detail elsewhere (Black, 2003, 2005) and will limit this discussion to a brief summary relevant to this article's focus on the role of accounting control fraud in bubbles and crises. Accounting control frauds normally control their boards of directors and cause their compensation to be based largely on short-term accounting gains and to be exceptionally large if the firm is highly "profitable." Accounting fraud guarantees extreme short-term profits while the bubble is inflating. Fraudulent CEOs use normal corporate mechanisms to convert firm assets to personal benefits on the basis of the firm's record "profits." This minimizes the risk that frauds will be detected or prosecuted. They can get rich enough through a year or two of accounting fraud to retire wealthy. The firm's failure does not mean that the fraud mechanism has failed. Fraudulent CEOs maximize their "take" by maximizing accounting "profits"—through means that often cause the firm to fail. They maximize their income by causing the lender to grow rapidly as the bubble hyperinflates, a strategy that often causes the firm to fail.

Why Individual Control Fraud Failures Can be Massive

It is easy to understand how the means of optimizing accounting control fraud cause crushingly costly individual failures. Accounting control frauds' business model maximizes failures and losses because:

- Making loans to uncreditworthy borrowers maximizes defaults
- Making loans to uncreditworthy borrowers on the basis of false representations of creditworthiness maximizes defaults
- Inflating the appraised "market value" of the home pledged to secure the loan maximizes losses upon default
- Growing extremely rapidly greatly increases the number of bad loans and eventual losses
- Extreme leverage and failing to provide meaningful loss reserves multiplies total losses
    - By funding extremely rapid growth
    - By setting the firm up for failure because it will have little capital to absorb losses

Other less obvious aspects of fraud optimization add greatly to the losses individual control frauds cause:

- Ending effective loan underwriting and suborning internal and external controls cripples the lender's ability to prevent *unintended* frauds
- Creating a Gresham's dynamic that degrades the ethics of the lender's officers and agents' ethics makes them more likely to engage in opportunistic frauds that the CEO does not know of or sanction because they are primarily for the officer's own benefit rather than the CEO's benefit (e.g., Enron's fraudulent CFO, Andrew Fastow)
- Accounting frauds' creation of guaranteed record short-term "profits" and hiding of real losses suborns and renders oxymoronic "private market discipline" and greatly delays regulatory action if the agency does not understand accounting control fraud schemes. This allows the control fraud to persist, and grow massively, for a number of years—producing extraordinarily expensive failures.
- The payment of extreme compensation to officers and to suborn "controls" leads to far more expensive failures by adding considerably to expenses

- Corrupt CEOs may exploit their power to cause further losses through abusing their power by creating conflicts of interest such as corporate loans to the CEO

- Corrupt CEOs often seek to gain status and fend off sanctions by using the firm's assets to make large political and charitable contributions—adding to expenses

Why Epidemics of Control Fraud Occur and Cause Recurrent, Intensifying Crises

At any given time, a small number of industries and assets are the best available setting for accounting control fraud. Optimization will lead to accounting fraud naturally clustering in these superior settings. When an environment creates strong incentives to act criminally, we term it a "criminogenic environment." Neither the creation of such an environment nor the initial clustering requires any conspiracy.

The factors that make a finance sector most criminogenic are the absence of effective regulation and the ability to invest in assets that lack a readily verifiable asset value. Unless those initial frauds are dealt with effectively by the regulators or prosecutors, they will produce record profits and other firms will mimic them. Those control frauds can be a combination of "opportunistic" and "reactive" (moral hazard). If entry is relatively easy, opportunistic control fraud is optimized. If the finance sector is suffering from severe distress, reactive control fraud is optimized. Both conditions can exist at the same time, as in the early years of the savings and loan (S&L) debacle.

When we fail to regulate or supervise financial firms effectively, we create a criminogenic environment because we, *de facto*, decriminalize accounting control fraud. Even the FBI, which has agents who specialize in white-collar crime investigations, cannot effectively prosecute a control fraud epidemic. The way to reverse a Gresham's dynamic is to take prompt action to ensure that cheaters do not prosper. Regulatory enforcement is often the quickest way to ensure that cheaters lose.

In the current crisis the nonprime housing sector provided the most criminogenic environment. It was overwhelmingly unregulated—unregulated lenders made nearly 80 percent of total nonprime loans.

> In 2005, 52% of subprime mortgages were originated by companies with no federal supervision, primarily mortgage brokers and standalone finance companies. Another 25% were made by finance companies that are units of bank-holding companies and thus indirectly supervised by the Federal Reserve; and 23% by regulated banks and thrifts. (Ip and Paletta, 2007)

The regulated sector was rendered ineffective by the appointment of regulatory leaders by the Bush administration who opposed (because they thought it unnecessary and harmful) regulation. They generally did not remove the regulations, but they largely ceased to enforce the rules— even when lenders they were supposed to regulate specialized in making "liar's loans." I refer to this process as "desupervision."

Nonprime loans also offered the best available (huge) criminogenic environment because it offered the potential for massive growth (nonprime loans peaked at roughly 40 percent of total home mortgage lending) and offered assets whose value could be inflated easily through accounting fraud and whose real losses could be hidden by refinancings made possible by the rapid inflation of the housing bubble that nonprime lending helped drive. Refinancings create fictional short-term fee income. (The net effect of refinancing at a higher loan level is the creation of a larger longer-term loss that, eventually, swamps the fee income.)

The initial clustering produces "learning effects." Other CEOs observe that the initial frauds' business practices produce guaranteed, record profits and minimal reported delinquencies and losses—followed by exceptional bonus payments to the officers. CFOs who fail to emulate these practices will fail to achieve exceptional bonuses and appreciation of their stock. More importantly, their CEOs will fail to come close to their maximum possible compensation. This produces a Gresham's dynamic where cheaters are guaranteed to prosper while honest CFOs will tend to be driven out of the marketplace.

I explained above why a lender cannot simply decide to grow rapidly in a mature field (such as home lending in the U.S.) by making honest loans. A lender that wants to take market share from rivals honestly will typically have to cut its interest rate on loans, and its rivals are likely to match that cut. The result is reduced profitability and only small increases in the quantity of home loans demanded. By loaning to the uncreditworthy, however, accounting control frauds are able to grow extremely rapidly and increase the interest rate and fees that they charge. In the case of U.S. housing lenders, the result was an immediate, large, and guaranteed surge in short-term "profits" and acted like a shift in the demand curve for housing outward from the origin—causing home prices to surge as well. Because accounting control frauds grow extremely rapidly to optimize their short-run "profits," they will generally continue to lend to uncreditworthy borrowers even as the bubble extends for years and hyperinflates.

The Gresham's dynamic and "learning effects" (and, more technically, the false market price signals that such lenders provide) combine to encourage even more firms to mimic the accounting control frauds' business practices as the bubble continues to inflate. The same dynamic greatly aids the coverup of the true losses because extending the life of the bubble and increasing its rate of inflation make it easy to cover-up loss recognition through the repeated refinancing of troubled loans. The ability of epidemics of accounting control fraud to hide such losses can fool regulators who do not understand accounting control frauds. The same dynamic makes "private market discipline" an oxymoron.

Epidemics of accounting control fraud create a dynamic that extends the life of bubbles and hyperinflates them. In the current crisis, when such a massive housing bubble finally bursts it will cause losses so great that many of the accounting control frauds will become insolvent and most recent purchasers of homes will suffer serious losses.

Three other factors related to the accounting control fraud epidemic exacerbated the ongoing crisis: CDO, credit default swaps (CDS), and accounting control frauds' unique ability to erode trust and cause financial markets to fail. By hiding nonprime loans' massive real losses, the epidemic of accounting control fraud made it commercially feasible to suborn the rating agencies and have the top tranches of CDOs backed even by liar's loans rated "AAA." These are the derivatives that played a key role in causing Fannie Mae and Freddie Mac to become insolvent. The rating agencies, therefore, acted like "vectors" spreading the nonprime mortgage fraud epidemic through much of the global economy.

CDS, which are typically (but inaccurately) referred to as "insurance," do not meet the requisites for insurance. The entity purchasing the guarantee does not have to have an insurable interest in the instrument that is the subject of the guarantee and the entity selling the guarantee does not have to establish reserves to ensure that it can honor the guarantee. AIG, a massive insurance company, was rendered insolvent by selling these guarantees to back nonprime mortgage assets without establishing reserves from which it could honor the guarantees. (The final section of this paper explains why the nonprime CDO and CDS markets could not have grown so massively without the endemic destruction of underwriting standards, controls, and professional ethics unleashed by the accounting control frauds that specialized in nonprime lending.)

At law, "deceit" is the defining element that distinguishes fraud from other forms of larceny. Fraudsters get the victim to trust them—and then betray that trust in order to gain something of value. As a result, accounting frauds by elite financial officers are the most powerful acid for eroding trust and causing financial markets to fail. The ongoing crisis saw the collapse of hundreds of financial markets. Regulators did not shut down these markets—bankers did, because they no longer trusted other bankers' asset valuations. Losses from fraudulently overvalued assets can be so large that even relatively small positions can be fatal to troubled banks in a crisis. Therefore, long before accounting control fraud becomes endemic it can cause financial markets to close.

The Epidemic of Nonprime Mortgage Fraud that Drove the Crisis

The FBI began to warn publicly in its congressional testimony in September 2004 that an "epidemic" of mortgage fraud was developing and that it would cause an economic crisis if it were not dealt with (Frieden, 2004). No one in the industry—regulators, ranks of investors or creditors, or law enforcement personnel—took effective action against the epidemic. Instead, the nonprime loan control fraud specialists exported their bad ethics and bad business practices throughout the global economy.

The latest FinCEN (2009) data show that the filing of mortgage fraud Suspicious Activity Reports (SARs) (their term for criminal referrals) for the first half of 2009 is running at roughly the same rate as the most recent data available for a full fiscal year—over 62,000. That is a staggering figure and the fact that the rate of criminal referrals for mortgage fraud has not declined even two years after the secondary market for nonprime loans collapsed in spring 2007 makes it more ominous. The FBI clears roughly 1000 mortgage fraud cases in a year, so it is clear that it has been overwhelmed by the epidemic and failed to prevent the economic crisis that it so aptly predicted in 2004.

But the total SARs figure is only a faint indication of the true incidence of mortgage fraud. Only federally insured and regulated depository institutions are required to file criminal referrals for mortgage fraud. Honest, unregulated lenders specializing in nonprime mortgage lending should, logically, aggressively file SARs. Deterring fraudulent borrowers should be one of their top priorities. Their failure to file SARs for mortgage fraud is not irrational—the last thing they want is to encourage the FBI to investigate their loans. Because unregulated lenders booked nearly 80 percent of nonprime loans (and did so without any regulatory quality standards), extrapolating from the SARs data to the total nonprime lending industry would require multiplying 62,000 by five.

Even that extrapolation would not capture the true incidence because it implicitly assumes that the regulated lenders (1) discover all mortgage frauds and (2) file SARs when they discover evidence of mortgage fraud. Neither assumption is warranted. The FBI estimates that regulated lenders detect roughly one-third of the cases of mortgage fraud at their institutions prior to loan disbursement.

> Indeed, according to a report on mortgage fraud released Thursday by the Financial Crimes Enforcement Network, a unit of the Treasury Department, only 31 percent of suspected fraud was detected before loan disbursements in the 12 months ended March 31, 2007. On stated income loans, only 19 percent of the cases of suspected fraud were detected before the loans were financed, versus 33.5 percent on more fully documented loans. (Morgenson, 2008)

The data also indicate that the typical regulated lender does not file SARs notifications when it discovers mortgage fraud. The FBI has reported that 80 percent of total mortgage fraud losses are caused by frauds in which lender personnel are involved.

> The FBI reports that, based on existing investigations, 80 percent of all reported fraud losses arise from fraud for profit schemes that involve industry insiders. (MBA, 2007a, pp. 5–6)

The FinCEN (2009) report on mortgage fraud SARs provides these facts essential to evaluating whether the regulators have been effective:

> In the first half of 2009, approximately 735 financial institutions submitted SARs, or about 50 more filers compared to the same period in 2008. The top 50 filers submitted 93 percent of all [mortgage fraud] SARs, consistent with the same 2008 filing period. However, SARs submitted by the top 10 filers increased from 64 percent to 72 percent.

Only a small percentage of mortgage lenders, 735 in total, file even a single criminal referral for mortgage fraud. Of the 735 that make at least one filing, only a small number file more than five referrals. A mere ten filers provide the FBI with almost three-quarters of all SARs mortgage fraud filings.

Putting these factors together, one can infer that the lowest estimate of the true annual incidence of mortgage fraud during the later years of the housing bubble would be 500,000.

A small sample review of nonprime loan files by Fitch, the smallest of the three large rating agencies, adds support for the view that fraud became endemic in nonprime mortgage lending.

> Fitch's analysts conducted an independent analysis of these files with the benefit of the full origination and servicing files. The result of the analysis was disconcerting at best, as there was the appearance of fraud or misrepresentation in almost every file. . . .
>
> [F]raud was not only present, but, in most cases, could have been identified with adequate underwriting, quality control and fraud prevention tools prior to the loan funding. Fitch believes that this targeted sampling of files was sufficient to determine that inadequate underwriting controls and, therefore, fraud is a factor in the defaults and losses on recent vintage pools. (Pendley, Costello, and Kelsch, 2007, p. 4)

Fitch also explained why these forms of mortgage fraud cause severe losses.

> For example, for an origination program that relies on owner occupancy to offset other risk factors, a borrower fraudulently stating its intent to occupy will dramatically alter the probability of the loan defaulting. When this scenario happens with a borrower who purchased the property as a short-term investment, based on the anticipation that the value would increase, the layering of risk is greatly multiplied. If the same borrower also misrepresented his income, and

cannot afford to pay the loan unless he successfully sells the property, the loan will almost certainly default and result in a loss, as there is no type of loss mitigation, including modification, which can rectify these issues. (Pendley et al., 2007, p. 4)

Other relatively small sample reviews also find extreme incidences of mortgage fraud and confirm the power of Gresham's dynamic. The testimony of Thomas J. Miller (Miller, 2007), Attorney General of Iowa, at a 2007 Federal Reserve Board hearing shows why fraud losses are enormous:

> Over the last several years, the subprime market has created a race to the bottom in which unethical actors have been handsomely rewarded for their misdeeds and ethical actors have lost market share. . . . The market incentives rewarded irresponsible lending and made it more difficult for responsible lenders to compete. Strong regulations will create an even playing field in which ethical actors are no longer punished. (p. 3)

> Despite the well documented performance struggles of 2006 vintage loans, originators continued to use products with the same characteristics in 2007. (note 2)

> [Many originators invent] non-existent occupations or income sources, or simply inflat[e] income totals to support loan applications. A review of 100 stated income loans by one lender found that a shocking 90% of the applications overstated income by 5% or more and almost 60% overstated income by more than 50%. Importantly, our investigations have found that most stated income fraud occurs at the suggestion and direction of the loan originator, not the consumer. (p. 10)

Fitch rightly emphasized that any reputable underwriting process by the nonprime lenders would have prevented the fraudulent loans from being funded by an honest lender. This finding is consistent with the view that the lenders were accounting control frauds. The obvious questions are (1) why did Fitch only conduct this study in November 2007—after the secondary market in subprime had collapsed and nonprime CDOs were no longer being created and (2) why would anyone have purchased the fraudulent nonprime loans from the originator (and the CDOs backed by the fraudulent loans) when any competent due diligence would have revealed the endemic fraud? The answer to both questions is the same—no one asked, and no one told because the entire immensely profitable scam would have collapsed had anyone done even rudimentary due diligence of a sample of the nonprime loan files. A S&P message illustrates this point.

> "Any request for loan level tapes is TOTALLY UNREASONABLE!!!. . . . Most investors don't have it and can't provide it. . . . we MUST produce a credit estimate. . . . It is your responsibility to provide those credit estimates and your responsibility to devise some method for doing so." (Emphasis in original). (E-mail from Frank Raiter to Richard Gugliada et al., March 20, 2001)

Let me translate a few terms that may not be clear and provide the setting. The professional credit rater at S&P has been assigned to provide a rating for a CDO backed by nonprime loans. He has requested the "tapes" that contain images of the documents in the underlying loan files so that he can review a sample of them to better evaluate their credit risk. His boss fires back an impassioned e-mail message denouncing his request. He is ordered not to seek the information on the loan files (making any effective evaluation of credit risk impossible). He is told that the "investors" (typically, investment banks) that purchased the nonprime loans and "pooled" them to create the CDO don't even have the loan tapes and therefore could not provide it. That almost certainly means that the investment bank that purchased the nonprime mortgage loans did so without reviewing a sample of the loan files. It also means that it is impossible for the investment bank creating and selling interests in the CDO to others to provide those buyers with the loan files for their review. Instead, the S&P rater is instructed by his boss to make up a rating through "some method." The rating, of course, has to be at least "AA" and was almost certainly "AAA."

The entire massive toxic market in nonprime CDOs was premised on no one ever looking at a sample of the loan files and discovering the embarrassing truth of endemic fraud led by lenders. If even one person actually competently reviewed a sample of the loans they (1) could not have been made by an honest lender, (2) they could not have been purchased by an honest investment bank, (3) they could not have been pooled to (supposedly) support a CDO, (4) they could not have received any positive rating, and (5) the CDOs backed by the fraudulent loans could not have been sold. That's why Fitch didn't look until after the secondary market had collapsed and there was no revenue to lose.

The fact that Fitch could identify the frauds simply through a file review without any investigation tells us something else about the accounting control frauds. They, correctly, determined that the risk of detection of their frauds was so minimal that it was not even worth the minimal cost of creating fictional, but credible, financial statements. They knew that the fix was in at every level because everyone in the finance industry selling the toxic product maximized his bonus by adopting a financial "don't ask; don't tell" policy.

The contrast with the S&L debacle, where roughly 1000 "priority" defendants were convicted of felonies, is stark. The FBI did not even begin to investigate the large nonprime lending specialists until the nonprime secondary market collapsed in spring 2007. The uninsured nonprime lending specialists began collapsing in 2006 when housing prices stalled and the ability to refinance bad loans to hide their losses began to end. It has been years, and not a single senior officer of a nonprime lending specialist has been indicted, much less convicted, of accounting/securities fraud. (Two Bear Stearns officials have been indicted for alleged false statements about the true financial condition of a hedge fund they managed.)

The FBI indicates that the difficulty is not the lack of criminal culpability on the part of the nonprime lending specialists, but rather acute "systems capacity" problems. Deputy Director John Pistole (2009) testified before the Senate on February 11, 2009:

> [I]t would be irresponsible to neglect mortgage fraud's impact on the U.S. housing and financial markets.
>
> The number of open FBI mortgage fraud investigations has risen from 881 in FY 2006 to more than 1,600 in FY 2008. In addition, the FBI has more than 530 open corporate fraud investigations, including 38 corporate fraud and financial institution matters directly related to the current financial crisis. These corporate and financial institution failure investigations involve financial statement manipulation, accounting fraud and insider trading. The increasing mortgage, corporate fraud, and financial institution failure case inventory is straining the FBI's limited White Collar Crime resources.
>
> In December 2008, the FBI dedicated resources to create the National Mortgage Fraud Team at FBI headquarters in Washington, D.C. The Team has the specific responsibility for all management of the mortgage fraud program at both the origination and corporate level. This Team will be assisting the field offices in addressing the mortgage fraud problem at all levels. The current financial crisis, however, has required the FBI to move resources from other white collar crime and criminal programs in order to appropriately address the crime problem. Since January 2007, the FBI has increased its agent and analyst manpower working mortgage fraud investigations. The Team provides tools to identify the most egregious mortgage fraud perpetrators, prioritize pending investigations, and provide information to evaluate where additional manpower is needed.
>
> While the FBI has increased the number of agents around the country who investigate mortgage fraud cases from 120 Special Agents in FY 2007 to 180 Special Agents in FY 2008.

The current epidemic of accounting control frauds has caused far greater damage than did their S&L counterparts, but the number of FBI agents assigned to deal with the current epidemic is roughly one-sixth the agents assigned to the investigations of the S&L control frauds.

REFERENCES

Akerlof, George A. (1970). "The Market for "Lemons": Quality Uncertainty and the Market Mechanism." *Quarterly Journal of Economics 84* (3), 488–500.

Akerlof, G., and Romer P. (1993). "Looting: The Economic Underworld of Bankruptcy for Profit." In W. Brainard and G. Perry (Eds.), *Brookings Papers on Economic Activity 2* (pp. 1–73). Washington, DC: Brookings Institution.

Best, A.M. (February, 2006). U.S. Banking Trends for 2005—Signaling End of Peak Industry Cycle. www.ambest.com/banks/reports/ambest-bankingtrends2005.pdf

Becker, G. (1968). "Crime and Punishment: An Economic Approach." *The Journal of Political Economy 76*, 169–217.

Black, W. (2000). "Control Fraud and Control Freaks." In H. Pontell and D. Shichor (Eds.), *Contemporary Issues in Crime and Criminal Justice* (pp. 67–80). Upper Saddle River, NJ: Prentice Hall.

Black, W. (March/April, 2003). "Reexamining the Law-and-Economics Theory of Corporate Governance." *Challenge 46*(2), 22–40.

Black, W. (2005). *The Best Way to Rob a Bank Is to Own One: How Corporate Executives and Politicians Looted the S&L Industry.* Austin: University of Texas Press.

Black, W. (December 1, 2009). "Bo Cutter's Indictment of the Finance Industry." Wall Street Pit. http://wallstreetpit.com/12572-bo-cutters-indictment-of-the-finance-industry

Black, W., Calavita, K., and Pontell, H. (1995). "The Savings and Loan Debacle of the 1980s: White-Collar Crime or Risky Business?" *Law and Policy 17*, 23–55.

BusinessWeek. (May 19, 2003). "Getting Money to Where It Hasn't Gone." http://www.businessweek.com/magazine/content/03_20/b3833125_mz020.htm

Calavita, K., Pontell, H., and Tillman, R. (1997). *Big Money Crime.* Berkeley: University of California Press.

Cressey, Donald R. (1973). *Other People's Money: A Study in the Social Psychology of Embezzlement.* Montclair, NJ: Patterson Smith.

Cressey, Donald R. (1953). *Other People's Money.* New York: Free Press.

Cutter, B. (November 24, 2009). "Keep Tim Geithner." *New Deal 2.0.* http://www.newdeal20.org/?p=6569

Easterbrook, F., and Fischel, D. (1991). *The Economic Structure of Corporate Law.* Cambridge, MA: Harvard University Press.

Financial Crimes Enforcement Network (FinCEN). (October 2009). "The SAR Activity Review." http://www.fincen.gov/news_room/rp/files/sar_tti_16.pdf

Frieden, J. (September 17, 2004). "FBI Warns of Mortgage Fraud 'Epidemic': Seeks to Head off 'Next S&L Crisis.'" CNN. http://www.cnn.com/2004/LAW/09/17/mortgage.fraud/

Geis, G. (1967). "White Collar Crime: The Heavy Electrical Equipment Antitrust Case of 1961." In Marshall B. Clinard and Richard Quinney (Eds.), *Criminal Behavior Systems: A Typology.* New York: Holt, Rinehart and Winston, p. 141.

Gormley, M. (November 1, 2007). "Cuomo: Appraisers Pressured to Inflate Subprime Mortgage Values." http://seattletimes.nwsource.com/html/businesstechnology/2003987769_webwamu01.html

Gottfredson, M. R., and Hirschi, T. (1990). *A General Theory of Crime.* Stanford, CA: Stanford University Press.

Harney, K. R. (February 3, 2007). "Appraisers under Pressure to Inflate Values." http://www.washingtonpost.com/wp-dyn/content/article/2007/02/02/AR2007020200712.html

Herrnstein, R.J., and Murray, C. 1994. *The Bell Curve.* New York: Free Press.

Ip, G., and Paletta, D. (March 22, 2007). "Regulators Scrutinized in Mortgage Meltdown." *The Wall Street Journal Online.* http://online.wsj.com/article/SB117449440555444249.html

Miller, T. J. (August 14, 2007). "Home Equity Lending Market Request for Comment." Docket No. OP-1288. http://www.iowa.gov/government/ag/latest_news/releases/aug_2007/Federal_Reserve_HOEPA.pdf

Mortgage Bankers Association. (2007a). "Mortgage Fraud: Strengthening Federal and State Mortgage Fraud Prevention Efforts." Tenth Periodic Case Report to the Mortgage Bankers Association. http://www.mbaa.org/files/News/InternalResource/57274_Study.pdf

Mortgage Bankers Association. (October 2007b). "Policy Position: The Importance of Accurate Appraisals Performed by Independent Appraisers." http://www.mbaa.org/Advocacy/IssuePapers/IndependentAppraisers.htm

Morgenson, G. (April 6, 2008). "Fair Game: A Road Not Taken by Lenders." http://www.nytimes.com/2008/04/06/business/06gret.html

National Commission on Financial Institution Reform, Recovery and Enforcement (NCFIRRE). (1993). *Origins and Causes of the S&L Debacle: A Blueprint for Reform.* A Report to the President and Congress of the United States. Washington, DC: Government Printing Office.

Office of Federal Housing Enterprise Oversight. (May 2006). "Report of the Special Examination of Fannie Mae." http://www.fanniemae.com/media/pdf/newsreleases/FNMSPECIALEXAM.pdf

Pendley, M. D., Costello, G., and Kelsch, M. (November 28, 2007). "The Impact of Poor Underwriting Practices and Fraud in Subprime RMBS Performance." *Fitch Ratings, U.S. Residential Mortgage Special Report.* http://www.securitization.net/pdf/Fitch/FraudReport_28Nov07.pdf

Pierce, J. (2004). Causes of the S&L Debacle. Unpublished paper presented at the annual meeting of the Allied Social Sciences Association. On file with author.

Pistole, J. (February 11, 2009). "The Need for Increased Fraud Enforcement in the Wake of the Economic Downturn." Testimony before the United States Senate Committee on the Judiciary. http://judiciary.senate.gov/hearings/testimony.cfm?id=3651&wit_id=7603

Pummer, C. (April 24, 2007). "Real-Estate Appraisers Feel Pressure to Inflate Home Values." *Market Watch.*

Wheeler, S., and Rothman, M. (1982). "The Organization as Weapon in White Collar Crime." *Michigan Law Review 80*(7), 1403–1426.

White, M. C. (August 5, 2009). "Rules to Regulate Home Appraisals Stymie Industry, Home Buyers." *The Washington Independent.* http://washingtonindependent.com/53788/rules-to-regulate-home-appraisals-stymie-industry-home-buyers

Wilson, J. Q., and Herrnstein R. (1985). *Crime and Human Nature.* New York: Simon and Shuster.

Woellert, L., and Kopecki, D. (October 22, 2008). "Moody's, S&P Employees Doubted Ratings, E-Mails Say." (Update 2). *Bloomberg.* http://www.bloomberg.com/apps/news?pid=newsarchive&sid=a2EMlP5s7iM0

12

Insider Trading

Patterns and Analysis

— *Elizabeth Szockyj and Gilbert Geis*

Introduction

Civil and criminal cases of insider trading involve persons, often in positions of power (Sutherland, 1949), who use nonpublic information that is generally gained from their corporate standing to serve their own financial interests or, at times, the financial interests of their clients, family, or friends. Insider trading is most frequently done in order to amass profits by trading in advance of takeover announcements. Significantly, the offense also often possesses the uncommon criminal quality of being committed not to gain money but to avoid losing it.

What Is Insider Trading?

Illegal insider trading occurs when a person who possesses nonpublic information trades in the securities market on the basis of that information. Generally, there are three broad categories of illegal insider trading: (1) The traditional definition includes trading or tipping by corporate officers, directors, and owners who, by doing so, violate a fiduciary duty to company shareholders; (2) The misappropriation theory, employed since the early 1980s and now endorsed by the U.S. Supreme Court, states that individuals outside of the corporation are prohibited from trading on confidential information if such trading breeches a fiduciary duty owed to the source

Source: Elizabeth Szockyj and Gilbert Geis, Insider Trading: Patterns and Analysis. *Journal of Criminal Justice*, Vol. 30, No. 4, pp. 273–286. Copyright © 2002 by Elsevier. Reprinted with permission.

of the information, typically the trader's employer (*United States v. O'Hagan*, 521 U.S. 642, 1997). The misappropriation theory was applied against a *Wall Street Journal* reporter who traded in advance of the printing of his business column (Winans, 1986); and (3) Anyone in possession of confidential information related to a takeover or merger is prohibited from trading.

The term "insider trading" entered the public lexicon in the 1980s. As the decade unfolded, increasing enforcement attention was directed at insider traders: Congress decreed stiff penalties, the Securities and Exchange Commission (SEC) came "down [on insider traders] with hobnail boots" (Noble, 1981, p. IV, 1), the Department of Justice began to prosecute the offense criminally, and the courts began to impose substantial monetary penalties and jail sentences on those convicted (Szockyj, 1993b). At the same time, there arose a scholarly counterforce that argued that sanctions against insider trading were economically counterproductive: "The only conceivable justification for banning it is that such trading involves the theft of valuable corporate property from its rightful owner," Macey (1991, p. 67) insists. For their part, proponents of a tough enforcement stance maintained that in the absence of intensive oversight to assure market integrity, the stock market would collapse and necessary capital would not be entrusted to it (for a summary of pro and con arguments, see Weng & Steinberg, 1996).

Despite the surge of interest in insider trading, very little is known about the characteristics of insider trading offenders or the elements of the offense beyond a few general details (see Dooley, 1980; Haddock & Macey, 1987; Meulbroek, 1992; Reichman, 1993; Tomasic, 1991). This article breaks into new substantive territory with a portrayal of the dimensions of insider trading as indicated by official records. These records, of course, tell only of what was discovered and acted against by enforcement agencies. Insider trading prosecutions, like those for most white-collar crimes, usually involve proactive strategies. To discover insider trading, the enforcement agency typically scrutinizes patterns of stock market trades and focuses on those that seem suspicious. Suspicion is most often aroused when there is a significantly higher volume of dealing in a particular stock a short time before news of a critical development brings about a considerable gain or loss in the price of the traded item. Enforcers obviously attend less assiduously to smaller transactions.

Theoretical Framework

The most prominent theoretical explanation of crime at the moment, Gottfredson and Hirschi's (1990) self-control theory, is promulgated as a general theory that purports to explain all types of crime. People with low self-control are risk-seeking, shortsighted, insensitive to others, and desire immediate gratification. These characteristics conflict with any long-term commitments to a job, marriage, family, or friends. Crime requires little skill or planning, according to this perspective, and criminals are versatile in the crimes they commit, not limiting themselves to one type of offense. Self-control is acquired early in life through effective child rearing practices. Consequently, low self-control is a product of poor parental monitoring of behavior, lack of parental recognition of deviance, and/or ineffective discipline for transgressions.

Self-control theory, has been, like so many earlier criminological formulations, particularly criticized for its failure to square with what is known about white-collar crime (Benson & Moore, 1992; Geis, 2000; Polk, 1991; Reed & Yeager, 1996; Steffensmeier, 1989). Critics of the theory almost uniformly point out that achievement of the standing that permits a person to engage in white-collar crimes clearly relates to gratification postponement, self-interested calculation, and restraint associated with awareness of the long-term consequences of illegal activities. Commentators often use insider trading as an exemplar when discussing the inadequacy of self-control theory in regard to white-collar crime: Polk, for example, notes that Gottfredson and Hirschi's general theory "would tell us that criminals do not specialize in one form of crime, thus today's burglar is yesterday's insider trader and tomorrow's rapist." Polk then asks: "Is this actually true for insider traders?" Available data indicate, Polk points out, that individuals such as Boesky (Stewart, 1991), Levine (1991), and Milken (Kornbluth, 1992) concentrated on financial crimes and that their illegal behaviors were not interchangeable with street offenses (Polk, 1991, p. 578). Similarly, Curran and Renzetti (1994, p. 217) note that "[n]o specialized knowledge is needed to write a bad check or to take money out of a cash register. It certainly cannot be claimed however, that specialized knowledge is not required to commit such crimes as insider trading" (see also Barlow, 1991, p. 236). The considerable use of insider trading to attack the theory is informative, but limited by the lack of available insider trading data.

Gottfredson and Hirschi's self-control theory could not be tested directly in this study, but only inferentially, since the data did not include an empirical measure of the level of self-control among either offenders or those with more or less equivalent opportunities who did not break the law. Nonetheless, official records of insider trading violations and crimes offered a particularly good opportunity to try to tease out data that would support or refute the various postulates of self-control theory.

Self-control theory offered several predictions that were examined in detail in the discussion section. First, illegal insider trading violations should be more common among lower-level employees than corporate officers or directors. Individuals who possess the least self-control should hold positions on the lowest rungs of the employment ladder since advancement up the corporate ladder requires a certain level of self-control. Second, insider traders should be repeat offenders, i.e., they should commit the offense on more than one occasion. Third, insider traders should be risk-seeking. Risky behavior would include tipping others since this activity increases the likelihood of detection. Consequently, insider traders should also be tippers, passing on the nonpublic information to others. Finally, insider trading should be an enterprise that requires minimal skills or expertise.

Methods

The data presented here were derived from civil charges filed by the SEC and criminal cases brought by the U.S. Department of Justice during the ten-year period from 1980 to 1989. The civil sample was made up of persons charged with insider trading under section 10(b) and 14(e) of the *Securities Exchange Act* (15 U.S.C. §78(j) and §78n(e)). Violations of section 14(e) and the associated SEC rule 14e-3h (17 C.F.R. §240.14c-3) dealt specifically with illegal trading in advance of tender offers related to matters such as mergers or acquisitions (for recent reviews of insider trading law, see Painter, Krawiec, & Williams, 1998; Pritchard, 1998). In criminal cases, defendants were typically charged with securities fraud under the criminal penalties section of the *Securities Exchange Act* or, to a lesser extent, with mail and wire fraud (18 U.S.C. §§1341, 1343), the catch-all federal statutes used to ensnare many forms of white-collar criminal behavior (Brickey, 1990; Coffee, 1988; Newman & Kidwell, 2000).

Since the SEC goes forward with only a small proportion of the cases that it reviews, those charged are persons most likely to have engaged in the illegal behavior. The sample therefore included a high number of true insider traders, a statement that could not be made concerning cases at the investigatory stage. Likewise, it would be less productive to examine only cases in which there was a guilty finding because insider trading charges were often settled without either an admission or denial of guilt.

Sources tapped to obtain a roster of persons charged during the decade studied were: publications of the American Law Institute–American Bar Foundation, the *Wall Street Journal*, the *SEC Reports and Decisions* accessed on LEXIS, and the SEC counsel's office. Some, but very likely only a few, cases have been missed. The unit of analysis was the defendant as opposed to the case. All defendants in any given case were included in the analysis so long as the actions of each comprised insider trading. The total number of persons studied came to 452. Approximately 94 percent of the defendants were male. The age and race of the defendants were seldom reported and consequently were not included in the analysis. Likewise, corporations or business firms charged with insider trading were not considered in the tabulations (twenty-eight corporations were charged civilly and three criminally for insider trading offenses).

The data on each defendant consisted of the following variables.

Occupation of the Accused

The occupations of the defendants were categorized according to whether the defendants worked in the corporate sector or the securities industry and according to their employment status, i.e., officers/ directors or lower-level employees. The officers/directors category included corporate directors, both former and current, business executives, such as presidents or vice-presidents, and others occupying positions deemed by the SEC to be prestigious enough to fit into the "officer" category. Defendants from either of these groups could tip others, often family members or friends, who formed another category. Infrequently, others, such as lawyers and law firm employees, psychiatrists, printers, and reporters became privy to inside information through their occupations.

Tipping

Defendants were either insiders in the company, temporary insiders—a category that refers to professionals such as investment bankers, lawyers, or accountants who were employed by the company on a temporary basis—or individuals who were tipped (i.e., tippees).

Recidivism

Frequency of trading activity refers to the number of occasions that the defendant took advantage of inside information and formed a measure of recidivism. Frequency was dichotomized into single or multiple occurrences. If the same company's shares were traded over several days on the basis of the same confidential information, then this was coded as a single occurrence of insider trading since the trades relied on the same inside knowledge. Recidivism occurred if the insider misappropriated nonpublic information more than once.

Illegal gain

The profit earned or loss avoided as determined by the SEC was recorded as a ratio level variable and later categorized. Loss avoidance referred to situations where defendants traded in advance of bad news which would drive the price of the stock down.

Type of Inside Information Used in the Trade

The type of inside information used related to the confidential information that the defendants relied on in anticipation of an increase or decrease of the price of the securities traded, for example, nonpublic knowledge of a merger.

Sentence

The type and the length of civil and criminal sanctions imposed were analyzed.

Results

First, the data on civil defendants were explored to indicate who was charged and what form of information was used in the trades. The data revealed several seemingly counterintuitive patterns regarding the "typical" insider trade and trader. Second, a comparison was drawn between defendants charged civilly and those charged criminally. Finally, the sentences imposed on insider traders were examined.

Portrait of an Insider Trader: Civil Cases

Occupation

The figures demonstrated that contrary to what the name of the charge implies, fewer than a third of the defendants actually were corporate officers or directors (see Table 1). The usual civil defendant was a relative or an associate of an insider (37.6 percent). Their occupation was not indicated in the records since, presumably, it was not related to the transactions that led to their prosecution. Most were tipped off about pending transactions. One insider might tip numerous individuals, who in turn tipped others. It was, primarily, the insiders and temporary insiders who breached their fiduciary duty by tipping or trading on confidential information.

Approximately a third of all defendants came from the business sector (31.5 percent), whereas only 18.2 percent of the defendants were from the securities industry. Corporate officers and directors, because of their position, were more likely to have access to material nonpublic information and were far more likely to be charged for trading on such information than their employees (84.2 percent of the business defendants were business officers or directors and only 15.8 percent were lower status employees). Defendants in the securities industry, on the other hand, were unlikely to be executives: securities employees such as brokers, dealers, and analysts (77.5 percent) were more likely than securities executives such as CEOs, vice presidents, and heads of departments (22.5 percent) to be insider trading defendants. Some of these lower-level securities employees acquired their inside information as a result of the illegal trades of their clients. When the clients were charged with insider trading, the brokers were snared as well. Other low-level market professionals traded on merger and acquisition information to which they were privy when they worked on details of the transactions.

In general, insider trading by market professionals was much more difficult to determine than that of business insiders because it was camouflaged within daily occupational activities (Katz, 1979). Arbitrageur Ivan Boesky escaped detection for years until Dennis Levine, who was a more minor player, cooperated with the authorities to provide evidence against him. Boesky then led investigators to junk bond king Michael Milken. Without these tips, the SEC would not have been able to penetrate the higher echelons of the securities business to apprehend insider traders.

The market professional had also been successful in influencing the definition of insider trading (see Reichman, 1992 for a discussion on the shaping of regulatory policy by those it was supposedly designed to keep in check). Only information that was directly communicated was regarded as insider trading, but confidential information could be conveyed quite subtly—and, presumably, legally—or, at least, beyond the ability of prosecutors to prove otherwise. Such information could be transmitted by nonverbal communications, such as "attitude, implication, enthusiasm, or a figurative wink" (Salbu, 1993, p. 320; see also Marcial, 1995, pp. 97–100). Mutual interdependence among those involved in the stock market made financially important disclosures, even if illegally premature, worthwhile quid pro quo chips in games played on Wall Street.

Tipping

Almost half (46.2 percent) of the insiders and temporary insiders did not seek to enrich only themselves; they shared the information they had with others. This was particularly true of temporary insiders, among whom 63.4 percent tipped others (chi-square is significant at $P < .001$). Embezzlers tended to be reluctant to reveal their illegal behavior to their family or friends (Cressey, 1953), but many insider traders showed no such hesitation. The information apparently was shared to enhance a relationship rather than to entice someone into law-breaking. Advance notice of a tender offer (67 percent) was most likely to generate tipping, probably because it involved the possibility for considerable profit (chi-square is significant at $P < .001$). In situations of potential loss, demands of loyalty to others, particularly if the insider had prompted family or friends to purchase shares in the first place, often would take precedence (see Szockyj, 1993a, for an example). That such an attachment to family and friends led to law-breaking rather than reduced it contradicts the postulate of social bonding theory (Hirschi, 1969), but might play upon the neutralization technique that Sykes and Matza (1957) identified as an "appeal to higher loyalties." Note that approximately 12 percent of the defendants did not themselves make any profits but rather only tipped others, though it was not known if the others were expected to reciprocate in some manner or were acting as fronts for the insiders (see Table 1 under Amount of profit/loss avoided). Perhaps they were aware of the risk to themselves of being caught but presumed that it would be more difficult for enforcers to detect others to whom they gave information. On the other hand, this result might reflect the kinds of cases that the SEC chose to pursue, particularly in terms of those with multiple rather than lone defendants.

Recidivism

Frequency of insider trading refers to the number of times that nonpublic information was exploited. Two-thirds (67.5 percent) of the defendants were charged with illegally trading on only one occasion—it was not known, however, how much they might have gotten away with earlier. Overall, there did not appear to be a pattern of illegal trading or a commitment to such behavior. If true, this was likely due to an absence of continuing opportunity: few persons often become aware of nonpublic material information. Defendants in the securities industry, who were most likely to encounter such information, were also most likely to be charged with multiple illegal trades (chi-square is significant at the $P < .001$ level).

Illegal gain

The gains (and losses avoided) from insider trading, with a median of US$25,800, were far from the enormous profits highlighted in cases which were attended to in the media. Nonetheless, the median insider trading profit was greater than the 1994 U.S. per capita personal income of US$21,699 (U.S. Bureau of Economic Analysis, 1996) and much greater than the average take in street crime. In 1993, the average loss due to a bank robbery was US$3308; a residential burglary netted US$1189, larceny theft US$504, and motor vehicle theft US$4808 (U.S. Department of Justice, 1994, p. 205).

Types of information traded

Persons both in the business (42 percent) and market (87.5 percent) sectors disproportionately traded on information regarding advance notice of takeovers and mergers. For those in the securities industry, this was the kind of valuable nonpublic information they were most likely to learn about. Business insiders, however, had opportunities to take advantage of a considerable range of confidential information. While they were less likely than market professionals to trade on tender offer information, this was still the most common type of insider information used illegally (chi-square significant at the $P < .001$ level). That they traded illegally most frequently in advance of tender offers might be due to the high expected profits from these rather infrequent business transactions (Terpstra, Reyes, & Bokor, 1991). It was also possible that they felt that any merger (particularly if their own company was the target) could jeopardize their job and their income and that they felt particularly compelled to act for what they defined as their fiscal salvation.

Cross-tabulation of the variables profit (above and below US$25,800) and type of information used (tender offer vs. other) failed to indicate that greater profits were made in illegal trades related to merger and acquisition information than on other types of information (chi-square is not significant, $P = .45$: a t test using profit as an interval level category resulted in a similar probability level). It had to be appreciated, however, that this method of analysis failed to take into account that profit gained was also a function of the initial amount invested and the number of trades. That is, individuals who illegally purchased ten shares would make less profit than those who illegally purchased a hundred shares of the same target-for-takeover company.

Trading on losses

Trades made to avoid losses represented an unusual form of criminal activity. Such trading occurred considerably more frequently (10.9 percent) than trading for gains (0.7 percent). If information regarding bankruptcy and reorganization was included, then the loss figure rose from 11 to 15 percent. There was no reliable base rate, however, for how frequently different forms of material information were available. The SEC annual reports noted that tender offers rose from ninety-two cases in 1983 to peak at 254 in 1988, then fell precipitously over the next few years (McLucas, Walsh, & Fountain, 1992). Figures for other types of information were more difficult to obtain. A search of press releases provided on LEXIS, using the key words "unexpected loss," "unexpected gain," "increased profit," and "increased loss," produced seventy-four items in 1988 mentioning profits and sixty-two on losses. Based on this check, there did not appear to be a large difference in the number of loss or gain announcements, suggesting that the greater trading on earnings losses was not a function of their more frequent occurrence.

Trading prior to losses also highlighted a quixotic aspect of the insider trading laws. Insiders might legally do nothing when they became aware that the company was positioned to make significant gains, and could still reap profits. Had they *not* known about the windfall, they could well have sold their stock in the ordinary course of a portfolio readjustment or because they were pressed for funds. The level playing field for stock transactions that the insider trading laws seek to promote will have a few irrepressible bumps in it.

When a corporation has bad financial news, there is considerable incentive to sell: what must be factored into the decision to violate insider trading statutes is the likelihood of being caught and the consequences of apprehension. At best, knowledge of the odds will be highly imperfect (in part because the enforcement inevitably is rather erratic). It is known, however, from psychological research that all things being equal, people prioritize the avoidance of loss ahead of the achievement of gain (Kahneman & Tversky, 1979; Tversky & Kahneman, 1990). Seyhun (1992, p. 162) found that as the penalties for insider trading escalated in the 1980s, "insiders . . . increasingly shifted to a strategy of bailing out before the bad news rather than buying on good news." In more colloquial terms, this phenomenon has been labeled "fear of falling" (Weisburd, Wheeler, Waring, & Bode, 1991).

Table 1.
Descriptive Characteristics of Insider Trading Defendants Charged Civilly[a]

Number charged (*N* = 452)

Occupation		*N*	%	Total *N*	Total %
Business	Officer/director	117	84.2		
	Employee	22	15.8		
	Total business			139	31.5
Securities	Officer/director	18	22.5		
	Employee	62	77.5		
	Total securities			80	18.2
Lawyer/firm employee				30	6.8
Other professions[b]				9	2.0
Friend/relative				166	37.6
Other[c]				17	3.9
Total				441	100

	Type of insider					
	Insider		Temporary insider[e]		Total	
Tipping[d,**]	*N*	%	*N*	%	*N*	%
No tip	80	63.5	26	36.6	106	53.8
Tip	46	36.5	45	63.4	91	46.2
Total	126	100	71	100	197	100

	Type of information					
	Tender offer		Other		Total	
Tipping	*N*	%	*N*	%	*N*	%
No tip	35	33.0	70	77.8	105	53.6
Tip	71	67.0	20	22.2	91	46.4
Total	106	100	90	100	196	100

	Occupation							
	Business		Securities		Other		Total	
Recidivism**	*N*	%	*N*	%	*N*	%	*N*	%
Single	126	90.6	40	50.0	129	58.1	295	66.9
Multiple	13	9.4	40	50.0	93	41.9	146	33.1
Total	139	100	80	100	222	100	441	100

Amount of profit/loss avoided[f]	*N*	%
No profits	49	12.3
1–10,000	64	16.0
10,001–25,000	85	21.3
25,001–50,000	45	11.3
50,001–100,000	69	17.3
Over 100,000	87	21.8
Total	399	100

Table 1. *(continued)*

Type of material information used	Business N	%	Securities N	%	Other N	%	Total N	%
Tender offers **	58	42.0	70	87.5	162	73.0	290	65.8
Earnings loss	30	21.7	2	2.5	16	6.8	48	10.9
Earnings gain	3	2.2	0		0		3	0.7
Bankruptcy/reorganization	9	6.5	0		8	3.6	17	3.9
Asset change[g]	30	21.7	4	5.0	5	2.3	39	8.8
Contents of article	1	0.7	3	3.8	17	7.7	21	4.8
Other[h]	7	5.1	1	1.3	15	6.8	23	5.2
Total	338	100	80	100	223	100	441	100.1

[a] All civil defendants and codefendants including those also prosecuted criminally, but excludes the twenty-eight companies/ firms charged civilly.

[b] Includes psychiatrists, printers, reporters, accountants.

[c] Includes business people unrelated to the company whose stock is traded.

[d] Excludes the seven cases of misappropriation where the original insider trader was unrelated to the business, e.g., a psychiatrist, reporter.

[e] This category includes investment bankers, lawyers, accountants, and others whose expertise is employed on a temporary basis by the corporation.

[f] Median profit was US$25,800 with a range of US$0–400 million. If the cases where no profits were made are excluded, the median is US$34,088 and the minimum is US$340.

[g] Includes loan approvals, contracts, and misrepresentation of assets.

[h] Includes government announcements (approvals and decisions), management change, and recapitalization.

** $P < .001$.

An alternate explanation is that trading on anticipated losses is easier to detect. Those who trade on losses have to trade on their own accounts, while they may locate nominees to take advantage of nonpublic information about the likelihood of a rise in a stock price.

Comparison of civil and criminal defendants

Civil and criminal defendants were compared since research on prosecutions of securities violations indicated that there existed an important filtering process in determinations of whether a person was proceeded against criminally or civilly (Hagan & Parker, 1985; Shapiro, 1985). Fewer defendants were charged criminally than civilly for insider trading. There were a number of reasons why criminal prosecution had been employed more sparingly. For one, to succeed in a criminal case, prosecutors must establish *mens rea*, showing that the alleged perpetrator knowingly and willfully violated the law (Carr, 2000). There was the further burden of demonstrating guilt beyond a reasonable doubt. In addition, presumed violators were much more likely to mount a spirited defense if they were charged criminally than if the proceedings involved less personal stigma. Also important was the fact that criminal cases were brought by the U.S. Department of Justice rather than the SEC. This meant that those who initiated the case had to turn it over to another agency which garnered much of the credit and which often had a different agenda than the SEC: the latter, for instance, might be interested in extending the reach of the law; the former only in chalking up a courtroom victory or, equally likely, negotiating a plea bargain.

Criminal defendants, as shown in Table 2, were more likely to come from the securities field (chi-square is significant at the $P < .001$ level), to be charged with trading on more than one occasion (chi-square is significant at the $P < .001$ level), to realize profits in excess of US$25,800 (chi-square is significant at the $P <.01$ level), to trade on tender offer information (chi-square is significant at the $P < .01$ level), and, finally, as insiders or temporary insiders, to be tippers (chi-square is significant at the $P < .01$ level). When all the variables were considered together in a logistic regression model, however, only the frequency of trades and occupation were the significant predictors (see Table 3). Compared to civil defendants, criminal defendants were more likely to have traded on two or more occasions ($P < .0001$). Being in business or in some other occupation than securities trading was associ-

Table 2.
Comparison of Insider Trading Defendants Charged Civilly and Criminally

		Civil[a]		Criminal[b]	
		N	%	*N*	%
Occupation**	Business	139	31.5	15	14.9
	Securities	80	18.2	43	42.6
	Other	222	50.3	43	42.6
	Total	441	100	101	101
Tipping*	No tip	106	53.8	13	28.9
	Tip	91	46.2	32	71.1
	Total	197	100	45	100
Recidivism**	Single Trade	305	67.5	24	23.5
	Multiple Trades	147	32.5	78	76.4
	Total	452	100	102	99.9
Amount of profit/loss avoided [c]*	Under US $25,800	200	50.1	24	31.2
	Over US $25,800	199	49.9	53	68.8
	Total	399	100	77	100
Material traded*	Tender offer	294	65.2	83	81.4
	Other	157	34.8	19	18.6
	Total	451	100	102	100

[a] There were 452 defendants and codefendants prosecuted civilly including those also prosecuted criminally, but excludes the twenty-eight companies/firms charged civilly.

[b] There were 102 defendants and codefendants prosecuted criminally including those also prosecuted civilly, but excludes the three companies/firms charged criminally.

[c] For criminal defendants, the median profit was US$50,000 with a range of US$0–50 million. If the cases where no profits were made are excluded, the median is US$94,000 and the minimum *is* US$500.

*$P < .01$.

**$P < .001$.

Table 3.
Logistic Regression Model of the Probability of Being Criminally Charged with Insider Trading

Variable	Coefficient	Standard error	P value
Constant	−2.4261**	0.4774	.0000
Frequency of trade (more than 1 = 1; single = 0)	1.4337**	0.299	.0000
Occupation	*		.0509
Business	−0.3555	0.4251	.4029
Other	−0.7405*	0.3072	.0159
Profit (over US $25,800 = 1; under US $25,800 = 0)	0.4937	0.2849	.0831
Information used (tender offer − 1; other − 0)	0.3460	0.3265	.2893
Model chi-square = 49.117, P<.001, df = 5, N = 466			

*P ≤ .05.
** P < .001.

ated with a decreased log odds of being charged criminally ($P = .05$). The amount of profit approached significance ($P = .08$), but the type of information used was not influential in differentiating who was charged criminally.

Securities professionals were the group most likely to be charged criminally. This finding conflicted with Shapiro's (1985) report that brokers were more likely to be handled administratively and less likely to be charged civilly and criminally for securities offenses than others. There were a number of possible explanations for this discrepancy. Insider trading by securities personnel might be seen to be more egregious than other crimes handled by the federal Department of Justice because they struck at the integrity of the marketplace. Since securities personnel had considerable opportunity to commit the offenses, their criminal prosecution might be seen as serving deterrent ends. Low-level securities defendants might also possess less economic, political, and legal support than others charged with insider trading. For example, the *Insider Trading and Security Fraud Enforcement Act of 1988* (98 Stat. 1264), passed during the time of notorious insider trading scandals, specified that securities firms must put in place written policies regarding the misuse of confidential information. There was no similar stipulation for the business community. Businesspeople were subject only to civil liability as "controlling persons" if they knowingly and recklessly failed to take appropriate measures to prevent offenses. As of 1990, only 25 percent of a random sample of thirty-seven corporate ethics codes from those available at the University of Michigan Career Resource Center showed company files that specifically warned against insider trading (Seyhun, 1992; see also Weinberger, 1990).

Sentencing

As depicted in Table 4, in civil cases, the typical sentence was an injunction, disgorgement of profits, and a fine of a similar amount as the

Table 4.
Sentencing of Insider Traders Charged Civilly

		Civil		Criminal	
		N	%	*N*	%
Plea	Without admitting or denying guilt	333	83.9	NA	
	Guilty/found guilty	31	7.8	89	89.9
	Found not guilty	19	4.8	3	3.0
	Dismissed	14	3.5	7	7.1
	Total	397	100	99	100
Prosecution route	Settlement	348	87.0	73	73.7
	Trial	34	8.5	19	19.2
	Dismissal	13	3.3	7	7.1
	Other[a]	5	1.3		
	Total	400	100.1	99	100
Disgorgement[b]	Yes	282	80.1	NA	
	No	70	19.9		
	Total	352	100		
Injunction	Yes	333	95.7	NA	
	No	15	4.3		
	Total	348	100		
Fine[c]	Yes	110	67.9	44	52.4
	No	52	32.1	40	47.6
	Total	162	100	84	100
Comparison of fine/profit[d]	Fine same as profit[e]	64	70.3	NA	
	Fine 2 × profit or more	9	9.9		
	Fine < profit	18	19.8		
	Total	91	100		
Probation[f]	Yes	NA		66	78.6
	No			18	21.4
	Total			84	100
Community service order[g]	Yes	NA		38	45.2
	No			46	54.8
	Total			84	100
Imprisonment[h]	Yes	NA		47	54.7
	No			39	45.3
	Total			86	100

[a] Includes default and summary judgment.

[b] One offender was charged with a tax violation, and consequently, disgorgement was not an applicable sentencing option. The median amount disgorged was US$30,849 with a range of US$340–500 million.

[c] The ITSA was passed in 1984, allowing courts to impose civil fines of up to triple the profits gained. In two cases, it was unclear whether the transaction occurred after the passage of the ITSA, and therefore, these two cases were not included in the tabulation. The tax case was also excluded. The median civil fine is US$26,502 with a range of US$1.386–50 million while the median criminal fine is US$10,000 with a range of US$1.0–200 million.

[d] Excludes those cases (*n* = 19) where the accused was fined but did not profit.

[e] Also includes fines higher than the profit, e.g., when interest is attached.

[f] The median probation sentence is thirty-six months with a range of twelve to seventy-two months.

[g] The median community service order was 300 days with a range of 200 to over 1,000 days.

[h] The median sentence was twelve months with a range of one month to ten years.

profits. Though insider traders generally did not admit guilt, they usually were enjoined (95.7 percent), ordered to disgorge profits (80.1 percent), and/or ordered to pay a fine (67.9 percent). The power to impose a fine double or triple the profits had not been exercised frequently (9.9 percent), though it was legislated in 1984 in the hope that it would prove to be an effective deterrent (U.S. House of Representatives, 1983). For 19.8 percent of the defendants, the fine was less than the profit that had been realized.

Additional sentencing options were available at the criminal level, where almost 55 percent of the defendants were sentenced to a period of incarceration. This imprisonment rate was comparable to that for bank embezzlers (55 percent in 1994) though somewhat less than for securities offenders sentenced in federal district courts (64 percent in 1994). Other white-collar offenders convicted or pleading before the same courts, however, showed a lower imprisonment rate (45 percent for bribery defendants, 38 percent for income tax fraud defendants, and 8 percent for antitrust defendants, Administrative Office of the United States Courts, 1995; for a similar conclusion, see Hagan & Nagel, 1982; Weisburd et al., 1991). This result should be interpreted cautiously, however, for, as Shapiro (1985) has noted, a filtering process tends to weed out cases at different rates for different white-collar crimes.

Discussion

Insider trading crimes call for interpretations that concentrate on the particular ingredients of this kind of criminal activity. Insider trading involves people and scenarios that differ in terms of how they might be interpreted theoretically. It might be argued that all the violations were prompted by greed, but what might well be the most profound of the nine statements in Sutherland's differential association theory was the one that reminded us that "While criminal behavior is an expression of general needs and values, it is not explained by these general needs and values, since noncriminal behavior is an expression of the same general needs and values" (Sutherland & Cressey, 1978, p. 82).

Insider trading differs from some law-breaking in the corporate world, such as antitrust crimes, which most directly advance the fortunes of the business entity rather than the perpetrator (Geis, 1998), though in some cases, insider trading will be undertaken to benefit securities brokerage firms (Zey, 1993, 1999). Insider trading can further be distinguished from embezzlement, where the employing firm is directly victimized (Cressey, 1953; Zietz, 1981) and from the "collective embezzlement" (Calavita, Pontell, & Tillman, 1997) that marked the savings and loan scandals. In the savings and loan cases, the banking institution was used by its owners as a tool to garner illegal profits. Insider trading does not deprive the company of its use of the information, only its exclusive use.

Similarly, the characteristics of insider traders could be distinguished from other white-collar offenders. Research by Weisburd et al. (1991), for example, showed that white-collar crime was found predominantly in middle management or the lower echelons of business. Such evidence conformed to the assumptions of self-control theory. In their study of white-collar crime prosecuted in the federal courts, Weisburd et al. found that only 16 percent of their sample of bank embezzlers were owners or officers, and only 55 percent were male (pp. 50–51). There was also evidence to suggest that theft was more frequent among employees in low status positions, although this might be dependent upon their length of service (Hollinger & Clark, 1983; Tucker, 1989). Insider traders came from a different background than employee thieves or embezzlers. Insider trading defendants were almost exclusively male, and were primarily composed of corporate officers and directors (and their tippees) who, one would suspect, had a considerable investment in their public persona.

These differences, however, might simply be an artifact of opportunity: lower-status business employees were not often privy to confidential corporate information. Defendants from the securities field, where confidential information was potentially available to a wider range of individuals, were more likely to have a lower status position as predicted by self-control theory. Securities defendants were also more likely than business defendants to recidivate. Half of these defendants committed more than one offense, whereas the vast majority of business defendants, composed primarily of corporate officers and directors who likely possessed greater self-control, illegally traded on only one occasion. The same was true for tipping behavior; 63.4 percent of the securities related offenders tipped others compared to only 36.5 percent of the business insiders.

The role played by opportunity, which was mentioned prominently but not explicated in self-control theory, was highly significant in explaining insider trading and was likely intertwined with motivation (also see Yeager & Reed, 1998). Research data demonstrated how persons so often committed crimes related to the position they occupied in the social structure. Accountants embezzle, inner-city youths steal automobiles and sell drugs, business people and securities professionals take advantage of confidential information by engaging in insider trading. Opportunities for the motivated offender were often guided by unanticipated circumstances. It was difficult, however, to determine whether the motivation preceded the opportunity or the perceived opportunity (plus whatever else played into the mixture) fueled the motive.

Another claim by the self-control theory was that offenders were risk-seeking. The literature on insider trading demonstrated that insider traders attempted to diminish their risk in the marketplace by trading on a "sure thing." Much like antitrust activities (Geis, 1967; Jamieson, 1994), insider trading served to increase the certainty of a profitable outcome. Market investors tended to be risk aversive, searching to minimize losses and to establish a certain level of control (Reichman, 1991). "Market participation depends, in some measure, on players' abilities to 'encapsulate' or 'frame' their risks, i.e., to transform uncertainty into more manageable, acceptable, and profitable risks" (Reichman, 1991, p. 264). Moreover, some insider trading defendants took steps to reduce detection, for example, by using off-shore accounts or by trading in nominee accounts. Rather than seeking action or risk, insider traders appeared to take illegal advantage of situations when they perceived minimal risk (also see Grasmick, Tittle, Bursik, & Arneklev, 1993).

One intriguing distinction stood out between insider trading and virtually all other forms of criminal behavior. This was the extent to which offenses involved tipping. Burglars, of course, sometimes receive information about particularly attractive targets. Their informants were likely to be people such as maintenance workers and rug cleaners who had legitimate access to a house they then cased. For their inside information, they ordinarily would receive a small percentage of the loot (Wright & Decker, 1994). In insider trading, a common scenario was for the possessor of fiscally valuable information to tell others how to cash in on that information or how to avoid a likely loss. Such behavior demonstrated an impulsiveness and risk-taking, which was consistent with a lack of self-control. Similarly, the tippees failed to exercise self-control by taking advantage of a lucrative financial opportunity. This situation was not far different from the chronic gossiper who could not resist passing along tidbits of information even though he or she knew that some harm might be done to others and the behavior might boomerang to cloud the messenger's image.

On the other hand, insider traders were not indiscreet, but selective in whom they confided in. The individuals tipped were primarily family members, friends, and associates and the act appeared to build, enhance, or stimulate relationships rather than interfere with them. This behavior ran contrary to the hedonistic traits that comprised the self-control theory, particularly in the case of the small fraction of defendants who tipped only and did not themselves trade.

The data provided support for the self-control theory in the area where the theory was most criticized by white-collar criminologists. The accepted wisdom was that insider trading exemplified the specialized expertise required for white-collar crime, but the data suggested otherwise. Unlike traditional theft or embezzlement, insider trading involved the use of information that was typically legitimately acquired as a consequence of one's occupational position. There were no goods to conceal or remove, no signatures to forge, and no surveillance equipment to bypass. The skills and technology used to steal information in corporate espionage, such as electronic eavesdropping or computer hacking, were not essential elements in the commission of insider trading. Only when an insider (or someone tipped by the insider) traded in the securities market on the basis of confidential information did an offense occur. It was the trade or the tip that the insider must conceal and not the possession of information.

Some insider traders might employ elaborate measures to cover up their illegal trades. For example, Dennis Levine cultivated a network of information sources, arranged an off-shore banking and trading account under a disguised identity, and prepared exculpatory documentation to justify his trading (Levine, 1991). The more typical occurrence, however, involved relatively little effort or skill. Tips were passed during the course of a telephone conversation with a relative or during a game of golf with an associate, while trades might be made in one's own account or in nominee accounts (Ricks, 1989; Stewart, 1991). Likewise, the friends and relatives receiving the tips did not require any specialized skills or training to trade on the basis of the information.

The thesis that the data seemed to support was that absence of self-control might be one of the factors that correlated with violation of the insider trading laws, particularly for the segment of insider traders from the securities industry. Yet, the insider trading data presented some interesting facets that Gottfredson and Hirschi's self-control theory did not take into account, such as the preference for loss avoidance and altruistic tipping. It might be noted in this regard that Collins and Schmidt (1993), administering various personality inventories to a large sample of white-collar offenders in federal prisons as well as a group of nonoffending white-collar persons, found that self-control, as defined by the California Personality Inventory (CPI) (Gough, 1987), did not significantly distinguish the two groups. At the same time, several other segments of the CPI—which the authors grouped under the heading of "social conscientious"—did differentiate them. Like most studies that involve incarcerated offenders, however, despite the authors' assurances, interpreters have to remain wary of the effect of imprisonment on responses to a personality test.

Conclusion

The data for this article were generated in regard to events that occurred during a decade in which greed was declared to be good, conspicuous consumption was in vogue, and the securities industry was awash in a sea of unprecedented growth. Detection of insider trading became a high priority with federal enforcement officials during these years. Social, political, and economic conditions of that time indicated, as they did with all time-bound criminological inquiry, that caution had to be observed when generalizing the findings into the 1990s and the twenty-first century, though there was little reason to believe that the conclusions were likely to have altered significantly in later years.

The findings told us about the manner in which white-collar criminals, such as insider traders, were dealt with by the legal system. Such persons predominantly were charged civilly, with penalties that most usually specified disgorgement of illegally acquired gains as well as a fine of the same amount. While the penalty might represent a financial strain for some defendants, insider traders were allowed to settle their cases without admitting or denying guilt and, for the most part, they avoided the stigma associated with a criminal conviction. Undoubtedly, the difficulty of proving violations beyond a reasonable doubt, the prospect of financial recovery of losses, and the very considerable skills of the defense bar involved in handling white-collar crimes (Mann, 1985) pressed prosecutors to file civil actions, considerations that did not prevail in regard to street crimes.

When insider traders were convicted or pleaded guilty in criminal proceedings, they were unlikely to be treated leniently. Though they were, so far as the record showed, usually first-time offenders, the amounts they stole were much greater than the typical haul of street criminals. In addition, the breach of trust might itself be viewed as notably serious (Shapiro, 1990). Clearly, the imprisonment rate for insider trading established it as a white-collar crime dealt with rather severely. Public opinion surveys indicated that such severity accorded with public sentiment (Rossi & Berk, 1997).

There exists a very large and important white-collar crime literature that ties such matters as the economic well-being of corporations to illegal behaviors such as antitrust violations (see, e.g., Simpson, 1986). Economists warmly recommend such studies, noting that they are "especially attractive because the indicators cited can be readily computed or accessed without gaining entry to the firms themselves" (Szwajkowski, 1985, p. 566). What is required, most certainly in the realm of studies of insider trading, however, is movement from the basic numerical picture, which is provided, into the minds and motives of those who engage in the behavior. Clues regarding what to look for are not wanting. This work, for instance, showed that those who transiently came across valuable inside information were more likely than long-term players to repeatedly use information illegally (cf., Geis, 1994). This was likely because they felt less loyalty to the organization they traduced, because they were not likely to have had further dealings with it, or because they felt their actions were less likely to be scrutinized.

For purposes of theory formulation, this article offers an array of information that existing general theories must absorb satisfactorily if they are to be supported. For another, it suggests that broadly defined criminal acts may often have to be split into more homogenous units for purposes of satisfactory theoretical interpretation, just as homicide may require subdivision into such distinct segments as infanticide, organized crime killing, and terrorist slaughters. For a third, the information put together here raises important follow-on questions that probably can best be answered by learning from offenders how they understood what they were doing, what they expected to accomplish, and what they presumed were their chances of being caught at it. Finally, it would suggest that criminological theory very likely has overreached the existent quality of available data, and criminologists might well retreat from general theories and perhaps even from theories of the middle-range, to explanations located at what might be called the lower-range, and then build upon these.

REFERENCES

Administrative Office of the United States Courts (1995). *Annual report of the director.* Washington, DC: U.S. Government Printing Office.

Barlow, H. D. (1991). Explaining crimes and analogous acts, or the unrestrained will grab at pleasure whenever they can. *Journal of Criminal Law and Criminology, 82,* 229–242.

Benson, M. L., & Moore, E. (1992). Are white-collar and common offenders the same?: an empirical and theoretical critique of a recently proposed General Theory of Crime. *Journal of Research in Crime and Delinquency, 29,* 251–272.

Brickey, K. F. (1990). *Corporate and white collar crime: cases and materials.* Boston: Little, Brown and Company.

Calavita, K., Pontell, H. N., & Tillman, R. H. (1997). *Big money crime: fraud and politics in the savings and loan crisis.* Berkeley: University of California Press.

Carr, B. J. (2000). Culpable intent required for all criminal insider trading convictions after *United States v. O'Hagan. Boston College Law Review, 40,* 1188–1218.

Coffee, J. C., Jr. (1988). Hush!: the criminal status of confidential information after McNally and Carpenter and the enduring problem of overcriminalization. *American Criminal Law Review, 26,* 121–154.

Collins, J. M., & Schmidt, F. L. (1993). Personality, integrity, and white-collar crime: a construct validity study. *Personnel Psychology, 46,* 295–311.

Cressey, D. R. (1953). *Other people's money: the social psychology of embezzlement.* New York: Free Press.

Curran, D. J., & Renzetti, C. M. (1994). *Theories of crime.* Boston: Allyn and Bacon.

Dooley, M. P. (1980). Enforcement of insider trading regulations. *Virginia Law Review, 66,* 1–80.

Geis, G. (1967). The heavy electrical equipment antitrust cases of 1961. In M. Clinard, & R. Quinney (Eds.), *Criminal behavior systems* (pp. 139–150). New York: Holt, Rinehart & Winston.

Geis, G. (1994). Trade secret theft as an analogue to treason. In T. R. Sarbin, R. M. Carney, & C. Eoyang (Eds.), *Citizen espionage: studies in trust and betrayal* (pp. 127–142). Westport, CT: Praeger.

Geis, G. (1998). Antitrust and organizational deviance. In P. A. Bamberger, & W. F. Sonnenstuhl (Eds.), *Research in the sociology of organizations: deviance in and of organizations* (pp. 71–100). Stamford, CT: JAI Press.

Geis, G. (2000). On the absence of self-control as the basis for a general theory of crime: a critique. *Theoretical Criminology, 4,* 35–53.

Gottfredson, M. R., & Hirschi, T. (1990). *A general theory of crime.* Stanford, CA: Stanford University Press.

Gough, H. G. (1987). *The California Psychological Inventory administrator's guide*. Palo Alto, CA: Consulting Psychological Press.

Grasmick, H. G., Tittle, C. R., Bursik, R. J., Jr., & Arneklev, B. J. (1993). Testing the core empirical implications of Gottfredson and Hirschi's general theory of crime. *Journal of Research in Crime and Delinquency, 30,* 5–29.

Haddock, D. D., & Macey, J. R. (1987). Regulation on demand: a private interest model, with an application to insider trading regulation. *Journal of Law and Economics, 30,* 311–352.

Hagan, J., & Nagel, I. (1982). White-collar crime, white-collar time: the sentencing of white-collar offenders in the southern district of New York. *American Criminal Law Review, 20,* 259–289.

Hagan, J., & Parker, P. (1985). White-collar crime and punishment: the class structure and legal sanctioning of securities violations. *American Sociological Review, 50,* 302–316.

Hirschi, T. (1969). *The causes of delinquency.* Berkeley: University of California Press.

Hollinger, R. C., & Clark, J. P. (1983). Deterrence in the workplace: perceived certainty, perceived severity, and employee theft. *Social Forces, 62,* 398–418.

Jamieson, K. M. (1994). *The organization of corporate crime: dynamics of antitrust violation.* Thousand Oaks, CA: Sage Publications.

Kahneman, D., & Tversky, A. (1979). Prospect theory: an analysis of decision under risk. *Econometrica, 47,* 263–291.

Katz, J. (1979). Legality and equality: plea bargaining in the prosecution of white-collar crime. *Law and Society Review, 13,* 431–459.

Kornbluth, J. (1992). *Highly confident: the crime and punishment of Michael Milken.* New York: Morrow.

Levine, D. B. (1991). *Inside out: an insider's account of Wall Street.* New York: Putnam's.

Macey, J. R. (1991). *Insider trading: economics, politics and policy.* Washington, DC: AEI Press.

Mann, K. (1985). *Defending white-collar crime: a portrait of attorneys at work.* New Haven, CT: Yale University Press.

Marcial, G. G. (1995). *Secrets of the street: the dark side of making money.* New York: McGraw-Hill.

McLucas, W. R., Walsh, J. H., & Fountain, L. L. (1992, November). Settlement of insider trading cases with the SEC. *Business Lawyer, 48,* 79–106.

Meulbroek, L. K. (1992). An empirical analysis of illegal insider trading. *Journal of Finance, 47,* 1661–1699.

Newman, S. A., & Kidwell, R. G. (2000). Mail and wire fraud. *American Criminal Law Review, 37,* 707–718.

Noble, K. B. (1981, October 26). S.E.C. chief plans insider trade curb. *New York Times, IV,* D1–D2.

Painter, R. W., Krawiec, K. D., & Williams, C. A. (1998). Don't ask, just tell: insider trading after *United States v. O'Hagan*. *Virginia Law Review, 84,* 153–228.

Polk, K. (1991). Review of *A General Theory of Crime*. *Crime and Delinquency, 37,* 575–581.

Pritchard, A. C. (1998). *United States v. O'Hagan:* Justice Powell's legacy of the law of insider trading. *Boston University Law Review, 78,* 13–58.

Reed, G. E., & Yeager, P. C. (1996). Organizational offending and neoclassical criminology: challenging the reach of a general theory of crime. *Criminology, 34,* 357–382.

Reichman, N. (1991). Regulating risky business: dilemmas in security regulation. *Law and Policy, 13,* 263–295.

Reichman, N. (1992). Moving backstage: uncovering the role of compliance practices in shaping regulatory policy. In M. B. Blankenship (Ed.), *Understanding corporate criminality* (pp. 244–268). New York: Garland.

Reichman, N. (1993). Insider trading. In M. Tonry, & A. J. Reiss (Eds.), *Beyond the law: crime in complex organizations* (pp. 55–96). Chicago: University of Chicago Press.

Ricks, T. E. (1989, July 21). Dangerous game: how 4 pals who mixed golf and stock tips landed in the rough. *Wall Street Journal, Al,* 6.

Rossi, P. H., & Berk, R. A. (1997). *Just punishments: federal sentencing guidelines and public views compared.* New York: Aldine de Gruyter.

Salbu, S. R. (1993). Tipper credibility, noninformational tipper trading, and abstention from trading: an analysis of gaps in insider trading law. *Washington Law Review, 68,* 307–350.

Seyhun, H. N. (1992). The effectiveness of the insider-trading sanctions. *Journal of Law and Economics, 35,* 149–182.

Shapiro, S. (1985). The road not taken: the elusive path to prosecution for white-collar crime offenders. *Law and Society Review, 19,* 195–217.

Shapiro, S. (1990). Collaring the crime, not the criminal: reconsidering the concept of white-collar crime. *American Sociological Review, 55,* 346–365.

Simpson, S. S. (1986). The decomposition of antitrust: testing a multi-level, longitudinal model of profit-squeeze. *American Sociological Review, 51,* 859–875.

Steffensmeier, D. J. (1989). On the causes of white-collar crime: an assessment of Hirschi and Gottfredson's claims. *Criminology, 27,* 345–358.

Stewart, J. B. (1991). *Den of thieves.* New York: Simon and Schuster.

Sutherland, E. H. (1949). *White collar crime.* New York: Dryden.

Sutherland, E. H., & Cressey, D. R. (1978). *Criminology.* (10th ed.). Philadelphia: Lippincott.

Sykes, G., & Matza, D. (1957). Techniques of neutralization: a theory of delinquency. *American Sociological Review, 22,* 664–670.

Szockyj, E. (1993a). Insider trading: the SEC meets Carl Karcher. *Annals of the American Academy of Political and Social Science, 525,* 46–58.

Szockyj, E. (1993b). *The law and insider trading: in search of a level playing field.* Buffalo, NY: William S. Hein.

Szwajkowski, E. (1985). Occupational illegality: theoretical integration and illustrative application. *Academy of Management Review, 10,* 558–567.

Terpstra, D. E., Reyes, M. G. C., & Bokor, D. W. (1991). Predictors of ethical decisions regarding insider trading. *Journal of Business Ethics, 10,* 699–710.

Tomasic, R. (1991). *Casino capitalism? Insider trading in Australia.* Canberra, ACT: Australian Institute of Criminology.

Tucker, J. (1989). Employee theft as social control. *Deviant Behavior, 10,* 319–334.

Tversky, A., & Kahneman, D. (1990). Rational choice and the framing of decision. In K. S. Cook, & M. Levi (Eds.), *The limits of rationality* (pp. 60–89). Chicago: University of Chicago Press.

U.S. Bureau of Economic Analysis (1996). *Survey of current business.* Washington, DC: BEA.

U.S. Department of Justice (1994). *Crime in the United States, 1993.* Washington, DC: Government Printing Office.

U.S. House of Representatives (1983). Committee on Energy and Commerce. *Insider Trading Sanctions Act of 1983.* Report No. 355. 98th Cong., 1st Sess.

Weinberger, A. M. (1990). Preventing insider trading violations: a survey of corporate compliance programs. *Securities Regulation Law Journal, 18,* 180–193.

Weisburd, D., Wheeler, S., Waring, E., & Bode, N. (1991). *Crimes of the middle classes: white-collar offenders in the federal courts.* New Haven, CT: Yale University Press.

Weng, W. K. S., & Steinberg, M. I. (1996). *Insider trading.* Boston: Little, Brown and Company.

Winans, R. F. (1986). *Trading secrets.* New York: St. Martin's Press.

Wright, R., & Decker, S. H. (1994). *Burglars on the job: Streetlife and residential break-ins.* Boston: Northeastern University Press.

Yeager, P. C., & Reed, G. E. (1998). Of corporate persons and straw men: a reply to Herbert, Green and Larragoite. *Criminology, 36,* 885–897.

Zey, M. (1993). *Banking on fraud: Drexel, junk bonds, and buyouts.* New York: Aldine de Gruyter.

Zey, M. (1999). The subsidiarization of the securities industry and the organization of securities fraud networks to return profits in the 1990s. *Work and Occupations, 26,* 50–76.

Zietz, D. (1981). *Women who embezzle or defraud: a study of convicted felons.* New York: Praeger.

Case Cited

United States v. O'Hagan, 521 U.S. 642 (1997).

Part 4

Other Forms of White-Collar Crime

The preceding sections addressed defining white-collar crime, corporate crimes, and Wall Street crimes. Corporate and Wall Street crimes have the most notoriety and result in the greatest amount of public condemnation—especially after the collapse of the mortgage industry, failure of the big banks, and Washington's bailout of large corporations. Nonetheless, it is important to remember that white-collar crime is generally associated with political and corporate elites who use their position to commit some type of crime—whether larceny, fraud, or the sale of inferior products or services. Even though white-collar crime is generally associated with corporations and the elite, it is not necessarily confined to this space. Indeed, white-collar crime can occur at the lowest levels of business, government, and society.

This section attempts to expand the concept beyond the corporate boardroom and to examine activities that normally are not associated with white-collar crime. Complicating this effort is that there is an overlap between white-collar crime and common criminals regarding some of these activities. For example, Heith Copes and Lynne Vieraitis examine identity theft. Identity theft is the fastest-growing crime in the United States and perhaps the world, and it is a modus operandi used by common criminals as well as elites. It is important to visualize white-collar crime more generally and expansively, since it enhances our understanding of several forms of criminality and crimes. If we examine white-collar crimes as common crime, we often fail to comprehend the crime's gravity and possible social impact. In some cases, these acts become labeled as minor crimes or inconsequential crimes, but in reality, they may have a graver impact on individuals and society. Here, we examine five other forms of white-collar crime: identity theft, political corruption, terrorism financing, Internet and crime, and environmental crime.

Copes and Vieraitis provide a descriptive examination of individuals who have committed identity theft. Essentially, they trace the methods that are used by criminals engaged in identity theft. They found that identity thieves come from varied backgrounds, demonstrating that the crime has inundated our society. The primary motivation for identity theft, like most other forms of crime, was money. Some people needed money to meet their daily needs, while others wanted to continue an extravagant lifestyle. Since there are numerous methods of obtaining identity information, the identity thieves were able to engage in the crime with little difficulty. This shows how alluring the crime is and how easily it can be perpetrated.

Political corruption is a constant systemic problem in US government whether at the national level or the local level. To a great extent, it is a pure form of white-collar crime since it most often involves powerful elites, politicians, and government heads—without question, it always involves an abuse of one's office or position. David Friedrichs identifies several forms of political corruption. Most importantly, he examines the subtleties of political corruption and their implications. For example, it is acceptable, legally but perhaps not morally, for lobbyists to provide politicians with campaign funds to sway votes for a project that will result in financial gain for the lobbyist's client. On the other hand, it is illegal for the lobbyist to give cash directly to the politician for his or her vote. Such distinctions must be understood to comprehend the scope and seriousness of political corruption. Friedrichs provides a foundation for this understanding.

Larry Gaines examines terrorist financing. Terrorist organizations, like businesses, must have the resources needed to carry out attacks and other related activities such as training, organizational maintenance, and logistic support. Today, terrorists are intertwined with transnational organized crime, governments, white-collar criminals, and common criminals such as drug traffickers. Gaines traces the flow of money to Osama bin Laden's operatives for the 9/11 attacks in New York and Washington, identifying many of the legitimate channels that were used to move the money. He also provides an overview of the mechanisms used by terrorist groups to acquire, move, and store money with much of these activities accomplished through *hawalas* or informal banking systems. Political corruption also plays a key role as a number of governments provide support or means to facilitate terrorists' financial activities.

The Internet has become indispensable to individuals, governments, and corporations across the globe. The Internet has ushered in globalization. It also facilitates new forms of criminality—cybercrimes. A number of crimes can be committed using the Internet including electronic piracy, counterfeiting, forgery, money laundering, and fraud. Moreover, the

Internet can be used by criminal cabals to communicate and coordinate a variety of criminal activities. Peter Grabosky examines how these crimes are being committed. He advises that we will see an exponential growth in these crimes in the future, given our relatively weak enforcement mechanisms and the many ways the Internet can be used to commit crime.

Significant and devastating environmental crimes have occurred, and some of these crimes are detailed in the last article in this section. Karen Clark notes that environmental crime frequently intersects with political corruption as corporations attempt to void or otherwise bypass environmental protection laws. These corporations also engage in strenuous lobbying to remove or change environmental regulations to enhance their profit and to the detriment of society, citizens, and the landscape. Even though today we are concerned with global climate change, there are numerous efforts to unleash corporations and industry for the pursuit of profit.

13

Understanding Identity Theft

Offenders' Accounts of Their Lives and Crimes

— *Heith Copes and Lynne M. Vieraitis*

The definition of white-collar crime has engendered much confusion and debate among criminologists since it was introduced nearly seven decades ago and agreement over conceptual boundaries has yet to be achieved. Perspectives on how best to conceptualize white-collar crime tend to fall into one of two camps, what Shover and Cullen (2008) refer to as the populist and patrician paradigms. The populist paradigm is perhaps best exemplified by the work of Sutherland who saw the respectable status of the perpetrators as the defining characteristic of white-collar crime. Those who take this perspective conceive of white-collar crime as involving the "illegal and harmful actions of elites and respectable members of society carried out . . . in the context of legitimate organizational or occupational activity" (Friedrichs, 2004, p. 5). When seen through this lens, white-collar crime evokes images of powerful elites who use their position to fraudulently obtain money and evade prosecution and elicits a critical, reform-oriented stance to research.

The patrician perspective of white-collar crime "takes a narrower, more technical, and less reform-oriented view of white-collar crime"

(Shover & Cullen, 2008, p. 156). Those who define white-collar crime from this perspective place emphasis on the characteristics of the crime rather than the characteristics of the criminal. The work carried out at the Yale Studies of White Collar Crime typifies this perspective (Weisburd, Wheeler, Waring, & Bode, 1991). By reviewing the presentence investigation reports of federal offenders, Weisburd et al. (1991) painted a portrait of white-collar offenders as mundane and ordinary. This camp points out that the notion of white-collar crime being committed only by elites is an exaggeration and, therefore, emphasis should be placed on "collaring the crime, not the criminal" (Shapiro, 1990). As Shapiro (1990) notes, researchers should be "exploring the modus operandi of their misdeeds and the ways in which they establish and exploit trust" (p. 363). Edelhertz (1970) suggests that white-collar crime is "an illegal act or series of illegal acts committed by nonphysical means and by concealment or guile, to obtain money or property, to avoid the payment or loss of money or property or to obtain business or personal advantage" (p. 3). Edelhertz (1970) makes clear the belief that "the character of white-collar crime must be found in its modus operandi and its objectives rather than in the nature of the offenders" (p. 4).

Regardless of whether one emphasizes the status of the offender (populist) or the nature of the crime (patrician), Friedrichs (2004, p. 4) notes that most criminologists who study white-collar crime agree that it occurs in a legitimate occupational context and is motivated by the goal of economic gain or occupational success. This issue was also raised by Newman (1958) who argued that "the chief criterion for a crime to be 'white-collar' is that it occurs as a part of, or a deviation from, the violator's occupational role" (p. 737). Typologies of white-collar crime also illuminate the difficulties in defining white-collar crime and classifying actors and/or actions as white-collar. Numerous typologies have emerged since Sutherland's (1949) *White Collar Crime* with some classifying types of white-collar crime based on the context in which the activity occurs, the status or position of the offender, the primary victims, the primary form of harm, or the legal classification of the offense (Friedrichs, 2004).

According to Braithwaite (1985), the most influential partition has been Clinard and Quinney's (1973) separation of white-collar crime into occupational and corporate crime. In doing so, the term *corporate crime* preserves the original definition of white-collar crime as delineated by Sutherland, but recognizes that lower level white-collar and even blue-collar workers commit crimes in the context of their occupations. Others have added forms of governmental crime, hybrid forms of white-collar crime (e.g., state-corporate crime, crimes of globalization, and finance crime), and "residual" forms such as technocrime and avocational crime (Friedrichs, 2004).

When labeling acts as *white-collar*, researchers typically use definitions from one of the two camps. But some crimes are hard to classify in either of these broad categories, which makes it difficult to determine the best conceptual lens with which to understand these crimes. Friedrichs

(2004, p. 187) argues that identity theft is a classic example of a hybrid form of white-collar crime based on the observation that a victim's identifying information is often taken by an employee and passed along to others. Thus, the employee and his/her actions may be classified as white-collar criminal and white-collar crime, respectively, but how does one classify the use of the identifying information that likely follows? Many perceive identity theft to be so sophisticated that it is committed predominantly by computer specialists, organized criminal networks, or sophisticated "hackers" who access such databases.[1] Others see it as a crime so mundane that it has become the crime of choice for those who have succumbed to the effects of methamphetamine addiction (Gayer, 2003). Thus, current discussions of identity theft focus either on drug addicted, unsophisticated mail thieves and dumpster divers, or more commonly on high-tech hackers and phishers. Such varied portrayals of the crime raise the question, is identity theft a white-collar crime? Our goals for this study are to contextualize previous research based on victimization surveys and law enforcement case files and to determine if identity theft should be treated as a white-collar offense using either of the two broad definitions. To do this we rely on the accounts of 59 federally convicted identity thieves to examine their personal backgrounds and the techniques they use to acquire identifying information and convert it into cash or goods.

Identity Theft in Context

Although it is difficult to gauge the extent of identity theft, it is possible to determine a general pattern of the crime by comparing the various attempts by public and private agencies to measure it. Numerous sources support the claim that identity theft rose considerably over the past decade. According to reports from the Federal Trade Commission (FTC), identity theft has been the most prevalent form of fraud committed in the United States for the past 7 years, comprising 36% of fraud complaints filed in the year 2006 (FTC, 2007). According to the Gartner Survey and the Privacy and American Business (P&AB, 2003) survey, the incidence of identity theft almost doubled from 2001 to 2002. The Social Security Administration's fraud hotline received approximately 65,000 reports of social security number misuse in 2001, more than a five-fold increase from the 11,000 reported in 1998 (U.S. General Accounting Office, 2002). Data from the FTC (2004) suggest that identity theft rose from 86,212 in 2000 to 214,905 in 2003, nearly a 250% increase. Recent data from the FTC indicate that identity theft reports have been relatively stable the past 3 years.

In 2007, the FTC released a report on estimates of the incidence and costs of identity theft. According to the report, approximately eight million people experienced identity theft in 2005 and total losses were nearly $16 billion (Synovate, 2007). According to the National Crime Victimization Survey (NCVS), in 2005, 6.4 million households, representing 5.5% of the households in the United States discovered that at least one member of the household had been the victim of identity theft during the previous 6 months. The estimated financial loss reported by victimized households was about $3.2 billion (Bureau of Justice Statistics [BJS], 2006). Regardless of how identity theft is measured, reports indicate that it is a growing and costly crime.

Identity Theft Offenders

Despite the creation of identity theft task forces throughout the country, clearance rates for identity theft are low. Available evidence suggests that offenders are seldom detected and rarely apprehended (Allison, Schuck, & Lersch, 2005; Gayer, 2003; Owens, 2004). The paucity of research on identity theft coupled with the low clearance rate makes it difficult to have a clear description of those who engage in this offense. To date only two studies have provided data on identity thieves, both rely on law enforcement files (e.g., closed cases or police reports). To gain an understanding of the type of individual who commits identity theft, Gordon, Rebovich, Choo, and Gordon (2007) examined closed U.S. Secret Service cases with an identity theft component from 2000 to 2006. They found that most offenders (42.5%) were between the ages of 25 and 34 years when the case was opened. And another one-third fell within the 35 to 49 years age group. Using data from a large metropolitan police department in Florida, Allison et al. (2005) found that offenders ranged in age from 28 to 49 years with a mean age of 32 years.

Both studies found similar patterns regarding race. Gordon et al. (2007) found that the majority of the offenders were Black (54%), with Whites and Hispanics accounting for 38% and 5% of offenders, respectively. Allison et al. (2005) found that the distribution of offenders was 69% Black, 27% White, and less than 1% were Hispanic or Asian. The two studies differed in terms of the gender of offenders. Gordon et al. (2007) found that nearly two-thirds of the offenders were male. Whereas, Allison et al. (2005) found that 63% of offenders were female.

Techniques of Identity Theft

To be successful at identity theft, would-be offenders must secure identifying information and convert it into goods or cash. Identity thieves have developed a number of techniques and strategies to do this. Researchers and law enforcement agencies have collected information, primarily from victimization surveys, on the techniques identity thieves commonly employ.

The first step in the successful commission of identity theft is to obtain personal information on the victim, which is relatively easy for offenders to do. Offenders obtain this information from wallets, purses, homes, cars, offices, and businesses or institutions that maintain customer, employee, patient, or student records (Newman, 2004). Social security numbers, which provide instant access to a person's personal information, are widely used for identification and account numbers by insurance companies, universities, cable television companies, military identification, and banks. The thief may steal a wallet or purse, work at a job that affords him/her access to credit records, may purchase the information from someone who does (e.g., employees who have access to credit reporting databases commonly available in auto dealerships, realtor's offices, banks, and other businesses that approve loans), or may find victims' information by stealing mail, sorting through the trash, or by searching the Internet (Davis & Stevenson, 2004; Lease & Burke, 2000; LoPucki, 2001; Newman, 2004).

Based on victim surveys, most offenders commit identity theft by obtaining a person's credit card information, which they use to forge a credit card in the victim's name and use it to make purchases (P&AB, 2003). According to the P&AB survey, 34% of victims reported that their information was obtained this way. In addition, 12% reported that someone stole or obtained a paper or computer record with their personal information on it, 11% said someone stole their wallet or purse; 10% said someone opened charge accounts in stores in their name; 7% said someone opened a bank account in their name or forged checks; 7% said someone got to their mail or mailbox; 5% said they lost their wallet or purse; 4% said someone went to a public record; and 3% said someone created false IDs to get government benefits or payments (P&AB, 2003).

Data from the FTC suggest that of those who knew how their information was obtained (43%), 16% said their information was stolen by someone they personally knew; 7% during a purchase or financial transaction; 5% reported their information was obtained from a stolen wallet or purse; 5% cited theft from a company that maintained their information; and 2% from the mail (Synovate, 2007). Other techniques have been identified such as organized rings in which a person is planted as an employee in a mortgage lender's office, doctor's office, or human resources department to more easily access information. Similarly, these groups will bribe insiders such as employees of banks, car dealerships, government, and hospitals to get the identifying information. Others have obtained credit card numbers by soliciting information using bogus e-mails (phishing) or simply by watching someone type in a calling card number or credit card number (Davis & Stevenson, 2004).

According to the FTC, the most common type of identity theft was credit card fraud followed by "other" identity theft, phone or utilities fraud, bank fraud (fraud involving checking and savings accounts and electronic fund transfers), employment-related fraud, government documents or benefits fraud, and loan fraud (FTC, 2007). Although not directly comparable due to differences in methodology, units of analysis, and definition of identity theft, data from the NCVS indicate that of the 6.4 million households reporting that at least one member of the household had been the victim of identity theft, the most common type was unauthorized use of existing credit cards (BJS, 2007).

Methods

The present study is based on data collected from interviews with 59 inmates incarcerated in U.S. federal prisons for identity theft or identity theft-related crimes. The interviews were conducted from March 2006 to February 2007. A purposive sampling strategy was employed to locate suitable participants, which involved an examination of newspapers and legal documents from across the United States. Lexis-Nexis News, an electronic database that organizes newspapers from around the United States by region and state, was used as the source for the newspapers. The Lexis-Nexis Legal Research database, containing decisions from all federal courts, and the Westlaw database, were also searched using the term *18 U.S.C. § 1028*, which is the U.S. federal statute for identity theft. Finally, the websites of U.S. Attorneys in all 93 U.S. districts were searched for press releases and indictments regarding individuals charged with identity theft.

The online Federal Bureau of Prisons Inmate Locator (www.bop.gov) was then used to determine whether the offenders identified during the earlier searches were housed in federal facilities at the time of the study. In total, this process yielded the names of 297 identity thieves. To sample participants, visits were made to the 14 correctional facilities that housed the largest number of inmates in each of the six regions defined by the Federal Bureau of Prisons (Western, North Central, South Central, North Eastern, Mid-Atlantic, and South Eastern). A total of 65 individuals who were incarcerated for identity theft, primarily aggravated identity theft, were interviewed. However, six interviews were excluded from the analysis because the offenders denied taking part in or having knowledge of the identity theft (if they had a codefendant) or because they committed fraud without stealing the victims' identities. The final sample consisted of 59 people who had engaged in identity theft.

Some argue that interviews with active, free-ranging offenders have numerous advantages over those with incarcerated offenders (Jacobs & Wright, 2006). Purportedly, findings based on inmate interviews may be biased because the participants are "unsuccessful," fearful of further legal sanctions, and likely to reconstruct their offenses in an overly rational manner. However, many of these claims against captive populations are overstated (Copes & Hochstetler, in press). In fact, a recent study examining target selection of burglars found a "striking similarity" between studies using free-ranging and prison-based samples

(Nee & Taylor 2000, p. 45). Little is gained by denying that the interview setting colors narratives or that conversations with social scientists are not different than what might be said elsewhere. Yet offenders appear to report similar patterns of behavior regardless of how they were originally contacted or where they were interviewed.

Semistructured interviews were used to explore offenders' life circumstances at the times of their crimes, their reasons for becoming involved in and continuing with identity theft, and the techniques they used to secure information to commit fraud and convert it into cash or goods. This style of interview allows the participants to discuss their crimes in their own words and with detail. Moreover, it allows the researcher to gain in-depth knowledge about the subject matter, in this case, the backgrounds and modus operandi of identity thieves.

The interviews took place in private rooms in the correctional facilities, such as offices, visiting rooms, and attorney–client rooms. For the majority of the interviews the authors interviewed as a pair, with one acting as lead and the other taking notes and ensuring that important questions were not left out. The one constant in the interview settings was that interviewers were alone with participants during the interview. Although correctional officers were nearby, they were unable to listen in on the conversations. This was important because participants may be hesitant to speak freely with the worry of staff overhearing the details of their lives and crimes. When possible, interviews were audio recorded and then transcribed verbatim. However, some wardens denied us permission to bring recording devices into their facilities and some offenders agreed to the interview only if it was not recorded. All but nine interviews were recorded. Detailed notes were taken during the interviews that were not recorded. The transcribed interviews and detailed notes taken from nonrecorded interviews were analyzed with QSR NVivo 7 (Richards, 1999). To ensure interrater reliability, the two authors read independently each transcript to identify common themes. The authors then convened to determine the overarching themes they had identified.

Background Characteristics of Identity Thieves

The common perception of identity thieves is that they are more akin to middle-class fraudsters than they are to street-level property offenders. That is, they hail disproportionately from the middle classes, they are college educated, and they have stable family lives. To determine if identity thieves resemble other fraudsters, various demographic characteristics including age, race, gender, employment status, and educational achievement were collected. In addition, offenders were asked about their socioeconomic status, family status, and criminal history.

Overall, it was found that identity theft was a democratic crime. Its participants came from all walks of life and had diverse criminal histories. In fact, they were just as likely to resemble persistent street thieves as they were middle-class fraudsters.

Gender, Race/Ethnicity, and Age

Table 1 shows the gender, race, and age distributions of the sample. The final sample of 59 inmates included 23 men and 36 women, which was consistent with the findings of Allison et al. (2005). However, the discrepancy in gender in our sample is likely due to our sampling strategy and the higher response rate from female inmates rather than the actual proportion of identity theft offenders. For example, the gender makeup of the full list of located identity thieves was more similar to that found by Gordon et al. (2007): 63% male and 37% female. The racial makeup of the sample was 44% White, 53% Black, and 3% other. The makeup for the full list of located inmates was 50% White, 46% Black, and 4% other. This is a higher percentage of White offenders than found by either Gordon et al. (2007) or Allison et al. (2005). Offenders in the sample ranged in age from 23 to 60 years with a mean age of 38 years. The majority of offenders were aged 25 to 34 (34%) or 35 to 44 (32%). Only 7% were aged 18 to 24 years and 5% were older than 55 years. The age distribution matches closely with the larger sampling pool and that found by Gordon et al. (2007) and Allison et al. (2005).

Table 1.
Gender, Race, and Age of Identity Thieves[a]

	Sampling Pool		Final Sample	
	N	Percentage	*N*	Percentage
Gender				
Male	187	63.0	23	39.0
Female	110	27.0	36	61.0
Race				
White	148	50.8	26	44.1
Black	137	46.1	31	52.5
Other	12	4.0	2	3.4
Age (Years)				
18–24	15	5.1	4	7.0
25–34	91	30.6	20	33.9
35–44	113	37.8	19	32.2
45–54	61	20.6	13	22.0
≥55	17	5.9	3	5.1

[a] Information collected from Bureau of Prisons Inmate Locator.

Table 2.
Employment Histories

	N	Percentage
Employed during lifetime		
Yes	47	79.7
No	3	5.1
Unknown	9	15.3
Employed during ID theft		
Yes	31	52.5
No	21	35.6
Unknown	7	11.9
Employment facilitated ID theft		
Yes	21	35.6
No	32	54.2
Unknown	6	10.2

Employment History

Most offenders had been employed at some point during their life-times (see Table 2). The diversity of jobs included day laborers, store clerks, nurses, and attorneys. At the time of their crimes 52.5% were employed and a total of 35.5% of the sample reported that their employ-ment facilitated the identity thefts. The majority of those who used their jobs to carry out their crimes committed mortgage fraud. Others worked at businesses that had access to credit cards and/or social security num-bers (e.g., department stores that granted credit or government agencies). These people used their position to obtain information and either used it themselves or sold it to others who then committed fraud. For instance, one offender worked as a junior recruiter for the National Guard and used his position to obtain identifying information. In his words:

> The military has [a form], which has all of your history on it, Social Security numbers, dates of birth, last known addresses that kind of stuff. And we use that to solicit people to come into the National Guard. . . . After I had gotten out [of the National Guard] I still had the information. . . . I had talked to some other people about how to get credit cards and stuff like that. Then I started, you know.

Not all used their positions to steal information; some used their employment to facilitate identity theft. For example, several worked at local Department of Motor Vehicles offices and used their position to help others obtain fraudulent identification. Most of them claimed that they sought employment at these places legitimately and then were approached by others to commit the fraud. Few said that they sought employment for the purposes of gaining easy access to sensitive information or to facilitate the thefts. Although the majority of thieves we spoke with did not commit identity theft through the course of their occupations, a significant number of offenders indicated that their past employment experience gave them insiders' knowledge that enabled them to carry out their crimes. This included knowledge of real estate transactions and how banks, credit agencies, and department stores operated and extended credit.

Criminal History

A total of 37 (63%) of the offenders reported that they had been arrested for crimes other than those for which they were currently incarcerated (see Table 3). Of those who had prior arrests most were for financial fraud or identity theft ($n = 26$) but drug use/sales ($n = 11$) and property crimes ($n = 13$) were also relatively common, which is consistent with Gordon et al.'s (2007) findings. A total of 26 had also been convicted of a crime. Again, most of these convictions were for financial fraud or identity theft ($n = 15$).

Table 3.
Criminal Histories

	N	Percentage
Prior arrest		
Yes	37	62.7
No	19	32.2
Unknown	3	5.1
Prior arrests by crime types [a]		
Property crime	13	35.1
Violent crime	4	10.8
Drug possession/sales	11	29.7
Fraud	19	51.4
ID theft	7	18.9
Other	3	8.1
Unknown	2	5.4
Prior convictions		
Yes	26	44.1
No	25	42.4
Unknown	8	13.6
Prior convictions by crime types [a]		
Property crime	5	19.2
Violent crime	2	7.7
Drug possession/sales	2	7.7
Fraud	13	50.0
ID theft	2	7.7
Other	1	3.8
Unknown	8	30.8

[a] For some categories percentages do not add up to 100% because some offenders reported more than one answer.

Researchers are unclear as to the degree that offenders specialize in particular crimes. Here again our sample showed diversity. Prior arrest patterns indicate that a large portion of them had engaged in various types of crime, including drug, property, and violent crimes. Yet the majority of them claimed that they only committed identity thefts or comparable frauds (e.g., check fraud). Although several offenders described having committed other crimes in the past, they stopped these other criminal endeavors because they could make more money through identity theft. For example, one offender said, "[selling drugs is] not the answer. That's not where the money is," and another, who switched from burglaries to identity theft, argued that, "[identity theft] is easier and you get the money, you know. You get a lot of money."

Inmates were also questioned about their prior drug use (see Table 4). A total of 34 (58%) had tried drugs in their lifetime, mostly marijuana, cocaine in various forms, and methamphetamine. Only 22 reported having been addicted to their drug of choice. Of those offenders who said that they were using drugs while committing identity theft, only 14 reported that the

Table 4.
Drug Histories

	N	Percentage
Drug use ever		
Yes	34	57.6
No	22	37.3
Unknown	3	5.1
Drug addiction		
Yes	22	37.3
No	31	52.5
Unknown	6	10.2
Drug use during ID theft		
Yes	25	42.4
No	31	52.5
Unknown	3	5.1
Type of drug used during theft[a]		
Cocaine (powder and crack)	10	40.0
Heroin	3	12.0
Marijuana	6	24.0
Prescription	1	4.0
Methamphetamine	7	28.0
Unknown	8	32.0
Drug use contributed to ID theft		
Yes	14	23.7
No	41	69.5
Unknown	4	6.8

[a] For some categories percentages do not add up to 100% because some offenders reported more than one answer.

drug use contributed to their identity thefts. Despite current claims about the link between methamphetamines and identity theft, only five of those with whom we spoke said that methamphetamine use directly contributed to their crimes. One respondent claimed, "I started smoking meth, then I stopped working, and then I started doing this for money." This finding is supported by Gordon et al. (2007).

Family Background, Marital Status, and Educational Attainment

To gain an understanding of their life experiences, offenders were asked to describe their past and current family situation (see Table 5). To assess social class a subjective measure was used by asking offenders to self-identify with a class based on their parents' occupations and lifestyles. When asked to describe their family's status growing up, most offenders classified their family background as either working-class (47.5%) or middle/upper-middle class (42.4%). Whereas a few of the parents of those who self-defined as working class made a living through crime, the majority said that their parents worked at jobs such as manual laborers. A typical response to what their families were like was, "Growing up, my mom was actually in prison. She was here actually for ten years and then my dad, like I said I don't know about him." Another replied:

> I had a rough background. Since I've been incarcerated, I've been able to reflect on everything that led me up to where I was a couple of years ago. Let's see. I'm a middle child of 5 girls and I'm from Chicago. My mother was a single parent. She was physically abused by my father. They were divorced when I was 4, but I remember the fights, you know? My mother was remarried. Her second husband had sexually molested me and that was like one time. I was 12 years old, but that never was able to be dealt with and I think I had a lot of anger starting at 11 years old that I held in. So my anger wanted to get back but I didn't know how.

Not all came from such humble beginnings, as over half claimed to hail from middle-class or upper middle-class families. The parents of those who self-defined as middle-class held jobs such as doctors, nurses, engineers, or other white-collar positions. When asked to describe their childhood one respondent said, "Typical middle-class. Both parents, actually my mother didn't work until the children were grown and out of the house (I have two younger sisters). My father's always been in law enforcement, he's also military, he's a colonel in the army." Another described, "[My] parents went to work and we went to school. . . . We had computers. Pretty much didn't want for anything."

Of those for which information was available, 39% came from broken homes, which is reflected in some of the above quotes. Most offenders were currently or had been married in their lifetimes: 25% of

Table 5.
Family Background, Marital Status, and Educational Attainment

	N	Percentage
Socioeconomic class		
Under/working class	28	47.5
Middle/upper-middle class	25	42.4
Unknown	6	10.2
Family background		
Broken	23	39.0
Intact	17	28.8
Unknown	19	32.2
Marital status		
Never married	19	32.2
Divorced/separated/widowed	21	35.6
Married	15	25.4
Unknown	4	6.8
Children		
Yes	44	74.6
No	11	18.6
Unknown	4	6.8
Educational attainment		
No high school diploma	9	15.3
High school diploma	10	16.9
Some college	19	32.2
College degree	12	20.3
Unknown	9	15.3

offenders were married, 30.5% were separated/divorced, 32.2% had never been married, and 5.1% were widowed. Divorces or separations were factors, among many, that instigated identity theft for 10 people. One female offender's remarks exemplify this process:

> I had gotten divorced, I was a single mom, and I was struggling. I was working, but I've worked for a number of years as an independent contractor doing medical transcription, and I lost some of my accounts. I was struggling with depression and dealing with a lot of things. I had met some ladies and we started talking and . . . we began to socialize and they said, "We do identity theft and we think you would do really good going into a bank and taking some money out. We can split that with you and you can have some money." I said okay and that's how I started.

Only one individual said that her thefts led to her divorce. Approximately 75% of offenders had children. With respect to educational achievement, the majority of offenders had had at least some college.

Based on the background characteristics of the identity thieves in our sample, it would be difficult to classify them as *white-collar* offenders.

They came from a variety of socioeconomic classes, occupations, and varied in their employment histories. Weisburd et al.'s (1991) study also reported a diversity of classes represented in their sample of white-collar offenders, with the majority hailing from the middle class. Thus, if one were to adhere to the populist perspective regarding the definition of white-collar crime, the majority of identity thieves in our sample would not be considered white-collar criminals; nor would their crimes be considered white-collar. The majority of offenders were not of high economic, social, or occupational status nor did most of them commit their thefts through the course of their occupation. In fact, most of the offenders who were employed at the time of their crimes did not use their positions to gain identifying information and commit identity theft.

Methods and Techniques of Identity Theft

Identity thieves use a variety of methods to acquire victims' personal information and convert that information into cash and/or goods. Data from victimization surveys and interviews with law enforcement officials have been used to describe the techniques identity thieves commonly employ to commit their crimes (Lease & Burke, 2000; Newman, 2004). In what follows we contextualize previous research on the topic by providing a description of the techniques participants used to commit identity theft.

Acquiring Information

When asked where the information came from nearly all were able to answer. However, some individuals worked in a group where other group members obtained the information. They claimed that they merely played their role in the crimes and chose not to ask too many questions. Those who did know where information came from did not specialize in a single method of procuring identifying information. Instead, they preferred to use a variety of strategies. Although some offenders acquired identities from their place of employment, mainly mortgage companies, the most common method of obtaining a victim's information was to buy it. Offenders in our sample bought identities from employees of various businesses and state agencies who had access to personal information such as name, address, date of birth, and social security number. Information was purchased from employees of banks, credit agencies, a state law enforcement agency, mortgage companies, state Departments of Motor Vehicles, hospitals, doctors' offices, a university, car dealerships, and furniture stores. One individual bought information from an employee of a state department of law enforcement. He described how he was able to do so:

I just happen to meet this lady that was a drug user. She smoked crack and worked for [law enforcement agency], so that told me that she could be bought. She was very discreet with it, but I knew that she had a weakness. Her weakness wasn't necessarily the crack, the weakness was the money from my part. I couldn't supply her with crack, but I could definitely give her the money to buy crack. So I would make her offers that she could not refuse as far as, "Look, I need you to go into the file for me, pull up some clean names for me."

He was not alone in the ability to locate employees willing to sell private information. According to one female identity thief, "It's so easy to get information and everybody has a price." Another said, "People are easily bought these days. You can get IDs anywhere. You can get IDs from a driver's license place if you find somebody corrupt working in there." When describing how she obtained information from a bank employee, one participant said:

[The bank employee] was willing to make some money too, so she had the good information. She would have the information that would allow me to have a copy of the signature card, passwords, work address, everything, everything that's legit.

Offenders who purchased information did so from persons they knew or who they were acquainted with "on the streets." As one male offender explained, "[people on the streets] knew what I was buying. I mean any city, there's always somebody buying some information." The majority of the people who were providing this information were drug users and/or petty street hustlers. The identity thieves bought information from other offenders who obtained it from burglaries, thefts from motor vehicles, prostitution, and pick-pocketing. For the most part, the participants did not know or care where their sellers obtained their information. As long as the information was good they asked no questions. When asked where the information came from one offender explained, "I didn't ask . . . they just said, 'Hey I got this and I got that.' And I said, 'Okay well here's a little bit of dope.' There you go."

Other individuals obtained information by using the mailbox method or searching trash cans. These offenders typically stole mail from small businesses such as insurance companies or from residential mailboxes in front of homes or apartments. Apartment complexes or other areas with rows of boxes in close proximity were popular targets. When asked where they got information, a female identity thief answered:

I would go into an apartment complex that would have the square boxes. There would be like 60 in one, because there's like a little community in there. You just pop it open and there's just all kinds of slots there. You just start taking it all out as fast as you can, real late at night, in the early morning like when people are just about ready to go to work.

Others simply drove through residential areas and pulled mail out. These offenders took steps to appear legitimate. One middle-class offender explained how he did this, "I usually had a flyer I was putting in the mailbox and I was dressed like I was getting a flyer out for these businesses so no I was never confronted." This strategy was similar to that used by residential burglars looking for a suitable home to break into (Wright & Decker, 1994). Mailboxes and trashcans for businesses that send out mail with personal information (account numbers, social security numbers, and date of birth) such as insurance companies were also popular targets. One offender, who paid people to get information for him, said, "I had a dude running into the banks and stealing the trashcans out the bank." Some would even steal from store cash registers to obtain credit and check information. Another offender would:

> Go to a department store register and pull out the under-box and pull out whatever they had for their credit receipts and stuff like that. They'd write social security number and date of birth on them. And pull that kind of stuff out.

Although most of the offenders interviewed did not know their victims, of those who did, half said that the victim willingly gave them the information in exchange for a cut of the profits. In these cases, the "victim" gave the offender information to commit the identity theft and then reported that their identity had been stolen. According to one, "What I did was I had got this guy's personal information, he actually willingly gave it to me." The other half used family members' information without their knowledge. One identity thief used a good friend and roommate's identity because of his high credit score. He explained:

> [He] moved into my home out of his apartment to save him money. And from there I just kept track of his credit. I kept track of what he was spending and his credit limits. From there whenever I needed to use his credit [I did]. . . . He just didn't know about it.

Another, who worked for a mortgage company, used her infant son's identity to buy property. In her words, "I bought another property in a false alias, I used my son's social security number and my maiden name and bought a property." Historically, deceased victims have been thought to be the targets of choice for identity thieves (Newman & McNally, 2005). Only two individuals used this type of information and one was a family member. Pontell, Brown, and Tosouni (2008) also found that only a limited number of people stole deceased people's identities.

Other methods of acquiring victims' information included various thefts (house and car burglary, purse-snatching). One individual claimed to have stolen mailbags from an unattended mail truck. Others conned or manipulated people to get their information. One individual set up a fake employment site to get information from job applicants. In his words:

> I put an ad in the newspaper, company in a new area, seeking
> employees. . . . I would write a synopsis up on the computer as to
> what the job was offering, the benefits. In the paper I always put
> excellent benefits and dental after ninety days, and I would take that
> and attach it to an employment application and put it in a folder. . . .
> Each person that filled out an application, I had a digital camera, I
> would take a picture of and I actually fashioned the application for
> the information that I needed. You know height, weight, color of eyes,
> date of birth, Social Security number. . . . Then I would take the appli-
> cations and screen the ones that were close to my makeup and shred
> the rest. I would take folders and I built the identities in case I needed
> one quick. So I would have the information, birth certificate, and
> Social Security card, everything you needed.

Another used the birth announcements in newspapers to get the
names of new parents and, posing as an insurance representative, called
the parents to get information for "billing purposes." Interestingly, the
offender made the phone calls from the waiting room of the hospitals
where the infants were born so that the name of the hospital would
appear on the victims' caller ID if they had it. Another offender used
rogue Internet sites to run background checks and order credit reports on
potential victims.

Converting Information

After they obtain a victim's information, the offender then has the
task of converting that information into cash or goods. Offenders used a
variety of methods to profit from the stolen identities including applying for credit cards in the victims' names (including major credit cards
and department stole credit cards), opening new bank accounts and
depositing counterfeit checks, withdrawing money from existing bank
accounts, applying for loans, and applying for public assistance programs. Identity thieves often used more than one technique when cashing in on their crimes.

The most common strategy for converting stolen identities into
cash was applying for credit cards. Offenders used the information to
order new credit cards. In a few cases the information was used to get
the credit card agency to issue a duplicate card on an existing account.
They used credit cards to buy merchandise for their own personal use, to
resell the merchandise to friends and/or acquaintances, or to return the
merchandise for cash. A typical response was, "you buying things so
that you could then sell it for cash or just items for yourself." Offenders
also used the checks that are routinely sent to credit card holders to
deposit in the victim's account and then withdraw cash or to open new
accounts. Offenders also applied for store credit cards such as department stores and home improvement stores. According to one offender
who used this technique:

> [I would] go to different department stores or most often it was Lowes or Home Depot, go in, fill out an application with all the information, and then receive instant credit in the amount from say $1,500 to $7,500. Every store is different. Every individual is different. And then at that time, I would purchase as much as that balance that I could at one time. So if it was $2,500, I would buy $2,500 worth of merchandise.

She went on to explain that sometimes she took orders from customers before making the fraudulent purchases or just sold them later. Gift cards were popular purchases. One participant explained, "I was buying like gift cards and things like that. . . . Gift cards were like money on the streets. People were buying them off me like hotcakes."

Another common strategy to profit from identity theft was to produce counterfeit checks. Offenders either made fraudulent checks on their own or knew someone who would produce these checks for them. Sometimes identity thieves would use the stolen identities to either open a new bank account as a way to deposit fraudulent checks or to withdraw money from an existing account. One offender described how she and her team would work this scam:

> They had fake checks deposited into the account. And because we were in Washington, I was required to go to Oregon because for [this bank], Washington, Idaho, Oregon, California are not on the same computer system. Every day you can make three transactions on an account without a flag coming up. So they would deposit monies into the account and for a two day period, he would drive me to Oregon and we would go to different bank branches and I would go in and I would withdraw money from the account and you could do three a day and so I would take $1,500 from each, so that'd be $4,500. . . . We would do 2 days at a bank, so we'd go to 6 different branches. Sometimes there would be a third day if there was still a balance on the account.

Another identity thief, who also worked in a group, described their process thus:

> There were some people in my cases that had fake ID and stuff like that. We use other people's names and stuff to go in [the bank] and cash checks. First they get your account, then they get your name and stuff. Make some ID and send a person in there to cash checks on your account.

Another offender, who acted as a ringleader, described how he would get a "writer" to cash checks from stolen identities:

> Say that the person already got an existing account. I would teach the [co-defendant] how to do the signature. I would let him do it couple of times, like send him in there and let him practice on it. Then once I feel like he got it down pat, I send them in there and let them cash checks in that person's name. . . . If the person got an account at any kind of bank, you ain't really got to go in there and cash a check, you

can go through the drive through. So, I send the [co-defendant] through the drive through with a rented car and just cash the check. But if the person doesn't have an account, what I'm going to do, I'll just take three grand and I'm going to go open up a checking account somewhere. And I just hit the branches around that area. . . . I might get ten pieces in one day, with that three grand in there.

Identity thieves also applied for and received loans with the stolen identities. The majority of those who applied for loans engaged in some type of mortgage fraud. These types of scams often involved using a victim's information to purchase homes for themselves. In one case, the offenders were buying houses and then renting them for a profit. Others applied for various auto loans, home equity loans, or personal loans.

When cashing checks in other people's names, applying for loans, or extracting money from the victim's bank account it was necessary to have fraudulent identification to pose as these individuals. Most commonly, offenders used the information to acquire or produce additional identity related documents such as driver's licenses or state identification cards. Some offenders created the cards themselves with software and materials (e.g., paper and ink purchased at office supply stores or given to them by an employee of a state Department of Motor Vehicles [DMV]). One participant described her process for making fraudulent identification:

We studied IDs. Then I went to the stamp shop, the paint shop, got the logos right and I know the [Bank] was one of the hardest banks for us to get money out, but when I found out about the logos, when I passed it through the black light, it became real easy. . . . I went to the stamp shop and bought a stamp and sat there for hours and hours with the colors and I made like seven different IDs before it come through under the black light.

Another claimed to have access to software that allowed them to produce realistic looking driver's licenses:

My friend, he made me the IDs and he was good at it and of course we have DMV program from people working at DMV and they get you the program. So we have DMV program. We even have real DMV holograms, backing, and the paper.

Several offenders claimed to get driver's licenses directly from the Department of Motor Vehicles either through fraud or by paying off employees. One prolific identity thief described how he obtained a driver's license from a small town DMV:

I was at a DMV and the lady said "something's not right." I said, "Yeah I don't understand why it's not coming up on your computer that I have a license." She goes, "Well, I think you did. I believe you did." And she gave me one anyway, because it was a transfer from another state.

Others used their contacts at their local DMVs to purchase driver's licenses. In these cases they would bring stolen information on the victim and present it to the compromised employee. Then the employee would process the information as if it were legitimate, resulting in a driver's license with the offender's photo but the victim's information.

Conclusion

The goals of the research presented here were to contextualize previous research on identity theft and to highlight the complexities in labeling the crime as white-collar. Our interviews with 59 offenders incarcerated in federal prisons revealed information about their backgrounds and the methods they employed to acquire information and convert it into cash and/or goods. Results show that identity thieves were a diverse group. The majority of them were between the ages of 25 and 44 years, have had at least some college, and were employed in a wide range of legitimate occupations. Although White offenders made up the largest proportion of offenders, Blacks were overrepresented in relation to their distribution in the population. In addition, offenders employed a variety of methods to both acquire information and convert it to cash. When seeking out identifying information, identity thieves were more likely to buy it from others. Those they purchased information from either obtained this information from their place of employment or through other crimes like burglaries. For those who obtained information on their own they typically did so by simple methods such as dumpster diving or stealing from mailboxes. Few in the sample used sophisticated computer technologies like phishing to obtain identities. When converting this information into cash the most common strategies were to apply for credit cards, apply for loans, or to counterfeit and/or forge checks.

Depending on which perspective one adheres to, identity theft may or may not be classified as a white-collar crime committed by white-collar offenders. Although the characteristics of our sample would seem to support the patrician view of white-collar crime that emphasizes the act rather than the populist view that emphasizes the actor, we find it difficult to categorize all identity theft as a white-collar crime. If one defines identity theft by the act itself, regardless of whether it occurs in an occupational context, then it would be included as a white-collar crime under the patrician perspective. Edelhertz (1970) suggests that white-collar crime is "an illegal act or series of illegal acts committed by nonphysical means and by concealment or guile, to obtain money or property, to avoid the payment or loss of money or property or to obtain business or personal advantage" (p. 3). Thus, if we ignore the offender's occupational position or social status we might conclude that identity theft is a white-collar crime.

If we take a more middle of the road position regarding the definition of white-collar crime, then some identity thieves can be classified as white-collar offenders, whereas others might best be classified as property offenders. If, as Friedrichs (2004) suggests, most criminologists support the basic assumption that white-collar crime must occur in the context of a legitimate occupation, identity theft is sometimes but not always white-collar crime. The majority of the offenders in our sample did not meet this requirement as many were either unemployed or, if employed, did not acquire information through their place of employment. We should reiterate however that many of them noted that they were able to engage in identity theft because of their knowledge gained from previous employment experiences. According to our findings, identity thieves include property offenders (e.g., those who acquire information from other street offenders or from employees of certain businesses) and white-collar offenders (e.g., employees who acquire information from their place of work).

Identity theft is often portrayed as a sophisticated crime committed by well-organized groups through the use of computers, and as such it is often portrayed as white-collar crime. Considering that the research on identity theft is rather limited and there are limitations to our own study (as discussed below) it is likely impossible to conclude that identity theft is a white-collar or even primarily a white-collar crime. But we should be careful not to overlook the fact that identity theft is committed by people from a wide range of classes and backgrounds. Based on the employment status of our sample of offenders, and the methods they used to acquire and convert identifying information, we do not advocate classifying it as a white-collar crime. It is best categorized as an economic crime committed by a wide range of people from diverse backgrounds through a variety of legitimate (e.g., mortgage broker) and illegitimate (e.g., burglar) occupations.

It should be noted that this project was designed to be a starting point for understanding identity theft from the offenders' perspectives. As such, the study does have limitations that should be addressed in future research on the topic. The primary limitation of the study is that it relied exclusively on interviews with federally convicted thieves. Although appropriate for an exploratory study, this type of sample does have its shortcomings. Generally, any sample based on convicted offenders may actually tell us more about enforcement patterns and priorities than about the actual distribution of crime (Jesilow, Pontell, & Geis, 1993). Those convicted at the federal level may not be characteristic of the typical identity thief. Federally convicted thieves may be responsible for unusually high monetary losses or have clear evidence against them making prosecution easier. However, the self-reported financial gains of those interviewed are comparable to reports from other researchers (BJS 2006; FTC, 2004; Gordon et al., 2007).

Our findings also suggest directions for future research. Expansion of the sample to include those convicted at the state level and those who are still active is warranted and desirable. Those charged and convicted at the federal level may not necessarily reflect the larger population of identity thieves for those reasons listed above. Expanding the sample accordingly would certainly increase our understanding of the problem. To address the problems associated with relying on data from federally convicted offenders, both state and federal prosecutors should be surveyed to assess the types of cases they handle. Questions may include those designed to ascertain the differences between the types of cases prosecutors accept for prosecution and those they decline and the types of cases that start at the state level and are picked up by federal prosecutors for processing. In addition, collecting data using a self-report questionnaire may provide relevant information about those who commit this crime. Doing so would allow for a considerably larger sample and would allow for quantifiable data, both of which were outside the reach of the current project. The information gleaned from the current research and from others could be used to develop an appropriate questionnaire.

Despite public perceptions of identity theft being a high-tech, computer driven crime, it is rather mundane and requires few technical skills. Identity thieves do not need to know how to hack into large, secure databases. They can simply dig through garbage or pay insiders for information. No particular group has a monopoly on the skills needed to be a capable identity thief. This should not be taken to dismiss or diminish the impact of large-scale, sophisticated identity theft organizations that do exploit modern information systems. These types of breaches do occur and exact considerably large costs to victims, but they are a rarity in comparison to the typical identity theft incident.

NOTE

[1] For a review and/or examination of the social construction of identity theft see Cole and Pontell (2006), Levi (2006, 2008), and Morris and Longmire (2008).

REFERENCES

Allison, S., Schuck, A., & Lersch, K. M. (2005). Exploring the crime of identity theft: Prevalence, clearance rates, and victim/offender characteristics. *Journal of Criminal Justice, 33*, 19–29.

Braithwaite, J. (1985). White collar crime. *Annual Review of Sociology, 11*, 1–25.

Bureau of Justice Statistics. (2006). *Identity theft, 2004*. Washington, DC: Government Printing Office.

Bureau of Justice Statistics. (2007). *Identity theft, 2005.* Washington, DC: Government Printing Office.

Clinard, M., & Quinney, R. (1973). *Criminal behavior systems: A typology* (2nd ed.). New York: Holt, Rinehart & Winston.

Cole, S. A., & Pontell, H. N. (2006). Don't be low hanging fruit: Identity theft as moral panic. In T. Monahan (Ed.), *Surveillance and security* (pp. 125–147). London: Routledge.

Copes, H., & Hochstetler, A. (2010). Interviewing the incarcerated: Promises and pitfalls. In Wim Bernasco (Ed.), *Offenders on offending: Learning About Crime from Criminals.* London: Willan.

Davis, K., & Stevenson, A. (2004). They've got your numbers. *Kiplinger's Personal Finance, 58,* 72–77.

Edelhertz, H. (1970). *The nature, impact, and prosecution of white-collar crime.* Washington, DC: U.S. Department of Justice, National Institute of Law Enforcement and Criminal Justice.

Federal Trade Commission. (2004). *National and state trends in fraud and identity theft January–December 2003.* Retrieved December 29, 2007, from http://www.ftc.gov/

Federal Trade Commission. (2007). *National and state trends in fraud and identity theft January–December 2006.* Retrieved December 29, 2007, from http://www.ftc.gov/

Friedrichs, D. O. (2004). *Trusted criminals* (2nd ed.). Belmont, CA: Wadsworth.

Gayer, J. (2003). *Policing privacy: Law enforcement's response to identity theft.* Los Angeles: CALPIRG.

Gordon, G. R., Rebovich, D., Choo, K. S., & Gordon, J. B. (2007). *Identity fraud trends and patterns: Building a data-based foundation for proactive enforcement.* Utica, NY: Center for Identity Management and Information Protection.

Jacobs, B., & Wright, R. (2006). *Street justice: Retaliation in the criminal underworld.* New York: Cambridge University Press.

Jesilow, P., Pontell, H., & Geis, G. (1993). *Prescription for profit: How doctors defraud Medicaid.* Berkley: University of California Press.

Lease, M. L., & Burke. T. W. (2000). Identity theft: A fast-growing crime. *FBI Law Enforcement Bulletin, 69,* 8–13.

Levi, M. (2006). The media construction of financial white-collar crimes. *British Journal of Criminology, 46,* 1037–1057.

Levi, M. (2008). Suite revenge? The shaping of folk devils and moral panics about white-collar crime. *British Journal of Criminology, 49,* 48–67.

LoPucki, L. M. (2001). Human identification theory and the identity theft problem. *Texas Law Review, 80,* 89–135.

Morris, R. G., & Longmire, D. R. (2008). Media constructions of identity theft. *Journal of Criminal Justice & Popular Culture, 15,* 76–93.

Nee, C., & Taylor, M. (2000). Examining burglars' target selection: Interview, experiment or ethnomethodology? *Psychology, Crime & Law, 6,* 45–59.

Newman, D. J. (1958). White-collar crime. *Law and Contemporary Problems, 23,* 735–753.

Newman, G. R. (2004). *Identity theft. Problem-oriented guides for police* (Problem-specific guide series. Guide No. 25). Washington, DC: U.S. Department of Justice, Office of Community Oriented Policing Services.

Newman, G. R., & McNally, M. (2005). *Identity theft literature review.* Washington, DC: U.S. Department of Justice, National Institute of Justice.

Owens, M. (2004). *Policing privacy: Michigan law enforcement officers on the challenges of tracking identity theft.* Ann Arbor: Public Interest Research Group in Michigan.

Pontell, H. N., Brown, G. C., & Tosouni, A. (2008). Stolen identities: A victim survey. In M. McNally & G. Newman (Eds.), *Perspectives on identity theft* (pp. 57–86). New York: Criminal Justice Press.

Privacy and American Business. (2003). *Identity theft: New survey and trend report.* Retrieved December 29, 2007, from http://www.bbbonline.org/idtheft/IDTheftSrvyAug03.pdf

Richards, L. (1999). *Using NVIVO in qualitative research.* London: Sage.

Shapiro, S. (1990). Collaring the crime, not the criminal: Reconsidering the concept of white-collar crime. *American Sociological Review, 55,* 346–365.

Shover, N., & Cullen, E. T. (2008). Studying and teaching white-collar crime: Populist and patrician perspectives. *Journal of Criminal Justice Education, 19,* 155–174.

Sutherland, E. (1949). *White-collar crime.* New York: Dryden.

Synovate. (2007). *Federal Trade Commission—2006 identity theft survey report.* Retrieved December 29, 2007, from www.ftc.gov/os/2007/11/SynovateFinalReportIDTheft2006.pdf

U.S. General Accounting Office. (2002). *Identity theft: Prevalence and cost appear to be growing.* Report to Congressional Requesters GAO-02–363. Washington, DC.

Weisburd, D., Wheeler, S., Waring, E., & Bode, N. (1991). *Crimes of the middle classes: White collar offenders in the federal courts.* New Haven, CT: Yale University Press.

Wright, R., & Decker, S. (1994). *Burglars on the job.* Boston: Northeastern University Press.

14

Political Corruption as White-Collar Crime

A Framework for the Theory and Policy

— *David O. Friedrichs*

1. Introduction

Political corruption has become a more visible issue of concern and interest in recent years, after some years of being somewhat less conspicuous in political, popular, and academic discourse (Williams & Beare 1999; Noonan 2004; Heineman & Heimann 2006). But what is the real meaning of this concern, and what kind of crime is political corruption? Various approaches are adopted with regard to political corruption, including theoretical, empirical, and policy-oriented ones. The premise here is that definitional, conceptual, and typological issues are especially challenging in relation to political corruption and must be addressed thoroughly to establish a coherent foundation for theories of corruption, empirical investigations of corruption, and the formulation of policy recommendations for responding to corruption. There are always those who express impatience with what they perceive to be "interminable" definitional discussions, and who call for getting on with the hands-on work of

Source: David O. Friedrichs, Political Corruption as White-Collar Crime: A Framework for the Theory and Policy. *Monthly Journal of Criminology and Criminal Law Reform*, 2(3). Copyright © 2007 by Wolters Kluwer. Reprinted with permission.

theory building, data collection, and the production of policy guidelines. This impatience may be understandable, but it is misplaced.

Indeed, one can adopt the position that the definitional discourse on corruption is the single most meaningful level on which political corruption can be addressed and, in the extreme case, the only meaningful level. On this view, political corruption is too complex and multifaceted a phenomenon to be explainable in terms of any theoretical construct; it cannot be investigated and measured empirically with any substantial degree of accuracy; and policies advocated in response to the problem of corruption are principally a "smoke screen" for some other agenda of those who promote them (Hindess 2005).

Here is one cautionary tale of the significance of attending to definitions. In 2005, the United States Supreme Court overturned the conviction of the Arthur Andersen accounting firm for shredding documents in the Enron case on the basis that the charge to the jury was improper (Greenhouse 2005). The late Chief Justice William Rehnquist incorporated several dictionary definitions of corruption into his opinion, to make the point that the jury charge's application of the term "to corrupt" was at odds with that to be found in the dictionary. As a consequence, a massive amount of trial preparation, and the time-consuming trial itself, was negated due to the failure to attend sufficiently to definitional issues.

Within criminology, much theoretical, empirical, and policy-related work has been compromised by confusion relating to key concepts. Edwin Sutherland is widely regarded as the single most important criminologist—at least among Americans—of the 20th century. Sutherland made seminal contributions to criminological theory, produced a tremendously influential textbook, and established the criminological study of white-collar crime. But Sutherland neglected to attend carefully to the matter of defining white-collar crime and, in fact, defined it somewhat differently during the decade that he published on this topic (Friedrichs 2007). As a consequence, Sutherland has been blamed for at least some of the enduring conceptual confusion that has plagued white-collar crime scholarship to this day. In 1996, the National White Collar Crime Center sponsored a workshop focused on addressing the definitional issues surrounding white-collar crime (Helmkamp, Ball & Townsend 1996). Although this workshop produced a provisional definition of white-collar crime, the term by now has become so much a part of popular and professional discourse, and is invoked in so many different ways, that it is really no longer possible to advance a single, uniform definition that will be universally adopted and applied. If the same problem surely exists in the realm of political corruption, it makes sense to address the definitional issues that underlie any further discussion of this topic.

My own work has focused on traditional forms of white-collar crime, but not on political corruption. However, I cannot help but reflect on the fact that some interest in this topic on my part extends far back. I recall producing a term paper on corrupt political bosses in American cities in high school for an American Government class in 1961. In my scholarly work of the past 15 years or so, I have addressed political corruption within the context of a more general discussion of what I have characterized as governmental crime. In the next section, I discuss briefly the circumstances under which I was recently drawn more deeply into consideration of issues surrounding political corruption, and some lessons learned from these circumstances.

2. Political Corruption in Israel and in Australia: Some Lessons Learned

In spring 2005, I was invited by Professor Leslie Sebba of Hebrew University to be one of two non-Israeli speakers at a Conference on "The Battle against Corruption by Senior Public Servants: Cultural, Social, Political, and Legal Perspectives," to be held at Hebrew University in June 2005 with co-sponsorship by the Israel Democracy Institute. This invitation prompted me to reflect more fully on the relationship of political corruption to the private-sector forms of white-collar crime, with the opening presentation I gave at the Conference providing the genesis for the present article. The conference was well-attended and was reported upon in the Israeli press, perhaps in part because 2 days before it began, the Israeli Knesset voted "no confidence" in the then-Prime Minister Ariel Sharon on the basis of allegations of corruption against him (Gilbert 2005). At the conference itself, the Attorney General of Israel, Menachem Mazuz, announced that he would not seek a criminal indictment against Sharon himself but would do so against one of his sons, Omri. This son was in fact subsequently convicted of criminal charges and sentenced to a term in prison; the start of the prison term was postponed due to the crippling stroke suffered by his father later that year.

The case of Israel as a political context within which corruption occurs brings into especially sharp relief one central paradox that can arise in such cases. Israel continues to contend with major on-going security issues, as it has for much of its existence (as this is being written in July 2006, it is engaged in acts of war on its southern and northern borders). And, in relation to its security, Israel contends with virtually unique geopolitical circumstances and policy choices. The Hebrew University conference on political corruption as well as the Attorney General's decision against prosecuting Prime Minister Sharon occurred during a period in which Sharon was directing a highly contentious and complex Israeli disengagement from the Gaza strip. For many observers, Sharon was uniquely positioned to pursue such disengagement, especially in light of his long record of tough-minded political stances and military actions against Palestinians. At the end of the day, the political and security-related issues, with so much at stake, take precedence over the pursuit of corruption charges.

This goes to a fundamental dilemma that arises in white-collar crime cases, but as a rule not in conventional crime cases. The pursuit of criminal charges against corporations, businesses, or those occupying high-status positions (e.g., physicians) can impact negatively—sometimes devastatingly so—against the realization of other socially desirable objectives. There is much less likely to be a downside to the pursuit of conventional crime cases, and far more often than not, it is politically attractive to pursue such cases. The social and political costs of criminally pursuing cases against someone like Sharon are exponentially greater than those involved in traditional white-collar crime cases. In a parallel vein, just as the political connections of white-collar offenders may offer them more protection against criminal charges than is typically true of conventional crime offenders, such connections are even more potent in the case of high-level government officials.

I might have left the topic of political corruption behind following my Israel experience, but it surfaced again for me in connection with a sabbatical in Australia in spring 2006. I provided my contacts at the Australian National University (ANU) with a number of possible topics for an invited lecture, and they chose the one on political corruption. This topic was almost certainly chosen because so much of the work of the Regulatory Network at ANU focuses in some way on the interface between public-sector and private-sector entities. Quite inevitably, corruption in various forms arises in the context of this interface. Whether corruption is better addressed within a legal or a regulatory framework is one of the questions that arise in this context.

Australia itself in the recent era has taken some pride in its publicly proclaimed status as one of the world's least corrupt countries (Bowman & Gilligan 2006). Of some 140 countries scored on the Transparency International Corruption Perceptions Indices Survey between 2000 and 2005, Australia scored between 13th and 8th *least* corrupt countries. However, this pride was severely compromised recently through the surfacing of a series of major corruption scandals, with the Australian Wheat Board (AWB) case arguably the most noteworthy of these (Kelly 2006; Wilson 2006). The passing along to Saddam Hussein and his representatives of several hundred million dollars in bribes in connection with the Oil-for-Food Program was the core feature of this scandal. Although the AWB itself is characterized as formally independent, it was widely alleged that the highest-level government officials (including Prime Minister John Howard) knew of or should have known of these bribes. For many commentators, the fact that the Howard government committed Australian military personnel (albeit in a limited way) to the "Operation Iraqi Freedom" coalition meant that these Australians might be killed or wounded by arms purchased by agents of Saddam Hussein with Australian bribe money. This seemed especially outrageous, and arguably a form of treason. But the Australian case also demonstrates that even in countries claiming relative freedom from corruption, the potential for such corruption occurring is always present and may arise at even the highest levels of government. One is reminded when such cases surface that measures of corruption are very much open to challenge, since we have no truly reliable way of knowing the proportional relationship between unexposed and publicly exposed corruption cases.

3. On the Core Vocabulary of Political Corruption

A basic premise of this article holds that the coherent criminological analysis of corruption should be grounded within a typological scheme and should apply key terms with care and consistency. Here I discuss selectively four core terms that are widely invoked in the analysis and discussion of political corruption, with the objective of identifying some especially consequential sources of conceptual confusion (Zimring & Johnson 2005). *Abuse of power* is the broadest charge associated with governmental crime, but it has been applied in quite diverse ways. Arguably its generic meaning is that a state (or agents of a state) assumes or exercises power it ought not to have. In the interest of clarity, it would be helpful if this term were limited to acts involved in maintaining and extending power—or basic violations of human rights—and not to the forms of political corruption centered on economic gain.

Then there is the term *corruption* itself. It has had many different meanings and has been invoked in quite different ways. In an earlier time, for example, it was especially applied to taking advantage of youth sexually or poisoning their minds (Heidenheimer 1977). Socrates, famously, was accused of corrupting the youth of Athens, although it is historically paradoxical that today his actions are typically regarded as admirable and virtuous.

Over time, the term corruption has increasingly been invoked in a political context, as is the case here. Even in this invocation, much historical and cross-cultural variation exists (Pardo 2004). An ethnocentric dimension is especially important to note, as political corruption has been disproportionately associated with ethnic minority politicians and governmental practices in developing countries (Nelken & Levi 1996). In some such countries, it seems that long-established and widely accepted pre-colonial practices came to be defined as corrupt in the colonial and postcolonial era (Gardiner 1993). Political corruption specifically has been applied most typically to the use of public office for private gain or for the benefit of a political party. In the narrow sense of the term, it is applied to a violation of a specific law. In a looser sense, it is applied to deviations from expected patterns of conduct within a political context.

Conceptions of political corruption may be discrete, continuous, or ascribed (i.e., some activity is either corrupt or not, or corruption is a matter of degree, or corruption is applied by those who have the power to do so to activities at odds with their interests). This ascribing dimension of corruption seems especially significant: How do certain acts get labeled corrupt? In an increasingly globalized world, the challenge of conceptualizing and understanding corruption beyond the framework of the nation-state becomes that much more imperative (Harris 2003). Within this context, James Williams and Margaret Beare (1999) have argued that recent claims by developed-world actors of an epidemic of corruption are best understood as a reframing (or redefining) of corruption relative to a transformed global economy. Transnational corporations have benefited historically from and been complicit in many forms of corruption. Accordingly, corruption only becomes an issue when it begins to work against their interests. Dave Whyte (forthcoming) has demonstrated persuasively that massive corruption has occurred in Iraq in the wake of its occupation by American (and "coalition") forces. This corruption has taken the form of awarding contracts to well-connected American companies that have enriched themselves with vastly fraudulent charges, "privatizing" the Iraqi economy to their own advantage while destroying many indigenous Iraqi businesses. As Whyte notes, the economic transformation of Iraq was rationalized in part as a means of eliminating the corrupt economy existing under Saddam Hussein.

Some other distinctions that can be found in the literature on corruption are worth attending to in the criminological analysis of corruption (Gardiner 1993). "Grand" corruption, on a large scale, is distinguished from petty forms of corruption. "Black" corruption—a form of corruption generally not tolerated by the citizenry—is distinguished from "white" corruption, which is quite broadly tolerated ("gray" corruption—tolerated by some factions but not others—falls in-between). It is worthwhile to compare the complex of variables involved in attitudes toward different forms of corruption and the parallels with different perceptions of private-sector forms of white-collar crime.

If both political corruption and white-collar crime generally are widely—and sometimes simply rhetorically and hypocritically—condemned and recognized to have significant dysfunctional aspects, claims are also put forth of functional dimensions of these activities. In the case of political corruption, some alleged functional dimensions include circumventing bureaucratic incompetence and inefficiency; attracting more able people to political and governmental offices by providing them with an opportunity to supplement official salaries; and opening up the political process to excluded groups (Gardiner 1993). The basic functionality of white-collar crime, on the other hand, is linked with the fact that profit and productivity generally can often be enhanced by violating laws and regulations. This "functionality" is one of the key dimensions of white-collar crime (including its political corruption form) that distinguishes it from conventional crime.

Arguably the most fundamental conceptual problem arising in the criminological analysis of political corruption is this: In the morally ambiguous world of politics, the distinctions between the legalized and illegal forms of political corruption—that is, the "honest graft" or "legal bribery" associated with political campaign fund-raising and lobbyist activities—is profoundly arbitrary (Nelken & Levi 1996). The political environment fosters corruption on many levels. The whole structure of public/private sector "interlocks," and the central role of lobbying can be characterized as inherently corrupt. Accordingly, addressing corruption exclusively in terms of criminal law-breaking is an exceptionally limited approach to corruption that fails to incorporate political practices demonstrably harmful to the citizens of a society. The criminological analysis of corruption has to specifically incorporate conceptions of crime both linked with and transcending violations of criminal law.

Bribery is a significant form of wrongdoing that has been underresearched by some lights, especially by criminologists. The formidable challenge of valid empirical inquiries on this topic surely goes a long way toward explaining this relative absence of research. Bribery is the most specific concept associated with corruption. For John Noonan (1984), author of "Bribes" (the most exhaustive study of this topic), bribery is "an inducement improperly influencing the performance of a public function meant to be gratuitously exercised." Although bribery is a legal concept, it has also been defined in moralistic and other terms. A fundamental problem with the concept of bribery parallels that of corruption generally: Much consequential bribery is in fact legal. On the other hand, not all forms of corruption—for example, nepotism, official theft, or conflict of interest actions—can be strictly classified as bribery. The laws of bribery—at least in the United States—are often ambiguous and even incoherent. For some commentators, this produces a risk of politically motivated prosecutions. Some parallel issues arise in the broader class of white-collar crimes: That is, the line of demarcation between legal versus illegal corporate, business, and professional practices can be quite blurred. While this problem is not wholly absent in the case of conventional forms of crime, it is far more pronounced in this realm. In this respect as well, political corruption has a generic relationship to white-collar crime.

Finally, the notion of *political scandal* is noteworthy in this context. Governmental crime generally, and political corruption specifically, is most likely to be exposed in the context of political scandal. The "exposers" of political corruption include informers and whistle-blowers, muckrakers and investigative reporters, public interest groups, politicians and political institutions, as well as criminal justice professionals and academics. Cross-cultural variations on these roles exist. For example, in Great Britain libel laws may inhibit media exposure of scandal. The motivations of those who expose and pursue corruption cases can be questioned (Nelken & Levi 1996). For example: Is it to overthrow incumbents? To advance their own profile and careers? To enhance the legitimacy of the system? To accommodate an aroused public? To protect public interests, or for principled reasons? Here too, the situation tends to parallel that of white-collar crime generally, while this range of motivations for exposure or reporting tends to be far less pronounced in the case of conventional forms of crime.

Conditions necessary for political scandals to surface include: a division of power, an absence of major external threats, and widely supported norms that are violated. The American "corporate scandals" of the early 2000s—beginning with the Enron case—also surfaced due in part to some parallel circumstances: an absence of corporate hegemony, an economy that was reasonably stable, and a perception of especially egregious corporate business practices driven by greed at the top. At the same time, the political dimensions of these corporate "scandals" tended to get marginalized. In effect, politicians (principally of a conservative orientation) were heavily lobbied, and "legally bribed" by Enron to block efforts to pass laws that might have prevented some of the egregious practices that led to the collapse of the corporation (Labaton 2002). Both political scandals and corporate scandals tend to focus principally on individual wrongdoers rather than on deeply embedded institutional practices. Furthermore, as an arguably paradoxical outcome of these scandals, they may convey the impression that the corruption or corporate crime has been addressed effectively. Altogether, the role of scandals is another link between political corruption and white-collar crime.

4. Political Corruption as a Cognate Form of White-Collar Crime

If there are a number of different approaches to the conceptualization of political corruption, I want to make the argument here that it is usefully conceived of as a cognate form of white-collar crime. The issue of political corruption has been, for the most part, addressed by historians, political scientists, and students of international affairs. It has been much less a focus of concern for sociologists and criminologists, although there are some notable exceptions to this proposition. Accordingly, one objective here is to situate the phenomenon of political corruption specifically within a criminological framework that, in turn, is based in some fundamental ways on sociological perspectives. But a sophisticated approach to the understanding of political corruption is inevitably interdisciplinary.

Especially in light of the definitional and conceptual confusion surrounding the concept of white-collar crime, the only coherent approach to this topic is typological. Sutherland did not formulate a typological approach to white-collar crime. His book "White Collar Crime" (1949) addressed crimes of corporations, but in early discussions of white-collar crime, he had invoked the notion of individuals in ordinary occupations who committed some offense within the context of that occupation as white-collar criminals. Sutherland (1949, 10 f., 232 f., 249 ff.) does make some allusions to "white-collar crime in politics," to the bribing of politicians, and the "fixing" of white-collar crime cases, and more generally to corporate influence within government and business/political ties that tend to shield corporations from "criminalization," but his book focuses wholly on the activities of the private sector. Furthermore, he focused on economic forms of wrongdoing wholly, and did not at all attend to corporate violence in the form of polluting the environment, creating unsafe working conditions, and marketing unsafe products.

The massively violent crimes of states, then, were wholly disregarded by Sutherland. It is rather remarkable to realize that during the 1940s—while Sutherland was working on his white-collar crime book—monumental crimes of states were taking place, most dramatically the Holocaust perpetrated by Nazi Germany. The surviving Nazi leadership was tried at Nuremberg primarily for waging crimes of war and for crimes against peace. Sutherland's book "White Collar Crime" does include a chapter entitled "War Crimes," but this focuses entirely on violations of wartime regulations by American businesses, their avoidance of war-related taxes, violations of embargoes, and revelations of war secrets to foreign countries by American corporations. Many references are made in this book to the National Labor Relations Board; none are made to the Nazi regime. And in the wake of Sutherland's pioneering work, the criminological investigation of white-collar crime, for several decades, continued to focus primarily if not exclusively on the economic offenses of corporations, small businesses, partnerships, and individuals within the context of legitimate occupations.

Marshall Clinard and Richard Quinney (1973), in the second edition of their influential book "Criminal Behavior Systems," clearly differentiated between corporate crime and occupational crime, and this distinction subsequently became standard within the field. Criminological attention to white-collar crime began to expand in the 1970s. Beginning during this period of time, some discussions of such crime incorporated forms of governmental crime, including political corruption. David Simons (2006) "Elite Deviance"—first published in 1982—exemplifies an approach to white-collar crime that explores both private-and public-sector wrongdoing in fairly equal measure. Simon adopts C. Wright Mills overall framework of the "power elite," with its attention to the interlocks or interconnections between public- and private-sector elites. Those who have studied public- and private-sector wrongdoing have sometimes used "deviance" in place of "crime" to characterize this wrongdoing. But the concept of deviance seems somewhat problematic to me in this context. This is so because much white-collar crime—including political corruption—conforms with the prevailing organizational or institutional norms. The notion of "deviants" is strongly associated in the public mind with those who have been colloquially referred to as "nuts, sluts, and perverts." And it is also indisputably true that the sociology of deviance has focused disproportionately on substance abusers, sex workers, the mentally ill, and so forth. A defense of the application of "deviance" to some of the activities of the powerful and privileged would surely stress that both public and professional consciousness must be attuned to the reality that those in such circumstances also "deviate." Accordingly, deviance is not restricted to "those people" at the margins, the disadvantaged and disempowered. Indisputably, political corruption deviates from something, and at a minimum from what the law or formally sanctioned norms require. But the application of the concept of deviance in this context risks deflecting attention from or obscuring the institutional sources, and the institutionalized character, of so much corruption.

5. A Typology of Crimes of States and Corruption

If the only coherent approach to white-collar crime generally is a typological approach, this is true of political corruption as well. Governmental crime, which encompasses crimes of the state and political white-collar crime, is the broad category under which political corruption can be subsumed. Such crime has not been a significant focus of criminological attention through most of the history of criminology, but more recently a growing number of criminologists have begun to attend to such crime (Green & Ward 2004; Rothe & Friedrichs 2006). In my approach, governmental crime is the public-sector equivalent of private-sector forms of white-collar crime, with crimes of states corresponding to crimes of corporations, and political white-collar crime (crimes of individual politicians) corresponding to occupational crime (or individuals within the context of legitimate private sector occupations). In the typology that I originally formulated in the first edition of "Trusted Criminals" (1996; now in its fourth edition, 2010), I categorized other manifestations of criminal activity as hybrid or marginal forms of white-collar crime, including: state-corporate crime, finance crime, enterprise crime, contrepreneurial crime, technocrime, and avocational crime. In the second edition of "Trusted Criminals" (2004), I added still another hybrid type, crimes of globalization. None of these types is synonymous with political white-collar crime, but all of these types of white-collar crime can be linked in differing degree with political corruption. It is my claim that it is useful to both identify the core attributes of these different types of crime and identify the points of intersection with political corruption. These links and intersections are addressed further on.

typologies

In my typological approach to crimes of the state, I differentiate between a criminal state, a repressive state, a corrupt state, and a negligent state. A *criminal state* is one whose central purpose is genocide or murder on a monumental scale; a *repressive state* is one that engages in human rights violations on a broad scale against at least a significant group within its borders; a *corrupt state* is one in which the central focus of the political leadership is on its own enrichment or that of its associates and cronies; and a *negligent state* is one that fails to address basic forms of suffering or deprivation among those within its borders that it has the resources to address. Admittedly, this is a highly abstract scheme, and some critics might well hold that it is simply invalid. While certainly conceding that this typology is problematic, I believe it is useful nevertheless to acknowledge some basic differences between the cases of Nazi Germany (a criminal state), apartheid South Africa (a repressive state), Suharto's Indonesia (a corrupt state), and Reagan's United States (a negligent state). These are hardly pure cases, with corruption—as just one example—surely a significant dimension of each of the illustrative cases but not necessarily the "core" attribute of the state. Admittedly, the concept of a negligent state—and the example of the United States in this context—is especially contentious. One might argue that some states—for example, Saddam Hussein's Iraq—manifested "core" projects of genocide, repression, corruption, and negligence in virtually equal measure, and accordingly cannot be classified meaningfully according to this scheme. Certainly those who hold a fundamentally hostile view of the United States—by some measures a growing number of people in the current era—might insist that the United States merits a parallel assessment, especially in historical terms. But, at a minimum, the typology introduced here provides a point of departure for analysis on the major different forms of harm perpetrated by, on behalf of, or through states.

Within the context of this article, the notion of "the corrupt state" obviously merits special attention. In addition to the case of Suharto's Indonesia cited above, the Philippines of Ferdinand and Imelda Marcos, the Zaire of Mobutu, and the Nicaragua of Somoza readily come to mind as relatively recent, historical manifestations of the corrupt state as defined here. Indeed, various existing African and Latin American countries might be classified this way. In the case of the United States, the most typical assessments acknowledge that corruption is hardly insignificant, but is principally concentrated in the hands of a finite number of individuals (i.e., "bad apples") and organizations. While no serious commentator would claim that personal enrichment of the top political leadership is the defining attribute of the American state, the claim that institutionalized, entrenched forms of political corruption are so deeply embedded within the American system that a designation of "corrupt state" is fully warranted (e.g., Etzioni 1988; Drew 2005; Hindess 2005). Certainly we have been provided with many documented manifestations of such entrenched corruption, and the inherently corrupting character of corporate lobbying initiatives is well established.

On the validity—or heuristic value—of the concept of the corrupt state one can pose the following questions: Is it justifiable to characterize a state as a "corrupt state," and, if so, what are the specific criteria for such a designation? Or should one simply treat political corruption within any state as a matter of a continuum? What are the specific conditions within a particular country or political system that facilitate massive corruption from the top? What is the nature of the relationship between "corrupt states" and lower-level forms of corruption? Although the interconnections between genocide and repression (as core projects of states) and corruption are not negligible, they will not be specifically explored here. But it seems worthwhile to note a basic interconnect between corrupt states and negligent states. After all, states—and political entities generally—have finite, not infinite, resources. When such resources are disproportionately directed toward those who have directly or indirectly bribed political leaders or decision-makers, then it follows that proportionally fewer resources are available to address conditions impacting negatively on those who are unable, or possibly unwilling, to engage in corrupt political influence. One recent catastrophe in the United States—the immense damage caused by Hurricane Katrina in the Gulf region and the virtual destruction of New Orleans—has been attributed at least partially to insufficient attention to and devotion of resources to the levees surrounding New Orleans (Brinkley 2006). In the case of the Turkish earthquake disasters of 1999 and 2003, Penny Green (2005) has shown that they are better understood in terms of political corruption that allowed for the building of unsafe structures in unsafe areas, rather than simply as "natural" events. Corruption accordingly is linked with political neglect of affirmative state duties toward citizens.

If the typology laid out above has value and validity, it follows that one needs to address systematically how criminal, repressive, corrupt, and negligent dimensions of states interact, reinforce, and in some cases work against each other.

6. Political Corruption in Relation to Hybrid and Marginal Forms of White-Collar Crime

The concept of state-corporate crime is surely useful in directing our attention to the cooperative character of many highly consequential forms of crime (Friedrichs 2002; Michalowski & Kramer 2007). In the broader application of corruption, such crime—insofar as it involves harmful activity at odds with the legitimate purposes of either states or corporations—meets the criteria. In the narrower sense of the term political corruption, with the private-sector party bribing the public-sector party, state-corporate crime does not necessarily involve direct inducements if mutual benefits are evident to both sides, as in the classic case of the Nazi state and the IG Farben corporation. But the "pure" cases of state-corporate crime—a cooperative coming together of state actors and corporate officers in a joint enterprise—can provide a point of departure for recognizing that: (1) In some cases, the state may be the dominant party, but in other cases the corporation may be the dominant party; and (2) in some cases, government officials (as opposed to "state interests") may be the primary beneficiary of the cooperative relationship. The latter case, strictly speaking, could be characterized as political white-collar crime-corporate crime. For example, in the Wedtech case of the 1980s, some well-connected politicians were bribed to steer major defense contracts to a company (in the Bronx, New York) not qualified to execute these contracts properly (Friedrichs 1996). But the awarding of these contracts to a minority company was also seen as producing broader political—and even state-related—benefits.

I am not seriously proposing the adoption of a cumbersome terminology to encompass all the possible permutations suggested here (e.g., also corporate-state crime and corporate-political white-collar crime). But I am making the argument that a criminological analysis of political corruption might usefully differentiate between different forms of corrupt relations between public and private sector entities and actors, taking also into account who dominates or initiates the transaction.

I have defined "crimes of globalization" as forms of harm emanating out of the policies and practices of international financial institutions (i.e., the World Bank and the International Monetary Fund) or international trade institutions (e.g., the World Trade Organization). These institutions have become powerful players in the global economy since their establishment (just after the end of World War II, in the case of the international financial institutions, and in 1995, in the case of the World Trade Organization). Yet these institutions function in fundamentally undemocratic ways, are not subject to meaningful, independent oversight, and have been almost wholly disregarded by criminologists (Friedrichs & Friedrichs 2002; Darrow 2003; Heineman & Heimann 2006). The World Bank claims to be combating corruption in developing countries, but many of its projects are viewed as disproportionately benefiting political and economic elites—and multinational corporations—and accordingly are inherently corrupt. The International Monetary Fund has begun to follow the lead of the World Bank in focusing on corruption, but the "structural adjustment" conditions that the International Monetary Fund imposes on countries in various ways tends to promote corruption (Linares 2005).

The establishment of Transparency International (TI) in 1993, by a former World Bank official, is a significant development in the global campaign against corruption. But, here too, some questions arise, especially on the index that ranks countries from *least* corrupt to *most* corrupt. Those at the bottom of the list are without exception developing or "third-world" countries. In light of both the definitional conundrums alluded to earlier, as well as the arguably insurmountable empirical problems with measuring corruption, the validity of any such index is highly problematic. The role of international financial institutions and international trade institutions as part of the "anticorruption industry" must be understood, then, in the context of the complicity of these institutions in the promotion of political corruption on various levels.

More briefly, interconnections between other hybrid and marginal forms of white-collar crime and corruption also arise. Finance crime refers to organizational and individual forms of white-collar crime with enormous stakes occurring in the world of high finance—for example, banks and investment banking houses, mutual funds, the insurance industry. In some cases, billions of dollars are lost by investors, clients, pensioners, and other parties. Since both institutions and individuals in these high-finance industries tend to make large-scale donations to the campaigns of politicians, they exercise significant influence over the laws regulating their activities and may enjoy some level of protection from investigation and prosecution when they do in fact violate laws. On the one hand, then, the financial services industry was able to lobby successfully for legislation (e. g., the Glass-Steagall Act) that facilitated massively profitable but inherently harmful manipulation of markets and securities. On the other hand, the celebrated case of Charles Keating and the "Keating Five" exemplifies the other aspect of political corruption in this realm (Friedrichs 2007). This case involved the head of a crooked savings and loan association on whose behalf five U.S. Senators to whom he had made substantial campaign donations pressured federal regulators to back off from their investigation of his activities. Many other cases of this nature could be identified.

Both enterprise crime (the intersection of syndicated crime and legitimate businesses) and contrepreneurial crime (swindles in the guise of legitimate business) have been characterized historically by significant levels of corruption of political officials. Space constraints do not allow for a more extended exploration of these interconnections. The key point here is that the study of political corruption has often been skewed toward characterizing it in terms of wrongdoing by state officials and officers when, in fact, it may be best framed as a cooperative public/private sector activity. In this sense, political corruption is most usefully conceptualized as—and studied as—a form of white-collar crime.

7. Conclusion

This article attempts to identify some of the core definitional, conceptual, and typological issues that must be addressed at the outset of any coherent criminological analysis of political corruption. In particular, it attempts to identify some of the principal intersections that both traditional and emerging hybrid forms of white-collar crime have with political corruption. No space was available here to explore the next challenge in refining a criminological approach to corruption: situating political corruption within the framework of an increasingly globalized, postmodern world. In such a world, sophisticated theories of and explanations for corruption are inevitably interdisciplinary and integrated—or multi-level—in form. Empirical criminological investigations of corruption contend with daunting challenges, but if they are to be undertaken, they must be grounded in such theories. In all respects, what has been learned about traditional forms of white-collar crime and the control of such crime should be useful in relation to understanding political corruption and its control. Ideally, then, the approach outlined here ultimately allows for the identification of optimal policy responses to the problem of political corruption.

REFERENCES

Bowman, D. & Gilligan, G. (2006). Collar colour? Gender and socioeconomic opinions about corruption. *Monash Business Review* 2, 30–35.

Brinkley, D. (2006). *The Great Deluge—Hurricane Katrina, New Orleans and the Mississippi Gulf Coast*. New York.

Clinard, M. B. & Quinney, R. (1973). *Criminal Behavior Systems: A Typology*. New York.

Darrow, M. (2003). *Between Light and Shadow: The World Bank, the International Monetary Fund, and International Human Rights Law*. Oxford.

Drew, E. (2005). Selling Washington. *The New York Review of Books* (June 23), 24–27.

Etzioni, A. (1988). *Capital Corruption: The New Attack on Democracy*. New Brunswick/NJ.

Friedrichs, D. O. (1996; 2004; 2007). *Trusted Criminals: White Collar Crime in Contemporary Society*. Belmont/CA.

Friedrichs, D. O. (2002). State-corporate crime in a globalized world: Myth or major challenge?, in: G.W. Potter (ed.), *Controversies in White Collar Crime*, 52–73. Cincinnati/OH.

Friedrichs, D. O. & Friedrichs, J. (2002). The World Bank and crimes of globalization: A case study. *Social Justice* 29, 13–36.

Gardiner, J. (1993). Defining corruption. *Corruption and Reform* 7, 111–124.

Gilbert, N. (2005). A day of stinging defeats for Sharon in the Knesset. *The Jerusalem Post* (June 15), 1.

Green, P. (2005). Disaster by design. *British Journal of Criminology* 45, 528–546.

Green, P. & Ward, T. (2004). *State Crime*. London.

Greenhouse, L. (2005). Justices reject auditor verdict in Enron scandal. *The New York Times* (June 1), 1.

Harris, R. (2003). *Political Corruption: In and Beyond the Nation State*. London.

Heidenheimer, A. J. (1977). Definitions, conceptions, and criteria of corruption, in: J. Douglas & J. Johnson (eds.), *Official Deviance*, 19–26. Philadelphia/PA.

Heineman, B. W., Jr. & Heimann, F. (2006). The long war against corruption. *Foreign Affairs* 85, 75–86.

Helmkamp, J., Ball, J. & Townsend, K. (1996) (eds.). *Definitional Dilemmas: Can and Should There Be a Universal Definition of White Collar Crime?* Morgantown/WV.

Hindess, B. (2005). Investigating international anti-corruption. *Third World Quarterly* 26, 1389–1398.

Labaton, S. (2002). Who, exactly, got us into this? *New York Times* (February 3), 3/1.

Kelly, P. (2006). Betrayal of the people. *The Weekend Australian* (February 18–19), 17, 22.

Linares, J. C. (2005). After the Argentine Crisis: Can the IMF prevent corruption in its lending? A model approach. *Richmond Journal of Global Law & Business* 5, 13–36.

Michalowski, R. & Kramer, R. (2007) (eds.). *State-Corporate Crime.* New Brunswick/NJ.

Nelken, D. & Levi, M. (1996). The corruption of politics and the politics of corruption: An overview. *Journal of Law & Society* 23, 1–17.

Noonan, J. T., Jr. (1984). *Bribes.* New York.

Noonan, J. T., Jr. (2004). Struggling against corruption, in: W. C. Heffernan & J. Kleinig (eds.), *Private and Public Corruption*, 227–238. Lanham/MD.

Pardo, I. (2004). Introduction: Corruption, morality, and the law, in: I. Pardo (ed.), *Between Morality and the Law: Corruption, Anthropology, and Comparative Society.* Aldershot/UK.

Rothe, D. L. & Friedrichs, D. O. (2006). The state of the criminology of crimes of the state. *Social Justice* 33/1, 147–161.

Simon, D. (2008). *Elite Deviance.* 9th ed. Boston/MA.

Sutherland, E. H. (1949). *White Collar Crime.* New York/Holt.

Whyte, D. (Forthcoming). The crimes of neo-liberal rule in occupied Iraq. *British Journal of Criminology.*

Williams, J. W. & Beare, M. E. (1999). The business of bribery: Globalization, economic liberalization, and the "problem" of corruption. *Crime, Law & Social Change* 32, 115–136.

Wilson, P. (2006). AWB puts our "least corrupt" tag at risk. *The Weekend Australian* (April 15–16), 6.

Zimring, F. E. & Johnson, D. T. (2005). On the comparative study of corruption. *British Journal of Criminology* 45, 793–809.

15

Terrorist Financing

The Intersection of Terrorism, White-Collar Crime, and Other Forms of Criminality

— *Larry Gaines*

The September 11, 2001, attacks on the World Trade Center in New York City and the Pentagon in northern Virginia changed the American political landscape. The attacks resulted in 3,030 deaths and numerous injuries. It was the most significant terrorist attack on the United States in our country's history, and it resulted in fear and panic among our populace. The American psyche was irrevocably altered. National security and the threat of terrorism became the most prominent issue in American politics and did not subside as the preeminent political issues until the 2008 economic recession. Even today, however, it remains a significant factor in politics, government, and citizens' worldviews. For example, fear of being a victim of a terrorist attack was ranked third behind victimization as a result of a home burglary and having your car stolen in terms of fear on a recent fear of crime survey. It ranked higher than a number of personal crimes such as robbery at home, mugging, sexual assault, or homicide (Said, 2009). These findings are perplexing considering the probability that any given city or jurisdiction being attacked by terrorists is next to zero. It ranked higher than homicide, even though approximately 18,000 Americans are murdered each year.

The 9/11 attacks spurred the federal government into action. The Department of Homeland Security was created and quickly became one of

An original article written for this publication.

the largest agencies in the federal government with approximately 200,000 employees. A number of other federal departments were given homeland security responsibilities. Individual states created new agencies devoted to responding to terrorist threats. Terrorist and homeland security issues such as border security, terrorist financing, and cyber terrorism became focal points for government policy makers and public debate. The National Commission on Terrorist Attacks was established to examine our national security failures and to make recommendations to improve security (National Commission, 2004).

The 9/11 Commission found that the 9/11 attacks cost al Qaeda between $400,000 and $500,000 dollars. Moreover, it was estimated that al Qaeda's annual expenditures were around $30 million (National Commission, 2004, pp. 169–170). For the most part, the 9/11 Commission could not determine the sources of al Qaeda's funding other than through charities and large donors. Further investigation has pointed to a variety of funding sources for al Qaeda and other terrorist organizations. It is reasoned that if we can reduce or throttle terrorist groups' funding and ability to move money, we can have a significant impact on their ability to attack. Thus, it is important to discover the sources of funding and money laundering operations for terrorist groups.

For the most part, the American homeland security and intelligence communities have been concerned with al Qaeda, which masterminded the 9/11 attacks, the 2000 attack on the USS Cole in Yemen, and the bombing attacks on U.S. Embassies in Tanzania and Kenya in 1998. However, it is important to note that there are dozens of terrorist organizations around the world. For example, Garu LaFree, Sue-Ming Yang, and Martha Crenshaw (2009) examined terrorist groups between 1970 and 2004 and identified 53 groups worldwide that were anti-American. Of this number, 47 had claimed or were strongly implicated in attacking America or American interests. Only one group, al Qaeda, was international in scope. There are numerous other terrorist groups whose focus is not the United States, e.g., the Shining Path in Peru, FARC in Colombia, Moro National Liberation Front in the Philippines, Liberation Tigers of Tamil in Sri Lanka, Uighar nationalists in China, ETA or Basque nationalists in Spain, and Kurdish Workers Party in Turkey to name a few. Essentially, there are terrorist groups in every region of the world and in most countries, and a number of groups are located in the United States. There are right-wing extremist groups and neo-Nazi groups who are racist and have called for the overthrow of the American government and have participated in numerous violent criminal activities. Several animal rights groups and ecoterrorists have been involved in terrorist activities including burning university buildings and destroying researchers' private property. Terrorism is an international problem and poses threats around the globe.

All terrorist groups have one thing in common—they must raise money in order to support their activities. Moreover, as they become larger and their agendas more ambitious, they must raise increasingly larger sums of money to support not only their terrorist activities but also their infrastructure. Fighters and their families must be paid; they must have large amounts of money to travel clandestinely and to purchase false documents; they must maintain training facilities; they must purchase weapons and bomb-making materials; and they need considerable resources to bribe government officials and avoid capture. As terrorist organizations increase in size, they begin to mirror complex organizations in terms of operations and expenditures. It results in their requiring a constant cash flow and multiple sources of income.

Terrorist groups, especially the larger ones, are organizations having many of the attributes of traditional organizations in our society. They have structure, division of labor, human resources issues, and leadership and management processes. Like other organizations, they operate within the confines of budgetary limitations. The availability of resources is one of the factors that limit their nefarious activities. Terrorist organizations like al Qaeda, Hamas, or FARC may have grandiose plans, but if they do not have the capital to place these plans in motion, their activities are curtailed. This is not to say that financing is the only limiting factor. Indeed, counter-measures enacted by governments and foes also have an impact. Nonetheless, financing is critical to terrorist organizations and their varied activities. Financing also serves as a weak link that can be attacked by governmental countermeasures.

Consequently, terrorist groups become involved in a variety of criminal activities to support themselves. That is, they must pursue available opportunities to raise funds, especially as they increase in size and desired objectives. Terrorism is a criminal act that often is facilitated by other criminal enterprises. Groups are involved in property and personal crimes, transnational organized crime, and white-collar crime. In the United States, law enforcement has investigated activities ranging from the sale of illicit drugs to coupon fraud to stolen baby formula to cigarette smuggling to pirated software (Olson, 2007, p. 2). The methods of raising funds often are dictated by opportunities. Larger, well-established terrorist groups often engage in a wider variety of fund-raising activities, and they are involved in more sophisticated activities.

Globalization and Terrorism

Globalization has had a profound impact on terrorism in a number of ways. First, it has resulted in a new information age whereby people across the globe have access to vast amounts of information. In poorer countries, it has allowed people to observe and comprehend the impact of capitalism and cultures that are antithetic to their own. They see these foreign cultures as intrusions or attacks on their way of life, resulting in resistance to and condemnation of the outside world. Using the vernacular of Samuel Huntington (1996), it has created a clash of the cultures. This to some extent helps to promote terrorism. Second, globalization has eliminated many borders and allowed terrorists to move more freely from one country to another, attacking perceived enemies in other countries. Finally, globalization has facilitated the free-flow of money across borders. For example, Sidney Weintraub (2002) estimated that more than $1 trillion a day is transferred via our international banking system. The sheer number of transfers makes it difficult for governments to ferret out transfers associated with terrorist groups. For example, some of the money used to finance the 9/11 attacks was wired to banks in California, New York, Florida, and Oklahoma (National Commission, 2004). Globalization has facilitated terrorist groups in the pursuit of their objectives and made counterterrorism measures more difficult.

U.S. Efforts to Counter Terrorist Financing

After the 9/11 attacks, the federal government and governments in other countries began to enact laws and regulations to "choke" terrorist financing and money laundering. The USA Patriot Act amended the Bank Secrecy Act and required financial institutions to practice "due diligence," which in essence required banks to create a paper trail of bank transfers. President George W. Bush issued an Executive Order freezing the assets of 27 different organizations that were suspected terrorist groups. A variety of federal agencies was given additional powers and mandates to investigate suspect money and transfers (Government Accounting Office, 2003). The Treasury Department increased the power of its Financial Crimes Enforcement Network (FinCEN) allowing investigators access to information about suspect bank accounts. The Federal Bureau of Investigation formed its Terrorist Financing Section and subsequently has assisted a number of countries including the United Arab Emirates, Pakistan, and Afghanistan in disrupting terrorist financing operations.

The United States, working with the G-8 nations, established the Financial Action Task Force on Money Laundering (FATF). Originally, FATF was concerned with money laundering associated with the narcotics trade, but the mission was expanded to counter terrorist financing. Today, FATF places pressure on noncomplying countries to strengthen their laws and enforcement of money laundering. A major problem, however, is that many nations, especially third-world nations, do not have the capacity to police their financial and banking systems. Nonetheless, there have been considerable efforts to tighten financial mechanisms to reduce terrorist financing.

As noted above, many terrorist organizations require large amounts of funds to operate. They have substantial expenses and require a steady, significant cash flow. Terrorist financing consists of three distinct mechanisms: 1) acquiring money, 2) moving money, and 3) storing money (Government Accounting Office, 2003).

Acquiring Money

Terrorist organizations use a variety of methods to acquire resources. They engage in a variety of criminal activities and, in some cases, operate legitimate businesses. The following are some of the primary methods used by terrorist organizations. Note that these activities are intertwined with low-level criminal crime, transnational organized crime, and white-collar crime.

Donor Support of Terrorism

There are numerous wealthy patrons of terrorism in the oil rich Middle East countries and Gulf States. Saudi Arabia is a primary donor country for al Qaeda and other terrorist groups (Winer, 2008; Prados and Blanchard, 2004). Osama bin Laden received some of the financing for the 9/11 attacks from patrons from the United Arab Emirates (National Commission on Terrorist Attacks upon the United States, 2004). In addition to the wealthy supporters, terrorists receive a substantial amount of money from imams at mosques who divert donations to terrorists or their facilitators. It is not known how much al Qaeda receives from wealthy donors. The U.N. Security Council (2002) estimated that individual wealthy donors provide the organization approximately $16 million annually. Given that al Qaeda's annual budget is approximately $30 million, it appears that donations account for approximately half of their financial needs. These donors likely provide considerable amounts to other terrorist organizations. A large portion of these funds probably travel through the international banking system, escaping detection by countries engaged in antiterrorism.

Criminal Activity

Terrorist groups around the world have a long history of using criminal activities such as robberies, extortion, and kidnapping to fund their activities. Criminal activities have long been part of terrorist groups' portfolio of activities in South and Central America. Today, Mexico is close to anarchy. Criminals and narco-terrorists routinely kill, kidnap, and extort money from citizens, politicians, and business people. The problem stems from Mexico's inability to police the wars between the various drug cartels that smuggle illegal drugs to the United States and other countries. The Mexican government, particularly the military, police, and armed forces are riddled with corruption. FARC, a terrorist group in Colombia, has a long history of kidnapping, holding, and ransoming people, especially foreigners. It was estimated that in 2008, the group was holding more than 700 people including 40 high-profile victims (BBC America, 2008). The Shining Path, a terrorist group in Peru, has also engaged in kidnapping. Kidnapping in the region has been used to supplement narco-terrorism activities. Terrorist groups and cells worldwide commonly participate in these criminal activities.

The narcotics trade represents an important business for terrorist organizations across the globe. There are numerous powerful transnational organized crime groups and terrorist organizations involved in narcotics trafficking in South and Central America. However, it is also prevalent in Asia and Africa. In 2000, the DEA estimated that Afghanistan produced over 70 percent of the world's opium. Many speculate that the Taliban, along with al Qaeda, began to raise funds from the opium trade after the United States and its allies invaded Afghanistan after the 9/11 attacks. For example, in 2007, the DEA arrested Mohammad Essa for conspiring to import $25 million worth of heroin from Afghanistan and Pakistan into the United States. He was a member of the Baz Mohammad trafficking organization, which is closely aligned with the Taliban and has provided them financial support (MacKinzie-Mulvey, 2007). The FBI (2002) has maintained that the al Qaeda network annually receives millions of dollars from the opium trade in Asia and Africa. Al Qaeda smuggles the opium through Central Asian countries to countries in East Africa. Given al Qaeda's wealth, world-wide organization, and financial demands or needs, it is very likely that the group is involved in the narcotics trade either directly or indirectly (Peters, 2009). Al Qaeda is not the only terrorist organization involved in narcotics trafficking. In 2002, federal agents broke up a methamphetamine ring in a dozen U.S. cities that funneled proceeds to Hezbollah (Kaplan, 2006).

Terrorism also results in unusual criminal opportunities. After the Khobar Towers bombing in Dharan, Saudi Arabia in 1996, a number of prominent Saudis met in Paris where they conspired to pay al Qaeda and bin Laden to refrain from mounting attacks in Saudi Arabia. It is alleged that the Saudi royal family has also made such payments (Lee, 2002). Whereas common criminals extort money from businesspersons and individuals, some terrorist groups extort money from countries and multinational conglomerates. When terrorists are able to solidify arrangements with governments or powerful groups, it provides opportunities for additional crimes, especially money laundering and the movement of terrorists from one country to another.

In some cases, terrorist groups resort to low-level criminal activities. The Terrorist Financing Section within the Federal Bureau of Investigation was involved in the investigation of a cigarette smuggling operation. In 2000, FBI agents made several raids in North Carolina and arrested members of a Hezbollah cell who were smuggling cigarettes from North Carolina to Michigan. They made weekly trips, and each trip netted them $3,000 to $10,000. Hezbollah members were able to raise several million dollars with their cigarette smuggling operation. Mohammed Yousef and Chawki Hammound used the proceeds to purchase and ship night-vision goggles, mine detection equipment, laser range finders, blasting caps, and other military hardware to Hezbollah operatives (Horwitz, 2004; Mutschke, 2000).

Another area of criminal activity that is pertinent to terrorism is identity theft and the fraudulent activities often associated with it. There are three concerns here. First, terrorists will attempt to steal or develop new identities to avoid government scrutiny. For example, their names may be on terrorist watch lists, and they obtain new identities to elude capture or to travel. They may obtain new identities while in foreign countries, complicating their discovery. For example, terrorists in the United States who enter using a student visa or a work visa may attempt to obtain false papers to facilitate their continued stay after the expiration of their visas. Second, they may attempt to obtain new documents so that they can blend into the social structure. Third, they may attempt to obtain documentation and provide the documents to others who have been denied entry or whose names are on watch lists.

Terrorists often obtain new identities in order to perpetrate fraud. Terrorists and terrorist cells must maintain themselves. In some cases, terrorists or their supporters will use identity theft to participate in welfare programs such as food stamps, unemployment benefits, or welfare. There are a number of entitlement programs; once in a program, one has little difficulty retaining benefits. Terrorists can use the money to maintain themselves while in the United States and, in some cases, use the money for terrorist causes. In other cases, they fraudulently obtain goods that can be used or converted to cash to maintain them.

The Jamaat Ul Fuqra, a terrorist group based in Pakistan having a number of American members, became involved in a wide variety of fraudulent activities in order to raise money to support their activities. The group declared Israel, the Nation of Islam, Hindus, Ansar Muslims, East Indians, Jews, Buddhists, and the United States as their enemies (Kane and Wall, 2005). In addition to being involved in several bombings, arsons, and murders, they committed fraud to support themselves. These activities included several American members fraudulently receiving worker's compensation, income tax evasion, identification fraud, and money laundering. In essence, they were using these activities to help sustain themselves and their terrorist group.

Terrorist groups are involved in a wide variety of crimes, and they are able to combine criminal activities with legitimate businesses or business fronts. They often are adept at identifying opportunities to raise money—they are involved in anything ranging from property crimes to white-collar crimes. Moreover, like transnational organized crime groups, they have networks and connections that help facilitate their criminal activities. This makes them resilient and difficult to identify.

Charities

A number of terrorist organizations have used charities to raise money. The Irish Republican Army had charities operating in the United States for decades to raise money to finance their attacks in Northern Ireland and England. Left-wing and right-wing groups worldwide solicit and accept donations to finance their operations. However, in the Muslim world, charities are more institutionalized. *Zakat*, or alms giving, is one of the five pillars of Islam—charity is a religious duty for all Muslims (Comras, 2005) and is practiced extensively, with numerous Muslim charities worldwide. Charities often have more influence than governments since they are able to provide scores of citizens with assistance.

Islamic-based charities are numerous and dispersed across the world. About one-fifth of all charitable organizations are Islamic, and they disperse several billion dollars annually (Looney, 2006). These charities have widespread acceptance in the Muslim world. They not only provide humanitarian aid but also reinforce Islamic religious and cultural philosophy. Charities are a tool by which to counter or reduce foreign influence on Islamic culture. They help to solidify xenophobic attitudes. Thus, charities are an important part of Islamic culture.

The plight of the Palestinian people has been a rallying point for many charities and givers. It has resulted in substantial donations primarily to Hamas (in Palestine) and Hezbollah (in Lebanon), two organizations that are recognized as terrorist groups. Other groups are also collecting money on behalf of the Palestinians. Many Muslims are angry over the United States invasion of Afghanistan and Iraq. Outrage in the Muslim world over these events has cemented the role of charities and has resulted in increased donations from the wealthy and poor. Many of these charities are legitimate, but some have collected or given money to terrorist organizations. Others serve to collect money solely for terrorist organizations. For example, the 9/11 Commission (2004) found that "entire charities under the control of al Qaeda operatives . . . may have wittingly participated in funneling money to al Qaeda" (p. 170).

Charities have been used extensively by bin Laden to obtain substantial resources for his al Qaeda organization.

> Standing orders were left by bin Laden to keep all transactions involving charitable groups in cash only . . . these NGOs [non-government organizations] were manipulated as a secret laundry to make al Qaeda's financial network virtually invisible. The charities would then create false documentation for the benefit of unwary donors, purportedly showing that the money had actually been spent on orphans or starving refugees. According to some former employers of these organizations, upwards of 50% of their total funding was secretly diverted to al-Qaeda and Osama bin Laden. (Kohlmann, 2006/7, pp. 2–3)

Charities have been successful in providing terrorist groups with a substantial amount of untraceable resources. They, to some extent, represent a repository for cash, which provides timely cash flow to terrorist organizations. The charities also serve other functions. Charities are effective in recruiting new jihadists. They emphasize the misery, repression, and injury suffered by Muslims and then solicit donations and "deeds." The deeds often include not only humanitarian assistance, but also actions—jihadist commitment, to remove the repressors or enemies and restore Islam to greatness (Kohlmann, 2006/7). The charities also facilitate international travel. Being associated with a charity allows members to obtain required travel documents more easily. Without the affiliation, it might be impossible to obtain the necessary documentation.

As noted, these charities exist throughout the world, including the United States. Investigators closed the Holy Land Foundation for Relief and Development (HLFRD) in Dallas, Texas. The proprietors were prosecuted on terrorism-related charges. It was estimated that the HLFRD raised $13 million in the United States in 2000, $6.3 million in 1999, and $5.8 million in 1998, claiming that the funds were for the care of needy Palestinians (Napoleoni, 2003). There was considerable evidence showing that a portion of this money went to Hamas (see Looney, 2006). The U.S. Department of Justice estimated that the charity provided $13 million to Hamas, a group that is on the United States' list of terrorist organizations. Although Hamas is involved in humanitarian activities in Palestine, it likely used some of this money for its attacks on Israel. It was estimated that the charity raised more than $57 million, but only reported $36.2 million to the U.S. Internal Revenue Service (*U.S. v. Holy Land Foundation for Relief and Development*, 2006). Interestingly, it took a multinational investigation, spanning eleven years, to close the HLFRD (Henifin, 2004).

In 2008, former Congressman Mark Siljander was indicted in Kansas City for lobbying for an Islamic charity that was funneling money to terrorists. Siljander received $50,000 from the Islamic American Relief Agency to lobby the Senate Finance Committee to have the charity removed from the panel's list of suspected terror fundraisers. The charity paid Siljander money that was fraudulently obtained from the United States government (Schmidt, 2008). These cases demonstrate the extensive and complicated nature of charity operations. They also demonstrate that terrorists are raising money on American soil using sophisticated techniques.

The United States and other countries have received substantial criticism for their efforts to close Islamic charities. Critics maintain that these charities provide a substantial amount of humanitarian service in areas that desperately need assistance. However, the problem remains that many of these charities are intermingled with terrorist organizations and activities, and it is extremely difficult to separate those that are genuinely providing humanitarian services from those that are funding terrorism. Even more problematic is that some of the charities do provide humanitarian aid while also funneling some of their resources to terrorist organizations. The United States government has adopted a policy that "it is better to be safe than sorry."

Internet Financing

Terrorist groups use the Internet for propaganda and recruiting purposes. Many groups, including al Qaeda, Hamas, and Hezbollah, also use the Internet to raise funds to support their activities and to transfer funds. The Internet provides inexpensive and efficient access to worldwide audiences. It also offers anonymity for both donors and recipients (Jacobson, 2009, p. 17) through a variety of techniques to hide Internet Protocol (IP) addresses. Funds can be transferred electronically through systems such as PayPal or through mobile payments using cell phones (p. 19).

Younis Tsouli may be the best known virtual terrorist (Jacobson, 2009); his Internet code name was "Irhabi 007" (terrorist 007). He began by uploading videos of terrorist activities to free Webhosting sites; al Qaeda soon began sending him videos to upload. As his activities increased, he needed more bandwidth than was offered on the free sites and needed to acquire the funds to purchase Web sites with more technical capabilities. He partnered with Tariq al-Daour (whom he never met—another example of the Internet erasing barriers of time and place) to purchase stolen credit card numbers on the Web. At the time of their arrest, al-Daour had 37,000 stolen credit card numbers on his computer, with which the two men had made $3.5 million fraudulent purchases. Tsouli used the stolen credit cards on 43 online gambling sites, conducting hundreds of transactions (Jacobson, 2009, p. 18). Winnings were transferred electronically to bank accounts, effectively laundering the funds acquired through the use of the stolen credit cards. Tsouli used the funds to register 180 Web sites.

Charities tied to terrorist organizations use the Internet for fundraising activities. Because they exist ostensibly for humanitarian purposes, many charities have Web sites that openly solicit funds. The U.S. Treasury Department in 2002 designated the Global Relief Foundation (GRF) as having ties to al Qaeda and the Taliban. The Web site for GRF said the charity was "organized exclusively for charitable, religious, education and scientific purposes including to establish, promote, and carry out relief and charitable activities, projects, organizations, institutions and funds" (Jacobson, 2009, p. 18). In 2008, the Treasury department added the al-Haramain Islamic Foundation to the list of organizations with ties to al Qaeda; it also has a Web site soliciting donations.

In March 2009, a Web site boasted about a deadly attack on coalition forces in Afghanistan. ThePlanet, the largest U.S. supplier of Webhosting, is located in Houston. It had rented space to a group for $70 a month (paid by credit card) and said it had no knowledge of links to the Taliban (Warrick and Rondeaux, 2009). For more than a year, the militant group used the site to encourage followers and to report suicide bombings, rocket attacks and raids against U.S. and allied troops. The numbers of anti-American extremists using U.S. technology companies continues to grow. U.S. Internet firms are known for their reliable, inexpensive service and easy access with virtual anonymity. Free Web Town is another Webhosting site run by Tulix Systems in Atlanta. A Taliban site there features regular updates about attacks on coalition forces and interviews with Taliban leaders.

Both Tulix and the Planet have policies that prevent airing violent messages, but they claim it is not always easy to spot militant activity. ThePlanet has nearly 16 million accounts; Tulix has more than 1 million. The companies cannot monitor every site but do investigate complaints and shut down any site violating company policies, which happened with the Web site in Houston. Changing domain names is so easy that the group reappeared under another name on ThePlanet's servers three days later (Warrick and Rondeaux, 2009).

Pakistan complained to U.S. officials about the use of North American Internet services by militants. An investigation of terrorism in Mumbai in 2008 had revealed that the attackers had communicated using Internet phone calls routed through another server based in Houston. Without international cooperation, there are limits to what governments can control. Many countries lack the technical capabilities to investigate online terrorist activity. In addition, there are debates about whether it is more valuable to allow the sites to continue and to monitor their activities for intelligence purposes or to shut them down to end the propaganda, solicitations, and communication. Laws have not kept pace with the available technology (Jacobson, 2009).

Terrorists and Suspect Businesses

Criminal groups have often used the money obtained from criminal enterprises to invest in legitimate businesses. In the United States, youth gangs have invested in car washes and automobile trim businesses using money derived from the drug trade (Decker, Bynum, and Weisel, 2004). Larger and more sophisticated groups often gravitate to large legitimate businesses since they often have the financing capital, and legitimate businesses are a good mechanism for laundering money. Al Qaeda has been involved in an assortment of businesses in several countries including mining, diamonds, trading firms, construction companies, an agricultural production and export company, and a furniture making company. For example, al Qaeda has been involved in the honey trading and export business. Honey is an important commodity in the Middle East, where it is routinely consumed and is an essential part of the culture. In some cases, the honey exportation business was used as a front by terrorist groups for smuggling guns, money, and drugs (Miller and Gerth, 2001). In 1998 the Clinton administration wanted to impose economic sanctions on Sudan because bin Laden had acquired 70 percent of Gum Arabic Ltd. that held 80 percent of a product (gum Arabic) widely used as a food stabilizer (Benesh, 2001). U.S. importers opposed the sanctions, arguing that the Sudanese would simply sell the product to the French, the second largest importer, and the French in turn would resell the product to American companies. These examples provide ample evidence of the intersection of business, terrorism, and white-collar crime.

Terrorist groups are also involved in a number of low level businesses, and they often use these businesses as a front to conduct criminal activities.

> According to FBI documents, a Madrid al Qaeda cell ran a home repair company that provided masonry, plastering, and electrical services, as well an enterprise that restored and resold dilapidated vehicles. The cell's activities also included a criminal repertoire—credit card and document fraud, as well as street crime such as home burglary and car theft. A Singapore-Malaysia al Qaeda cell sold medical supplies and computer software but also engaged in bank robberies, violent assaults, and kidnappings. (Lee, 2002, p. 11)

As discussed previously, terrorist groups are involved in a variety of legitimate enterprises. In some cases, the businesses are formed to provide financing for the terrorist group; in other cases, they front the conduct of criminal activities that facilitate terrorist actions. It is difficult to identify or distinguish the legitimate businesses from those that serve terrorist needs.

Moving or Laundering Money

As noted above, the acquiring of funds is just part of the terrorist financial equation. Once funds are raised, they must be moved to where those funds are needed. If a cell in Somalia needs considerable resources to conduct an activity, it may require the movement of funds from a number of other countries. Governments have placed restrictions on the flow of money and capital. There are now numerous agencies that monitor the flow of money in an effort to intercept terrorist funds.

Generally speaking, money laundering refers to moving money derived illegitimately into the economic system so that it will appear to be legitimate. Drug trafficking and organized crime organizations generally are most interested in laundering money. They attempt to incorporate their tainted gains in the economy so that it can be used without coming to the attention of authorities. Government entities constantly monitor financial transactions for money laundering activities. To a large extent, terrorist organizations are not interested in laundering money. They are not necessarily interested in moving it back into the economy; it will be spent on illicit activities, which negates the need to make it appear legitimate. They are, however, interested in moving it without detection from one location to another to meet situational demands.

There are several ways in which terrorists move and, in some cases, launder their money: 1) precious commodities such as gold and diamonds, 2) banking and wire transfers, 3) informal banking or hawala, and 4) bulk cash. Terrorists, when engaging in their financial operations, also work with or interact with other players such as transnational organized crime groups, supporters of terrorist organizations or causes, and corrupt government officials.

Precious Commodities

Precious commodities represent a funding source for terrorist groups, and they are a convenient method by which to move large sums of money.

> Diamonds, it should be noted, are a particularly attractive commodity for smuggling operatives. They don't set off alarms at airports, they can't be sniffed by dogs, they are easy to hide, and are highly convertible to cash. Also, diamonds have a high value-to-weight ratio: a pound of average quality diamonds is valued at approximately $225,000. A pound of $100 dollar bills is worth in the neighborhood of $45,000, and a pound of gold, at $300 an ounce, is worth $4,800. (Lee, 2002, p. 12)

It appears that Osama bin Laden has used precious stones to raise money and to move it from one country to another. He supposedly obtained millions of dollars over a three-year period through the transportation of precious stones. Abdullah Ahmed Abdullah, a top bin Laden advisor, was in contact with diamond dealers who represented Sierra Leone's Revolutionary Front in 1998 and bought uncut diamonds. Al Qaeda operatives then transported the diamonds to Europe and other countries where they were sold for sizable profits (Farah, 2001). In another case, two al Qaeda companies, Tanzanite King and Black Giant, exported large quantities of uncut tanzanite from Kenya to Hong Kong, enabling al Qaeda to make large amounts of money (Block and Pearl, 2001). It is likely that terrorist organizations across the world use precious commodities to move and bank their assets. Given the complexity and scope of the commodities trade, it is extremely difficult to trace these assets.

Banking and Wire Transfers

Terrorists frequently wire money from one bank account to another. American and Western banks often have strict controls over such transactions, while banks in many third-world and Middle-Eastern countries often have insufficient control or enforcement mechanisms. Moreover, some of these banks willingly facilitate these transfers for ideological reasons or profits. The FBI tracked $90,000 in wire transfers from the United Arab Emirates to New York and Florida bank accounts. The money was accessed by the 9/11 hijackers (FBI, 2002). After the 9/11 attacks, the federal government passed a number of laws and regulations restricting bank transfers and providing oversight for such transactions. The United States government has been active in pursuing illegitimate funds. The U.S. Treasury Department fined the U.S. arm of UBS AG $100 million for funneling $5 billion to countries such as Cuba, Iran, and Libya, and the Riggs Bank was fined $25 million for failing to report unusual transactions (Weiss, 2005). The amounts of these fines demonstrate the amount of illicit monies that are being transferred or laundered by financial institutions. These actions also demonstrate that numerous legitimate banks have substantially and willingly been involved in terrorists' financial networks in the past. It is unclear to what extent they may still be involved in these activities.

Banks in Muslim countries operate differently from Western banks. First, there is weak governmental oversight of banks in these countries, as well as in a number of other developing countries. This results in many transactions not being scrutinized by any government regulators, which allows terrorist organizations to transfer money with relative ease. Moreover, under Sharia or Islamic Law, banks and customers are prohibited from making interest. The money made by banks generally is used for internal projects or given to charities (Basile, 2009). Many of these banks have Sharia Boards who allocate some of these excess funds to charities; it is very likely that some of this money ultimately is transferred to terrorist organizations through charities.

Money Brokers or Hawaladars

The roots of Hawala—a system of transmitting money without moving money—go back centuries (Dickman, 2008). It exists as an alternative remittance system and operates parallel to banking or financial channels. The root h-w-l in Arabic means "change" and "transform" (Jost and Sandhu, n.d.). Hawala is a major remittance system used around the world. A hawala operator is a hawaladar. Unlike traditional banking, hawala involves no negotiable instruments. Transfers take place based on communications between members of a network of hawaladars. "Hawala provides a means of transmitting value across national borders without any movements of money taking place, which means there is no record or way to trace the transactions" (Taylor, 2007).

A simple hawala consists of four steps (see Razavy, 2006). Essentially, someone desiring to send money to a person in another country contacts a hawaladar who then contacts a hawaladar in the destination country who delivers the funds to the intended recipient without the funds leaving the originating country. This results in a deficit between the two hawaladars. The accounts are settled at some point in the future—frequently when someone in the destination country wants to send funds to someone in the originating country. Very few elements of the hawala are recorded, making it difficult to determine the number of transfers, the transmitters, and the beneficiaries. Although hawaladars keep track of their transactions, their system is idiosyncratic, and any records are maintained only briefly (Olson, 2007, p. 4).

Hawala has a number of advantages. It allows funds to be transferred within a very short time, sometimes in a matter of minutes. There are no written records of the transfers; all actions are made on an informal and cash basis, skirting taxes and government scrutiny. Those participating in hawala money transfers remain anonymous since the transfers are usually conducted using coded passwords. The system is resilient and unaffected by economic downturns or war. Finally, hawalas are a less expensive means for people to transfer money as compared to the international banking system, especially when small amounts of money are being transferred.

Hundreds or thousands of Hawala transactions are bundled together over weeks or months. Midlevel hawaladars act as clearing houses for small scale operators; larger hawaladars act as clearing houses for those in the middle. Dubai has become one of the world's centers of the hawala transfer system. At the megalevel in Dubai, the minimum units of trade in each hawala swap are valued at 100,000 pounds (Bowers, 2009, p. 380). International financial institutions estimate annual hawala transfers at approximately $2 trillion dollars, representing 2 percent of international financial transactions (Olson, 2007, p. 4). Sander (2003) found that in 2002, $80 billion was remitted through hawala by people living in developing countries. It represented the second largest flow of capital to these countries behind foreign investment. Officials in Pakistan estimated that at least $7 billion enters that country each year through this alternative remittance system (Lee, 2002).

The hawala system is used by numerous people for all sorts of transactions. It is used primarily by average people, but the system also is being used to transfer funds for terrorist activities. Al Qaeda has an extensive network across the globe, and the organization likely uses hawalas to transfer monies from one country to another without the transfers being detected. Other organizations are also using this system. For example, Colombian drug lords are using the hawala system to launder approximately $5 billion annually. U.S. officials note that thus far they have had little luck in tracing the transactions or seizing assets. In another case, in 2002, approximately 390,000 kilograms of U.S. honey was shipped to the United Arab Emirates, Saudi Arabia, and Kuwait. The importers in those countries paid 35 percent over the U.S. price or cost (over invoicing) yielding funds in excess of $257,000. It could not be determined if the money was used for terrorist activities in the United States, but two of the honey exporting companies were on a terrorist list (Lee, 2002). According to the FBI, some of the money used to finance the 9/11 attacks was transferred to the United States using hawalas (GAO, 2003).

The hawala system presents a significant challenge to U.S. and world authorities who are attempting to reduce terrorist financing. While the concept of hawala is fairly straightforward, the roles it plays internationally are not.

> Is it a valuable remittance tool or is it a national security threat? The answer, as frustrating as it may be, is that it is both. And, it is precisely this duality—simultaneously an affordable remittance option to the unbanked and nefarious funding vehicle to terrorists and money launderers—that makes regulation both so tricky and so unattractive to politicians. There is, understandably, a reluctance in poorer countries to close the tap through which vital monies flow. But, there is an equally compelling, or perhaps more compelling, security interest in favor of regulating these informal channels (Bowers, 2009, p. 387).

Storing or Banking Money

The above sections describe the methods by which terrorist organizations acquire and move money. Al Qaeda and other terrorist organizations accumulate varying amounts of wealth; in al Qaeda's case, millions of dollars, since its annual budget is approximately $30 million. As noted, these terrorist organizations as a result of these activities accumulate cash and numerous products such as agricultural goods, precious gems and metals, and disposable goods. These goods represent financial resources, but they are not necessarily fluid; they cannot be converted to cash quickly to finance an operation or to sustain a cell. Terrorist organizations develop a business model whereby they estimate their cash flow needs and develop a timely process or methods to convert these goods into cash. The hawalas likely are used for some of this conversion. It is also likely that terrorist organizations retain large amounts of cash. They thus have readily accessible funds without the risk of seizure by governments, which might occur if the money were deposited in banks. Terrorists also accumulate goods such as diamonds and precious metals that can be sold fairly quickly.

Conclusion

Terrorist organizations are involved in a wide variety of criminal activities as well as legitimate businesses. They must be involved in a smorgasbord of such activities to raise funds for their attacks and other activities such as sustaining terrorist cells. They often have significant expenses, especially the larger organizations. They must maintain supply lines, train fighters, pay their employees, purchase weapons and equipment (for example, night-vision goggles, cameras and scopes, surveying equipment, global positioning systems, and mine and metal detectors), and sometimes pay fighters' families. This becomes fairly problematic as these organizations grow in size and become more geographically dispersed. It requires substantial funding and support.

Typically, when terrorism is discussed, little consideration is given to white-collar crime. This is because we tend to focus on the acts of terrorism or the violent acts terrorists perpetrate as opposed to the task of maintaining the terrorist organization—terrorist financing. Both perspectives are equally important, and we may be more successful in countering terrorism by attacking its funding as opposed to trying to prevent individual acts of terrorism. Nonetheless, it can be demonstrated that terrorists are involved in a number of white-collar crimes ranging from smuggling to securities fraud. Moreover, they develop relations with other criminal organizations, corrupt governments, and corrupt government officials, especially transnational organized crime, to perpetrate crimes. In many cases they are sophisticated, which expands the variety and number of crimes they commit. Their levels of sophistication also make enforcement or intervention more difficult.

For the most part, terrorists are involved in raising money, moving or laundering money, and storing money. They have developed numerous mechanisms for these purposes. As noted, they are involved in a wide variety of crimes. They move money via informal banking systems, by purchasing commodities, and through banks in countries that assure anonymity. A number of international banks are duplicitous and assist terrorists for financial reasons or political ideology. In many cases, these nonviolent crimes go unnoticed; there are no obvious victims. Even though the United States and other countries have adopted policies to police terrorist financing, many gaps exist. The international community must constantly develop more effective strategies to reduce terrorist organizations' funding streams. It also requires greater cooperation among all nations if terrorist financing is to be substantially reduced. Moreover, terrorist organizations are resilient, and when governments enact countermeasures, the terrorist groups often will devise new strategies for financing their operations.

REFERENCES

Basile, M. (2009). "Going to the source: Why al Qaeda's financial network is likely to withstand the current war on terrorism financing." In *Terrorism and Counterterrorism*, R. Howard, R. Sawyer, and N. Bajema, eds. pp. 530–547. New York: McGraw-Hill.

Benesh, P. (2001). "Did U.S. need for obscure Sudan export help bin Laden?" *Investor's Business Daily*, 21.

BBC America (2008). *New Kidnappings in Colombia.* http://news.bbc.co.uk/2/hi/americas/7188509.stm

Block, R. and D. Pearl (2001). "Underground trade: Much smuggled gem called tanzanite helps bin Laden supporters—bought and sold by militants near mine, stones often end up at Mideast souks—deal making at the mosque." *The Wall Street Journal*, (November 18): p. A1.

Charles B. Bowers, "Hawala, money laundering, and terrorism finance: Micro-lending as an end to illicit remittance." *Denver Journal of International Law and Policy*, Vol. 37, 3, Summer 2009, pp. 379–419. http://law.du.edu/documents/djilp/37No3/Hawala-Money-Laundering-Terrorism-Finance-Micro-Lending-End-Illicit-Remittance-Charles-B-Bowers.pdf

Comras, V. (2005). "Al Qaeda finances and funding to affiliated groups." *Strategic Insights*, 4(1).

Decker, S., T. Bynum, and D. Weisel (2004). "A tale of two cities: Gangs as organized crime groups. In *American Youth Gangs at the Millennium*, F. Esbensen, S. Tibbetts, and L. Gaines, eds. pp. 247–274. Long Grove, IL: Waveland.

Diekman, P. A. M. (2008) *Protecting Financial Market Integrity: Roles and Responsibilities of Auditors*. Netherlands: Kluwer. http://publishing.eur.nl/ir/repub/asset/12353/10125590–HANDEL.pdf

Farah, D. (2001). "Al Qaeda cash tied to diamond trade, sale of gems from Sierra Leone; rebels raised millions." *The Washington Post*, (November 2): p. A1.

Federal Bureau of Investigation (2002). "Financing of terrorism and terrorist acts and related money laundering." *Briefing*, (September 30).

Government Accounting Office (2003). *Terrorist Financing: U.S. Agencies Should Systematically Assess Terrorists' Use of Alternative Financing Mechanisms*. Washington, DC: Author.

Henifin, D. (2004). *What Took So Long? Closing the Holy Land Foundation: A Case Study in Counterterrorism*. A paper presented at the National War College.

Horwitz, S. (2004). "Cigarette smuggling linked to terrorism." *The Washington Post*, (June 8): A1.

Huntington, S. (1996). *The Clash of Civilizations and the Remaking of World Order*. New York: Simon & Schuster.

Jacobson, M. (2009, June). "Terrorist financing on the Internet." *CTC Sentinel* 2(6).

Jost, P. M. and H. S. Sandhu. "The hawala alternative remittance system and its role in money laundering." Financial Crimes Enforcement Network. http://www.ustreas.gov/offices/enforcement/key-issues/hawala/FinCEN-Hawala-rpt.pdf

Kane, J. and A. Wall. (2005). *Identifying the Links between White Collar-Crime and Terrorism*. Washington, DC: U.S. Department of Justice.

Kaplan, K. (2006). "Tracking down terrorist financing." *Council on Foreign Affairs*, (April 4). http://www.cfr.org/publication/10356/

Kohlmann, E. (2006/7). *The Role of Islamic Charities in International Terrorist Recruitment and Financing.*" Copenhagen: Danish Institute for International Studies.

LaFree, G., S. Yang, and M. Crenshaw (2009). "Trajectories of terrorism: Attack patterns of foreign groups that have targeted the United States, 1970–2004." *Criminology & Public Policy*, 8(3): 445–473.

Lee, R. (2002). *Terrorist Financing: The U.S. and International Response*. Washington, DC: Congressional Research Service.

Looney, R. (2006). "The mirage of terrorist financing: The case of Islamic charities." *Strategic Insights*, 5(3).

McCusker, R. (2005). "Underground banking: Legitimate remittance network or money laundering system?" *Trends & Issues in Crime and Criminal Justice*, (No. 300). Sydney: Australian Institute of Criminology.

MacKinzie-Mulvey, E. (2007). "United States announces arrest of Taliban-linked Afghan heroin trafficker on charges of conspiring to import million of dollars worth of heroin." *DEA News Release*, http://www.usdoj.gov/dea/pubs/states/newsrel/nyc051107a.html

Miller, J. and J. Gerth (2001). "Trade in honey is said to provide money and cover for bin Laden." *The New York Times*, (October 11): A1.

Mutschke, R. (2000). "Threats posed by the convergence of organized crime, drug traffickers, and terrorism." Testimony of the Assistant Director, Criminal Intelligence Directorate, International Criminal Police Organization-Interpol, before the U.S. Judiciary Committee, Sub-Committee on Crime (December 13).

Napoleoni, L. (2003). *Modern Jihad: Tracing the Dollars behind the Terror Networks*. Sterling, VA: Pluto Press.

National Commission on Terrorist Attacks upon the United States (2004). *The 9/11 Commission Report*. New York: W.W. Norton. http://www.gpoaccess.gov/9/11/index.html

Olson, Dean T. (2007, February). "Financing terror." *FBI Law Enforcement Bulletin*. http://www.au.af.mil/au/awc/awcgate/fbi/financing_terror.pdf

Peters, G. (2009). *Seeds of Terror: How Heroin is Bankrolling the Taliban and Al Quaeda*. New York: Thomas Dunne Books.

Prados, A. and C. Blanchard (2004). *Saudi Arabia: Terrorist Financing Issues*. Washington, DC: Congressional Research Service.

Razavy, M. (2006). "Hawala: An underground haven for terrorists or social phenomenon?" *Crime, Law & Social Change*, 44: 277–299.

Said, L. (2009) "Two in three Americans worry about identity theft." Gallup Organization. http://www.gallup.com/poll/123713/two-in-three-americans-worry-about-identity-theft.aspx

Sander, C. (2003). *Migrant Remittances to Developing Countries*. London: Bannrock Consulting. http://www.dai.com/pdf/Migrant_Remittances_to_Developing_Countries.pdf

Schmidt, R. (2008). "Ex-Rep Rick Siljander indicted." *The Los Angeles Times*, (January 17). http://www.latimes.com/news/nationworld/nation/la-na-indict17jan17,1,1025865.story?track=rss

Taylor, J. B. (2007). *Global Financial Warriors: The Untold Story of International Finance in the Post-9–11 World*. New York: W.W. Norton.

United Nations Security Council (2002). *Second Report of the Monitoring Group Established Pursuant to Security Council Resolution 1363 (2001) and Extended by Resolution 1390 (2002)*. (August 22): p.3.

United States v. Holy Land Foundation for Relief and Development, 470 F3d 572 (2006).

Warrick, J. and C. Rondeaux. (April 9, 2009), "Extremist web sites are using U.S. HOSTS." *Washington Post*. http://www.washingtonpost.com/wp-dyn/content/article/2009/04/08/AR2009040804378.html

Weintraub, S. (2002). "Disrupting the financing of terrorism." *The Washington Quarterly*, 25(1): 53–60.

Weiss, M. (2005).Terrorist Financing: The 9/11 Commission Recommendation. *CRS Report for Congress*. Washington, DC: Congressional Research Service.

Winer, J. (2008). "Countering terrorist finance: A work, mostly in progress." *Annals of the American Academy of Political and Social Science*, 618: 112–132.

16

The Internet, Technology, and Organized Crime

— *Peter Grabosky*

Introduction

When scholars and law enforcement officials think of organized crime, they instinctively think about stereotypical organizations committing certain types of crime. The classic monolithic, pyramidal organization such as the Yakuza, triads, or the Italian mafia engaged in extortion or in the delivery of illicit services, come immediately to mind.

However, the nature of organizational life is changing, for criminal organizations no less than for legitimate ones. Monolithic, hierarchical, formal organizations still exist, but organizational form is becoming increasingly diverse. So too are the activities that criminal organizations engage in. To a significant extent, these trends are both the products of rapid developments in information and communications technology. *Internet crime*

This article looks at the exploitation of digital technology in furtherance of organized crime. It first addresses the concept of criminal organization, and suggests the desirability of a more expansive construction to accommodate the evolution and diversification of organizational forms in the modern era. It then looks at various types of high tech crime that have

Source: Peter Grabosky, The Internet, Technology, and Organized Crime. *Asian Journal of Criminology*, Vol. 2, No. 2, pp. 145–161. Copyright © 2007 by Springer Science. Reprinted with permission.

been committed by organizations, with particular reference to those operating in Asia. It concludes with a few suggestions for the prevention and control of organized crime in the digital age.

On Organizations

Morphology

Legitimate organizations look very different today from the way they appeared a century ago (if indeed they existed that long in the past and have survived). What were once vertically integrated organizations have shed functions, preferring to contract out specific tasks to specialist service providers, rather than deliver everything using in-house resources. In recent years, the term "virtual organization" has been coined to refer to networked entities in general, or to those organizations that outsource a significant amount of activity.

While a few criminal organizations still fit the classic monolithic, hierarchical, formal model, analysts began a decade ago to observe emerging variations (Halstead 1998). Much organized criminal activity became recognized as the collective work of loose coalitions of groups, collaborating with each other from time to time to achieve certain objectives. Today, the term "network" has become more familiar than "family" to describe organized crime. As discussed below, such networks are involved in activities as diverse as drug trafficking, software piracy, credit card fraud, and the distribution of child pornography.

less mafia style, more impersonal

In some cases, small groups of youths engage in online activity much as they would on the street; "hanging out" and showing off to each other. While much adolescent behavior in either setting is an innocent manifestation of youthful exuberance, some is not so innocent. Youth congregate in cyberspace, as they do on the street, for illicit fun and for illegal profit. Their organizational structure resembles more that of kids "messing around" in physical space, than that of an organized crime group. Drug newsgroups attract people interested in the manufacture of synthetic illicit drugs (Schneider 2003). To the extent that these relationships become institutionalized, new organizational forms are created. Contact made in chatrooms between people who have never met each other (and may never meet each other) in physical space can evolve into hacker groups (Legion of Doom), piracy or "warez" groups (Drink or Die), and child pornography rings (Wonderland).

Longevity

The lifecycle of organizations has also become more varied. Some organizations are stable and enduring, like the Vatican or the University of Oxford. Others transform themselves, adapting to dramatically changing circumstances. The Hong Kong Police of today is substantially different from the Hong Kong Police of 1925. Some organizations have come into existence only recently, to exploit a new opportunity. Google, Inc. was first incorporated as recently as 1998. Other organizations are short lived, coming into existence for a particular purpose, and then disbanding. Consider the Sydney Organizing Committee of the Olympic Games, which was established to oversee the 2000 Summer Olympics. It exists no longer.

Some organizations are extremely short lived. One of the more recent manifestations of the evanescent organization is the "flash mob" (Wasik 2006), otherwise unrelated individuals who engage in "swarming," "the unexpected gathering of large numbers of people in particular public locales" (White 2006, p. 1). The communications processes that underlie such gatherings need not involve high technology, word of mouth can suffice. But one can easily appreciate how swarming can be facilitated by the Internet, or by digital telephony. Flash mobs have begun to appear in Asia (Nicholson 2005). Although much of the activity in question relates to shopping or other harmless recreation (CRIENGLISH.com 2006), Rheingold (2002, p. 157) suggests that protests coordinated by cell phone helped bring down the Estrada [Philippines] government in 2001. Vanderbilt (2004) suggests that sudden Falun Gong assemblies may also be orchestrated by mobile telephone.

Dimensions of Cybercrime

It has become common to classify cybercrime according to three dimensions: computers as the instrument of crime; computers as the target of criminal activity; and computers as incidental to criminal activity. This classification is not perfect, and some discrete offenses cut across conceptual boundaries. Computers may be used to attack other computers, for example. As such, they are both the instruments and the targets of an offense.

Crime itself is a moveable feast, politically and socially constructed, and often changing. If a certain act is not prohibited by law, it is not a crime. And prohibitions can vary over time and space. Although defined as criminal in many other places, the dissemination of a computer virus was not a crime under the law of the Philippines in May 2000, when the ILOVEYOU virus was released. Soon thereafter, the Philippine Government enacted criminal legislation to prohibit such activity. Today, the electronic dissemination of material promoting Falun Gong would offend against the laws of China, but not those of Canada.

Cybercrime and organized crime are not identical. As Williams (2002) observed, most cybercrime is the work of individuals, and most organized crime still occurs in the physical world. One of the most noteworthy characteristics of digital technology is the way it can empower individuals. For example, in 2001, a 15-year-old Canadian boy succeeded in singlehandedly accessing a number of university computers in the United States from his home in Montreal, and directing their computing power against major websites such as Yahoo and Amazon.com.

Of course, digital technology can empower organizations, too. Let us look at some basic types of cybercrime that are committed by organizations.

Electronic Piracy, Counterfeiting and Forgery

Digital technology permits the perfect reproduction of text, images, video and sound, and multimedia combinations of these. Unauthorized reproduction of copyrighted material is thus greatly facilitated. The original digital pirates embraced the ideology that information should be free, and distributed digital content free of charge as an act of protest. But the commercial potential of pirated content was not lost on others. While individuals are perfectly capable of reproducing copyrighted material singlehandedly, criminal organizations began to engage in this activity on a large scale, particularly in East Asia, where pirated software and compact discs are now all but ubiquitous. Although most piracy today uses digital technology, the means of reproduction and dissemination are often physical (Curtis et al. 2003; Priest 2006; US Department of Justice 2007).

Offenders obtain a product, remove its embedded copy protections, make multiple copies, and distribute them through markets and retail outlets. The US Department of Justice (2005) noted that "Release groups are hierarchical, highly-structured organizations with leadership positions that control day-to-day operations, recruit new members, and manage the group's various computer archive sites."

Pirated CDs and DVDs may be found in any Asian city. Data from just one investigation are illustrative of industrial-scale piracy. In August 2000, Malaysian investigators raided a factory, seizing 100 CD stampers, 200,000 counterfeit CDs and 20 PCs, worth an estimated US$480 million (Smith and Urbas 2001, p. 58).

Because they stand to lose the most from this type of crime, the software and entertainment industries have urged governments around the world to respond forcefully to piracy. Many states have responded accordingly. Operation FastLink was a major investigation that resulted in 120 simultaneous searches in 11 countries, in April 2004. Among the targets of the investigation were a Singaporean man and his brother, who were charged with conspiring to obtain "cracked" copies of software and entertainment products by downloading them for a fee from a server managed by a "warez" group, for mass production and eventual sale. The accused was convicted in Singapore and sentenced to 15 months imprisonment (Parsky 2005). Here we see an example of a functionally differentiated criminal network, where the physical manufacturer of pirated goods had a commercial relationship with IT specialists.

Forgery

Similarly, the digital reproduction of official documents facilitates subsequent criminal behavior. Scanning and laser printing technologies can be used to produce false passports for illicit border crossings (Goodell 2002). Here again, organizational arrangements are networked, rather than hierarchical. The manufacturers of false passports stick to what they do best. They sell their products to middlemen, who on-sell them to others, be they terrorists, traffickers, or smugglers. Burrell (1999) observed that sophisticated forgers based in Bangkok and Kuala Lumpur were offering their products to criminal "facilitators" based in China, India, Pakistan and Sri Lanka, who in turn were offering travel packages to Britain for about GBP7,000.

False passports and other identity documents can be used in furtherance of fraud. Bank accounts may be established upon presentation of a passport and driver's license. And, of course, credit cards themselves may be manufactured.

Credit Card Fraud

Digital technology permits the capture, on or offline, of credit card details. For some years now, physical skimming of credit card details has been achieved using a hand-held scanner. This often entailed the complicity of employees in retail establishments, restaurants, and hotels. Counterfeit cards have been produced using the captured credit card details, personal computers, embossing machines and forged holograms. Members of the Chinese gang, Wo Hop To, were involved in a counterfeit credit card ring in California in 1994, using computers, laminators, and embossing equipment to produce the counterfeit cards. Hologram manufacture is itself a specialized activity. Hong Kong, Taiwan and China have been identified as centers of illicit hologram manufacture for over a decade (Slotter 1997). The products are then sold to card counterfeiters.

Now, credit card details may be captured remotely, either in transmission, or by unauthorized access to a database in which these data reside. These can be on-sold and even advertised on the World Wide Web. Captured credit card details can be used for online purchases or in the manufacture of counterfeit cards. One organization, whose members referred to themselves as "Shadowcrew," managed a password protected website which served as a marketplace for stolen credit card details and other identity information.

Other organized credit card fraud can occur in physical space on a more limited scale. In January 2007, authorities in Thailand arrested three Sri Lankan men and seized 5,000 fake cards at Phuket. Many of the cards contained valid details of British cardholders. The men were reported to have been making frequent withdrawals from ATMs in the area (Radio Australia 2007).

The proliferation of credit cards in China is providing unprecedented opportunities for credit card fraud in that country. Obtaining a card is relatively easy, and individuals, alone or in concert, may obtain multiple cards and use them for illicit purposes. One group of four people posted recruitment advertisements in newspapers, collected personal data from those who responded, and used the data to obtain 39 cards, which they then used to purchase goods worth over 410,000 yuan (China.org 2007).

Communications in Furtherance of Criminal Conspiracies

A decade ago, Grabosky and Smith (1998) noted that cocaine traffickers were using management information systems, satellite communications for global positioning, and encryption (p. 198). One group of organized criminals in Colombia was able to identify the telephone numbers from which calls were made to the US Embassy with a view to determining the identity of persons cooperating with US drug enforcement personnel (Ramo 1996). The new millennium has seen continuing criminal exploitation of digital technology. Criminal organizations, like all organizations, have become dependent upon digital technology for routine communications and record keeping. The Awn Sect [accused of mass killing in Tokyo subway] made extensive use of Internet technologies for communications and recruitment (Ortis and Evans 2003, p. 563).

Digital technology can also be used to create "temporary organizations." Not all swarming is undertaken with criminal intent. The digital orchestration of collective action may be done for amusement and recreation. But other swarming can occur in furtherance of crime. Violent demonstrations during the 1999 meeting of the World Trade Organization in Seattle were coordinated using digital technology, including live Internet feeds (Sullivan 2001, pp. 120–123). It has been suggested that mobile phone text messages were used by right wing white supremacist groups to foment a riot at a Sydney beach in 2005 (Poynting 2006, p. 86). Mobile telephony has also been used to organize group sexual assaults (Finnane 2002). An alleged attempt in Hong Kong led to a criminal conviction (Wong 2006).

Digital technology can also be used to organize unrelated third parties to harass or stalk a victim. Malaysian Police reported a number of incidents in 2001 where women's personal information had been posted on the Internet. In one case, a man in Malaysia allegedly dialed into a Singapore-based website and posted a sex-for-hire advert that included the telephone number of his estranged wife. She subsequently received obscene telephone calls from Singapore, Thailand, and Brazil (Reuters 2001).

Child Pornography

Digital technology lends itself perfectly to the production and unobtrusive dissemination of child pornography, a crime in most countries

around the world. In addition, the technology greatly assists in concealing this activity from the attention of law enforcement or other adversary
interests. Even more dramatic is the manner in which digital technologies
facilitate the dissemination of the content in question almost instanta-
neously to many recipients, over vast distances. The introduction of this
technology has dramatically enhanced the amount of material available
to those who would access child pornography, as well as the speed and
privacy with which it may be accessed.

[handwritten margin note: internet increased crime because it made access to child pornography easier]

Production and distribution of child pornography is hardly the
exclusive province of sole offenders, and can be a collective, organized
endeavor. Chatrooms frequented by aficionados of child pornography
allow people of like mind, widely dispersed geographically, to congregate in cyberspace. Private bulletin boards involving access control and
requiring authentication limit participation to those in possession of a
valid password, thereby excluding uninvited visitors. Technologies of
pseudonymity and anonymity enable one to create a false identity, or to
otherwise conceal one's identity altogether. It is possible for participants
in these criminal organizations never to have met face to face, and not to
know each other (Grant et al. 1997).

One of the first major investigations of Internet child pornography
was Operation Cathedral. The investigation targeted the Wonderland
Club, an international network with members in at least 14 nations ranging from Europe to North America to Australia. The physical location of
servers was periodically rotated in order to avoid detection, and access to
the system was password-protected. The investigation resulted in
approximately 100 arrests around the world in 1998.

At the end of 2001, German police conducted a search on a citizen
suspected of offenses related to child pornography. It became apparent
that the suspect had been exchanging incriminating material over an
Internet Relay Chat (IRC) channel. He subsequently provided police with
the nicknames of some of his correspondents. The resulting investigation,
Operation Artus, led to the execution of seven search warrants in the US
and 30 simultaneous searches in 10 foreign countries, including Japan.

The increasing commercialization of child pornography has led to
the involvement of credit card payment processing companies to manage
the revenue generated by product sales. In 2004, a major investigation
called Operation Falcon led to indictments against two companies as well
as a number of individuals (Ashcroft 2004).

Electronic Funds Transfer Fraud

In the early 1990s, Vladimir Levin, a young man in St. Petersburg,
Russia, succeeded in obtaining unauthorized access to the servers of
Citibank in the United States. His intrusion was undetected. He then
enlisted a number of accomplices to establish accounts in financial insti-

tutions around the world. Levin proceeded to transfer funds from the accounts of legitimate Citibank account holders into the accounts of his confederates (Goldstone and Shave 1999).

Nigerian Advance Fee Fraud

In the 1990s, many people in the world's more affluent nations began receiving letters from Nigeria seeking assistance in transferring funds out of the country, and offering a sizeable commission to those willing to help. Persons expressing an interest in the activity were soon asked to send a "handling fee" in advance. Those who did never saw their money again. The more gullible among them were persuaded to part with additional fees, before realizing that they had been duped. Hundreds of thousands of overtures of this nature were sent through the post, a daunting logistical exercise that invariably required a degree of organization. The advent of fax machines made the sending of advance fee fraud solicitations somewhat less labor intensive, but electronic mail made it even more so. Fraudsters are now able to communicate with millions of prospective victims at the speed of light and at negligible cost (Smith et al. 1999). Although one can almost achieve this singlehandedly, advance fee fraud solicitation is a popular activity of West African organized criminal networks, based in Africa, the US, or in European countries with a large west African population (Buchanan and Grant 2001).

Other Fraud

Hill (2005, p. 109) suggests that some Yakuza have been involved in Internet frauds involving false or excessive billing charges to visitors to pornographic and other websites. He notes that the Yakuza members themselves may not be acting as "webmasters," but rather providing protection to the technicians. McMullan and Perrier (2007) describe the division of labor involved in various forms of fraud against electronic gaming technologies. Teams of three individuals will drive to a business with video lottery terminals. Two "players" will clandestinely transmit images of the video screen to an accomplice who remains in the car with a computer programmed to reveal how close the terminal is to paying out (see also Mitnick and Simon 2005, Chapter 1).

On-line Dealing in Illicit Products

Most Internet users, unless they have invested in very effective spam filters, have received emails advertising pharmaceutical products for sale. These may be nonexistent or inert, in which case the overture is fraudulent. They may be counterfeit. Or they may be the genuine article, otherwise obtainable through a doctor's prescription. Whatever the case, such practices violate the laws of many countries (Forman et al. 2006).

Offenses of this nature may be perpetrated by a sole individual, but more often than not, particularly when they involve counterfeit or controlled substances, they will involve some form of organization. One Internet drug marketing organization was allegedly run by two Indian nationals, who repackaged controlled substances that had been physically smuggled into the US and used online pharmacy websites to distribute millions of dosage units throughout the world. Indictments issued in the US in 2005 sought the forfeiture of 41 bank accounts, in the US, Cyprus, India, Singapore, the Channel Islands, Isle of Man, Nevis, Antigua, and Ireland. See, e.g., *US v Bansal et al.* US District Court (Eastern District of Pennsylvania) http://www.npr.org/programs/morning/features/2005/june/onlinerx/indictment.pdf (visited 31 December 2006).

Money Laundering

Concealing the origin of ill-gotten gains has proven to be a challenge for criminal organizations in recent years, especially since the international community has intensified its efforts to monitor cash transactions. Nevertheless, digital technology facilitates money laundering, as it does legitimate financial transactions, by allowing money to move around the world at the speed of light. When electronic transfers are routed through jurisdictions whose transaction reporting regulations are less than rigorous, the "money trail" may be lost.

Money launderers may take advantage of otherwise legitimate online services, such as auctions, where a buyer and a seller may collude in transferring one or more "phantom" items at a designated price. The proceeds of crime are thus transformed into cash apparently derived from the sale of a purportedly legitimate product. Online gambling services (in jurisdictions where they are legal) may also be used in furtherance of money laundering. A bettor may establish an account with a service provider using proceeds of crime, and then cash out his account, with the funds deemed to be gambling winnings.

Money launderers may also recruit unwitting accomplices. Students, for example, or other individuals responding to advertisements to "earn money while working from home," may be recruited to assist in the electronic transfer of funds offshore, in individual amounts below the threshold of cash transaction reporting surveillance. These accomplices, who are known as "mules," receive a small fee for their services.

The advent of electronic cash and its implications for concealing the proceeds of crime was noted more than a decade ago (Wahlert 1996). Today, some offenders favor the services of e-gold and similar providers who may not yet be covered by the cash transaction reporting regimes of all countries.

Industrial Espionage

In the competitive global economy of the twenty-first century, obtaining a competitor's trade secrets, and other economic information of a sensitive nature, can be extremely lucrative. Depending on the methods employed, it can also be extremely illegal (Nasheri 2005). Traditional espionage techniques, such as infiltrating a company's workforce or poaching an employee entrusted with sensitive information, are now complemented by high-tech methods. Given that much, if not most, information today exists in digital form, industrial espionage will have its digital manifestations. Web-based research through open sources may be legitimate. But the insertion of a Trojan horse or backdoor into a competitor's computer network is quite another matter. Digital technology allows unobtrusive access to acquisition of, and storage and transfer of vast quantities of information. The vulnerability of wireless technology and of Internet telephony to industrial espionage goes without saying. Today, digital cameras have become a standard feature on many mobile telephones.

It is not surprising, therefore, to learn that "several foreign companies" have become world leaders in the use of cybertools to collect sensitive US technology and economic information [Office of the (US) National Counterintelligence Executive 2006, v]. Presumably, several US companies and government intelligence services have developed similar proficiencies (Sheptycki 2000, p. 13). Governments themselves are capable of considerable organized crime (Chambliss 1989).

The global economy is indeed a jungle. According to US authorities,

> In early 2005, a British programmer sold customized copies of his spy software to three Israeli private investigation firms. These firms, in turn, worked for a number of blue-chip Isreali (sic) firms, which allegedly used the software to spy on dozens of their international competitors, including at least one major high tech firm. The software tempted victims into installing it by posing as a package of confidential documents delivered via e-mail. Once installed, the software recorded every keystroke and collected business documents and e-mails on a victim's personal computer and transmitted information to a server computer registered in London (Office of the National Counterintelligence Executive 2006, p. 10).

Intelligence and Counterintelligence

One of the first great stories in the annals of cybercrime, the "Cuckoo's Egg" case, involved a German hacker, engaged by the Soviet KGB, who in 1986 obtained access to computer systems of defense installations in the United States (Stoll 1989). This was by no means the last attempt to obtain state secrets online. US authorities report that foreign intelligence services "clandestinely employ commercial firms in technology collection activities" (Office of the (US) National Counterintelligence Executive 2006, p. 7). In July 2006, The Associated Press reported the US State Department had experienced "large scale computer break-ins worldwide" that appeared to target information on China and North Korea (Associated Press 2006).

Denial of Service

We have already noted the exploits of Mafiaboy, the 15-year-old Canadian who singlehandedly organized a distributed denial of service attack against Amazon.com, Yahoo, and other e-commerce sites in 2001. Before the capacity to create robot networks or "Botnets" became widespread, denial of service attacks took the form of "mail bombing." This entailed a coordinated "blitz" of e-mail messages or website hits against the target computer or system. In sufficient volume, this would slow a system down, or make it difficult (if not impossible) for legitimate users to obtain access. During the Kosovo conflict at the end of the 1990s, hackers from Belgrade directed an attack against NATO servers, saturating the system (Denning 2000). In March 2001, hackers based in South Korea caused the crash of a website at the Japanese Ministry of Education in protest against a newly approved history textbook (BBC News 2001). Some have suggested that attacks targeting Falun Gong websites hosted in North America and the United Kingdom have been sponsored by the Chinese Government (Ortis and Evans 2003, p. 562).

Terrorist Organizations and Cyberspace

Traditionally, organized crime has existed to make a profit. Although feelings of belonging may motivate some participants in organized crime, the raison d'être of organized crime is money. It was fashionable for organized crime to be differentiated from terrorist organizations, whose objectives were political not financial.

This distinction is somewhat artificial. Most terrorist activity is certainly organized. And it is usually, if not always, criminal. Moreover, one sees examples of terrorist organizations engaging in more traditional criminal activity in order to raise revenue. Similarly, one sees organized crime groups diversifying into terrorist activity. For example, an investigation of a Chicago street gang in the 1990s revealed a plan to attack a commercial airliner with a shoulder-launched missile on behalf of the Libyan Government (US Department of Justice 1997, p. 11). Makarenko (2004) speaks of a "crime-terror continuum" in which terrorist and criminal groups have begun to share common organizational features, and to learn from each other.

Denning (2000, p. 10) offers a precise definition of cyber terrorism: "unlawful attacks against computers, networks and the information stored therein when done to intimidate or coerce a government or its people in furtherance of political or social objectives." There have been a few documented cyber attacks against critical infrastructure, but most of these have been the work of lone adventurers rather than criminal organizations. One does, however, see digital technology employed in furtherance of terrestrial terrorist activities, among them intelligence collection. High-resolution satellite images of every city in the world are available on the Internet (see http://earth.google.com/).

Digital technology greatly facilitates communications among terrorists, and between terrorists and a wider public. The Internet and World Wide Web are ideally suited to communications across widely dispersed elements of a network (Givner-Forbes and Shwery 2007). In addition, terrorist groups may communicate directly to a general worldwide audience, or to specialist target audiences, bypassing journalistic editing and government censorship. This may include inflammatory hate speech intended to legitimize violence against specified adversaries.

The Internet may also be used as an instrument of psychological warfare by terrorist groups. By generating anomalous patterns of message traffic they can give the erroneous impression that an operation may be imminent. This form of tactical deception referred to as "chatter" may distract law enforcement and intelligence services from true terrorist activity.

Another form of psychological warfare can involve general or specific threats or displays of force. Webcasts of hostages, and even hostage executions and bombings, can reach the world. These may be coupled with threats against nationals of specific countries who may be identified with causes anathema to the terrorist organization (see http://news.xinhuanet.com/english/2004-06/27/xinsimple_08060127073520206981.jpg (visited 16 January 2007).

Terrorist groups may raise funds through charity and other front organizations, or they may actively seek to recruit new members. Webcasts that celebrate martyrdom may be particularly useful in attracting the attention of prospective suicide bombers. Terrorists can also resort to conventional cybercrime in order to raise money. It has been reported that Imam Samudra, the alleged mastermind of the Bali bombings in 2002, had attempted credit card fraud to help finance his operations. More generally, he has encouraged jihadists to engage in widespread credit card fraud against US targets. A chapter in his autobiography contains basic advice and identified Indonesian language websites where readers could go for further instruction (Sipress 2004).

Terrorist groups may also use the Internet and the Web for instructional purposes, to teach attack techniques and skills. For example, an alleged Al Qaeda Training Manual (in English translation), seized during a raid on suspect premises in the United Kingdom, was posted on the website of the US Department of Justice (Thomas 2003; Cilluffo 2007).

Varieties of Criminal Organizations in Cyberspace

From the previous discussion, it is possible to differentiate between forms of criminal organization in cyberspace. First, there are the more traditional criminal organizations that use digital technology in furtherance of their traditional practices (such as the Yakuza interface with Internet fraud and Colombian cocaine traffickers using encryption).

Second, there are those organizations that have come into existence in cyberspace, and whose organizational activities occur almost exclusively in the online environment. Examples of the latter include the Drink or Die piracy conspiracy, the Wonderland child pornography ring, and The Shadowcrew identity theft organization.

Third, there are those organizations that exist for otherwise legitimate purposes, but which become corrupted, engaging in criminal conduct because their principals have chosen to lead them down a corrupt path. Vaughan (1983) describes how a large pharmacy chain used a computer-generated double-billing scheme to overcharge governments for health insurance reimbursements. Alternatively, otherwise legitimate institutions (such as some in the finance sector) may be infiltrated by criminal elements (Carwile and Hollis 2004). Organized crime groups might seek to place a member in an organization, or corrupt a previously legitimate member. They in turn could provide access to systems or could disclose account details, facilitating check counterfeiting or fraudulent electronic funds transfers (McDonell 1998).

The nation state can also be placed in this category. Such offenders would include not only the government of North Korea, which uses digital technology in the alleged production and laundering of counterfeit currency (Perl 2005), but the US government, which has allegedly conducted telecommunications interception without obtaining a warrant (Sims 2006).

One might also create ostensibly legitimate organizations as a front for criminal activity. The Bank of Credit and Commerce International (BCCI) could perhaps be regarded as such an organization (Passas 1996). In the digital age, a criminal entrepreneur might, for example, become an Internet service provider, in order to allow criminal communications to avoid hindrance or scrutiny that might otherwise be directed against them. The Awn Shinrikyo sect recruited computer scientists and engineers and actually controlled a software company serving clients in business and government (Ortis and Evans 2003, p. 563).

Finally, there are the more ephemeral organizations that exist only briefly, then disperse. Swarming for the purpose of creating mass disturbance, organized stalking, and mail bombing were cited as examples.

Explaining Organized Cybercrime

Cybercrime, like crime in general, can be explained by the conjunction of three conditions: a supply of motivated offenders, the availability of suitable targets or victims, and the absence of capable guardians; someone to mind the store, so to speak.

Most organized crime, in terrestrial space or in cyberspace, is driven by greed. Greed is an enduring part of the human behavioral repertoire, and is likely to remain so. While there is easy money to be made, there will be no dearth of people, acting singly or in concert with others, seeking to try their hand.

Criminal opportunities are both enduring and evolving. As noted above, the standard fare of organized crime entails the provision of illicit goods and services, and extortion. As long as there is a demand for illicit products or services, there will be those criminal entrepreneurs prepared to meet that demand. When opportunities are foreclosed by such public policies as decriminalization or regulation, such as is the case in some countries with gambling and the sex industry, criminal organizations tend to adapt and seek out new profitable ventures. Digital technologies have created both new opportunities (such as electronic funds transfer fraud) and new techniques for exploiting old opportunities (such as extortion).

The exponential growth in connectivity means that in the developed world at least, nearly everything depends on software. Digital technology enhances the capacity of organizations to maintain themselves. The pervasiveness of digital technology is such that soon there will be elements of digital technology at nearly every crime scene in physical space. Every new application of digital technology presents an opportunity for criminal exploitation.

The advent of multi-player role-playing games has also given rise to a variety of criminal opportunities. Choo et al. (2007) note how these increasingly popular simulations may invite theft and fraud relating to digital property, not to mention creating new opportunities for money laundering and clandestine criminal communications.

Guardianship can be exercised by individuals or by technological means. Every individual or organization with significant assets to protect will have not only a vigilant systems administrator, but also will have invested in the appropriate security technology. The capacity of the modern state to provide capable guardianship is limited. It is not possible to place a police officer next to every computer. The prevention of cybercrime is a task that must be shared by governments, citizens, and institutions of civil society alike.

Trends in Cybercrime

Cybercrime in general and organized cybercrime in particular is following three basic trends: sophistication, commercialization, and integration.

Sophistication

The growing sophistication of computer criminals is manifest in their nimbleness and adaptability. Every new technology and every new application is quickly exploited. The widespread availability of cryptography beginning in the 1990s was a boon to legitimate electronic commerce, because it enabled the transmission of credit card details beyond the reach of most criminals. But cryptography was available to criminals too, and enabled criminal conspiracies to proceed beyond the reach of law enforcement. The advent of wireless technology was quickly accompanied by criminal use of the technology to obtain unauthorized access to computer systems.

Commercialization

At the dawn of the digital age, much computer crime took place for fun, rather than for profit. The distribution of child pornography occurred in the context of a barter economy. Other computer criminals were motivated by the intellectual challenge, adventure, or by rebellious spirit, rather than by mercenary considerations. Practitioners of digital piracy gave products away, rather than selling them. Virus writers regarded their activity as an art form rather than as a way to make a living. Today, the services of accomplished hackers are available for hire; a criminal group can rent robot networks for use in spamming, or denial of service attacks, or extortion, and digital piracy has become big business.

Integration

Organized criminal activities in the digital age now often entail a sequence of discrete criminal acts. Unauthorized access to a computer system may be the predicate to theft of personal financial information, which can then be used further in online credit-card or funds-transfer fraud. The offense of extortion may include such distinct elements as the use of the Internet to communicate an extortion threat, unauthorized access to computer systems, theft of and damage to computer systems, and the use of electronic funds transfer to receive an extortion payment.

The Borderless Nature of Cyberspace

One of the more distinctive characteristics of cybercrime is that it can be committed from one country to another, as easily as it can from the house next door. This poses significant challenges to those who are responsible for identifying by whom and from where a crime was committed, to those who would investigate an alleged crime, and to those who would bring a case to court (Sussmann 1999).

Asia as a Setting for Cybercrime

By the year 2015, half of the world's online population will reside in two countries: China and India. The takeup of digital technology in Asia over the coming decade will be nothing short of dramatic. In all probability, the growth of online commerce will follow a parallel trend. This will provide unprecedented numbers of potential victims and prospective offenders.

Responding to Cybercrime

The Transnational Implications of Organized Crime in Cyberspace

We have noted that cybercrime can be committed by individuals or groups alike, as easily from across the globe as from across town. And some organizations themselves transcend national borders. As is the case with terrestrial transnational organized crime, the effective control of transnational cybercrime requires a degree of cooperation between countries. The foundation for this cooperation requires a degree of legislative uniformity, common priorities, and adequate investigative capacity.

Organized cybercrime has proven to be a daunting challenge for law enforcement, but not an insurmountable one. One could cite a number of successful investigations, not only within a given jurisdiction, but also investigations of cross-national criminal activity, involving law enforcement agencies from many countries. There have been a number of successful cross-national investigations of organized cybercrime groups. Among many others, these include:

- Operation Cathedral, an investigation of the Wonderland child pornography club, culminating in 107 arrests in 12 countries in 1998.
- Operation Buccaneer, a 14-month undercover operation against the Drink or Die piracy group that resulted in simultaneous raids in seven countries in 2001.
- Operation Firewall, an investigation across nine countries that targeted the Shadowcrew credit card and ID fraud.
- Operation Site Down, an investigation of copyright piracy resulting in 90 searches in 11 countries in 2005.

Essential to successful interdiction of cross-national organized cybercrime are three factors:

- Legislative harmony
- A framework of law enforcement cooperation
- The capacity to investigate and, if necessary, to prosecute

Bullwinkel (2005) has provided a detailed and useful roadmap. The first steps in this direction were taken by the G-8 and by the Council of Europe, whose cybercrime convention has served as a legislative and policy model for a number of non-European nations, including Australia and

Japan (Broadhurst 2006). The UN Convention Against Transnational Crime provides a further framework.

More recently, countries in the Asian region have focused their attention on cooperation in furtherance of cybercrime control. ASEAN Ministers have met periodically to reaffirm their commitment. In 2006 The ASEAN Regional Forum published a statement on combating cybercrime, that called, inter alia, for countries to establish an appropriate legislative foundation to:

- establish an ARF-wide network of Computer Security Incident Response Teams;
- identify national cyber security units and increase coordination among national agencies;
- develop national watch, warning, and incident response capabilities;
- collaborate with international and regional agencies for cyber investigation and collection and sharing of cyber evidence;
- conduct training/ technology transfer and counter-measures, especially digital forensics;
- encourage private sector partnership with the government in the field of information security and fighting cybercrime; and
- encourage private sector partnership with the government in the field of information security and fighting cybercrime (ASEAN Regional Forum 2006).

Conclusion—The Future of Organized Crime and Digital Technology

It is essential to adapt one's systems of substantive criminal law, criminal procedure, and evidence, to be able to cope with the criminal exploitation of emerging technologies. Because the global nature of cyberspace means that a significant amount of high technology crime will be committed across national borders, this will include the laws relating to jurisdiction, mutual legal assistance, and extradition. It may also include the laws relating to remote cross-border searches by officials in one country, through a networked environment, to data that are physically located in another.

It is also important for criminal justice professionals to remain abreast of developments in technology so that they are able effectively to investigate, prosecute, and adjudicate high tech crimes.

The nature of digital technology is such that a great deal of knowledge and expertise resides outside the public sector, across a range of industries such as software, IT security, Internet service providers, and accounting firms. The most effective response to organized crime in the digital age is to harness the potential contributions of these industries.

Organized criminal exploitation of digital technology has been driven by two factors: as traditional opportunities begin to wane, because of decriminalization or policy changes that create a more hostile climate, organized criminals have sought new worlds to conquer.

For those organized criminals choosing to stick to their traditional activities, digital technologies have presented new more efficient means of going about their usual business. Because accounting systems of most large organizations are now automated, much white collar crime is committed with computers.

Developments in technology have also "created" new organized criminals and new criminal organizations. Many individuals who practice digital piracy or online sharemarket manipulation, for example, had no prior criminal history. Armed simply with the skills necessary to engage in the acts in question, they have seen their opportunities and have taken them. But organizations can be corrupted for criminal purposes as well. The practice of traditional organized crime groups operating behind "front companies" long predates the digital age. And companies can be created explicitly for the purpose of engaging in criminal activity.

There seems little doubt that all organizations, legitimate and criminal, will depend increasingly on digital technology for their continued existence. Digital technology will become increasingly pervasive, surrounding us all, to the extent that much like electricity today, we take it for granted.

But as new technological developments occur, we can be confident that criminals, organized or otherwise, will be poised to exploit them. The challenge, then, is to design technologies that are robust in the sense that their legitimate use is minimally constrained, but their illegitimate use prevented or discouraged. This, of course, will not always be possible.

REFERENCES

ASEAN Regional Forum (2006). Statement on cooperation in fighting cyber attack and terrorist misuse of cyber space of the thirteenth ASEAN Regional Forum 2006. http://globalwarming.mofa.go.jp/region/asia-paci/asean/conference/arf/state0607-3.html (visited 18 September 2007).

Ashcroft, J. (2004). Statement of Attorney General John Ashcroft on the Regpay Child Pornography Indictment. http://www.usdoj.gov/opa/pr/2004/January/04_ag_021.htm (visited 18 September 2007).

Associated Press (2006). State Department Suffers Computer Break-Ins. 11 July 2006. http://www.usatoday.com/news/washington/2006-07-11-state-department_x.htm (visited 18 September 2007).

BBC News (2001). Attack on Japan ministry website. http://news.bbc.co.uk/hi/english/world/asia-pacific/newsid 1252000/1252965.stm (visited 18 September 2007).

Broadhurst, R. G. (2006). Developments in the global law enforcement of cyber-crime. *Policing: An International Journal of Police Strategies and Management, 29*(3), 408–433.

Buchanan, J., & Grant, A. (2001). Investigating and prosecuting Nigerian fraud. *United States Attorneys' Bulletin*, November 2001, 39–47.

Bullwinkel, J. (2005). International cooperation in combating cyber-crime in Asia: Existing mechanisms and new approaches. In R. Broadhurst & P. Grabosky (Eds.), *Cybercrime: The challenge in Asia* (pp. 269–302). Hong Kong: Hong Kong University Press.

Burrell, I. (1999). Asian trade in illegal immigration is uncovered. *The Independent*, 27 December. http:// news.independent.co.uk/world/asia/article287888.ece (visited 18 September 2007).

Carwile, K. P., & Hollis, V. (2004). The mob: From 42nd street to Wall Street. *Journal of Financial Crime, 11*(4), 325–341.

Chambliss, W. (1989). State organized crime. *Criminology, 27*(2), 183–208.

China.org (2007). Banking Authority Addresses Credit Card Fraud. http:// www.china.org.cn/english/BAT/ 140063.htm (visited 18 September 2007).

Choo, K.-K. R., Smith, R. G., & McCusker, R. (2007). Future directions in technology-enabled crime: 2007–09. Research and Public Policy Series No. 78. Australian Institute of Criminology, Canberra. http://www.aic.gov.au/publications/rpp/78/ (visited 18 September 2007).

Cilluffo, F. J. (2007). The internet: A portal to violent Islamist extremism. Testimony to the Homeland Security and Governmental Affairs Committee, United States Senate, May 3, 2007. http://hsgac.senate.gov/_files/050307Cilluffo.pdf (visited 18 September 2007).

CRIENGLISH.com (2006). Flashmob of 12 Proposed to One Girl in Beijing. CRIENGLISH.com, 3 September (visited 18 September 2007).

Curtis, G. E., Elan, S., Hudson, R., & Kollars, N. (2003). *Transnational activities of Chinese crime organizations*. Federal Research Division, Library of Congress, Washington. http://www.loc.gov/rr/frd/pdf-files/ChineseOrgCrime.pdf (visited 18 September 2007).

Denning, D. (2000). Cyberterrorism. Testimony before the special oversight panel on terrorism, Committee on Armed Services, U.S. House of Representatives, May 23, 2000. http://www.cs.georgetown.edu/-denning/infosec/cyberterror.html (Visited 18 September 2007).

Finnane, M. (2002) Sentencing judgment, Judge Michael John Finnane QC *Regina v H.* The District Court of New South Wales, Criminal Jurisdiction, Friday, 23 August 2002 01/11/0877. http://www.abc.net.au/ 4corners/stories/s676658.htm (visited 18 September 2007).

Forman, R. F., Woody, G. E., McLellan, T., & Lynch, K. G. (2006). The availability of web sites offering to sell opioid medications without prescriptions. *American Journal of Psychiatry, 163*(7), 1233–1238.

Givner-Forbes, R., & Shwery, C. (2007). Mapping the electronic Jihad: An outline of the virtual Jihadi Community. RSIS Commentaries 33/2007. http://www.rsis.edu.sg/ publications/Perspective/ RSIS0332007.pdf (visited 18 September 2007).

Goldstone, D., & Shave, B. (1999). International dimensions of crimes in cyberspace. *Fordham International Law Journal, 22*, 1924–1971.

Goodell, J. (2002). How to fake a passport. *The New York Times Magazine*, February 10, 2002. http://query.nytimes.com/gst/fullpage.html?sec=travel&res= 980CE6D6133DF933A25751C0A9649C8B63 (visited 18 September 2007).

Grabosky, P. N., & Smith, R. G. (1998). *Crime in the digital age*. New Brunswick, NJ: Transaction Publishers, and Sydney: Federation Press.

Grant, A., David, F., & Grabosky, P. (1997). Child pornography in the digital age. *Transnational Organized Crime, 3*(4), 171–188.

Halstead, B. (1998). The use of models in the analysis of organized crime and development of policy. *Transnational Organized Crime, 4*(1), 1–24.

Hill, P. (2005). The changing face of the Yakuza. In M. Galeotti (Ed.), *Global crime today* (pp. 97–116). Abingdon: Routledge.

Makarenko, T. (2004). The crime-terror continuum: Tracing the interplay between transnational organized crime and terrorism. *Global Crime, 6*(1), 129–145.

McDonell, R. (1998). Money laundering methodologies and international and regional countermeasures. Paper presented at a conference convened by the Australian Institute of Criminology, Sydney, 7–8 May. http://www.aic.gov.au/conferences/gambling/mcdonnell.pdf (visited 18 September 2007).

McMullan, J., & Perrier, D. (2007). The security of gambling and gambling with security: Hacking, law enforcement and public policy. *International Gambling Studies, 7*(1), 43–58.

Mitnick, K., & Simon, W. (2005). *The art of intrusion.* Indianapolis: Wiley Publishing.

Nasheri, H. (2005). *Economic espionage and industrial spying.* Cambridge: Cambridge University Press.

Nicholson, J. A. (2005). Flash! Mobs in the age of mobile connectivity. *The Fibreculture Journal, 6.* http://www.journal.fibreculture.org/issue6/index.html (visited 18 September 2007).

Office of the National Counterintelligence Executive (2006). *Annual Report to Congress on Foreign Economic Collection and Industrial Espionage 2005.* Office of the Director of National Intelligence, Washington. http://www.ncix.gov/publications/reports/fecie_all/FECIE_2005.pdf (visited 19 October 2007).

Ortis, C., & Evans, P. (2003). The internet and Asia-Pacific security: Old conflicts and new behaviour. *The Pacific Review, 16*(4), 549–572.

Patsky, L. H. (2005). Statement before the subcommittee on oversight of government management, the federal workforce, and the District of Columbia, Committee on Homeland Security and Governmental Affairs United States Senate, June 14, 2005. http://www.usdoj.gov/criminal/ cybercrime/PatskyIPtestimony061405.htm (visited 18 September 2007).

Passas, N. (1996). The genesis of the BCCI scandal. *Journal of Law and Society, 23*(1), 57–72.

Perl, R. (2005). State crime: The North Korean drug trade. In M. Galeotti (Ed.), *Global crime today* (pp. 117–128). Abingdon: Routledge.

Poynting, S. (2006). What caused the Cronulla riot? *Race & Class, 48*(1), 85–92.

Priest, E. (2006). The future of music and film piracy in China. *Berkeley Technology Law Journal, 21,* 795–871.

Radio Australia (2007). Thai authorities uncover massive credit card fraud, 8 January. http://www. radioaustralia.net.au/news/stories/s1822746.htm (visited 15 January 2007).

Ramo, J. C. (1996). Crime Online. *Time Digital,* September 23, pp. 28–32.

Reuters (2001) Internet sex offer puts Malaysian husband in jail. http://www.newsbits.net/2001/20010404.htm (visited 18 September 2007).

Rheingold, H. (2002). *Smart mobs: The next social revolution.* New York: Perseus Publishing.

Schneider, J. L. (2003). Hiding in plain sight: An exploration of the activities of a drug's newsgroup. *Howard Journal of Criminal Justice, 42*(4), 372–389.

Sheptycki, J. (2000). Introduction. In J. Sheptycki (Ed.), *Issues in transnational policing* (pp 1–20). London: Routledge.

Sims, J. C. (2006). What NSA is doing and why it's illegal. *Hastings Constitutional Law Quarterly, 33* (2&3), 101–136.

Sipress, A. (2004). An Indonesian's prison memoir takes holy war into cyberspace: In sign of new threat, Militant Offers Tips on Credit Card Fraud. *Washington Post,* 14 December, A19. http://www.washingtonpost.com/wp-dyn/articles/A62095-2004Dec13.html (visited 18 September 2007).

Slotter, K. (1997). Plastic payments: Trends in credit card fraud. *FBI Law Enforcement Bulletin.* http://www. fbi.gov/publications/leb/1997/june971.htm (visited 18 September 2007).

Smith, R. G., Holmes, M., & Kaufmann, P. (1999). Nigerian advance fee fraud. *Trends and Issues in Crime and Criminal Justice, 121.* Australian Institute of Criminology, Canberra. http://www.aic.gov.au/ publications/tandi/ti121.pdf (visited 18 September 2007).

Smith, R. G., & Urbas, G. (2001). Controlling fraud on the internet: A CAPA persepective. Research and public policy series no. 39. Australian Institute of Criminology, Canberra. http://www.aic.gov.au/publications/rpp/39/ (visited 18 September 2007).

Stoll, C. (1989). *The cuckoo's egg.* New York: Pocket Books.

Sullivan, J. P. (2001). Gangs, hooligans, and anarchists: The vanguard of netwar in the streets. In D. F. Ronfeldt & J. Arquilla (Eds.), *Networks and netwars: The future of terror, crime, and militancy* (pp. 99–126). Santa Monica, CA: RAND Corporation.

Sussmann, M. (1999). The critical challenges from international high-tech and computer related crime at the millennium. *Duke Journal of Comparative and International Law, 9,* 451–489.

Thomas, T. L. (2003). Al Qaeda and the Internet: The danger of cyberplanning. *Parameters, 33*(1), 112–123. http://carlisle-www.army.mil/usawc/Parameters/03spring/thomas.htm (visited 18 September 2007).

US Department of Justice (1997). The Office of Enforcement Operations—its role in the area of electronic surveillance. *US Attorneys' Bulletin, 45*(5), 8–18. http://www.usdoj.gov/usao/eousa/foia_reading_room/usab4505.pdf (visited 18 September 2007).

US Department of Justice (2005). First U.S. Convictions in Largest Ever Multinational Investigation of Internet Piracy (March 8). http://www.usdoj.gov/criminal/cybercrime/kleinbergPlea.htm (visited 18 September 2007).

US Department of Justice (2007). Operation Buccaneer. http://www.cybercrime.gov/ob/OBorg&pr.htm (visited 18 September 2007).

Vanderbilt, T. (2004). Follow the crowd: Tom Vanderbilt on new-model flash mobs. *ArtForum.* http://findarticles.com/p/articles/mi_m0268/is_10_42/ai_n6205876/pg_1 (visited 18 September 2007).

Vaughan, D. (1983). *Controlling unlawful organizational behavior: Social structure and corporate misconduct.* Chicago: University of Chicago Press.

Wahlert, G. (1996). Implications of the move to a cashless society: Law enforcement. In A. Graycar & P. Grabosky (Eds.), *Money laundering in the 21st century: Risks and countermeasures.* Canberra: Australian Institute of Criminology. http://www.aic.gov.au/publications/rpp/02/rpp02-03.html (visited 18 September 2007).

Wasik, B. (2006). My crowd: Or, phase 5. *Harper's Magazine,* March 2006, 56–66.

White, R. (2006). Swarming and the social dynamics of group violence. *Trends and Issues in Crime and Criminal Justice, 326.* Canberra: Australian Institute of Criminology. http://www.aic.gov.au/publications/tandi2/tandi326.html (visited 18 September 2007).

Williams, P. (2002). Organized crime and cyber-crime: Implications for business. http://www.cert.org/archive/pdf/cybercrime-business.pdf (visited 18 September 2007).

Wong, A. (2006). Flash mob rape case conviction. *The Standard,* 21 September. http://www.thestandard.com.hk/news_detail.asp?pp_cat=11&art_id=27735&sid=10022367&con_type=3 (visited 18 September 2007).

17

Environmental Crimes

— Karen K. Clark

Introduction

An environmental crime can be defined generally as an act that is outlawed, typically on the grounds that it causes deterioration to our natural surroundings, detracts from the quality of life, and poses health risks to those who are directly or indirectly impacted by the consequences of the illegal behavior. Environmental crimes differ from the historic common-law prohibitions and constitute a new and evolving area of both criminology and jurisprudence. For persons concerned with white-collar crime, environmental offenses provide a significant topic to study. They are most often committed by persons in positions of power and authority while performing their occupational roles. This includes governmental organizations and their agents. For example, the departments of energy, defense, and the interior are linked to activities that create the largest sources of hazardous waste that permeates soil and water systems throughout the nation.

The dropping of atomic bombs on the Japanese cities of Hiroshima and Nagasaki by the American military could be regarded as the most horrendous environmental crime in human history (although often excepted or excused as proactive self-defense). The uncertainty regarding how we label the atomic attacks indicates definitional problems surrounding the concept of environmental crime. Consider another example. Should smoking be considered an environmental crime even though there is no statutory ban against it? There also are problems determining guilt. Who should be charged criminally if a corporation uses asbestos to insulate newly-built houses or schools? Are the school districts or school boards criminally liable for hiring contractors who violate regulations?

An original article written for this publication.

Enforcement issues are similarly complicated. Is it better to use a soft approach that assumes offender goodwill and a desire to remedy the wrong rapidly, or is a tough approach employing heavy fines and possible prison or jail time preferable? Presumably the tactic adopted will depend on particular circumstances, but we do not as yet clearly understand all the various elements that should feed into the enforcement arrangements.

The mismanagement of waste that results from cost-cutting measures causes long-term damage to the environment. A classic example is the El Toro Marine Corps Air Station in Lake Forest, California, which was declared a Superfund site in 1990 after the discovery of a plume of trichloroethylene (TCE), a known carcinogen used for degreasing aircraft, extending 3 miles to the west of the base in 1985 (O'Dowd, 2010). The military base was decommissioned in 1999. The military improperly disposed of hazardous waste including TCE through the 1990s in amounts up to 100 times the legal limit established by the Environmental Protection Agency (EPA) in 1974 (O'Dowd, 2009). The estimated time frame for remediation is 50 years.

There are 130 military bases on the EPA Superfund list. Camp Lejeune in North Carolina exposed as many as 1 million people living on the base to water contaminated with TCE, tetrachloroethylene (PCE), benzene, and other volatile chemicals from 1957 to 1987 (Barrett, 2010). Although there is no generalized governmental regulatory policy to notify veterans and dependents of possible exposure to toxic contaminants, the *National Defense Authorization Act (NDAA) of 2007* required the Defense Department to contact veterans through the Internal Revenue Service and tell them about the exposure at Camp Lejeune. There is no presumption that any diseases are the result of the contamination; each case is judged individually. Chronic exposure to TCE and PCE can cause kidney, esophageal, bladder, breast, and lung cancer (VA Health Care, 2010).

The military's disregard for long-standing environmental laws such as the Resource Conservation and Recovery Act (RCRA), established in 1976 to track the life cycle of hazardous waste, compromised the water and soil qualities of Marine bases and of neighboring communities. There has been no criminal prosecution despite violations of RCRA, the Clean Water Act of 1977, and other environmental statutes. People who worked on the bases have contracted cancers and died prematurely. Government agents were not held criminally accountable for compromising the environment, and taxpayers were left with a tremendous financial burden.

Toxic Waste: Love Canal

Environmental crimes today are most often associated with toxic or hazardous waste dumping and leaks. Two of the most notorious examples are Love Canal in New York and Bhopal in India. Both cases reflect malfeasance that resulted in significant levels of human and environmental harm. The seeds for the Love Canal disaster were sown in 1942. The Hooker Chemical Company began filling an abandoned canal with 22,000 tons of hazardous waste. The waste was placed in fifty-five gallon drums and covered with soil. Hooker then sold the land to the Niagara Falls School Board in 1953. The land was eventually developed into a residential community, which sat atop the buried hazardous waste for more than twenty-two years. In 1975 and 1976 heavy precipitation caused the hazardous waste containers to rise to the surface. Contaminants began oozing into the basement walls of homes. Soon, in-ground pools began to rise. New York authorities declared a state of emergency in 1978 and relocated 238 families. The remaining residents were left to cohabit with the toxins that continued to surface throughout their community.

In 1980 the EPA sent two investigators to determine the extent of the Love Canal contamination. By this time, it had become clear to all Love Canal residents that their health had been compromised due to exposure to the hazardous waste. An epidemiological assessment revealed that for every thirty-six Love Canal residents tested, eleven had chromosomal abnormalities. The residents were outraged that the government had failed to protect them. Their anger was so fervent that they took the two EPA officials hostage, declaring that they would hold them until the federal government declared a federal state of emergency at Love Canal. It took the government less than two days to do so, thereby enabling 710 additional families to be relocated. The long-term impact of Love Canal was the formalization of the Superfund Site program, formally known as the Comprehensive Environmental Response, Compensation and Liability Act (CERCLA) of 1980. This legislation enables the EPA to act to identify corporations or entities responsible for hazardous waste contamination. The EPA can require those parties to bear the cost of environmental remediation and clean up. When a party cannot be identified or cannot pay for the remediation, the taxpayer is left with the financial burden of toxic waste removal. Some of the public funds used to remediate sites are garnered through taxation of chemical and petroleum companies. Unfortunately, an estimated twenty percent of Superfund sites are U.S. military installations. Given the government's ownership of these lands, the public inevitably ends up bearing the costs for many Superfund sites.

Bhopal and Union Carbide— an Unprosecuted Crime

In December 1984, toxic methyl isocyanate (MIC) leaked from a pesticide plant in Bhopal in central India. An explosion at the manufacturing plant operated by Union Carbide India Limited, a subsidiary of Union Carbide, released the gas into the atmosphere. The plant was jointly owned by Union Carbide (based in Danbury, Connecticut) and the government of India. Union Carbide Corporation was one of the companies that had produced Agent Orange (a controversial defoliant and herbicide used in the Vietnam War). The plant in Bhopal was a cost-saving measure. In India, Union Carbide did not have to pay union wages or abide by American environmental laws. It wasn't that India lacked environmental laws. By 1974 it had enacted the Water Act, which established the Central Pollution Control Board and the Station Pollution Control Board. In addition, the Air Act of 1977 was passed to address control and prevention of air pollution. Union Carbide, however, took advantage of the lack of effective enforcement of these laws (Kaur, 2006, p. 97).

By the company's own admission, the Union Carbide engineers used untested technology when designing and constructing the chemical manufacturing plant. Engineers in India repeatedly alerted Union Carbide officials in Connecticut as to the failings of the construction materials and specifications for the Bhopal plant. The company's top managers insisted that its engineers ignore these warnings. As a direct result of this corporate decision, more than 7,000 people died immediately and another 15,000 over the next 20 years (Amnesty International, 2010b). More than 500,000 people were exposed to the toxic gas (Mehta, 2009). The site remains contaminated more than 25 years after the accident, and 10 to 30 people die every month from exposure to the 425 tons of hazardous waste that have not been removed.

Warren Anderson, the head of Union Carbide when the disaster occurred, and two officials of Union Carbide India Limited were arrested four days after the explosion. After being released on bail following intervention by the U.S. embassy, Anderson left India and never returned (Amnesty International, 2009a). Union Carbide reached a settlement with India in 1989 to pay $470 million to Bhopal residents. The Indian Supreme Court upheld the settlement in 1991 and dismissed outstanding petitions seeking a review of the settlement. The families of the dead received an average of $2,200; the wounded received $550 (Mehta, 2009). Union Carbide sold its Indian subsidiary and moved out of India in 1994. Dow Chemical (which produced napalm for the Vietnam War) bought Union Carbide in 2001 and has consistently maintained that it bears no responsibility for Union Carbide's Bhopal disaster—that the $470 million settlement ended any obligations. However, Dow accepted asbestos-related liabilities of Union Carbide in the United States that were incurred as far back as 1972. In response to Dow's sponsorship on Earth Day in 2010 of a program (Dow Live Earth Run for Water) to raise global awareness about safe drinking water, Audrey Gaughran, Director of Global Issues for Amnesty International stated:

> Bhopal raises fundamental questions about the accountability of corporations and the capacity and willingness of governments to address corporate-related human rights abuses. For years the govern-

ment of India, Union Carbide Corporation [UCC], and Dow have played "pass the parcel" over the issue of responsibility, while the people of Bhopal have struggled to obtain even basic relief such as clean water. Companies must understand that they cannot escape responsibility for human rights abuses in one area by engaging in positive action elsewhere. Human rights abuses cannot be "offset" by corporate good works. . . . The only way for Dow and UCC to finally put the legacy of Bhopal to rest is to work with the affected communities and government of India to fully, and effectively, address the human rights impact of the disaster. (Amnesty International, 2010a)

Generations of children have been born with significant abnormalities, and the environment remains significantly contaminated—creating additional health problems. Corporate negligence contributed to the disaster. The pesticide plant stored the chemical in bulk rather than smaller barrels without adequate safety mechanisms. In addition, there was no emergency plan to warn local communities if a leak occurred, although emergency plans existed for facilities in the United States. While thousands were dying in Bhopal from exposure to 54,000 pounds of MIC, company officials denied that MIC was toxic. Union Carbide did not provide a list of reaction products to make treating victims more effective, even though it did provide a detailed list after a gas leak in West Virginia in 1985. Although Union Carbide provided some support for relief operations after the explosion, it also sought to limit its compensation responsibilities and left Bhopal without cleaning up the factory site, leaving victims to cope with the contamination (Amnesty International, 2009b).

In 2003, the Indian government asked the United States to extradite Warren Anderson—11 years after a similar request in 1992. The United States government rejected the request in 2004. In response to an appeal by a victim's group, an Indian court issued another arrest warrant on July 31, 2009. A Union Carbide spokesman stated that despite the terrible consequences of the explosion, it was senseless to criminalize a tragedy that no one could have foreseen. He added that Union Carbide had no role in operating the plant at the time of the explosion because India's government required the factory to be managed and operated by employees of Union Carbide India Limited. "Despite the fact that it did not operate the plant, Union Carbide never attempted to escape responsibility for the disaster. Union Carbide immediately accepted moral responsibility for the tragedy and also provided substantial monetary and medical aid to the victims" (Associated Press, 2009).

Criminal charges had been filed against officials of Union Carbide India Limited in 1987. After a protracted court battle that lasted longer than 25 years, the Indian court finally convicted eight senior officials (one posthumously). Originally charged with culpable homicide (maximum sentence 10 years), the officials were convicted of death by negligence (maximum sentence 2 years) after India's Supreme Court reduced the charges. Death by negligence is most frequently used in deaths involving a car accident, prompting an advocate for the disaster victims to describe the verdict as "the world's worst industrial disaster reduced to a traffic accident" (Polgreen and Humar, 2010). The Bhopal disaster is a stark reminder that the interests of the poor are frequently sacrificed to the pursuit of development and that safety regulations are only as effective as their enforcement (Burke, 2009).

White-collar Crime and the Environment

Love Canal and Bhopal are classic examples of environmental crimes not only because of the extensive environmental degradation through failure to comply with regulations but also because they both demonstrate the link between corporate greed and the exploitation of poverty, indigenous populations' rights, human health, and natural resources. The cases highlight the fact that the theoretical underpinnings of environmental criminology relate to social justice, disparities created by globalization, and inequalities based on gender and race (White, 2008, p. 14).

Environmental crimes have been linked to social inequalities. As multiple studies indicate, "Differential victimization [is] evident with respect to the siting of toxic waste dumps, extreme air pollution, chemical accidents [and] access to safe clean drinking water" (White, 2008, p. 16). One of the earliest studies linking disparities between environmental degradation and minority populations was conducted by the U.S. General Accounting Office in 1983. The study evaluated associations between locations of toxic waste dumps and socio-economic factors and race, and concluded that "blacks make up the majority of the population in three of the four communities where the landfills are located" (Lynch and Stretesky, 2007, p. 257). The large corporations that dominate the means of production enjoy the profits derived from the exploitation of natural resources while compromising the health of workers and nearby residents through the contamination of air and water. Environmental crimes are reframed often as worker or consumer issues as well as corporate wrongdoings (White, 2008, p. 38).

As with other white-collar crimes, environmental crime is diffuse. Both the victims and the physical space impacted are spread across regions, time, and borders. The victims are often unknown, and the crime may go undetected for years. As an example, pesticides may be illegally dumped underground. Over time, precipitation and fluctuation in water tables cause the pesticide to permeate aquifers and ponds downstream. Populations dependent on the water and aquatic life absorb the pesticide through ingestion. Their water and quality of life are compromised because of the negligent behavior of someone who never had direct contact with them. The intention of the individuals who illegally dispose of toxic material is to maximize profits while minimizing costs. By failing to adhere to environmental standards that require physical treatment and perhaps incineration of hazardous waste to be followed by biological remediation of the waste site, companies drastically reduce their costs. Unfortunately, those living and working in impacted environments often pay with their health and their lives—and taxpayers often find themselves financially responsible for the cleanup.

Confusing the Issues
by Distracting the Consumers

Under the administration of President George W. Bush, the line between legal and illegal shifted dramatically with the deregulation of many of the laws protecting the environment. Similar to the "greenwashing" of companies (see Dow's clean water initiative above), the Bush administration sought advice from the Luntz Research Company (a "message-development firm") on how to promote an environmentally friendly image. Luntz produced a sixteen-page memorandum (the "Luntz Memo") that outlined specific phrases and terms to be used by the president and conservative Republicans to sound—but not necessarily to be—supportive of environmental issues (Devine, 2004, p. 6). The memorandum promoted the term "climate change" in place of "global warming" in order to make the problem sound less frightening. "The Luntz Memo also provides a list of proven warm and fuzzy words, such as 'common sense' and 'balance' which the memo encourages Republicans to use as often as possible when discussing the environment" (Devine, 2004, p. 6). Words such as "crime," "prison," and "guilty" were notably absent in the Luntz recommendations.

The Bush administration was so successful at having the Luntz suggestions adopted that they advanced two environmental legislative efforts: the Clear Skies Initiative, proposed in February 2002, and the Healthy Forests Initiative, proposed in August 2002. The Clear Skies Initiative sought to reduce the impacts of the 1990 Clean Air Act by allowing larger emissions of sulfur dioxide, nitrous oxides, and mercury, three of the largest pollutants produced by coal-burning power plants. It would also increase the permissible levels of ozone emissions, a primary pollutant in photochemical smog. The proponents of the Clear Skies Initiative argued for a cap-and-trade system whereby corporations could emit more pollutants than were allowed under EPA regulations, and companies that emitted fewer pollutants could sell or trade their allotment to the heavy polluters—thereby creating a balance of air emissions. Those in favor of this initiative argued that the Clean Air Act had set standards that were unachievable and that the cap-and-trade system would promote "clear skies" while allowing for large air polluters to adapt newer technologies.

However, those who argued for the reduction in air pollution standards failed to acknowledge publicly that the original Clean Air Act already had a cap-and-trade program. The only ascertainable difference between the Clean Air Act and the Clear Skies Initiative was the amount of emissions allowed for the largest polluters. Under the Clear Skies Initiatives, an extra 35 million tons of sulfur dioxide and nitrous oxide could be released before 2012, and an additional 248 million tons of mercury by 2020 (U.S. Senate Committee on Environment and Public Works, 2003).

Opponents to the bill argued that it was written largely by those in the industry who were most responsible for air pollution and that it would increase pollution substantially. The initiative was killed by the Senate in March 2005. The Clear Skies Initiative was anything but a promotion of clear or clean skies. This is but one demonstration of how the industrial elite can mitigate criminality by persuading those in power to alter regulations. Under the Clean Air Act, large pollution-emitting power plants were being fined $37,500 per violation for exceeding the allowed level of air pollutant release. For companies like the Mojave Generating Station (located near Laughlin, Nevada, and providing power to Los Angeles), administrative penalties forced its closure after a judge found the plant had 40,000 violations in less than a decade (Tullis, 2009, p. 24).

The Healthy Forests Initiative was referred to by environmental conservation groups as the "no tree left behind" measure. The proposed legislation would violate the Roadless Area Conservation Rule proposed by President Clinton and put into effect in January 2001. The Roadless Rule prevented new road construction and logging in 58.5 million acres of national forests. Aside from attempting to protect the last American forests, its proposal stemmed from the fact that roads that had already been constructed were proving to be an economic burden to the taxpayer.

> An astronomical road maintenance backlog, a continually failing timber program, and a poor record of financial accountability has resulted in billions of American taxpayer dollars wasted, largely at the behest of timber companies who rely on government roads in remote areas to facilitate deforestation of public lands. (Heritage Forests Campaign, 2003)

Politicians refer to commercial logging as an approach that can prevent forest fires, despite scientists' assertions that fires are a natural and healthy part of forest ecosystems. Further, the clear-cut method employed by commercial logging companies increases the number and intensity of forest fires. Additionally, the taxpayers spend approximately two billion dollars a year subsidizing the timber industry. Taxpayers fund illegal roads, timber mills, and deforestation so that commercial timber companies can garner substantial profits. The annual cost of two billion dollars does not include the expense of mitigating environmental damage that results from poor forest-management practices such as the suppression of

fire. The impact isn't just the removal of public assets that were established to benefit multiple generations. Failure to maintain forests leads to
poor water and air quality as well as diminished opportunities for recreation. The government pays subsidies to an industry that provides significant financial campaign contributions to garner favorable treatment.

The Roadless Rule hardly inconvenienced many timber companies
between 2001 and 2009. They continued to build roads and retrieve timber in western states, assuming that the Bush administration would win
its court cases. These illegal actions, supported by the U.S. Forest Service,
exacerbated citizen confusion. The Healthy Forests Initiative was written
to increase road building and logging by streamlining access to govern-
ment-owned lands by private industry. The term "healthy forests" was
used to promote the idea of environmental support when in fact the initiative would diminish the viability of forests and increase harm to
human populations living within the vicinity of public lands.

In 2009 President Barack Obama acted to close the roads that were
illegally constructed during the Bush years. Many of those who referred
to themselves as "teabaggers," protestors against the Obama administration, were objecting to the closure of these roads in Nevada, one of the
states impacted by the 2005 ruling. A few citizens wanted to be able to
access the illegally constructed roads for their own benefit. When Obama
put a stop to continued commercial logging that was possible only by
accessing the illegal roads, some citizens were upset by the loss of access
to these illegal roads. The failure of the U.S. Forest Service to abide by
federal law perpetuated the notion that any manipulation of public land
by private enterprises and even private citizens would be tolerated.
Those who profited from the increased activities on these lands were private timber, mining, and oil companies while the public, which was heavily subsidizing these activities, was being told that the illegal actions were
being taken for their benefit.

Televised Trickery

General Electric (GE) has created more Superfund sites than any
other company in the United States. The company unveiled a $90 million
"Ecoimagination" advertising campaign in 2005 to demonstrate commitment to efficient sources of energy, reduced emissions, and clean water.
GE is one of many companies that engage in the dissemination of misleading information to present a positive public image and to conceal
abuse of the environment. As Gaughran noted regarding Dow's sponsorship of "Run for Water": "Sponsoring an event that highlights water
scarcity while ignoring ongoing problems with access to clean water and
medical care, amongst other issues, in Bhopal is at best hypocrisy, at
worst, a flagrant attempt by Dow to try to whitewash its image"

(Amnesty International, 2010a). The National Broadcasting Corporation (NBC), a subsidiary of GE, runs advertisements that portray its parent as a "green company" that earnestly pursues alternative fuel technologies.

Television-based news sources, in deference to their paid corporate sponsors, reliably fail to air stories that are politically threatening or controversial, using the pretense of promoting national security or interest. Stories covering environmental disasters are aired, yet scientific findings linking these disasters to global warming are not. The politicalization of scientific studies and their findings are the direct result of corporate influence on commercial media. Controversies thereby frequently are generated in the newsroom rather than through the scientific community. It is when the authorities invoke the criminal law that the media are likely to attend more carefully to the threat from environmental crimes.

Ultimately the impact of media manipulation lies in what does or doesn't get listed as an environmental crime. Public perception of environmental exploitation is directly tied to what is covered by the media. Portrayals of corporate support of conservation mitigate corporate liability. This, combined with absorbed messages of "unavoidable" and "undeveloped technologies" put forth by companies when defending malfeasance, further confuses consumers. The demand for compliance with environmental regulations is therefore imposed on only the most egregious offenders. Environmental harm rather than environmental crime becomes a cost of doing business. Harm, regardless of legal classification, meets Edwin Sutherland's definition of white-collar crime. As one set of writers has noted:

> The difference between a regulatory law and a crime is not found in the degree of harm but in how effectively opposing interests organize to represent an interpretation that they wish to codify. And, because law is a political process that unequally represents the interests of various groups in society, it cannot be taken as an objective measure of harm. (Lynch and Stretesky, 2007, p. 251)

Ivory and the Illegal Wildlife Trade

Some valuable wildlife species are pushed closer to extinction due to the lucrative illegal trafficking in animal skins, feathers, body parts, and pet trade. A classic example is the illegal sale of ivory. Ivory trade was banned in 1989 due to the killing of 50% of the African elephant population every ten years. In 2006, 180 tons of elephant tusks were smuggled out of Africa. The illegal trade and trafficking of wildlife generates approximately $20 billion annually. An endangered South American macaw can garner up to $100,000 while a python can cost $30,000 (Bergman, 2009, p. 40). The illegal trafficking of wildlife follows closely behind the illegal trafficking of drugs and weapons in terms of volume and profit.

The United States and China are the largest importers of endangered and illegally trafficked animals and their parts. The United States attracts much of the illegal trade through a demand for exotic pets and skins. The Chinese believe several endangered species have medicinal or aphrodisiac value. The gall bladders of bears and rhinoceros horns are in demand on the black market in China.

One of the disturbing trends of the illegal trafficking of wildlife is its association with illegal drug smuggling. The United States-Mexico border is the center point for narcotics smuggling; it is also the route crossed for trade in rare and endangered species from South America. Several Mexican drug cartels have "narco zoos"—private zoos stocked with exotic animals acquired with money from narcotic sales. According to Patricia Patron, the head of Mexico's Environmental Protection Agency, the leaders of Mexico's criminal underworld have narco zoos as a demonstration of power. A raid on a drug mansion in 2008 "in an upscale Mexico City neighborhood netted a menagerie of two lions, two Bengal tigers, two black jaguars and a monkey—all of them well-fed and likely tended to by a personal veterinarian" (Rosenburg, 2009).

Asbestos and the EPA's Most Wanted

[handwritten: white collar crime?]

Asbestos was a commonly used industrial material in the twentieth century; more than 3,000 consumer and industrial products on the market at that time contained asbestos. Asbestos was commonly used in public buildings and workplaces for soundproofing, fireproofing, and insulation. Millions of people are still exposed at home or in their workplace to the asbestos that remains in use—for example, the attic insulation in 30 million American homes (Environmental Working Group, 2007). The highest asbestos use and exposure was in the mid-1970s; workers exposed to asbestos on the job brought home the dust and exposed their wives and children. Asbestos diseases have a 20- to 50-year latency period. Individuals exposed in the 1960s and 1970s are still at risk of dying from the exposure. Ten thousand Americans die each year (almost 30 deaths per day) from diseases caused by asbestos.

Inhaling asbestos fibers has been linked to pulmonary problems such as asthma, asbestosis, and mesothelioma (a lethal cancer that attacks the membranes around the lungs, heart, and abdominal cavity). All industrial countries now regulate asbestos exposure in the workplace. The Occupational Safety and Health Administration (OSHA) started regulating exposure limits in the United States in 1971. Throughout the 1970s, as the dangers of asbestos were better understood, the exposure limit was lowered. The Consumer Product Safety Commission (CPSC) banned the use of asbestos in wallboard patching compounds and gas fireplaces in 1970 because of the danger of asbestos fibers being released into the environment. The EPA banned all new uses of asbestos in 1989, although previous uses were grandfathered. The EPA also established regulations that require school systems to inspect buildings for the presence of damaged asbestos and to eliminate or reduce asbestos exposure to occupants by removing the asbestos or encasing it (National Cancer Institute, n.d.).

Asbestos removal has become a thriving industry in the United States. Although there are strict removal and disposal laws, many companies skirt the regulations to profit from the public's desire to remove the hazard. The Clean Air Act requires that workers wear safety gear and masks and that the asbestos be strictly contained. The federal government has prosecuted dozens of violations of the Act, often involving contractors who hire undocumented workers and provide no training or protection and ignore other safety regulations in removing the asbestos. Contractors who ignore the regulations commit an environmental crime that exposes countless people to potentially fatal diseases (York, 2004). AAR Contractor, Inc. of Albany was an asbestos-removal company that made millions of dollars removing asbestos from 1,555 buildings without proper safety precautions. The buildings included churches, private homes, elementary schools, banks, hospitals, universities, nursing homes—and the New York State Department of Labor Building, which houses the state's office of asbestos control. The contractors exposed countless people, especially their employees, to health risks. The Salvagnos, who owned the company, were sentenced to federal prison and fined $23 million in 2004. The prison terms (25 years for the son, and almost 20 years for the father) were the longest ever handed down for an environmental crime.

Defendants charged with environmental crimes sometimes flee to avoid prosecution. The EPA has a "most wanted" list for current fugitives. Albania Deleon, convicted in 2008 on 28 felony charges, is on the list. She created Environmental Compliance Training in Methuen, Massachusetts, in 2001 to train and certify asbestos removal workers. According to EPA records, Deleon sold hundreds of certificates to workers who never received training. Several were workers who were employed by Deleon's other business, Methuen Abatement Staffing, which offers asbestos removal services. Deleon not only committed fraud but she compromised the health of workers, many of whom were illegal in the United States and were unaware of environmental regulations and workplace protections.

Lawsuits related to asbestos exposure continue. The W. R. Grace Company and seven officials were indicted in February 2005 for knowingly spreading disease-causing asbestos for two generations in Libby, Montana (Johnson, 2007). Two hundred people died and more than 1,200 people in the small mining town and surrounding areas showed signs of lung problems linked to asbestos at the mine operated for almost 30 years by Grace (Anez, 2005). Most of the people with health issues had not worked at the mine; they had contacted asbestos fibers away from the site. The EPA declared the area a Superfund site, and Grace filed for bankruptcy protection. According to a report issued by U.S. Supreme Court Chief Justice John G. Roberts, "The federal trial courts' civil docket grew by three percent [in 2009]. Much of the increase was a consequence of a national increase in personal injury cases related to asbestos" (Liptak, 2010, p. A19).

Awash in Electronic Waste

According to European Union law, electronic equipment cannot leave Europe unless it is reusable. Officials in the United Kingdom have investigated several cases of illegal shipping of electronic waste to Africa. On June 5, 2009, the British Environment Agency, the Metropolitan Police of London, and the Essex Police conducted a raid and seized 500 storage and shipping containers outbound to Africa. Containers were filled with electronic waste that was not reusable. In a statement made by Chris Smith, the Environment Agency's national enforcement service project manager, the electronic equipment was scheduled "to be stripped down for raw materials under appalling conditions in Africa" (*Waste Management News*, 2009). Similarly an article in the *Sydney Morning Herald* reported that illegal shipments of electronic waste from residential communities in Australia were bound for China.

The United States and Canada have been equally complicit in the illegal exportation of electronic waste. Approximately 80% of the waste given to recyclers does not get recycled on the North American continent. Instead, the waste is exported in order to circumvent environmental regulations. In June 2009, the EPA filed a complaint and compliance order against Earth Ecycle, a company that recycles cathode ray tubes from old televisions and computer monitors. The EPA cited Earth Ecycle owner Jeffrey Nixon for shipping seven containers of electronic waste scheduled for recycling in the United States to Africa. Global shifting of electronic and hazardous waste to developing countries to ignore regulations and to generate profits has led to studies of the impact on the health of those, usually children, who sift through the waste without any physical protection. The Seattle-based Basel Action Network, an environmental watchdog group named after the 1989 Basel Convention that monitors the international movement and disposal of hazardous waste, cites studies conducted in Guiyu, China. This area receives vast amounts of electronic waste and, as consequence, has some of the highest levels of dioxin, lead, and other cancer-causing pollutants ever recorded (Basel Action Network Press Release, 2009).

Mineral King Valley

The Sierra Club, an environmental organization, sued the Department of the Interior and its secretary, Roger C. B. Morton, in 1972 to prevent the private development of the Mineral King Valley, a wilderness area in the Sierra Nevada Mountains in Tulare County, California. The property was adjacent to the Sequoia National Forest. In 1965 Walt Disney Enterprises, Inc. sent a proposal to the US Forest Service, which managed the land, to develop motels, restaurants, and recreational facilities on 80 acres of the valley. In order for the public to access the resort, the state of California would have to construct a twenty mile highway and establish a high voltage power line to distribute electricity to the newly developed area, pending an approval by the Department of the Interior. The Sierra Club moved to stop the development by taking legal action against the government agency.

The Sierra Club was a petitioner based on "special interest in the conservation and sound maintenance of the national parks, game refuges, and forests of the country" (Stone, 1974, p. 61). Attorneys for the Sierra Club argued that the proposed Disney development "would destroy or otherwise affect the scenery, natural and historic objects, and wildlife of the park and would impair the enjoyment of the park for future generations" (Stone, 1974, p. 65). The Sierra Club won its initial case against the Department of the Interior but lost under appeal. The case was eventually heard by the U.S. Supreme Court in 1972 (*Sierra Club v. Morton*, 405 U.S.727 (1972)). The court, by a vote of four to three due to two abstentions, ruled that the Sierra Club did not have legal standing to sue.

This case is cited often as one of the first environmental law cases. Although the Sierra Club failed in its objective, the idea that an environmental group may sue on behalf of a wilderness area became a new legal paradigm. Not long after the Sierra Club lost, new cases against the government brought by various private groups altered the course of environmental law. Eventually, organizations such as the Sierra Club, the Environmental Defense Fund, and the National Resources Defense Council would successfully bring cases against both developers and government agencies to trial. Although such cases prevented unimpeded development and exploitation of public resources, the environmental groups were mostly successful in litigation that addressed the harms caused to people, not the harm or potential harm endured solely by ecological systems. Even the banning of DDT (dichlorodiphenyltrichloroethane, a pesticide with widespread use throughout the US) was achieved by its link to cancer in people. The impacts of DDT on watersheds and bird populations were critical to environmentally conscious individuals like Rachel Carson, a biologist for the U.S. Fish and Wildlife Service who wrote about DDT effects in her 1962 book *Silent Spring*. The government, however, was persuaded to ban DDT only after the impact on human health was established.

Conclusion

Private enterprises that profit from exploitation of natural resources are able to fund campaigns and to influence legislators. As a result, many environmental regulations are weak, poorly enforced, and regularly subject to repeal. Crimes against the environment degrade wildlife species, ecosystems, and people's well-being. As resources and environments become increasingly intermingled under the effects of globalization of trade and climate change, it becomes increasingly important to recognize and address the consequences of environmental crimes.

Environmental degradation creates negative economic impacts. Aside from the increase in human health-care costs, remediation of impacted areas and removal of hazardous waste, future development and recreation are limited by present and past resource exploitation. The manipulation of environmental restrictions by large, financially powerful corporations and the government agencies they influence reflect many white-collar crime paradigms. Future generations are left to pay, in this case both financially as well as physically, for the effects of voraciousness. Government representatives use their positions of power to acquiesce to the demands of those whose short-term profits exceed the needs of long-term sustainability. Compromise of societal well-being, animals, plants, water, air, and soil become concessions exchanged for enhanced proceeds. The study of environmental crime has the potential to raise awareness about harms to ecological systems as well as to humans. It will identify the complicity of those in authority charged with protecting people and the environment whose lack of action permits companies to profit at the expense of the public—in violation of laws and regulations. Efforts to enforce compliance can also reveal problems in the construction of laws and regulations that do little to safeguard resources, despite claims of conservation and communal rewards.

REFERENCES

Amnesty International (2010a). "Dow cannot run from the legacy of Bhopal by sponsoring 'run for water' events." April 16. http://www.amnesty.org/en/news-and-updates/dow-cannot-run-legacy-bhopal-sponsoring-run-water-events-2010-04-16

Amnesty International (2010b). "DOW Chemical Company (DOW), Union Carbide Corporation and the Bhopal communities in India." http://www.amnestyusa.org/business-and-human-rights/dow-chemical/page.do?id=1101668

Amnesty International (2009a). "Bhopal: Justice delayed, justice denied." December: pp. 3-4.

Amnesty International (2009b). "India: Dodging responsibility: Corporations, governments and the Bhopal disaster." May 28. http://www.amnesty.org/en/library/info/ASA20/002/2009/en

Anez, Bob (February 8, 2005), "Indictment charges W. R. Grace over asbestos." *U.S.A. Today*. http://www.usatoday.com/money/industries/manufacturing/2005-02-08-grace-asbestos_x.htm

Associated Press (2009). "Company defends chief in Bhopal disaster." *The New York Times*, August 2. http://www.nytimes.com/2009/08/03/business/global/03bhopal.html?_r=1&html

Barrett, Barbara (2010). "Marines fight for help after years of bad water." *Chicago Tribune*, June 21: 14. http://www.chicagotribune.com/health/sc-nw-lejeune-water-0621-20100621,0,1138117.story

Bergman, Charles (2009). "Wildlife trafficking." *Smithsonian*, December: pp. 34-41.

Burke, Jason (2010) "Bhopal campaigners condemn 'insulting' sentences over disaster." *The Guardian*, June 7. http://www.guardian.co.uk/world/2010/jun/07/bhopal-disaster-india-sentences

Burns, Ronald G. and Lynch, Michael K. (2004). *Environmental crime: A Sourcebook*. New York: LFB Scholarly Publishing.

Carson, Rachel (1962). *Silent spring*. Boston: Houghton Mifflin.

Cassidy, Kevin M. (2009). "The role of motive in white collar environmental crimes." *Natural Resources and Environment*, 23: 37–41.

Dean, Cornelia (2009). "A list of the most wanted, by the EPA." *New York Times*, April 5: A9.

Devine, Robert S. (2004). *Bush versus the environment*. New York: Random House.

Environmental Working Group (2007–2009). "The asbestos epidemic." http://ewg.org/sites/asbestos/facts/fact1.php

Frank, Nancy (1985). *Crimes against health and safety*. New York: Harrow and Heston.

Gaynor, Kevin A. and Bartman, Thomas R. (1999). "Criminal enforcement of environmental laws." *Colorado Journal of International Environmental Law and Policy*, 10: 19–52.

Harrell, Martin, Lisa, Joseph K., and Votaw, Catherine L. (2009). "Federal environmental crime: A different kind of 'white collar' prosecution." *Natural Resources and Environment*, 23: 3–8.

Heminway, Diane (2001). "The 20th anniversary of Love Canal: Lessons learned." *Buffalo Environmental Law Journal*, 8: 3–10.

Johnson, Carrie (July 13, 2007). "Asbestos evidentiary ruling goes against Grace." http://www.washingtonpost.com/wp-dyn/content/article/2007/07/12/AR2007071201799.html

Kaur, Gurkirat (2006). *Environmental crime*. New Delhi, India: Shree Publishers and Distributions.

Liptak, Adam (2010). "A busy year for judiciary, Roberts says." *New York Times*, January 1: A19.

Lynch, Michael J. and Stretesky, Paul (2007). "Green criminology in the United States." In (Beirne, P. and South, N., Eds). *Issues in green criminology: Confronting harms against environments, humanity and other animals*. Portland, OR: Willan Publishing.

Mehta, Suketu (2009). "A cloud still hangs over Bhopal." *The New York Times*, December 2. http://www.nytimes.com/2009/12/03/opinion/03mehta.html?_r=1

National Cancer Institute, "Asbestos exposure and cancer risk." http://www.cancer.gov/cancertopics/factsheet/Risk/asbestos

O'Dowd, Robert (2010). "It's all about 'the green'." *Salem-News.com*, January 2. http://www.salem-news.com/articles/january022010/green_marines_ro.php

O'Dowd, Robert (2009). "Navy sealed El Toro wells without thorough inspection." *Salem-News.com*, May 7. http://www.salem-news.com/articles/may072009/el_toro_wells_5-1-09.php

Periconi, James J. (2009). "The state of environmental crimes prosecutions in New York." *Natural Resources and Environment*, 23: 11–16.

Polgreen, Lydia and Kumar, Hari (2010) "Eight former executives guilty in '84 Bhopal chemical leak." *New York Times*, June 7. http://www.nytimes.com/2010/06/08/world/asia/08bhopal.html

Report by the Interpol Pollution Crime Working Group. October 21, 2009. http://www.interpol.int/Public/EnvironmentalCrime/Default.asp. Retrieved on December 15, 2009.

Revesz, Richard L. (1997). *Foundations of environmental law and policy.* New York: Oxford University Press.

Rosenbaum, Walter A. (2002). *Environmental politics and policy* (5th ed.). Washington, DC: CQ Press.

Rosenburg, Mica (2009). "Exotic animals trapped in net of Mexican drug trade." *Reuters* (February 5).

Schoenbrod, David (2005). *Saving our environment from Washington: How Congress grabs power, shirks responsibility, and shortchanges the people.* New Haven, CT: Yale University Press.

Sierra Club v. Morton, 405 U.S.727 (1972).

Szasz, Andrew (1994). *Ecopopulism: Toxic waste and the movement for environmental justice.* Minneapolis: University of Minnesota Press.

Stone, Christopher D. (1974) *Should trees have standing? Toward legal rights for natural objects.* Los Altos, CA: William Kaufmann, Inc.

Tullis, Paul (2010). "The west without coal." *Sierra Magazine*, 95: 22–27.

Unknown Author (2003). "Administration opens millions of acres of wild forests to development." *Heritage Forests Campaign*, March 21.

Unknown Author (2005). "Clearer skies." *New York Times*, March 12.

Unknown Author (2009). "Catastrophic e-waste fuels global toxic dump." *Sydney Morning Herald*, November 14.

Unknown Author (2009). "EPA files legal action against exporter of e-waste following toxic trade watchdog investigation." *Basel Action Network Press Release*, June 11.

Unknown Author (2009). "Large-scale raids on suspected illegal WEEE exports." *Waste Management News*, June 8.

U.S. Senate Committee on Environment and Public Works, Subcommittee on Clean Air, Climate Change, and Nuclear Safety (2003). Hearing on S. 385, "Clear Skies Act of 2003," April 8.

VA Health Care (2010). "Camp Lejeune water contamination." Fact Sheet 16-9, May 10. http://www4.va.gov/healtheligibility/Library/pubs/CampLejeuneWaterContamination/CampLejeuneWaterContamination.pdf

Weiss, Edith Brown (Ed.) (1992). *Environmental change and international law: New challenges and dimensions.* Tokyo, Japan: United Nations University Press.

White, Rob (2008). *Crimes against nature: Environmental criminology and ecological justice.* Portland, OR: Willan Publishing.

York, Michelle (December 24, 2004), "Father and son get long terms in defective asbestos removal." *New York Times* http://query.nytimes.com/gst/fullpage.html?res=9A06E1DD1E30F937A15751C1A9629C8B63

Part 5

Social Response

Social response to white-collar crimes is often different than the response to other lawbreaking for several reasons. In many cases, the perpetrators do not seem to be violent. White-collar crimes are more complex than street crimes and are harder to prove; offenders often can afford a strong legal defense. The publicity and public outcry in most white-collar cases are more muted than in the case of violent crimes. The public usually does not identify with the victims of white-collar crime, frequently assuming the victims were as driven by greed as the perpetrators of the financial crimes. However, in the wake of the major corporate and financial crimes of the first decade of the twenty-first century, public attitudes and public opinion became more critical of and often even hostile toward white-collar offenders.

Francis Cullen, Jennifer Hartman, and Cheryl Jonson describe how public attitudes that until the 1960s did not pay attention to the crime of the upper world have changed. The major financial scandals of the last four decades have convinced the public that high-profile, white-collar offenders are indeed "bad guys"—motivated only by greed without concern for the harm they cause victims and ultimately society. This change in attitude opens the way for more severe punishment than was common previously for white-collar offenses. The authors wonder whether this new attitude will deflect attention away from the sources of white-collar offending that are embedded in the social structure of our society.

Michael Levi, the prolific British scholar, compares the sentencing patterns of the United Kingdom and the United States. He focuses on a particular set of crimes—*frauds*—that are often associated with white-collar crime. His findings indicate clear differences between the United Kingdom, where most fraud offenders get off comparatively lightly, and the United States, where sentencing is considerably harsher than it was before the Enron case in 2001. The Sarbanes-Oxley Act was enacted after the Enron fraud was exposed and created tougher sentencing guidelines.

Andrea Schoepfer and Nicole Piquero provide an informative review of the antitrust laws. Their article explains the rationale behind these laws beginning with the Sherman Act of 1890, which regulated commercial activity in a capitalist free market economy. The authors analyze an interesting exception of the application of these laws involving one of the favorite US pastimes—baseball. Schoepfer and Piquero give an historical account of the antitrust exemption for MLB (Major League Baseball) as demonstrated by the "reserve clause" in players' contracts. The situation changed somewhat in 1975 when the clause was abolished; the players' union won free agency with the Curt Flood Act in 1998. In reality, however, some aspects of antitrust exemption are still in effect in professional baseball.

John Heeren wrote the final article for this collection, which focuses on the victims of white-collar crime. He explores the ambiguities involved in the definitional concept of white-collar crime and how it reflects on studying the victims of white-collar crime. The systematic study of white-collar crime victims and white-collar crime victimization is inhibited by the difficulties in obtaining reliable data; the extent of white-collar crime is not clearly measured by the Uniform Crime Report or by official victimization surveys. Heeren explores the various types of victims, such as individual victims versus large groups victimized by corporations. He also discusses how the public views white-collar victims and treats them differently than victims of street crimes.

18

Bad Guys

Why the Public Supports Punishing White-Collar Offenders

— *Francis T. Cullen,*
   Jennifer L. Hartman, and
   Cheryl Lero Jonson

As Igo (2007) illuminates, the invention in the 1930s of the scientific national opinion poll—especially by Gallup and Roper—made it possible to capture how "the American public" felt about a range of issues. In a nation that was socially diverse and that spread from the Atlantic to the Pacific Ocean, this was a remarkable and important accomplishment. For the first time, it was possible to monitor continuously "Americans' attitudes and beliefs" and thereby present an "ongoing constitution of 'the public' through anonymously expressed views" (pp. 130–131). Polling data in turn contributed to the creation of a "mass society" by calculating what the "average American" believed—a standard against which individuals could now check their views.

The emerging power of opinion polls rested on two features. First, the poll was scientific, which provided it with legitimacy, and its predictions proved largely accurate, which provided it with practical utility (e.g., predicting election results). Second, the poll was parsimonious; it was able to reduce the views of millions of Americans to a single number (e.g., "70%" favored a candidate or a policy). But the opinion poll also

Source: Francis T. Cullen, Jennifer L. Hartman, and Cheryl Lero Jonson, Bad Guys: Why the Public Supports Punishing White-Collar Offenders. *Crime, Law and Social Change*, Vol. 51, No. 1, pp. 31–44. Copyright © 2009 by Springer Science. Reprinted with permission.

carried a special danger. Once taken, the poll potentially exerts an independent influence. It not only reflects but also helps to construct social reality. Thus, when published, polling results are taken as accurate portrayals of what the American public believes—portrayals not easily challenged and that can be cited in favor of specific policy positions.

This phenomenon burdens understandings about crime attitudes. The repeated publication of national polls showing that a high percentage of respondents (70% or more) support harsher courts and capital punishment has created the view that Americans are rigidly punitive toward crime. This research—and the social reality it constructs—has been cited, including by the U.S. Supreme Court in death penalty cases, as showing that the public endorses a "get tough" approach to crime control. More sophisticated research, however, has shown that although harboring punitive sentiments, members of the public temper their support for harsh sanctions when given more information about the offender and when given a wider array of sentencing options (Cullen, Fisher, & Applegate, 2000; Roberts & Stalans, 1997; Turner, Cullen, Sundt, & Applegate, 1997). Studies also reveal strong support for rehabilitation programs, especially for youths (Cullen et al., 2000; Cullen, Vose, Jonson, & Unnever, 2007).

Although less apparent, national opinion polls also have communicated a more subtle message about what constitutes "crime." Although exceptions exist, these surveys have primarily asked about what should be done to street offenders, such as "those convicted of murder." Other times, the public has been asked whether crime made them afraid to walk outside their house at night. These questions are legitimate, but they are also limiting and consequential. They focus attention on some domains of offending—street crimes—while diverting it away from other domains—including white-collar crime. They provide data that encourage concern about traditional criminality by suggesting that it is feared and merits stringent punishment. Meanwhile, they provide few hints about public sentiments toward lawlessness in the upperworld. Thus, whereas death penalty polls have been conducted regularly for decades, there is no comparable survey that reports, year in and year out, that 70% (or some percentage) of the American public believes that white-collar crooks should be locked up.

Knowing "what the public thinks" about white-collar crime has long concerned scholars (see, e.g., Ross, 1907; Sutherland 1983 [1949]). Over the years, many scholars have attempted to raise public consciousness about the crimes of the rich and powerful. Implicit in their writings is the notion that the public is unaware of the true harms exacted by white-collar lawlessness. Scholars have worried that unless the public were outraged by these wayward acts, it would be difficult to persuade policy-makers to bring white-collar offenders within the reach of the criminal law. Public opinion has thus been depicted as a potential barrier to the control of upperworld lawlessness.

Assessing these issues is complicated by the relative lack of data on public opinion about white-collar crime. To be sure, a small body of solid criminological studies exists and attitudinal data can be culled from other sources (Evans, Cullen, & Dubeck, 1993). But in comparison to the extant literature on public opinion about street crime (Roberts & Stalans, 1997), the research on white-collar crime is sparse. Reasonable conclusions can be derived, but they are not fully free from a measure of speculation.

With this caveat stated, it seems possible to trace the evolution in public opinion about white-collar offending. Although attitudinal swings can be found, many key features of public views toward street crime and its punishment have remained relatively stable over the past few decades (Cullen, Pealer, Fisher, Applegate, & Santana, 2002; Cullen, Vose, Jonson, & Unnever, 2007; Unnever, Cullen, & Jonson, 2008). By contrast, we propose that public opinion about white-collar crime has been marked by important transformations. In this regard, we contend that the evolution in attitudes can be divided, in rough terms, into three periods. The first period, before 1970, was characterized by a relative inattention to white-collar crime. The second period, from 1970 to 2000, produced a remarkable shift in awareness about and the willingness to sanction upperworld lawlessness. The third period, from 2000 to the present, continued earlier trends but solidified a narrative about white-collar offenders that depicted them as "bad guys." This social construction of the white-collar criminal has salient public policy implications—some potentially favorable, some potentially problematic.

Period I: Inattention

Throughout the first three-quarters of the 1900s, the study of white-collar crime remained largely on the periphery of American criminology (Cullen & Benson, 1993). As marginal men and women of their discipline, scholars had the challenge of persuading observers that their object of inquiry—white-collar crime—was a serious social problem. Toward this end, by probing a number of celebrated scandals, they were able to unmask not only the huge financial costs of these offenses but also the ways in which illegal practices endangered lives (e.g., marketing of defective products). As such, they engaged in a brand of advocacy research that often mixed science with a clear reformist impulse.

A particularly galling fact was that white-collar offenders often committed their harmful acts with impunity. Many shady practices were not formally outlawed, and others were simply never prosecuted. White-collar crooks thus lived beyond the reach of the criminal law. Deterrence was undermined and, still worse, a fundamental injustice persisted: offenses committed in the community streets were met with arrest and incarceration, whereas those committed in corporate suites were met with legal immunity and profit. As Reiman (1979) titled his book, "the rich get richer and the poor get prison."

Just how could this be? Politics, of course, is one answer; those with power are able to deflect the criminal law from attacking their interests. But scholars also pointed to another consideration. The public just did not understand the dangers of white-collar crime. People might be outraged episodically by revelations of an egregious scheme or scandal, but they did not see such lawlessness as endemic to the nation. Public ignorance about and apathy toward upperworld criminality thus was seen as a major barrier to moving elected officials to use the criminal law to crack down on white-collar crime. As Conklin (1977) noted three decades ago, "The issue of public norms and attitudes toward business crime has long formed a central part of the debate over whether white-collar crime should be considered criminal in the same way as are such offenses as murder and rape" (p. 16).

E. A. Ross (1907) was perhaps the first to voice these concerns in a compelling way. In *Sin and Society,* he warned that the United States was experiencing a cultural lag in that its laws and public sentiments were not consistent with the new threats posed by advancing industrial capitalism. An invidious feature of the "new sins" in society was that they could victimize citizens without their knowledge. The business leader was able to make unethical but profitable decisions "leagues or months away from the evil he causes. Upon his gentlemanly presence the eventual blood and tears do not obtrude themselves" (pp. 10–11). Indeed, "the current methods of annexing property of others are characterized by a pleasing indirectness and refinement" (p. 8). The public thus remains unaware or unconcerned about these victimizing practices. "Surpass as their misdeeds may in meanness and cruelty," observed Ross, "there has not yet been enough time to store up strong emotions about them; and so the sight of them does not let loose the flood of wrath and abhorrence that rushes down upon the long-attainted sins" (p. 47).

As a consequence, these "criminaloids"—as Ross called them (p. 45)—are accorded a "shocking leniency" by the public (p. 46). "The real weakness in the moral position of Americans," noted Ross, "is not their attitude toward the plain criminal, but their attitude toward the quasi-criminal" (p. 46). This false consciousness had to change for the criminal law to be updated to address the threats posed by the new industrial order. *Sin and Society* was a call to action—a tract meant to educate the public and to spike their moral outrage.

Although using less vivid language, Edwin Sutherland (1983 [1949]) made a similar argument in *White Collar Crime.* For Sutherland, this lawlessness flourished because of differential social organization favorable to crime. Companies are organized effectively for crime; through differential association they impart the criminal definitions (especially "rationalizations") and techniques that allow officials to take advantage of opportunities to profit illegally under the veil of secrecy. Accordingly, "violations of law by corporations are deliberate and organized crimes" (p. 239).

In contrast, Sutherland (1940) complained that the public was not aroused by white-collar crime. This contributed to their being "socially disorganized" in the face of corporate lawlessness (1983 [1949], p. 255). For one thing, "the victims of corporate crimes are seldom in a position to fight against the management of the corporation" (p. 237). Thus, consumers are "scattered," "unorganized," and lack "objective information," whereas stockholders "seldom know the complex procedures of the corporations which they own" (p. 235). More broadly, the general public "does not think of the businessman as a criminal because the person does not fit the stereotype of criminal" (p. 232). In essence, the respectability of company officials—their status and power within their community—insulates them against being designated as a traditional offender. Similar to Ross, Sutherland thus urged the public to recognize the toll exacted by white-collar crime—to change its attitudes and to fight back:

> This calls for a clear-cut opposition between the public and the government, on the one side, and the businessmen who violate the law, on the other. This clear-cut opposition does not exist and the absence of this opposition is evidence of the lack of organization against white collar crime. What is, in theory, a war loses much of its conflict because of the fraternization between the two forces. White collar crimes continue because of this lack of organization on the part of the public. (p. 257)

As Conklin (1977) notes, it was commonly accepted by scholars into the 1970s that the public was inattentive to white-collar crime. "There is widespread acceptance of the view," he observed, "that the public is 'condoning, indifferent, or ambivalent' toward business crime" (p. 17). For example, in its state-of-the-field review, the President's Commission on Law Enforcement and Administration of Justice (1968, p. 158) concluded that "the public tends to be indifferent to business crime or even to sympathize with the offenders who have been caught." Again, this inattention was decried by most scholars who wished to stir up the public to demand equal justice for white-collar thieves and thugs. A smaller group of scholars, however, was not dismayed that traditional street crimes received more condemnation (Kadish, 1977). Still, they too agreed that citizens did not worry much about upperworld offending. Thus, in *Thinking About Crime*, James Q. Wilson (1975) stated that he would not focus on white-collar offending. In part, this decision reflected his "conviction, which I believe is the conviction of most citizens, that predatory street crime is a far more serious matter than consumer fraud (and) antitrust violations" (p. xx).

However, this reigning consensus that the public cared little about white-collar crime was likely overdrawn. Although studies at the time were limited, Conklin's (1977, p. 32) research review led him to conclude

that "there is a greater degree of public condemnation of business violations than is thought to exist by those who claim that the public is apa-
thetic to or tolerant of business crime." For example, an early study by
Newman (1957) examined public responses to six violations of food laws
(e.g., adulterated food) based on cases taken from the files of the Federal
District Attorney. Although not recommending sentences as long as traditional street crimes (e.g., burglary), 78% of the respondents endorsed
harsher penalties than the court had handed out. There was little reluctance, in short, to impose criminal sanctions (see also Hartung, 1953).
Similarly, Gibbons (1969) would later find that residents from the San
Francisco area favored sending a company official to prison who engaged
in an antitrust violation (70% supported incarceration) or in false advertising (43%). These figures were comparable to sentences endorsed for
auto theft (70%) and assault (48%). And a national poll in 1969 discovered
that the public thought that "a manufacturer of unsafe automobiles is
worse than a mugger (69% to 22%)" and that "a businessman who illegally fixes prices is worse than a burglar (54% to 28%)" (*Time*, 1969, p. 26).

In the end, most Americans before and around 1970 were not so
unconcerned about white-collar crime that they believed that such offenses
should go unpunished. If prompted by a survey to think about a company
official who fixes prices or sells a defective product—that is, if given a list
of offenses and asked what should be done—they would prescribe some
punishment. Still, their concern was circumscribed. As Conklin (1977, p.
33) observed, "they are rarely indignant or militant in their expression of
their condemnation of business crime." Further, it is not clear that upperworld criminality was of much salience in their everyday lives. Although
not morally approving of such conduct, they did not pay it much attention.
This conclusion gains credence from a 1972 survey of college students by
Reed and Reed (1975). In their study, only 42% "said that they had read or
heard about white collar crime" and only 32% "gave an acceptable definition of white collar crime" (p. 282). According to Reed and Reed, "knowledge of white collar crime was not very widespread. . . . The majority were
either ignorant of its existence or incapable of defining it" (p. 290).

Period II: Rising Attention

Serious criminological study of white-collar crime blossomed in the
mid-1970s and then rapidly accelerated into the 1980s (Cullen & Benson,
1993). Although only a modest slice of this scholarly enterprise, a meaningful body of research was published that aimed to illuminate public views
on the control of upperworld criminality (see, e.g., Cullen, Clark, Link,
Mathers, Niedospial, & Sheahan, 1985; Cullen, Link & Polanzi, 1982; Cullen, Mathers, Clark, & Cullen, 1983; Frank, Cullen, Travis, & Borntrager,
1989; Goff & Nason-Clark, 1989; Grabosky, Braithwaite, & Wilson, 1987;

Hans & Ermann, 1989; Schrager & Short, 1980; see also Evans, Cullen, & Dubeck, 1993). Taken together, these investigations yielded three fairly firm conclusions.

First, people were increasingly aware of white-collar crime. The concept had entered the public lexicon and could be used in conversation and in newspaper headlines without explanation. Not surprisingly, citizens now viewed these offenses more seriously than they had a decade previously. Second, similar to their reactions to street crimes, respondents accorded different levels of seriousness and severity of punishment depending on the nature of the white-collar offense. Disapproval was greatest when illegal acts involved clear culpability or recklessness and high levels of harm (e.g., enormous amounts of money misappropriated; violence to workers or consumers). Third, there was no reluctance to bring white-collar offenders—whether individuals or corporate entities—within the reach of the criminal law. One study, for example, found that nearly 9 in 10 respondents agreed with the statement, "White-collar criminals have gotten off too easily for too many years; they deserve to be sent to jail for their crimes just like everyone else" (Cullen et al., 1985, p. 485). These and similar results prompted commentators to speak of the myth of community tolerance toward white-collar crime (Grabosky et al., p. 33).

This research on public attitudes was important precisely because of the longstanding claims that Americans were indifferent to white-collar crime and thus that the moral imperative to control this criminality was lacking. It had been believed that the respectability of upperworld offenders insulated them from the stigma of "criminal" attaching to them—that their contributions as an upstanding citizen of the community somehow gave them a free pass to break the law in the workplace. But the public opinion research that accumulated by the mid-1980s punctured the notion that the criminal immunity enjoyed by white-collar offenders was the will of the people—that it was somehow a case of democracy taking its course. Instead, as willingness to sanction the rich and powerful revealed itself, it was clear that the public no longer could be blamed for the failure to punish white-collar crime (Cullen et al., 1983). Instead, obstacles to prosecution would have to be traced to other factors, including the ability of white-collar actors to use their money and influence to undermine the use of the criminal law against them.

Regardless, it was clear that public attitudes toward white-collar crime had been fundamentally changed. Inattention had been replaced by rising attention and, in some instances, by outright indignation. What brought Americans to the point of readily supporting the punishment of white-collar offenders? Four main factors can be suggested.

First, from the mid-1960s to the mid-1970s, there was a precipitous decline in public confidence in "big" business. Thus, between 1966 and 1971, confidence in those running "major companies" fell from 55% to just 27% (Lipset & Schneider, 1983a, p. 43). According to Lipset and Sch-neider (1983a), this anti-business sentiment was part of a broader confi-dence gap or legitimacy crisis that damaged the trust in government and in other major social institutions. Its origins can be traced to a series of disastrous events, starting around 1965, that included "the Vietnam War, protest movements, Watergate, exposés of corruption in high places, and urban violence" (Lipset & Schneider, 1983b, p. 44, see also Levi & Stoker, 2000). In this context, people were less likely to embrace the once san-guine view that what was good for General Motors was good for Amer-ica. By the 1980s, the public assumed that "business people . . . will act in a socially responsible way only when the public interest coincides with their self-interest" (Lipset & Schneider, 1983a, p. 382). Polls showed that a strong majority of the public believed that "individuals and corporations (often) commit white-collar crimes to make a dishonest profit for them-selves or their companies" (*Public Opinion*, 1986, p. 22). A widespread belief existed that corporate executives were dishonest. Only 16% rated executives' honesty and ethics as "high" or "very high" (Gallup Poll, 1988, p. 19). Such mistrust and animus likely served to fuel punitive senti-ments toward white-collar crime.

Second and related, the civil rights movement of the 1960s and beyond fostered a growing concern about "equal justice." Campaigns for "law and order" and a "war on crime" swept increasing numbers of the disadvantaged into the nation's prisons. This reality prompted charges of social injustice and the accusation that the state wished to use the criminal law to repress the poor and people of color. It was a short step to question why impoverished burglars and robbers should go to prison but not affluent price-fixers and embezzlers. Basic fairness now seemed to com-pel the state to get tough with offenders wearing white-collars. To protect its legitimacy, the state did move in the direction of expanding the use of the criminal law against corporations (Cullen, Cavender, Maakestad, & Benson, 2006; see also Benson & Cullen, 1998).

Third, dramatic changes occurred in the public's conceptions of acceptable risk. In the days of Ross and to an extent Sutherland, deaths from natural and human-made hazards were not uncommon. Physical harm from disease, from the workplace, and from use of products was often seen as an inherent feature of everyday life. The advance of science and technology, however, created expectations that such dangers were controllable and preventable. When illness, injury, or death now trans-pired, there was a tendency to search for culpability.

Who had displayed reckless or wanton disregard for human well-being? Who ignored the evidence of danger? Who chose to make a buck rather than take reasonable steps to protect the vulnerable? For corpora-tions in particular, there was a more exacting standard of liability. Vic-tims of corporate malfeasance clamored for "total justice"—not excuses but legal redress and compensation for the avoidable harms visited upon them (Friedman, 1985). If companies caused illness by polluting the water, injury by allowing an unsafe workplace, or death by marketing a defective product, they were seen as culpable for these acts (Cullen et al., 2006). In this context, calls to criminally sanction wayward corporations were seen as eminently justifiable.

Fourth, beginning in the 1970s, there was a growth of investigative reporting—in the newspapers and on television (e.g., *60 Minutes*). Suddenly, instances of white-collar malfeasance were not hidden from view but highly publicized. Corporate executives smugly denying any wrongdoing while on camera were often then juxtaposed to internal company memoranda revealing a guilty mind and to victims enduring shattered lives. Professional status was now accorded to reporters who could uncover crime and corruption in high places. Juicy revelations of misconduct were published "above the fold" in newspapers; even on local news stations, "I-Team" stories were given the lead. The resulting repeated disclosures of upperworld scandals helped to fuel cynicism and to remove inhibitions about punishing supposedly "respectable" executives and politicians.

Taken together, these factors created an era in which attention toward white-collar crime rose precipitously. In fact, some commentators have argued that the multifaceted attention given to this criminality—from news reporters, scholars, prosecutors, and the public—created a "social movement against white-collar crime" (Cullen et al., 2006; Katz, 1980; see also Benson & Cullen, 1998). Much of this movement was symbolic—episodic crackdowns on selected offenses followed by political posturing (with cameras flashing) and rhetoric about the importance of equal justice before the law. Still, more substantive changes also occurred, including the expansion of the criminal law to cover a broader range of white-collar offenses and the creation of special units to investigate and prosecute environmental and workplace crimes (Benson & Cullen, 1998; Cullen et al., 2006). Regardless, in retrospect, it is clear that the kind of public ignorance of upperworld "sins" that Ross and Sutherland had decried was a relic of a more naïve and trusting period. By the turn of the twenty-first century, Americans cast a suspicious eye toward the rich and powerful and were prepared to send them off to prison if given a compelling reason for doing so.

Period III: Transformed Attention

A central premise of this essay is that whereas Americans once did not support (or only weakly) supported punishing white-collar criminals, this is no longer the case. In the last three decades of the twentieth century, social and political events coalesced to create a movement against upperworld criminality. As its prevalence and the magnitude of its harm were publicized, the public became aware of white-collar crime and critical of offenders in white-collars. Confidence in businesses and in other institutions declined, while concern for equal justice escalated. This confluence created a special problem for the government. For the state to protect its own declining legitimacy, it had to show a concerned public that it was not beholden to corporate interests. It had to prove that it understood the need for victims to be accorded "total justice." As a result, the state created space for the expanded use of the criminal law against white-collar miscreants. In doing so, it revealed that crime occurred across classes and that no offender was above the law. Even if these prosecutions were more symbolic than substantive—after all, most resources were still devoted to repressing the crimes of the disadvantaged—their occurrence did much to cement in the public consciousness that white-collar offending was serious and deserving of criminal sanctions. It seems unlikely, therefore, that public attitudes will ever return to the point of indifference toward white-collar crime once decried by Ross and Sutherland. They have changed—likely for good and firmly in the direction of supporting the punishment of upperworld criminality (for a summary of these points, see Table 1).

A recent round of studies reinforces the conclusion that the public has little tolerance for white-collar crime and is willing to bring it within the reach of the criminal law (see, e.g., Holtfreter, Van Slyke, Bratton, & Gertz, 2008; Kane & Wall, 2005; Piquero, Carmichael, & Piquero, 2008; Rebovich, Lane, Jiandani, & Hage, 2000; Schoepfer, Carmichael, & Piquero, 2007; Unnever, Benson, & Cullen, 2008). To be sure, street crimes,

Table 1.

Components of Americans' Punitiveness toward White-Collar Criminals

Component	Why Americans did not support punishing white-collar criminals	Why Americans do support punishing white-collar criminals
General awareness of white-collar crime	Unaware; embrace a lower-class image of crime	Increasingly aware; the movement against white-collar crime
Awareness of harm from white-collar crime	Unaware	Magnitude publicized
Confidence in business	High	Low
Concern for equal justice	Low	High; need to justify racial oppression
Cost to the State of not punishing white-collar offenders	Low	High; loss of legitimacy
Total justice—victim salience	Low	High
Typification of the white-collar offender	Good Guys—like "us"; not really a criminal; someone to empathize with	Bad Guys—unlike "us"; rational; greedy; exploitive
Mitigation of culpability	A "good citizen"; contributes to the community	More culpable; affluence makes crime less warranted; betrayer of trust

especially violent transgressions, trigger punitive responses. Even so, clear evidence exists that the public continues to perceive many white-collar crimes to be as serious as street offenses, wants to devote more resources to the control of lawlessness in the upperworld, and wishes to get tough with company officials who break the law. For example, one poll revealed that compared to street crime, "nearly two-thirds of the sample (60.9%) felt that the federal government should devote equal or more resources to enforcing and preventing white-collar crime" (Holtfreter et al., p. 53). In another national survey, the respondents rated bank embezzlement as more serious than a handbag robbery (54.4% to 27.4%; 18.2% rated them as equally serious), and rated knowingly shipping diseased meat that caused a serious illness as more serious than committing a robbery at gunpoint that caused serious injury (42.0% to 38.8%; 19.2% as equally serious) (Piquero et al., p. 298). And still another national poll found that when asked, Do you support or oppose stricter penalties, including longer prison terms and high fines, for corporate executives who conceal their company's true financial condition?, 94% responded either support strongly (77.7%) or somewhat support (16.3%) (Unnever et al., p. 175).

Other polls reveal the persistence of a confidence gap toward corporate and other institutional leaders. Thus, in a 2006 Gallup Poll, a national sample was asked how much confidence they had in sixteen institutions in American society. Big business and Health Maintenance Organizations (HMOs) ranked at the bottom of the list; only 18% and 15% of the respondents, respectively, expressed a great deal or quite a lot of confidence in them. Congress ranked right above them in fourteenth place, with 19%—a finding that showed little trust in the state as well (Saad, 2006). Still, another development is perhaps equally salient: the emergence in the polls of distrust not only of corporations but specifically of individual executives.

Thus, a recent poll found that more than 8 in 10 Americans believe that "CEOs of large American companies are compensated too much." In the same survey, the respondents were asked about the ethics of CEOs. Nobody in the sample selected "always ethical," and only one in three selected "mostly ethical." By contrast, 44% chose "not too ethical" and 12% chose "not ethical at all" (6% were unsure) (*Los Angeles Times*/Bloomberg Poll, 2007). In another national poll, two in every three sample members stated that they believed that "most American corporate executives" were "dishonest" (CBS News Poll, 2002). A *Time/CNN* Poll (2002, pp. 18–19), carrying the title "Losing Faith in Corporate America," found that 71% of the public believed that "the typical CEO" is less honest and ethical than the "average person." Members of this sample also were more likely to rate the "moral and ethical standards" of "CEOs of major corporations" as "fair or poor" (72%) than as "good or excellent" (21%). Similarly, when asked in another study whether they could trust "the executives in charge of major companies in this country," 3 in 4 Americans stated either "only some of the time" (52%) or "hardly ever" (23%). Only 1% could say "always." The same survey asked about "cases of wrongdoing among chief executives of corporations." Fifty percent responded that this was a "widespread problem in which many business executives are taking advantage of a system that is failing." Only 40% said that it was a case of a "few corrupt individuals" (10% responded "don't know") (*Los Angeles Times* Poll, 2004). And to cite but one other example, 7 in 10 Americans stated that corporate executives deserved "a lot" of the blame for "recent corporate scandals like Enron, WorldCom, and Tyco." Less blame was attributed to corporate boards of directors (59%), accounting firms (49%), government regulators (35%), Wall Street firms (33%), and the U.S. Congress (20%) (*Newsweek* Poll, 2002).

As this final polling question suggests, these anti-executives sentiments likely were inflated by the wave of corporate crime scandals that rocked the United States in the first part of this century (Cullen et al., 2006). It is possible, therefore, that these polling results may reflect a temporary bump upward in public condemnation. But as Lipset and Schneider (1983a) observe, a series of high-profile scandals can create a largely permanent change in people's attitudes. Although speculative, we propose that such a fundamental transformation has occurred.

The nature of the media coverage in these cases is important. Corporate executives were portrayed as immensely wealthy—living lavishly—but still pilfering the company treasury and luring people through false financial information to make foolish investments. Meanwhile, unsuspecting victims—including many average citizens holding stock in the company—were cast into economic ruin, as they lost life savings, places to live, and retirement funds. Thus, the coverage employed a "vocabulary of deviance" to describe offenders and used the "personalization of harm" to describe victims (see Swigert & Farrell, 1980, p. 181; see also Cavender & Mulcahy, 1998). Corporate executives—such as Kenneth Lay and Jeffrey Skilling at Enron—were poster boys for what was wrong with big business in America. They inspired little sympathy and many calls to lock them up and throw away the key.

Symptomatic of the press coverage was an account in the *New York Times* called "Corporate Scandals: A User's Guide," which described various cases, published pictures of executives under legal scrutiny, and noted how many indictments and guilty pleas had been achieved by prosecutors (Kirkpatrick, 2003). Similarly, in a *Time* (2002) story titled "Corporate Greed: Heroes to Heels," major financial scandals were listed, accompanied by photos of the companies' executives. The story asked, "How bad are they?" The options were "thoroughly rotten," "strong stench," and "a little fishy."

It is instructive that in the major corporate scandal of the early 1960s—a major price-fixing scheme involving General Electric—a book about the case was called *The Gentlemen Conspirators* (Fuller, 1962; see also Geis, 1967). Such a benign title would never be found today; rather, contemporary exposés carry labels such as *The Predators' Ball* (Bruck, 1988) and *Infectious Greed* (Partnoy, 2003). Indeed, as has long been the case with street offenders (Unnever & Cullen, 2008), there has been a powerful "typification" of the white-collar offender as a "bad guy" whose greed and amorality drives him (or her) to harm vulnerable victims with little remorse (cf. Feld, 1999). This is E. A. Ross's "criminaloid" now written into the public consciousness. It reminds us of DiIulio's (1995) use of the term "super-predators" to describe juvenile offenders—those who exist in an environment of "moral poverty" and who wantonly victimize with no sense of empathy for those they harm.

These considerations allow us to flesh out the final points in Table 1 as to why Americans want to punish white-collar crime. We now have entered a period of not only more attention but also transformed attention about upperworld illegality. Such offenders are viewed no longer as respectable members of the community who are "like us" but as greedy, arrogant, and heartless. There is little to mitigate their culpability when their acts are self-serving and risk ruining the very community in which they reside. They are "bad guys." And bad guys deserve to go to prison.

Conclusion

Having just passed the 100th anniversary of the publication of *Sin and Society*, it is perhaps appropriate to reflect on what E. A. Ross would say about today's public opinion toward white-collar crime. He had warned that "the criminaloid flourishes until the growth of morality overtakes the growth of opportunity to prey" (Ross, 1907, p. 69). Ross might well be pleased that Americans now see corrupt business leaders as "bad guys"— as individuals clearly capable of doing wrong and who deserve to be held accountable. The breastplate righteousness has been stripped away. White-collar offenders are being seen for who they are: criminaloids.

Most contemporary criminologists will greet the heightened awareness of white-collar crime as a positive development. Similar to Ross, they want the public to be outraged by upperworld illegalities and to support expanding the criminal law to control such acts. Public opinion is not always sufficient to prompt political elites to enact get-tough policies (Beckett, 1997), but it does provide a context in which criminal trials will be populated with jurors sympathetic to the state's case and in which securing convictions of the rich and powerful might earn prosecutors favorable publicity and higher office (Cullen et al., 2006). It is clear that the legitimacy of prosecuting and sending to prison white-collar offenders is no longer in question. Sentences in high-profile corporate crime cases now frequently exceed twenty-five years in prison, with convicted CEOs facing the prospect of spending the remainder of their lives behind bars (Farrell, 2005; 2006). These sentences typically are greeted with applause. The bad guys have received their just deserts (Mullins, 2007).

Still, thoughtful scholars might retain two reservations about the depiction of white-collar offenders as "bad guys." First, it encourages a blood lust among the public that leads them to embrace inordinately lengthy prison sentences. The logic is that "if robbers can spend twenty years in prison, so can corporate swindlers." What is lost in this juxtaposition is the more fundamental question of whether anyone—save the truly dangerous and heinous criminals—should be sent to prison for two decades. Public support for getting tough on predatory white-collar offenders may inadvertently bolster the legitimacy of getting tough on all offenders. A more reasoned stance that argues for the judicious use of imprisonment might be preferred.

Second, the focus on individual "bad guys" and their punishment potentially deflects attention away from the structural and political conditions that made many of the most egregious scandals possible (Rossoff, Pontell, & Tillman, 2004). Parading just-convicted executives before the camera as they leave the courthouse is good drama. It has the symbolic value of emphasizing that criminals of any collar stand some risk of conviction. And such events may have a deterrent effect, even if mainly temporary. Even so, the punishment of "bad guys" does not illuminate how government and business leaders at times conspire to create conditions that not only enrich companies but also create enticing criminal opportunities. The savings and loan scandal, Enron, and the recent spate of exploitative sub-prime loans given to those seeking to own homes are all examples of costly swindles that could not have occurred under more scrupulous regulation and monitoring. Perhaps the next stage in the education of the American public lies in their being alerted to the reality that most "bad guys" in white-collar cannot victimize on a grand scale unless powerful actors in society allow them to do so.

REFERENCES

Beckett, K. (1997). *Making crime pay: Law and order in contemporary American politics.* New York: Oxford University Press.

Benson, M. L., & Cullen, F. T. (1998). *Combating corporate crime: Local prosecutors at work.* Boston: Northeastern University Press.

Bruck, C. (1988). *The predators' ball: The inside story of Drexel Burnham and the rise of the junk bond raiders.* New York: Penguin Books.

Cavender, G., & Mulcahy, A. (1998). Trial by fire: Media construction of corporate deviance. *Justice Quarterly, 15,* 697–717.

CBS News Poll (2002, July 8–9). Retrieved June 20, 2007, from http://www.PollingReport.com.

Conklin, J. E. (1977). *Illegal but not criminal: Business crime in America.* Englewood Cliffs, NJ: Prentice-Hall.

Cullen, F. T., & Benson, M. L. (1993). White-collar crime: Holding a mirror to the core. *Journal of Criminal Justice Education, 4,* 325–347.

Cullen, F. T., Cavender, G., Maakestad, W. J., & Benson, M. L. (2006). *Corporate crime under attack: The fight to criminalize business violence* (2nd ed.). Newark, NJ: Lexis/Nexis-Anderson.

Cullen, F. T., Clark, G. A., Link, B. G., Mathers, R. A., Niedospial, J. L., & Sheahan, M. (1985). Dissecting white-collar crime: Offense type and punitiveness. *International Journal of Comparative and Applied Criminal Justice, 9,* 17–28.

Cullen, F. T., Fisher, B. S., & Applegate, B. K. (2000). Public opinion about punishment and corrections. In M. Tonry (Ed.), *Crime and justice: A review of research* (vol. 27, pp. 1–79). Chicago: University of Chicago Press.

Cullen, F. T., Link, B. G., & Polanzi, C. W. (1982). The seriousness of crime revisited: Have attitudes toward white-collar crime changed? *Criminology, 29,* 83–102.

Cullen, F. T., Mathers, R. A., Clark, G. A., & Cullen, J. B. (1983). Public support for punishing white-collar crime: Blaming the victim revisited. *Journal of Criminal Justice, 11,* 481–493.

Cullen, F. T., Pealer, J. A., Fisher, B. S., Applegate, B. K., & Santana, S. A. (2002). Public support for correctional rehabilitation in America: Change or consistency. In J. V. Roberts & M. Hough (Eds.), *Changing attitudes in punishment: Public opinion, crime, and justice* (pp. 128–147). Devon, UK: Willan.

Cullen, F. T., Vose, B. A., Jonson, C. L., & Unnever, J. D. (2007). Public support for early intervention: Is child saving a habit of the heart? *Victims and Offenders, 2,* 109–124.

DiIulio, J. J., Jr. (1995, November 27). The coming of the super-predators. *The Weekly Standard,* pp. 23–28.

Evans, T. D., Cullen, F. T., & Dubeck, P. J. (1993). Public perceptions of corporate crime. In M. B. Blankenship (Ed.), *Understanding corporate criminality* (pp. 85–114). New York: Garland.

Farrell, G. (2005, July 14). Ebbers gets 25 years for fraud at WorldCom. *USA Today,* p. 1B.

Farrell, G. (2006, May 26). Lay, Skilling found guilty: Both men could spend the rest of their lives in prison. *USA Today,* p. 1B.

Feld, B. C. (1999). *Bad kids: Race and the transformation of the juvenile court.* New York: Oxford University Press.

Frank, J., Cullen, F. T., Travis III, L. F., & Borntrager, J. L. (1989). Sanctioning corporate crime: How do business executives and the public compare? *American Journal of Criminal Justice, 13,* 139–169.

Friedman, L. M. (1985). *Total justice.* New York: Russell Sage Foundation.

Fuller, J. G. (1962). *The gentlemen conspirators: The story of price-fixing in the electrical industry.* New York: Grove.

Gallup Poll. (1988, December). *Honesty and ethical standards* (Report No. 279, pp. 1–40). Princeton, NJ: Author.

Geis, G. (1967). The heavy electrical equipment conspiracy cases of 1961. In M. B. Clinard & R. Quinney (Eds.), *Criminal behavior systems.* New York: Holt, Rinehart and Winston.

Gibbons, D. C. (1969). Crime and punishment: A study of social attitudes. *Social Forces, 47,* 391–397.

Goff, C., & Nason-Clark, N. (1989). The seriousness of crime in Fredericton, New Brunswick: Perceptions toward white-collar crime. *Canadian Journal of Criminology, 31,* 19–34.

Grabosky, P. N., Braithwaite, J. B., & Wilson, P. R. (1987). The myth of community tolerance toward white-collar crime. *Australian and New Zealand Journal of Criminology, 20,* 33–44.

Hans, V. P., & Ermann, D. (1989). Responses to corporate versus individual wrongdoing. *Law and Human Behavior, 13,* 151–166.

Hartung, F. E. (1953). Common and discrete values. *Journal of Social Psychology, 38*, 3–22.

Holtfreter, K., Van Slyke, S., Bratton, J., & Gertz, M. (2008). Public perceptions of white-collar crime and punishment. *Journal of Criminal Justice, 36*, 50–60.

Igo, S. E. (2007). *The averaged American: Surveys, citizens, and the making of a mass public.* Cambridge, MA: Harvard University Press.

Kadish, S. (1977). Some observations on the use of criminal sanctions in enforcing economic regulations. *University of Chicago Law Review, 30*, 423–449.

Kane, J., & Wall, A. D. (2005). *The 2005 national public survey on white collar crime.* Fairmont, WV: National White Collar Crime Center.

Katz, J. (1980). The social movement against white-collar crime. In E. Bittner & S. Messinger (Eds.), *Criminology review yearbook* (vol. 2, pp. 161–184). Beverly Hills, CA: Sage.

Kirkpatrick, D. D. (2003, May 11). Corporate scandals: A user's guide. *New York Times,* p. WK 2.

Levi, M., & Stoker, L. (2000). Political trust and trustworthiness. *Annual Review of Political Science, 3*, 475–507.

Lipset, S. M., & Schneider, W. (1983a). *The confidence gap: Business, labor, and government in the public mind.* New York: Free.

Lipset, S. M., & Schneider, W. (1983b). Confidence in confidence measures. *Public Opinion, 6*(4), 42–44.

Los Angeles Times Poll (2004, March 27–30). Retrieved June 20, 2007, from http://www.PollingReport.com.

Los Angeles Times/Bloomberg Poll (2007, June 7–10). Retrieved June 20, 2007, from http://www.PollingReport.com.

Mullins, L. (2007, May–June). Enter a hellish place. *The American.* Retrieved March 17, 2007, from http://www.American.Com/archive/2007/May-June-magazinecontents.

Newman, D. P. (1957). Public attitudes toward a form of white collar crime. *Social Problems, 4*, 228–232.

Newsweek Poll (2002, July 18–19). Retrieved June 20, 2007, from http://www.PollingReport.com.

Partnoy, F. (2003). *Infectious greed: How deceit and risk corrupted the financial markets.* New York: Time Books.

Piquero, N. L., Carmichael, S., & Piquero, A. R. (2008). Research note: Assessing the perceived seriousness of white-collar and street crime. *Crime and Delinquency, 54*, 291–312.

President's Commission on Law Enforcement and Administration of Justice (1968). *Challenge of crime in a free society.* New York: Avon.

Public Opinion (1986, November–December). Opinion roundup: An erosion of ethics? pp. 21–28.

Rebovich, D. J., Lane, J., Jiandani, J., & Hage, S. (2000). *The national public survey on white collar crime.* Morgantown, WV: National White Collar Crime Center.

Reed, J. P., & Reed, R. S. (1975). Doctor, lawyer, Indian chief: Old rhymes and new on white collar crime. *International Journal of Criminology and Penology, 3*, 275–293.

Reiman, J. H. (1979). *The rich get richer and the poor get prison: Ideology, class, and criminal justice.* New York: Wiley.

Roberts, J. V., & Stalans, L. J. (1997). *Public opinion, crime, and criminal justice.* Boulder, CO: Westview.

Ross, E. A. (1907). *Sin and society: An analysis of latter-day iniquity.* New York: Harper and Row.

Rossoff, S. M., Pontell, H. N., & Tillman, R. H. (2004). *Profit without honor: White-collar crime and the looting of America* (3rd ed.). Upper Saddle River, NJ: Prentice Hall.

Saad, L. (2006). *Military still tops in public confidence: HMOs and big business garner little trust.* Princeton, NJ: Gallup Organization.

Schoepfer, A., Carmichael, S., & Piquero, N. L. (2007). Do perceptions of punishment vary between white-collar and street crimes? *Journal of Criminal Justice, 35,* 151–163.

Schrager, L. S., & Short Jr., J. F. (1980). How serious a crime? Perceptions of organizational and common crimes. In G. Geis & E. Stotland (Eds.), *White-collar crime: Theory and research* (pp. 14–31). Beverly Hills, CA: Sage.

Sutherland, E. H. (1940). White-collar criminality. *American Sociological Review, 5,* 1–11.

Sutherland, E. H. (1983 [1949]). *White-collar crime: The uncut version.* New Haven, CT: Yale University Press.

Swigert, V., & Farrell, R. (1980–1981). Corporate homicide: Definitional processes in the creation of deviance. *Law and Society Review, 15,* 161–182.

Time (1969, June 6). Changing morality: The two Americas—A *Time*-Louis Harris Poll, pp. 26 27.

Time (2002, June 17). Corporate greed: Heroes to heels, p. 48.

Time/CNN Poll (2002, July 22). Losing faith in corporate America, pp. 18–19.

Turner, M. G., Cullen, F. T., Sundt, J. L., & Applegate, B. K. (1997). Public tolerance for community-based sanctions. *Prison Journal, 77,* 6–26.

Unnever, J. D., Benson, M. L., & Cullen, F. T. (2008). Public support for getting tough on corporate crime: Racial and political divides. *Journal of Research in Crime and Delinquency, 45,* 163–190.

Unnever, J. D., & Cullen, F. T. (2008). Toward a theory of individual differences in punitiveness: The salience of empathetic identification. Unpublished paper, University of South Florida, Sarasota.

Unnever, J. D., Cullen, F. T., & Jonson, C. L. (2008). Race, racism, and support for capital punishment. In M. Tonry (Ed.), *Crime and justice: A review of research* (vol. 37, pp. 45–96). Chicago: University of Chicago Press.

Wilson, J. Q. (1975). *Thinking about crime.* New York: Vintage.

19

Sentencing Frauds

A Comparative Perspective

— *Michael Levi*

1. Introduction

Analysis of the sentencing of different crimes and "sorts of people" brings into sharp relief tensions between:

1. backwards-looking reflections of the gravity of offenses (what is usually called "letting the punishment fit the crime"),

2. forwards-looking focus on the risks and consequences of *future* harm, and

3. social fairness in the treatment of offenders of different social statuses.

This article examines a sub-set of crimes—*frauds*—that are often associated with "white-collar crime" but are actually committed by a broad range of social types ranging from the poor and marginalized (social security) through blue-collar petty and "organized" offenders (check, credit card and small-scale insurance frauds, some of which are used to finance terrorist attacks or small groups) to major swindles by elites or by professional confidence tricksters that take years to commit. Shapiro's title (1990) famously suggested that we collar the crime, not the criminal, but there is no need here to review those wider debates about the importance of social status to financial crimes. Rather, the aim is to explore some key features of

Source: Michael Levi, Sentencing Frauds: A Comparative Perspective. *Monthly Journal of Criminology and Criminal Law Reform*, Vol. 2, No. 3. Copyright © 2007 by Wolters Kluwer. Reprinted with permission.

the sentencing of "serious frauds" in a limited comparative context, concentrating upon the UK and US, where more comprehensive data are available (at least in the English language), to show how the dilemmas referred to above are played out in the context of their national legal systems, norms and cultures. If this complicates some ideologically oversimplified models of crime control, then this is a positive contribution to comparative criminology and criminal justice, and it is hoped that this will stimulate others to develop a comparative approach in a wider range of countries and types of society than I have been able to cover in this article.

One reason why people may be interested in fraud sentencing is to test (or affirm!) the lenient treatment of the powerful (Reiman 2006). A traditional difficulty in analyses of the fairness or bias of sentencing is that people who reach the sentencing stage are those who have not been filtered out earlier by conscious or unconscious discretionary decision-making. In the particular case of fraud, even in countries that in principle operate the "legality principle" rather than the Anglo-Saxon "opportunity principle" of prosecution, the availability of non-criminal alternatives such as regulatory/administrative law sanctions (or, in some cases, suppression of allegations!) means that we have to be careful in our interpretations of sentencing practices to take account of unprosecuted *potential* criminal cases (Shapiro 1985) whose rationale may be absent or ambiguous in interpretation. Thus, it is not obvious how we adjudicate between hypotheses that (1) there is a bias against prosecuting the powerful and (2) inequality is an accidental, unintended product of wider criminal justice processes such as plea bargaining that are uneven in their application (Katz 1979). Here, provided that we have some empirical baseline, comparative analysis, insider "whistle-blowing" and changes in prosecutorial conduct over time (e.g., at times of "moral panic" about corruption or white-collar crimes, or efforts to get rid of elite rivals) may help us. We might also, where possible, take account of those cases pursued by advice and civil injunctions, in accordance with the future-oriented model positively advocated by regulation advocates (see Hawkins 2002). With these methodological caveats, let us examine sanctioning processes.

The distinguishing character of fraud is that it is, in essence, a *means* of generating gains to which we are not entitled legally. If past harm and future risks are pointing in the same direction, the sentencing task is relatively simple (though fairness *between* offenders may still be an issue). However, in some frauds, the harm may be great but future risks may be small (unless the offenders can commit crimes via nominees or, more colloquially, via "front men." Another source of controversy lies in whether judges (and indeed "society" and "the" media) have under-valued the seriousness of some or all types of fraud. Yet another may arise from the social position of the perpetrator—whether social elite or organized criminal—that may also (a) actually have and/or (b) *defensibly have* an impact on social judgments of culpability and of harmfulness,[1] as well as on judicial perceptions of the impact of conviction and sentence on offenders. The aim of this study is to bring together some relevant evidence about fraud sentencing, nowhere coherently compiled,[2] and to relate these to principles of sentencing. The sentencing system cannot cure or substitute for these prior resource and efficiency factors, and deterrence relies more on perceived probability of conviction than on sanction severity. However it is important to bear in mind that neither probability nor severity is a continuous variable affecting deterrence;[3] and some important consequences for high-status offenders—though for by no means all fraudsters even in Serious Fraud Office cases—arise from conviction or even bad publicity alone, irrespective of sentence level. For this sub-set of fraudsters, "the process is the punishment." Sentencing research has not been systematically applied in the context of frauds and fraudsters, but fraudsters likely to vary on a broad and not clearly demarcated scale, depending on whether they are:

1. people with no other criminal involvements who intentionally or recklessly commit offenses in the context of their businesses;

2. specialist fraudsters who do not commit other types of offense; or

3. multi-offense-type, persistent or organized criminals.

It seems plausible that for the first category, the crucial sentence points influencing guilty pleas and deterrence are (a) whether they will go to prison or not and (b) (a much harder point to specify) whether they expect, *at the time(s) when offenses are contemplated*, that they will go to prison for some period that really concerns them more than the alternative. The alternative might be personal or corporate bankruptcy; in which case, the temptation to take a chance might be greater. For the second category, the "tipping point" for deterrence is whether, in their minds, expected probability of conviction is high enough and sentences are long enough to outweigh the benefits from crime. For the third, the comparison is usually of conviction and imprisonment risks between fraud and other types of crime that the offenders would be likely to commit. In addition, some fraudsters (and money launderers providing services to criminals)—for example, professional people such as accountants, notaries and lawyers—may be caught up on the fringes of "organized crime groups" without themselves readily falling into this category, as when they facilitate corporate vehicles or specific transactions for major criminals.

Wheeler, Mann & Sarat (1988)[4] have noted what (based on interviews with US Federal judges in the 1970s) they term the "paradox of leniency and severity" in the sentencing of white-collar crimes. On the one hand, judges generally do regard the breach of trust by people in high positions as deeply reprehensible (except where it can plausibly be portrayed as inadvertent); on the other, they are normally faced with sentencing people for whom the offense is "out-of-character" (i.e., they have not been convicted previously[5]) and who have often lost a well-paid job simply as a consequence of conviction or even for breach of in-house rules. In some cases, not only are their circumstances reduced but also—where authorization is mandatory—they may be prevented by the fact of conviction or disciplinary sanctions alone from committing the offense again—at least directly in their own names. This is a very rare situation for judges in substantial crimes for gain. Normally, people who come up for sentence in armed robbery, hi-jacking or major commercial burglaries have a string of previous convictions or have been portrayed by the police and the media as a cunning "Mr. Big." The latter can always be given a long sentence for being a mastermind, but this does not happen to fraudsters, except in some Missing Trader Intra-Community, Value-Added Tax Carousel or bankruptcy frauds connected with organized crime syndicates (Levi 1981). Judges are torn, then, between concern to reflect the seriousness of the crime and human concern about the "fall from grace" of the offender, for they can imagine how they would feel were they in his (or, more rarely, her) position. Judges may sometimes see white-collar defendants as being more affected by social degradation than they actually are: But errors can be made in either direction. One area where there are few parallels with most "ordinary" offenders is that professional sanctions can also create the possibility of incapacitation without custody. However, here, too, it is important to make distinctions *within* fraud: It is much harder to cut off bankruptcy and credit card fraudsters from crime opportunities so readily as people who need authorization as "fit and proper persons" to practice their professions; and though some payments to social security fraudsters can be cut off, other opportunities to defraud might be available to them. Street and household crimes, of course, are open to all.

2. Comparative Statistics for Custody Rate and Length of Custodial Sentences for Fraud and Forgery and Other Acquisitive Crimes

The comparability issue is particularly difficult, because popular, media, and political constructions of harm prioritize offenses involving actual, threatened or perceived threatened violence and both burglary and, especially, robbery contain those elements. Moreover, fraud offenders—particular those committed by individual or corporate elites—typically have fewer previous convictions than is the norm for other offenses and in a system where prior criminality (or convictions) is important, this makes a big difference. There is no obvious metric for balancing very large sums obtained by fraud (or theft) against violence (though we implicitly do so in current practice and in the way we talk about the "fairness" of sentences). It is difficult to steal non-violently very large amounts of money or property *without* an abuse of trust (e.g., the Bank of England employees who in the early 1990s stole from Bank cages millions of pounds in notes that were supposed to have been destroyed could not have done this without being employees). The best comparison for fraud and forgery is theft and handling but, in both cases, the aggregate statistics are comprised of very large numbers of smaller cases, though "small" in fraud is often seen in relation to multi-million pound cases rather than in relation to much smaller average values in thefts and burglaries.

Sentencing statistics show that there has been a slight decrease 1994–2004 in the average custodial sentence length (ACSL) for fraud and forgery and theft and handling. The ACSL for fraud and forgery fell from 11.1 months in 1994 to 9.2 months in 2004. The ACSL for theft and handling stolen goods fell from 6.5 months in 1994 to 4.3 months in 2004. The average sentence length for burglary has increased, from 11.4 months to 17.5 by 2004. The average sentence length for robbery was 39.8 months in 1994 and 38.4 months in 2004.

3. A Victim-Based Typology of Sentencing in Serious Fraud Office Cases

The UK Serious Fraud Office (SFO) deals with the top layer of "serious or complex frauds" other than tax frauds. However, it only deals with about 15 trials annually, so the total of fraudsters sentenced is not large, and given that many involve multiple defendants, there is significant within-case variation that makes presenting average sentences a little misleading. One might take the "top sentence" in each case as a better indicator, though there are issues about whether sentencing theorists or practitioners have properly conceptualized the importance of support roles (and the deterrence of potential supporters who may be necessary to fraud commission or may be potential whistle-blowers).

Altogether, counting suspended sentences as zero (since none were known to be activated), the 109 persons convicted in SFO cases 2000–2005 received an average of 31.7 months imprisonment. Out of the 53 *cases* in which convictions were obtained in this period, the average sentence of the *most severely sentenced* person per case was 37.7 months imprisonment. Eight persons received sentences longer than 5 years; 19 people received 4–5 year sentences; 22 people (mostly co-defendants in cases where others were imprisoned) received non-custodial sentences; the median sentence was 3 years imprisonment. In terms of time actually served, the real sentences are likely to be half of the formal sentences imposed.

It might be helpful to relate sentencing in serious fraud cases to the types of victim involved: I have reconstructed this into a format that I think is helpful, though this cannot serve satisfactorily as a framework for explaining sentencing—since factors such as amount of money, plea (and stage at which plea was offered) and previous convictions are relevant to sentence but are not available. The categories I initially chose are frauds against:

1. government (including the EU);
2. consumers (e.g., intellectual property by deceiving that goods are genuine);
3. trade creditors;
4. financial services firms;
5. general public investors;
6. business investors;
7. market abuse (including insider dealing);
8. procurement fraud/bribery.

However, after reviewing the SFO cases 2000–2006, I have collapsed some of these categories, though there are a few cases in which, for example, an investment fraud also defrauds trade creditors. One could add permutations including frauds by employees and/or outsiders, frauds against UK/non-UK persons and the social status/prior convictions/prior business record of offenders, which may be relevant to sentence. Previous conviction data are not usually available, but previous experience suggests that few offenders in SFO cases have prior records; in many cases, the amounts involved are also unavailable, but they should be at the high end of the seriousness scale (over € 1.5 million as a minimum) to qualify as SFO cases in the vetting process when the SFO decides whether or not to take a case. It should also be noted that, in most cases, the guilty pleas are quite late in the day and, if the contemporary advice of the sentencing council were to be followed, this would mean very little sentence discount for them. It is not possible within the confines of this brief review to examine the sub-text behind these last-minute plea changes, but—absent the desire to save privately paid defense costs—their offering and acceptance by the prosecution and judge implies that some benefit was received.

For frauds against business creditors, the average was 27.4 months; investment frauds against business investors, 37.7 months; investment frauds on individuals, 40.4 months; market abuse, 12 months (though in one of the two cases, all four defendants received suspended prison sentences, showing how distorted averages can be); procurement fraud/corruption, 19.9 months; and frauds on government, 36.8 months (but only three cases). In 17 cases (about a third), at least one defendant was disqualified from company directorship, for an average of over 7 years. This reflects not just legal powers but also a belief that this is an appropriate financial punishment (reducing future earnings) and will be effective as incapacitation. The latter is an open question: It certainly would affect those who need to play an upfront role as a director, but the extent of "shadow directorships" among those subject to disqualification is unknown and very difficult to discover even in principle.[6]

4. Sentencing in Tax Fraud Cases

To provide some historical perspective for comparison, in 1990–91, 59 people were convicted for VAT (Value Added Tax) fraud, and received sentences between 6 months and 7.5 years and fines totaling £ 405,615; the 63 cases that HM Customs & Excise dealt with by compounding[7] netted £ 4.8 million in "fines" and saved the trial costs as well as freeing up investigation officers for other enquiries. Inland Revenue statistics for this period were less penetrable, for they stated nothing about sentences. The most recent data, supplied by HM Revenue and Customs (HMRC) and the Revenue and Customs Prosecutions Office (RCPO), suggest that there were 24 prison sentences in income tax, new tax credit and VAT fraud cases, plus 106 prison sentences for excise fraud in the most recent tax year, 2005–2006. During 2005–06, there were six successful prosecutions for MTIC fraud, resulting in 18 convictions with sentences totaling 72 years imprisonment. HMRC also took action against 29 companies involved in MTIC fraud resulting in £ 9.4 million being recovered or frozen. VAT and MTIC (Missing Trader Intra-Community) frauds have become so high-profile within the UK and Europe generally during 2006 that one would expect sentencing to rise substantially because of changes in the perception of its harmfulness to the UK economy and society—thus in January 2007, one 54 million carousel fraudster was sentenced to 15 years imprisonment (and co-defendants sentenced to 4.5 years and a suspended jail sentence):

Direct Tax Cases 2005–06

New Tax Credit – (relatively low value) volume work + Grabiner (Shadow Economy):

In the 3 months to 12/31/05, there were 40 cases proceeded with leading to:

Imprisonment – 3 cases

Suspended Sentences – 3

Community Punishment/Service Orders – 20

Fines – 8

Compensation Orders – 2

Curfew Orders – 1

Other—Costs only – 1

Complex Business (more organized, large scale frauds):

Prosecutions yr to date 05/06 (including 3 cases where there were 2 defendants or more):

Total 15 cases, ranging from a Community Punishment Order for 240 hours to 12.5 years custody:

Custody Order – 1

Suspended Sentence – 2

CPO – 1

Fines – 3

Custodial sentences – 9 including Confiscation Orders in 4 cases

Indirect Tax and Duties Year to Date 2005/06

Excise cases:

Imprisonment	< 2 yrs = 87
	2–4 yrs = 19
Guilty—no sentencing details = 9	
Suspended Sentences = 13	
Fines range from £ 100 – £ 38 K = 141	
Conditional Discharge = 9	
Community Punishment/Service Orders = 44	
Curfew Orders = 2	
Abscondees = 6	

VAT cases:

Imprisonment	< 3 yrs = 2
	3–4 yrs = 4
	4–5 yrs = 6
Guilty—no sentencing details = 5	
Suspended Sentences = 2	
Fines range from £ 75 – £ 24 K = 68	
Conditional Discharge = 9	
Compensation Orders = 1	
Abscondees = 2	

5. Approaches to Sentencing

Unlike many continental European jurisdictions, there is no unitary prosecution authority in the UK: bankruptcy offenses, social security frauds and tax frauds are prosecuted by specialist bodies separate from the Crown Prosecution Service that handles all police-investigated cases and from the Serious Fraud Office that handles the top tier of non-tax frauds. Although the need to be human rights-compliant has brought them procedurally much closer, there has been a major difference historically between utilitarian and retributivist approaches to criminal justice and to sentencing, with the compliance model of corporate and individual misconduct (e.g., in financial services) aiming to maximize social utility irrespective of differential treatment of cases, while the traditional criminal justice model has a simpler approach of punishing for past behavior that disregards economic or social cost-benefit analysis. Even within the arena of fraud, one finds big differences in the extent to which prosecution follows detection, which does not relate to either evidence-led harm or culpability but rather to investigative and prosecutorial difficulties, departmental traditions and resources, the possibilities of compensation and penalties being paid, imagery of evil, et cetera. Despite shifts in policy—for example, arising from the merger of the Inland Revenue and

Customs & Excise into Her Majesty's Revenue and Customs and into the separate Revenue and Customs Prosecutions Office (RCPO)—these differential inter-fraud prosecution risks are very hard to justify other than on purely pragmatic grounds. We shall discuss the array of nonconviction-based sanctions that can have both a retributive and an incapacitating effect on those affected. Whether these or any other penalties have much of a *general* deterrent effect has not been demonstrated.

In retributivism, there are two dimensions of sentencing—harm and culpability—around which various aggravating and mitigating factors are clustered. As regards the harm of fraud (collective, singular) or of frauds (types of—but how to classify for these purposes?), the courts have been fairly silent except in relation to "abuse of trust" as an aggravating factor warranting a higher sentence. In general sentencing guidelines, the targeting of "vulnerable victims" is another aggravating factor, but the question is what counts as vulnerability in relation to frauds? Wasik (1998, 116)[8] argues that corporate victims generally are less harmed than are other categories of victim, but without some measurement criteria, this is no more than a plausible assertion, even disregarding the distress caused to bank staff when there is a robbery or a staff kidnapping. In a sense, his generalization is a tautology, since a business can feel no direct pain: only its staff, directors, and shareholders can do so. A priori, one would expect greater impact/harm where there is an element of being deceived while making a personal judgment, and/or where victims feel foolish in the eyes of their peers (if the latter should come to know). There are potential implications for personal careers of individual victims (such as Finance/HR Directors) from being conned in a corporate setting, but these have not been analyzed in any discussions of sentencing, which tend to focus on offenders rather than victims.

In practice, not always consciously, the politics of media anathematization—"evil offenders" or "deserving victims"—may have an impact on sentences by incorporation into the denunciatory function of punishment. However, retributivists state that harm aggravation and mitigation cannot properly apply on the basis of an individualized reaction to a particular crime, because offenders must take victims as they find them. Nevertheless, some classes of victim may be held to be especially vulnerable, and small businesses have been so treated by the English Court of Appeal in relation to burglary and robbery, since they cannot afford to take the kinds of precautions that larger firms can, they keep substantial quantities of cash and they have long opening hours.[9] Other general categories such as elderly persons are treated as especially vulnerable: Though this has not been the subject of judicial rulings, in the case of fraud, one might argue that they have less working time to recoup their losses and therefore that the severity of harm might typically (though not invariably) be greater (contrariwise, they have a shorter period to live and thus may have less time to suffer a lower standard of living). How one translates broken dreams and damaged expectations (and bribery, domestic and transnational) into standardized criteria—especially monetary value—might be a matter of some dispute, but damage to mental and physical health has been measured more prosaically by health economists in terms of QUALYS (Dubourg Hamed 2005).

The issue of fraud sentencing has received little systematic attention in England and Wales, perhaps because comparatively few high social profile major corporate cases have reached that stage here, and it is has not hitherto been a priority for the Sentencing Council, though there is some "read-across" from the general principles set out in its work on seriousness and on sentence discounts for guilty pleas. In this respect, England and Wales is unlike the US, where the US Sentencing Commission (2003) was specifically tasked post-Enron to review white-collar crime sentencing, and where the US sentencing statistics generate more readily analyzable data. No countries present sentencing data in a particularly illuminating way for the purpose of testing the relationship between sentence and the sorts of victims harmed—the understandable result of their using legal rather than victim or behavioral categories as a method of classification. We hear most about the high-profile cases, but it is easy to get these and the aggregate US sentences for white-collar crimes out of context. American sentencing levels (and imprisonment per capita population) are so much higher than anywhere in Europe that it is tempting to advocate using sentence ratios for fraud versus other crimes rather than to look at fraud sentences in isolation. On the other hand, for a sub-set of fraud offenders—business elites—it might be defensible to think of deterrence or retribution in isolation from other sentences, since the substitute would seldom be other forms of offending (however, the symbolic nature of sentencing as a gesture of moral and social censure cannot be so isolated, since even if social elites saw a short prison sentence as agonizing, the public and their earthly representatives—the media—might see it differently). For those habitual offenders in a position to commit frauds of particular types, on the other hand, the relative consequences of conviction may stimulate a shift towards/away from particular offenses.[10] When looking at the relative attractiveness of plausible crimes, one might have to think here in terms of clusters of transferable skills and contacts possessed by different offenders: Not just bank directors but also junior staff may find it easy to commit fraud while in post but once dismissed—depending in how transparent their employment history is—they may find it very difficult to reoffend.

It is also a mistake to homogenize the category of white-collar offenses: The federalization of US criminal law (e.g., "wire fraud") means that many minor cases are included in the US data, concealing the high-end sentences in both mean and median sentences. This broad spread led Weisburd, Wheeler, Waring & Bode (1991) to characterize the Federal cases they examined as "crimes of the middle classes" as opposed to upper classes, though a significant proportion of offenders were blue-collar in background, so even this narrows the description.[11] Hence, the longer average and median sentences for embezzlement and tax offenses in the Southern District of New York—where the big Wall Street cases tend to be handled—compared with the Federal system nationally in 2003: though these averages of under 2 years are still not long compared with sentences in the well-publicized scandal cases, and for all the rhetoric about deterrence, are little different from British fraud sentencing. However, not all major frauds are prosecuted federally, and there is more scope for departure from guidelines in the State system.

Alone among the Western nations—both common and civil code— the traditional British view has been that the prosecution should stay out of the sentencing process and neither advocate a particular sentence nor proactively refer judges to any precedents for sentence (unless asked). Some might argue that law and order issues have become sufficiently politicized already without adding to the levels of emotion by pressuring prosecutors (who are neither elected nor political appointees in the UK) to "stand up for victims." However, this passive stance may promote departures from guidelines by failing to alert judges to sentencing norms. What is clear is that the general level of sentences in the US Federal and other Sentencing Guidelines has a powerful effect on the earlier decision stages, including plea negotiation, "proffers" and the new trend toward "deferred prosecutions" used to elicit changes within institutions that, if prosecuted, might lose their licenses (e. g., KPMG in the tax shelter case). It is unlikely that senior staff and companies such as AIG, Arthur Andersen, Enron and WorldCom—or, in US tax prosecutions, conceivably KPMG—would have cooperated with the prosecutors or settled tax/SEC/New York cases if it were not for the prospect of lengthy prison sentences plus no sentencing discount unless they both confess first and implicate others. It is inconceivable that so many people in Enron would have been prosecuted or pleaded guilty were that case to have happened in the UK. This is stimulated by the pressures placed on businesses that wish to avoid indictment or to reduce financial penalties not to pay their staff's criminal defense costs for fear of being viewed as "uncooperative" within the controversial Thompson guidelines,[12] which mean that corporations do not receive credit for cooperation if they are not deemed by the prosecutors to be behaving appropriately.[13] The "Prisoner's Dilemma" model has been incorporated into administrative penalties for cartel and allied offenses at the British and European Commission as well as American level. Equity apart, much may depend on how plausible it is that fraudsters (of what "types" and in what contexts?) are part of some wider offender/rule-violator networks, and there is no extant analysis of this issue.

The importance of the super-tough sentences in generating compliance can be overstated, even if one considered that this was a sufficient principled justification for imposing them. If white-collar defendants' prime motivation is to avoid a conviction that will have serious career consequences and/or public stigma, then unless they feel they have little or no chance of avoiding conviction (in which case, the benefit to prosecutors is correspondingly lower except at a very early stage), the expected sentence levels on not guilty pleas may be relatively unimportant unless they are very high (as Jamie Olis found when sentenced to 24 years without parole in the Dynegy case, which was re-sentenced to 6 years in 2006 after a successful appeal).[14] As Kenneth Mann's (1985) valuable (if dated) US Federal study of white-collar defenses in pre-guidelines days shows, the system of "proffering" and informal discussions with prosecutors occurred in the context of there being assets to trade: But given variations in types of fraudster, it must be considered carefully whether this model is readily transferable to the UK offender sets and if so, to whom. It might be expected to work best where there are rings of offenders or Enron-style hierarchies to unravel. The application of this model to other European jurisdictions is even more questionable.

6. Fraud Sentencing in Continental Europe and in the US

It is the US that the UK commonly looks to when reviewing sentencing elsewhere, partly for linguistic reasons but also, as in other criminal justice policy transfers, because they are considered to be culturally closest as a capitalist economy. Information on fraud sentencing in Scotland is sparse, though in 2004–5, Scottish Prison Statistics show that the average sentence for those imprisoned for fraud was just under 7 months: four people received 4 years or longer; three got 2–4 years imprisonment; and 25, from 6–24 months.

Systematic research on European fraud sentencing practices is absent. However my informal consultations led to response from a Dutch colleague, who noted:

> High-level fraud cases with "respectable" in the dock usually end with a "conditional" prison term (or on parole) and a community service order. Lower class fraudsters (like koppelbazen) go to prison, but rarely get more than 2 years. The Ahold fraudsters are just on trial for "cooking the books." The offenders in the building scandal (cartel forming, documentary fraud and corruption + participation in a criminal organization) received probation plus fine. One investment fraudster (about € 120 million damages) is in pre-trial custody and I predict an 18-month sentence, of which 8 months will be on probation minus pre-trial detention term. One can get statistics from the Central Statistics Office if one searches on the legal articles "documentary fraud" and "tax fraud." But given the low public and political interest, these statistics have never been requested.

In May 2006, a Dutch court subsequently fined Cees van der Hoeven, Ahold's former chief executive, and A. Michiel Meurs, its former finance

chief, € 225,000 each after convicting them of fraud, but it rejected prosecutors' request to imprison them, giving them both 9-month sentences
suspended for 2 years. Jan Andreae, former executive board member in
charge of Ahold's European operations, was sentenced to 4 months in jail,
suspended for 2 years, and was fined € 120 million. Ahold had overstated
its earnings by more than $1 billion from 1999 to 2002, mostly by inflating
sales at its U.S. Foodservice unit.

In Sweden, where sentencing generally is not severe by UK standards, a former chief executive of Sweden's biggest insurance group Skandia, was, in May 2006, sentenced to 2 years in prison for agreeing to large
bonuses for executives without board approval, a case that had aroused
serious cultural concern in Sweden. Petersson, who was chief executive of
the group from 1997 to 2003, had removed a ceiling on an executive bonus
program without authorization in 2000, which led to executives receiving
an extra SKr 156 m (€ 21 m) in payments. Petersson had not been a beneficiary of the bonus program. "Lars-Eric Petersson was not authorized to
take away the ceiling ... by doing so, he abused his position of trust in
Skandia, causing damage to Skandia itself," the court said. The court found
no evidence to support a second charge that Petersson had increased his
pension by SKr 37 m, also without board approval, and rejected the prosecutor's request to ban Petersson from holding other industry positions.

Huber (2003, 32–33) noted in her review of the way that Germany
dealt with economic crimes:

> Sanctioning practice in white-collar cases is difficult to establish,
> because the statistic does not indicate any details as to certain sectors
> of white-collar crimes. However, fines are prevailing, 80 to 90% of the
> sentences are fines when it come to the regular white collar offenses
> contained in the Penal Code: bankruptcy and environmental offenses,
> handling of employers salaries. When a prison sentence is imposed at
> all it is mostly suspended; in less than 10% of sentences for offenses
> that count for economic crime the imprisonment was unconditional.
> Out of the additional penalties contained in the Penal Code only pro-
> hibition to work in one's profession (SS 70 ff. StGB) is of certain signif-
> icance though the preventive potential of this measure is considered
> to be high. Forfeiture and confiscation of assets and objects however
> (§§ 73 ff. StGB) are used more often (food and wine laws, copyright
> law). Further to mention is the fine against collective entities for
> breaches of competition law. Under § 30 OWiG the amount of the fine
> can be three times as high as the advantage reached by the offense or
> violation of regulatory rules (OWiG) [Examples are fines of 284 Mil-
> lion against the producers of power cable who entered into a cartel, or
> against the producer of traffic signs of 3.7 Million].

> A characteristic of the economic chambers is the generally lower tariff
> than that we find in judgments of the regular courts. In particular
> when one compares the penalties after a full trial and those that are
> the consequence of a guilty plea, the inconsistency is most striking.

In the first of the Parmalat trials, in Milan in 2005, 11 defendants pleaded guilty in "plea bargains." The longest sentence, 2 years and 6 months, was given to Fausto Tonna, a former chief financial officer. Gian Paolo Zini, a lawyer who set up some offshore companies that were used to hide billions of dollars in debt and losses, was given 2 years. However, these sentences may be served in the community, a decision to be made by another judge.

Also convicted were two other former chief financial officers, Luciano Del Soldato and Alberto Ferraris, as well as internal auditors and former board members. Two of those sentenced are related to Parmalat's founder and former chairman, Calisto Tanzi: Stefano Tanzi, his son, and Giovanni Tanzi, his brother, both former board members. They were both sentenced to one year and 11 months in prison.

The sentences in the more prominent American cases are set out in the box overleaf, in descending order except where co-defendants are sentenced. One important feature of US Sentencing Guidelines is the impact of assistance to the prosecutor on downwards variation in sentence. Noteworthy here are comments (11 July 2006) by the 11th Circuit Court of Appeals in the case of *United States v. Martin* (Michael Martin), which for the second time ruled that the sentence issued by the district court was insufficient, despite the defendant providing cooperation. The court decided that a huge departure from the guidelines for cooperation leading to an ultimate sentence of 7 days imprisonment for a multi-billion dollar securities fraud was unreasonable. Martin, a former chief financial officer of HealthSouth provided evidence against Richard Scrushy at his HealthSouth related trial, in which Scrushy was found not guilty. Despite this cooperation, the government argued that a 23 level departure was unreasonable. The appellate court found the sentence "shockingly short," and the fact that Richard Scrushy was found not guilty at this trial[15] was not relevant to determining the appropriate sentence for Martin (who also forfeited $2.375 million dollars). On 12 September 2006, he was given 36 months imprisonment at his re-sentencing hearing.

In May 2006, HealthSouth itself agreed to a deal with the Department of Justice under which it agreed to accept responsibility for crimes committed by its executives, must pay $3 million to the United States Postal Inspection Service's consumer fraud division, enact more stringent internal controls and commit no other illegal acts for 3 years. In essence, the company is on probation until 2009. Otherwise, prosecutors stated, the firm would have been pushed into bankruptcy. In 2006, HealthSouth agreed to pay the Securities and Exchange Commission and other civil litigants more than $500 million in cash and shares; plus more than $350 million to settle suits for Medicare fraud.

It is apparent that US sentences are typically far longer than would have occurred in the UK, but it is important to appreciate that this is a relatively recent phenomenon since the turn of the 21st century, reflecting the perceived need for deterrence for prevalent offenses as well as strong feelings of retribution towards persons and companies that have caused serious harm.

US White-Collar Crime Sentences
Bernard J. Ebbers *WorldCom* Chief executive CASE: Masterminding an $11 billion accounting fraud SENTENCE, IN YEARS: 25 (confirmed on appeal July 2006)
Scott D. Sullivan *WorldCom* Chief financial officer PLEADED GUILTY: Leading role in $11 billion accounting fraud SENTENCE, IN YEARS: 5
L. Dennis Kozlowski *Tyco* Chief executive CONVICTED: Looting the company and deceiving investors SENTENCE, IN YEARS: 8.3–25
Mark H. Swartz *Tyco* Chief financial officer CONVICTED: Looting the company and deceiving investors SENTENCE, IN YEARS: 8.3–25
Timothy J. Rigas *Adelphia* Chief financial officer CONVICTED: Looting the company and lying to investors and regulators SENTENCE, IN YEARS: 20
John J. Rigas *Adelphia* Founder and chairman CONVICTED: Looting the company and lying to investors and regulators SENTENCE, IN YEARS: 15
Martin R. Frankel Financier PLEADED GUILTY: Looting insurance companies and racketeering SENTENCE, IN YEARS: 16.7
Reed Slatkin Money manager PLEADED GUILTY: Stealing hundreds of millions from investors SENTENCE, IN YEARS: 14
Alan B. Bond *Albriond* Capital Money manager PLEADED GUILTY: Stealing from investors and taking kickbacks from brokers SENTENCE, IN YEARS: 12.5
Franklin C. Brown *Rite Aid* Vice Chairman CONVICTED: Played a leading role in accounting scandal SENTENCE, IN YEARS: 10
Martin L. Grass *Rite Aid* Chief executive CONVICTED: Accounting scandal that inflated the value of the company SENTENCE, IN YEARS: 8
Andrew S. Fastow *Enron* Chief financial officer PLEADED GUILTY: Inflating the company's value and defrauding the company SENTENCE, IN YEARS: 10 (+ wife, Lea Fastow, sentenced to one year for tax misdemeanor)
Ben F. Glisan Jr. *Enron* Treasurer PLEADED GUILTY: Manipulating the company's financial statements SENTENCE, IN YEARS: 5
E. Kirk Shelton *CUC International* Vice Chairman CONVICTED: Conspiracy and fraud to inflate the company's value SENTENCE, IN YEARS: 10

Robert E. Brennan *First Jersey Securities* Founder
CONVICTED: Money laundering and bankruptcy fraud
SENTENCE, IN YEARS: 9.2

John M. Rusnak *Allfirst* Financial Currency trader
PLEADED GUILTY: Hiding $691 million in trading losses over 5 years
SENTENCE, IN YEARS: 7.5

Samuel D. Waksal *ImClone Systems* Founder, chief executive
PLEADED GUILTY: Securities fraud and perjury
SENTENCE, IN YEARS: 7

Jamie Ohs *Dynegy* Mid-level executive
CONVICTED: Falsifying the company's books to hide a $300 million loan
SENTENCE, IN YEARS: 6 (following successful appeal against 24 years, on grounds of harm estimation)

Ex hypothesi, whether regulatory sanctions (or formal monitoring) really deter fraudsters depends on what "sort of people" they are. Let us look at the sort of variation I have in mind. Criminologists are broadly agreed that among the factors influencing involvement in crime are:

1. personal values (though it is astonishing how readily ethical values can be reconciled with financial self-interest via rationalizations);

2. attachment to the social networks of respectability (which degree of attachment regulators and judges may misinterpret or be misled about); and

3. expectations of being sanctioned—prosecuted, convicted and punished both in formal (exclusion from the profession or from contractor lists) and in informal terms (being snubbed by friends, losing business contacts through imputed disreputability, etc.).

Even the most unpleasant tycoons accused of white-collar crime generally want others to think that they are not crooks. Part of the "techniques of delinquency" of those who do offend are beliefs—prevalent among offenders generally—that their acts cause no real harm to anyone: hence, the importance of the imagery of seriousness in the media and among those whose opinions they may value, though the ingenious can always differentiate their contemplated or past acts as belonging to the lower range of harmful or even harmless actions.

But the symbolic and practical messages that are sent out to white-collar offenders may have an impact on deterrence as well as retribution and shaming: hence, the controversy over the Queen Mother shaking hands at a Covent Garden fund-raising party with Guinness convict Gerald Ronson while he was on parole, and the tendency of the media to treat fraud as a glamour issue rather than emphasizing harm to victims.

Stigma, or perceptions of the emotional and social trauma likely to be experienced by white-collar offenders as a result of conviction per se, may play an important role in judges' views about the appropriateness of sentence, though other factors may submerge its practical effect. Though it may be impossible to determine until after the fact whether shaming is going to be reintegrative or disintegrative—a serious problem for the explanatory power of his model—Braithwaite (1989) has plausibly argued that reintegrative shaming is the key to successful crime control.

A very large proportion of top UK executives—88% in 1994 (though it is not claimed that these respondents are a representative sample)— stated in an Ernst & Young survey that they would react vigorously in terms of refusing to do business with people convicted of fraud (though they were more tolerant of tax fraud). A substantial majority stated consistently in successive surveys that they would also avoid socially those convicted of fraud against other people and investors. Indeed, over a third stated that they would avoid them even if merely suspected of such frauds. But the effects of this depend on how much intending or more vaguely potential fraudsters care about such reactions. The issue of time also has to be taken into account: Stigma may be intense for a few weeks, but except for media targets for lifetime condemnation, if they tough it out, the media soon lose interest. Moreover, if the stigmatized are useful to others in business or politics, then unless they are disqualified from business legally, they will re-emerge because of *realpolitik*.

American economists Karpoff & Lott (1993, 758 f.) observe that "the reputational cost of corporate fraud is large and constitutes most of the cost incurred by firms accused or convicted of fraud." Despite their very unsophisticated model of organizational functioning, the sound points remain that there are indeed reputational effects partly independent of formal sanctions (though publicity is partly a function of the sort of sentence imposed or expected to be imposed); and we should be wary about the imposition of more punishment than is needed to regulate the activity "sensibly" (unless one is a retributivist). However, the authors and the other economists they cite take no note of the symbolic values of (a) fairness vis-á-vis penalties in non-white-collar crime cases and (b) maintaining or generating general confidence in investment among the "little people" who, whatever their importance as a proportion of stock owners, may own only a small proportion of the total securities, and whose discontent that "white-collar crooks are getting away with it" may not show up in share prices—mass consumer boycotts are rare—but may show up in politician's minds. The issue of fairness across types of crime never enters into the analysis.

It is hard to disentangle the pure reputational effects from those connected with expected financial and legal losses (as well as the diversion of executives' time) from sanctions. Thus, hypothetically, if it were not for internationalization of share markets, one might expect smaller price falls in high-penalty countries like the US than in low-penalty ones like the UK used to be.

But the implications may depend on the type of firm also: After the head of research was suspended for "alleged misconduct," which the company inaccurately stated did not involve its drugs trials or fraud, hi-tech drugs company British Bios share prices lost £ 100 million (18% of their value), and dropped dramatically, after he "went public" with claims of misrepresentation of the drugs' prospects. And this happened without any hint of criminal or even regulatory action: It was the market's estimate that the executives could not be trusted and the drugs would not make as heavy profits as they had expected previously.

However, treating such stock price and reputational damage as relevant to retribution does widen the gap between the formal punishment imposed on those companies and their stockholding directors, on the one hand, and the street criminal who has little salient reputation to be injured and no "tradeability" for the market to judge, on the other (though there may be analogies in terms of creditworthiness to drugs suppliers or trustworthiness to "fences," for example). Furthermore, to the extent that the loss of share value takes account of expected direct fines, a reduction in that part of the punishment would reduce the value loss. The fairness argument makes it hard to isolate the kinds of crimes that appear in the *Financial Times, Frankfurter Allgemeine Zeitung* or the *Wall Street Journal* from the kind that more commonly appear in the tabloids such as *Bild Zeitung* and in the television news.

The morally neutralizing effect of money anyway gives many persons who might still be stigmatized by traditional élites the capacity to elude such stigma while living in some luxury. The ease and anonymity of international travel makes social exile to more tolerant social circles abroad less isolating than it would have been in former times, while modern technology such as air conditioning, power generators and chilled transportation of fresh food makes the reproduction of physical comfort an easy matter wherever in the globe one lives. The longing for "home" may be more a problem for working class professional criminals and their families "on the run" from Interpol warrants than for businesspeople, but such longings may be variable culturally, even if "fish and chips," "bratwurst," "korma" and "sushi" (as well as more refined food, beer, and wines) are available in most of the world now.

Avoiding cultural imperialism, the conceptualization of what shaming might be expected to achieve nonetheless remains obscure. Is it primarily social pressure to impact on social prestige (in which case, this has to be affected or cared about, the latter implying some psychodynamic effect analogous to guilt but injected situationally from the outside rather than from the internalized super ego)? Or is it some commercial incapacitation that operates through social mechanisms?

Whatever the case, part of the effect of shaming depends on how much the particular business wants to continue operating. Few pre-planned fraudsters will care, unless the publicity somehow incapacitates them—after all, they have already successfully neutralized their crimes to their own ethical satisfaction, and though confrontation by the views of others may shake those neutralizations, they may regard this still as unrealistic or hypocritical. Those who turn to fraud when their businesses are about to go bust may not care anyway, for they are focused narrowly on "staying alive" or "saving a few pennies for my wife and children" (though there are likely to be personality and cognitive dimensions here). The main people who care about shaming are (a) those whose social lives are embedded and are sufficiently distanced to appreciate the impact, and (b) those who fear that they may be excluded economically from markets. This, for example, is doubtless what propelled activity to redress "mis-selling" by the UK pensions industry, which feared corporate exclusion from lucrative new markets (even so, almost all priority cases accepted offers of redress). Hundreds of firms were fined for failing to comply with review guidance, but the naming and shaming of large firms has had an effect.

The capacity to boost shame in contemporary societies is limited not just by the partial reactions of business and political elites (e.g., in the UK, to the "fat cat" allegations about gross overpayment to directors, especially to directors of privatized utilities), but also by the ability of the sociopathic to enjoy themselves in isolation from their censurers. In this sense, issues such as the move from ascribed to achieved status are important, as are the motivations of the fraudsters in the first place.

7. Concluding Comments

If offenders perceive that they will have both a low chance of conviction and a light sentence for complex, multi-jurisdictional frauds obtaining sums of money that are vast compared with other types of crime for gain, then unless this shift is an intentional policy objective (as a choice between evils), this is cause for reflection on existing sentencing practices, but it is also cause for reflection on the "justice gap" in fraud. The relativities as between fraud and other sentences are salient, especially (in the deterrence mode) to those choosing between different crime types within their capacities, but also to justice between different sets of both offenders and victims. On the expectations and beliefs of both sets, we have little information, so the systematic information is not yet there to make any clear evidence-based decisions as to potential impact of sentencing upon different sorts of fraudster. Nor, following the "corporate death" of Arthur Andersen, do we have any clear idea of whether the "deferred prosecutions" currently fashionable in the US carry with them a credible threat that will produce either special or general deterrence (though the mandated organizational reforms ought to lead to better behavior in the future, if the diagnosis of the causes of misconduct is accurate, the collateral damage from the collapse of major international institutions might be immense). How does this model adapt to those European and other jurisdictions that do not have corporate criminal liability or a system that allows for corporate or individual pentiti to be exculpated or to receive a formally lower negotiated sentence? Should there be an approximated/harmonized set of punishments for European VAT carousel fraudsters, and where should it be anchored?

Perhaps it is appropriate to end with Lewis Carroll (1865/1984, 87) and the interchange between the Cheshire Cat and Alice in Wonderland:

> "Would you tell me, please, which way I ought to go from here?" "That depends a good deal on where you want to get to," said the Cat. "I don't much care where . . .", said Alice. "Then it doesn't matter which way you go," said the Cat. ". . . so long as I get somewhere," Alice added as an explanation. "Oh, you're sure to do that," said the Cat, "if you only walk long enough."

At a normative level, to adapt from the Cheshire Cat, it is helpful if we decide what we want from the sanctioning process and whether our actions are likely to move fraud and fraudsters—generally or of particular types—in the right direction!

REFERENCES

Braithwaite, J. (1989). *Crime, Shame, and Reintegration*. Cambridge, UK.

Carroll, L. (1984). *Alice's Adventures in Wonderland*. 2nd ed. Harmondsworth, UK.

Duh, S. (2005). *The Infiltration of the New York's Financial Market by Organised Crime: Pressures and Controls*. Cardiff University Ph.D.

Dubourg, R. & Hamed, J. (2005). *The Economic and Social Costs of Crime against Individuals and Households 2003/04*. Home Office Online Report 30/05.

Hawkins, K. (2002). *Law as a Last Resort*. Oxford, UK.

von Hirsch, A. (1993). *Censure and Sanctions*. Oxford, UK.

Huber, B. (2003). The tribunal for serious fraud: The continental European experience. *Journal of Financial Crime* 11(1), 2837.

Karpoff, J. & Lott, J. (1993) The reputational penalty firms bear from committing criminal fraud. *Journal of Law and Economics* 36, 757–802.

Katz, J. (1979). Legality and equality: Plea bargaining in the prosecution of white-collar and common crimes. *Law and Society Review* 13, 431–459.

Levi, M. (1981). *The Phantom Capitalists*. 1st ed. London.

Mann, K. (1985). *Defending White-Collar Crime: A Portrait of Attorneys at Work*. New Haven.

Pollack, B. & Murphy Johnson, D. (2006). Commentary: Sufficient, But Not Greater Than Necessary: Sentencing Fraud After Olins, Andrews Litigation, March, Appendix 4.

Reiman, J. (2006). *The Rich Get Richer and the Poor Get Prison*. 8th ed. New York.

Shapiro, S. (1990). Collaring the crime, not the criminal: Liberating the concept of white-collar crime. *American Sociological Review* 55, 346–364.

Shapiro, S. (1985). The road not taken: The elusive path to criminal prosecution for white-collar offenders. *Law and Society Review* 19(2): 179–218.

Simpson, S. (2002). *Corporate Crime, Law, and Social Control.* Cambridge, UK.

US Sentencing Commission (2003). *Increased Penalties Under the Sarbanes-Oxley Act of 2002,* Report to Congress.

Wasik, M. (1998). Crime seriousness and the offender-victim relationship in sentencing, in A. Ashworth & M. Wasik (eds.), *Fundamentals of Sentencing Theory,* 103–128. Oxford, UK.

Weisburd, D., Wheeler, S., Waring, E. & Bode, N. (1991). *Crimes of the Middle Classes: White-Collar Offenders in the Federal Courts.* New Haven, CT.

Wheeler, S., Mann, K & Sarat, A. (1988). Sitting in Judgment. New Haven.

NOTES

[1] Some retributivists might think it inappropriate to take involvement in "organized crime" into account, because the harmfulness of "the act" is not a judgment about the harmfulness of the setting of which the person committing it is a part. Yet, if the previous convictions of the individual are relevant to sentence (as some—e.g., von Hirsch 1993—believe), why not also the gang/group setting of which the individual is willingly a part? This might affect the sentencing of those types of frauds linked to organized groups, such as some payment card and Value-Added Tax (sales tax) frauds.

[2] The information compiled by government may be taken as an indicator—albeit also a legacy—of what government now and in the past considered to be important. By this criterion, the sentencing of serious fraud has never been seen as anyone's core or even subsidiary business.

[3] That is, we do not know scientifically the extent to which it makes a difference to deterrence whether a fraudster gets a 3-, 4- or 10-year sentence, but it seems implausible from general sentencing research or commonsense that a jump from a suspended to a 2-year jail sentence will have the same or less effect than a jump from a 2- to a 4-year sentence, etcetera. Likewise, there will be differences in the risk appetite of businesspeople contemplating offenses, and we do not know the "tipping point" at which perceived probabilities of detection will deter, nor what fraudsters believe about those risks, which will vary by type of offense as well as personality.

[4] See, for a more general discussion of corporate crime sanctions, Simpson (2002).

[5] Though they may have had prior regulatory violations for which they and/or their firms have been sanctioned or dealt with "by advice" but which are not normally admissible as evidence of bad character. In the US, this might raise constitutional issues in the same way that introducing evidence of harm that has not met the criminal standard in the eyes of a jury or has not been admitted by the accused. The Attorney General and the British courts may in the future have to consider whether such "facts" are incompatible with the Human Rights Act in the UK.

[6] If the companies to which they are shadow directors get into visible trouble, there may be a reasonable chance that their involvement will be uncovered (if there are financial traces or if anyone informs against them). However, we may overestimate the extent to which director disqualification and even de-authorization from financial services actually incapacitate.

[7] Compounding refers to a situation in which a suspect taxpayer voluntarily makes an offer on his or her initiative to a VAT investigating officer, though this voluntariness usually occurs within a context in which a criminal prosecution and the collateral damage consequent upon it is seen by the volunteer as the next step in the process.

Unlike many pleas of guilty "on the courthouse steps" in criminal cases, this usually happens at an early stage in the process, saving more investigative and legal costs as well as scarce investigative resources (see www.hmrc.gov.uk/manuals/bimmanual/BIM31610.htm).

8 See also the essays by Bottoms and by Ashworth & Player in the same volume.

9 See Attorney General's Reference (no 9 of 1990) (1990)12 Cr. App. R. (S) 7; Attorney General's Reference (Nos. 23 & 24 of 1996) [1997] 1 Cdr App. R. (S) 174

10 A Cardiff University doctoral study by Diih (2005) documents via wiretaps the way that some American-Italian Mafia families in New York were encouraged to move into securities fraud from their "normal" forms of racketeering by the low sentences and big profits of the Boesky/Milken frauds of the 1980s. However, this was also induced by the "push" factor from tough RICO prosecutions and sentences.

11 It seems plausible that "outsider" fraudsters would be more blue-collar or connected with "organized crime," whereas insiders are more middle and occasionally upper class. Whether this is relevant to sentence is an open question.

12 [Editor's note: On January 20 2003, Deputy Attorney General Larry Thompson issued a policy memorandum to all Justice Department prosecutors entitled "Principles of Federal Prosecution of Business Organizations." Known as the "Thompson Memo," the document directed the approach to corporate criminal prosecutions, explaining that there would be increased scrutiny of the authenticity of a corporation's cooperation. The memo announced an increased emphasis on two topics: corporate cooperation with government investigations and evaluation of the effectiveness of corporate governance measures (whether corporate policies, in fact, deter, detect, and disclose violations or law or regulations). The application of the guidelines in the Thompson Memo have provoked strong reactions. Some believe it threatens the foundation of our system of justice by moving power from the courts and juries to the Department of Justice; others applaud it as an effective way to save our market system from itself. See, for example, Wray, Christopher A. and Robert K. Hur (2006). "Corporate Criminal Prosecution in a Post-Enron World: The Thompson Memo in Theory And Practice." *American Law Review*, Vol. 43, pp. 1095–1096, 1106, 1188. Retrieved from http://www.kslaw.com/library/practicearea/Post-Enron.pdf]

13 Stating that the government "let its zeal get in the way of its judgment" and "violated the Constitution it is sworn to defend," Southern District of New York Judge Lewis Kaplan in *United States v. Stein*, S1 05 Crim. 0888, found that prosecutors had violated the Fifth and Sixth amendments by "causing *KPMG* to cut off legal fees and other defense costs upon indictment" (see, e.g., *New York Law Journal*, 28 June 2006; www.law.com/jsp/article.jsp?id=1151399128531). He was highly critical of prosecutors' interpretation of the Thompson guidelines as oppressive. It is likely that this case will be appealed.

14 The technicalities of this are unimportant to a British audience (see Pollack & Murphy Johnson 2006). Part of Olis' appeal rested on the unconstitutionality of what amounted to trial without jury in an American context, the judge using estimates of harm that had not been considered by the jury when reaching its verdict.

15 He was later found guilty (with the former Governor of Alabama) of bribery and mail fraud, involving paying the then Governor $500,000 in laundered money to obtain a seat on a state regulatory board governing HealthSouth. He had not been sentenced by January 2007; see www.usdoj.gov/criminal/press_room/press_releases/2006_4667_06-29-06-ScrushyConvicted.pdf

20

Understanding Antitrust Offenses

An Examination of Major League Baseball's Modern-Day Monopoly

— *Andrea Schoepfer and Nicole Leeper Piquero*

Almost everyone is familiar with the Parker Brothers real estate trading board-game, Monopoly, where the object of the game is to "amass the greatest fortune in money and property" and the player who does so is deemed the winner. While the game provides for hours of entertainment for those playing, the gravity of this kind of behavior for the American marketplace was identified early in American history when Congress passed the Sherman Antitrust Act of 1890. Clearly, then as now, anticompetitive behavior in the marketplace is not regarded as child's play. Over the years, legislation continued to be refined and developed to curb unfair and deceptive trade practices in order to ensure a free market society.

Antitrust laws are designed to regulate all forms of commerce across all industries—from the earliest case of the Standard Oil Company to more recent cases such as that of Microsoft—where both criminal and civil lawsuits are filed or are threatened to be filed against companies who engage in unfair competitive practices against their competitors. Across all spectrums of business, the underlying capitalist view is free competition and the prevention of behaviors that lead to a restraint in trade. As such, competition must be fair and open to all companies or

An original article written for this publication.

parties who wish to get in the game and compete. In other words, the playing field should be level to all potential competitors, unless, of course, the playing field of interest is a baseball diamond.

America's pastime—baseball, a game that many Americans enjoy every year from April until the "hunt for" October, may not seem, at first, to have a connection with antitrust laws and the business world, but the business of professional baseball occupies a unique place in the antitrust law discussion. Major League Baseball (MLB), unlike the other major American professional sports (e.g., National Football League, National Basketball Association, and the National Hockey League), is exempt from antitrust laws.[1] In this article, we first review the evolution of antitrust laws in the United States and then describe how MLB became a modern-day monopoly.

History of Antitrust Legislation in the United States

The post-Civil War era in the United States was characterized by rapid business growth and expansion, particularly in the railroad, steel, sugar, tobacco, lead, and oil industries. Many of the firms within these industries joined together as "trusts" or holding companies in order to reduce competition.[2] At the time, there were various intrastate antimonopoly laws (beginning with Alabama in 1883). However, these existing laws were quite limited in that they were focused on a very precise jurisdiction—that is, within single state boundaries. Since most of the major industries (i.e., oil, steel, and tobacco) were involved in interstate commerce and expanding beyond a single state's borders, the intrastate laws had little impact. In 1887, Congress took the first step in attempting to regulate big industry power across state borders by establishing the Interstate Commerce Commission (ICC) specifically designed to regulate the railroad industry. However, as with the intrastate laws, early enforcement was minimal.[3]

As power, cooperation, and voracity among these trusts grew stronger, public skepticism and distrust of big industries grew commensurately. Newspapers frequently published stories of the abuses associated with monopolies and the widening gap between the upper and lower social classes due to the "greed and excessive power" held by the industrial trusts.[4] In response to this growing public outrage, President Benjamin Harrison called for a federal law to regulate trusts and industrial combinations. Meanwhile, the Republican Senator of Ohio, John Sherman, introduced the first antitrust bill to the Senate Finance Committee.[5] Legislative debates on the form and content of his antitrust bill proceeded for two years, and the Sherman Antitrust Act became law on July 2, 1890. Interestingly, the U.S. Congress felt so strongly about restoring a free market economy in which competition leads to the best outcome for consumers, that there was only one vote against the act.[6]

The purpose of the Sherman Antitrust Act (15 U.S.C. §1–2) was to prohibit monopolies and restore competition to the market economy. The act states that "Every contract, combination in the form of trust or otherwise, or conspiracy, in restraint of trade or commerce among the several States, or with foreign nations, is declared to be illegal," and "Every person who shall monopolize, or attempt to monopolize, or combine or conspire with any other person or persons, to monopolize any part of the trade or commerce . . . shall be deemed guilty of a felony." In other words, the act allowed Congress to regulate interstate commerce by declaring contracts, combinations, and/or conspiracies in restraint of interstate and foreign trade by corporations or individuals illegal. Originally, those found in violation of the act were subject to a maximum penalty of $5,000 fine and one-year imprisonment. Over the years, the maximum penalties have increased; currently, the maximum penalty is $10 million for a corporation, $350,000 for an individual, and/or three years imprisonment.

Unfortunately, just like the prior state antimonopoly laws, the Sherman Antitrust Act received minimal enforcement when first enacted. In fact, less than two antitrust cases were filed per year from 1890 to 1904, due largely to the fact that Congress did not specifically fund antitrust enforcement.[7] Jurisdiction over antitrust cases was given to the attorney general rather than to a separate agency until 1904 when Congress funded five full-time antitrust lawyers for the Department of Justice, thus creating the Antitrust Division.[8]

The first U.S. Supreme Court case to find a Sherman Act violation was *U.S. v. Trans-Missouri Freight Association*[9] filed in January 1892 and decided by the Supreme Court in March 1897. The Supreme Court found that the railroad companies named in the petition had illegally entered into an agreement in which they formed themselves into an association for the purpose of affecting railroad traffic rates. The Sherman Act continued to gain momentum until the Supreme Court invoked the "Rule of Reason" doctrine in the 1911 Standard Oil and American Tobacco cases, thus further limiting the scope of the Sherman Act.[10] The reasonableness doctrine declared that not all restraints of trade were necessarily illegal; it was only the "unreasonable" restraints of trade that were prohibited. Unfortunately there were no guidelines as to when restraints of trade were either reasonable or unreasonable. In the 1911 reasonableness doctrine decision, the Supreme Court ruled that "the law does not make mere size [of the corporation] an offense"; however, the Supreme Court reversed its decision in 1945 and declared that corporate size and structure were indeed adequate justifications for initiating antitrust action.[11]

Since the inception of the Sherman Antitrust Act of 1890, the United States has enacted several additional antitrust legislations, much of which built on the Sherman Act. For example, in 1914 President Woodrow Wilson announced an antitrust initiative; in response, Congress passed both the Federal Trade and Commission Act and the Clayton Act. The Federal Trade and Commission Act prohibits unfair competition in interstate business but carries no criminal penalties. The act also established the Federal Trade Commission (FTC) to hold jurisdiction over violations of the act. Similarly, the Clayton Act is a civil statute that also carries no criminal penalties. The Clayton Act, while established in 1914, was significantly amended in 1950 by the Cellar-Kefauver Act. The Clayton Act prohibits mergers and acquisitions that are likely to reduce competition and increase prices for consumers. The Clayton Act also requires all companies above a certain size to notify the Department of Justice's Antitrust Division and the FTC about any mergers they may be considering. Furthermore, the act allows private parties injured by an antitrust violation to sue in federal court for up to three times the actual damages plus court costs. Due to vague writing in the original legislation, the Cellar-Kefauver Act of 1950 was enacted to close the asset acquisitions loophole as it applies to vertical, conglomerate, as well as horizontal mergers.[12]

According to the Department of Justice, the Sherman Act, the Federal Trade Commission Act, and the Clayton Act are the three most influential federal antitrust laws in U.S. history. However, several other antitrust legislations have been passed since 1914. One of the more interesting lesser known acts was the National Industrial Recovery Act (NIRA) of 1933. In order to stimulate the economy after the Great Depression, Congress passed the NIRA to promote business consolidation, which of course was in complete opposition to the Sherman Antitrust Act. Shortly after the NIRA proved to be unsuccessful at reviving the economy, the Supreme Court ruled it unconstitutional.[13]

In 1936, the Robinson-Patman Act amended Section 2 of the Clayton Act by allowing criminal sanctioning of predatory pricing practices. Then in 1937, the Miller-Tydings Act was passed to benefit certain businesses by exempting them from Sherman Act prosecutions. The Magnuson-Moss FTC Improvement Act of 1974 expanded FTC powers from policing to being able to make rules and sanction violators. And in 1976, the Hart-Scott-Rodino Antitrust Improvement Act allowed state attorneys general to file antitrust cases on behalf of state residents and requires pending mergers and acquisitions to be reported and reviewed by the government.

As with most governmental involvement with corporations, support for antitrust regulations ebbed and flowed with the respective political administrations and United States Supreme Court rulings. After 1950, the Supreme Court played a large role in antitrust doctrine. Similar to political outlooks on corporations, the Court generally took one of two opposing views on the capitalist market system in the United States. On one hand, markets were seen as fragile and easily protected through public action (deterrence style of corporate control). The other view was that business competition was healthy and the market would fix itself;

therefore, public intervention was not necessary (compliance style of corporate control). During the 1950s through the late 1960s, the Court generally took the former stance and aggressively intervened in antitrust before switching to the latter style by cutting back on their interventions in the late 1970s. The Court returned to their aggressive stance once more in the late 1980s through the 1990s then switched back to the more passive approach in the late 1990s. These ebbs and flows on Supreme Court interventions against antitrust actions may help explain the case of professional organized sports' run in the antitrust realm.

A Modern-Day Monopoly: Major League Baseball

In 1922, Major League Baseball (MLB) gained a unique status in American business. It was an industry that became—and to this day remains—exempt from antitrust laws. In order to understand the lawsuit that earned MLB this exemption and what allows the monopolistic situation to prosper, we will review the creation of professional baseball leagues and subsequent lawsuits that addressed the antitrust exemption. We conclude with a review of how this exemption is being taken advantage of by MLB generally and by its commissioner, Allan H. "Bud" Selig, in particular.

In January 1903, the first two established leagues—the American League of Professional Base Ball Clubs and the National League of Professional Base Ball Clubs—joined to form Major League Baseball. One of the central components of this newly formed baseball league was the inclusion of a "reserve clause" included in all contracts between the league and players. The reserve clause in players' contracts basically bound the player to the organization that first signed him. The player could only play professional baseball for the club that originally signed him unless the club decided to trade or sell him to another team. Teams could decide to trade or sell players without input or even knowledge from the player who would be affected.

John T. Powers of Chicago along with other entrepreneurs established a new baseball league, calling it the Federal League (FL), in 1913. At the end of the first year (August 2, 1913), the FL voted to expand and have franchises in Eastern cities, which was an area dominated by MLB teams. For the 1914 and 1915 seasons, the FL was comprised of eight teams: Baltimore Terrapins, Brooklyn Tip-Tops, Buffalo Blues, Chicago Whalers, Indianapolis Hoosiers,[14] Kansas City Packers, Pittsburgh Rebels, and St. Louis Terriers. As such, the FL was competing with MLB for talented baseball players and did so by offering larger salaries and the promise of no reserve clause in their contracts with the FL. By 1915, the FL filed a lawsuit suing MLB for violation of antitrust laws because the reserve clause in players' contracts allowed them to monopolize the hiring of professional baseball players. Eventually, after a two-year dispute, the FL and MLB reached a "peace treaty" at a meeting held in Cincinnati. As part of the agreement, the FL agreed to dissolve the league and MLB would compensate the FL $600,000 which was to be dispersed among all FL owners. Due to the agreement, the FL antitrust lawsuit was dismissed on February 7, 1916 by mutual consent from both parties.

On September 20, 1917, the Federal Baseball Club of Baltimore, the Terrapins, sued MLB arguing that the National League and the American League (and other owners from FL who agreed to the peace treaty) were engaging in anticompetitive practices in an attempt to create a monopoly in baseball by squeezing out the FL. At first, the Baltimore Terrapins successfully won their lawsuit; however, the decision was reversed on appeal. The case appeared before the U.S. Supreme Court in 1922.[15] The 9–0 ruling (with Justice Oliver Wendell Holmes writing the opinion) upheld the appellate court ruling, essentially arguing that baseball was a "game" or an "exhibition" and not interstate commerce; that it was not a good or service being transported from one state to another and thus was not subject to antitrust laws.[16] As such, MLB earned a unique status by becoming exempt from antitrust laws.

Since the 1922 U.S. Supreme Court ruling, several attempts have been made to rid MLB of the antitrust exemption. Both tries specifically targeted the reserve clause in players' contracts with professional baseball and had their cases argued before the U.S. Supreme Court. Unfortunately, neither attempt was successful. In 1953, the U.S. Supreme Court heard the case of George Toolson who was suing the New York Yankees organization for violating antitrust laws because of the reserve clause in his contract with the team.[17] Toolson filed suit after the Yankees renewed the contract between him and their Newark minor league team only to turn around and then trade him to another team without his knowledge or approval. The Court, in a 7-2 unsigned ruling, upheld the antitrust exemption for MLB noting, "We think that if there are evils in this field which now warrant application to it of the antitrust laws it should be by legislation." In essence, the Court would not overturn the 1922 ruling allowing the antitrust exemption for MLB but did suggest and encourage that the introduction of new legislation by Congress could change the exemption status.

A similar situation arose concerning St. Louis Cardinals seven-time Golden Glove outfielder, Curt Flood. After learning that the Cardinals traded him as part of a multi-player deal to the Philadelphia Phillies, Flood refused to sign with the new organization and wished to sign with a different organization; however, he was unable to do so because of the reserve clause in his contract with the Cardinals. Flood appealed to Bowie Kuhn, who was then the commissioner of baseball. He asked Kuhn to allow him to become a free agent in order to make his own contract with a new team. Kuhn sided with the Cardinals. Flood, not wanting to move to Philadelphia for a variety of personal and business-related reasons, filed an antitrust lawsuit against MLB and Commissioner Kuhn. In 1972, the U.S. Supreme Court heard Flood's case; in a 5-3 opinion written by Justice Harry Blackmun, the Court upheld Flood's trade. Once again, the Court refused to overturn the antitrust exemption.[18] While his lawsuit was moving through the criminal justice system, Flood still refused to play baseball for the Philadelphia Phillies and sat out the entire season. At the end of that season, the Phillies organization decided to sell Flood to another team, the Washington Senators. After an abbreviated period of time with the Washington team, Flood chose to retire from professional baseball before the end of the 1971 season.

While neither Toolson nor Flood was successful in winning their antitrust lawsuits targeting the reserve clause of MLB, they did help pave the way for other players to earn their freedom. In 1976, just a few short years after Flood's retirement from professional baseball, the players union was successful in winning free agency for the other professional baseball players through a collective bargaining agreement with MLB owners. The new agreement stated that after six years in the league, players could negotiate with other teams when their original contract expired. As a result of free agency, which essentially established a free-market economy where players could sell their services to the highest bidder, the salaries of professional baseball players rose dramatically.

Perhaps a small sense of redemption came for Curt Flood in 1998 when President William J. Clinton signed into law, The Curt Flood Act, which removed the antitrust exemption for MLB in labor relation issues. Of course, the new legislation mattered little in the day-to-day operation of professional baseball for two reasons. First, the free agency status established some twenty-two years earlier as part of the players' union collective bargaining agreement already addressed the wrongs associated with this specific issue. Second, the U.S. Supreme Court ruled in 1996 that unionized players could not file antitrust lawsuits, arguing that the antitrust exemption would apply only to non-unionized players.[19] In other words, players' associations and unions would have to dissolve before antitrust lawsuits could be filed against any professional sporting league including MLB. Therefore, the newly passed legislation was more symbolic than functional in breaking down the antitrust exemption for MLB.

The 1998 federal Curt Flood legislation did not remove antitrust exemption from professional baseball across the board but rather removed it from one tiny, very narrow aspect of the game, player employment issues. Other aspects of the business, such as team relocation and league expansion issues, were still protected from antitrust laws. Team relocation has been at the heart of the most recent debate against the antitrust exemption of MLB.[20] The antitrust exemption gives unparalleled power to MLB and specifically to its commissioner, Bud Selig, who acquired the position in 1992 and was elected as permanent Commissioner in 1998, in determining whether or not a baseball franchise can

relocate from city to city. Essentially, MLB constitutes a relocation committee, whose committee members are handpicked by Selig, to investigate
the potential costs (e.g., impact on other franchises) and success (e.g.,
securing a new state of the art stadium) of relocating an already existing
team to another city who places a "bid" to be considered as the new location. Then, in order to approve the relocation of a team, the owners of all
thirty baseball teams must vote with at least 75% in favor of the relocation.

It took over thirty years before a relocation was approved for a professional baseball franchise. Washington, DC, lost its baseball franchise in
1971. Robert Short, the owner of the then Washington Senators, moved his
team to Arlington, Texas, to become the Texas Rangers. While MLB has
expanded since that time, it had not allowed any relocation. Commissioner
Bud Selig announced on September 29, 2004, that the Montreal Expos
would relocate to Washington DC and begin playing in the 2005 baseball
season. They would become the Washington Nationals because the Texas
Ranger franchise still held the rights to the name "Washington Senators."

While MLB experienced a thirty-year lull in relocation of teams, the
same is not true for other major professional sports, which do not enjoy the
antitrust exemption status of MLB. Since Al Davis, the owner of the Oakland
Raiders in the National Football League (NFL), filed and won his antitrust
legal suit against the NFL permitting him to move his football franchise after
the 1981 season from Oakland, California, to Los Angeles, California, there
have been numerous team relocations in the NFL, as well as within the
National Basketball Association (NBA) and the National Hockey League
(NHL). Both the NFL and the NBA have had seven teams relocate since 1978
and the NHL nine teams since the league expanded in 1967.[21]

Much controversy surrounded the relocation of MLB's Montreal
Expos to Washington, DC. The process took nearly two years to be investigated, in large part due to Commissioner Bud Selig's reluctance to
change the thirty-year old precedent of non-relocation but also due to the
number of locations interested in being considered. Along with the
nation's capital, six other sites were bidding for the possible relocation of
the Montreal Expos. These locations included: Northern Virginia (near
Dulles airport); Norfolk, Virginia; Portland, Oregon; Las Vegas, Nevada;
as well as Monterrey, Mexico; and San Juan, Puerto Rico. All of the locations hoping for the relocation of the ball club had to promise a new state
of the art, publicly financed stadium. One other serious hurdle to the
Washington DC as well as the Northern Virginia potential location was
their proximity to the already existing team the Baltimore Orioles. Peter
Angelos, the owner of the Baltimore Orioles, argued against the relocation to either of the two sites because it could diminish his fan base, thus
negatively impacting the Orioles' bottom line. Ultimately, an agreement
was reached between Angelos and MLB which permitted the relocation
of the Expos to Washington, DC. The agreement included a financial settlement paid directly to Angelos, plus it granted him broadcast privileges.

Bud Selig's tenure as Commissioner has been tumultuous. Since becoming the commissioner in 1992, there have been conflict-of-interest issues. He owns the Milwaukee Brewers. The other three professional sporting leagues do not permit the commissioner to own a team. Selig became a team owner in 1970 when he bought (along with other investors) the Seattle Pilots and relocated them to Milwaukee as the Brewers. However, it is important to note that he withdrew from day-to-day operations of the Brewers' organization, stopped receiving his annual salary, and placed his ownership into a blind trust when he became the commissioner. The Brewers were not, however, the only baseball team in which Selig had a vested interest. In February 2002, he and the other twenty-eight team owners agreed to buy the Montreal Expos for $120 million, thus allowing MLB to operate, run, and manage one of its own franchises for a period of time.

Facing a serious economically deteriorating situation, MLB owners tried to renegotiate the collective bargaining agreement between themselves and the players' association with the expiration of the existing contract. The owners were demanding the players agree to a salary cap in order to help stabilize the economic situation. The players absolutely refused. The lack of a compromise resulted in a players strike beginning on August 12, 1994. The strike lasted 232 days. Almost 2,000 games—including the playoffs and the 1994 World Series—were not played. The strike ended when a federal judge issued an injunction against the owners, and baseball resumed April 25, 2005, under the conditions of the expired contract. The financial situation has not improved despite the owners and the players reaching a new collective bargaining agreement. In fact, owners still report losing money every year since the strike over a decade ago.

Given the unstable economic situation of MLB, the baseball team owners changed MLB's constitution agreeing in January of 2000 to allow Commissioner Bud Selig the unprecedented authority to rule over baseball economic issues—including all issues dealing with collective bargaining. In addition, he was granted the authority to remove or suspend anyone including team owners who did not act in the best interest of MLB.[22] These powers would not be passed on to Selig's successors but rather would expire at the end of his term. Selig introduced several strategies and changes to enhance baseball and keep the fans coming to the ballpark. These changes included: establishing inter-league play, a wild-card playoff system, enhanced revenue sharing among the team owners, as well as raising the possibility of eliminating two franchises, the Montreal Expos and the Minnesota Twins, who were not profitable. Ultimately, the elimination of the two franchises never occurred. Instead, the Expos were relocated to the nation's capital and the Twins began playing in a new $545 million stadium in 2010 (almost 65% financed by taxpayers).[23]

Conclusions

As previously discussed, antitrust laws were originally designed to regulate economic competition and are particularly relevant for a free market economy such as is present in the United States. However, despite the fact that MLB is a $3.5 billion industry, U.S. Supreme Court precedence and the failure of the legislature to enact laws against its anticompetitive behavior allows MLB to continue to carve and maintain horizontal restraints or regional monopolies across the United States.[24]

Interestingly, four years after Toolson's 1953 Supreme Court case in which the antitrust exemption was upheld, the same Supreme Court ruled in *Radovich v. National Football League* that the NFL was a business and thus subject to antitrust regulations.[25] Justice Tom C. Clark noted that the only reason baseball remained exempt was because of the precedent set in the 1922 case, yet they refused to use this precedent when ruling on the NFL case. The court ruled that "the volume of interstate business involved in organized professional football places it within the provisions of the [Antitrust] Act" (p. 452). In fact, Justice Clark even stated that if the court were "considering the question of baseball for the first time upon a clean slate we would have no doubts" about holding baseball to the same antitrust standards other professional sports were being held (p. 452). Essentially, the majority opinion stated that if they had the chance to do it all over again, baseball would not be exempt from antitrust legislation. Yet when the Supreme Court heard Curt Flood's case in 1972, fifteen years after the NFL case, the court upheld the baseball antitrust exemption once more.

In the dissenting opinion in the Radovich case (just as in the 1953 Toolson case), Justices Harlan and Brennan noted that the court should not be making distinctions between baseball and other professional sports and should leave all future decisions on antitrust to Congress.[26] Interestingly, in 1951, Congress introduced four bills that would extend the baseball rule to other professional organized sports; none of the four bills were enacted.[27] Congress has considered possible legislation regarding baseball more than 60 times since 1950, sixteen times since 1990, without acting to regulate MLB.[28]

Since no court decision or legislation has reversed the exemption, MLB has been able to maintain and use its antitrust law exemption status any way it sees fit. While the U.S. Supreme Court had the opportunity to overturn the Court's early exemption status on two different occasions, it refused to do so. Both of these cases and the conflicting rulings regarding other organized professional sports occurred during the Supreme Court's aggressive enforcement period, thus possibly explaining why other sports were not held to the same standards. While this does not explain why MLB's status was not changed, MLB was originally granted antitrust exemption in a time when the United States was still fine-tuning antitrust legislation and was not aggressively enforcing antitrust actions. Since 1972, the highest court of the land has not heard a professional sports antitrust case—not because cases have not been filed but because the Court refuses to hear them.[29] In 1999, the Supreme Court unanimously denied the attorney general of Minnesota, Mike Hatch, the opportunity to present his antitrust case against MLB. His argument was that Commissioner Bud Selig and team owners were abusing the antitrust exemption in order to extort public funds to have new baseball stadiums built. In doing so, team owners would threaten local and state governments that they would relocate the local team if funds were not raised to build a new state of the art stadium. Specifically, Carl Pohlad, owner of the Minnesota Twins, had announced he would sell the team to North Carolina if a new, publicly financed stadium was not built—and Commissioner Selig said MLB would approve the move.[30]

Baseball owners are some of the wealthiest people in the United States. MLB has a powerful lobby and makes donations to a number of Congressional candidates. Factoring in the emotional attachment to the game of baseball in addition to political support, it is not difficult to understand why no legislation has changed baseball's exemption from antitrust laws—even though the exemption has been costly.

> Baseball's monopoly allows it to artificially restrict the number of franchises and to treat cities without teams as assets of the league. As a consequence, cities and states compete against each other, leading to exorbitant stadium-financing packages and sweetheart leases. Further, when state governments become involved in financially supporting stadium construction, they often must simultaneously support parallel pork projects elsewhere in the state to secure the necessary votes in the legislature.[31]

In sum, MLB appears to have only one, albeit small, strike against them in that they are no longer exempt from antitrust laws with regard to player negotiations. So with the count in their favor—with still two strikes to go—the question remains if and when they will ever be held accountable to the same antitrust laws as other businesses. Until that time, MLB will undoubtedly continue to "play ball!" without antitrust restrictions.

NOTES

[1] It is important to note that there have been a couple of antitrust exemptions exercised for the other major professional sports leagues; however, these were designed to ensure the long-term (financial) vitality of the existing leagues. For example, the Sports Broadcasting Act of 1961 grants all major league sports (including MLB) an antitrust exemption by allowing each respective league to pool their separate broadcasting rights to sell to a single purchaser. Additionally, the Football Merger Act of 1966 permitted the merger between the two professional leagues, the Ameri-

can Football League and the National Football League, into one major professional football league (which would retain the name "National Football League"). Thereby, Congress granted an antitrust exemption to professional football by allowing the merger of two competing football leagues.

2 Perhaps the most famous of these trusts was the Standard Oil Company headed by John D. Rockefeller; see Friedrichs, D. O. *Trusted Criminals* (Belmont, CA: Cengage 2010).

3 Sherman, R. *Antitrust Policies and Issues* (Reading, MA: Addison-Wesley, 1978).

4 Jamieson, K. M. *The Organization of Corporate Crime: Dynamics of Antitrust Violation* (Thousand Oaks, CA: Sage, 1994), p. 28.

5 Weaver, S. *Decision to Prosecute: Organization and Public Policy in the Antitrust Division* (Cambridge, MA: MIT Press, 1977).

6 U.S. Department of Justice (2005) Antitrust Division, http://www.usdoj.gov/atr/.

7 U.S. Department of Justice (2005) Antitrust Division, http://www.usdoj.gov/atr/.

8 Jamieson, *The Organization of Corporate Crime.*

9 *United States v. Trans-Missouri Freight Association*, 166 U.S. 290 no. 67 (1897).

10 *Standard Oil Co. v. United States*, 221 U.S. 1 (1911) and *United States v. American Tobacco Co.*, 221 U.S. 106 (1911)

11 *United States v. Aluminum Company of America*, 148, F.2d 416, 448 (1945).

12 Simpson, S. S. "Strategy, Structure, and Corporate Crime: The Historical Context of Anticompetive Behavior" in *New Directions in Criminological Theory: Advances in Criminological Theory, Volume 4*, eds. W. S. Laufer and F. Adler (New Brunswick, NJ: Transaction, 1993).

13 Sherman, R. *Antitrust Policies and Issues.* (Reading, MA: Addison-Wesley, 1978).

14 In 1915, the team was moved from Indianapolis to Newark to become the Newark Peppers.

15 *Federal Club v. National League*, 259 U.S. 200 (1922).

16 It is noteworthy to point out that Chief Justice William Howard Taft was the brother of the former Cubs owner, Charles Taft.

17 *Toolson v. New York Yankees, Inc.*, 346 U.S. 356 (1953).

18 *Flood v. Kuhn*, 407 U.S. 258 (1972).

19 *Brown v. Pro Football Inc.*, 518 U.S. 231 (1996).

20 Fainaru, S. (2004) "Expos for Sale: Team Becomes Pawn of Selig," *Washington Post*, 28 June, sec. A, p. 1, 14–15. *Sports Illustrated* (2001) "Ain't Nobody's Business: Why Antitrust Exemption is Important to Baseball Owners," Sports Illustrated.com: A CNN website, http://sportsillustrated.cnn.com/baseball/news/2001/12/05/antitrust_owners_ap/.

21 Greenberg, D. (2002) "Baseball's Con Game," Slate MSN, http://slate.msn.com/id/2068290.

22 Fainaru, S. (2004) "The Last Cartel: How Baseball Does Business," *Washington Post*, 27 June, sec. A, p. 1, 12–13.

23 Mark Yost (2010), "If They Build It, You Will Pay." *The Wall Street Journal* http://online.wsj.com/article/SB10001424052702304017404575165760977036190.html

24 Fainaru, S. (2004) "Angelos, Selig Last Men Standing in D.C.'s Way," *Washington Post*, 29 June, sec. A., p. 1, 8–9; Simpson, S. S. "Strategy, Structure, and Corporate Crime: The Historical Context of Anticompetive Behavior" in *New Directions in Criminological Theory: Advances in Criminological Theory, Volume 4*, eds. W. S. Laufer and F. Adler (New Brunswick, NJ: Transaction, 1993).

25 *Radovich v. National Football League*, 352 U.S. 445 (1957). Retrieved from http://caselaw.lp.findlaw.com/scripts/getcase.pl?court=us&vol=352&invol=445

26 Similar rulings were also reached in *United States v. International Boxing Club*, 348
    U.S. 236 (1955) and *United States v. Shubert*, 348 U.S. 222 (1955).
27 *Radovich v. National Football League*, 352 U.S. 445 (1957), footnote 7.
28 Andrew Zimbalist (2003) *May the Best Team Win: Baseball Economics and Public Policy.*
    Washington, DC: Brookings Institution, p. 135.
29 On May 24, 2010, the U.S. Supreme Court ruled in *American Needle, Inc. v. National Foot-
    ball League Et Al* (No. 08–661) that the NFL must be considered 32 separate teams rather
    than one entity when selling branded items such as jerseys and caps. The League had
    requested broad antitrust law protection, but the Court reversed a lower court ruling
    throwing out the antitrust suit initiated by a competitor to Reebok. American Needle
    alleged that all the teams in the NFL worked together to exclude companies from mak-
    ing licensed items because it had given Reebok an exclusive 10-year license. The case
    was sent back to the lower courts to be reconsidered.
30 Zimbalist, p. 22. Carl Pohlad died in 2009; his net worth was estimated at $3.6 billion.
31 Zimbalist, p. 139.

21

White-Collar Crime and Its Victims

— *John W. Heeren*

In spite of the well-known conceptual ambiguities of Sutherland's "white-collar crime," it has proven to be a surprisingly fertile category. Interest and research in political corruption, professional malpractice and malfeasance, charitable fraud, occupational crime, organizational crime, and strictly criminal organizations operating as businesses have been added to the original focus on business or corporate crime. In addition, successive economic and technological changes since the Sutherland era have brought forth new arenas for white-collar offenses. This is evident in the new opportunities for fraudulent acts with the advent of television (e.g., rigged quiz shows), computerized marketing (e.g., "personalized" mailings), Internet communication (e.g., phishing), and the global spread of capitalism (e.g., outsourcing pollution). Unfortunately, the growth and metamorphosis of white-collar crime has made the problem of definitions and related concepts even more jarring. It seems difficult to find a single thread that unites all that falls under the white-collar crime heading.

Parallel to these problems of conceiving white-collar crime and criminals, the victims of these offenses also have proven difficult to delineate. The original discussion by Sutherland (1940) describes victims as "weak." Business leaders and professionally respectable strata were seen as victimizing the vulnerable lower strata who were unorganized and lacking in technical knowledge. However appealing this may be as a moral tale, it does not comport with the patterns of embezzlement or consumer insurance fraud in which individuals from the middle and lower strata take advantage of large financial and insurance organizations

An original article written for this publication.

through violations of trust (Weisburd et al., 1991; Holtfreter, 2005; Lesch and Byars, 2008). Moreover, the victims of "elite" crime have often been elite themselves, e.g., large corporations and wealthy investors (Levi, 1992). For this discussion, we will attempt to articulate the general patterns that have been identified by researchers, while also noting the exceptions to those patterns.

Understanding White-Collar Crime and Its Victims

There appear to be two contradictory emphases in definitions of white-collar crime. The one deriving from Sutherland (1940) focuses on the criminal aspect; the other, most fully articulated by Shapiro (1990), is more concerned with the nature of the white-collar offense itself. Although I agree with the "populist" perspective (Shover and Cullen, 2008) that the offenses in question are most harmfully committed by those at the top of society, it seems that the elements of the crime are the more appropriate starting point. In this light, violations of trust are likely to be the central element of white-collar crime (Shapiro, 1990). A key ingredient for this violation is deception, but there are other ways besides deceit in which occupational responsibility can be violated. For example, a professional can misuse property that s/he is expected to protect or guard for another person. If the owner of the property is underaged or not mentally competent, then deceit may not be needed. Subsequently, of course, deception may be called for if the misappropriation is likely to be revealed.

There are several elements that this conception of white-collar offenses includes, beginning with intent, then the act as a violation of rules, and, finally, ending with harm. Without intent, accidental or involuntary pollution or food adulteration may occur, but this would not generally be considered a crime, even when some penalty may be exacted. With respect to the act that violates a rule, criminal offenses are one expression of this; however, the violation might also be a breach of administrative, regulatory, or civil law. Harm of some sort, the varieties of which will be detailed below, is also a necessary part of the offense. Deception is the typical means or device by which the harm is done to victims. However, if the deception is not accompanied by some material advantage to the offender and loss to the victim, then we are likely to see the deceit as parallel to "tact" or "flattery." When deception is an element of the trust violation, it really entails duplicity toward victims. That is, the offender must be aware of the true state of things represented and know that the information or story that they are providing is false, misleading, or incomplete.

As difficult as it is to define white-collar crime without putting many offenses in a residual category, a unitary account of white-collar victims is equally problematic. For certain types of white-collar crimes, researchers have found that the victim often suffers very little harm (Croall, 2009; Shichor, 1998; Friedrichs, 2010). That is, the actual harm may be so indirect and diffuse that victims are quite unaware of it. Consumer fraud illustrates this type of white-collar crime. When a manufacturer packages a bit less volume or weight than the label promises, few victims are likely to notice or be much affected by the offense. For the manufacturer, however, the incremental profit can be quite substantial when calculated over the large number of victims. This type of impersonalized mass victimization that is often unrecognized by victims is most common in consumer, environmental, and safety offenses. However, a seemingly minor offense can eventually have a much larger impact on victims. For example, pollution can become highly toxic over time, and safety violations can lead to death. Examples of great magnitude can be seen in the 1972 Buffalo Creek disaster (Erikson, 1976), Hooker Chemical's pollution of Love Canal (Mokhiber, 1988), or the 1992 fire at the Imperial chicken processing plant in North Carolina (Rosoff, Pontell, and Tillman, 2002).

Moreover, with some forms of white-collar victimization, such as investment scams, the impact on victims is likely to be anything but minor. Here, the number of victims per offense may be smaller, but the financial burden of individual victims can be quite grave and the media have been ready to embrace retirees and other vulnerable groups as the victims (Levi, 2006). Nor are large entities immune from great harm through white-collar offenses. While the massive failure and subsequent bailout of Savings and Loan institutions in the U.S. in the late 1980s was not completely the result of white-collar crime, a substantial component of fraudulent and criminal activity did lead to the failure of hundreds of financial institutions and costs to taxpayers in the hundreds of billions of dollars (Rosoff, Pontell, and Tillman, 2002). The scope of harm in this and parallel instances contrasts directly with other white-collar crime that causes minimal harm to largely invisible victims.

Another common conception is that many victims of white-collar crime share some responsibility for their victimization (Shichor, 1998; Titus, 2001; Friedrichs, 2010). Andrew Karmen (2010) discusses a continuum of responsibility of victims of conventional crime, from the "completely innocent" person who is cautious and resists being exploited to the "fully responsible" victim who invites victimization. The latter end of the continuum can be expressed as a "victim-blaming" mentality (Croall, 2007). By failing to recognize that a free market economy embraces the concept of caveat emptor ("buyer beware"), victims could be viewed as insufficiently assessing risk prior to buying or investing in any product (Shichor, 1998). Moreover, the key motivation that is seen as animating white-collar victims is often greed (Trahan, Marquart, and Mullings, 2005; Shupe, 1991). It is in the pursuit of "exorbitant returns" and the "never-ending pursuit of money" entailed in the American

Dream that victims are brought to their "deserved" financial fate (Shupe, 1991; Trahan, Marquart, and Mullings, 2005). Finally, the fact that some victims, especially of investment frauds, are relatively affluent often means that there is even less sympathy for the harm they suffer. "They should have known better," seems to be the prevailing attitude. Once again, there is an element of truth in these views of victims, but it only seems to apply to *some* victims in *some* situations.

When one considers the victimization that occurs with environmental pollution, safety rules in the work setting, or food adulterants, choice plays a very minimal role in becoming a victim. Nobody can really expect that the ordinary person could check out potential risks in their environment, independently assess problems with existing safety precautions, or apply laboratory standards to all foods consumed. To entertain that image is to regard the human actor as a scientist who goes about his or her daily affairs with an attitude of doubt. As Harold Garfinkel (1963; 1967) showed many years ago, to take the scientific attitude out of the lab and into the real world profoundly disturbs the everyday processes of interaction and makes daily living anomic. The "rationality" of our action is severely limited in ordinary situations. Moreover, even with respect to such a rational activity as investing for one's retirement, it is reasonable to accept some statements made by investment agents at face value. After all, a typical investment prospectus will say that, "Past performance of the fund is not a guarantee of future results." In addition, there is evidence that investors who are risk-averse are carefully nurtured by fraudulent schemes (Shichor, Sechrest, and Doocy, 2001). One British investment fraud assuaged the concerns of potential investors by noting that the fund was "as safe as the Bank of England" (Levi, 2006: 1042). It is also probably inaccurate to think that investors necessarily pursue the highest return/highest risk option. Many seem to be more attracted to opportunities that are safe and show some balance of risk and return (Shupe, 1991; Shichor, Sechrest, and Doocy, 2001; Shover, Fox, and Mills, 1994).

In a broader sense, one can raise questions about how decisions on purchases or investments are actually made. Many of those decisions seem to be made on the basis of rational economic considerations. What is often described in the white-collar crime literature as greed approximates the model of rational economic decision-making—i.e., maximizing profit with some consideration to avoiding risk. This would seem to conform to the ideal of *homo economicus*. For example, the clients of one investment scam are described as having discussed their possible investment in a fraudulent scheme with others, including "experts" (Shichor, Sechrest, and Doocy, 2001). As many investment frauds and Ponzi schemes are known to work through affinity groups, people are encouraged to invest through those they trust. This often includes people of the same ethnic background, fellow employees, retirees, and church members and even religious officials (SEC, 2006; Shupe, 1991). Respect for authority, good citizenship, and compassion can also play a significant role in economic decisions (Titus, 2001).

Moreover, most fraudulent schemes have gone to great lengths to assure investors that their contributions are secure and their profits real. For example, Bernard L. Madoff Securities LLC, the recent and largest Ponzi scheme yet, was skillfully managed by Madoff and others. The investment fund began in the early 1990s and lasted for almost twenty years, using the authority of longevity to add to its reputation. As a one-time chair of NASDAQ, Madoff also had a solid personal reputation. He promised clients that he would invest in common stocks in the S&P 100 Index, but that he would outperform the index by a "split strike conversion" investment strategy. He made sure that reports to clients would closely mimic the price movements of the S&P 100 and sent false trading confirmations to clients. Madoff says that his clients had "no way of knowing by reviewing these documents that I had never engaged in transactions represented on the statements" (CNNMoney.com, 2009). Finally, when agencies, such as the Securities and Exchange Commission charged with investigating and certifying investment advisors, have put their stamp of approval on a business, consumers generally accept the approval as sufficient proof that the investments are real and safe. Madoff passed an SEC review in 2006. This vetting provided validation; some of the largest contributors to Madoff's fund were European banks and wealthy, sophisticated investors, such as Henry Kaufman, the former chief economist at Salomon Brothers (*Wall Street Journal*, 2009). With the success of a Ponzi scheme on the scale of the one perpetrated by Madoff, it is difficult to entertain the notion that investor/victims are typically so greedy that they ignore relevant risks.

A third generalization that is prominent in the literature on victims of white-collar crime is that they are very reluctant to report their victimization to authorities (Reisig and Holtfreter, 2007; Kane and Wall, 2006). This is attributed in part to the generally small losses sustained (Titus, Heinzelmann, and Boyle, 1995; Croall, 2001; Croall, 2009; Greenlee et al., 2007), the amount of time involved in complaints (Levi, 1992), the difficult prospect of getting any of one's losses returned (Shichor, Sechrest, and Doocy, 2001; Shover, Fox, and Mills, 1994; Nerenberg, 2000), and the lack of awareness as to the relevant agency that one should alert (Nerenberg, 2000). Michael Levi (1992: 192) provides support for the importance of the element of compensation. His research indicates that the most important motive for reporting frauds is to get the money back. One consequence of this concern for restitution is that well over half of those who have lost money do seem to attempt to get it back from credit card companies or the person or company involved in the fraud (Kane and Wall, 2006). Other reasons for not reporting have to do with the self-blame associated with having been victimized and the embarrassment of being duped (Levi, 1992; Shover, Fox, and Mills, 1994; Shichor, Sechrest, and Doocy, 2001). The organizational counterpart to this embarrassment is the attempt to avoid bad publicity. Nonprofit organizations, for example, fearing the impact of scandal on future donations, tend to avoid prosecuting smaller losses and those that are least likely to result in conviction; many losses are handled by internal discipline (Greenlee et al., 2007). For commercial organizations, it appears that larger frauds are the most likely to be publicly prosecuted (Levi, 1992). However, there are some indications that in one area, that of insurance companies dealing with consumer insurance fraud, there is a tendency to not wait for state enforcement; instead, these companies have greatly expanded their own anti-fraud activities (Lesch and Byars, 2008).

As noted, another relevant issue with regard to reporting fraud is the question of the proper agency for handling the complaint. Several surveys have found that substantial proportions of respondents did not know the relevant agency to which they should report an attempted fraud. A 1992 survey on telemarketing fraud found that only one-third of the sample knew whom to contact with respect to whether an offer was legitimate; later surveys found similarly that two-thirds of respondents could not name any agency protecting people from telephone fraud (Titus and Gover, 2001). Representatives of people responsible for preventing elder financial crime (local and federal law enforcement agencies, civil justice officials, and other elder advocates) admitted during a roundtable discussion that there are often overlapping spheres of legal responsibility that prevent effective protection (Nerenberg, 2000). The following were among the problems mentioned: an unclear line between civil and criminal matters, inadequate coordination of various jurisdictions of victims and offenders, lack of legal expertise on the part of local law enforcement, the complexity of the crimes entailing many victims, lax oversight of guardianship and restitution efforts, and the dissipation of assets as a case slowly moves through the legal system.

The lack of expertise element is also supported by a National White Collar Crime Center (NW3C, 2004) survey of local, state, and federal legal authorities and people involved in intellectual property-based commerce. Lack of understanding of "intellectual property rights" on the part of investigators, prosecutors and judges was cited as a central obstacle to enforcement. It is not surprising, then, that victims often do not find legal authorities to be helpful and fault them for efforts on behalf of the victim (Moore and Mills, 1990; Shichor, Sechrest, and Doocy, 2001). One Florida survey found that being a recent fraud victim was significantly associated with diminished confidence in legal authorities (Reisig and Holtfreter, 2007). Given the fact that state authorities have at times increased the sense of victimization of those who have experienced losses through fraud (Shover, Fox, and Mills, 1994), one more reason might be added to why white-collar victims may not report their victimization.

The Extent of White-Collar Victimization: Some Survey and Other Data

One important dimension to consider about white-collar crime is how pervasive it is. This is important not only for understanding the shifting contours of crime in American society but also for informing public decisions about where social control efforts should be directed. The two traditional government efforts at measuring the shape and size of criminal victimization are the Uniform Crime Reports (UCR) of the FBI and the National Crime Victimization Surveys (NCVS) done by Bureau of Justice Statistics. Because the NCVS uses information from victims, it would be an ideal tool for measuring white-collar victimization. Unfortunately, the survey focuses on traditional street crimes only and provides little or no useful information for our purposes. The UCR, by contrast, relies on reports provided by local law enforcement agencies about crimes, including arrestees, victims, etc. But, because most white-collar offenses are not reported to local law enforcement, the data are likely to be radically incomplete (Barnett, 2002). The implication of patterns of offense reporting is that most information about white-collar crime will inevitably have to be brought together from the diverse agencies that do supervise the prosecution of the variety of offenses that constitute white-collar crime.

The most useful source of information, however, does attempt to cover the whole gamut of white-collar victimization. Sponsored by the U.S. Department of Justice and carried out by the nonprofit organization, The National White Collar Crime Center (NW3C), the survey investigates white-collar crime by interviewing a nationally representative sample of U.S. adults who might have been victims of these crimes. In addition to investigating the experiences of victims, it inquires about their reporting of offenses to official and other agencies and about how seriously respondents view white-collar misdeeds. The most recent version of this survey was conducted in 2005 and is referred to as the National Public Survey on White Collar Crime (Kane and Wall, 2006). A most important finding of the survey was that, in the six years since the original NW3C survey, there was a notable increase in victimization, with 46.5% reporting a victim in the household versus 36% for the earlier period. Well over half of the respondents (62.5%) reported being a white-collar crime victim at some time in their lives. Not surprisingly, the strongest growth in offenses occurred with respect to Internet-mediated crime, including credit card fraud, monetary losses in cyberspace, and illegitimate e-mails. However, the traditional offenses such as "unnecessary repairs" were still fairly common, with the most common being "billed for a product or service at a price higher than originally quoted" (price lie). Among other significant findings was the small proportion (30%) of victims who reported the crime to authorities, the much larger group (57%) among the total sample who felt that the government should devote more resources to controlling white-collar crime, and the rating of several white-collar offenses as more serious than acts of nonlethal violence.

While the NW3C data above give a good sense of the perspective of victims, it is also possible to look at white-collar crime victimization through official sources. In addition to the violent and property offenses contained in Part I of the Uniform Crime Reports, the FBI also gathers arrest data on some of the offenses commonly seen as white-collar crimes. Three of these Part II offenses are relevant here: embezzlement, forgery/counterfeiting, ar.d fraud. Because the number of agencies contributing to the UCR data has fluctuated annually by as much as 20%, precise estimates of these offenses are not possible. However, there are about 13–14,000 arrests for embezzlement each year; about 85–90,000 arrests for forgery/counterfeiting; and about 200-300,000 arrests for fraud each year (NW3C, 2008). In addition, the Transactional Records Access Clearinghouse (TRAC) site at Syracuse University provides information about federal white-collar prosecutions from all of the major U.S. government agencies. Over the past twenty years, the number of these prosecutions has varied between 8–10,000, with the peak being in the mid-1990s. The offenses currently most commonly prosecuted at the federal level are defrauding a financial institution and identity theft (TRAC, 2009). While each of these sources gives only limited information about the extent of white-collar victimization, they seem to confirm the observations that many victims do not report offenses to authorities and, further, that many cases are not fully prosecuted.

While not encompassing all white-collar crime, other surveys have focused on consumer fraud and identity theft. The consumer fraud surveys sponsored by the Federal Trade Commission provide insight on the extent of one kind of white-collar crime victimization. The most recent survey, administered in late 2005, inquired about the consumer/victim experiences in a nationally representative sample of 3808 U.S. adults (Anderson, 2007). Researchers found that 13.5% of respondents (equivalent to 30.2 million consumers) had been victimized in the previous year by one of the fourteen specific or two more general frauds covered by the survey. Since respondents on average experienced 1.6 incidents in the prior year, the total number of incidents (extrapolating from the sample to the U.S. population) was 48.7 million. The most common frauds were paying for something never received (3.1% of the sample, equal to 6.9 million U.S. consumers) and being billed for a product not purchased (2.4% of respondents, or 5.2 million consumers). Although most of the dollar losses were small, generally under $100, there was an increase between 2003 and 2005 in the percentage of victims who paid for something they never received.

With respect to identity theft, the Federal Trade Commission has found it to be the most widely reported white-collar offense, with 312,000 complaints registered in 2008 (FTC, 2009). Separate surveys by the FTC have found that an estimated 8–10 million U.S. adults feel that they have been identity theft victims (Synovate, 2003; Synovate, 2007). A recent initiative toward including identity theft issues in the National Crime Victimization Survey, the first such "white-collar offense" to be included in this survey of record, found that 3% of U.S. households (approximately 3.6 million households) had experienced identity theft in the previous 6-month period (Baum, 2006).

As noted in our introductory remarks, organizations can also be victims of white-collar crime. Of course, organizations are typically collective proxies for some other group that has a claim on the assets of the organization. For business entities, this is usually either private owners or stockholders. In the case of government, successful frauds against the organization are reflected in losses to the taxpayers. For nonprofits, any losses sustained through fraud or theft has an impact on the population the charitable organization intends to serve. Nevertheless, when the loss occurs in the context of the organization, the offense often falls under the heading of occupational fraud, where the offender misuses organizational resources for his/her personal advantage. This kind of offense has been the central focus of the periodic *Report to the Nation on Occupational Fraud and Abuse* produced by the Association of Certified Fraud Examiners (ACFE). The most recent *Report* was published in 2008 and was compiled from 959 cases of occupational fraud investigated by ACFE over a 26-month period. Parallel to the Uniform Crime Reports of the FBI, this report uses "crimes reported" as its data, while recognizing that much occupational fraud is never reported or is handled internally by the organization (ACFE, 2008). This selection bias has to be kept in mind when noting the apparent costliness of the occupational frauds studied. The median loss was $175,000; in one-quarter of the cases, the losses were at least $1 million. Again, based on the cases they have seen, the CFEs who contributed to this report estimate that about 7% of annual organizational revenue is lost to fraud. When applied to the Gross Domestic Product of the U.S., this would amount to $994 billion in losses. The most common occupational offenses within organizations were corruption (bribery, conflicts of interest, illegal gratuities, etc.) and fraudulent billing. The most likely victims of such fraud were smaller companies, those privately held, and those involved in banking and financial services. However, the largest median losses ($800,000) were sustained by organizations in the field of telecommunications. In spite of the problems of sample selection bias, the 2008 ACFE *Report* provides the best available insight into organizational victims of white-collar crime.

Explaining White-Collar Crime Victimization

An important consideration in understanding any crime is the range of factors that seem to be related to victimization. This is crucial not only to a full account of the occurrence of the offense, but also to societal efforts made to identify vulnerabilities and prevent or control that crime. In light of this, many studies of white-collar crime have attempted to delineate the characteristics of victims as well as looking at any other facilitants of the criminal activity. The task of specifying the distinctive demographic or other characteristics of victims is not a simple one, especially since the quality of data on victims varies significantly. Moreover, the wide variation among white-collar offenses and the attendant variety of victims adds to the complexity. The preferred data would be a nationally representative sample that included non-victims as well as victims. Some research derives from this kind of sampling; most does not. When the research begins with a population of victims, several issues can be raised about how useful it is. The first problem is that no population includes *all* victims, since, as noted above, victims are often not aware of being victimized at all or may consider the harm so small as to ignore their victim status. Then, whatever the population of victims might be, what kind of bias comes into play when drawing a sample for purposes of research? From all the available or identified victims, who will decide to participate? Who will refuse to do so? What are the differences between these two groups? Similar problems, though perhaps more serious, arise from using a sample of complainants. How do these complainants differ from victims in general? For example, if there are indeed some 8–10 million victims of identity theft, what conclusions can one draw about their demographic makeup based on a thousand cases of complaints? There are other lessons to be gained from studying the experiences of complainants, but ascertaining victim characteristics may not be that useful.

There are several surveys based on nationally representative samples that can be very helpful in ascertaining victim characteristics. One of these is the "National Public Survey on White Collar Crime" mentioned above. Having assessed several variables as predictors of victimization, their results are mixed. In predicting individual victimization in the prior year, the only significant relationships were with use of the Internet and residing in an urban area. When the focus shifts to lifetime individual victimization, the variables that proved to be important, along with Internet use, were being white, being male, and having a higher income. When the concern shifts to a person being victimized more than once over their lifetime, the predictor variables of greatest significance are being non-white, being older and Internet use. The only common factor here is utilizing the Internet. This is not particularly surprising since many of the eleven white-collar victimization opportunities used in the survey were likely to come to the victim through the Internet. More important, however, is the observation made by the authors of the survey that white-collar crime is such a heterogeneous category that it is perhaps unrealistic to expect much consistency in the pattern of victim characteristics. The best chance of finding such patterns may call for examining more narrowly defined crime types (Kane and Wall, 2006: 13).

If we compare the 21 offenses comprising "personal fraud" in one survey (Titus, Heinzelmann, and Boyle, 1995) with the 16 offenses comprising "consumer fraud" in a Federal Trade Commission survey (Anderson, 2007), we do find considerable overlap in crime categories. Many of the same offenses (e.g., work-at-home schemes, free prizes, credit repair, membership billing, price fraud, etc.) appear in both surveys; the major differences between the offenses were the result of differences in the time frames in which they were completed (the Titus, Heinzelmann, and Boyle research was done in 1991, while the Federal Trade Commission research was done in 2005). Given the similarity of offenses in these nationally representative surveys, what are their findings on victim characteristics?

The 1991 research (Titus, Heinzelmann, and Boyle, 1995) found only two victim characteristics that were linked to the experience of victimization. One of these was age, with older people being likely to have few or no contacts with fraudsters. Second, with respect to education, those at the extremes of education (no high school diploma, graduate college degree) were least vulnerable to fraud. However, once a person with these characteristics did encounter a fraud attempt, the age or educational factor did not protect them from succumbing to the attempt.

The Federal Trade Commission survey (Anderson, 2007) found that Hispanics and African-Americans were more likely to experience frauds but that these differences disappeared once age, education, and comfort with debt were brought into consideration. Specifically, the minority samples tended to be younger, had less education, and reported having more debt than they could handle. These three elements were associated with experiencing more fraud. In addition, older consumers were less likely to be victims of the frauds covered by the research. These studies together seem to confirm, with some minor differences, that age and education are two of the key variables in explaining victimization.

Identity theft is another white-collar offense that has received sustained attention by researchers. Unfortunately, the nationally representative study of identity theft commissioned by the FTC (Synovate, 2007) did not attempt to break down the results by victim categories. However, the study on identity theft carried out by the Bureau of Justice Statistics (Baum, 2006) as a component of the NCVS, did look at victim characteristics. Specifically, it was found that identity theft was more likely among households headed by the youngest group (18–24), by the those in the highest income category ($75,000+), and by urban/suburban rather than rural households.

Other researchers have made arguments about victim characteristics that they think are particularly important. For example, there have been a number of papers written on the distinctive victimization of women in white-collar crime (Gerber and Weeks, 1992; Szockyj and Fox, 1996; Croall, 2001). However, these arguments are often punctuated by qualifications noting that men, too, have been perhaps equally victimized. For instance, in discussing lax safety for women working in sweatshops, Jurg Gerber and Susan Weeks (1992: 331) mention that "the victims of the resulting accidents have been women and men alike." Hazel Croall (2001: 70), in discussing workplace harms to women, adds, "This is not to underestimate the dangers to male workers . . . indeed, most victims of death in the workplace . . . have been men . . ." It is certainly true that decisions about controlling female fertility or enhancing feminine attractiveness are especially going to impact women as consumers. Yet, this observation does not show gender to be a key factor across a wide range of white-collar crimes.

Beyond the case for women, parallel claims have been made about other distinctive groups of victims. Anson Shupe (1991: 45), for one, suggests that Mormons are "particularly gullible" when they encounter fraudulent business schemes. His suggestion is that the Mormon emphasis on material success and trust in fellow Mormons, sometimes to the point of being naive, "set them up to be duped" (48). This line of analysis seems to ignore the role that affinity groups play in both legitimate and illegitimate investment schemes. Insofar as people make choices in economic matters, they tend to rely on those they know and trust in making those decisions. Sometimes those who are trusted do not deserve that trust. Both gender and religion seem to fit well with particular cases of white-collar crime but do not really reflect any essential vulnerability or causal factors for white-collar crime victimization in general. Their role in a "lifestyle exposure" or "routine activities" approach to victimization (Miethe and Meier, 1994) does seem worth exploring.

The Impact of White-Collar Crime

Another matter that needs to be addressed is that of the consequences of white-collar offenses in the lives of victims. As noted above, the typical effect of white-collar crime is a small loss, often unrecognized, that is spread over a large number of victims. For the offender, the result may represent substantial cost-savings, income, or profit, in spite of the apparently negligible impact on individual victims. In looking, then, at the forms and magnitude of the losses suffered by victims, it will be important to consider whether the individual impact is as small as expected. In our discussion of the harm experienced by victims, it will be useful to distinguish the personal from the organizational and societal impact. David Shichor (1989) has shown the application of Sellin and Wolfgang's (1964) classification of victims of conventional crime—primary (personal), secondary (organizational) and tertiary (societal)—to white-collar crime. Yet, whether the organization is a profit-oriented corporation, a government entity, or a charitable nonprofit, the ultimate victim of fraud or other white-collar crimes usually has to be seen at the individual level. In other words, a corporation may suffer direct financial harm, but stockholders are the ultimate though indirect victims. Or, governments may be the immediate and direct victims of fraud or corruption, but taxpayers or citizens pay the eventual price of those offenses. In the discussion that follows, the concern will be for the types of harms resulting from white-collar crimes, the size of that victimization, and the impact at different personal and organizational levels.

If homicide and assault are considered the most serious offenses due to their harms to life and limb, it is not difficult to find parallel white-collar offenses that must be considered equally grave as threats to health. While common fraud is unlikely to be the underlying offense leading to life-threatening victim costs, one can identify dangerous products and practices being promulgated with accompanying violations of trust that well illustrate the potential hazards of white-collar crime. Foremost among these instances is tobacco use, which has for decades been marketed by corporations that denied the scientific evidence of the harms of smoking. Such public denials by tobacco executives of the addictive and harmful nature of smoking were made even as internal documents of their companies portrayed a different reality. Tobacco officials knew nicotine to be addictive, made sure it was a sufficiently potent ingredient, and refused to consider removing cancer-causing and other harmful components delivered by cigarettes (Rosoff, Pontell, and Tillman, 2002). The sad result is that tobacco use is the leading preventable cause of mortality in the United States—over 400,000 deaths annually (CDC, 2009).

Similar, yet smaller, outcomes appear when one looks at the marketing of the antidepressant, Prozac. The manufacturer of this medication, Eli Lilly, had done research in the late 1980s that showed increased activation for users of the drug, when compared to more conventional antidepressants. This activation is thought to increase anxiety, agitation, and hostility. Yet, when compared to other similar drugs, Prozac was also known to increase suicide attempts. When Joseph Wesbecker, a patient taking Prozac, killed eight people and then himself, Lilly suppressed their research on the negative effects of the drug. Indeed, when it emerged again in 2005, the pages of the research were stamped "CONFIDENTIAL" and "FENTRESS," the name of one of Wesbecker's victims (Watkins, 2005). One research psychopharmacologist, Dr. David Healy, suggests that Prozac is responsible for thousands of suicides (Giombetti, 2002).

The tobacco and antidepressant cases are unusual in their toll on health. The more common physical impact of white-collar offenses occurs in a localized or time-limited crisis, with a much smaller cost to life and health. For example, workplace injuries and even death may occur at one site or during a particular period; however, as the harm increases, the prospect of financial or legal costs or bad publicity make it clear that practices and products must be revised or removed. Or, products, once launched into the marketplace, may be found to have harmful defects. While their withdrawal may be resisted at first by the sponsoring corporation, eventually the costs make clear that this is the only feasible strategy.

Two cases illustrate the process. In 1980 Procter & Gamble, one of the largest consumer products companies in the U.S., began wide distribution of a new kind of superabsorbent tampon made out of synthetics rather than cotton like its competitors. This product, called Rely, had been test-marketed for five years, during which time Procter & Gamble had received 100 complaints per month about problems associated with use. Most troublesome ultimately were the cases of toxic shock syndrome, leading to about 50 deaths and over a thousand nonfatal illnesses shortly after the wide introduction of the product to consumers in early 1980. Under threat from the federal Centers for Disease Control and the Food and Drug Administration, Procter & Gamble withdrew Rely from the market in September of 1980 (Rosoff, Pontell, and Tillman, 2002). In the second case, the Ford Motor Company introduced the Pinto into the subcompact automobile market in the 1970s. Prior to production the company became aware of a problem with the fuel system which could lead to fiery explosions in the event of a rear-end collision. Rather than investing $11 per car to fix the design flaw, Ford executives decided it would be more cost-effective to pay claims against the company (at $200,000 per death and $67,000 per injury) for crashes than to retool production. Not only were their liability estimates starkly awry (one serious injury case alone resulted in a $127 million award), but the U.S. Department of Transportation concluded that the Pinto was unsafe and had to be recalled.

While not perhaps as important as the impact to health and life, the financial costs of white-collar crime are substantial. Moreover, because these latter harms are commonly stated in terms of currency (usually, dollars or pounds), they permit the easier comparison of "suite" and "street" offenses. As noted earlier, the typical loss is small and adds up significantly over hundreds, thousands, or even millions of cases. A study, cited earlier, of white-collar crime victimization using a representative sample found that the mean loss per episode of personal fraud was $216 (Titus, Heinzelmann, and Boyle, 1995). However, when projected to the U.S. population, the collective loss was about $40 billion. The Federal Trade Commission (Anderson, 2007) arrived at similar estimates more than a decade later. Most fraud victims had small losses, generally under $500 and a median loss of only $60. Yet, when multiplied by over 30 million victims and 48 million incidents nationally, the loss estimate balloons into the billions. The study on identity theft showed the mean loss of all cases to be $1,290, with a median loss of $400 (Baum, 2006). On a national scale, this projects to $3.2 billion.

Other national estimates of financial harm are somewhat higher. For instance, the U.S. Chamber of Commerce produced a figure as early as the mid-1970s of $40 billion lost to a range of what are predominantly white-collar offenses (Rosoff, Pontell, and Tillman, 2002). At about the same time, Congressional estimates of white-collar crime costs, excluding safety and environmental harms, were about $75–100 billion. If we take inflation into account, the current losses would exceed $200 billion. Limiting the scope of losses just to telemarketing fraud, the suspected loss in 1995 was already up to $40 billion. Compared to the $3.2 billion cited above for identity theft costs, the Federal Trade Commission arrived at a figure of $15.6 billion lost to identity theft in 2006 (Synovate, 2007). In a separate analysis, Kip Schlegel (2000) suggests that as much as a trillion dollars of white-collar crime occurs annually in the U.S. The wide variation in these estimates done by different agencies and experts in different eras shows the considerable degree of imprecision that characterizes such studies. However, what seems undeniable is that the cost of white-collar crime to individuals is greater than that which accompanies conventional crime. For example, one early attempt to assess the total cost of conventional crime found that combined losses from property theft and damage, cash losses, medical expenses, wages foregone by virtue of being a victim of all traditional crimes except homicide came to an aggregate figure of $17.6 billion (Klaus, 1994). A more recent report by the FBI (2008) on crime in the U.S. showed that the direct amount lost due to all property crimes in 2007 was $17.6 billion.

When the focus shifts from the impact of white-collar crime on individuals to its impact on organizations, the waters become much more difficult to navigate. There are few sample surveys that produce neat proportions of those victimized and those untouched by fraud. Nor does there seem to be the same kind of transparency in agency reports of organizational victims. Part of this may reflect the complex nature of the fraudulent schemes used against organizations; rarely are these offenses as simple as the "false advertising" or "unnecessary repairs" to which individuals succumb. A second reason is the reluctance of businesses or nonprofits to subject their losses to public view. Government's losses may be more publicly documented, but there remains an issue of the proportion of those harms that are actually discovered. Finally, there is also the problem of readily identifying the level of victim where the greatest harm is suffered. For instance, in securities and investment fraud we have noted that, though businesses may suffer losses, the ultimate though indirect victims are investors. Yet, investors themselves are often other organizations, e.g., pension funds, investor groups, banks, charitable agencies. A glance at the list of victims of Bernard Madoff's hedge fund shows numerous European banks with losses in the millions (*Wall Street Journal*, 2009). In some instances, also, the harm is shared by individuals and organizations, e.g., if identity theft entails credit card losses, the individual may be liable for the first $50, then the card issuer absorbs the remaining loss.

One of the rare sample studies that investigated corporate victims found that in the previous five years one-third of the largest U.K. companies had experienced a loss of at least £50,000; the average loss among this subsample was over £200,000 (Levi, 1992). These losses may seem great, but Levi does add the cogent point that these losses have to be seen in light of the large resources available to these corporations. In an international sample, it was further reported that three-fourths of the corporate respondents had suffered a loss through fraud in the previous five years; one-fourth of these victims lost more that US$1 million in total over that period (Levi, 2001). Probably the best information source on fraud and its costs to organizations in the U.S. is the *2008 Report to the Nation On Occupational Fraud and Abuse* of the Association of Certified Fraud Examiners (ACFE, 2008). To assess the costs of fraud, the Report asked the CFEs who participated in their survey to estimate how much loss to fraud occurred in the economy. Based on their first-hand knowledge of fraudulent cases, these participants opine that about 7% of the economy entailed fraud; this would amount to about $994 billion. This estimate is clearly weakened by being based on a 6% response rate (959 of 16,606 distributed) and soliciting an opinion about a factual matter. Yet, the Report is more valuable on other counts, especially the description of the CFEs recent cases. It tells us, for example, that the frequency of fraud is greater in private than public companies and that the losses are larger in business than they are in government or nonprofits. The median loss for private companies was $248,000, while the median loss for government was $100,000.

Other agencies provide partial insights on the problem of white-collar crimes in selected areas of the economy. For example, the FBI suggests that about $2 billion is lost annually to fraud against financial institutions; this derives from check fraud, check kiting, counterfeit checks, counterfeit negotiable instruments, and mortgage loan fraud (FBI, 2007). On a larger scale, estimates of the loss to health care fraud for 2003 range from $51 billion to $171 billion (NW3C 2008). The immediate victims here are the government (i.e., taxpayers) or insurance companies (i.e., shareholders). Also relatively high are the estimates of insurance fraud committed by consumers against the property-casualty insurers. The losses here were estimated to be about $20 billion in the mid-1990s (Lesch and Byars, 2008). In general, then, losses by organizations to white-collar offenses seem to be widely variable. However, by most standards the losses are substantial and are likely to have a negative effect on the economy as a whole.

In addition to the health and financial harms, there are psychological and social costs associated with white-collar crime. Although the emotional effects of victimization are quite variable, several studies have documented serious trauma for significant proportions of victims. Perhaps the most common reaction where some degree of victim facilitation occurs was self-blame, embarrassment, and a loss of self-esteem (Shichor, Sechrest, and Doocy, 2001; Levi, 2001; Shover, Fox, and Mills, 1994). Yet, the self-blaming does not preclude considerable anger and disappointment about their predicament (Shichor, Sechrest, and Doocy, 2001; Pontell, Brown, and Tosouni, 2008). Where the victim is less likely to be responsible for their losses, such as the case of identity theft, the response is more likely to entail psychological stress. The central precipitants of stress with respect to identity theft are the extensive time and effort needed to resolve unforeseen problems, the feelings of "violation," and the experience of harassment by credit agencies (Pontell, Brown, and Tosouni, 2008; Newman and McNally, 2005; Synovate, 2007). It is interesting that these psychological effects can be relatively long-lasting (Shover, Fox, and Mills, 1994) and be unrelated to whether financial compensation was awarded (Levi, 1992). In terms of mental health consequences, studies have shown that the stress of victimization can lead to depression and anxiety (Ganzini, McFarland, and Bloom, 1990).

Among the social costs of white-collar crime, the harm most frequently investigated by researchers is the loss of faith in economic and governmental leaders. While it is true that victims have little or no confidence in the organization that exploited them and want to see them punished (Shichor, Sechrest, and Doocy, 2001), this does not seem to generalize to other financial or commercial institutions. In part, this seems to be related to the self-blame noted above and the tendency to personalize responsibility for the fraud (Shover, Fox, and Mills, 1994). This may, however, be changing if public opinion polling is any indication. Recent polling on corporations and their executives show a decline in public esteem. "Big business" is ranked second from the bottom among sixteen institutions when the public is asked about their level of confidence in segments of American society (Cullen, Hartman, and Jonson, 2008). Another poll found that two-thirds of respondents felt that most corporate executives were "dishonest" and a slightly higher percentage felt that executives deserved a lot of the blame for "recent corporate scandals" (Cullen, Hartman, and Jonson, 2008). Government and other institutions of control and enforcement tend to get somewhat negative assessments as well. The immediate agency dealt with in the course of the fraud gets generally low marks (Reisig and Holtfreter, 2007; Shover, Fox, and Mills, 1994; Newman and McNally, 2005). However, this negative view of government may be getting more generalized. One of the victims of the Madoff Investment fraud said, "It feels like a nightmare that we can't wake up from. SIPC [Securities Investor Protection Corporation] insurance has been refused, we have been threatened with 'clawback suits' . . . . We have lost all faith in our government, in the ability of the SEC to honestly regulate the securities markets, in the integrity of . . . our elected representatives who . . . advocated deregulating Wall Street" (McCoy, 2009).

Conclusion

If one element of white-collar crime seems most notable today, it is the growth that is occurring in this area. First, the growth is apparent in certain indicators of increasing criminality, including: significant and sometimes dramatic hikes in mortgage fraud (FBI, 2009), credit card fraud and associated losses (Kane and Wall, 2006; Newman and McNally, 2005), corporate fraud (Kane and Wall 2006), Internet crime (Internet Crime Complaint Center, 2009), consumer fraud (FTC, 2008), identity theft (FTC, 2009), and general white-collar crime (Kane and Wall, 2006). While there is considerable overlap in these statistical measures, the underlying reality is one of growth. In addition to increasing numbers, it seems that the each new "worst case" that comes along quickly trumps the previous record. Ponzi schemes were believed to be of limited duration and to involve losses in millions of dollars (Rosoff, Pontell, and Tillman, 2002) until the Madoff debacle, which lasted over two decades with tens of billions lost. Moreover, the taxpayer bailout of the recent mortgage meltdown, fueled in part by fraud (HUD, 2009) makes the Savings and Loan crisis of the late 1980s pale by comparison. Another expression of growth can be found in new technologies and economic trends as sources of new opportunities for white-collar offenses. The advent of computers and other new modes of communication, Internet commerce, and economic globalization all contribute to linking with new potential victims for possible exploitation. Finally, along with the other forms of growth, there seems to be a growing public awareness of the threats of white-collar crime and a developing consciousness of its perpetrators (Cullen, Hartman, and Jonson, 2008).

Even though victimization has been extended in the forms noted above, there does not appear to be a parallel concern with effectively controlling or preventing this predation. Instead, the most common patterns seen are that victims do not know to whom they can turn for help, do not get the kind of assistance they seek, and control agencies often seem to make things worse (Nerenberg 2000; Shichor, Sechrest, and Doocy, 2001; Shover, Fox, and Mills, 1994). The result is that the majority of victims do not report their victimization to a crime control agency (Kane and Wall, 2006). Although certain federal agencies such as the FBI, SEC and the FTC have recently become more active on the enforcement front, there is a need for more assistance at the level of local and state law enforcement and coordination of agency efforts (Nerenberg, 2000). Moreover, it should be possible to develop some "best practices" that could be disseminated in order to control white-collar victimization. For example, it appears that frauds are more likely to be discovered and ultimately controlled through "tips" that insiders can provide (ACFE, 2008; Leap, 2007). Since this kind of whistle-blowing is not widespread or generally accepted in organizations, some consideration should be given to how corporate and governmental cultures might be shifted toward providing a more favorable climate for this control mechanism. Until the efforts of social control come to match the increasing concern on the part of the public and the increasing attention of the media, white-collar victimization will continue to ravage modern society.

REFERENCES

Anderson, Keith B. (2007). *Consumer Fraud in the United States: The Second FTC Survey.* Washington, DC: Federal Trade Commission.

Association of Certified Fraud Examiners, Inc. (2008). *Report to the Nation on Occupational Fraud and Abuse.* Austin, TX: Association of Certified Fraud Examiners, Inc.

Barnett, Cynthia. (2002). "Measurement of White-Collar Crime Using Uniform Crime Reporting (UCR) Data." Washington DC: Federal Bureau of Investigation.

Baum, Katrina. (2006). *Identity Theft 2004: First Estimates from the National Crime Victimization Survey.* Washington, DC: Bureau of Justice Statistics.

CDC. (2009). "Tobacco-Related Mortality." Smoking and Tobacco Use Fact Sheet. Atlanta, GA: Centers for Disease Control and Prevention.

CNNMoney.com. (2009). "Read What Madoff Told The Judge." March 12, 2009. Retrieved from http://money.cnn.com/2009/03/12/news/newsmakers/madoff_transcript/index.htm

Croall, Hazel. (2001). *Understanding White Collar Crime.* Buckingham, England: Open University Press.

———. (2007). "Victims of White-Collar and Corporate Crime." In Pamela Davis, Peter Francis, and Chris Greer (Eds.), *Victims, Crime, and Society* (pp. 78–108). Los Angeles: Sage Publications.

———. (2009). "White Collar Crime, Consumers and Victimization." *Crime, Law and Social Change* 51: 127–146.

Cullen, Francis T., Jennifer L. Hartman, and Cheryl Lero Jonson. (2008). "Bad Guys: Why the Public Supports Punishing White-Collar Offenders." *Crime, Law and Social Change* 51: 31–44.

Erikson, Kai T. (1976). *Everything in its Path: Destruction of Community in the Buffalo Creek Flood.* New York: Simon and Schuster.

FBI. (2007). "Financial Institution Fraud and Failure Report: Fiscal Years (FY) 2006 and 2007." Washington, DC: Federal Bureau of Investigation.

———. (2008). "Property Crime." *Uniform Crime Report: Crime in the United States, 2007.* Washington, DC: Federal Bureau of Investigation.

———. (2009). "2008 Mortgage Fraud Report: Year in Review." Washington, DC: Federal Bureau of Investigation.

FTC. (2008). "FTC Releases List of Top Consumer Fraud Complaints in 2007." Washington, DC: Federal Trade Commission. Retrieved from http://www.ftc.gov/opa/2008/02/fraud.shtm

———. (2009). *Consumer Sentinel Network Data Book for January–December 2008.* Washington, DC: Federal Trade Commission.

Friedrichs, David O. (2010). *Trusted Criminals: White Collar Crime in Contemporary Society*, 4th ed. Belmont, CA: Wadsworth Cengage Learning.

Ganzini, Linda, Bentson McFarland, and Joseph Bloom. (1990). "Victims of Fraud: Comparing Victims of White Collar and Violent Crime." *Bulletin of the American Academy of Psychiatry and Law* 18: 55–63.

Garfinkel, Harold. (1963). "A Conception of, and Experiments with, 'Trust' as a Condition of Stable Concerted Actions." In O. J. Harvey (Ed.), *Motivation and Social Interaction* (pp. 187–238). New York: Ronald Press.

———. (1967). *Studies in Ethnomethodology.* Englewood Cliffs, NJ: Prentice-Hall.

Gerber, Jurg, and Susan L. Weeks. (1992). "Women as Victims of Corporate Crime: A Call for Research on a Neglected Topic." *Deviant Behavior* 13: 325–347.

Giombetti, Rick. (2002). "Prozac, Suicide and Dr. Healy." *Counterpunch* March 20. Retrieved from http://www.counterpunch.org/prozacsuicide.html

Greenlee, Janet, Mary Fischer, Teresa Gordon, and Elizabeth Keating. (2007). "An Investigation of Fraud in Nonprofit Organizations: Occurrences and Deterrents." *Voluntary Sector Quarterly* 36: 676–694.

Holtfreter, Kristy. (2005). "Is Occupational Fraud 'Typical' White-Collar Crime? A Comparison of Individual and Organizational Characteristics." *Journal of Criminal Justice* 33: 353–365.

HUD. (2009). "Interim Report to the Congress on the Root Cause of the Foreclosure Crisis." Washington, DC: Housing and Urban Development. Retrieved from http://www.huduser.org/Publications/PDF/int_Foreclosure_rpt_congress.pdf

Internet Crime Complaint Center. (2009). "2008 Internet Crime Report." Washington, DC: Internet Crime Complaint Center. Retrieved from http://www.ic3.gov/media/annualreport/2008_IC3Report.pdf

Kane, John, and April D. Wall. (2006). *The 2005 National Public Survey on White Collar Crime.* Fairmont, WV: National White Collar Crime Center.

Karmen, Andrew. (2010). *Crime Victims: An Introduction to Victimology*, 7th ed. Belmont CA: Wadsworth Cengage Learning.

Klaus, Patsy A. (1994, February). "The Costs of Crime to Victims: Crime Data Brief." Washington, DC: Bureau of Justice Statistics, NCJ 145865. Retrieved from http://bjs.ojp.usdoj.gov/content/pub/ascii/COCTV.TXT

Leap, Terry L. (2007). *Dishonest Dollars: The Dynamics of White Collar Crime.* Ithaca, NY: Cornell University Press.

Lesch, William C., and Bruce Byars. (2008). "Consumer Insurance Fraud in the US Property-Casualty Industry." *Journal of Financial Crimes* 15: 411–431.

Levi, Michael. (1992). "White Collar Crime Victimization." In Kip Schlegel and David Weisburd (Eds.), *White Collar Crime Reconsidered* (pp. 169–193). Boston, MA: Northeastern University Press.

———. (2001). "Transnational White-Collar Crime: Some Explorations of Victim Impact." In Henry N. Pontell and David Shichor (Eds.) *Contemporary Issues in Crime and Criminal Justice: Essays in Honor of Gilbert Geis* (pp. 341–359). Upper Saddle River, NJ: Prentice-Hall.

———. (2006). "The Media Construction of Financial White-Collar Crimes." *The British Journal of Criminology* 46(6): 1037–1057.

McCoy, Kevin. (2009). "Ponzi Victims' Anger Now Shifts from Madoff to SEC, SIPC." *USA Today*, June 29, 2009. Retrieved from http://www.usatoday.com/money/industries/brokerage/2009-06-29-madoff-victims-outrage-sec-sipc_N.htm

Miethe, Terance D., and Robert F. Meier. (1994). *Crime and Its Social Context: Toward an Integrated Theory of Offenders, Victims, and Situations.* Albany: State University of New York Press.

Mokhiber, Russell. (1988). *Corporate Crime and Violence: Big Business Power and the Abuse of the Public Trust.* San Francisco: Sierra Club Books.

Moore, Elizabeth, and Michael Mills. (1990). "The Neglected Victims and Unexamined Costs of White Collar Crime." *Crime & Delinquency* 36: 408–418.

NW3C. (2004). "Intellectual Property and White-Collar Crime: Report of Issues, Trends and Problems for Future Research." Fairmont, WV: National White Collar Crime Center. Retrieved from http://www.ncjrs.gov/pdffiles1/nij/grants/208135.pdf

———. (2008). "White Collar Crime Statistics." Fairmont, WV: National White Collar Crime Center. Retrieved from http://www.nw3c.org/research/site_files.cfm?mode=r

Nerenberg, Lisa. (2000). "Forgotten Victims of Financial Crime and Abuse: Facing the Challenge." *Journal of Elder Abuse and Neglect* 12: 49–74.

Newman, Graeme R., and Megan M. McNally. (2005). *Identity Theft Literature Review.* Washington, DC: National Institute of Justice.

Pontell, Henry N., Gregory C. Brown, and Anastasia Tosouni. (2008). "Stolen Identities: A Victim Survey." *Crime Prevention Studies* 23: 57–85.

Reisig, Michael D., and Kristy Holtfreter. (2007). "Fraud Victimization and Confidence in Florida's Legal Authorities." *Journal of Financial Crime* 14: 113–126.

Rosoff, Stephen M., Henry N. Pontell, and Robert Tillman. (2002). *Profit Without Honor: White-Collar Crime and the Looting of America.* Upper Saddle River, NJ: Prentice Hall.

Schlegel, Kip. (2000). "Transnational Crime: Implications for Local Law Enforcement." *Journal of Contemporary Criminal Justice* 16: 365–385.

Securities and Exchanges Commission SEC. (2006). "Affinity Fraud: How to Avoid Investment Scams that Target Groups." Retrieved from http://www.sec.gov/investor/pubs/affinity.htm

Sellin, Thorsten, and Marvin E. Wolfgang. (1964). *The Measurement of Delinquency.* New York: Wiley.

Shapiro, Susan P. (1990). "Collaring the Crime, Not the Criminal: Reconsidering the Concept of White-Collar Crime." *American Sociological Review* 55: 346–365.

Shichor, David. (1989). "Corporate Deviance and Corporate Victimization: A Review and Some Elaborations." *International Review of Victimology* 1: 67–88.

———. (1998). "Victimology and the Victims of White Collar Crime." In Hans-Dieter Schwind, Edwin Kube, and Hans-Heiner Kuehne (Eds.), *Festschrift fuer Hans Joachim Schneider* (pp. 332–351). Berlin: Walter De Gruyter.

Shichor, David, Dale Sechrest, and Jeff Doocy. (2001). "Victims of Investment Fraud." In Henry N. Pontell and David Shichor (Eds.), *Contemporary Issues in Crime and Criminal Justice: Essays in Honor of Gilbert Geis* (pp. 81–96). Upper Saddle River, NJ: Prentice-Hall.

Shover, Neal, and Francis Cullen. (2008). "Studying and Teaching White-Collar Crime: Populist and Patrician Perspectives." *Journal of Criminal Justice Education* 19: 155–174.

Shover, Neal, Greer L. Fox, and Michael Mills. (1994). "Long-Term Consequences of Victimization by White-Collar Crime." *Justice Quarterly* 11: 75–98.

Shupe, Anson. (1991). *The Darker Side of Virtue: Corruption, Scandal, and the Mormon Empire.* Buffalo, NY: Prometheus Books.

Sutherland, Edwin H. (1940). "White-Collar Criminality." *American Sociological Review* 5: 1–12.

Synovate. (2003). *Federal Trade Commission 2003 Identity Theft Survey report.* McLean, VA: Synovate.

———. (2007). *Federal Trade Commission 2006 Identity Theft Survey Report.* Mclean, VA: Synovate.

Szockyj, Elizabeth, and James G. Fox. (1996). *Corporate Victimization of Women.* Boston: Northeastern University Press.

Titus, Richard M. (2001). "Personal Fraud and Its Victims." In Neal Shover and John Paul Wright (Eds.), *Crimes of Privilege: Readings in White-Collar Crime* (pp. 57–67). New York: Oxford.

Titus, Richard M., and Angela R. Gover. (2001). "Personal Fraud: The Victims and the Scams." *Crime Prevention Studies* 12: 133–152.

Titus, Richard M., Fred Heinzelmann, and John M. Boyle. (1995). "Victimization of Persons by Fraud." *Crime & Delinquency* 41: 54–72.

TRAC. (2009). *White Collar Crime Prosecutions Filed, Year to Date, 2009.* (Report). Syracuse, NY: Transactional Records Access Clearinghouse. Syracuse University. Retrieved from http://trac.syr.edu/tracreports/bulletins/white_collar_crime/monthlyapr09/fil

Trahan, Adam, James W. Marquart, and Janet Mullings. (2005). "Fraud and the American Dream: Toward an Understanding of Fraud Victimization." *Deviant Behavior.* 26: 601–620.

United States Bureau of Justice Statistics. (1994). *National Crime Victimization Survey.* Washington, DC: U.S. Department of Justice, Bureau of Justice Statistics.

Wall Street Journal (2009). "Madoff's Victims." March 6, 2009. *Wall Street Journal.* Retrieved from http://s.wsj.net/public/resources/documents/st_madoff_victims_20081215.html

Watkins, Tom. (2005). "Papers Indicate Firm Knew Possible Suicide Risk." CNN January, 3. Retrieved from http://www.cnn.com/2005/HEALTH/01/03/prozac.documents/index.html

Weisburd, David, Stanton Wheeler, Elin Waring, and Nancy Bode. (1991). *Crimes of the Middle Classes: White-Collar Offenders in the Offenders in the Federal Courts.* New Haven, CT: Yale University Press.